CW01081220

UPHILL RACERS

UPHILL RACERS

THE HISTORY OF BRITISH SPEED HILL CLIMBING

CHRIS MASON

Foreword by JIM THOMSON

BOOKMARQUE
PUBLISHING
Minster Lovell · Oxfordshire

To Haydn

First published December 1990

© Chris Mason 1990

This work is published with the assistance of the Michael Sedgwick Memorial Trust.
Founded in the memory of the famous motoring researcher and author Michael Sedgwick (1926-1983),
the Trust is a registered charity to encourage new research and recording of motoring history.
   Suggestions for future projects, and donations, should be sent to the Honorary Secretary of the
Michael Sedgwick Memorial Trust, c/o The John Montagu Building, Beaulieu, Hampshire SO42 7ZN, England.

British Library Cataloguing in Publication Data
Mason, Christopher, *1948–*
   Uphill racers : the history of British speed hill climbing.
   1. Great Britain. Racing cars. Hill-climbing, history
   I. Title
   396.720941

ISBN 1–870519–08–6

Page layout by John Rose
Edited by T. C. Colverson
Text keyed on an Amstrad PC by Kim Giles
Disc conversion by Daily Information, Oxford
Typeset by Bookmarque Publishing
Set in 10 on 12 point Times Roman
Photographic screens by Martin & Gail Verity
Printed on Fineblade Smooth 115gsm
Published by Bookmarque Publishing · Minster Lovell & New Yatt · Oxfordshire
Printed and bound by Butler & Tanner Ltd · Frome · Somerset

CONTENTS

PHOTOGRAPHS & CAPTIONS IN THIS BOOK

Where two or more photographs appear on a page, the captions (in descending order) relate to the photographs on a left-to-right basis.

ACKNOWLEDGEMENTS

Without the support of Jim Thomson and John Rose this book just would not have happened. No matter how long one has been involved in the sport as a journalist and publicist, a full appreciation of what is involved in speed hill climbing can be gained only from the driving seat. I am therefore deeply indebted to Haydn Spedding and John Walker for entrusting their valuable E-type Jaguars to me, with strict instructions to fling them around the landscape as hard as judgement and nerve would allow.

Many people and organisations have been tremendously helpful and encouraging in pulling together the text and photographs. Those who contributed facts, reminiscences or valuable encouragement to help me with the text include: Mike Wilson, Richard Chapman, George Ritchie, Jack Davidson, Mike Hayhurst (Longton and District Motor Club), Geoff and Sue Ward (Bugatti Owners Club), Mark Joseland, the late Walter Gibbs and Alec Pine (Midland Automobile Club), David Swan, A. F. Rivers Fletcher, Ron Smith, Patsy Burt, Tom Leake and Dave Parr (Hagley and District Light Car Club), Hugh Dunsterville, Bill Goodman, P. R. Silverstone (The *Buckler Car Register*), David Greeney, A.M. Dowler, the late Austen May, Steve Butterworth, Colin Rawlinson, H. R. Evans, Mrs M. Lambert, Neil Loxton, Jon Derisley, Percy and Margaret Duff (Westmorland Motor Club), Keith Merry, Marcus Pye, Andrew D. Birrell (Lothian Car Club), John Meredith, Robin Boucher, Bryan Saull, D. Mitchell, Roger Thacker, Brian Joscelyne and Alan Archer (Aston Martin Owners Club), Doug Nye, Gordon Watson, Simon Taylor, Tom Grimshaw, Dick Mayo (Bristol Motor Cycle and Light Car Club), Linda Gallagher (Longleat House), and T. Barnes. A number of magazine editors have generously given me space to appeal for reminiscences and photographs, with Bill Boddy of *Motor Sport* and Tony Dron of *Classic Cars*, in particular, taking a much appreciated interest in the project. And that does not include the scores of hill climb drivers and officials whom I have been privileged to know over many years and who were providing me with copy all the while.

Longer and better memories than mine would still be deeply indebted to secondary sources, so in order to produce a credible history of the sport I have consulted *The Motor*, *The Autocar*, *Motor Sport*, *Autosport*, and *Speed Scene*, extensively. My own collection of motoring literature is fairly extensive, but my task was made much easier when Mick Osborne of The British Library Lending Division took the trouble to set up the facility for me to consult the Division's extensive runs of pre-1940 volumes of the leading motoring magazines at Boston Spa, conveniently near my home.

Haymarket Magazines Limited has kindly allowed me to quote from material published in *The Autocar*, *Autosport*, and *Old Motor* (now *Classic & Sportscar*), while Reed Business Publishing Limited has extended the same facility for material published in *The Motor*.

Motoring and motor sport is fortunate in the quality and quantity of its literature, although books on speed hill climbing have not been numerous. Invaluable works for specifically hill climb matters are: C.A.N. May, *Shelsley Walsh* (Foulis, 1946); C.A.N. May, *Speed Hill-Climb* (Foulis, 1962); John Bolster, *Specials* (Foulis, 1949); T. R. Nicholson, *Sprint* (David & Charles, 1969); Raymond Mays, *Split Seconds* (Foulis, 1951); Harold C. Hasting (Ed.), *Seventy Years of Shelsley Walsh* (Midland Automobile Club, 1976); and Peter Hull, (Ed.), *Prescott Speed Hill Climb* (Bugatti Owners Club,

1988). I have referred fleetingly to many other works, especially marque histories, not primarily dealing with hill climbing, and at the risk of offending many worthy authors I have to record a special debt to three invaluable and seminal works: G. N. Georgano (Ed.), *The Complete Encyclopaedia of Motorcars* (Ebury Press, 3rd edition, 1982); William Boddy, *The History of Brooklands Motor Course 1906-1940* (Grenville, 2nd edition, 1979) and David Weguelin, *ERA: The History of English Racing Automobiles Limited* (White Mouse Editions, 1980).

A book like *Uphill Racers* would be sadly incomplete without some good photographs and although a small number of my own pictures are included, some far better photographers have gone to a lot of trouble to provide many of the illustrations. Many other people have generously loaned or given precious prints or negatives from their own private collections for consideration. In this context Mike Kettlewell, Bob Light, Rivers Fletcher, Bruce Grant-Braham, Bob Cooper, Bill Henderson, Haydn Spedding, Alec Pine (Midland Automobile Club), Frank Hall and Brian Demaus, in particular, have been generous with their time and pictures, quite beyond the call of duty. I am further indebted for pictures to Richard Chapman (some real gems from the 1932 season), David Swan, Ron Smith, Patsy Burt, Bill Goodman, W.E. Avory, Michael Ware and Philip Scott (National Motor Museum), John Park, Louis Klemantaski, Peter Gaskell, Jim Tiller, Jeff Bloxham (*Autosport*), Brian Foley, Percy and Margaret Duff (Westmorland Motor Club), Clive Pearce, Tom Grimshaw and T. Barnes.

Photographs used are all individually credited. When two names appear, the first is that of the original photographer where this is different from that of the person who supplied the picture. Some older pictures have been used of which the original photographer is unknown. I humbly apologise to anyone who has not been credited who should have been. I must further thank my colleagues Ken Baldwin, Mike Braham, Celia Madden and Lily Etherington for the time spent running off prints from a large number of negatives, and Irene Carle and Viv Hurst for occasionally helping out with typing. Tom Colverson was a valued disciplinarian when it came to sorting out some of the inconsistencies, grammatical horrors and stylistic shortcomings in my manuscript. Last, but not least, a big thank you to Kim Giles for keying the text onto disc.

I am grateful for the assistance of The Michael Sedgwick Memorial Trust in enabling us to use many of the photographs dating from the sport's earlier days.

Chris Mason
Riccall, York, 1990

FOREWORD

This is a most enjoyable collation of facts about one of the friendliest sports in the UK, which has been put together over a number of years by Chris Mason and will, I hope, give a great amount of pleasure to the many followers of motor sport.

This book is written with the intention of covering historical facts right from the earliest days of hill climbing, but I am sure the reader will recognise that it has been written by an enthusiast who has more than a little knowledge of the sport.

Jim Thomson (November 1990)
Managing Director
Guyson International Limited

PREFACE

I may be using an old cliché but I was really hooked on speed hill climbing from an early age. My father, a keen and knowledgeable motorist, first took me to the hill climb at Barbon Manor – the only speed event of consequence near our Kendal home – in May 1953. Although I was not yet five years old, cars were already ousting teddy bears in my affections, and even before the competition runs started I was deeply impressed.

In those days, the Westmorland Motor Club, primarily a motorcycle-orientated club, was a decade away from RAC Championship status and although Barbon was already a notable happening on the Westmorland sporting and social calendar, it was only a minor matter in the great motoring scheme of things. Of course, I knew nothing of this as I gazed on the array of noisy, smoky, pungent-smelling and terrifyingly fast cars – the like of which I had never before seen. I stood in the paddock with my father, lost in awe and wonderment. That was when I got carried away...

My temporary point of vantage was just in front of a rope defining the edge of the paddock. Unbeknown to anyone, least of all the offending driver, a tender car had backed up to the extent of neatly hooking the boundary rope over its tow bar. The driver chose this moment to drive away, taking the rope with him – and one four-year-old boy who had been smartly 'dead-legged' by the suddenly taut rope! Forward motion was not maintained for long before the car stopped, but my father was horrified. I suspect that he was less concerned about the painful-looking red weals appearing on the backs of my legs than about the likely possibility that his son and heir would scream the place down and demand to be taken home forthwith, thereby spoiling his whole day. He needn't have worried as, to my young mind, this was clearly just another strange part of this whole exciting world of motor racing!

I have missed only half-a-dozen-or-so Barbons since, and it gave me enormous pleasure when, over thirty years later, I first won a very modest 'pot' there driving Haydn Spedding's E-type Jaguar. In between, I was fortunate to become actively involved in motor sport as an *Autosport* correspondent, than a hill climb publicist and press officer, before becoming, thanks to Haydn's great trust and generosity, a regular competitor.

The idea to write the history of speed hill climbing stemmed from conversations I had with Jim Thomson and his sister Jean back in 1976/77 when I was working as the Championship Press Officer for the BARC Series, which was then sponsored by the Thomsons' Guyson business. No serious attempt has been made to chronicle the sport's history since the publication of Austen May's excellent *Speed Hill-Climb* in 1962 and Tim Nicholson's *Sprint* in 1969, and even they covered only parts of the sport's history. Speed hill climbing has an exceptionally long history in a form perfectly recognisable to modern eyes. It imposes special disciplines and encourages great technical ingenuity and driving skill, yet remains great fun for all concerned. In this commercial age it also remains an amateur sport in the truest sense. Considerable car manufacturer interest in the early days, when British circuit racing did not extend beyond Brooklands (at least on the British mainland), actually lent a more commercial air to the sport in the nineteen-twenties than occurs today. This is not to say that speed hill climbing has been slow to attract business sponsorship. It has not, for many companies lend their names to events, championships and individual competitors. Happily, the proprietors and senior managers of many sponsoring companies are hill climb enthusiasts, see sponsorship in modest terms and have had no wish to change the character of the sport. That has been an immensely valuable attitude and is typified, for example, by Guyson's involvement.

Guyson's international business in the manufacture of industrial cleaning and refinishing equipment has grown immensely from the modest Otley, West Yorkshire-based, family business which Jim and Jean Thomson inherited. Jim is quick to point out the commercial benefits which have accrued from his company's enduring identification with the sport. At heart, though, Jim is an enthusiast. He has been a hill climb competitor since the nineteen-fifties and it has given him great satisfaction to see his sons James and Tim achieve eminence as drivers in recent years. He wanted to see the sport with a decent historical record and one which finally dispelled the irritating impression held by the uninitiated that speed hill climbing was something to do with 'mud plugging', as in sporting trials.

By the early nineteen-eighties Jim had persuaded me that I could and should write a history and I buckled down to researching and writing it. It has proved to be a fairly big task and one which has greatly increased my already considerable respect for acknowledged motor sporting historians of the calibre of Denis Jenkinson and Doug Nye.

Even with Guyson's enthusiastic support I still needed a publisher and as such was remarkably fortunate when Mike Kettlewell put me in touch with John Rose of Bookmarque Publishing. John's confidence, enthusiasm and assistance has been vital in bringing the project to fruition.

I should emphasise that while Jim Thomson graciously accepted the invitation to write the Foreword and was eager to contribute his useful appendix on hostelries with hill climb associations, he has never sought to prescribe or to influence the content of the text. Put another way, the mistakes and opinionated value judgements are all mine. I have striven to be as accurate and as objective as possible, checking anything which I believed to be suspect, but I'm quite sure that errors remain lurking to be discovered on the day following publication. I can only apologise and urge all aficionados to buy enough copies to merit a second, corrected, edition! I have been actively involved with hill climbs for a mere twenty years so inevitably I have had to deal with much that happened before my time. My fitness to write this book was further put into question in my own mind when I queried the accuracy of something in a report of a Harewood meeting in the early nineteen-seventies, only to realise that I myself had written the suspect report in the first place. However, if readers derive from reading *Uphill Racers* a fraction of the enjoyment I have had from the sport I will feel that the task has been thoroughly worthwhile.

Readers must be left to judge whether I have adopted the right approach for *Uphill Racers*, but I should perhaps draw attention to a couple of points of style. This splendid branch of British motor sport has been variously titled 'Speed hill climbing', 'Speed hill-climbing', 'Speed hillclimbing', and even 'Speedclimbing'. I have chosen the first of the styles because 'Speed' is the essential ingredient and 'hill climb' is the form used at Shelsley Walsh and Prescott. What is good enough for these august hills is good enough for me. Secondly, I have preferred the term 'Best Time of Day' (BTD) to the often-used 'Fastest Time of Day' (FTD), no matter who uses 'FTD'! Someone once said that time is constant and neither fast nor slow. You can have a fastest speed but not a fastest time.

Chris Mason
Riccall, York, 1990

INTRODUCTION

Motor Sport is very similar to athletics. It is a composite of many very different disciplines and types of event. Just as the Mile, 100 Yards (Metres) and Marathon have tended to overshadow other athletic events, so Grand Prix circuit racing, motorcycle road racing and special stage rallying have tended to attract the most widespread popular and media attention in the motor sporting world.

Yet other kinds of motor sport have gained and retained a solid following over many years, and none more deservedly so than British speed hill climbing. Ever since a 325 yard section of mostly 1 in 9 to 1 in 12 gradient on Petersham Hill was incorporated in the Automobile Club of Great Britain and Ireland's (ACGBI) General Efficiency Trials of June 1899, this aspect of motor sport has had a keen following in these islands. Over ninety years later, speed hill climbing remains one of the healthiest branches of the sport with full entry lists of varied and well-prepared machinery, an almost total lack of controversy, modest but rarely intrusive commercial sponsorship, and an exceptionally high level of sportsmanship between competitors.

As later chapters will reveal, it was not always so!

The essentials of speed hill climbing are simple. The object is to climb a timed stretch of well-surfaced hill road, preferably including a good variety of tricky corners, in the minimum possible time. Sadly, there are still those outside the sport who confuse speed hill climbing with 'mud plugging' trials on unsurfaced slopes. A multitude of classes enables virtually any type of competition car to compete against comparable vehicles, and the Britishness of the sport, as opposed to the Continental version of the same discipline, lies primarily in the shortness of the acclivities tackled. Honest competition between driver plus car versus the clock has been the norm for many years, but in the early days, before the First World War, many regarded speed hill climbing as a way of demonstrating to a sceptical populace that the motor car was a truly practical and efficient conveyance. Hence organisers of hill climb competitions tended to give great importance to awards won on one of many formulae of a Byzantine complexity undreamt of even by the organisers of the Le Mans 24 Hour Sports Car Race. The result was the paralytically slow progress of pathetically underpowered and overladen touring cars, 'competing' for *The Formula Award*. The increasingly large crowds of interested, if often ill-disciplined, spectators soon tired of this worthy but dull form of demonstration and concentrated on the dramatic battle for Best Time of Day between stripped competition machinery driven by the leading drivers of the day. The pattern was set.

The growing problem of safety on events which were almost all taking place over unclosed (in any formal sense) public roads led to the Royal Automobile Club ban on such events in 1925 after a fairly minor but widely publicised accident at Kop Hill, near Princes Risborough. Thereafter events took place on private land, as they had done at Shelsley Walsh ever since 1905. That ban in 1925 is doubly remarkable. It marked the end of a frenetic and exciting era in the sport's long history, but it also marked the last occasion when the basic rules and regulations of the sport were changed. Ever since then speed hill climbing has evolved naturally with little or no outside intervention apart from the enforced hiatus caused by the Second World War.

The type of car favoured by those seeking outright Best Time of Day has developed without periodic changes of Formula and the fortunes of the favoured types of car have waxed and waned just

When this Little Star was climbing Dinmore Hill in the 1904 Small Car Trials, there were many who still needed convincing that a modest motor car like this was a practical proposition for climbing hills at all.
NATIONAL MOTOR MUSEUM

as naturally as the ideal compromise between power, torque, handling, weight distribution, traction and agility has been sought. That is one of the most remarkable features of hill climbing, especially since 1945, when most other types of motor sport have been the subject of bewilderingly frequent and arbitrary eligibility regulation changes.

So what has kept the sport going over so long a period? What attracts competitors, officials and sometimes large crowds of spectators to a sport which today offers no Grand Prix 'names', little prize money, and can never offer the wheel to wheel dicing of circuit racing?

Back in 1929 *The Autocar* waxed lyrical when describing the appeal of Shelsley Walsh, then virtually alone in providing top class hill climbing. The 5,000 spectators enjoyed:

> Sunlight and shadow. The scream of racing engines, the haze of exhaust, the pungent smell of alcohol, slow cars and sleek, speedy cars flitting up between the trees with the green fields and woods far below. Weeks of work for less than a minute, perhaps, of skilful work with gear lever and wheel on a tricky, snaking hill.

While the cynical reader of today might be forgiven for thinking that not all the alcohol went into the petrol tank in the vicinity of this writer, it is a fact that hill climbing has often attracted a rather lyrical following, perhaps drawn by the sylvan settings which form the backdrop of many events.

Then there are the mathematicians, the coldly logical types for whom the perfectionist purity of hill climbing appeals.

In 1972 the organisers at Shelsley Walsh, the Midland Automobile Club (MAC), invited suggestions for improving the appeal of this most famous of all climbs, and one respondent was Mr A. M. Dowler, of London. While taking into account all factors in a closely reasoned survey, Mr Dowler emphasised the cerebal appeal of motor sport, stressing:

> The purely intellectual activity of deciding how to tackle a particular hill or circuit with a particular car in particular conditions. The decisions to be taken will include gear-change and braking points, whether certain bends can be taken flat or not and, above all, what line should be followed through each bend. Complicated relations exist between these points and it is this that renders the problem with which the driver is confronted so interesting.

Mr Dowler then continued to explain why, in this intellectual activity, hill climbing had the edge of circuit racing.

…here hill-climbing has the advantage over circuit racing for two reasons. First, the fact that only one car is in action at any one time means that each driver is free to choose his own line and general approach without regard to those of his rivals. Accordingly, the spectator can see how each driver considers that the problems affronted by the hill should be tackled and, what is more, the prompt announcement of the time for the run enables the spectator to judge, at least to some extent, not only the wisdom of the driver in making the decisions and his skill in carrying them out, but his own wisdom. In other words, the spectator can identify himself to a considerable extent with the drivers by considering how he would tackle the various problems and then comparing the fortunes of drivers whose approach approximates more closely to his own with the fortunes of drivers who adopt radically different approaches. It does not matter in the least that the spectator himself would not have the experience, skill or courage to put his own scheme into execution.

So what is it all about? A romantic, latter day evocation of Homeric achievement in a pastoral British setting, or an exercise in minimising a certain space-integral subject to a set of extremely complicated constraints? Probably a bit of both, but in 1976 the author tried to summarise the sport's appeal in an article in *Autosport*, and judging from the response this piece generated from active competitors, it was perhaps fairly close to the mark for many. Although the examples referred to in the piece date it, its gist seems as valid now as when it was written.

The challenge of Shelsley Walsh, a deceptively simple looking course where it is not easy to excel, despite its 'power course' reputation, has remained essentially unchanged since the sport's earliest days. In 1925 it took 55.05s for John Joyce to reach the finish line, over an unsealed surface, in his very special lightweight AC.
MIDLAND AUTOMOBILE CLUB

An infinitely better surface, twin rear wheels and a supercharged JAP engine helped Dick Henderson to a 35.84s BTD in August 1957.
MIDLAND AUTOMOBILE CLUB

Why the interest? What's the appeal of an event where, for an entry fee of £6-£7, a driver has about three to five minutes highly concentrated driving – including practice? A limited amount of sponsorship has come into hillclimbing (sic), notably from Castrol, Shell, Guyson International and Woking Motors in event/championship sponsorship, and from firms as diverse as Fenny Marine, Grünhalle Lager, Waring & Gillow, and Wendy Wools, with individual competitors. But most concerned in hillclimbing are aiming only for competitive relaxation. The atmosphere in the paddocks is therefore more relaxed and informal than is often the case at race meetings. The leading contenders in the RAC Hillclimb Championship are usually to be found congregating around each other's multi-thousand-pound machinery, helping each other out (there have been many occasions over the years where a crash or mechanical derangement has resulted in a driver being lent an arch-rival's car), and generally behaving in a truly *civilised* manner – not that this lessens the competition on the hill.

Hillclimbing is a sport for perfectionists. The very limited amount of time on the hill means that to be in with a chance of an award a driver must have a perfectly prepared and developed car, and cannot afford a single mistake on the hill when an event is often won by a few hundredths of a second. It is very evident that 'rock-ape' driving and 'bodged' cars are few and far between and singularly unsuccessful. During the 1950s it did seem that the optimum hillclimb car had been evolved in the form of the Cooper-JAP, but for some years now there has been great competition between nimble F2-type cars and the very powerful yet relatively cumbersome F5000 and F1 machinery. Is the 3.4-litre Cosworth GA-engined Grünhalle Lager March 76 A of Chris Cramer the long-term answer? Or will it fall between two stools?

Those drivers seriously chasing the RAC Championship naturally receive a lot of attention – after all they are usually the fastest men in the fastest cars – but for the scores of other competitors at major meetings there are classes to be won, points to be scored in the RAC Leaders or Guyson/BARC Championships (which cater for fast drivers irrespective of the classes in which they compete), and, by modern standards, a minimum of pettifogging regulations to trip them up. Although entry fees are by no means insignificant for the clubman, running expenses tend to be much lower than in other forms of motor sport, by virtue of the short competitive distances involved. Driveshafts are about the only components which take a more than average amount of punishment!

Harewood has certainly had the odd 10,000-plus crowd, and, I believe, so has Shelsley in recent years, and in fact hill climbing has at least as much to offer to the spectator as special stage rallying for instance. To start with, most hill climbs are in areas of beautiful scenery (Prescott, Harewood, Barbon, Doune and Bouley Bay spring to mind immediately), which makes for greater co-operation from the less enthusiastic side of the family. The cars range from slightly modified road cars up through a nostalgic collection of older competition cars to the very latest equipment from March, Modus, Ralt and Pilbeam – all of which can be examined more closely at most venues than is generally the case at major circuit meetings.

As for those people who insist that there is little spectacle in hillclimbing, they obviously haven't seen a F1 car driven in anger up what amounts to an English country lane. For spectacle, I think that's in the Blomqvist or Mikkola class!

The hill climb scene of the 'seventies and 'eighties is the result of decades of evolution, much of it almost imperceptible except in hindsight, and over several years. Later chapters in this book describe the factors which have directed that evolution.

Speed hill climbing is of course a close relation of sprinting on the flat. Many competitors still take in both types of event as a matter of course. Yet in recent years in particular, and despite the RAC's National Sprint Championship having its own band of regular contenders, the sprints rarely achieve great stature or seem to possess that elusive 'atmosphere' or 'charisma'. Only the historic Brighton Speed Trials and the end-of-season occasion at Weston-Super-Mare are undoubted exceptions.

One other characteristic of British speed hill climbing is particularly noteworthy: insularity. Since the earliest years of competition motoring there have been major hill climbs on the European mainland. Daunting climbs such as La Turbie, Mont Ventoux, Gaisberg, Freiburg-Schauinsland, Trento-Bondone and Ollon-Villars spring to mind. Before the Second World War, teams of the stature of Auto Union, Daimler-Benz, and Scuderia Ferrari contested some of these alpine 'Bergpreis' events. In 1957 the FIA re-instituted a European Mountain Championship, and before its stature declined in the later nineteen-sixties, this series, confined to sports cars up to 2-litres in capacity, attracted Porsche, Borgward, Ferrari and Abarth among its factory contestants.

Yet there has been remarkably little crossflow between the British events and the Continental climbs. In 1930 Shelsley Walsh formed a round in the European Championship for the first time, and Hans Stück – the 'Bergmeister' – brought over his Austro-Daimler and broke the course record in a famous climb. He returned in 1936 with a short chassis Auto Union, amid tremendous excitement and anticipation, but was defeated by the Worcestershire rain and the car's relative lack of agility. The next time a European Mountain Champion competed in a British hill climb was in 1964 when Edgar Barth ran a flat eight Porsche Spyder at Prescott. A few British drivers, including Raymond Mays, Ken Wharton, Peter Westbury, Patsy Burt and David Franklin have tackled the European climbs, often with considerable success, but have not done so consistently.

This situation has come about because of the shortness and sinuousness of the British climbs, which have not really suited the European Championship cars, while the club weekend atmosphere over here

Eleven years later and Peter Lawson was fully exploiting four-wheel-drive and modern Grand Prix car technology to clock 31.37s at Shelsley, on his way to the RAC Hill Climb Championship. Twenty years on and the record stood at 26.08s.
MIDLAND AUTOMOBILE CLUB

The growth of commercial sponsorship in the early nineteen-seventies did not change the sport's basic character. This well-sponsored line-up is at Doune in 1980. Malcolm Dungworth's Waring & Gillow Pilbeam is in the foreground, while Malcolm and mechanic Steve Oyibo relax at the rear of the car.
BILL HENDERSON

has had little to offer to Continental works teams. Conversely, since most British hill climb competitors are very much spare time racers few could afford the time or money for a serious Continental campaign. Although Shelsley was given European Championship rounds before the Second World War, it is probably no exaggeration to regard these as little more than a gesture, rather in the manner of Indianapolis being accorded World Drivers Championship status from 1950 to 1958. No British round in the European Mountain Championship has been held since the Second World War.

Hill climbing can be very spectacular. Martin Bolsover's controlled power slide round Barbon's hairpin in 1983, in the Guyson Pilbeam MP51 was awe-inspiring.
BOB COOPER

Although they are beyond the scope of this work, hill climb events have been and continue to be held all over the world, or at least in most places where competitive motoring exists; in the USA (especially the legendary Pike's Peak climb), Canada, Australia, South Africa, Ceylon (now Sri Lanka), and New Zealand to name but a few countries. But in Britain they have a character all their own, with a 'full time' following who do not regard hill climbs as something to do on a weekend when there are no circuit races to compete in. Hill climbers certainly see Britain too. No other national motor sporting championship visits as many parts of the British Isles as the RAC Motor Sport Association's Hill Climb Championship. Although Tholt-y-Will in the Isle of Man is no longer on the schedule, our premier series visits most parts of England, Scotland, Northern Ireland, Jersey and Guernsey during the course of the year.

A few British hill climbers have enjoyed tackling the long Continental hill climbs. Here, Patsy Burt tackles the Trento-Bondone climb during 1961 in her Porsche; a car which excelled in these tough events, but was over-engineered for the short, sharp British climbs with far smoother roads.
ATTUAL FOTO
via PATSY BURT AND RON SMITH

CHAPTER ONE

THE FORM EVOLVES
(1899-1914)

LIKE so many motor sporting 'firsts', the first-ever recorded speed hill climb took place in France, at Chanteloup, in November 1898. But Britain was not so far behind. On 9 June 1899, around forty competitors converged on Petersham Hill, Richmond-upon-Thames, for a timed distance of 325 yards and with a maximum gradient of 1 in 9.

The climb formed part of a larger event, the General Efficiency Trials of the Automobile Club of Great Britain and Ireland (ACGBI). This club, the forerunner of the Royal Automobile Club, instigated these trials, incorporating a road run over several days and a straight 1½ miles speed trial. Run less than three years after the notorious Red Flag regulations had been repealed, and with a 12 mph open road speed limit in force, the event aimed to show how efficient and practical the motor car was becoming. These were true pioneering days when the vast majority of the populace needed a lot of convincing that the motor car was neither a rich man's impractical toy, nor the dangerous machination of deranged inventors.

There was no question of closing the road for the climb to take place but then the speeds of the laden vehicles up the stiffish gradient rarely exceeded the speed limit. Flying starts were permitted and the average speed over the measured distance rather than elapsed times was the deciding factor. In fact, only a Barrière tricycle infringed the law of the land at 14 mph. An equally obscure device, an Electrical Undertaking Dog-Cart managed 11 mph while the fastest proper car was the 6 hp Paris-Marseilles Panhard-Levassor of the Hon. Charles Stewart Rolls which managed 8.75 mph. If nothing else, the event provided an early lesson in the importance of power-to-weight ratios, and for some years what we would now regard as conventional cars were often beaten by light tricycles in hill climbs.

To be truthful the most exciting feature of the Petersham Hill event was the *descent* after the finish where speeds were considerably in excess of the vehicles' braking capabilities. A star performer was the intrepid occupant of a Tourist three-wheeler (a Bollée-type device) who was able to halt the thing only by gripping the offside front wheel! Frederick Lanchester also raised a few eyebrows as he arrested his already considerably developed Lanchester Spirit Passenger Phaeton prototype from an estimated 18 mph to considerable audible accompaniment.

At least one far-sighted individual saw the possibilities after Petersham Hill. Selwyn Francis Edge, racing driver, entrepreneur and the greatest motoring propogandist of his age, wrote to the motoring press proposing an independent open hill climb contest on Westerham Hill, between Westerham and Bromley, in Kent. This was to be a wholly sporting and, hopefully, international contest. Edge, whose grasp of the importance of publicity would be the envy of many of today's marketing and public relations practitioners, was on to something: 'I feel sure that a test of this sort, which could be witnessed by a large number of people, held on a Saturday afternoon, would create wonderful amusement'.

Notwithstanding Edge's suggestion, the next hill climb was another 'proving' trial, held on Mucklow Hill, Halesowen, in January 1900. All the precedents were still to be established at this time and the, to modern minds, unseasonal date came about because the event was laid on for the benefit of the light cars and motorcycles exhibiting at the 4th Birmingham Midland Cycle and Motor Show. Since the climb was held in snow, over a tortuous and steep course – naturally without benefit of a sealed surface – the whole thing must have resembled a sporting trial rather more closely than a speed

hill climb. Since the winning Mors 'Petit Duc' (a little 850cc flat-twin with handlebar steering) needed 9m 2.4s for the one mile timed distance, the 12 mph speed limit was not abused! Runner-up to the French-built car was a single-cylinder, 3½ hp Wolseley, driven by the firm's General Manager, Herbert Austin.

These were truly pioneering days, when every aspect of the form of events had yet to evolve. The nearest precedents were seen by many to lie in the horse racing world. Back in 1896 there was even a proposal to hold a 'Two Thousand Guineas Contest' for 'The Motor Derby'. The idea was abortive, but even by 1907, the first year of racing at Brooklands, the rules and the terminology were basically equestrian, even down to the drivers racing in coloured silks. As the time went by and motor sport evolved a tradition of its own the derivations became less marked but terms such as 'Paddock', 'Clerk of the Course', 'Steward', and 'Handicap' have never been improved upon.

The ACGBI, which by early 1900 could count some 600 members, stepped in during March of that year with an attempt to provide a binding set of competition rules. All events had to have permits and any ACGBI member competing in a non-registered event would forfeit his membership. Like all other norms, sub-division into classes by cubic capacity and vehicle function had yet to be established. This first code of rules advocated classes by weight within three categories of driver: private individuals; manufacturers' agents; and 'paid drivers and artisans'.

Not surprisingly, the major event of 1900 was another, more ambitious, proving event: the ACGBI's Thousand Mile Trial, run in April and May. This time there were four timed climbs on the route. These comprised 2½ miles of Taddington Hill, Buxton: 9 miles of bleak Shap Fell (for many years a daunting winter obstacle on the A6 road between Kendal and Penrith); Dunmail Raise, between Grasmere and Keswick (another celebrated northern main road hill); and Birkhill, near Moffatt. Regarded as a hill climbing contest, the event was a duel between the Hon. C. S. Rolls, now mounted on a 12 hp Panhard; and one of the effective little Ariel Tricycles. Honours were shared with the Ariel ahead over Taddington and Shap and Rolls taking the honours on Dunmail and Birkhill. Rolls's Dunmail climb, with full complement of passengers, including one stretch of 1 in 8.6, at a highly illegal 20.54 mph, was particularly noteworthy. Although strictly outside the scope of this work, drivers on the Trial also had a rare opportunity to compete on private ground. This was the first speed trial over the Duke of Portland's estate road in Welbeck Park, Nottinghamshire – Clipstone Drive. Some idea of the progress then reached in automobile engineering can be gained from Rolls's winning speed over the two-way flying mile, which was 37.63 mph.

That Summer two independent 'sporting' climbs were held, on Westerham Hill (a mere 208 yards but with 1 in 6.25 gradient) by the Catford Cycle Club; and on Tilburstowe Hill, Godstone Green, in Surrey. The fastest English-built car extant, the new 16 hp Paris-Toulouse Napier of S. F. Edge, was the star attraction at Westerham, but after an unsatisfactory practice climb the untried car was withdrawn. Edge contented himself with romping up at 22.22 mph on an Ariel tricycle, soundly thrashing the other two cars competing, including Henry Weguelin's 12 hp racing Panhard. There were eight competing cars, classified by price, at Tilburstowe, on 7 July, just one week after Westerham. This climb was, as was usually the case, open to tricycles as well, and was held under the auspices of the English Motor Club, formerly the Motor Car Club, and a known 'front' organisation for the wholly commercial and entrepreneurial activities of Harry J. Lawson who made such determined efforts to corner the fledgling British motor industry.

History repeated itself at Tilburstowe with a 6 hp De Dion Tricycle, ridden by Charles Jarrott, setting the fastest speed of 25.8 mph over the timed 972 yards. Fastest of the 'conventional' cars was Edge in the 16 hp Napier (18.39 mph), who just shaded out Weguelin's Panhard (17.86 mph). The premier award was actually made on the basis of a formula which took into account weight, price and speed, and was secured by O. E. Lord's 12 hp Peugeot.

By 1901, there were signs of the ACGBI's hold over British motoring sport weakening as the Motor Union – a semi-detached adjunct of the ACGBI, primarily motivated by the need to counter discrimination against motorists in the Law Courts – gathered strength, and regional motor clubs proliferated. Apart from the English MC, at least four independent clubs ran speed hill climbs in 1901: the Reading AC on Peppard Village Hill; the Scottish AC, a series of climbs during a 500 mile reliability trial; the Midland AC on Gorcott Hill, on the Birmingham-to-Alcester road; and the Nottingham AC on Broughton Hill, Kettleby, on the Nottingham-to-Melton Mowbray road. Faced by what looks suspiciously like the inevitable, the ACGBI dropped its compulsory registration of drivers and vehicles and no longer insisted on an ACGBI-appointed handicapper at other than ACGBI events.

Another sign of the times was that the senior club, hitherto rather reluctant to see competitive events in any light other than proving trials, ran an independent hill climb on Dashwood Hill in May. A fair climb over 1,434 yards, with the steepest gradient increasing to 1 in 9.8, this event marked an early success for the English Daimler. The best performances were put up by the Hon. John Montagu, later Lord Montagu, in 24 and 12 hp versions of the marque. No times nor speeds were published because the ACGBI was already becoming sensitive to public opinion, or rather to the opinion of the non-motoring public, who could not be expected to look favourably on blatant infringements of the law of the land.

Although originally formed in 1893 by F. R. Simms to exploit the German Daimler patents in Britain, and briefly forming part of the ephemeral Harry Lawson empire, the Daimler Motor Syndicate was now very much a marque in its own right, with the production of increasingly formidable four-cylinder machines. It was in an early 12 hp edition that Montagu made history in the 1899 Paris-Ostend race, when he became the first Briton to compete abroad in a British-built car.

Certainly the most exciting climb of the year was the English MC event at Tilburstowe in June, where the automotive progress accomplished since the previous July was startling. D. Napier and Son Ltd, then of Acton, were a long-established precision engineering firm, but it was only in 1899 that Montague Napier, aided and abetted by his cycling friend S. F. Edge, started to experiment with motor cars. The company made rapid headway and with Edge as Napier's sole distributor (through his Motor Power Company), racing team leader, and publicist, the headlines were not long in coming. The 1900 4.9 litre, 16 hp four-cylinder was one thing, but in 1901 Edge turned up at Tilburstowe with a 50 hp monster. This chain-driven, armoured-woodframe two-tonner, boasted a 17,157cc four-cylinder engine developing 103 bhp at 800 rpm, and was aimed at the Paris-Bordeaux race. Edge fought it up Tilburstowe at 37.72 mph, to which Mark Mayhew's 20 hp Panhard – formidable enough – could respond with only 29.48 mph. The entry of no fewer than 37 included one of the revolutionary new 35 hp Mercedes and Jarrott's 16 hp Panhard, from which much was expected. The apparently undistinguished performance of the latter was explained by *The Autocar*:

> The difference in times of Mr. Mayhew's 20 hp and Mr. Jarrott's 16 hp Panhard is wider than would seem to be warranted by the difference of four horsepower, but the fact that Mr. Jarrott was badly interfered with on the 1 in 11 section by an old lady who selected the very moment of his passing to rush across the road must be taken into consideration.

Thus was emphasised the problems inherent in running events over 'open' roads even with the tacit agreement of local authorities – problems which were magnified by the total unfamiliarity of an interested local populace with such powerful machines, and with judging their speeds.

Other notable occurrences of the year included the BTD at Kettleby (Broughton Hill) by Daimler employee Percy Richardson, driving an 18 hp model, and the first-ever hill climb organised by the Midland Automobile Club, at Gorcott Hill, on 5 October. A timed furlong, which included eight bends, still favoured the Arial tricycles in an entry which included club founder members Frank Lanchester and Herbert Austin. A. E. Crowdy's 8 hp Darracq was the fastest car, but again prudence dictated no announcements of speeds or times.

Hill climbing activity in 1902 was quite overshadowed by the ACGBI's Bexhill Speed Trials on 19 May, held over Earl de la Warr's specially prepared De la Warr Parade. This event was tremendously successful apart from an enduring dispute over the infringement of a local citizen's right of way, and signified a number of firsts. It was the first of the great tradition of seaside speed trials, the first time a special motor course had been employed in Britain, the first time a representative international entry had competed in Britain – the list included Serpollet, Georges-Richard, Baras, Gabriel, Mercier, Jarrott, Rolls, de Knyff, Girardot, Edge, Mayhew, Baron Henri de Rothschild and Alfred Harmsworth – and the first major British victory for a steam car, that of Leon Serpollet. That was to be of particular significance in hill climbs, where the steamer's excellent torque gave an 'unfair' advantage in the short-distance events.

In fact, a steam car, a 4½ hp Locomobile, had already given the petrol-engined ranks a fright at the ACGBI's February climb at Petersham Hill. On this occasion Mr Ginder's Locomobile ascended at 16.5 mph, faster than Edge's 16 hp Napier and two 16 hp Panhards, but beaten by a 20 hp Milnes-Daimler. Not to be confused with the Coventry make, this was a German Daimler, bodied and marketed by the Shropshire firm, G. F. Milnes & Co Ltd.

Of particular significance was the same club's event at Dashwood Hill on 10 May. Still courting respectability, the ACGBI ran this as part of a petrol consumption trial, and they were able to welcome a most distinguished and influential guest riding down as passenger in the Hon. John Montagu's 20 hp Daimler. This was no less a personage than Arthur Balfour, the Prime Minister. An atmosphere of mature responsibility was vital, so the action of Montague Graham-White in descending the hill in his 28 hp Mors at an estimated 60 mph – with a 12 mph speed limit in force – in front of the PM was almost unbelievably stupid. Graham-White was disqualified from the event and suspended from future competitions, but the matter did not end there. When the ACGBI returned to Dashwood Hill in July, it was only to find that the 20 would-be competitors were confronted with a Sergeant and twelve Constables with orders to take the particulars of all those who exceeded 12 mph. The meeting was promptly abandoned.

Notwithstanding the excesses of Graham-White, it was becoming harder for even benevolent local constabularies to overlook the speed limit infringements. When cars were only capable of climbing timed hills at speeds which were barely in excess of the limit, a blind eye could easily be turned. The growing power of the latest offerings from Napier, Daimler, Panhard, Mors, Mercedes, and so on, made the infringements far from marginal.

Nevertheless, climbs were taking place outside the increasingly difficult South East. In June the active Scottish AC ran an event up Glenlude Hill (better known as Paddy Slacks), Innerleithen, a one mile course where top honours fell, appropriately, to a Scottish car, the 9 hp Argyll of the make's founder, Alex Govan. In August, the Yorkshire Automobile Club staged the first climb in Yorkshire, a modern stronghold of hill climbing, at Harewood, near Leeds. This was not over the modern Stockton Farm course, but was up Harewood Bank on the Leeds-to-Harrogate road, and it was said that competitors were outnumbered by plain clothes policemen!

The ACGBI tried again on River Hill, on the Tunbridge Wells-to-Sevenoaks road, as part of their 650 Mile Reliability Trial, and announced that no marks would be given anyone climbing the hill between 12 and 15 mph, and for anyone climbing in excess of this figure would be excluded altogether. As the event progressed this public relations-inspired regulation seemed to have been forgotten. A Gardner-Serpollet steamer was adjudged fastest at 16.84 mph, while later the same day, and still forming part of the same Trial, competitors tackled Westerham Hill where a 20 hp Wolseley ascended at 12.34 mph. All fairly modest for 1902.

The Midland Automobile Club returned to Gorcott Hill in October (they also ran a climb at Weatheroak Hill in November) and employed a different ploy to avoid prosecution. They lengthened the timed distance by an undisclosed amount and announced times not speeds. They attracted a good entry too which is less surprising given the MAC's geographical and membership base at the heart of the new British motor manufacturing industry. Best Time of the Day went to A. Harvey du Cros's monstrous 70 hp Panhard, with 63.8s, from A. E. Crowdy's 45 hp Wolseley. Herbert Austin's smaller, 20 hp, Wolseley and George Lanchester's 10 hp Lanchester were among the class winners.

Anyone who cherishes the impressions of speed hill climbing as a bastion of good hearted sportsmanship, unmarred by controversy, would have been sadly disillusioned had he been involved with the sport in 1903. The endemic legal problem of running fundamentally illegal events on unclosed roads, depending on the goodwill of the many who felt that the law was an ass anyway, was just the start. During the year, the 'unfair' competition of steam cars, the difficulty of coming up with a handicap formula which did not give an advantage to that particular handicapper's vested interest, the growing incidence of racing machines masquerading as touring cars, and the domination of 'trade' entries were all subjects which generated a lot of heat.

The season – the message seemed to be getting through that hill climbs during the Winter months were not a particularly sensible proposition – began in bizarre fashion at Dashwood Hill where the ACGBI ran an eliminating trial for the all-important Gordon Bennett Trophy race on 27 April. Bizarre? Well, the event was run at 4 o'clock in the morning to avoid the unwelcome attentions of the law. Dominated by Napiers, it was the 45 hp version in the hands of C. S. Rolls (still at that time a London agent for the French Panhard concern) which put up the best performance on the aggregate of three climbs, but it was the similar car of J.W. Stocks which eventually formed part of the British Gordon Bennett team.

A succession of steam car successes at the Sheffield AC's Padley Wood, Grindleford Bridge Hill (Locomobile), the Scottish AC Kirkfield Bank event (Gardner-Serpollet), and at Peppard Hill (Gard-

S. F. Edge's fearsome-looking 50 hp Napier at Dashwood Hill in 1902. It was no longer sufficient merely to climb successfully, for racing cars were now becoming frighteningly fast in relation to their roadholding capabilities.
NATIONAL MOTOR MUSEUM

ner Serpollet) were followed by more controversial happenings at the MAC's latest venue. Run on 25 July, this climb by the active MAC who were rapidly achieving a position of pre-eminence in hill climbing, was held on Sun Rising Hill, between Banbury and Stratford-upon-Avon. The 1,000 yards timed section included about a quarter of that distance over a gradient steeper than 1 in 8, and even worse, the competitors were also faced with a stop and restart test on a 1 in 6.75 incline. Three out of twenty fully laden cars failed to reach the top altogether, but Cecil Edge (S. F.'s brother) romped up in a 20 hp Napier, in 1m 55.8s, way ahead of the 20 hp MMC (a near-Panhard, built in Coventry, and another residue of the Harry Lawson empire) driven by George Iden, MMC's works manager, which needed 2m 21.8s for the same task. There were dark allegations that Edge's car was fitted with one of the 1902 racing Napier engines. The MAC held another climb at the same hill in September, won by J. A. Holder's 24 hp Panhard, but this time cars started with a standing start on a 1 in 9 gradient, only 400 yards of the steepest section were included and a 'secret formula' was again employed to arrive at a winner on handicap. Sun Rising has left at least one important legacy. Right up to the present day the MAC's rising sun motif provides a lasting reminder of these early and experimental days.

By now smaller club hill climbs were proliferating and were held at such diverse places as Grimsthorpe Castle (Lincolnshire AC); Hill Cliff Lane, Turnditch (Derby & District AC); Hindhead Hill (West Surrey AC); Kettleby Hill (Nottingham AC); Hermitage Hill, Bridgenorth (Wolverhampton & District AC); and at Offley Hill, Hitchin (Cambridge University AC). The ACGBI ran another Reliability Trial in September, with a 10 hp Gardner-Serpollet steam car reigning supreme up all four timed climbs.

The Irish too gained there first taste of speed hill climbing during the ACGBI's Irish Fortnight in July. Ballybannon Hill, Castlewellen, was the chosen venue and Campbell Muir's 60 hp Mercedes (32.4s) won a battle of the giants with C. S. Rolls's 70 hp Mors (33.8s). The latter gained recompense before the end of the month, however, with victory at Killorglin Hill, between Killarney and Tralee, this time at the wheel of an even more powerful 80 hp Mors. In October a rather more parochial Irish climb was held on Glendhu Hill, in the foothills of the Dublin Mountains, organised by the Irish AC, with success falling to William Goff's 12 hp Napier from the 10 hp Siddeley of Irish pioneer motor sportsman, Walter Sexton.

By 1903, Selwyn Francis Edge (leading British racing driver and publicist) had an 80 hp Napier at his disposal.
NATIONAL MOTOR MUSEUM

The trends which were becoming apparent in 1903, continued apace the following year. Whatever the difficulties encountered in organising speed hill climbs, they were becoming increasingly popular – as was motor sport as a whole. There were about 26 climbs held on the British mainland, plus one in the Isle of Man (Gordon Bennett eliminating trial, won by S. F. Edge's 80 hp Napier) and one in Ireland (Glendhu Hill, won by Goff again, this time in a 20 hp Clément).

New events meant new hills, and to the 'old favourites' could be added Woodcock Hill (Elstree-to-Barnet road); Pot Bank, Harrogate; Dinmore Hill (Hereford-to-Leominster road); Frome's Hill (Hereford-to-Worcester road); Aston Hill, Tring; Detling; Gatacre; South Harting (Chichester-Petersfield-North Marden road); Hazlewood Hill (Duffield-to-Belper road); Sulham Hill, Reading; Bully Hill (Market Rasen-to-Grimsby road); Rockingham Hill, Nottingham; Yearby Bank, Stockton; Thonock Hill, Gainsborough; and Bridehead, Dorchester. All these climbs hosted events for the first time – formally organised ones anyway – and two of them, Aston Hill and South Harting, were to gain lasting fame.

First major talking point of the year, however, arose long before competitors made there way to the Nottingham AC's Kettleby Hill on 12 March, for the first climb of the year. On 1 January, the Motor Car Act came into force. Since this new legislation replaced the 12 mph universal speed limit with one of 20 mph, it might seem to be a source of at least limited rejoicing to motorists. Not so, for the old limit was enforced in a patchy and generally lax manner while car owners were assured that the new limit was to be rigorously enforced. What's more the new licencing regulations which formed part of the Act ensured that any car could be traced all too easily, even if the speeding motorist did succeed in shaking off the probably bicycle-mounted guardian of the law.

The Woodcock Hill Climb, held in May, actually formed part of the Scottish AC's Glasgow to London Trial, and was notable mainly for a formula for arriving at a winner on handicap which would have taxed even a modern computer. A conclusion was to be arrived at after taking into account unladen weight, length and height of the hill, velocity of the car, piston area, number of cylinders, stroke, lowest gear ratio and even road wheel diameter. This almost wilful complexity still did not take into account the apparently obvious factors of price, horsepower and cylinder capacity!

A rather more significant innovation was introduced at the Nottingham AC's second event of the year at Kettleby on 28 May. This was the institution of closed-to-club members and 'open' classes. The object of the exercise was to keep the trade entrants from winning all the trophies. The idea had a limited success in meetings of dual status, but failed at 'closed' meetings where trade entrants gained entries by the simple expedient of joining the organising club. The Kettleby event was dominated by the Napier 'steamroller' with S. F. Edge's 80 hp four-cylinder defeating the smaller Napiers of Mark Mayhew and Clifford Earp.

The Yorkshire AC's tortuous 1 in 7 climb of Pot Bank, between Beckwithshaw and Killinghall, held on 2 July, was notable for two things: one was an important innovation in the form of electrical timing and telephone installation between the start and finish, and the other was the first significant win for Yorkshire driver Albert Farnell, at the wheel of a 28 hp Daimler.

When the MAC returned to Sun Rising on 23 July they scotched one area of controversy by specifically excluding steam cars. They still had a near riot on their hands though. Source of the trouble was S. F. Edge's innocuous-seeming 20 hp Napier, supposedly a touring car. His Best Time of Day in 2m 48.2s and reluctance to reveal what went on under the bonnet refuelled allegations that the car was either a 1903 Gordon Bennett racer, suitably re-bodied as a touring car, or that the engine was the new prototype six-cylinder. In fact, Edge's 1.4s advantage over Daimler General Manager, Ernest Instone's 28 hp Daimler was deceptively small for the wily Edge had been baulked during his climb.

This problem of what constituted a racing or touring car was not to be resolved easily. The term 'sports car' had not been coined let alone defined, and even racing cars, as designed for the Gordon Bennett Trophy races or the great inter city races, differed fundamentally from the larger touring machines only in their increasingly large engines and their sketchy bodywork. What's more, it was positively fashionable among the wealthy to buy a racing car, such as a '60' Mercedes, and rebody it with something more suitable for touring in the grand manner.

While the attention focused on Edge's victorious Napier, the close observer would have noted that no fewer than four of the powerful but unquestionably touring Daimlers beat the de Rothschild '60' Mercedes. These chain-driven, four-cylinder Daimlers, complete with the newly fluted radiator header tanks, were among the first of a new line from the Coventry company which were to achieve a surprisingly dominant position in hill climbs until the Daimler concern abandoned these effective though rather rough-running and conservative machines for the unsporting refinement of sleeve valves in 1909.

Both Aston Hill[1] and South Harting had small beginnings in 1904. It was the Hertfordshire AC who arranged to run an event up the three quarters of a mile of the former, running over a public road but through the estate of Alfred de Rothschild, near Tring. With a 1 in 9 average gradient, but not too tortuous a course, the climb was a fast one for the increasingly powerful cars which were now available. As at Pot Bank a telephone was installed to relay results so there was no delay in learning of Edge's BTD (87.6s) in the notorious '20' Napier.

South Harting was the second of two venues chosen by the Portsmouth Naval Club for a two-part event in October. Climbing up through the estate of the Hon. Turnour Featherstonehaugh of Uppark, although again actually a public road, South Harting's gradient was 1 in 6.7 at its steepest but averaged out at 1 in 12. J. D. Siddeley, who was to replace Herbert Austin as General Manager at Wolseley the following year, made short work of the hill in 65.6s, driving a 40 hp Mercedes,

Although real road racing on the British mainland remained as far away as ever in 1905, the popularity of motor sport was growing. The first-ever climb at Shelsley Walsh, the first-ever Brighton Speed Trials, and the first-ever sand race meeting (at Filey, Yorkshire), were all important landmarks of a year when around thirty-four speed hill climbs were run, including three in Ireland.

Yet still there was the establishment's ambivalent attitude to speed on the public road. The ACGBI had another go at regulating the sport and announced that no elapsed times were to be published by member clubs. Classes differentiated by weight were recognised but price classes were favoured. All meetings, whether of 'open' or 'closed' status, were to need a permit, and all these regulations were presented to affiliated clubs as a *fait accomplit*. The result was instant revolt and after a meeting of the Motor Union clubs in Leeds, in June, the ACGBI backed off and everyone proceeded very much as before. The inconsistencies of attitude prevalent at the time are well illustrated by the pronouncement of *The Automotor Journal* which went so far as to advocate a total ban on public road sprints, although 'Hill-climbing competitions…of course are not races at all but merely tests of horsepower and efficiency of transmission'.

---

1   The Aston Martin Owners Club Archivist, Alan Archer, points out that the course which has been widely known to later generations as Aston Clinton was always referred to contemporarily as Aston Hill. The village of Aston Clinton is nearby. The often repeated legend that Lionel Martin named the Aston Martin car after Aston Clinton is therefore not strictly correct. The location thus marked was Aston Hill and not the nearby community of Aston Clinton.

Ernest Instone's soon-to-be-victorious Daimler 'weighs in' at Martley before the first-ever event at Shelsley Walsh on 12 August 1905.
MIDLAND AUTOMOBILE CLUB

Shelsley Walsh

While the arrival of hill climbing to the wooded Worcestershire slopes of Shelsley Walsh created a tremendous stir, the MAC's inaugural meeting at Court House, Shelsley Walsh, by courtesy of the tenant, Mr Claude Taylor, was just one event where the increasingly powerful 30/40 hp (7.2 litre) and 35 hp (8.5 litre) Daimlers were victorious. More nimble than the 'monsters' which held sway in the most important straight line speed trials, but still formidably fast, the Coventry cars were fastest at Kettleby (Daimler agent Frank Bolton in a 30/40); the MAC's June climb at the rather undemanding Middle Hill House, Broadway (a tie between Ernest Instone and Percy Martin with 'works' 35 hp models); South Harting (Edward Manville's 30/40 hp from Instone); and Shelsley Walsh (Instone, at 77.6s, from A. Birtwhistle in 78.2s, and Percy Martin in 89.0s).

Straw boaters abound as Dr Slaney's 12 hp Wilson-Pilcher prepares for the first Shelsley climb. His time of 172.4s was actually fifteenth BTD from the thirty-nine actual starters. Some of the climbs must have seemed very tedious.
NATIONAL MOTOR MUSEUM

The ACGBI were in charge at South Harting on 10 June and attracted 49 entries for a rare event run according to their unpopular new rules. No times or speeds were issued and classes were divided by price, one winner being Louis Coatelen in an 8/10 hp, four-cylinder Humber. In a year of landmark events, further history was made on 8 July when G. S. Seccombe's 12 hp Wolseley won the first Welsh hill climb, a 'closed' event with no fewer than 42 entries organised by the South Wales & Monmouthshire AC, at Buttrill's Hill, Barry. In contrast, the Hertfordshire AC could attract only 9 starters at Aston Hill, of which the fastest was Tom Thorneycroft's latest 24 hp Thorneycroft, from Basingstoke.

But it was Shelsley Walsh which caught the imagination then as now. After fairly strenuous attempts by the MAC to find a suitable course on private land, the slightly over 1,000 yards of Shelsley – rough, steep (1 in 6.26 at its worst), narrow and featuring a severe ess-bend – were secured and an excellent entry of 38 cars presented themselves. The event was well run, Mr Taylor's hospitality exemplary, and the domination of the Daimlers headed by Instone's was broken only by the results on formula (based on a calculation including time, horsepower and weight). In a run which must have tried the patience of all concerned, G. Patterson's 6 hp De Dion, painfully heavily laden, triumphed in a resounding 289.6s! Even contemporarily it appeared to be all too easy to overlook these 'important' formula competitions, which sometimes carried an event's supposedly premier award. Their continuation was assured for many years to come as they gave manufacturers and agents without fast cars a chance to win something, kept alive the ACGBI's desire to emphasis the serious, development side of motor sport, and brought organising clubs the entry fees of many who might not otherwise bother to enter.

Naturally, competitors in the formula competition had to have their cars weighed under controlled conditions. At Shelsley in 1905 that involved a trip to the public weighbridge at nearby Martley, although for some later meetings the RAC installed, at the considerable cost of around £100, a portable weighbridge at Shelsley itself. Everyone crammed their cars with as many passengers and as much ballast as possible and there were allegations that at least one competitor had fitted an extra fuel tank which mysteriously leaked water all the way to the start line, by which time it was totally empty and considerably lighter! Those liquid-cooled brakes fitted to 1981 Grand Prix cars would appear to have had a spiritual ancestor.

This kind of gamesmanship, which was also running to some furtive practising at some venues – no official practice was normally allowed – disgusted some of the old school, such as Charles Jarrott, but it was only to be expected. Growing popular interest in speed events made them more attractive still to the motor trade which sought to show the latest cars to best effect. Entry lists were dominated by 'works' or 'agents' entries of makes which could improve their sales prospects drastically with competition success, probably far more so than is possible today.

For the next two years, hill climbing was on an apparently-ever-rising wave of popularity. There were around 47 climbs on the British mainland in 1906, and another 7 in Ireland. The following year the figures had increased further to 64 and 8 respectively. Yet the seeds of a decline were apparent. Hitherto, only short-distance speed trials, the principal ones on seaside promenades, on northern beaches, and on Clipstone Drive, provided a true alternative in Britain, but when Brooklands opened in 1907, there was the option of track racing at last, at least for those in the Southern counties. Crowd control problems remained unsolved, and at Frome's Hill in May 1907, a Rex motorcycle, after setting BTD, hit a spectating labourer, apparently because the pulling-up area after the climb was too short. Fortunately, the man's injuries were not serious: merely bad luck on the driver concerned, but indicative of the conditions under which the less-well-regulated events were run. A run at Aston Hill in June 1906 by Frederick Coleman's formidable, if conventional-looking, White steam car was ruined by the intervention of a hay cart and then by some misguided officials. The tolerance of local authorities was also strained at times. For example, the police presence spoilt the competition at the North Hertfordshire AC's event at Gravel Hill, Hexton, in May 1906, while residents' complaints and police intervention put paid to Southsea MC's Kidd's Hill Climb in June 1907. In April of the same year, *The Autocar* actually went so far as to complain that there were simply too many hill climbs, suggesting that there should be no more than about six big 'open' events during the season. Scant notice was taken.

These were but straws in the wind. Overall, these were years of expansion and innovation, mostly of rather more serious character than the idea of running a four-in-hand for comparison at the Essex MC/South Hertfordshire AC Lippiett's Hill event in Epping Forest in April 1906, with unrecorded results, or the spectacle of a British Thomson-Houston petrol-electric bus competing at that all-too-lively Frome's Hill event in 1907. Progress must have been distinctly sedate since the bus was 8 *minutes* slower than the class-winning 40 hp Berliet, a large French car along Mercedes lines.

The innovations came thick and fast. Both Derby & District AC (Hill Cliff Lane) and the Nottingham AC (Oakamoor) ran climbs in May 1906 which instituted official practice runs to decide the all important handicap formula. Barely a month later the now almost universal classification by cubic capacity was instituted for the first time, not at one of the established major events, but at the North Eastern Automobile Association's meeting at Ragpath Slide, Lanchester. There were only 15 starters, but they contested 2.0-, 3.0-, 4.0-, 5.0- and 6.0-litre classes. Very steep and run in heavy rain, the climb was almost a washout, being re-run on 7 July before 1,500 well-disciplined spectators. G. S. Barwick's 30 hp Daimler won on both occasions.

Three notable new venues were used for the first time in the same year. The North East Lancashire AC were fortunate to gain the use of the spectacular 1 in 10 climb of Rivington Pike, Horwich, on the estate of Sir William Lever, on 25 July. A kilometre in length, and set at the Eastern edge of industrial Lancashire, the hill was a fast one and gave BTD to A. Birtwhistle's 35 hp Daimler in just 67.6s, from a 40/50 Wolseley. On 8 September it was the turn of the Manchester MC to hold a well-supported meeting on the famous Snake Pass, on the Glossop-to-Ashopton road across the Southern Pennines. This brought a new name to the fore, that of the wealthy Stockport textile engineer, Joseph Higginson, who set BTD in a rather unlikely 30/50 La Buire. This 7.5-litre, chain-drive, French car was conservative to the point of obsolescence, yet it was a winner in Higginson's skilful hands. Three weeks later a small meeting was held in Scotland, up the beautiful if bleak climb out of Glen Croe – Rest and be Thankful. A '60' Mercedes took the honours on a road which was to become a modern hill climb classic over forty years later. Tim Nicholson, who carried out such meticulous research for his book *Sprint* (David & Charles, 1969), points out that this upsurge of hill climb activity in the North, and particularly in the industrial Lancashire/Yorkshire region, was encouraged by the entrepreneurial and manufacturing establishment who were in sharp contrast to the powerful, and often still motorphobic, landed classes of the Home Counties.

Returning to the more important 'open' climbs of this busy period, the first major climb in 1906 was at Hertfordshire AC's 1,289 yard Frome's Hill, where the gradient steepened to a stiffish 1-in-7 maximum. The regulations allowed touring cars up to 35 hp, while specifically excluding steamers, and drew 53 starters. No times were published (as per ACGBI advice) but the seemingly inevitable 30/40 hp Daimler came off best, while the rather unexciting but deceptively effective 2.7 litre, side valve, 12/16 hp Talbot scored an early success in a distinguished career by tying for the formula award.

The first of the legendary Shelsley rain contrived to mar the enjoyment of the RAC's second annual visit, while the sum of £50 had been spent in easing the severity of the first bend after the start. Steam cars were not excluded this time and it was Frederick Coleman's White, rated at just 18 hp, climbing in 80.6s, which was fastest, beating a row of Daimlers headed by 1905 winner, Instone. Further interest centred on the defeat of Cecil Edge's 60 hp Napier, hampered by a three-speed gearbox, by the sliding 50 hp version of the intrepid Miss Dorothy Levitt. This doughty lady had made a memorable spectacle at the Brighton Speed Trials the previous year when she fought her 80 hp Napier down the course, sacrificing no feminity by wearing a tulle gown.

The ACGBI's own meeting at South Harting drew 64 starters, with classes determined by chassis price. Coleman won again, but this time from Miss Levitt's Napier and Edward Manville's Daimler. Instone followed this by climbing Aston Hill (Herts County AC) faster than G. D. Powell's Daimler and the Levitt Napier. Coleman was defeated by the hay cart! In this succession of events early existence of what we would now call the hill climb circus was already apparent. Apart from Coleman's White, the fastest cars still tended to be rather large, if effective, Edwardian fast tourers, which were well-made, but distinctly conservative in design. However, signs of smaller, more efficient, thing to come were apparent in the growing number of class wins and formula successes by the 12/16 Talbot, especially in the hands of works driver H. G. Day, and by Victor Riley's little 1,034 vee-twin Riley.

The ACGBI became the Royal Automobile Club (RAC) early in 1907 and got off to a good start by coming up with a simple formula suitable for adoption at hill climb and sprint events, classifying cars

Steam cars enjoyed a brief success and, despite a low horsepower rating, Frederick Coleman's White steamer provided formidable opposition to the big Daimlers in 1905/1906.
NATIONAL MOTOR MUSEUM

by RAC horsepower where the hp figure was arrived at by multiplying the square of the bore by the number of cylinders. This was of great assistance to clubs who had never really come up with a satisfactory basis for dividing the entry. Another RAC invention, Colonel Holden's handicapping formula, was also adopted by some clubs, perhaps unwisely, for it definitely strayed into the realms of higher mathematics.

Frome's Hill, hosting the RAC/Herefordshire AC 'Open' climb on 3 May 1907, drew a phenomenal 110 entries but the crowd problems effectively put paid to this venue. Among the more predictable class winners – Day, Riley, Holder's Daimler – was the 24/28 Métallurgique of Oscar Cüpper. On the way to becoming the premier Belgian make, this rapid 'big four', had such refinements as a steel frame and a live axle, and with its good performance and elegant Vanden Plas touring coachwork was to earn itself a minor vogue in Britain.

Two significant climbs took place on 10 July – bad clashes were not uncommon by this time – with the RAC and the Sussex County AC co-promoting at South Harting with support and 'The Yellow Trophy' from the yellow-covered *The Automotor Journal*, and the Manchester AC in command at Werneth Low, Hyde. Cecil Edge brought success to the by now Acton-based Napier concern in the former, driving one of the 60 hp, 7.7 litre six-cylinder cars to beat A. E. Harrison's Mercedes-based Ariel-Simplex and the still-formidable White steamer of Frederick Coleman. The spectacle was at least matched at Werneth Low where La Buire agent H. Holingdrake (35/50) defeated Birtwhistle's 8.5 litre 35/45 Daimler, only to be vanquished himself by the remarkable Higginson, wrestling the monstrous 80 hp (13.6 litre) version of the La Buire.

Despite rain at Shelsley Walsh, and despite a slight lengthening again of the course (by 8 yards to 1,000 yards), the RAC saw the course record slashed by over 10 seconds, to 67.2s, by the big 80 hp Berliet of J. E. Hutton, which was 2.2s clear of Cecil Edge's Napier. Winner on formula, still an award of major significance to the trade, was V. Stokes's 20/24 hp Talbot. This was truly the age of the great Edwardian fast touring car, and this was underlined at Aston Hill (Hertfordshire AC), where Guy Lewis's 120 hp Mercedes was victorious, and at Caerphilly, where the Cardiff MC held the first Welsh 'open' climb on 11 September. This time a 60 hp Napier was on top, with Sidney Smith at the wheel.

Opposition mounts

If 1907 had seen growing challenges to the popularity of hill climbing – popular hostility to events on public roads, growing concern by the motor trade at the cost of competing, Brooklands, internecine strife between the RAC and the Motor Union – it had still been something of a peak year. For the next few years the factors tending against the sport outweighed the enthusiasm of those who wanted to compete, organise or merely spectate. The decline was not dramatic at first. There were still some 52 events organised in 1908, plus 6 in Ireland. But in 1909 there were but 41, with another 5 on the Emerald Isle, and in 1910 the respective figures fell to a mere 23 and 3 – fewer than in 1904. Only in 1911 did the position improve, marginally, when 27 climbs, plus a lone event in Ireland, were held.

It was not just speed hill climbing, and the closely related road sprints, which suffered during this period. A slump in the demand for the products of the motor industry made itself felt in 1908, and manufacturer interest in motor sport declined. Even the Grand Prix itself was in abeyance between the 1908 event and the 1912 revival. Some of the richer motor sportsmen were also finding a new field to conquer, too – the budding science of powered flight, a fascination with drew away Rolls and Graham-White to name but two.

The most serious obstacle to hill climbing, though, remained the necessity to run most events on the public road. The opposition of public authorities and influential local landowners to this quasi-legal activity grew by the year. Hill climbing had true novelty value, but drew faster and more dangerous cars, and larger and seemingly chronically ill-disciplined crowds of spectators. The problem was especially acute in the South-Eastern counties where there were few rural fastnesses where the sport could continue without causing unrest among a rather conservative establishment. Needless to say, many of the sport's less-responsible adherents did nothing to enhance the sport's image. Too many sloppily-run events, the abuse of 'closed' events which could be run without an RAC permit and which sometimes had the character of 'open' meetings in everything but name, and illicit practising all served to fire up the opposition. Sixty years later, the supporters of road rallying faced depressingly similar problems.

The casualties came thick and fast, with the RAC, even then treading a wary course in an effort to present a truly responsible face to authority, doing little to campaign actively for the sport. Even in 1907, police activity or the threat of legal penalties, forced the abandonment of climbs at Kidd's Hill, Birdlip, Frome's Hill, and an event to be organised at an undisclosed Sussex County club venue.

While the RAC continued to organise long-distance reliability trials – a Thousand Miles Trial in 1908 – these were of decreasing interest to the competitively-minded, and the club's stance meant that no climb was run at South Harting that year. In May, the local rural district council forbade the Herefordshire AC the use of Frome's Hill. By 1909, the Motor Union, hitherto and active campaigner for the motoring interest, went so far as to say: '...hillclimbs have ceased to attract'. It is a fact that new sporting cars were now tending to be developed at Brooklands, but the Motor Union, which was itself to merge with the RAC in 1910, was exaggerating a little. Nevertheless, by 1910 the nadir had been reached. Noted venues including Aston Hill, Frome's, the Bexhill Speed Trials, South Harting, Rivington Pike, Caerphilly, Ragpath Slide, and Grindleford Bridge had been abandoned and such esoteric activities as flexibility trials, slow-driving contests, gymkhanas and speed-judging were all the rage. Then in the spring of that year, the RAC went so far as to ban the promotion of 'open' hill climbs on public roads unless the specific approval of the local authorities had been secured. The verdict of *The Motor* summed up the prevailing mood:

Until there can be discovered a hill so steep that fast speeds upon it on the part of touring cars are impossible, or some other practical means of limiting speed whilst encouraging progress can be found, the attitude of the RAC towards open hill-climbs on the high road is to be commended and supported to the full by all reasonable people. The prejudices of the public and of the local authorities against speed per se is, of course, unreasonable, and it will take time to prove to them that speed and dangerous driving are not synonymous terms. But whilst these objections are held by those able to inflict unfair penalties, motorists must be content to keep the facts about hill-climbing and speed capabilities of the modern motorcar to themselves unless special permission to close the highway for traffic can be obtained, or some exceptional opportunity such as the use of a hard foreshore presents itself. There can be no harm in an event confined to members of a single club, but, even in the case of such an event, care should be taken to prevent members from using extremely fast cars lent by makers and others for the purpose of scoring a win.

By June 1911, while surveying the parlous state of motor sport as a whole, *The Autocar* dolefully declared:

Hillclimbs have gradually dwindled until only a few remain... racing pure and simple has centred on Brooklands, with but one exception... the great Northern race meeting (Satburn).

In fact, during this rather depressing period there *was* some good hill climbing competition, especially in the North and at Shelsley Walsh, where the RAC had the great advantage of being able to run events on private land. Already a leading hill climb club, the Midland Automobile Club, became indisputably pre-eminent during these years. There was rapid technical development, too, with the large, rather rough running, and by no means advanced sporting cars which were epitomised by the big Daimlers, being overtaken by smaller, lighter machines which handled better and had the advantage of much more flexible and higher revving engines.

The Hertfordshire AC did run a major climb at Aston Hill on 11 July 1908, drawing a moderate 37 starters, and forbidding practising on pain of instant disqualification. Victory went to S. F. Edge's '60' Napier, a reminder perhaps that although Daimlers had an enviable record in hill climbing, the Napier marque was still the premier British sporting car in a wider context, with Edge still spearheading the company's marketing efforts. The 20 hp L-head-engined Vauxhall, designed by Laurence Pomeroy, and driven by Vauxhall's Joint Managing Director, Percy Kidner, won its class while J. Hedges' 15 hp Talbot won on handicap. Both these cars had distinguished themselves in the just-completed RAC Two Thousand Mile Trial, with the Vauxhall making the best performance. Pomeroy's Vauxhall, on which Harry Ricardo's influence was also marked, was revolutionary and was the forerunner of a truly great line. A 3 litre engine with a far less extreme bore/stroke ratio than was hitherto fashionable (91 x 120.6mm), a five bearing crankshaft, efficient gas flow and carefully lightened reciprocating parts permitted the extraction of a commendable 38 bhp at a remarkably high (for 1908) 2,500 rpm. Although the chassis design was far less radical, this free-revving power, allied to well-chosen gear ratios, made the car a formidable hill climber.

A fashionably-attired and attentive audience watch a 9 hp Vee-Twin Riley tackle Sun Rising Hill in 1908.
NATIONAL MOTOR MUSEUM

Not unexpectedly, Kidner was best on formula at Shelsley a fortnight later, but on this climb where sheer power has always been most desirable, the old order remained firmly on top. The record fell again after a brave and spectacular climb by H. C. Tryon, who clocked 65.4s with a '60' Napier. Tryon had been one of the support drivers for S. F. Edge the previous year during the so successful 24 hour record run at Brooklands. This time the Daimlers were beaten by the six-cylinder Napier, although both G. S. Barwick (68.2s) and Instone (71.4s) were now equipped with the ultimate 10½ litre, 58 hp version of the successful four-cylinder car.

The other major climb of the year was the Lancashire AC's event at Rivington Pike, where the timed section appears to have been somewhat shorter than that employed in 1906, but where an excellent entry of 49 contested classes differentiated by horsepower. There were 'open' and 'closed' handicaps and a significant innovation was the use of the best of two runs to decide the awards, as is now the normal pattern. Overall, it was another Napier benefit with W. Watson beating S. F. Edge by 48.6s to 49.0s, both in 60 hp cars. Edge had some compensation in taking a class win with a 40 hp car while other successes fell to Victor Riley's 12 hp, 2 litre Riley (still a vee-twin); C. Bertrand's little French 16/18 Zédel; Kidner's inevitable 20 hp Vauxhall; Cüpper's 26 hp Métallurgique; J. Dootson's 4½ litre, 25 hp Talbot; Albert Farnell's 30 hp Daimler, and Hollingdrake's 40 hp La Buire. There was nothing provincial about the entry at Rivington Pike.

Abbreviated as it was, the 1909 hill climb season was slow getting under way and although held on 26 June (only a month earlier than the previous year), it was Rivington Pike, this time co-promoted with the Manchester AC, which provided the first big encounter. The entry was not to the same standard this time but that detracts little from Joseph Higginson's BTD with the immense 80 hp La Buire. A Daimler, said to be a '30/40', was only third on time. One of the freakish, ultra long stroke (100 x 250mm), 1963cc, single-cylinder Sizaure-Naudin roadsters won its class, and so did Vauxhall factory driver A. J. Hancock, in outstanding fashion, with his 20 hp model; and the 40 hp Crossley of G. H. Woods. Designed by former Daimler designer, J. S. Critchley, these Gorton, Manchester-built cars were shaft-driven, but otherwise were conventional in design – very much in the Mercedes/Daimler tradition – and would be eclipsed by the A.V. Reeves-designed, 4 litre, 20 hp model of 1910.

A disappointingly small field of 23 cars presented themselves at Shelsley Walsh on 17 July, and although H. C. Holder achieved BTD in his 58 hp Daimler he was 3 seconds outside Tryon's record and was run fairly close by the increasingly formidable Vauxhalls of Hancock (20 hp) and Kidner (24 hp). The latter's more powerful version might have been challenging for victory if it had not been hampered by less-than-ideal gear ratios.

Dorothy Levitt was one of the first women to compete successfully in British motor sport. Here, this brave and accomplished young lady poses at the wheel of a 26 hp Napier at Brooklands.
NATIONAL MOTOR MUSEUM

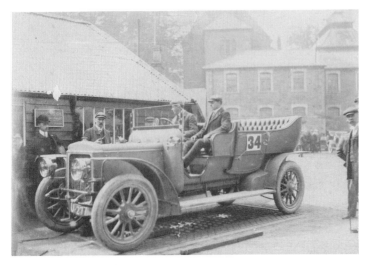

Strong, reliable and powerful, and a rather conservative design, the big Edwardian Daimlers were formidable hill climbers. This is a 45 hp example on the weighbridge at Pateley Bridge.
NATIONAL MOTOR MUSEUM

Christopher Bird raises the dust in spectacular fashion as he powers his 65 hp Napier to second BTD at Shelsley in 1911. The rear seat passenger looks terrified!
MIDLAND AUTOMOBILE CLUB

A rare success for one of the 60 hp, 1908 Grand Prix Austins was scored by Sir Hickman Bacon at the Lincolnshire AC's Syston Park climb while there was a truly local success at the Sheffield & District AC's meeting at Grindleford Bridge – victory for Percy Richardson in the by-no-means sporting 45 hp Sheffield-Simplex. Built at Tinsley, Sheffield, this refined and luxurious six-cylinder car was fitted with two gears only. Bottom was an emergency 'low' and the whole idea was to build a car which cut out the tricky-to-master chore of gear changing. This may have been the only occasion when a speed hill climb was won in top gear only!

On the same day as the Sheffield-Simplex 'demonstration', the mainstream of the hill climb fraternity converged on Aston Hill, where there were more class successes for Hancock and Kidner in the Vauxhalls. The Yorkshire AC organised a big 'open' climb at Pateley Bridge in September, but it poured with rain and proceedings were frequently interrupted to allow the passage of farm carts and flocks of sheep. The club had omitted to note that their chosen date was market day! Top honours went to W. Bradwell's 1908 TT Hutton (alias a four-cylinder Napier, running incognito because Napier did not want to tarnish their reputation for six-cylinder smoothness). Both here, where he beat Kidner, and at Aston Hill, where he dead-heated with him, H. F. Bayliss's 16/20 Sunbeam, an early example of Louis Coatalen's design work, was prominent and here was yet another increasingly efficient, moderate-sized, sporting tourer which was making its presence felt. In the same category was the fairly conventional, well-made and rather expensive 2.8 litre, 15 hp Star, built in Wolverhampton. Several class successes were gained during the year in the hands of Richard Lisle, but he gained greatest fame when he won the Wolverhampton & District AC 'stop and restart' climb at Harley Bank outright. It was said that the rugged Star attained an almost incredible 4,000 rpm during this performance, which rounded off a season which was by no means an outstanding one even if technical advances were striking among the smaller cars. One other noteworthy occurence during the year was the MAC's experiment in running a very small, closed to club, meeting in September at Shelsley. This was not repeated again until 1926.

Although a Hertfordshire County AC 'closed' meeting, won by a 40/50 Rolls-Royce from a trio of Vauxhalls, was run at Aston Hill in 1910, a lack of interest from the trade killed off the projected 'open' climb in September.

Biggest meetings in this depleted season were at the inevitable Shelsley Walsh on 2 July, and at Pateley Bridge on 17 September. Climbing up through the Worcestershire woods, H. C. Holder's 58 hp Daimler repeated his previous year's success, but his time of 69.0s was 0.6s further still from Tryon's record. Holder's nearest challenger was the 65 hp Napier of a relative newcomer, Christopher Bird, from whom Shelsley had much more to hear. In the efficiency stakes, otherwise the formula competition, Richard Lisle's 12 hp Star put one over the works Vauxhalls of Hancock and Kidner. The former's 20 hp model did go on to win outright at Pateley Bridge, a noteable success, even though there were but 25 starters, and a TT Hutton actually set BTD. In the minor climbs which still studded the calendar, regular wins were being recorded by both Bird and the Crossleys driven by G. H. Woods.

Although 1911 was to prove a turning point in the sport's fortunes, it was not always readily apparent. There was even a threat hanging over Shelsley Walsh, for the estate was up for sale.

However, the year had some bright spots, including a first event for cars at Kop Hill, near Princes Risborough. Previously used for motorcycles, the Motor Cycling Club held an event there for touring cars up to 30 hp, on 13 May, as an experiment. Although it was a rather low-key affair, with victory going to the rather unlikely vertical twin, 10/12 Phoenix of its instigator, J. van Hooydonck, the roughly ¾ mile climb clearly had potential. Although there was a maximum gradient of 1 in 5, there were no really sharp corners and the faster cars would definitely be spectacular over the loose macadam surface. Another new hill was found by the Sutton Coldfield AC, namely Coalport Hill, Ironbridge. This was a tricky one, steep with sharp bends in its 1,000 yards, and witnessed much bank-swiping. Bird's successful Napier won while Charles Jarrott's former riding mechanic, Cecil Bianchi, won a class on formula in a 12/14 hp Crossley.

Quite apart from the sale threat, Shelsley on 10 June was marred by the incursion of thoughtless spectators on the course. In those pre-Leslie Wilson days the organisation at Shelsley showed signs of strain at times, and this was one of them. There was an air of *déja vu* about the results, with Holder achieving his hat trick. He did it in style, for the 58 hp Daimler tore up in 62.2s – lopping 3.2s of the 1908 record – to round off Shelsley's Daimler era in the best possible way. Second and third fastest were Bird's Napier and Holder again, this time in a 40 hp Austin. Formula winner was Hancock, who thoroughly outwitted Frederick Lanchester's calculations with his efficient 16 hp Vauxhall. After a fair amount of argument, the Vauxhall's engine was stripped to confirm that the bore was indeed 90mm. This was one of the team of 3 litre cars prepared for the 1910 Prince Henry Trials – so important for the early development of what we now understand as the sports car – and was now developed to produce around 60 bhp at 2,800 rpm. The celebrated Mr Lanchester then withdrew with his equally celebrated rotary slide rule to concoct another formula!

Bereft of Rivington Pike, the Manchester AC found a new hill, Cornist Hall, for their July climb, but the new venue found very little favour. The road was over-cambered, and the close proximity to the finish of a right-angle bend and a farm gateway combined to make the whole thing pretty dicey. Under these conditions it was no surprise to see G. H. Woods excel with the effective 4 litre, 20 hp Crossley, a safe and manageable machine, but even he was beaten by the courageous Higginson, whose ascent in the 80/100 La Buire, snaking from side to side of the road, was terrifying to behold.

A month later, Higginson did it again at Pateley Bridge where his arch-rival Woods was disqualified for failing to weigh in. Often the 'bridesmaid', Woods had to accept second once again, this time to Bird's Napier, at Beacon Hill, Woodhouse Eaves, on 2 September. This, too, was a new hill, promoted by the Leicestershire AC, as an East Midlands replacement for the old Kettleby venue. Measuring 1,433 yards, the hill was popular, being fair and lacking in the freakish features which were frowned upon by competitors.

The year ended with the last of the big Edwardians – Bird's Napier, Higginson's La Buire, Holder's Daimler – all still holding their own against the new generation of smaller, more effecient, and more truly sporting machinery from Vauxhall, Talbot, Sunbeam, Crossley, Star and Calthorpe. But it was with the latter type of car that technical development was being concentrated, and where the manufacturer interest was highest. Therein lay the future.

The Cyclecar Emerges

Motor sport as a whole was strongly on the upturn during the last three years before the great 1914-18 conflict turned minds to grimmer things. The Grand Prix was revived in 1912 and international motor racing attained a magnificent climax at Lyons in July 1914, when one of the all-time great Grands Prix took place just a few weeks before the outbreak of the First World War. At a lesser level, but still arousing considerable international publicity and manufacterer interest, Voiturette (Coupe de l'Auto) and even cyclecar racing took off as design trends moved away from the early racing monsters and encouraged the efficient employment of modestly sized engines.

In Britain, the success of the Wolverhampton-based Sunbeams in the (Coupe de l'Auto) race of 1912 was one significant factor in the stimulation of new interest in motor sport. Manufacturer participation, spearheaded by Vauxhall, Sunbeam and Talbot – all builders of high-quality, medium-sized cars – increased as market conditions improved. The development of practical, if still rather expensive, light cars by Singer, Rover, Riley, Humber and many more aspiring manufacturers, made motoring less remote to more people. Then in the last years of the Edwardian era the cyclecar, crude and primitive though so many were, finally brought a sort of motorcar within reach of at least some of the masses. Brooklands, too, was gaining in stature, and overall, the motorcar attained a degree of maturity.

In the sphere of hill climbing, more manufacturers joined battle – there were perhaps twenty involved by 1913, double the number of 1910 – and although not all the old complaints were dead, slightly more and generally better-organised meetings were held. The upsurge was not dramatic. There were probably 33 'organised' hill climb events in 1912, yet the total was only some 25 (plus one in Ireland) the following year, while 32 (and 2 Irish meetings) were held before the hostilities called a halt at the end of August 1914. The meetings that were held included a higher percentage of 'open' events than in recent years, and organisers gradually abandoned the rather unconvincing insistence that hill climbs were all about proving the efficiency of touring cars. This element remained, but it was secondary to the theme of *competition* between machinery modified, if not built, for speed. A significant step was taken by the RAC in 1913 in waiving the rule that cars had to ascend Shelsley fully laden, although the formula event remained for the benefit of those who could not compete on sheer speed. While more -moderately-sized sporting cars, with Austro-Daimler, Arrol-Johnston, Straker-Squire and DFP among them joined the pacesetters from Luton, Wolverhampton and North Kensington in providing the mounts for the most successful drivers, the cyclecar began to make itself felt: not perhaps in 1912, but certainly the following year and in 1914, and especially in the form of the three-wheeled Morgan and the four-wheeled GN of Messrs Godfrey and Nash, the cyclecar became a force to consider on the hills. Handleability and the best use of moderate power had gradually prevailed over brute engine size but now new possibilities had opened up. The importance of a high power-to-weight ratio was becoming apparent.

Much of this was still in the future when the 1912 season opened, but the mood was optimistic, with competition returning to both Aston Hill and to Rivington Pike. The Essex MC's 'closed' affair at Aston Hill was modest enough with Pearce-Jones's 1910 Vauxhall 'Prince Henry' team car easily defeating A. P. Howard's 15.9 hp Calthorpe. A cyclecar class was introduced as an experiment but there were no takers. There was nothing parochial about the Lancashire AC/Manchester AC return to Rivington Pike, though. Cars were still being disqualified for not being standard enough, and there were many who still felt that the appearance of racing cars would discourage more than it would attract, yet overall battle was rejoined by Higginson's mighty La Buire and Woods's deceptively rapid 20 hp Crossley. The Stockport driver, Higginson, held the upper hand with a 50.8s run and these two began a season of duels with the honours shared evenly. Although they were not always in direct competition, Woods set BTD at Aston Hill, Caerphilly, Beacon Hill, Heydon Bridge (twice), Ambergate, Clipstone Drive (Sprint), and Styal Kop, while Higginson was victorious at Rivington Pike, Shelsley Walsh, Heyden Bridge, Pateley Bridge and Hazlewood. This was long before there were any hill climb championships of course, but had there been, then these two would have fought hard for top honours that year.

There were still public relations problems to be overcome, and especially in the South-Eastern Counties. The Kent police caused the cancellation of the Kent AC's meeting at Yorks Hill, Sevenoaks.

On the other hand, the Hertfordshire County & Aero Club were given clearance to go ahead with the first 'open' event at Aston Hill since 1909. There was much eager anticipation before this major meeting on 8 June, but in the meantime a newcomer in an unfamiliar make of car had netted a modest success at the MCC's closed climb at Aston Rowant in Buckinghamshire. The car was the French DFP, a well-made 2 litre car with a respectable 55 mph available from a soundly-designed four-cylinder engine which would run up to 2,500 rpm. It was driven by Walter Owen Bentley, who, with his brother 'H M', held the British agency for the car. 'W O' had already developed the little 10/15 hp machine to the point were 70 mph was now available. Bentley was to score several successes with the marque DFP in 1913/14 and in the latter year pioneered the use of aluminium alloy pistons.

There were just 46 actual starters at Aston Hill and a time of 58.6s over the now one-kilometre timed distance was enough to give Woods BTD over a pair of the superb 5.8 litre, single overhead camshaft, 27/80 'Prince Henry' Austro-Daimlers – arguably the best of all the Edwardian sporting tourers. It may have been an 'open' meeting, but it wasn't all totally serious: Bentley, for one, succeeded in winning his class accompanied by his excited 'joy-riding' financée, Leonie! (even a competitor as serious as Lisle once ascended Shelsley 'co-driven' by his large dog). Other class successes fell to the Austro-Daimlers, the curious friction-drive GWK (with rear-mounted, vertical twin Coventry-Simplex engine) cyclecar of C. M. Keiller, R. S. Mitchell's 15 hp Straker-Squire, and the inevitable H. G. Day (Talbot 12).

Joseph Higginson gave the Shelsley Walsh spectators a thrill when he wrestled the 13,619cc La Buire up the already famous hill (whose future seemed secure once more) in 68.8s – not fast enough to beat Holder's record, but a second faster than his nearest challenger, O. Tholander's 27/80 Austro-Daimler. Holder had to be content with third in the 40 hp Austin, while the Formula of Merit fell to Bianchi's successful Crossley.

Glorious weather and a large, fashionably attired crowd graced the South Wales AC/Cardiff MC 'open' at Caerphilly, and they saw Woods defeat F. T. Burgess's 15.9 hp Calthorpe by 2.2s, while another of the intrepid lady competitors who were beginning to appear in this male-dominated sport, Miss Laura Starkey, won a closed class with a 12/16 Sunbeam.

Although one wonders at the strict legality of it, there is one example of a local authority formally closing a road for a speed hill climb during this period, and only one. This unique event was the Leicestershire AC's climb at Beacon Hil, Woodhouse Eaves, and was interesting in several ways. For one thing it was probably the first occasion when a 'historic' class was run in a speed event. 'Veteran' was the term used, and to be eligible cars had to be but four years old. Development was rapid indeed in those years. The meeting also gave a graphic demonstration of the pitch of development attained by the Crossley of G. H. Woods. His 59.6s climb beat Christopher Bird's Coupe de l'Auto Sunbeam, albeit by only 0.4s, and Louis Coatalen in the actual Coupe-winning car. There was another class win too for Laura Starkey. The year virtually concluded with another Woods win at the much-used Manchester AC, Heyden Bridge climb (on the Woodhead to Huddersfield road in the Pennines). This time his task was not so hard, because Higginson's La Buire departed from the fray in suitably spectacular fashion with a seized piston.

In sharp contrast to these truly competitive goings on, the newly established journal *The Light Car and Cyclecar* promoted a climb of the 'freak' (and all but unclimbable) Alms Hill, Stonor, Henley, in the depths of the January winter. This was in the old tradition of a proving trial rather than a speed competition, and as such has little bearing on the history of the speed hill climb. It was, however, a true ancestor of the modern sporting trial.

Influenced by the noticeable trend towards permitting overtly racing cars into hill climbs, some showing marked Brooklands track-racing characteristics, and the plethora of new light cars and cyclecars (around 70 different makes of cyclecar were in production of some sort in 1912/13), the 1913 season was a most exciting one. The Lancashire AC had the honour of staging the first major event, on Waddington Fells, near Clitheroe, and opted to divide the entries by cubic capacity. The rather curious limits were at 1,639cc, 2,458cc and 3,769cc, with a further category for cyclecars. Since the latter was won on time and formula by a 10/12 hp Calthorpe, the definition of cyclecar appears to have been somewhat broad. The day was wet but there was plenty of excitement among the 27 entries in the 'open' competition, climaxing in the dramatic, sliding BTD from Joseph Higginson. He beat Cecil Bianchi's 15 hp Crossley for the honour but he was not driving the old La Buire. Out to crack the record at Shelsley, above all else, Higginson obtained from Vauxhall, a prototype Pomeroy-designed car which was the forerunner of the famed 30/98. A logical progression from the refined lines of Edwardian sports tourers which had stemmed from the 3 litre 'Prince Henry' cars, this lightened sprint car was fitted with a new 98 x 150mm, 4½ litre engine and was already a formidable performer.

Thanks to the efforts of Woods and Bianchi, among others, the Crossley marque had gained a fair reputation for sporting characteristics and a tuned version of the side-valve, 2.6 litre '15' was actually named the Shelsley Model in honour of Crossley's hill climb exploits – the first but by no means the last time that that celebrated hill was chosen for a model name. Nevertheless, a Crossley, even a 20/25 model in Bianchi's capable hands, was no match for the new Vauxhall. Watched by a crowd which included the famed singer Dame Nellie Melba, the Hertfordshire AC's climb at Aston Hill drew a good 48-car entry. The record fell to a 4½ litre Vauxhall – this time a works car in the hands of A. J. Hancock.

*Typical Edwardian garden
party atmosphere. A Crossley
(right) is prominent in this
scene at Aston Hill in 1913.*
NATIONAL MOTOR MUSEUM

*Joseph Higginson starts his
run to a 55.2s Shelsley Walsh
course record on 7 June 1913,
in his Pomeroy-designed
Vauxhall prototype, which was
the direct ancestor of so many
fine sporting cars. Passengers
were no longer obligatory.*
MIDLAND AUTOMOBILE CLUB

*V. A. Barber-Lomax handles
his 20 hp Vauxhall with aplomb
at Shelsley in 1913.*
NATIONAL MOTOR MUSEUM

A superb entry was the reward for the RAC's decision to waive the necessity of running fully-laden cars at Shelsley Walsh on 7 June. On a day when contemporaries noted the advances in roadholding and driving skill, the course record fell no fewer than seven times, although these figures are not strictly comparable with what went before – but then nor were the cars. When the dust had settled Higginson had indeed achieved his ambition with the new Vauxhall. The new record stood at 55.2s, a sobering contrast to the 67.6s recorded by H. C. Ansell's dated 58 hp Daimler, which was the runner-up in the same class. Nearest to Higginson, though, was Talbot works driver Leslie Hands in the very special development 25 hp car (101 x 140 mm engine developing around 130 bhp at 3,500 rpm, in a 12 hp chassis) which was similar to the Brooklands record car of Percy Lambert. Hands managed 57.2s, just 1.2s less than Christopher Bird's big 25/30 Sunbeam, and with Hancock's Vauxhall a lowly fourth. Apart from the Daimler, longer memories were also evoked by A. W. Tate's 1908 chain-drive 60 hp Mercedes. This took charge and bulldozed about 10 yards of iron railings with little noticeable effect on the Mercedes but a lot on the fence! Despite the loss of a hub cap which was innovatively replaced by a chunk of bread to separate oil and dust, the old car took a second climb, living evidence of the progress in automobile design in just five years.

A fortnight later many of the same competitors had made their way down to Caerphilly, where Hancock gained some recompense with a 64.6s BTD. Perhaps he was a little fortunate for Hands managed 73.4s with the handicap of a burst tyre. Mrs W. G. Morel distinguished herself with a pair of class wins in a 26/60 Métallurgique, but William Morris did not distinguish himself with a slow ascent in his 10 hp Morris Oxford.

The growing interest in cyclecars manifested itself in the Cyclecar Club's first climb at South Harting (in use for the first time since 1907) on 28 June. This club, the forerunner of the Junior Car Club and the modern British Automobile Racing Club, began its long association with hill climbing shortly after the foundation of the club. Fastest with 93.4s was the single-seater Morgan three-wheeler of A.W. Lambert. Among the class winners were the single-cylinder, air-cooled Chota, designed and

By 1913 new makes of sporting cars were taking over: this is a 12/16 hp Sunbeam at Caerphilly.
NATIONAL MOTOR MUSEUM

built by J. F. Buckingham; the hero of the Amiens Cyclecar Grand Prix and future travel writer, W. G. McMinnies (Morgan); and the practical vee-twin GN of Archie Frazer Nash. Among those defeated by the latter was a former racing cyclist called Lionel Martin, driving a 10 hp Singer in those pre-Aston Martin days.

Returning to the mainstream of 1913 hill climbing, the now traditional climb at Pateley Bridge, promoted by the Yorkshire AC, brought another Vauxhall versus Talbot battle, more cars running in racing trim, and another new record. Only an enforced delay, while a flock of sheep passed by, interrupted a fine day's sport. Hands, this time driving Lambert's Brooklands Talbot, set BTD from Higginson, who was unlucky to suffer a blown tyre. Hands was also third, now driving Day's usual 25 hp Talbot.

It had been a good year but still the sport had its darker side. The Leicestershire AC's Beacon Hill meeting in July was marred by uncontrolled (uncontrollable?) crowds and a horrifying accident when Higginson, at around 60 mph, was confronted by an old lady wandering about on the road. He spun wildly, sending the errant pedestrian head over heels, although happily without serious injury. All the while the Vauxhall's gyrations were watched by a fascinated young boy called Raymond Mays. From near-tragedy to farce: a non-competing charabanc ground to a hopeless halt on the hill and demanded a (leisurely) full-scale service before vehicle and equally mulish driver could be persuaded to the top.

Talbot was another make to come to the fore before the outbreak of war in 1914. Leslie Hands' winning margin here at Caerphilly in his formidable 25/50 hp model was a resounding 5.4s.
NATIONAL MOTOR MUSEUM

Through all this Percy Lambert's Talbot scored a notable BTD (49s) with Higginson (not on his gyratory run) on 51.4s and Woods's Crossley 10 seconds slower. Such is progress.

The year had also seen a resumption of hill climbing in Ireland after a year's gap, when the Irish section of the Society of Motor Manufacturers and Traders (SMMT) held an event up 1⅛ miles of Craigantlet Hill, near Belfast. Future tractor manufacturer Harry Ferguson (25 hp Vauxhall) won his first event on a hill which still hosts a round of Britain's premier RAC Championship.

In that final summer of the Edwardian age, that of 1914, the emphasis in hill climbing swung towards the light car and the even more humble cyclecar. The popularity of the new breed of small cars prompted the RAC to hold its first road event since 1908, purely for light cars, and incorporating 11 timed climbs. Of these, 7 went to Westall's 10 hp, four-cylinder AC, and 4 to Rollason's 10 hp Singer. There was a cyclecar class again at Aston Hill on 16 May, where Lionel Martin's familiar Singer was beaten by 3.8s by J. F. Buckingham's Buckingham (née Chota), which now boasted a 12 hp, belt-drive vee-twin engine to power just 6¾ cwt of motorcar. This Coventry-built car never achieved the lasting success of GN or Morgan, but it was a formidable performer in hill climbs. BTD overall went to Leslie Hands whose works Talbot 25/50 took professionalism forward another step by arriving in a transporter van. This works Talbot was actually the ultimate development of this well-designed side-valve, four-cylinder line, featuring a lengthened 150mm stroke.

The Inter-Varsity Hill Climb at Kop, which became something of an institution in post-war years, had exceedingly modest beginnings on 23 May, when a mere 9 cars competed against each other on the wet and slippery chalk surface. That T. S. Coates' 10 hp Singer defeated J. W. Read's ex-Hancock 25 hp Vauxhall says a lot for the conditions and for Coates' driving, and perhaps for Read's caution.

Talbot was again in the ascendant at Waddington Pike, held the same day, with Hands taking BTD (46s) and H. G. Day's 20/30 winning on formula. Buckingham was best on both time and formula in the cyclecar category and there was an early success in his class for the burly Humphrey Cook in an equally burly 120 hp Isotta-Fraschini.

The formidable 25/50 Talbot was really into a winning streak, for Hands lifted another important BTD at Caerphilly, where his 66.6s winning climb was 5.4s faster than R. S. Mitchell's 15/20 Straker-Squire, which was often prominent, if unable to match the racing 4½ litre cars. This situation repeated itself when crowds at the Leicestershire AC's Beacon Hill event were treated to the sight of no less than Algy Lee-Guinness, newly returned from Lyons, with a pukka twin ohc Grand Prix team Sunbeam, dispose of Roy Fedden's 15/20 Straker-Squire to the tune of nearly 10 seconds.

Cyclecar development was proceeding apace and the evidence was clear when the Light Car Club returned to South Harting on 18 July. The fastest time came down to 85s, with the honour falling to J. V. Carden's Teddington-built Carden, a single-seater with rear-mounted, single-cylinder engine. Carden was 5.8s swifter than another single-seater, a new GN driven by Archie Frazer Nash. This was 'Kim', designed as a pure racing car for the projected Dangerfield Trophy in the Isle of Man, which

In 1913 Crossley became the first manufacturer to name a car after a British hill climb. This is a Crossley Shelsley Model, pictured at Shelsley.
NATIONAL MOTOR MUSEUM

Although rare in Britain, the Alpen Type Austro-Daimler was a fine example of a superior Edwardian sporting car, with a first class hill climbing performance. This photograph was taken during the 1914 Austrian Alpine Trials on the Turracherhöhe, just before Britain's Teutonic opposition became altogether more serious.
NATIONAL MOTOR MUSEUM

never took place because of the outbreak of war. Frazer Nash employed the familiar GN cyclecar ash frame, complete with wire and bobbin steering. The vee-twin, 1,086cc GN power unit benefitted from a more robust crankshaft and crankcase, and brass rather than bronze cylinder heads. Drive was through a production-type belt transmission. Weight of the whole car was pared to the absolute minimum. The car's most striking feature was the exceptionally narrow single-seater bodywork. Almost a parody of contemporary Brooklands track cars such as Lambert's Talbot, this sharp-prowed lightweight's appearance was startling. Its potential was barely tapped in 1914, but it and the Carden clearly showed what could be done with the new breed of cyclecar.

There were many other small events that summer as the war clouds gathered. Events often ran in a very informal manner for every motor sport event was no longer a big occasion, such was the sport's growth. The cyclecars were showing a performance which belied their mechanical crudity. A typical example was the Easter Monday climb held by the motorcycle-minded Westmorland MCC, up the steep Greyhound hill. Running to this day under the west coast main railway line, to the east of Kendal, this five-eighths of a mile climb with 1 in 8 gradient, failed to daunt Buckingham – whose formidable vehicle could even defeat a GP Morgan on occasion.

Sadly, with young men concerned now with enlisting rather than racing cars, there were but 4 car entries for the Coventry & Warwickshire MC's meeting at Style Kop (near Rugeley and not to be confused with the better known Kop Hill, near Princes Risborough). William Morris took a rather empty win in his 10 hp Morris Oxford. Other meetings, including Shelsley, were naturally cancelled and, as Britain went to war, hill climbing became just a memory to savour and a hope for the future in the grim days to come.

CHAPTER TWO

AN EARLY VINTAGE
(1919-1925)

THE period between the resumption of motor sport in 1919 and the abrupt end to public road hill climbing in 1925 has been referred to as a Golden Age. It was certainly exciting: technical developments continued apace, and all the while the sport's public – competitors and spectators – increased sharply. Manufacturers continued to use the sport to prove and develop their latest machinery, and more particularly to gain kudos and resulting sales.

On the other hand, a true Golden Age surely implies a mature prosperity amid a sense of profound security. These hectic years did not have that. The vast majority of hill climbs still took place on the public road. Any of these events, local affairs or the major fixtures at Kop, South Harting, Aston Hill, Spread Eagle or Sutton Bank alike, could have been halted at a stroke if too many complaints were lodged with the local Watch Committees of the Constabulary. Organisers usually came to informal agreements with the local Chief Constable for his officers to help to regulate proceedings although the roads remained nominally open. And more than once there was the proverbial awkward and uncompromising farmer, accompanied by stock or hay cart, who would insist on his right of passage to prove that the road was open! And since there remained an overall open road speed limit of 20 mph in force until 1926, the constables were not encouraged to bring their stop watches with them.

Worse still, the increasingly large crowds of spectators could only be encouraged and cajoled into avoiding standing in dangerous places and even wandering around on the road in close proximity to speeding cars. They could not be *ordered* off the public highway. That was the Sword of Damocles which hung by a thread over the sport until a major controversy blew up after a serious incident involving spectators. On 28 March 1925 the thread snapped and an era ended virtually overnight.

There were other signs of immaturity too. Organisation was still patchy. There was little consistency in the regulations as issued for successive events, and by 1923 the crowded hill climb and sprint calendar was chaotic. Clashing events were legion. Large entry lists were garnered for some meetings while others were cancelled through lack of entries, as often as not through poor co-ordination and amateurishness in its worst sense. Trade competitors became increasingly frustrated at risking their commercial investments for no direct material return at meetings run by amateurs, where the trade entries pulled in the crowds, yet were sometimes regarded by the 'gentlemen' as having an unfair advantage. Conversely, the private club members were just as bitter at entering for a 'closed' meeting only to find some works driver cleaning up all the awards after joining the organising club for the occasion. As we shall see there were serious attempts to resolve this problem but it was not solved by regulation.

No, this was no Golden Age, but it was an exciting, rather wild, and often highly spectacular adolescence for hill climbing. Crowds of 4,000 to 5,000 regularly made their way to the fairly out-of-the-way venues where the new breed of stars – Archie Frazer-Nash (he was known as plain Archie Nash before the War), Malcolm Campbell, George Bedford, Raymond Mays, John Joyce, Mathew Park, Cyril Paul and Humphrey Cook – were ascending faster and faster in their increasingly specialised cars. Certainly the rather tedious formula events remained on the day's card, contested by such worthy vehicles as Austin 20s, Humber 8/18s, Morris Cowleys and their often less worthy commercial competitors. But it was the 'racers' which everyone really came to see, and as these few short years passed, the pace quickened noticeably.

Of course, this was not entirely new. After the pre-First World War revival around 1911/12, hill climbing became far less the preserve of lightened sporting tourers and far more the province, at least where Best Time of Day was concerned, of racing machinery from companies such as Sunbeam, Talbot, and Vauxhall. Yet these were cars which were not so very different from sporting cars for the open road. After all, they were usually developed for competition over long distances over poor road surfaces. Yet by the last couple of years before hostilities a far more highly developed more specialised machine was evolving. Perhaps the stimulus was the presence of Brooklands which encouraged high speeds, wind-cheating bodywork and the pursuit of narrower objectives. Then again, the cyclecar boom concentrated other fertile minds into devising drastic ways of extracting the maximum performance potential from (literally) very little. Archie Frazer-Nash's 'Kim' was the obvious pioneer; a single-seater, a pure sprint car with excellent acceleration permitted by light weight and a highly tuned, if small, engine.

In many ways the 1919 to 1925 era was just an extension to the last pre-1914 years, with more experience and science being enlisted into preparing ever more potent sprint machinery. Certainly, in ultimate terms a Grand Prix or Indianapolis Sunbeam or TT Vauxhall usually had the edge over the purpose-built sprint cars with their basically prosaic origins and generally under 1500cc power units, but it was becoming a very close thing by 1923/24.

What was not keeping pace with engine and indeed chassis development was either road surfaces or tyre performance. Towards the end of this remarkable era the spectacle of the fastest cars bucking and sliding their way up the untarred and sometimes fairly rough hills was truly frightening, the more so as narrow, high pressure, beaded-edge tyres increasingly frequently burst under the strain, with spectacular though happily never fatal results.

A measure of the advances in sprint car design during these years is most graphically represented by the drastic reduction in the record times for the most singular hill climb of all. This was the Brooklands Test Hill. It was never used for a formal hill climb event, although it was included in some other milder forms of non-racing competition at the busy Weybridge track, but the honour of holding the record carried much prestige and provided a reliable benchmark for what was achieveable in terms of a straight, uphill burst.

This approximately 350 feet long, paved, steep gradient (1 in 4 maximum), had been built in 1909 for the benefit of the motor industry's testers. The first post-Armistice record for the Test Hill fell in September 1920, to Major Pearce-Jones, driving a 30/98 Vauxhall in 9.66s, an average speed of 24.86 mph. By the end of 1925 that figure had been slashed to 7.691s, 31.227 mph, by Archie Frazer-Nash. In the meantime others such as Bertie Kensington-Moir (Straker-Squire and Aston Martin), John Joyce (AC), Frank Halford (Aston Martin) and L. A. Cushman (Frazer Nash) had all held the honour, but none more often than the indefatigable AFN, who smashed the record six times in all. During just five years over 20 per cent of that rapid enough 1920 time of Pearce-Jones's had been lopped off – a fair measure of the progress in achieving high power-to-weight ratios, allied to excellent traction and effective gearing.

The times set on the Brooklands Test Hill also serve to emphasise the technical development which was accomplished specifically on the light car in the early nineteen-twenties. The cyclecar boom survived into the postwar mood of euphoria but the harsh economic realities of 1920/21, weariness with the crudity and discomfort of these primitive machines, and the arrival of the altogether more sophisticated Austin Seven in 1922 soon saw the bottom drop out of the market for the cyclecar. The best of the breed, the GN (although both Godfrey and Frazer-Nash left the firm in 1922) and the three-wheeled Morgan kept going. The latter with a unique appeal, survived quite strongly right up to and even after the 1939-45 War. For the less sporting-minded, small car motoring no longer demanded actual physical hardship, and the growing affordability of habitable light cars ensured a growing market. When the Government imposed an annual horse power tax (in the 1920 Finance Act) calculated on the RAC Formula, the incentive to develop better light cars was further heightened. In 1921, with the cyclecar past its peak of popularity, an incredible 71 makes exhibited under-1,500cc cars at the Olympia Motor Show. Alas, many would not survive for long.

Similarly, in the competition field the emphasis on the smaller car, and more especially on the under-1,500cc 'Light Car' grew strongly. Manufacturers, eager to prove the quality of their offerings, were keen to contest suitable events. The French revived the Voiturette category in 1920, at Le Mans, not for 3-litre cars as hitherto, but for 1,400cc machines initially, and for 1500s in later years. At home, the Cyclecar Club changed its name in 1919 to the Junior Car Club, reflecting a broader sphere of interest, and was becoming a major force, successfully promoting England's first International long-distance race: the 200 miles Race at Brooklands, in October 1921, for under 1,500cc cars. Moreover, the third and most vigorous of the 'big three' motoring journals, *The Light Car and Cycle Car*, founded as such in 1913, concentrated wholly on the under 1500s.

In hill climb events, an up-to-1500cc class became almost universal, even when other divisions were still more frequently made into 'open', 'closed', 'touring', 'racing', 'time', and 'formula' categories. Often taking advantage of the availability of proprietary engines – British Anzani and Coventry-Simplex, for example – a whole new breed of light, sporting cars appeared. By 1921/22 the term 'sports car' came into increasingly common usage to describe those cars whose performance took priority over other considerations. Most of these cars were not in the running for Best Time of the Day at hill climbs, but they became increasingly common among the supporting cast of enthusiastic club-men. The 10hp Calthorpe, Hillman Speed Model, Riley 11/40 Redwing, 10/30, 10/40 and 12/50 Alvis, side-valve Aston Martin and four-cylinder Frazer Nash were typical of the breed. While it conformed to the type in terms of size and purpose, the Type 13 Brescia Bugatti, which was complex, formidable and distinctly expensive, was really in a category of its own.

The 16-valve Bugattis were doubly unusual for if we may discount the abortive Crossley-Bugatti project, they were about the only non-British make to excel in the hill climbs of this period. Cars built in the 'enemy' countries of 1914-18 were specifically excluded from British events, so that ruled out Austro-Daimler and Mercedes for example. Since Molsheim is in Alscace, disputed territory between France and Germany for decades, even the Bugattis became 'friendly' only through the terms of the November 1918 Armistice! American cars, and especially the fairly light, cheap fours as exemplified by the Hudson Essex, held a brief vogue thanks to their relatively large, torquey engine and giving value for money. But their popularity waned as they ceased to be at all competitive against more sophisticated British cars, and when the imposition of the McKenna Duties effectively raised the prices in Britain of American cars, interest in them faded away. Most important of all, though, was the simple fact that there were so many *good* British sporting cars available during the nineteen-twenties – it was the Vintage era after all – that there was little incentive to look further afield for a competitive car at a reasonable price.

This significant era began tamely enough, in 1919 when the first few post-war hill climbs were held. Many enthusiasts were keen to begin where they had left off in 1914 but manufacturers were less eager. The priority was to switch back from wartime activity to private car production, to be ready to meet a terrific demand for new cars, and especially cheap ones, which had been damned up for so long. In these circumstances competition was just an unwelcome complication which diverted money and effort. Only when the commercial going became tougher in 1920/21 did the need for publicity and technical development through competition become most urgent once again. The Society of Motor Manufacturers and Traders (SMMT) was almost unanimously opposed to supporting the resumption of motor sport in 1919/20. Naturally, this reasoning did not apply to those men who were car enthusiasts first and motor manufacturers second, men like Archie Frazer-Nash, H. O. Godfrey, W. C. Bentley, and Lionel Martin. The first two were still further improving their successful GN Cyclecar, whereas Bentley and Martin were making only their first tentative steps as car makers.

The resumption began very modestly on 14 June 1919, when the Middlesex County AC ran a small hill climb at Hand Post Hill. F. H. W. Church's Vauxhall, apparently one of the extremely rare 1914 30/98 models, took a fairly predictable BTD in 50s, which was 15s less than the winner of the 1,500cc category, S. J. Prevost's Morris Cowley.

It was very different when the newly renamed Junior Car Club returned to South Harting, for this was one of the highlights of the rather sparse 1919 motor sporting year, generating much publicity and interest, despite its nominally 'closed' status. The entry from the light car and cyclecar exponents for whom the meeting catered was large. But even with a 1,500cc capacity limit the JCC Committee felt that it was prudent not to publish times in case public opinion set against the sport as it had threatened to do at times before the war. Much to the Committee's consternation and embarrassment, *The Motor* printed the times anyway! Lack of driving experience was all too noticeable at this meeting. The old hands were obviously rusty after the long lay-off while a whole new generation were eagerly, if not as yet skilfully, pitting themselves in competition for the first time. Bad starts and clumsy gearchanges were as rife as the military titles prefixing the drivers' names.

The day belonged to the GN marque, and especially to Captain Archie Frazer-Nash. He began by leading a trio of production GNs to win the 'touring' cyclecar division. Other 'touring' successes fell to Wadham's 9.5 hp Standard (on formula) and Stead's 10 hp four-cylinder AC, but the real excitement came with the racing cars. Looking much the same as it had in 1914, complete with the narrow, tapered aluminium body, 'Kim' was victorious in Frazer-Nash's hands. In fact, although the car retained the 1086cc vee-twin engine in a basically production-type chassis, much development had already taken place. The old belt transmission had given way to the chain and dog principle which was to serve the much more sophisticated Frazer Nashes so well for so long. The suspension was newly modified too, although the principle of the quarter-elliptic springing was retained. Runner-up to AFN was none other than his business partner, Ron Godfrey, who was campaigning one of the latest GN Vitesse models. This was the recipe as before but with less weight (about 7½ cwt) and even fewer creature comforts than the touring Légère version. Hard on Godfrey's heels came the first representative of the new order of sporting light cars, Hillman works driver George Bedford in the first of the neat, polished aluminium-bodied, four-cylinder, side-valve-engined, Speed Models; and Captain Coates in a 10 hp Singer that had been built for the 1914 Tourist Trophy which was never held.

Although there were several significant speed trials held that summer, there were only two more hill climbs of note. Style Kop had been the venue for the last pre-war hill climb and with the Sutton Coldfield & Mid-Warwickshire AC (another name change) in charge, saw one of the first post-war events. Both Godfrey and H. Underwood's 10 hp Calthorpe (another of the well-made, if conventional four-cylinder, side-valve-engined models which were capable of effective performance) lifted class awards, but fastest of all was pre-war star Leslie Hands in a works 25 hp Talbot.

In some contrast was the Southend & District AC's event at a new hill, Bottledown, between Little Bursted and Billericay, in Essex. Leading drivers and cars were absent from this rather parochial affair, but the American 'invasion' was most evident. Burrows' Studebaker climbed in 40s, and Jones's eight-cylinder Knight came nearest with 41.6s. Third, and a pleasing success for a lady driver, was the 24 hp Brasier of Miss Ivy Cummings. Sadly, what should have been the first northern climb, at Pateley Bridge, on 4 September, had to be cancelled when the Yorkshire, Manchester and Lancashire AC, who were to promote the event jointly, received insufficient entries.

If 1919 was but a prelude, the sport returned with a vengeance in 1920. This was the year when racing returned to Brooklands, when racing on the sands at Southport began, when 22 hill climb events were held, many of high quality, and when several new venues were found. The year had its dark side too. Although over 300 entries were received for a Liverpool MC speed trial, near Birkenhead, there were still several cancellations including important northern fixtures at Pateley Bridge (again) and Waddington Pike. Over in Ireland, the 'troubles' ensured that there would be no hill climbs (or indeed any other speed events) until the Ulster Division of the Motor Trade Association ran a climb at Red Brae, in 1924.

Long before he became indelibly associated with Thinwall bearings and Vanwall Grand Prix cars, Tony Vandervell was a successful hill climb contender with this 25/50 hp Talbot, seen here at Brooklands.
NATIONAL MOTOR MUSEUM

Kop Hill was not new but the Essex MC established a new tradition in holding the first of the year's major events at the Princes Risborough course on 27 March. Worried by the possibility of public nuisance caused by illicit practising before the event, the club revealed the venue only 24 hours before it was held. Limited to touring cars up to and over 1,500cc, the meeting introduced another innovation – more than one car on the hill at once. Although this practice is commonplace today, it seems risky for 1920 in what was about the fastest climb in use at a time when marshalling and spectator control on these unclosed roads remained only partially effective. Bearing in mind the club's concern about illegal practising, and notwithstanding an admirable desire to cut out long delays between runs, this seems an odd decision to make. 'Touring' or not, there were some suspiciously sporty cars running. Fastest, with a 15.3s winning margin, was a young Royal Army Service Corps Lieutenant, C. A. 'Tony' Vandervell, who had been invalided out of the forces after a serious bout of 'flu during the infamous 1918/19 epidemic. Business success with Thinwall Bearings and the World Championship triumph of the Grand Prix car were far in the future when this rather wild young man slid his way to the top of Kop Hill with a stripped 25/50 hp Talbot which boasted an engine suspiciously like that from Percy Lambert's 1913 Brooklands 100 miles in the hour car. This formidable car had been purchased from car dealer and Lloyds uderwriter Malcolm (later Sir Malcolm) Campbell, who was ironically next fastest. Campbell was driving a much less powerful 12 hp Talbot, although the application of the name 'Bluebird' to the car suggests that it was not entirely standard. His decisive win on formula is a little suggestive, too.

The inevitable GN, this time in the hands of Douglas Hawkes, scored a worthy third BTD while a class win fell to the energetic and invariably charming Captain Noel Macklin – later of Silver Hawk, Invicta and Railton fame, and father of Grand Prix driver Lance Macklin. This was a pleasing success, for Macklin was then a partner in the Cricklewood-based Eric-Campbell concern which was building a simple little Coventry-Simplex-engined sporting light car. It was with one of these that he defeated no less than Major Lefrère, the British Bugatti agent who was driving an early, clover-leaf-bodied 16 valve Bugatti, of the type which had created a lot of interest at Olympia the previous Autumn.

Thanks to the previous year's Pateley Bridge cancellation, June's Huddersfield MC climb at Hill Moor Road, Meltham, was the first significant post-war climb in the North. The winning margin, this time with Harold F. Clay's 30/98 Vauxhall on top, was again great, with no less than 31.8s in hand over a 25 hp Talbot in the hands of Yorkshire newcomer, Eddie Hall. Clay also won on formula but among the classes the cheap Americans were in evidence. Time and formula awards fell to the euphoniously named Drysdale Kilburn (Essex), and more class successes went to J. Harold Clay (H. F.'s brother driving an Essex) and the 30 hp Hudson of Mr. A. Dawson. The latter really competed in style, directing operations from the rear seat while the wheel was taken by his liveried chauffeur. The spirit of an earlier age was clearly not entirely dead!

Even at this early stage some organisers contrived to have clashing dates. On the same day most of the leading Southern drivers were exploring a new and very short – 400 yards with a maximum gradient of around 1 in 9 – course in Essex. This was Thundersley Church, near Hadleigh and although many leading names competed, it was all a little chaotic with spectators all over the road, and many inexperienced drivers finding the whole affair rather fraught, which also goes for the promoting Southend and DAC. The ever cheerful, and equally invariably pipe-smoking Archie Frazer Nash made a terrifying ascent, snaking and sliding 'Kim' to great effect with but one hand. All the while the other hand was fully employed waving errant spectators out of the way. His 20.8s BTD may have owed as much to sheer courage and bravado as to technical superiority, but it had Campbell's Talbot and Hawkes' 10 hp Morgan well beaten. Macklin took another class win with the effective little Eric-Campbell, as did the six-cylinder, 25.4 hp Chalmers of J. H. Burrows, and a further GN success went the way of one of the three competitive members of the Keddie family; Maitland in this case.

One date which was eagerly awaited was 3 July, when the Midland AC returned for the first time since 1913 to Shelsley Walsh, always one of the most prestigious and better-organised affairs. In fact, there were just 33 entries but all the 'best' people were there and many lesser lights were doubtless put off by the swingeing 20-guinea entry fee for non-members. One of the lesser lights among the competitors was one Leslie Wilson in a tiny Le Zèbre light car. Actually, he had just taken over the MAC's Secretarial duties, in succession to Cedric Type and T. H. Ryland, and was on the threshold of a career which was to make him the best known and most respected hill climb organiser of all time.

Centre of attraction for the large crowd, who were to be drenched by torrential rain during the latter part of the day, was the arrival of the most powerful works Sunbeam yet seen. Driven by Christopher Bird, this was one of the two 4.9 litre, four valves per cylinder, six cylinder cars built originally for the 1916 Indianapolis race. After further development, they had gone over for the 1919 edition of the American race only to be withdrawn just before the event. Oversize engines, insufficient testing and inferior straightline speed were all rumoured, but no official reason was given for their default. At this time Sunbeam was in the throes of the complicated merger with Talbot and the French Darracq concern to form the cumbersome STD combine. The Wolverhampton Sunbeam company's active competition programme emerged unaffected and it was the North Kensington-based Clement-Talbot marque which now rarely figured among the factory entries. However, since the Suresnes arm of the group was entrusted with the STD *voiturette* racing programme under the name Talbot-Darracq, the Talbot name was not lost to the competition world even if it was now pronounced 'Talbo' in the French manner.

Christopher Bird's six-cylinder Indianapolis Sunbeam throws up an immense cloud of dust on 3 July 1920 as he records the first Shelsley BTD since 1913.
MIDLAND AUTOMOBILE CLUB

To return to Shelsley, Bird's Sunbeam developed some 156 bhp at 3,200 rpm, but had unsuitable gear ratios and Bird himself was out of practice, yet the combination roared up in 58.6s. This was 3.4s outside Higginson's 1913 record but it was enough for Best Time of Day. Two competitors shared second place on 60.2s, but neither achieved the time in the 'open' class. G. D. Pearce-Jones's stripped 30/98 Vauxhall set the time first in the 'closed' class, but the unofficial 'Man of the Meeting' was Frazer Nash, who somehow matched this time in the Light Car category, on a streaming wet road at the end of the meeting. Since Vandervell had earlier set a 60.4s time it was all rather close behind the victorious Sunbeam. L. T. King's Austin 20, in winning the 'open' formula competition, set something of a precedent for these stripped touring cars which were then the mainstay of Herbert Austin's production.

That climb by Frazer Nash was a classic and was vividly described by the contemporary motoring press who were at last covering hill climbs as exciting competitions rather than baldly listing results as they had tended to do before the 1914-18 war. *The Autocar*'s report on AFN's ascent has often been quoted but no excuse is needed to reprint a passage which encapsulates the drama and the appeal of the as-yet-unchristened Shelsley Special:

Standing at the S bend the crackle of the open exhaust of the little two-cylinder engine was plainly audible as the GN waited the word to go. Then followed a screaming rattle of acutely sharp explosions, altering in tempo, slowing and quickening as the driver negotiated the various bends or changed gear. The car unseen, the varying sound was dramatic. Each change in note suggested violent skidding, rushes up banking, and all kinds of disastrous imaginings. Yet the rapid increase of intensity made it evident that the car was climbing at prodigious speed, and the feeling grew that it would be advisable to climb higher up the natural grandstands, formed by the banks of the bend, in order to be safe from this infuriated reptile. With an ear-splitting din, the shining torpedo rushed round, skidded a little on the straight, and disappeared like a flash round the second bend, with a volley of sound, to a dashing finish. As an example of fine driving this performance was magnificent. Obviously capable of yet greater speed, the little car was held just to the limit within which it could be kept on the road.

After this, the meeting at Style Kop a fortnight later was all rather low key, with just 14 entries for the Sutton Coldfield & North Birmingham AC's 'closed' meeting. The club had changed its name yet again, the definitive wording now producing the SUNBAC initials by which it has been known ever since. Small or not, there were some fast cars competing and none faster than Ron Godfrey's winning GN 'Bluebottle', which climbed 4.8s faster than George Bedford's now well-developed Hillman 'Mercury', and with Macklin third in his new 10/35 hp, 1,357cc side-valve Silver Hawk. He had parted company with the Eric-Campbell concern and was now promoting this similar but more uncompromisingly sporting car of his own, fitted with a particularly dashing polished aluminium body. Godfrey's 'Bluebottle' was less radical than 'Kim'. Recognisably a GN, this was a much modified pre-war, belt-drive car, and was second only to 'Kim' in performance.

'The South Harting Hill-climb is now firmly established as the classic light car event of the year, and attracted no fewer than 71 entries last Saturday...' So began *The Motor*'s report on the JCC's big meeting on 24 July, run over the now famous chalky climb near Midhurst. The JCC vied with the MAC for responsible and effective organisation and new measures for 1920 included a class for 'sports cars' and meticulous scrutineering for cars entered in the touring category. The meeting was another GN benefit with 'Kim' taking two wins, including BTD at 64.6s for the ¾-mile, 1 in 6¼ maximum-gradient incline. Godfrey's 'Bluebottle' was next up and an early class success was secured by Kaye Don in one of the curious little Tamplin cyclecars. These Staines-built devices, fitted with a centrally-mounted 980cc JAP engine achieved some commercial success despite some dubious features including a tandem two-seater body constructed from fibreboard. Former GN driver, Douglas Hawkes, was now Morgan mounted, but at South Harting he was overtaken by mechanical catastrophe. *The Motor*'s graphic description needs no elaboration:

Then Mr. W. D. Hawkes made a beautiful start on his spidery Morgan, which waltzed fantastically around corners and was altogether surpassing itself when, with a detonation which drowned even its own piercing exhaust note, the whole near-side cylinder flew clean off! It cavorted ungainly up in the air some 10 or 12 feet with a length of exhaust pipe making it appear like some sort of deadly grenade. For what rhyme or reason the debacle happened even the driver knows not. The break was in the skirt, and pieces flew round like bits of shrapnel, luckily without hurt to anyone. Mr. H. R. Godfrey made a clean but fast climb after the highly excited crowd had been cleared off the road near Mr. Hawke's Morgan...

Sadly, only a week later 'Kim' was crashed very heavily at Brooklands. Frazer Nash was hospitalised with a broken collar bone, and a lengthy rebuilding programme, involving a new steel chassis, was needed before the car was to be re-born as 'Kim II'.

In the meantime, interest switched Northwards with two major climbs on new hills in Yorkshire held during August. Holme Ross, a 1¼-mile stretch of the Holme to Woodhead Road, near Holmfirth, with a maximum gradient of 1 in 8.77, was the chosen venue for the Bradford AC's match against their neighbours from Huddersfield and Halifax, on 7 August. Although he had competed at Brooklands before the war, Malcolm Campbell had only recently taken to hill climbs with the 12 hp Talbot, but he was already a formidable contender. His 95s climb of the hill which was a testing one, featuring 5 major bends, beat Harold F. Clay's 30/98 and Eddie Hall's Talbot for BTD. Campbell's winning time was achieved only after carrying out an important change to the car's weight distribution. He removed an anvil and a sandbag from the rear of the car! Truly 'development' still sometimes owed more to enthusiasm than to science. In the same vein, the passenger in Rippon's Hudson was very energetic in his attempt to assist his driver. Unfortunately, he was leaning out of the wrong side on the bend!

Although Sutton Bank, between Thirsk and Helmsley, on the edge of the North York Moors, had been included in the 1914 Light Car Trial, it was new for a true speed hill climb when the York & DMC staged an event there two weeks later. Victory fell to Harold F. Clay's Essex in 118.6s for the nine-tenths of a mile climb which was steep – 1 in 3.9 at its steepest – and included several bends.

Yet another new hill used that year was Spread Eagle. On the Shaftesbury to Blandford road at Melbury, this seven-tenths of a mile hill was both loose and bumpy. Since it was also fast it was pretty spectacular despite a stiffish gradient of up to 1 in 6. The Hampshire AC were in charge and the overall winner was Bertie Kensington-Moir in the touring-based Straker-Squire which is still a familiar car in VSCC events today. His 56.4s time was 5.2s faster than Campbell, but an unofficial fastest of all was Pearce-Jones's very rapid Vauxhall. He made a mistake on his first climb but shot up in 51.2s on a second run at the end of the meeting, which did not count for awards. The problems of scrutineering were tackled again at this meeting, with all stripped touring cars having to compete in the 'open' class.

A full description of all the minor meetings which were again becoming commonplace would be tedious to most readers, but during the year significant BTDs were set by Macklin (at a Kop climb in May), Bedford (Style Kop) and Frazer Nash (Pebble Combe). A meeting at Rhubina Hill in South Wales was ostensibly won by Charles Sgonina in a 1914 TT Humber, the same Charles Sgonina who was still club racing until the late nineteen-sixties. In fact, however, although entered by him, the car was driven by his brother.

Around 37 properly organised hill climbs took place in 1921, so if 1920 had seemed fairly busy, the new season demonstrated the extent to which the sport was regaining its momentum. A real hill climb (and sprint) 'circus' was coming into being, with some drivers, and especially those with trade interests, taking in meetings almost every weekend, all over the country.

Precursor of so many hill climb and sprint specials, 'Kim II' is seen here after its major rebuild. Archie Frazer-Nash is at the wheel here at Sutton Bank.
DEMAUS TRANSPORT PHOTOGRAPHICS

Enter Raymond Mays

First to make his mark was a young Cambridge undergraduate from a Lincolnshire wool family, Raymond Mays. Aided by an old Oundle school friend, Amherst Villiers, Mays had obtained and started to modify a Hillman Speed Model. Despite going faster in second gear than in top (around 62 mph as opposed to 55 mph!) through being over-geared, the car was responsive to tuning and careful preparation. Around 80 mph was eventually extracted form the car which, inspired by the example of Bedford's 'Mercury', Mays christened 'Quicksilver' and ran with polished aluminium bodywork which was so fashionable at the time. Mays' Best Time of Day at the opening Inter-Varsity Aston Hill climb (now over only 750 yards rather than the ¾-mile course of 1904), 0.3s faster than R. M. Hamilton's GN, was a copybook start to a remarkable career.

Nevertheless, 1921 was Archie Frazer Nash's year. 'Kim II' used the engine out of the Brooklands wreck but with a new chassis, although the concept of this narrow, light and exceptionally nervous – not to say twitchy – machine remained unchanged. It appeared first at Kop in April, when the Essex MC had again kept the meeting secret until a day before. Since the hill was so well-known by now, this seemed a fairly pointless exercise. It was another GN-dominated meeting with the little cyclecars winning three out of six classes on time. AFN duly took BTD with a record-breaking 34.6s climb to show that 'Kim' was back with a vengeance while Godfrey won two classes. Tony Vandervell contrived to run his potent Talbot as both a touring and a racing car and as well as winning two classes, his 35.4s best was a second BTD. Significantly, there was a class for four-cylinder, water-cooled cars up to 1,500cc which was run purely to provide at least one 'open' class which a GN could not win! In a rare hill climb appearance (he didn't like them), Henry Segrave won this in his T13 Bugatti, a former Coupe des Voiturettes team car, in 39.8s, by 1s from Bedford's familiar Hillman. Once again the Austin 20s dominated on formula, A. H. Pass (later of Pass and Joyce fame), winning with the better-known Felix Scriven only third.

Frazer Nash was very quickly back into a winning run, following up his Kop success with BTDs at Sutton Bank (where he won four classes), and again at Kop in May, at the Oxford MC meeting. He was slower this time, climbing in 38.8s, but the opposition was weaker than in April and he had 8.4s in hand over another driver of amateur status whose family fortunes depended on the textile industry, Humphrey Cook. At this stage Cook's 30/98 Vauxhall, named 'Rouge et Noir', although stripped, remained fairly standard. This formidable sporting car showed its prowess by winning a class while climbing almost entirely in third gear.

May was an exceptionally budy month with several clashes. Taking advantage of Frazer Nash going to the ACU's Western Centre meeting at Chatcombe Pitch, near Cheltenham, George Bedford went North, to Style Kop, on the 21st and achieved a 31.8s BTD from a field which contained two drivers who would be indelibly associated later with the Jaguar marque: R. M. V. 'Soapy' Sutton (Hillman) and S. H. 'Sammy' Newsome (Calthorpe). The Chatcombe Pitch meeting was one where the emphasis was rather more on the motorcycles, and AFN had no real opposition, winning both car classes, with Captain Arthur Waite's Austin 20 and Major Oates's single-seater-bodied 11.9 hp Lagonda the best of the rest.

Not all meetings were major affairs, and one of the lesser happenings was a Banbury MC/Oxford MC 'closed' event on Crondown Hill, which is on the Deddington-to-Chipping Norton road. It was remarkable only in that it provided an early BTD for Humphrey Cook and what is thought to be the first meeting between Cook and Raymond Mays, an association which was to come to its full flowering in the ERA project of the nineteen-thirties.

A feature of most hill climbs was the number of cars which were competing in several classes and where the time taken on just one run often counted for more than one class. This meant that a really fast small car could be entered in every class possible and just about sweep the board – like AFN was wont to do. This rather irritating and certainly unfair practice lingered on in smaller events in particular until well after the Second World War, but it really got out of hand in the early 'twenties. Since entries were duplicated in this way it also accounts for some apparently large entry lists which, in reality, consisted of many fewer cars than there appeared to be at first sight.

However, this explanation only partly accounts for the incredible 600 entries at Thundersley Church on 28 May. The Essex County and Southend AC were prone to over-ambitious events, but really excelled themselves this time by throwing open the entry to just about everything on wheels, contesting

8 'open' and 'closed' classes, with inumerable sub-divisions. It was chaotic, with racing cars interspersed with landaulettes. The height of lunacy was attained when a removal van decisively defeated an omnibus. Through it all Malcolm Campbell flung his recently acquired pre-war Grand Prix Peugeot to a 19.8s BTD, with Godfrey's 'Bluebottle' on 21.6s. There were a couple of wins for Leon Cushman's increasingly fast 'trade' T13 Bugatti, and an early success for Bentley works tester Frank Clement in W.O.'s new 3-litre, ohc, four-cylinder sports car.

Early in June, Frazer Nash took 'Kim II' up to Holme Moss where the Bradford and Huddersfield MC had garnered a good entry. However, AFN's run of success was temporarily halted when 'Kim' twitched once too often and landed in a ditch. This left a surprise 92s BTD to C. H. Mitchell in Colonel Hoyle's old 1908 'Four-Inch TT' Hutton which had been successful in hill climbs pre-1914. Mitchell succeeded in defeating a field which included Segrave (in a 1914 TT Sunbeam, 93.2s), George Bedford (94.6s), Humphrey Cook (97.4s) and Harold F. Clay (99s).

The situation was back to normal, though, at South Harting two weeks later for the JCC's blue riband event, with 'Kim II' winning both racing classes on its way to BTD. Two class second places, one on formula, were secured by the new make, Aston Martin, ahead of Cushman's Bugatti no less. Lionel Martin had split with his erstwhile partner Robert Bamford at the end of the war and, aided by former Coventry-Simplex draughtsman, S. Robb, and the loyal Jack Addis, was embarking on the protracted development of his new 1,500cc, side-valve-engined, high-quality sports car for production in a tiny workshop in Kensington. With the 'Aston' in the name derived from Aston Hill, it was only appropriate that the prototypes should appear in hill climbs. Already successful at Brooklands in May, the car – it was probably AM 270, the second prototype – was driven on this occasion by Miles Thomas, then a young motoring journalist but with a great motor industry and aviation career ahead of him, by the end of which he would be Lord Thomas of Remenham.

Frazer Nash had to give best to Malcolm Campbell at Hampshire AC's Spread Eagle meeting, an event which had gained considerably in stature since the previous year. Although he also drove the smaller 15 hp Talbot, Campbell's outright success was at the wheel of a very stark 25/50 model and his 46.4s BTD was 2s clear of 'Kim II'. Cook managed a more-than-respectable 49.8s climb in the increasingly rapid 'Rouge et Noir' while a class win on formula fell to another new Aston Martin. This was a brand-new staggered-seat racing car, still with side-valves, and christened 'Bunny' by Martin's effervescent second wife Katherine. The driver was Bertie Kensington-Moir, who had joined the little Kensington concern from Zenith Carburettors, and whose lean (and usually laughing) presence was no stranger to competition. He was already familiar at the wheel of the Straker-Squire, a make promoted by his uncle.

Lionel Martin climbs Kop Hill in the prototype Aston Martin, AM 270, with spectators worryingly close to the road. For several years Lionel and his friends competed at every possible event, ringing the changes most confusingly with the same handful of early Aston Martins.

DEMAUS TRANSPORT PHOTOGRAPHICS

It is perhaps a tribute to the quirky, intensely individualistic and generally highly temperamental, competition cars of the day that so many were given pet names. There was really no such thing as a production racing car until Ettore Bugatti's Type 35 models came along, so each car had a 'personality' all of its own.

There had been no works Vauxhalls seen in sprint events since the war, but in July, the Luton concern returned to the fray at Aston Hill, for the Hertfordshire AC meeting. They weren't new cars, but E. Swain's 1914 4½ litre Grand Prix car was rapid enough to set BTD. Humphrey Cook's best time of 48.8s was only 1.6s slower than Swain, though, and Cook had the satisfaction of beating Hancock's works-entered 30/98, to complete a clean sweep for Luton.

Cook set another Best Time of Day when the Leicestershire AC revived the Beacon Hill meeting on 3 September, when his 48.4s predictably beat Felix Scriven's Austin 20 and Lionel Martin, who edged out Raymond Mays. The latter's rapid little Hillman now benefitted from a rather special Zenith carburettor set-up which had been arranged through Kensington-Moir before he left the company. The car was now good enough to give Mays fourth place in the Light Car class at Shelsley a week later when the Bourne driver made his début on the Worcestershire slopes.

Five thousand spectators turned up for the MAC's showpiece meeting, the last really important climb of the season. The Leslie Wilson régime had affected a number of changes since the previous year, not least reducing the non-members' entry fee to 15 guineas, which was still a lot of money for one run and no practice. So once again there was a high-grade entry, but numbering only 33 in total. Many of those 5,000(?CM) spectators received a nasty shock too when they were invited to pay up 5 shillings (25p) for admission, plus another shilling for a programme, with unaccompanied ladies admitted for just 2 shillings (10p). Fortunately, it was a superb meeting so the hubbub which greeted this unnanounced imposition of admission charges was short-lived. Nevertheless, several near-accidents caused by the cars, which were now becoming much faster, aroused some concern.

Sunbeam turned out in force with Bird in the old Indianapolis car which had set BTD the previous year, and Count Louis Zborowski and former Talbot driver H. G. Day with two new straight-eight, 3 litre Grand Prix cars. This time the silver 4.9 litre six was properly geared and Bird thundered up in a stunning new 52.2s course record. In contrast, the new GP cars were unimpressive, mainly because they were set up for road racing and were hopelessly slow off the starting line, although much faster on the higher slopes. Day managed 62.8s while the exuberant and fabuously wealthy Zborowski had to be content with 65.4s. Bird's closest challenger was Mathew Park's works Vauxhall – rather more GP than 30/98 in performance – with a 54.4s which was just 0.4s faster than Archie Frazer Nash who was really up against it with this kind of opposition on a 'power' hill. Nonetheless, such was the advance over 1920, that all three were under the previous record, with Humphrey Cook next up with a 57.0s climb in 'Rouge et Noir'. With other notables such as Vandervell (winner of 'closed' event on time), Cushman, Barber-Lomax's fast 30/98, Scriven, Mays, J. Harold Clay and A. C. 'Bert' Bertelli (Enfield-Allday) providing the supporting cast, it had been a fine meeting. It also showed that while even AFN could not match the bigger, and much more expensive, road and track racing-orientated works cars from Sunbeam and Vauxhall, the new breed of lightweights were running them pretty close, thanks to intensive development for the more specialised sprint events.

During the year Frazer Nash had also won hill climbs at Bore Hill and Kingsdown Hill (Bath), while Ron Godfrey added wins at Haynes Park and Kop (including 4 class wins) to the GN tally. Cook won at Aston Hill, and Bedford at Penkridge Park although the Hillman was now becoming a little breathless against growing opposition, while for a change Garrowby Hill, in East Yorkshire, provided a deserved win on time for Felix Scriven's big Austin 20.

If 1921 had been Archie Frazer Nash's year, the following season saw honours fairly evenly divided, but with increasing success going the way of the skilful, ambitious but always thoughtful Raymond Mays. He had made a good impression with the rather upright Hillman 'Quicksilver', complete with flambuoyant 'QS' monogram on the side of the cockpit, but he and his close associate Amherst Villiers were well aware of the Hillman's limitations. In an incredibly bold, even rash, move, for the Mays family's financial resources were by no means unlimited, the youthful Lincolnshire driver ordered one of the very latest pattern of Type 13 Bugattis. These 16-valve, ohc, four-cylinder machines, available as T13, T22 and T23 models with three different wheelbases and coachwork ranging from stark racing pattern to something more suitable for fast touring, had pre-war origins and had been available in Britain since 1919. They were regarded as the aristocrats of the light car world. Since scoring a notable Voiturette racing victory at Brescia in 1921, the shortest (2 metre wheelbase), starkest and fastest (with ball-bearing camshaft engine) version took the name 'Brescia' and over the 1921/22 close season the first three of these to come to Britain were ordered by experienced Bugatti driver Cushman, Yorkshireman Eddie Hall, and by Mays. In order to help pay for this expensive machine Mays took the modern approach of seeking, and obtaining, trade support from Englebert tyres, Lodge sparking plugs and Speedwell oil.

Cushman had his 'Brescia' ready in time for the opening Essex MC Kop climb on 25 March and won four classes with it, although he was not a contender for BTD at a well-supported meeting which featured a 50 yards flying start and no fewer than eighteen classes involving the sort of widespread duplication of entries which was becoming the norm. Overall, it was a day for the big cars with a spectacular 26.8s Best Time of Day to extrovert Count Zborowski driving a new acquisition, the 1919 Indianapolis Ballot which Anglophile Frenchman Jean Chassagne had driven at Brooklands back in 1920. Runner-up was another car built for the American race, one of the big Sunbeams, which Tony Vandervell took up in 27.2s (a reward from STD for his sterling performances with his 25/50 hp Talbot?). Then there was quite a gap to Frank Clement's impressive 3-litre Bentley (31.2s) and the irrepressible Frazer Nash (31.4s). The absurdity of the class duplications was underlined when W. F. Millward's fast Charron-Laycock contrived to win no fewer than 12 on formula! More significant category wins fell to Godfrey's 'Bluebottle' (two), Cook's now more streamlined E-type 30/98 Vauxhall 'Rouge et Noir', and Aston Martin-mounted Kensington-Moir and a man whose wealth (from South African mining interests) and enthusiasm matched even Zborowski's. This was Wolf Barnato, driving a rather unsuitable Hispano-Suiza.

The GN was still able to hold its own, however, and this was shown at Staxton Bank, the Scarborough and DMC's choice of venue, some seven miles from the sea on the Great Driffield Road. On a day when the road was particularly slippery, and when a spectator was hurt by a competitor's out-of-control three-wheeler, Captain Trubie Moore's GN 'Vitesse' came out on top ahead of Bugattis, Vauxhalls and the remarkably fast Hodgson of H. Hodgson. This Leeds-built car was conventional enough, with four-cylinder Anzani motivation, but was remarkably well-prepared and in fact was the forerunner of a small series of sports cars built in the mid-twenties.

'Kim II' was back on top at a couple of sharply contrasting meetings in April and May. Frazer Nash's sheer competitiveness and commercial interests combined to have him competing in probably more events than anyone else, including some odd ones. The Bradford MC and DCC's 'freak' hill climb (we would call it a trials hill) at Rosedale Abbey Bank was certainly one of these but AFN remained undefeated by this notorious hill. Then there was the oddly named Laindon Two Church Hill, on the Billericay to Gravesend road.

The Essex County & Southend AC had seemingly learnt little from the previous year's Thundersley Church episode because this time they accepted around 1,000 entries in 23 classes, each with 4 or 5 subdivisions! This rather bizarre event, which must surely have had the largest entry list on record, was won by Frazer Nash in a snappy 28.6s but he only won 3 classes. Cushman, beating Mays similar new Bugatti, lifted 5, and Major Charles Coe's well-developed 30/98 Vauxhall, 5 more. Maitland Keddie had to be content with 3 wins in his early 10/30 Alvis, while even Barnato won a couple with the Hispano.

Raymond Mays makes his Shelsley début in 1921, in his Hillman Speed Model 'Quicksilver'.
DEMAUS TRANSPORT PHOTOGRAPHICS

Eddie Hall was a prolific hill climb class winner over almost two decades. He was one of the first British Bugatti drivers. His T13 'Brescia' model is photographed at Shelsley.
NATIONAL MOTOR MUSEUM

Emphasising the interest in the development of the light car, the Royal Scottish Automobile Club (RSAC) revived the idea of a long-distance road trial in June, specially for the up-to-1500s. This included six timed climbs of such Scottish favourites as Tummel Bridge, Cairn O'Mount, Rest-and-be-Thankful, Little Gruinard, Glendoe and Loch-na-Craig. The entry included men of the calibre of H. G. Day (8/18 Talbot), Richard Lisle (11.9 hp Star) and C. Harvey (10/30 Alvis) but until it was forced out with magnet failure, the most impressive on the hills was Walsgrove's 11 hp Riley.

A mere three weeks after the Laindon extravaganza, the Essex County & Southend crowd were in action again, this time with a rare handicap climb at Bottledown Hill. The result was rather satisfying, too, with Frazer Nash tying for the premier award with Miss Riddie's Alvis.

Rather more serious was the revival of the excellent custom of the South Wales AC 'weekend' over the 28/29 June, with the Caerphilly hill climb on the Saturday and racing on the sands at Porthcawl the following day. Caerphilly belonged to Kensington-Moir, for on a wet and slippery course he set the best time overall in the big 4-litre Straker-Squire and also cleaned up three classes with 'Bunny', the staggered two-seater, side-valve Aston Martin. Raymond Mays was becoming more formidable with the Bugatti, to which he and Villiers were ministering with total lack of awe, and he won his class, as did Enfield-Allday co-designer Bertelli, and the fast and much modified Morris Cowley Sports of A. E. Keen.

Mays went one better a couple of days later at an atrociously wet Dean Hill where burst tyres and buckled wheels were all too prevalent as many drivers came into contact with roadside scenery as they struggled to control their sliding cars. The meeting was a JCC (South West Centre) affair and Mays took BTD. The opposition was stronger, though, on the following day (this was a particularly hectic holiday week) when the Hampshire AC garnered a fine entry at the popular Spread Eagle Hill. The 'Brescia' was already beginning to rev like no standard T13 but a 53.8s time was good enough only for third overall. The man on top was Malcolm Campbell, not Talbot-mounted but in one of the big Sunbeams. His 41s record was too much for even Frazer Nash (48.6s), while Mays's 53.8s had the edge over the formidable Vauxhalls of Coe (55.4s) amd Cook (56.4s).

Campbell made it two records in less than a week when he took the Sunbeam to a Holme Moss record in a shattering 80.8s (7.8s faster than Harold F. Clay at the wheel of a 1914 Grand Prix Vauxhall), and with Frazer Nash and Eddie Hall's Bugatti best of the smaller cars. Mays was missing from the entry for he had gone to the clashing JCC Saltersford Church, near Macclesfield, climb. When he saw the 1,200 yards climb, complete with 1 in 4.4 gradient, he may have regretted that decision, but undaunted he set another BTD on a hill which several competitors could not climb at all.

Tarmacadam surfacing where there was a risk of the track breaking up, a widened gateway at the summit, undergrowth cleared away and spectator banks railed off, all emphasised that the MAC were not resting on their laurels at Shelsley Walsh. Held earlier than in 1921, on 29 July, the meeting again drew a fine entry and a big crowd, but the loose and dusty surface probably accounted for the lack of a new record. Chris Bird was out for a hat trick of Shelsley wins in the Indianapolis Sunbeam but 54s was the best he could attain on the one and only climb, and he failed to set a BTD by just 0.2s. That was all the more remarkable as his sliding car clouted a bank on the way up and finished with one broken halfshaft. Bird's conqueror was Vauxhall works driver Matthew Park in a car new to hill climbing but one which was to be very successful over many years, the 3-litre car which had recently made a not-too-successful début in the Tourist Trophy. One of three built, Park's car represented the zenith of Vauxhall competition car design. Instantly recognisable by the prominent, cone-shaped cowls before driver and passenger, the TT Vauxhalls were the work of C. E. King (chassis design after Pomeroy had gone to Daimler) and Harry Ricardo (engine). The advanced 2 ohc, 4 valve per cylinder, engines were developing around 130 bhp on a petrol-alcohol mixture fuel, while the most notable feature of the chassis design was the four wheel braking by pressurised servo-operated rods and cables. At 22½ cwts, Park's bright red racer was no lightweight, but his 53.8s climb demonstrated the car's potential with good preparation.

With his 30/98 Vauxhall bearing a bodily resemblance to a 1914 GP car, Humphrey Cook recorded a commendable 56.8s, but he was only 0.4s up on Kensington-Moir's game 'Bunny'. Even so, the inevitable Frazer Nash almost stole the show by contriving to reach the finish in 64.2s with one tyre burst and another wheel buckled after a bank storming episode en route! Cushman's Bugatti was a bit disappointing at 62s while Mays, who arrived with high hopes, crept over the finish line a demoralis-

Mathew Park sets a 53.8s BTD at Shelsley in 1922 in a TT Vauxhall, one of three such cars which were to be highly significant in hill climbing.
MIDLAND AUTOMOBILE CLUB

ing 78.6s after leaving the start. The explanation was the presence of a bluebottle – the winged variety, not a piece of GN – in the carburettor!

Mays made up for this disappointment with his biggest win yet when, in September, he set a 59.8s BTD at the JCC's big South Harting meeting. Since he beat Frazer Nash, Hawkes's Morgan (with both cylinders firmly attached to the car this year), and Cushman to do it, it was a truly significant win. Unlike at Shelsley, competitors had more than one run (in different classes) and this time it was 'Kim II's' turn to suffer a blocked carburettor jet, although AFN's earlier 62.2s climb was good enough for second BTD.

Hill climbing had generally followed a similar pattern to the previous year, with around 36 climbs, plus those on the Scottish Light Car Trial, but straight sprint meetings seemed to be gaining over them in popularity. There was also the threatening noises coming from both the Commissioner of Police and the RAC about the dangers of racing powerful cars up narrow, sinuous hills between large numbers of still often unruly spectators. The RAC went so far as to propose to grant permits only to established events for the following year. Like so many other slightly nervy proposals made by the sport's governing body, this came to nought.

The by no means inexhaustible supply of entries for hill climbs was underlined when, after one postponement for this reason, the Hertfordshire AC drew only 37 entries for the last of the year's major climbs, the Aston Hill 'open' in September. NM 1795, Park's Shelsley-winning TT Vauxhall, was out again and the deep-throated red car set another BTD in 48s. It was another narrow victory, however, for Frank Clement's Bentley and Humphrey Cook's Vauxhall tied on 48.6s. Mays won his class, Lionel Martin won three and Kensington-Moir had a scare when 'Bunny' had two tyres burst, fortunately without serious harm to anyone.

During the year many of the minor events had also been won by the same people who were tending to dominate the bigger meetings. Mays took top honours at Chatcombe Pitch, Kop and Why Not Hill, while Godfrey also had a win at Kop. Frazer Nash won at Colne, while Hodgson was very successful in Northern events in his rapid Anzani-engined creation, winning at Sutton Bank and Garrowby. Moore lifted another GN success at Pateley Bridge, but Bedford's Hillman, rather outclassed by now in bigger meetings, still took a brace of wins at Edge Hill and Why Not Hill.

Then, as now, the RAC was constantly lobbied by the often conflicting interest groups within the sport. During the early days, when the Motor Union was a major power in the land and was seen to represent the interests of the provincial clubs, the supreme position of the RAC was neither secure nor even universally recognised. Whatever its shortcomings, by 1922 it was the sport's unchallenged regulating authority in Britain, and over the 1922/23 winter a serious attempt was made to resolve the long-standing grievances surrounding 'closed' meetings.

Above all the RAC sought to maintain hill climbing's 'respectability' in the eyes of the wider public and, secondarily, sought to ensure that the interests of those who had the greatest material stake in the sport, the competing manufacturers, were upheld. The RAC's rules provided a framework for reasonably well regulated events and the issue of the necessary permit to hold an 'open' meeting was natur-

Malcolm Campbell enjoyed considerable success in 1922 with the old 4.9 six-cylinder Sunbeam. Here he climbs at Caerphilly.
NATIONAL MOTOR MUSEUM

Although rather outclassed now in bigger events, George Bedford still dominated some smaller meetings in his highly developed Hillman Speed Model. This is at Spread Eagle in 1922.
NATIONAL MOTOR MUSEUM

ally conditional upon those rules being adhered to. The snag was that 'closed' meetings did not need a permit and, effectively, were beyond RAC control.

So, in February 1923 the RAC announced, via a rather tactlessly high-handed missive to member clubs, that in future permits *would* be needed for 'closed' meetings. What is more, competitors would be eligible to run in 'closed' meetings only if they were already members of the organising club before the publication of regulations for the meeting in question. This was intended to stop trade entries 'pot hunting' at small meetings by the simple expedient of joining the club concerned just in order to compete at a given meeting. This wasn't too unpopular with trade entrants who would rather compete at a smaller number of more important meetings, but who felt that they had to spend money on competing as often as possible in order to score over competitors who would otherwise gain a commercial advantage over them. The real howls of anguish came from the clubs who were afraid that they would lose a crowd-pulling star driver from their 'closed' promotion if the new rule was carried through, and who, in any case, were understandably disgruntled at the rather high-handed way the change had been communicated to them without prior consultation. In the end the RAC compromised. The permits for 'closed' fixtures remained, but a concession was allowed over club membership. Henceforth, members could join up to three weeks before a 'closed' meeting in order to be eligible to compete.

Climax on public roads

Once the heat was taken out of this debate, everyone could look forward to another busy season. Approximately 43 hill climbs were actually held during the year, and when the Brooklands meetings, many level ground sprint events (including a modest revival of the Brighton Speed Trials) and several important and attractive Continental fixtures were taken into account, chronic fixture congestion with many serious date clashes ensued. At the end of the season the RAC announced that it would make serious efforts to help organising clubs to avoid the worst excesses of this problem in 1924.

The Inter-Varsity event at Aston Hill was again the prelude to the season and brought success to the Vauxhall 30/98 of R. F. Summers, who was later to become one of the first customers for the side-valve Aston Martin. Just 0.4s off the pace of his 45.5s BTD came the 2-litre Ballot of J. Lucas Scudamore, while the Light Car class winner was H. S. Eaton's GN, whose 1922 200 Mile Race ohc engine propelled it up in 48.8s. Although not very significant in terms of the mainstream of top-class hill climbing in 1923, this meeting gave a pretty fair impression of the sort of car a wealthy young undergraduate might aspire to in this year. Also noticeable was the erection or iron railings lining the course, for the protection of the spectators, a move which was rather les popular with the competitors who would certainly come off worst if they hit these substantial railings.

Before March was out the season was under way with a vengeance, with the Essex MC holding their 'open'/'closed' meeting at Kop on the 23rd. Fastest of all the public road climbs, Kop attracted a good and varied field headed by a formidable refugee from Brooklands track. This was the 20,508cc Maybach aero-engined Isotta-Maybach of the equally exotically-named L. C. G. M. Le Champion, a well-known habitué of the Weybridge concrete. This much modified, pre-war, chain-drive Isotta-Fraschini was a fairly typical example of the type of monstrous hybrid which did well at Brooklands in the early twenties. It was an inexpensive (due to the ready availability of redundant aviation engines) way for the brave to attain high speed. Popular on the track and in straight-line speed events, these immense machines were hardly suited to the more sinuous hill climbs, but Kop was a possibility. In fact, Le Champion's spectacular effort ws good enough for second BTD, beaten by a combination which was to prove to be *the* dominant factor of the year. After two years of exemplary success in his well-prepared E-type, Humphrey Cook had been able to obtain from Vauxhall one of the three TT cars, the number 2 TT car driven to third place by Osborne Payne. The 1922 performance of Park at Shelsley and Aston Hill in the sister car, NM 1795, suggested that Cook was on to a winner. Originally red, the car was now repainted black and red and was dubbed 'Rouge et Noir II', and a 29.8s climb was good enough for the Kop BTD, with an average speed of over 70 mph. The usual proliferation of classes resulted in 8 wins to Cushman, 6 to Mays, 5 to Cook and single successes to Frazer Nash and to Clement's Bentley. The old hands were still on top.

The leading names would meet again at Kop a month later, the ACU's South Midland Centre were in charge, but in the meantime minor events threw up some interesting results. A rare, but not unprecedented, BTD for a woman competitor, fell to Miss Ivy Cummings at the North West London MC's

Road surfaces in the early nineteen-twenties were usually pretty poor, bearing a close resemblance to those of modern forest rally stages. The analogy is particularly appropriate here as Archie Frazer-Nash ('Kim II') rounds the Sutton Bank hairpin, on the edge of the latterday Yorkshire forests.
DEMAUS TRANSPORT PHOTOGRAPHICS

climb at Waterworks Hill. One of the bravest and best of the female competitors of the time, she was at the wheel of the big 5-litre, chain-drive Bugatti 'Black Bess', a four-cylinder racer sold in 1913 by Bugatti to the French aviator Roland Garros. Second in class at the same meeting was Captain George Eyston with the 16 valve, twin-overhead-camshaft-engined Aston Martin which had been one of the 1922 Strasbourg GP cars. Further North, in Scotland, where most events were now run under ACU permits as the RSAC insisted on the unpopular measure of limiting competing cars to 1,600cc or under, the Glasgow MC ran their climb up the steep (maximum 1 in 5) Dalgrain Brae, near Sorn. Best Time of Day fell to one of the sporty new 2-litre ohc Beardmores, built in Glasgow, and driven by A. Francis. Scottish makes had not really figured prominently in hill climbs since the early days of Argyll and Arrol-Johnston, but the Beardmore – which had only begun production in 1920 with solid cars of no particular sporting pretension – was to be noted well South of the Border before long. Taking rather

Kop was fairly straight and very fast. Spectators appear oblivious to the danger as an early Aston Martin, possibly fitted with the rear bodywork of a delightfully named 'Coal Scuttle', speeds past.
NATIONAL MOTOR MUSEUM

more than twice as long to ascend, yet still taking a second in class, was an Austin Seven, possibly giving its driver, G. Evans, the distinction of being the first man to hill climb the immortal Seven.

The return match at Kop on 28 April gave the same result, but this time Humphrey Cook lopped 2 seconds off his winning time, and his 27.8s run was well clear of Mays (31.8s), Ivy Cummings (33.6s), and Eaton's fast GN (34.2s). Mays was still campaigning his Brescia Bugatti with his increasingly demanding perfectionism, allied to boundless optimism, triumphing over prudence where mechanical and financial considerations were concerned. He and Villiers had embarked on a development programme which saw the T13 being endowed with special high-compression pistons from Specialloid, a duel fuel supply suitable for road or competition use – the latter calling for a special brew of fuel called RD2 – and astronomical revs! By the end of the season the 1922 figure of 4,000 to 4,300 rpm maximum had been increased to 6,000 rpm. Fair reliability was achieved by the time that serious bearing and fuel supply problems, which would have daunted lesser mortals, had been overcome. Fortunately, Mays was becoming adept at wringing support from trade suppliers who were beginning to feel fairly sure that Mays would give them a worthwhile return in terms of promotable success.

Not yet in the same league as Mays, was a class winner at the JCC's Northern Centre event at Saltersford. He was Basil Davenport, from Macclesfield, and he was just starting with a contraption which, if it had not born a striking physical resemblance to 'Kim II', could have been dismissed altogether. How wrong appearances can be! Inspired by Frazer Nash's achievements with a car which was fairly inexpensive, Davenport bought a GN chassis from AFN, who took plenty of GN parts with him when he left the company in 1922, and after converting it to central-steering, fitted the prototype 1,086cc, ohc, vee-twin 'Vitesse' engine. A similar but even slimmer body to that of 'Kim II' was cobbled up, and for a total financial outlay of about £110, the young Davenport had a racer, albeit a scruffy one, which nobody took seriously for a while.

Humphrey Cook was the man to beat. He scored his hat trick of big wins at Aston Hill, when the Hertfordshire County AC held their 'open' meeting on 12 May. Despite the presence of factory Vauxhalls in the hands of Park (TT car) and Swain (supposedly a touring 23/60 but with remarkable speed), Cook was supreme with his 46.4s BTD, decisively faster than Swain (48.2s), Park (48.4s), Frank Clement (49.2s), and Mays with the fastest of the smaller cars (49.6s). As usual the Aston Martin boys were playing a variety of musical chairs with the assortment of mainly competition cars which were still virtually the entire production of the little Kensington works. This time Major Frank Halford, who was later to build the Halford Special Grand Prix car round an Aston Martin chassis, figured prominently with a 52.6s climb in 'Bunny'.

For 1923, Humphrey Cook obtained a sister TT Vauxhall to Park's successful mount. Painted the familiar red and black and dubbed 'Rouge et Noir II', the car helped Cook to more success.
NATIONAL MOTOR MUSEUM

After the excesses of the previous two years, the Essex County & Southend club opted for single-class entries at Laindon, and drew a paltry 30 entries. They still hadn't learned all the lessons though, for the absence of a finishing banner caused much confusion and a near-catastrophe. Brooklands star, J. G. Parry Thomas entered his self-designed and developed 7.26-litre, straight-eight Leyland Eight track car, and this immensely powerful machine caused havoc at the finish when the great Welsh driver misjudged where this was located and finally came to a shuddering halt after hitting two motor-cycles and running over a policeman's foot! He still set joint third BTD with Eaton's more suitable GN, while honours fell to John Joyce's AC from Cushman's Bugatti. Joyce's car was the highly developed 1,500cc ohc single-seater with which he had covered a record 101.39 miles in the hour at Brooklands the previous November. Originally commissioned by Harry Hawker, and enthusiastically backed by arch publicist S. F. Edge (who now headed the Thames Ditton AC concern), this car was a serious proposition with around 77 bhp from its Weller-designed four-cylinder engine, to propel barely 9 cwt of copiously lightened motor car, even if eight attempts were needed before sufficient reliability could be obtained to set that Brooklands hour record for a 1500.

There seemed to be no stopping Humphrey Cook. More BTD's followed at Holme Moss (despite particularly unruly spectators encroaching on the road) and at Caerphilly where success was gained despite ramming the bank and causing some damage to the car. What *The Autocar* called 'one of the accepted classic events of the year', the Hamphire AC's Spread Eagle meeting took place on 7 July and Cook did it again: BTD in 43s. He also had a bad fright when having a run in the always rather unstable and virtually brakeless Aston Martin track car 'Razor Blade'. He all but cleaned up the cart of a farmer who was intent on proving that the road was indeed open to the general public! Although busy with the development of his new four-cylinder Frazer Nash sports car, AFN was still campaigning 'Kim II' with success, and his 44s climb was good enough for second BTD, 0.6s faster than Joyce who won on formula, and 0.8s clear of Parry Thomas who was having another go with the rather unwieldy Leyland.

By now Mays and Villiers were getting over the development problems with the highly modified Bugatti and there was a pleasing Best Time of Day on 14 July, at Angel Bank. Mays's 27.8s was well beyond the reach of moderate opposition but a noteworthy 34.8s from A. E. Keen showed what you could do to develop a Morris Cowley, this car now being endowed with a special single-seater body. There is nothing new about one-make events, and the organisers of this meeting, SUNBAC, ran a class specially reserved for Ford cars. The JCC had done the same for GWK's once at South Harting.

In fact, the 1923 edition of JCC's South Harting fixture was a little inferior by this club's high standards, with a rather poor entry competing. This may well have had something to do with the announcement that only relative times within the classes would be published – yet one more attempt to allay public fears and hostility about speed on the public road. Some big names were running, though,

Eddie Hall flings Aston Martin 'Bunny' up Aston Hill, in 1923, with scant regard for any fine distinctions between road and verge.
DEMAUS TRANSPORT PHOTOGRAPHICS

George Eyston was another notable personality to take his turn with the early Aston Martins. This is one of the 2 ohc Strasbourg cars at South Harting.
DEMAUS TRANSPORT PHOTOGRAPHICS

and it was a good day for Bugattis with wins for Cushman and Hall, the latter beating Archie Frazer Nash by 0.4s, while Captain C. M. (Maurice) Harvey's works Alvis also garnered a couple of classes. Although the GN's and Morgans were still prominent, it was notable that fewer and fewer other cyclecars were now appearing. The arrival of relatively refined four-cylinder light cars had rendered the cyclecar concept all but redundant. Apart from running 'Kim II', AFN also competed in his new four-cylinder, 8.7 hp Ruby-engined Frazer Nash sports car, although with the Ruby engine performance was still fairly modest.

The defensive attitude of the JCC in not announcing actual times was not mere paranoia, for behind the intense competition and the obvious bonhomie of the 'circus' of regular entrants there was considerable disquiet. On the same day in August both the Edinburgh and DMC hill climb at Whitbridge Hill and a speed trial much further South had to be abadoned when the police intervened and made it clear that the law would be upheld to the letter. Trouble of a different kind afflicted the Kent AC when they tried to put Bugattis into a separate class at Sharnden Hill, near Mayfield. Since trade interests were prominent among Bugatti-mounted competitors, and since a win over only other entrants with the same type of car was meaningless in terms of publicity, there was an outcry from those affected so the idea was dropped. As ever, clubs were grappling with the thankless task of balancing the interests of the trade, the top drivers with often the most expensive cars (the very ones the spectators come to see) and those of the relatively impecunious competitor who, however skilful, was going to be outclassed.

Problems apart, everybody looked forward to Shelsley where a high-grade entry arrived to do battle before a reported 5,000 spectators. Leslie Wilson and the MAC had instituted a new class structure which at last abandoned the not very satisfactory 'open'/'closed'/unlimited/Light Car divisions of previous years. Instead, cars were categorised by engine capacity, with class divisions at 750cc, 1,100cc, 1,500cc, 2-litres, and 3-litres.

Although hardly in the running for outright honours, Captain Arthur Waite, with a fairly standard Austin Seven, climbed in a most satisfactory 75.5s, enough to win the 'baby' class. The eagerly awaited 1,500cc class duel between a very determined Mays and Frazer Nash – both sawing away at the enormous steering wheels connected to high-geared steering which characterised the sprint cars of the period – went decisively to the super-tuned Bugatti, 52.8s to 54.8s. Cyril Paul brought the ohc Beardmore South and his 56.2s climb was too much for hte 2-litre class opposition headed by the Reading-built HE, driven by designer R. J. Sully (60.8s). With both Park and Cook in TT Vauxhalls much was expected in the 3-litre class but this was one 1923 event where things went wrong for Cook. The servo-assisted brakes locked at the Esses after a good start and 'Rouge et Noir II' spun to a standstill. Park fairly flew up but his 52.9s was still and elusive 0.1s away from Mays' time in the phenomenal little Bugatti, once an initially announced figure of 52.8s was corrected. Malcolm Campbell was not experienced on this so deceptive hill, so a workmanlike and class-winning 54.8s was pretty fair with the big Indianapolis Sunbeam which he had by now bought from STD's Louis Coatalen. The previous year Miss Heath's 14 hp Sunbeam had won Shelsley's first-ever Ladies' Prize, but in 1923 the MAC actually instituted a separate class for women. Miss Roper's AC won on time (71.4s) while the winner on formula was a regular and modestly successful competitor, Miss Winifred Pink, who drove Lionel Martin's now wire-wheeled prototype Aston Martin, AM 270, with Martin himself in the rear pasenger seat. So far, Bird's 1921 record remained unbeaten, but Mays had another, 'unofficial', run in a team contest. The result was a shattering 51.9s – convincing testimony to Mays's driving skill, Villier's tuning ability and the general advance in the state of the art with the Light Car. Although this extra run could not be counted as an official record it made little difference to the celebrations. It was a superb achievement but it would have been fairer had the two TT Vauxhalls had another run.

After this anything else was rather anti-climactic, and a grand total of 9 entries at Kop for the Essex MC meeting in October did nothing to inspire. Everyone won at least two awards! Frank Clement's stripped and track-bodied Bentley took BTD honours, beating Paul and Mays, although it was Paul who had the last word by setting BTD at Thundersley Church on 20 October to round off a very long season.

Before a large crowd made their way to Kop on 29 March, 1924, *The Autocar* had already published dire warnings about the safety of onlookers at hill climbs and the serious implications of another accident involving spectators. But the attention of others was on more competitive matters. Although he was not ready to compete at Kop, Raymond Mays was preparing for a major offensive with *two* T13 Bugattis. His exploits had greatly impressed Ettore Bugatti himself and after inviting the Lincolnshire driver to Molsheim, *Le Patron* provided Mays – still an amateur driver, remember – with a new Brescia, to the latest factory specification although nothing like as highly developed as the older car which now rejoiced in the name 'Cordon Rouge'. It was named after the champagne imported by G. H. Mumm & Co., who gladly gave permission to use the name and 'sponsored' the enterprising Mays to the tune of three dozen bottles of the stuff. The idea was for the older car to carry on more or less where it had left off in the sports car classes prior to another of the radical Villiers development programmes being set in motion.

In fact, by July 'Cordon Rouge' was pulling an astonishing 6,400 rpm on an 8 to 1 compression ratio, and was developing 80 bhp. Since the standard Brescia produced around 40 bhp at a safe 3,800 rpm, the magnitude of the achievement can be gauged. As ever, the Essex MC drew an excellent entry for the opening Kop event, and in the absence of Mays, the bigger car were in command. Cook's TT Vauxhall was unbeatable on 29s (by the other cars anyway – overall BTD went to Freddie Dixon's Harley-Davidson motorcycle), but he was pursued by the heavy metal of Dario Resta (works Indianapolis Sunbeam), Zborowski (1919 Indianapolis Ballot), and Howey in the sister Leyland Eight to Parry Thomas's car. Fastest of the smaller cars was Joyce's lightweight AC (32.4s), but only 0.2s gaps separated him, Eddie Hall in the track Aston Martin 'Razor Blade', and Paul's rapid Beardmore.

Both Hall (Sutton Bank) and Paul (Angel Bank) soon opened their winning accounts with triumphs in streaming wet conditions in a rather damp Spring. For the second successive year, Richard Summers won the Inter-Varsity event, this time at Kop, with his 30/98 Vauxhall, but he was only 0.6s up on one of the new Frazer Nashes, driven by the Hon. Brian Lewis, then at the beginning of a distinguished motor racing career. The RAC ran another long distance Small Car Trial, in May, taking in eleven timed hills in Wales. Nevertheless, this event – in which the premier award fell to Chinery's Gwynne – served to confirm how far this kind of event and the main stream of hill climb events had diverged.

Over 3,000 spectators flocked to Aston Hill on 17 May for the second major climb of the year, this time under the aegis of the Hertfordshire AC. The big attraction was one of the latest 2-litre Grand Prix Sunbeams, driven by Dario Resta. The timed distance at Aston Hill was 1,400 yards at that juncture so records were difficult to compare, but Resta's winning time of 44.6s was highly significant. Mays, driving 'Cordon Rouge' recorded 46.6s, Cook with the TT Vauxhall, 47.8s, and Eddie Hall, now at the wheel of 'Bunny', 48.8s. Resta's winning margin with a new 2-litre road racer which was by no means as light as some of the sprint cars needed some explanation. Inspired by the formidable Grand Prix Fiats of 1923, Sunbeam had developed their new six-cylinder engine to be boosted by a Roots-type supercharger, in an installation designed by Captain Jack Irving. The result was 138 bhp at 5,500 rpm: rather more than the unsupercharged, 3-litre TT Vauxhall in 'standard' form. This dramatically successful arrival of the 'blower' on the hill climb scene set everyone thinking, not least Villiers and Cook.

Resta repeated the lesson at a treacherously wet South Harting a fortnight later. This time the Sunbeam's winning margin over Cook's Vauxhall was all of 3.4s, with the supercharged car climbing in 25.8s. One of the much campaigned Aston Martins, the ex-Eyston 200 Mile Race car, suffered disas-

Noel Beardsell's effective Anzani-engined Hodgson awaits its turn at Shelsley in 1923.
DEMAUS TRANSPORT PHOTOGRAPHICS

The blackboard says it all. Dario Resta won at South Harting in May 1924, driving a supercharged 2.0 Grand Prix Sunbeam. The supercharger had arrived in hill climbing.
NATIONAL MOTOR MUSEUM

ter when Robin Morgan had a tyre blow out and the car crashed into a bank with devastating force, although both car and driver lived to fight another day. In marked contrast to the professionalism of the Sunbeam team and their superb new Grand Prix car was the laudable, but not too successful attempt by the promoting Surbiton and Ealing Motor Clubs to keep spectators up to date regarding times set via a chalked blackboard carried (too fast) up the hill in a Vauxhall.

The pace was really hectic in 1924, a fact which was well illustrated when the course record fell no fewer than seven times at Spread Eagle on 28 June. The day really belonged to Raymond Mays who contrived to win six classes with 'Cordon Rouge' and 'Cordon Bleu', and set the final record with the former car at 38.6s. This domination obviously embarrassed the organising Hampshire AC because they asked Mays for some of their trophies back so that they could award them to someone else! Nearest to the super-tuned 'Cordon Rouge' was the big Sunbeam of Campbell (39.8s), with John Joyce flinging the lightweight AC racer up in an even 40s. Some way adrift of the battle for BTD but significant nonetheless was a defeat for Gordon England (Austin Seven, 54.8s), at the hands of Miss Ivy Cummings, who was now at the wheel of one of the new 1,100cc four-cylinder Frazer Nashes. At this time Gordon England was giving the works Austin team much to think about as his own development programme on the little 750 Austin ensured that he was at least a match for the factory entries.

Given good weather, a new course record at Shelsley was a near certainty, and expectations were not disappointed. It was not Mays to whom the honour fell, but Cyril Paul with the remarkably fast Beardmore. By this time the car was always a front runner, but on this occasion everything 'clicked'. Paul's skill and judgement were perfect but the decisive factor may have been the car's gearing – not an easy compromise at Shelsley. The Beardmore was set up perfectly, with exceptional speed on the final straight, and the result was the new record at 50.5s.

Mays had plenty to be proud of too for he contrived to take both Brescias up in the same time of 50.8s, over a second under his 1923 unofficial record with 'Cordon Rouge'. Mays's time was also equalled by the most consistently successful of all the early Aston Martins, 'Bunny', with Eddie Hall driving. There were no works Sunbeams competing this time, and with Cook's TT Vauxhall beaten into fourth BTD (52.8s), ahead of Joyce's AC (53.2s), the smaller cars were certainly in the ascendant. King's Brooklands Austin Seven won the 'baby' class while Miss Pink reinforced a good day for Astons by winning four awards on formula with AM 270. One driver was dismissed in a contemporary report as having 'wobbled somewhat alarmingly', but the competitor, on his first visit to Shelsley, was Basil Davenport, who was raising a few eyebrows with his curious driving style whereby he gripped the large steering wheel of his neo-'Kim' GN near the top with both hands, seeming to change direction by means of sharp tugs at the wheel.

Not surprisingly, given the increase in speeds over the previous year, there were several hectic tyre-

One week after setting a 50.5s Shelsley record in 1924 with the Beardmore, Cyril Paul set second BTD at Caerphilly, sharing the honour with Raymond Mays who set his time in his Bugatti 'Cordon Bleu', before it snapped a halfshaft in dramatic fashion.
DEMAUS TRANSPORT PHOTOGRAPHICS

bursting incidents. A new 12/50 Alvis, driven by Major Harvey was one such although he did contrive to finish his run. Even more spectacular was the departure from the course of J. A. Hall, who had now bought 'Kim II' from AFN, who was fully occupied with his new Frazer Nashes and finding that his old GN sprint car was no longer as competitive as hitherto. Hall was said to have cleared the heads of several spectators as he left the road.

Just one week later most of the 'aces' were down in South Wales for the popular Welsh Weekend.

A classic picture: Raymond Mays does the original 'double take' as the rear wheel of his Bugatti 'Cordon Bleu' makes a bid for freedom at Caerphilly in 1924.
NATIONAL MOTOR MUSEUM

Again there was no surprise with Kensington-Moir setting a spirited 61.4s BTD with the rather special sprint hill climb Bentley, often driven by Clement, with both Mays and Paul on 63.2s, Cook on 64.4s, just 0.4s ahead of a 30/98-mounted Park (at Caerphilly for the first time), and Joyce on 65s. Mays was lucky to finish so high up for he had both Brescias break during the day. 'Cordon Rouge' disgraced itself by stripping a gear on the starting line while 'Cordon Bleu' at least managed one run before snapping a halfshaft and tossing off the nearside rear wheel in a moment recorded for posterity in an oft-published photograph, which even made the *Sunday Times* Colour Magazine in 1982! The expression on the face of the immaculately-attired (as always) Mays is priceless.

'Cordon Bleu' was a four-wheeler again at South Harting, a week later, when the JCC repeated the public relations ploy of announcing relative times only. This time Mays had 2.4s in hand over his nearest rival, Hall in 'Bunny', with Joyce in third place. The 1100cc battle was almost as interesting with J.A. Hall in 'Kim II' (although Hall also ran one of the new Ruby-engined Frazer Nashes) defeating Brian Lewis's fast Ruby 'Nash by only one second, with Davenport four seconds slower still.

The final full scale confrontation in this busy season – approximately 53 hill climbs including those on the Welsh Light Car Trial – came at Holme Moss, where the Bradford and Huddersfield clubs drew a record entry with many amateurs encouraged by the institution of a handicap competition, and enjoyed a fine September day.

It was another fraught day for Mays, but one ending in triumph. Apart from running 'Cordon Bleu', he had been invited to try Peter Gurney's TT Vauxhall. Racing 'Cordon Bleu' for the last time, he had a terrifying moment when the throttle stuck open and he left the road, the wide open throttle causing serious mechanical damage. He also had the Vauxhall catch fire at the first attempt! Undeterred, Mays tried again and an impressive 75s record for the course ensued, beating even Humphrey Cook himself (78.8s). Nobody else got under 80s, with Eddie Hall (80.8s), T. Moore's special Horstmann (81.2s) and Paul (81.6s), all closely matched.

Raymond Mays looks awfully vulnerable in his Bugatti 'Cordon Bleu' at Holme Moss in 1924. He was lucky to avoid a major accident when his throttle jammed open, causing him to veer off the road.
DEMAUS TRANSPORT PHOTOGRAPHICS

Before catastrophe intervened, Major Coe, in his Alfa Romeo RL Targa Florio, races past the Kop spectators massed on the very edge of the road in March 1925.
DEMAUS TRANSPORT PHOTOGRAPHICS

As was becoming customary during the Winter months, *The Autocar* was full of gloom regarding the future of hill climbing. The Boxing Day issue (no 'bumper' two-week Christmas numbers then to give magazine staff and printers an extended holiday) aired all the old complaints such as domination by works cars (since both Mays and Cook were strictly amateurs this was a big generalisation), erratic timing arrangements, lack of consistency in the means adopted by clubs to calculate formula results, the equally inconsistent interpretations of what was meant by 'touring', 'sports' and 'racing' cars, the abuses of weighing-in arrangements, and cost of entry fees (normally £2 or £3 except at the much more expensive Shelsley Walsh). All this was significant but not crucial. The really serious concern remained the risk of accidents involving spectators on public road events. A recent court case where a spectator injured by a competing motorcyclist in a public road event had been awarded damages was a worrying precedent.

The concern grew to new levels before the 1925 season even began, with protests growing in volume and influence. Public road speed events were banned in Worcestershire, Warwickshire and Staffordshire. But a real and permanent solution to this chronic problem seemed to be at hand. A Bill

One of the works 2.0 Grand Prix Sunbeams passed into the hands of the talented May Cunliffe, who did well with it for several seasons. She poses here with Bill Perkins of Sunbeam.
NATIONAL MOTOR MUSEUM

'Rouge et Noir', Humphrey Cook's immensely successful 30/98 Vauxhall in its most developed form.
DEMAUS TRANSPORT PHOTOGRAPHICS

was in preparation to go before Parliament to permit the closing of public roads for motor competitions, in the same manner as was done in Northern Ireland and the Isle of Man.

Looking ahead, the biggest news was that Raymond Mays, whose ambitious programme was rather more than his financial reources could stand, even with trade backing, had sold both his Brescias. 'Cordon Bleu' was rebuilt and sold to a novice, a Cambridge undergraduate named Francis Giveen, who Mays undertook to assist in gaining experience with this by-no-means-easy car. 'Cordon Rouge' was de-tuned and went to F. B. Taylor. During 1924, Mays had actually competed twice with a TT Vauxhall, for he had raced Peter Gurney's car at a Kop meeting, scoring second BTD to Joyce's AC, but it was not one of these cars he had in mind for 1925. Impressed with S. F. Edge's programme with John Joyce, he came to an arrangement with the publicity-conscious Edge to run a new AC which would be supercharged, with Villiers working on this installation as he was in a plan to supercharge Cook's TT Vauxhall.

An enormous entry of 221, including many motorcycles, augured well for the Essex MC when they arrived at Kop on 28 March 1925. Scrutineering was strict, and the only problem seemed to be a particularly large crowd who obstinately, and often extremely rudely, refused to obey marshals' instructions to retire to safer vantage points. They were particularly thick, in both senses, at the very fast top right hand bend of the hill. Mays's new AC was not yet ready so he came along to help Giveen, who did not inspire confidence. He had already had one testing accident and seemed to have very little awareness of the limits and dangers of his very fast car. In a nutshell, he seemed to be 'speed happy'.

Early in the meeting a motorcyclist had crashed, injuring only himself, but narrowly missing several spectators. In the competition proper, there was no matching Henry Segrave who was driving a works 2-litre, supercharged, Grand Prix Sunbeam. The time was 28.8s, but Joyce was fairly close with the AC, while Archie Frazer Nash climbed in 30.6s with one of his new generation Frazer Nashes. A wild climb by Giveen stopped the clock at 31.2s, and he seemed totally unaware of the havoc he had created along the way. He had shot off the road on the last right-hander, bounced along the track, and back on to the road again, without pause. Unfortunately he struck a spectator during the excursion, breaking one of his legs. This point on the course was where the fastest cars habitually became airborne, and attracted a big crowd. Fortunately, by the time Giveen arrived that crowd had thinned considerably, otherwise the accident could have had even more serious results. The injured spectator had been one of those who had been asked to move several times during the meeting, but had ignored the exhortations of the marshals, so really he had only himself to blame. However, with a number of competitors still to run, including Major Harvey's brand new supercharged Alvis, fitted for the first time in competition with front wheel drive, the RAC Steward stepped in and called a halt to the meeting.

The moment that many had feared had come. The Bill due to go before Parliament was too late and it was never pursued. The RAC atted swiftly to pre-empt even greater hostility being levelled at motor sport. On 2 April it announced a total ban on the issue of permits for public road speed events, a ban which remained in force until a special Act of Parliament enabled the streets of Birmingham to be closed for the first Super prix in 1986. Astonishingly, the York & District MC pressed on with the organisation of their climb at Sutton Bank on 10 April, laying themselves open to serious criticism. But right from the start spectators were obstructing the course and the meeting was rapidly abandoned.

Thus, abruptly, hill climbing's early vintage was over. There was only Shelsley Walsh to look forward to. For the rest it was the alternative of racing at Brooklands or beach racing.

It is doubly ironic that the accident at Kop happened just when a legal solution to the problem of public road events was at hand, and that the fateful incident came about at least partly by reason of the purchase of Mays's car by someone psychologically unsuited to the task in hand. Unwittingly, one of the sport's most popular stars had contributed to the demise of Kop, Aston Hill, South Harting, Spread Eagle, Holme Moss, Sutton Bank and all the other hills where he had helped to popularise the sport.

Taking the period 1919 to 1925 as a whole, Raymond Mays looms large through his driving skill and the mechanical ingenuity of his friend Amherst Villiers, but also to Mays's own flare for publicity. His own autobiography, *Split Seconds* (edited by Dennis May), published by Foulis in 1951, came after a number of articles in the specialist press which for the first time explained the special techniques needed to achieve success in hill climbs. On the other hand, so much material is available on Mays's exploits, and was so even in the nineteen twenties, it would be easy to exaggerate his successes, considerable though they are, during this period. The record shows that he scored 14 major BTDs in hill climbs from 1921 until the end of 1924. This was actually two less than the total netted from 1919 to 1924 by Archie Frazer Nash, although AFN, through his own ingenuity in developing 'Kim II', probably had less consistent opposition in the earlier years when he scored the majority of his outright successes. Nobody else exceeded 10 major hill climb BTD runs, although Humphrey Cook, a fine driver and a true gentleman amateur, came close with 9, and achieved near total domination of the 1923 season, his first with the TT Vauxhall.

Perhaps the final irony of that last meeting at Kop was that an era of tremendous spirit, enthusiasm and ingenuity in developing a new breed of nervous, highly-tuned, sprint cars was rounded off by victory for a Grand Prix driver who did not like hill climbs, driving a thoroughbred road racer.

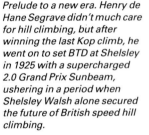

Prelude to a new era. Henry de Hane Segrave didn't much care for hill climbing, but after winning the last Kop climb, he went on to set BTD at Shelsley in 1925 with a supercharged 2.0 Grand Prix Sunbeam, ushering in a period when Shelsley Walsh alone secured the future of British speed hill climbing.

CHAPTER THREE
SHELSLEY SUPREME
(1925-1939)

I T is not beyond the bounds of possibility that if Shelsley Walsh had not been such a respected and thoroughly successful motor sporting venue, and the Midland Automobile Club such efficient hill climb organisers, then the sport of British speed hill climbing might have just faded away in the later nineteen-twenties.

At a stroke, the RAC's entirely understandable if precipitous ban had wiped every hill climb event from the calendar except for the solitary exception of Shelsley, the one event which was run on private ground. It was the greatest of good fortune that that one survivor happened to be the event which was already regarded as *primus inter pares* among speed hill climb venues. Leaving aside 'freak' hill climbs run by a number of Northern clubs at Post Hill, Dalton Bank and Hepolite Scar – we would call them trials hills with their gradients around the 1 in 1½ mark to catch out the competitors who were not already inhibited by the rocky surfaces – and such enjoyable but definitely small-time affairs as those at Ewelme Bank, Dancer's End, Chalfont St Peter, and Backwell; Shelsley Walsh stood alone until the Bugatti Owners Club began to develop Prescott in 1937/38.

Even without the ban there may well have been a lean patch in the later nineteen-twenties when the depressing realities of economic slump loomed ever more serious. Most branches of motor sport, up to and including Grand Prix racing declined into a rather formless collection of *formule libre* races. A mere 17 cars actually started the 1930 Le Mans 24 Hour sports car race, although this lamentable fact was forgotten after the great Bentley versus Mercedes duel. At home there remained Brooklands and a fair number of assorted speed trials and sand races of foreshores, promenades and the occasional private road such as the Race Hill at Lewes.

But even here the tendency was towards decline, hastened by further official discouragement. In 1926 the Board of Trade, which had responsibility for the foreshore round these islands, reacted to increasingly strident complaints against the noise and crowds which were inseparable from sand racing and threatened to withhold permission for future events. A couple of meetings were called off and this became another branch of motor sport which seemed to be running on borrowed time, at least in the South of the country. That piece of official discouragement came in March 1926. Less than two months later the SMMT, always ambivalent in its attitude to the competitive side of motoring, ruled that in future its member companies should not officially contest *any* motor sporting events, except for a few recognised 'classics'. A strong body of opinion within the motor industry's representative body believed that motor sport served no useful purpose whatsoever! For 1926 only two sprint events had the SMMT's seal of approval: the Northern sand race meeting at Saltburn (cancelled because of the General Strike and not run again as a major meeting) and the 'Open' meeting at Shelsley Walsh.

All these negative factors served to concentrate attention on Shelsley Walsh, where Leslie Wilson and his colleagues in the MAC rose to the occasion by continually honing the running of their events to a sharpness which ensured their enduring appeal. From 1926 two meetings were held each year, one 'Open' (with SMMT trade support) and one 'Amateur'. In fact, with the much reduced number of manufacturers actually contesting hill climbs the entry lists for the racing classes for the two meetings were pretty similar in most years. This was truly the age of amateurism which firmly established the genuinely sporting atmosphere of hill climbs which is still valued highly today.

Shelsley Walsh was a social as well as a competitive institution in the nineteen-thirties. Centre of attention for this fashionably-attired gathering on the steps of the Swan Hotel, Tenbury Wells, in 1930 are Hans Stuck (front row, second from left) and Rudolf Caracciola (front row, fourth from left).
DEMAUS TRANSPORT PHOTOGRAPHICS

This happy group was pictured at the Swan Hotel rather later in the 'thirties. Freddie Dixon is on the extreme left, Fay Taylor and Joe Findon are also prominent in the front row next to Leslie and Mrs Wilson.
DEMAUS TRANSPORT PHOTOGRAPHICS

As a European Hill Climbing Championship round in the early nineteen-thirties, Shelsley attracted some exotic foreign entries. This is Tort's supercharged, straight-eight Nacional Pescara, which achieved a commendable fourth BTD in 1931, behind team-mate Zanelli.
DEMAUS TRANSPORT PHOTOGRAPHICS

Shelsley Walsh became a fixture on the motoring calendar around which other activities were simply re-arranged! Like the Motor Show – or in later years, the Donington Grand Prix – Shelsley became one of those social and competitive landmarks by which one gauged the passing of the season. It became an institution. As the later nineteen-twenties and nineteen-thirties passed, many of the essential characteristics of post-Second World War hill climbing were established. Ironic though it may seem, with only one major venue and with motor sport as a whole only gathering new momentum around 1933/34, this was truly a first golden age for hill climbing.

The new impetus, away from the wooded Worcestershire slopes, was very gradual. In 1929 the Oxford University CC held a small 'Inter-Varsity'-type climb at Ewelme Downe, while over in Ulster a fine entry tackled the revived Craigantlet climb near Belfast, when the Ulster Automobile Club shrewdley ran the event as a curtain raiser for the following week's Ulster Tourist Trophy. The Berkhamstead & DMC began running meetings at Dancer's End in 1930, while the following year the recently formed Bugatti Owners Club started holding hill climbs up the 1,000 yards or so of loose-surfaced roadway on an incomplete housing estate at Chalfont St Peter. As the 'thirties advanced, Backwell, Joel Park, Bo'ness, Prescott, Great Auclum and Trengwainton all joined the list of active venues, even though only Prescott, a few miles outside Cheltenham, aspired to the same league as Shelsley.

Of course, motor sport as a whole advanced in the second part of the inter-war period. The abolition of the hated 20 mph overall open road speed limit in 1930 greatly increased the scope for the milder forms of open road competition. Rallies, usually comprising a mixture of relatively easy navigation, none too fierce driving, gymkhana-like driving tests and Concours d'Elégance, gained favour with those who liked to combine a little motoring with their social lives. Regularity trials, involving the sort of hills which were more 'freak' than 'speed' burgeoned in popularity. At least partly responsible for this new competitive interest among so many new clubmen was the ready availability of relatively cheap sporting cars which did not demand the stoic single-mindedness of a GN or a Morgan. If the Austin Seven introduced motoring to the British masses in 1922, then certainly the MG Midget introduced sporting motoring to the many in 1929, although to be fair more than a few had already discovered that you could do quite sporting things with an Austin Seven long before that. By the mid-nineteen-thirties flotillas of small MGs, Wolseley Hornets, Singers, Rileys, the more expensive and specialised Frazer Nashes, and the aristocratic Aston Martins provided the backbone of many club events of varied character.

Even pure circuit racing was expanding. Brooklands, for so long the sole racing circuit on the mainland, was joined in 1933 by Donington Park, near Derby, a true road circuit which was soon 'poaching' major events away from the more artificial environment of Weybridge. In 1937 the London County Council began to promote race meetings on a specially constructed and very tight road circuit around the grounds of the old Crystal Palace in South London. Further afield, but still on British soil, a magnificent series of Tourist Trophy races were held on the closed public roads around Newtownards in Northern Ireland, from 1928 to 1936. Further major Irish road races were run in Dublin's Phoenix Park and elsewhere and an important Light Car race was run on the Isle of Man in 1936, and again in 1937. By the latter year the old problem of fixture congestion was a real problem once again. Abroad, Grand Prix racing attained a new level of spectacle with the German-dominated 750 Kilogramme maximum weight formula of 1934 to 1937. Light Car or Voiturette (1,500cc) racing became extremely popular, and the French led a renewed interest in sports car racing in the later nineteen-thirties.

But for British hill climb enthusiasts the centrepiece was, and remained, Shelsley Walsh. The MAC's meetings so dominated hill climbing between 1925 and 1939, that it is reasonable to consider events there in isolation before considering other happenings elsewhere. During these years Shelsley and hill climbing were almost interchangeable terms.

Hill climb chroniclers of earlier years, including Raymond Mays and Austen May, stressed the keen air of anticipation and the eager enthusiasm among competitors and officials, as they gathered in the area before Shelsley meetings. The atmosphere at hotels such as *The Swan* at Tenbury Wells, for long a kind of unofficial hill climb HQ, and *The Crown* in Worcester, was not unlike the beginning of term at one of the heartier public schools, with old friends renewing acquaintance, new posessions being eagerly examined, and 'new boys' being carefully scrutinised. Long before he worked with Mays and the ERA team, A. F. Rivers Fletcher remembers ticking off the weeks to the next Shelsley meeting, like so many others, with ill-concealed impatience.

Given its unique position in contemporary motor sport, Shelsley's promoters, the MAC, could have been forgiven for resting on their laurels. Nothing could be further from the case. New improvements to the course and its surroundings or innovations in the way the events were run cropped up virtually every year. By the late nineteen-thirties the format of the modern, nineteen-eighties, hill climbs was perfectly recognisable, shorn only of the plethora of annual championships, which are so widespread today.

Not surprisingly the improvements made for the 1925 event majored on safety. Spectators who had previously been able to watch proceedings from either side of the course, now had to cross the track, under the benign but firm guidance of members of the Worcestershire Constabulary, at a point on the second right-hand curve. This feature immediately became known as The Crossing. It has always retained that name, even though spectators have long since ceased to use the left-hand side of the course at all. There had also been much clearing of trees, cutting of pathways and steps, and barriers erected to keep bystanders and competitors safely apart. A scoreboard at the 'S' Bend, manned by Boy Scouts, further assisted people to keep track of what was going on.

With but one isolated exception there had always been just one meeting each year, but in 1926 the MAC staged two climbs, an 'Amateur' event in July (without SMMT trade support) and an 'Open' meeting in September. Competitors at last had the opportunity for an additional official competitive run in 1927, despite misgivings about running 56 competitors through twice in reasonable time. The

Basil Davenport's deceptively scruffy and disreputable-looking GN 'Spyder', which set an astonishing seven successive BTDs at Shelsley. This was the quintessential Shelsley Special and after retirement in 1931 (soon after this picture was taken), re-emerged into competition again in 1946.
DEMAUS TRANSPORT PHOTOGRAPHICS

next major innovation came in 1929 when the 'Open' meeting incorporated a well-supported class, run on formula, for cars which had run in the previous week's Ulster Tourist Trophy. In fact, this was the last time a formula competition really received much attention, for Shelsley was becoming more and more an outright speed contest unfettered by a motor industry which was taking less interest in speed events.

Shelsley's stature received a major boost in 1930 when the 'Open' meeting was accorded the honour of counting for the European Hill-climbing Championship for the first time. Geographical isolation and its unrepresentative nature among all the long European mountain climbs, meant that there was never a large Continental entry, but since Stuck, Caracciola, Zanelli, Luigi Villoresi, Baumer and Kohlrausch all competed at least once, the quality was there even if the numbers were low. Conversely, a few Englishmen – notably Raymond Mays, Richard Seaman, Reggie Tongue and Charles Martin (all ERA mounted) – successfully took in the odd Continental hill climb as part of a European racing programme. Also most significant in 1930 was a big improvement in the track surface. The hill was grouted with small flints, then sprayed with bitumen and water.

An innovation of a very different kind came in 1932 when for the first time the BBC covered a motor sporting event with a live outside broadcast. The experiment, with a commentary by F. J. 'Eric' Findon (then editor of *The Lightcar*, and Major Vernon Brook, was a great success and laid the foundations for all the radio and television commentaries which have followed over the years. One idea was not pursued, though, when mooted that year. This was the plan to lengthen the course by about a third of a mile at the top of the hill, employing a second 'S' bend. This decision enables the MAC to make its proud claim to have the world's oldest motoring event still run on its original course.

A new Members' Enclosure below the 'S' Bend and the consequent move to allow the public into the former Members' Enclosure, at the prime viewing point on the outside of the exit to the first part of the 'S', in exchange for an additional half-crown (12½ pence) on top of the five-bob (25 pence) course admission, was a popular move in 1933. The MAC were now granted two 'Open' permits, so in this year the 'Amateur' meeting was upgraded.

By 1935 (the thirtieth anniversary of the first meeting) prize money was an established tradition, but with the prize for BTD increased to £250 in May, modern-day competitors may wince a little. That would be an above average sum for a hill climb BTD today, even without taking inflation into account.

It had long been accepted that most people came to Shelsley with the performance of the racing cars, untrammelled by regulations and road equipment, uppermost in their minds. In 1936 the engine capacity classes were divided simply into supercharged and unsupercharged categories, superseding the old sports/racing division, although there remained awards for the fastest fully-equipped sports cars. Then the following year the trees in the orchard Paddock were felled, a much-needed hard surface was laid, and the now familiar stalls were erected for undercover fettling of the machinery: a welcome move after the downpours of 1936.

Throughout all these years the focus of attention was always on the battle for Best Time of the Day, and if the weather was co-operative, the efforts to smash the all-time course record. Over the fifteen-year period that coveted and prestigious record, which counted for far more than any such record today in a wider motor sporting context, was reduced from 50.5s to just 37.37s, and was held by six men: Cyril Paul (the 1924 record holder); the Macclesfield 'Specialist' Basil Davenport, who successfully bettered his own figures three times; Raymond Mays (four times a record holder in these years

Raymond Mays was Britain's best-known racing driver in 1932 at the time this photograph was taken. The passenger in his 'second string' sports Invicta is his longtime collaborator Peter Berthon.
RICHARD CHAPMAN

alone); the Austrian *bergmeister* Hans Stuck; the enormously talented Whitney Straight (twice); and the enigmatic Fane. The latter, born A. F. Agabeg and a naturalised Englishman, changed his name to A. F. P. Fane, and since the 'F' also stood for Fane he tended to be referred to as just that.

Perhaps rather surprisingly, only three other drivers strictly set BTDs without holding the record. They were the Grand Prix star Segrave, the by no means young and often underrated Earl Howe, and another of the 'Specialists', R. G. J. 'Dick' Nash. 'Strictly', because that prolific hill climb class winner, Eddie Hall, had climbed fastest in his 30/98 Vauxhall when the 1926 'Amateur' meeting was abandoned because of bad weather. However, the racing class was postponed and run as part of the September meeting, an odd situation where Basil Davenport had the unusual experience of theoretically setting two BTDs in one day! Counting both of these successes, Davenport achieved the remarkable record of seven successive Best Times of Day, and all with the same car, the deceptively scruffy and disreputable looking GN 'Spider', which was once refused admission to the Paddock by a policeman who could not believe that such a tatty contraption could be a legitimate competitor!

But even Davenport's record must take second place to that of Raymond Mays who left Shelsley Walsh with the Best Time of Day no fewer than thirteen times between 1925 and 1939. During these years Mays overcame many setbacks – especially financial – to become Britain's best-known racing driver and, aided by a close team of talented associates, the inspiration behind the immortal ERA. Despite an incurable tendency to tackle the over-ambitious, a charateristic fuelled by unquenchable optimism, Mays usually succeeded in the end. In the words of Rivers Fletcher, who worked with Mays

1926 was Basil Davenport's year at Shelsley with BTD at both meetings and a new 48.8s record.
MIDLAND AUTOMOBILE CLUB

Raymond Mays and Peter Berthon return down the hill after setting a 45.6s Shelsley record in 1929. The Vauxhall Villiers Special is fitted for the first time with trendsetting twin rear wheels.
DEMAUS TRANSPORT PHOTOGRAPHICS

for 30 years: 'Above all, Ray had tremendous drive, energy and determination to do what he wished to do'. Most important too was his enormous charm and persuasiveness, allied to meticulous concern to give good value to all to whom he was indebted, which ensured that his key friendships with Amherst Villiers, Peter Berthon, Humphrey Cook, Murray Jamieson and Reid Railton were both close and enduring.

Returning to 1925 and the sport-starved aftermath of the Kop incident, it was no surprise that a large crowd made their way to Shelsley on 23 May. Cyril Paul's record remained intact but few would have been disappointed with the spectacle. Dressed in a lounge suit but wearing (unusually for the nineteen-twenties) a peaked crash helmet, Britain's number one driver of the day, Henry Segrave, made his one and only competitive climb of Shelsley Walsh, driving one of the rebuilt 1924 Grand Prix Sunbeams, as at Kop. His typically polished climb in 53.8s was unbeaten, but just 0.4s clear of a tie for second place between Maurice Harvey's FWD Alvis – destined for the JCC's 200 Mile Race at Brooklands and running without a body on this occasion – and the 2-litre, four-cylinder Mercedes 'Targa Florio' of E. A. Mayner. A disconnected advance-retard control dropped Raymond Mays's new supercharged AC from the reckoning, but Davenport was coming into contention. He had obtained the unique 1½-litre vee twin GN engine out of Archie Frazer Nash's long wheelbase Brooklands car 'Mowgli', and was only 0.4s slower than Harvey and Mayner, despite a monumental engine blow-up at a highly risky 5,000 rpm just before the finish.

Torrential rain at the first 'Amateur' climb in July 1926 meant that the rather wild young Davenport with his homely racer (gross financial outlay now standing at £135), had to wait until September for further improvements.

The wait was well worthwhile. Sixty competitors gathered on a sunny afternoon for what appeared to be a very open contest. Record holder Cyril Paul had obtained the use of one of the supercharged Grand Prix Sunbeams, now two years old, while Raymond Mays had been lent J. Harold Clay's ex-Park TT Vauxhall which was a former Shelsley record holder. In fact, this was to be Mays's only competition appearance of the year for his career was at a low ebb. The AC engine had failed to stand up to the stresses imposed by Villiers's experiments in supercharging it, and the necessary development would have been prohibitively expensive. In fact, Mays's financial resources were seriously over-extended in the attempt and he spent most of 1926 working in the family business, recouping the losses. Villiers had also been working on a project to supercharge Humphrey Cook's TT Vauxhall, but the burly 'gentleman driver' had lost interest and Villiers's efforts were now being channelled into his own engineering consultancy business, with the emphasis on supercharging aero engines.

The efforts of Paul and Mays in relatively unfamiliar cars were commendable for both broke the existing record, Mays (impressed with the old Vauxhall) in 49.4s and Paul in 50.6s, but they were decisively beaten by Davenport who, tugging at the wheel of the GN in characteristic style, shot up in 48.8s. Over the winter Davenport had fitted lightweight pistons and JAP connecting rods to the 'Mowgli' engine to enable the big twin to survive at high revs, and he again proved that the Frazer Nash recipe of low weight, good traction and reasonable power was a formidable combination for short-distance events. What nobody could have foreseen at the time was that this relatively impecunious driver/mechanic, aided only by advice from the scholarly Dr G. F. Mucklow (later Professor of Engineering at the Unversity of Birmingham), would remain unbeaten at Shelsley until September, 1929.

Shelsley Specials Supreme
The track was still damp for the July 'Amateur' meeting in 1927 – the first occasion when two competitive runs counted – but a 50s climb by Davenport was enough to defeat a good 51.2s run by Raymond Mays who was now at the wheel of the ex-Mayner Mercedes, which had been provided by the Managing Director of the British Mercedes importer, Frank Seddon. The Mercedes had suffered from fuel starvation on the fist climb and Mays had found reverse gear, momentarily, on his 51.2s second run, so he may well have been able to go faster given better fortune. As it was, his time was matched by E. L. F. Mucklow (brother of the Doctor), Davenport's 'teammate' in his consistently rapid 1100cc 'Akela' GN-based car.

A thoroughly wet day spoilt the prospects for September when the soaking course was opened by the Le Mans-winning Bentley with Sammy Davis and Doctor Benjafield 'up'. Although the courageous and skilful May Cunliffe fought her supercharged, lightweight-bodied 3-litre Bentley up in 53.4s and Sunbeam mechanic W R Perkins climbed in a careful 55.0s in one of the versatile 4-litre V12 Sunbeams which had broken the Land Speed Record in Segrave's hands the previous year, the battle was really between Davenport and Mays. Despite the pouring rain they both managed to break the record! Mays took the ear-splitting Mercedes up in 48.2s but Davenport somehow contrived to lop a whole second off his record, leaving it at 47.8s. Since the previous year, the engine of 'Spyder' had been further modified and now boasted new cams giving greater valve overlap, lighter valves, a new crankcase (after another blow-up) and connecting rods, alcohol fuel, a raised 8 to 1 compression ratio, and two big 40mm Solex carburettors. The results speak volumes for the effectiveness of Davenport's largely trial-and-error development.

The weather relented in 1928 and Davenport broke the record both in May (46.8s) and in July (46.2s). The former was probably his easiest BTD at Shelsley for he had no less than 3.6s advantage over his nearest challenger, Mucklow in the single-seater GN which had once been Ron Godfrey's 200 Mile Race mount. Third was the redoubtable May Cunliffe (51.2s), now the owner of one of the 1924 GP Sunbeams. In July, to which month the 'Open' meeting had been brought forward, there was a new challenger, however. Mays had bought the ex-Cook TT Vauxhall, together with the discarded Villiers supercharger set-up from Jack Barclay who had raced the car at Brooklands since buying it from Cook.

Together with Villiers and future ERA and BRM designer Peter Berthon, Mays was embarking on an ambitious development programme on a type of car which he admired enormously, and all three of which he had driven. Now repainted white, with the legend 'Vauxhall Villiers Special' on the side, this revived veteran had an appreciative audience of six thousand people, including the Prime Minister, Stanley Baldwin, accompanied by his daughter Betty. Mays, with Peter Berthon in the passenger seat, persuaded the deep-noted Vauxhall to the top in 48.0s which was a promising start, but not yet a match for Davenport. Also under 50s were the consistent Mucklow (49.4s) and none other than Archie Frazer Nash (49.6s) in a new, low-built, supercharged Anzani ohc-engined device. The car's road-hugging appearance accounted for AFN's departure from his more usual Kiplingesque pet names to christen the car 'The Slug'.

Earl Howe's patrician taste in cars would satisfy the most fastidious. This stunning 1931 paddock line-up features (left to right) 1926/27 Grand Prix Delage, ex-Varzi Alfa Romeo 6C/1750 and ex-Caracciola Mercedes-Benz 38/250.
NATIONAL MOTOR MUSEUM

Battle was renewed in May 1929 with the Mays team concentrating on further developing the Vauxhall Villiers, and ensuring that the difficult-to-service engine could cope with higher boost pressure. Mays brought his time down to 47.8s, but Davenport was still ahead with another 46.2s climb. The 'Open' meeting went back to its more customary September date and this time Mays had a secret weapon – twin rear wheels. The task in transmitting the car's 250 plus bhp to the road was a formidable one, and Amherst Villiers had the brainwave of doubling the tyre contact area by the (theoretically) simple expedient of mounting two sets of wheels on specially fabricated hubs. It worked and set the fashion for twin rear wheels for sprint events which was to remain until well after the Second World War. The first run had the time down to 46.2s – matching Davenport's record – and the second, superbly controlled, climb clocked 45.6s. The record belonged to Mays at last. Meanwhile, Davenport recorded 47s on his first climb but had 'Spyder' break on the second. The pursuit was not that far

behind either, for J. D. Jevons' 2.0 Bugatti T35C howled up in 47.6s, Frazer Nash shot up in 48s and 'Scrap' Thistlethwayte did well to conduct his monstrous 7.1 litre, Mercedes-Benz 38/250 up in 49.6s. But all their efforts were shaded by Earl Howe, who forced another 38/250, the actual car with which Caracciola had won the recent Tourist Trophy, to the summit in 47.6s, a superb effort in a very large car which was hardly tailor-made for the narrow and sinuous confines of Shelsley.

Born Francis Richard Henry Penn Curzon into a most distinguished family, Earl Howe came to motor sport in 1928 at the advanced age of 44 after having already accomplished a notable career as an MP and Government Whip when he was Viscount Curzon. Only his regular appearances before

*Eager anticipation...
Jean Bugatti prepares to tackle
Shelsley in 1932 in the four-
wheel-drive T53.*
RICHARD CHAPMAN

*Disaster... the stricken Bugatti
after the crash in practice
which kept the MAC's star
entry from competing in the
July 1932 meeting.*
RICHARD CHAPMAN

magistrates on speeding charges gave a clue to his later career. 'The Old Man', characterised by his ubiquitous flat cap and his immaculately-turned-out blue and silver cars, was to become the sport's 'elder statesman' and valued ambassador, but he was first and foremost a very fine competition driver, and this early sports car record-breaking Shelsley climb provided clear proof.

The near continuous development and rebuilding programme carried out on the Vauxhall Villiers prevented Mays from running in July 1930 when the 'Open' meeting was brought forward to fit in with the schedule for the European Championship for which Shelsley was to count for the first time. With the course resurfaced for the occasion, the weather set fair, and the arrival of Hans Stuck with his unblown Austro-Daimler (thought to be bored out to 4,255cc from the standard 2,994cc of the 19/100) and Rudi Caracciola's latest Mercedes 38/250 with bigger supercharger, the scene was set for a great occasion. Davenport, heading the 'home' side, rose to it and the familiar thumps and bangs from the twin-cylinder car filled the course for a mere 44.6s, well under Mays's record. But there was no answer for the purpose-built, rather high and old-fashioned-looking Austro-Daimler and its *Bergmeister* driver, who had driven it around 1,000 miles to compete. Taking great armfuls of lock on the enormous steering wheel, Stuck shattered the opposition with 42.8s – on both runs! Caracciola broke the sports car record with the theoretically unsuitable 38/250 (46.8s), and a promising 47s was recorded by young industrialist David Brown. The future owner of the Aston Martin and Lagonda marques had bought another of the TT Vauxhalls from Jack Barclay (the ex-Park/Clay car), and this too now boasted a Villiers supercharger.

By September, Mays was again ready for the fray with the Vauxhall almost unrecognisable with new bodywork shorn of the Vauxhall flutes and with the sinister-looking addition of a machine-gun-like intercooler emerging from the side of the squared-up bonnet. Now developing almost 300 bhp but with the weight up from some 22 cwt to around a ton and a half, this remarkable car came close to Stuck's record with 43s in practice. Sadly, race Saturday was very wet and although Mays set BTD, the time was a disappointing 46.4s.

The 1931 'Open' meeting again counted for the European Championship and two exotic, if seemingly unlikely, challengers came over from Barcelona. They were the Enrique de Pescara/Edmond Moglia-designed Nacional Pescaras, supercharged ohc straight eight competition sports cars, developing some 180 bhp from their 2.8 litres. They arrived late, their mechanics were exhausted, and drivers Zanelli and Tort had no experience of Shelsley, yet the cars' performance was highly creditable.

*By July 1932, when it was
beaten by Lord Howe's Bugatti
T35B, Mays' Villiers
Supercharge – as it was now
known – was virtually
unrecognisable as the 1922 TT
Vauxhall from which Mays,
Amherst Villiers and Peter
Berthon had developed it.*
RICHARD CHAPMAN

Zaneilli managed 44.4s and Tort 44.6s, beaten only by Mays and Dick Nash. Re-christened the Villiers Supercharge, the big Vauxhall climbed in 43.6s but Dick Nash was three-tenths faster still to score his first Shelsley BTD in the 'Terror', a true special in the Frazer-Nash tradition.

Basically a short-wheelbase version of the old 'Mowgli' chassis, but much altered and fitted with a Powerplus-supercharged side-valve Anzani engine, the 'Terror' had been developed by Nash to a pitch where at least 80 bhp was achieved with a unusually good mid-range torque. The car was perfect for Nash's sliding 'dirt track' technique. Basil Davenport had fitted front wheel brakes to 'Spyder' but his 46.2s climb was beaten by another special, the 100 bhp Becke Powerplus of 'Bill' van der Becke (45s). This low-slung and stubby looking machine was also GN-based but Becke, who was an employee of the SU Carburettor Company at the time, used a most unusual engine. This was a Powerplus-supercharged version of the ohc Wolseley Moth unit of 1,351cc.

Further 1931 attempts to beat Stuck's demoralising record were ruled out by wretched weather in September. Davenport, who was soon to retire from the scene, again had a poor day, suffering a slight accident on his second ascent, and the main issue was again fought out between Mays and Nash. This time it was the Villiers Supercharge which came out on top with 46s to the 'Terror's 46.7s.

Yet another Continental challenge appeared for the July meeting in 1932, the four-wheel-drive Bugatti T53. Employing the 4.9-litre T50-type engine in an all-new chassis, clothed in an oddly unattractive and dated-looking body, the T53 was definitely in the experimental category. Only two were built and Ettore Bugatti sent his young son Jean over to Shelsly with one. It is now part of the Shelsley folklore that after a meteoric practice run, in a time which Leslie Wilson always refused to divulge, Bugatti crashed the difficult-to-handle car and had to content himself with competing in a smart T55 sports car in the event proper. His practice performance and the subsequent telephone 'confession' to his father – of matching animation – overshadowed the rest of the meeting.

This was a pity, for the outright victory fell to a road racing thoroughbred, the Bugatti T35B of the skilful Earl Howe. Although not a record, Howe's 44s BTD in the wailing French car was a superb effort to which Mays could reply with ony 44.6s. It was quite a Bugatti occasion for Noel Carr's red ex-Chiron T35C – generally driven in terrifyingly wild style or as the polite contemporary journalists used to say: 'always a shade too dashing' – climbed in 45.6s, 0.4s less than road racer Norman Black in the ex-Birkin GP Maserati 2500. Dick Nash had an off day and even lost the 1500cc class to yet another Bugatti, that of Jack Lemon Burton.

Mays was in serious gearbox trouble in September and the Villiers Supercharge was a non-starter. This was disappointing but nobody could be bored by a battle for supremacy between Carr and Nash, two of the most spectacular drivers in all Shelsley's history. Dick Nash made it with 43.2s but the Birmingham businessman's dark red Bugatti was only 0.4s slower. Also impressive was the Horton

A fine photograph of Raymond Mays entering the Esses in July 1932 – the Villiers Supercharge watched by a typically large crowd.
RICHARD CHAPMAN

Special of Birmingham brewer, Ron Horton, who recorded 44.8s. With the aid of Robin Jackson, Horton had built his special, unusually, from *new* Frazer Nash parts, originally using a twin-cylinder JAP engine. The latter had been replaced for 1932 with one of the new four-cylinder, twin ohc, supercharged 1100cc Alta units developed by Geoffrey Taylor.

For the first time, both the 1933 events were accorded 'Open' status, but in May wet weather again ruled out serious attempts on Stuck's long-standing record. Although he now had a potent new supercharged Riley on the stocks, Mays was still campaigning the complex and temperamental Villiers Supercharge. It was still competitive too as his 44.8s BTD emphasises. Nash came nearest with 45.6s in a new car, dubbed the 'Spook'. He has sold the 'Terror' to Mancunian J. Allan Arnold (who had little joy with it), and had built up his new challenger on similar Frazer Nash lines with the motive power coming from the single ohc Anzani engine out of the 'Slug'. Carr was not far away on 46s while two rapid newcomers to the racing classes were Italian visitor Count Gigi Premoli, who took his big supercharged Maserati-Bugatti up in 47.2s, and a young American undergraduate at Cambridge, Whitney Straight, who had bought the ex-Birkin GP Maserati and recorded 47.8s. Straight had actually competed at Shelsley two years earlier, as a teenager, in a sports Riley.

After standing for so long, Stuck's celebrated record – the only outright Shelsley record held by a visiting Continental – was beaten no fewer than four times in September, 1933. The first man to do so was a delighted Raymond Mays with his new, much modified Riley 12/6, which was rapidly dubbed 'The White Riley' as it was liveried in the familiar Mays colours of white body with blue upholstery. Preoccupations elsewhere had caused Amherst Villiers to sell his interest in the Villiers Supercharge to Mays but the latter was not left bereft of supercharging expertise. Austin employee T. Murray Jamieson, who had learnt much from working with Villiers, now played a major and increasing role in the Mays team, together with the former RAF officer Peter Berthon, Humphrey Cook and Victor Riley. The latter enthusiastically allowed Mays to have one of the latest Riley 12/6 chassis to do with as he thought fit as long as it still remained recognisably a Riley – and it broke the Shelsley record! The result was a much-modified 1½ litre Riley engine, retaining the characteristic twin high-mounted camshafts, but with a new Jamieson-designed crankshaft and a supercharger on the Roots principle among the many departures from standard. With around 150 bhp delivered for transmission through

'Composite with JAP engine'.
An early, 1932, shot of John
Bolster nearing the finish at
Shelsley with the then 981cc
'Bloody Mary'.
DEMAUS TRANSPORT PHOTOGRAPHICS

Barbara Skinner (later Mrs
John Bolster) chats with Elsie
'Bill' Wisdom, while sat in her
Morris Minor-based Skinner
Special.
DEMAUS TRANSPORT PHOTOGRAPHICS

the twin rear wheels in a car far lighter than the old Vauxhall, expectations were high. The record fell in 42.2s but Mays had little time to celebrate before the brilliant Whitney Straight gunned the Maserati (one of the last of the two-seater Grand Prix cars) away from the 'S' bend to clock an astounding 41.4s. Although he was slower in the Riley on his second climb, Mays then achieved another triumph by persuading the difficult old Villiers Supercharge up in 42.3s, under the Stuck figure and the temperamental old warrior's best time yet. But the day belonged to Straight. On his second climb he chipped another 0.2s off his time, to leave the new record at 41.2s, a tremendous performance for one with so little experience. Although a little overshadowed by this great duel, Dick Nash put in another spectacular dirt-track-style run to record a fine 43s with the 'Spook'.

The wealthy Straight decided to leave Cambridge and organise a professional international racing team with a fleet of new Grand Prix Maseratis for 1934, and he returned to Shelsley in May with the latest 2.9 litre 8CM model with modified bodywork to his specification. The result was another record, in just 40s. The possibilities suggested by the Riley had led to Humphrey Cook agreeing to finance a serious international Voiturette racing team of single-seaters developed from the Riley technology, and although the first ERA was not ready to run in May, Mays brought the Riley which, understandably, had not had a lot of attention of late. A best time of 42.8s was still good enough for second BTD ahead of Scotsman Thomas Fotheringham who sprung a 43s surprise with his blue 2-litre Bugatti, and an astonishing 43.2s run by Eddie Hall in the supercharged MG Magnette sports car, which was faster than the Grand Prix Bugattis of Earl Howe and Lindsay Eccles, and the increasingly effective special of the extrovert John Bolster.

Although the thoroughbred (and expensive) racing car now seemed to have the upper hand, the band of 'Shelsley Special' builders (so-called because they tended to build their machines with the primary aim of having as much fun as possible at Shelsley Walsh, although most of them ran elsewhere too) was as active as ever. This was particularly apparent in the corner of the Paddock filled by the families Bolster (John and brother Richard) and Skinner (father Carl who was the 'S' of SU carburettors, son Peter and daughter Barbara who was to become Mrs John Bolster), and their collection of specials. The Skinner Specials were characterised by rather unlikely Morris Minor origins while the Bolster efforts involved an increasing number of JAP-engines! John Bolster, recovered from a nasty roll over at the May 1933 meeting, was back in successful action later the same year with his 981cc, side-valve JAP-engined, ash-framed, GN suspended device. Titled 'composite with JAP engine' by the uncomprehending tax man, 'Mary' or 'The Tudor Queen' by coy journalists in a less permissive age than the present day, and plain 'Bloody Mary' by everyone else, Bolster's pride and joy gained an extra unsupercharged JAP engine for 1934 and a 44.2s 2-litre class win was the immediate result, beating even Noel Carr's thoroughbred Bugattti

Mays and the ERA

Unfortunately it was wet in September when battle was rejoined with Mays arriving with two new ERAs, the original R1, running in 1½-litre Voiturette trim, and the 2-litre R3, racing for the first time (the more familiar R1A and R3A suffixes were only applied when the B-type appeared in 1935). Although not designed primarily as hill climb cars it was inconceivable that they would not do well at Mays's beloved Shelsley. They did and a new chapter in the course's distinguished history opened

In May 1935, Sir Malcolm Campbell returned to Shelsley with one of the 4.0 V12 Sunbeams and won the 5-litre class.
DEMAUS TRANSPORT PHOTOGRAPHICS

At the May 1935 meeting, Pat Driscoll in one of the works side-valve-engined Austin Seven single-seaters was over a second faster than Campbell.
MIDLAND AUTOMOBILE CLUB

Wet weather ruined Hans Stuck's return to Shelsley in 1936 with the short-chassis V16 Auto Union. Only Stuck's immense skill kept the difficult rear-engined machine under control for a praiseworthy 45.2s; well down on May's 41.6s BTD. On a dry road...?
MIDLAND AUTOMOBILE CLUB
via BOB COOPER

with the twin rear-wheeled 2-litre car setting BTD in 44.0s, a mere 0.2s better than Whitney Straight, and the 1½-litre car lifting the 1,500cc class in 46s. This meeting was the last time that Straight competed at Shelsley, for after a brief but very successful motor racing career he moved on, gaining lasting distinction as an industrialist.

With Straight gone and the development of the ERA — jointly to the credit of Peter Berthon, Murray Jamieson and Reid Railton of the Brooklands firm of Thomson and Taylor (who built the chassis) — continuing apace, 1935 belonged to Mays and the high-built ERAs. Although the chassis technology was basically that of the early-'thirties Italian school, the combination of the 230 bhp Jamieson/Roots-blown 2-litre Riley-based engine, coupled to the effective Wilson pre-selector gearbox, and mounted in a car weighing only some 14½ cwt — and driven by Mays — was truly something. In May, at the

30th anniversary meeting where Sir Malcolm Campbell, who had been knighted for his Land Speed Record achievements, returned to climb in 44.4s in the old V12 Sunbeam 'Tiger', Mays at last cracked the 40s mark with a scintillating 39.6s in R3. Then to rub it in he achieved a remarkable 39.8s with the 1,500cc R1! Nobody came near these times although highly significant was the performance of Pat Driscoll in one of the little side-valve-engined works Austin Seven single-seaters. His 43.4s time was actually faster than Richard Shuttleworth's Alfa Romeo Monoposto Tipo B.

In September, Mays again returned with two ERAs: a new R4B with the latest Thomson and Taylor chassis modifications and the 2-litre engine, and R1A. He took BTD and second BTD once again. The 39.6s in R4B, the first incarnation of what was to become the most successful hill climb car of all time, equalled the record while Mays's best in R1A was 40.4s. Again nobody approached these times although Charlie Martin (T51) set the fastest Bugatti time yet (42.8s) and was tied with Frazer Nash works driver Fane. The latter was now driving the two-stage supercharged Gough-engined single-seater built by the Aldingtons (who had controlled Frazer Nash since 1929) for Adrian Thorpe, and was becoming increasingly formidable.

Midland Automobile Club supporters are always quick to refute any suggestion that Shelsley has more than its fair share of wet meetings. The statistics back them up but there is no doubt about the weather in 1936: it was vile, both in May and September. In the case of the European Championship round in May this was a near tragedy, for a large crowd turned out to see the legendary Hans Stuck return with perhaps the most fabulous hill climb car of all, the short chassis, 5.3-litre V16 Auto Union. The vast rear-engined machine was a real handful at Shelsley, and in the wet it was terrifying. Only the immense skill of Stuck enabled a respectable, if bitterly disappointing, time of 45.2s to be returned. Mays had a 1½-litre engine in R4B this time (now developing about 185 bhp on 12 lbs boost) but he still set BTD with 41.6s to the 42.6s second BTD which was shared by Fane (despite the Frazer Nash jumping out of gear) and the German driver, Walter Baumer, who was outstanding in one of the little side-valve-engined Austins.

It was wetter than ever in September and the meeting was mainly notable for the total domination by the ERA marque, with the Bourne firm's customers joining in for a 1-2-3-4 result. Mays, thought to have been driving the new R12B with 2-litre engine, set BTD of course, in 43.91s, and was runner-up with the 1½-litre-engined R4B. Next up were the privateers Dennis Scribbans (R9B) and Peter Whitehead (R10B). New timing apparatus now permitted times to be quoted to one-hundredth of a second, thereby making ties less likely.

Several leading competitors had an almighty rush to 'make' the June 1937 Shelsley as they had been competing in the important RAC international Light Car Race on the Isle of Man on the preceding Thursday. Mays was among them and his rather breathless arrival in Worcestershire was accompanied by just one car, the former R4B, now re-designated R4C and fitted with a revamped chassis to incorporate Porsche-designed independent front suspension and with the 1½-litre engine fitted with the enormous Zöller supercharger which intruded into the cockpit area. The effectiveness of the re-hash was emphasised when Mays cracked the record once more for a 39.06s BTD. Nobody else looked like getting under the 40s mark. Outstanding was the 40.83s by former trials driver Bert Hadley in the superb little twin-overhead camshaft, 750cc Austin single-seater which had first appeared the previous year. This, the ultimate expression of the British tradition for competition 750s, was designed by Murray Jamieson and three examples were built by Austin for factory use, with no expense spared. The successor to the earlier, highly-stressed side-valve 750s, this exquisite little 'tool room racer' bore no relation to the production Sevens and used a Jamieson/Roots-blown twin ohc engine which revved to 7,800 rpm in original form and was developing around 100 bhp even in 1937. In an age when the established pacesetters in motor racing were usually Continental, it is worth remembering that these little gems had one of the highest specific outputs of any contemporary racing machine. With a dry weight under 10 cwt (Lord Austin even chose his drivers: Hadley, Pat Driscoll, Charles Goodacre and Charlie Dodson, with light weight in mind), the car was easily the fastest 750 yet to ascend Shelsley. Even the formidable Fane (40.89s) was beaten. Italian road racer Luigi Villoresi also brought his Maserati 6CM down from Douglas but his 44.29s best climb was achieved in the face of unfamiliarity with Shelsley's deceptively tricky slopes and unsuitable gearing. His right arm cocked in habitual fashion to clear the offside rear wheel, John Bolster flung 'Bloody Mary' up still faster to become the fastest unsupercharged runner in a splendid 42.24s.

Tool room racer. Bert Hadley flings one of the 2ohc 750cc Austin single-seaters through the Esses. These advanced and superbly-engineered cars were far removed from the average Shelsley Special and were truly Grand Prix cars in miniature.
DEMAUS TRANSPORT PHOTOGRAPHICS

Built originally for Adrian Thorpe, the works single-seater Frazer Nash set a 38.77s Shelsley Walsh record in September 1937, in the capable hands of A. F. P. Fane. Not too reliable in circuit racing, this car was formidable at Shelsley, appropriately enough as the chassis was based on the Shelsley sports model.
MIDLAND AUTOMOBILE CLUB

The September meeting was likened by *The Autocar* to Hamlet without the Prince of Denmark, for Raymond Mays reluctantly decided to compete at the clashing Phoenix Park, Dublin, race as he was intent on chasing points for the BRDC Gold Star competition, but his absence seemed to inspire everyone else and times were very fast. In ideal weather, Fane excelled and slithered the single-seater Frazer Nash – closely related to the 'chain gang' sports cars which were just being supplanted by the Frazer Nash-BMW 328 models – to a remarkable new 38.77s record. There was one ERA present to uphold fully the honour of Bourne: the red painted R3A, now in the capable hands of road racer Charles Martin. Less potent than the Zöller-blown R4C, this former works car was on good from. So was Martin, who broke the elusive 40s barrier with a resounding 39.68s. For the rest, Kenneth Evans achieved a noteworthy 40.39s in his Alfa Romeo Monoposto, while the little Austins were quicker than ever, with Charles Goodacre (40.70s) just shading out Hadley (40.74s). There was a new challenger among the Shelsley Specials too (by now there was a major trophy for the fastest of this breed at Shelsley). Joe Fry, a member of the Bristol family who were a major force in the chocolate industry, clocked 42.58s in the new 'Freikaiserwagen'. The brainchild of the Fry cousins, Joe and David, Bristolian Special builder Dick Caesar, and Brooklands preparation expert Robin Jackson, the 'Freik' was rather more scientific than the average Shelsley Special and in original form employed a 70 bhp unsupercharged air-cooled, vee-twin Blackburne engine, mounted behind the driver in similar position to the celebrated Auto Union (hence the Teutonic rendering of the names of Fry and Caesar in the device's name) in a chassis which comprised the familiar assortment of GN and Morgan bits.

One of the very few leading British drivers not to compete at Shelsley pre-1939 was 'B Bira' (until 1939 the British-based Siamese Prince Birabongse raced on an RAC licence and was a BRDC member, and indeed a triple Gold Star winner), but he did enter for the May meeting in 1938. Sadly, no suitable car could be readied in time and the confrontation with his arch-rival on the track, Raymond Mays, did not materialise. Instead, the 'society' followers could devote their energies to following the fortunes of the Yorkshire woman flier, Amy Johnson, in Fane's sports Frazer Nash-BMW 328. Mays returned with a sprint engine in R4D, another rebuild of R4C around a completely new frame and with further modified front suspension and brakes. Despite becoming airborne in a rather alarming moment, he set another BTD, although his time of 38.90s remained just outside Fane's record. The astonishing Hadley sped up in 40.09s to better even Fane (40.13s), and the addition of a Marshall supercharger to the 'Freikaiserwagen' helped Joe Fry to bring his time down to 41.52s. This compared well with the 41.25s achieved by the experienced Earl Howe, now at the wheel of the Zöller-blown ERA R8C which he owned but which formed part of the works team.

Come September and Mays re-asserted his superiority with yet another course record, in a mere 37.86s. There were no challengers to the powerful 2-litre R4D but the Birmingham mechanic/driver Bert Hadley came even closer to breaking 40s in the little Austin with a tantalising 40.05s second BTD, while an impressive Barrie Goodwin brought his time down to 40.36s in another of the effective Frazer Nash single-seaters. This was originally a two-seater Shelsley model, and was converted for Tim Davies (who raced under the pseudonym Dudley Folland) and which had passed through the hands of MAC President Sammy Newsome before being bought by Goodwin.

The war clouds were gathering ominously when the first 1939 meeting was held on 3 June before a small crowd which was – almost unheard of – not even large enough for the meeting to break even financially. Those who were able to come saw Raymond Mays smash the record one more time in the black R4D, which was now being run as a formidable freelance effort by Mays after an (eventually) amicable parting with Cook and the ERA company. The new time was 37.37s, with Fane nearest on 38.82s. Bob Ansell (of the Midlands Brewing family) went well in his 1½-litre ERA R9B (ex-Scribbans) to be third with 40.53s, just a whisker ahead of Hadley (40.56s). There was more spectacle when two 750-Kilogramme Formula Grand Prix cars, the 3.8-litre Alfa Romeo 8C-35 of the Swiss Hans Ruesch and the 3.3-litre Bugatti T59 of Arthur Baron were matched against each other. The 41.14s from the supremely elegant French car was enough to beat the bulky ex-Scuderia Ferrari Alfa with which Ruesch ascended in 41.71s.

War was declared before another Shelsley could be held so Mays, a star performer on the hill since the early nineteen-twenties, remained firmly on top, aided by a car which was perfectly suited to the hill. Only two other drivers, Fane and Charlie Martin shared the honour of having climbed the 1,000 yards in less than 40s.

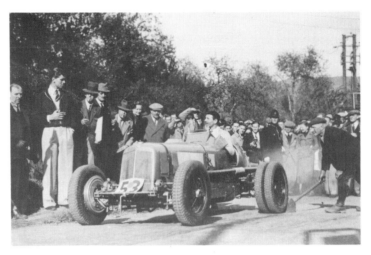

By 1935 Raymond Mays was back on top, running both 1.5 and 2.0 ERAs. This is R3 record-breaking in May.
DEMAUS TRANSPORT PHOTOGRAPHICS

The battle for the Shelsley record captured the attention of racing enthusiasts in the nineteen-thirties like no other hill climb honour before or since, but it was by no means the only focus of attention at Shelsley where the honour of being fastest Shelsley Special, fastest sports car driver, ladies' record holder or best 750/850, in particular, earned considerable prestige. The trophies to be won were plentiful, but with so many entries received that qualifying runs were needed for the first time in 1937, there were still many competitors who had little chance of winning anything, yet they enjoyed the sporting and social occasion which was Shelsley just as much as their more fêted rivals.

Many of the 'Specialists' came into this category, even though the most effective Shelsley Specials were capable of matching the times of expensive thoroughbreds which were not developed primarily for the slopes of Shelsley Walsh. One could easily divide the racing car entries into two loose groups: the relatively well-to-do with their professionally-maintained road-racing machinery (and including the small number of factory entries from the likes of ERA and Austin); and the usually rather-hard-up Special builders who tended to do most of their own mechanical work. They were often guided more by intuition and optimism than by textbook engineering, and were assisted only by unpaid friends and relations. The 'Specialists' were particularly thick on the ground before meetings in the environs of the *Crown Hotel*, Worcester, for that esteemed hostelry boasted undercover accommodation where it was possible to work on cars. There was certainly intense rivalry between the owners of each type of car, but it did nothing to detract from the sociable and mutually helpful atmosphere which prevailed. The bones of contention which were all too frequent in the 'professional' days of hill climbing were happily absent from Shelsley during the nineteen-thirties.

Something Special

The prowess of the fastest of the Shelsley Specials and their drivers/builders has already been covered in the battle for the Shelsley record, so no further elaboration is needed on 'Spider', the Villiers Supercharge (unusual in that it only *became* a Shelsley Special and was certainly *not* a cheap car), the 'Spook', the 'Terror' (and Dick Nash's third Frazer Nash-based Special, the 'Union Special' which was good for 43s climbs), 'Bloody Mary' and the 'Freikaiserwagen'. But there were many others.

The most common feature among the Specials was a chassis which owed at least something to Frazer Nash or GN origins, while bodywork tended to be sketchy or even non-existent. Engines had to be cheap and torquey, tended to be between 1,100 and 2,000cc in capacity (the former size was especially popular), and the whole lot had to be extremely light. Strength and reliability were less common. Fairly typical was the AC-Nash, once an Anzani-engined Brooklands car run by Christopher le Strange Metcalfe. This Frazer Nash-based car ran at Shelsley for the first time in 1936 in the hands of Peter Neil, who substituted one of the 2-litre, six-cylinder Weller-designed AC engines for the worn out Anzani. In total contrast was the Appleton Special which John Appleton and Zillwood 'Sinbad' Milledge developed into a regular 1,100cc class winner, characterised by both speed and an ear-splitting noise! Originally a sports two-seater Maserati with the unsuccessul 1,100cc straight eight from Modena, this became a lightened and beautifully-bodied single-seater with Riley power. By the time development of the high-boost, 180 plus bhp, supercharged engine was complete in the later 'thirties, the car was an international class record holder, which broke the Brooklands Mountain Circuit record for its class. Always impeccably prepared, the car was said by the owner to have cost some £5,000 in all.

A much earlier device, more in the Frazer Nash/Davenport vein, was the Avon-JAP. Built in 1926 this employed a GN frame and since one of the builders was Vivien Prestwich of J.A. Prestwich Ltd (H. E. Walters was his co-builder), JAP engines were naturally used, a water-cooled 750 alternating with an air-cooled 996. Although it had been driven by both Kaye Don and Clive Lones, its finest Shelsley performances came in July, 1930 when Ron Horton won the up-to-1100cc class with it.

The Bolsters were among the most inveterate of Special builders, and the famous 'Mary' was only the most successful of many. Not satisfied with two engines, John Bolster contrived to fit four JAP vee-twins in a steel channel-section chassis for 1938. Despite a nightmare collection of linkages and gearings and rather frightening handling, development was proceeding surprisingly well when war broke out. Brother Richard began with a fairly straightforward little GN single-seater. The old 1100cc sohc GN unit was then replaced by a Powerplus supercharged MG Magna engine, before Richard too went in for multiplication with four Rudge dirt-track motorcycle engines. A 4-litre Hudson straight eight in a Frazer Nash/GN chassis was on the stocks when the war came.

Great friends of the Bolsters were the Skinners. Father Carl rebuilt a Morris Minor with lightened body and with the engine Zöller-supercharged to develop a fairly amazing 60 bhp. With this, Peter Skinner won the 850cc class at Shelsley in 1933, and when a similar car was built up for Peter's sister Barbara in 1934 she promptly broke the Ladies' Record with it. Not content with this the Skinners somehow persuaded a 4.2-litre Hudson 'eight' into the 6ft 6in wheelbase of Peter's car for 1937, and although the resulting concoction was distinctly twitchy, the power/weight ratio of 138 bhp/12½ cwt helped Peter to a 41.22s climb in 1938 which stood as a record for unsupercharged Shelsley Specials for some years.

Ingenuity was the hall mark of H. D. Carlmark whose fairly orthodox GN-JAP gained some success

'Twin rear wheels at the front'. Typical of the ingenuity of those who built Shelsley Specials was 'Dorcas II'. BSA front-wheel-drive components were employed by the Glegg brothers, Gordon and Donald. This is a 1932 picture and two years later they were experimenting with a primitive four-wheel-drive arrangement.
RICHARD CHAPMAN

in the early 'thirties. However, the owner wasn't satisfied with that and experimented with such radical departures from the norm as mounting the trusty JAP behind the driver, attaching a Fiat 500 front end on the GN chassis, and even running with no rear suspension whatsoever! Barry Woodall was another JAP user, competing in the later nineteen-thirties with the ohv, water-cooled vee-twin mounted in what had begun life as a Morgan three-wheeler. A JAP engine, this time a potent Eric Fernihough-prepared version, appeared in the various permutations on the 'Dorcas' theme by the Glegg brothers, Gordon and Donal. After starting with an Austin Seven chassis, they plumped for a front-wheel-drive BSA set up, 'with twin rear wheels at the front'.

By 1934 the Gleggs had gone one better with a primitive form of four-wheel drive, employing immensely long chains which tended to self-destruct fairly often. Another Special builder to devise something really ambitious was the extrovert engineer Robert Waddy who built a particularly curious and astonishingly small device in a shed at Brooklands. This was 'Fuzzi' which comprised a sort of spaceframe of light-section tubes, Porsche-pattern all-independent suspension, and a 500cc JAP dirt-track engine mounted at both ends. Sadly, although 'Fuzzi' held the road fairly well, Waddy had a bad accident with it at a speed trial and was seriously injured.

The 'GNAT' of E. G. Sharp belonged to an earlier era and was almost wholly GN. An 1100cc class winner at Shelsley in 1930 using a much-modified pushrod GN engine, the 'GNAT' bore a close resemblance to 'Kim'and 'Spyder', and in fact Sharp was a close associate of Messrs Davenport and Mucklow. Sharp initially ran the car without bodywork (as did Teddy Wilkes with the rather later, and always immaculately-turned-out, Wilkes-GN), but eventually fitted a narrow single-seater shell *à la* 'Kim'.

Until 1932, W.E. Harker had raced a very effective Austin Seven, complete with Villiers supercharger. In that year Harker produced another Austin-based chassis but with two Austin Seven engines mounted on a common crankcase. Unfortunately, Harker hurt himself in a crash during practice with the car at Shelsley, and the chassis was a write-off. A heavier French Lombard chassis was substituted, and later still, more powerful MG cylinder blocks were employed to offset the extra weight.

Familiar at modern Vintage Sports Car Club race meetings is 'Salome', a sort of four-wheeled Morgan three-wheeler with JAP motivation. When Jan Breyer built it there was not a vestige of bodywork on it! Geoffrey Sumner (Sumner-JAP, which began life as a GN 'Vitesse'), Clive Lones ('Tiger Cat', a JAP-powered Morgan/GN concoction which this successful Welsh former Morgan racer introduced in 1936), and Jack Moor (GN-based 'Wasp' with yellow and black striped tail, evolved from an ex-Trubie Moore GN 'Vitesse' bought in 1923) were yet more devotees of the traditional Shelsley Special.

Very different, and altogether more scientific, was the Lightweight Special which, after a long gestation period, appeared in 1939. This was the brainchild of Austin engineer and one-time 'Ulster' Austin Seven racer Alec Issigonis (now best-known as the designer of the post-war Morris Minor and the epochal Mini) and his friend George Dowson. Way ahead of its time, the beautifully-built Lightweight featured a full monocoque chassis, all-independent suspension and, at this early stage in its career, a Murray Jamieson-specification side-valve Austin racing engine. After the war a lighter, sohc engine (an experimental Nuffield unit) was fitted. The replacement developed more power but sorely tried the transmission. Despite the 'works' connections and its professional looking appearance, this was no factory-built car and was a truly prophetic indication of the Issigonis genius.

You can see the smoke but you have to imagine the noise. This is Rupert Instone's GN 'Martyr'. Like most Shelsley Specials this one evolved over the years and this particular 1932 picture shows the car still with its two-seater body. The engine is the seemingly inevitable 996cc vee-twin JAP and the front axle once graced Dick Nash's 'The Terror'.
RICHARD CHAPMAN

There were others too, an astonishing diversity of Specials, many of them undoubtedly primitive, misguidedly engineered, even perilous, but all of them great fun for their enthusiastic owners. Two splendid quotations, one about John Bolster and one by the man himself, evoke perfectly the sort of carefree spirit which kept that band of optimists, the Shelsley Specialists, going. When *The Autocar* reported on the June 1937 meeting, the tale ran:

> There was a pause, as though to marshal spectators more carefully, officials made as though to climb trees, and then, with an almost indescribable noise, the famous 'Mary' appeared, but alas, feebly, Bolster's pantomime confirming the fact! Returning to the Paddock the car was then held up in the air by one wheel, the erring engine traced, found to have its timing wrong, corrected. And then the machine put up a tremendous climb and fourth fastest time, literally being held on the road by will-power and travelling quite a considerable distance more than the official thousand yards.

Many years later, in an article in *Old Motor* (March 1982), John recalled the performances of Jack Moor:

> … one of the pioneers of GN specials was dear old Jack (Moses) Moor, and the things that happened to his cars were unprintable. On one occasion he was seen to throw away the steering wheel while taking the S bend at high speed, regaining control by grabbing the remaining stumps of the spokes. Jack's cars were all called *Wasp*, and painted to resemble that insect, but this brought him no luck. There was the time when his valve gear was seen to dismantle itself, halfway up the hill, the parts disappearing among the branches of the trees.
>
> Jack Moor's funniest disaster was in the days when one was started by a flag. Jack was on the starting line, with his engine revving, when suddenly his clutch spigot bush seized and he made an involuntary getaway. Scattering the marshals he roared off up the hill, but, being a gentleman, he shouted, "goodbye!"

Fast Ladies

While the fluctuating fortunes of the Shelsley Specials provided one sub-plot in the between-the-wars period, another, of growing interest as the 'thirties progressed was the competition for the honour of being Shelsley's fastest woman competitor. Even in the early nineteen-twenties several women drivers often ran in hill climbs, and that's leaving aside pioneers like Dorothy Levitt. With the obvious exception of Ivy Cummings, most contented themselves with driving the smaller sporting cars with formula classes in mind. Winifred Pink was particularly successful in one of the early Aston Martins while Doris Heath and Lilian Roper were other regular contenders.

One of the most skilful and brave of these sporting ladies was May Cunliffe who made a big impression at the September 1927 meeting by flinging her lightened and stripped 3-litre Bentley, complete with supercharger, up Shelsley in a spectacular 53.4s. The big and still very heavy Bentley was not ideally suited to Shelsley and this performance, the fastest yet by a woman, was outstanding. Yet she

In 1938 Shelsley was climbed by Britain's most celebrated woman pilot, Amy Johnson, who drove Fane's Frazer Nash-BMW. Her time of 49.57s was most respectable.
MIDLAND AUTOMOBILE CLUB

did even better the following May after acquiring one of the 1924 2-litre GP Sunbeams. Her 51.2s climb was actually third BTD. Tragically, it was in this car that her father, acting as riding mechanic, was killed in a roll-over on Southport Sands. May Cunliffe returned to Shelsley in 1936, by now as Mrs Millington (her son, Tim, became well known as the author of a book on tuning Hillman Imps and who today is head of Peugeot-Talbot special tuning department), with a sports Alta. Unfortunately, she lost control after the finish line and in the ensuing crash she badly broke her jaw. A sad postscript to the career of a courageous lady.

May Cunliffe's record stood for some years and the next really 'fast' lady to tackle Shelsley was 'Bill' Wisdom, otherwise Elsie, wife of motoring journalist Tommy Wisdom, and a regular Brooklands racer. Her sports Frazer Nash, a particularly rapid TT Replica with blower, recorded 54.4s to win the Ladies' Cup in September 1930. By the following year her husband was breaking 50s with the same car and 'Bill' was not far behind, lopping 2.4s off her 1930 time in September. In June 1932 she had further reduced her time to 51.6s – so close to May Cunliffe's record.

The 'Amateur' meeting of 1932 saw the arrival of a teenager at the wheel of an as yet fairly 'normal' Morris Minor sports. This was Barbara Skinner, but although she won the Ladies' Cup her 56.6s time did not threaten the record.

A formidable new contender emerged in May 1933 in the shape of an Irish (via Australia) girl, Fay Taylour, who had already gained fame as a motorcycle dirt-track rider. She had at her disposal one of the formidable new MG K3 Magnettes, one of the actual cars which had just returned from a successful foray in the Mille Miglia. With this Fay managed to equal that elusive 51.2s time, but she did not win the Ladies' Cup as on this occasion it was not considered ladylike to drive supercharged (like the MG) or racing cars – or something! Instead the 'official' award went to Cynthia Sedgwick in a Frazer Nash. This was a popular type of car with the women, for Mrs Arlene Needham, Midge Wilby, Mrs

Doreen Evans was probably a faster driver than either of her enthusiastic brothers, Kenneth and Denis. Doreen is pictured in the MG R-type.
MIDLAND AUTOMOBILE CLUB

Gripper and Miss McOstrich were others to join the 'Chain Gang'. Lucky win or not in May, when the September meeting came round it was Miss Sedgwick who was in fine form with the TT Replica and her Ladies' Cup was secondary to a new Ladies' Record, at long last, in a resounding 48s.

But this was one record which did not last for long, for at the very next meeting the now more experienced Barbara Skinner, well able to tame the phenomenal output from her Morris Minor Special, shot up in 47.6s. It was wet in September 1934, and although she won again, she had to be content with 50.6s. Battle was rejoined in earnest at the Thirtieth Anniversary Meeting in May 1935, with Miss Skinner driving a modified Q-type MG Midget, a pure competition car with Zöller supercharger opposed by Doreen Evans who went one better with the latest, independently-suspended, R-type MG Midget, a purpose-built single-seater, but with the same Zöller-blown 750cc engine. On the very edge of control, Doreen, sister of Dennis and Kenneth Evans and arguably the fastest of the whole family, took the record in 45.4s, although Barbara Skinner also broke her old time.

By the time September came round the Bellevue Garage, Wandsworth driver, Doreen Evans, and her 'Wilkie' Wilkinson-tuned MG had become Mrs A. G. Phipps, and she now faced opposition not only from Barbara Skinner in both MG and Morris, but also from successful circuit racer Kay Petre. The latter, petite and always immaculately attired, had managed to obtain the use of Mays's 'White Riley', but since she had proved herself well able to hammer a 10-litre Delage round Brooklands, she was well up to handling the formidable Riley. The ensuing battle, which was settled only after a run-off caused by a tie when both Mrs Phipps and Mrs Petre recorded 44.8s, was a highlight of the day. Barbara Skinner was not able to match their times on this occasion, and honours finally fell to Kay Petre with the remarkable time of 43.8s. The 'White Riley', incidentally, was now smartly turned out in powder blue, the favoured Petre colour.

The atrocious weather ruled out any records in 1936 but Mrs Petre slithered the Riley to a worthy 47.17s in September. For 1937, the record holder switched to one of the side-valve works Austin single-seaters but at the Spring meeting she was beaten by the 45.96s from Mrs Barbara Bolster (née Skinner) in the Morris. Kay Petre soon became used to the high revving little Austin, however, and in September she went up to rather more than the already dauntingly high 9,500 rpm of the highly stressed Austin to smash her own record with 43.78s. Another fine effort on the same day came from Miss Joan Richmond who recorded 44.88s in the difficult little 'Fuzzi' of Robert Waddy, rapidly coming to terms with twin engines and four-wheel drive.

During the 'thirties as many as eighteen women competed at Shelsley in one meeting, far more than could be expected today, and the competition was fierce, but Kay Petre's Austin record stood until the very last pre-war meeting in 1939 when former MG driver Dorothy Stanley Turner arrived for the first time with an ex-Johnny Wakefield 1½-litre Alta single-seater. After a rapid first climb in the 45s bracket, she put in an impeccable second run to clock a record 43.40s.

Sports cars

Ever since the early days when there were many complaints from bored spectators about the tedium of watching slow and overloaded touring cars contesting the formula awards, the MAC were well aware that even most of the sports cars could sometimes amount to little more than a prelude to the racing car runs. Nevertheless, there was considerable prestige attached to setting the best sports car times.

One driver could be said to have dominated the sports car classes over the years, and that was the experienced and so methodical Yorkshireman Eddie Hall. Although he only ever set BTD once, in his 30/98 Vauxhall at the wet 1926 'Amateur' meeting, Eddie scored more class wins at Shelsley between 1925 and 1939 than any driver bar Raymond Mays – 26 (including 3 tied wins) against the 31 of Mays. Many people seem to remember Eddie's epic drives in the Tourist Trophy but rather overlook his many other successes during a long and varied career which was managed by his ultra-organised and efficient wife Joan. There is a close parallel with the post-war career of Bob and Joan Gerard. Over the years he won at Shelsley with the 30/98, Cricklewood and Derby Bentleys, and Montlhéry C-type and K3 Magnette MGs.

Other regular sports car class winners included the 30/98 of Ronnie Hughes, the mighty Mercedes of Earl Howe, the touring Bugatti T30 of G. Fairrie (there were Touring classes at the 'Amateur' meetings), Sammy Newsome in Lea Francis and SS100, Leslie Bachelier's lovely Bugatti T55 and Forrest Lycett's famous 8-litre Bentley, which achieved 44.08s in 1938. The latter's wins actually

Eddie Hall nears the Shelsley finish line, driving bare-headed as usual, in his twin-rear-wheeled MG Magnette in stripped racing trim
DEMAUS TRANSPORT PHOTOGRAPHICS

A. F. P. Fane won the MAG Sports Challenge Trophy for sports cars, conforming to the Automobile Club de France regulations, with the sophisticated Frazer Nash-BMW 328 in 49.51s during 1936. By 1938 he had reduced this time to 46.12s
DEMAUS TRANSPORT PHOTOGRAPHICS

came in the big racing class in the years after sports car classes as such were dropped, the stripped and much-modified monster seldom encountering opposition worthy of it. In fact, the really big cars were not best suited to Shelsley, sheer size and weight offsetting the power. This makes the performances of the deceptively agile Mercedes 38/250s of Caracciola, Howe and 'Scrap' Thistlethwayte all the more meritorious, while a particularly daunting sight was that of Whitney Straight running his Gurney

Earl Howe was another regular class winner at Shelsley with his superb stable of sports and racing cars. He won his class at the very wet September 1930 meeting in his Bugatti T43.
DEMAUS TRANSPORT PHOTOGRAPHICS

Nutting-bodied 8-litre Bentley coupé (unusually fitted with pre-selector gearbox) in 1933. The big car keeled over at the 'S' bend like some giant ocean liner!

The outright sports car record for the hill was successively reduced as follows: 56.6s (Hall, Vauxhall, July 1926); 53.4s (H. F. Clay, Mercedes 36/220, July 1928); 47.6s (Howe, Mercedes, September 1929); 46.8s (Caracciola, Mercedes, July 1930, and equalled by Howe in July 1931); 45.6s (Raymond Mays, 4½-litre Meadows-engined Invicta, provided by Sir Noel Macklin, late of Eric Campbell and Silver Hawk, September 1932); and 43.2s (Hall, MG Magnette, June 1934). Hall's time in the supercharged K3 – what a later age of enthusiasts would call a sports-racer – was not bettered after the abandonment of sports car classes in 1936. Nevertheless, there were still people running in sports cars, competing for the MAC's Challenge Trophy for road-equipped cars. Prominent were the Frazer Nash-BMW 328s (especially when driven by Fane), Charles Follett's Railton (Reid Railton's early application of an American Hudson engine in a light British chassis), and the Le Mans-type Talbot-Darracq of Ian Connell which recorded a fine 43.76s in June 1939.

With the ready availability of sports versions of the Austin Seven there was considerable support for the 750cc class, where the capacity was raised to 850cc in 1931 to let in the M-type MGs. However, this category soon became the preserve of Eddie Hall with his C-type MG Midget, although if he was otherwise occupied the much-modified Austin of R. F. Turner, a particularly successful driver in the early Donington Park race meetings, took top honours. In sharp contrast, the first stirring of interest in historic racing cars led to a class for pre-1914 racing cars being instigated in 1938, competing for a trophy presented by Forrest Lycett. This was won on all three occasions by Anthony Heal in his 1910 10-litre Fiat, which recorded a splendid 47.96s in May 1938.

By comparison with Shelsley Walsh, other hill climb happenings of the period seem rather secondary, at least until the arrival of Prescott in 1938. In the later nineteen-twenties there was little that was even secondary. One such isolated event was run in March 1926 as an Inter Varsity climb. The venue was Henley Park, Henley-on-Thames, on the land of Captain Hamilton. The event was run over a measured distance of 605 yards, with a maximum gradient of 1 in 8. A Cambridge undergraduate, H. Marineau set the BTD in 31.4s, driving the ubiquitous 30/98 Vauxhall.

Away from Shelsley there were no speed hill climbs of significance until 1929 when the scheduling of the revived event at Craigantlet, in Ulster, on 10 August, produced a big occasion attended by an estimated 20,000 people. The reason was simple. The meeting was arranged as a curtain-raiser to the Tourist Trophy on the nearby Ards circuit and attracted a strong entry, including TT cars, although, unlike the old Gordon Bennett preliminary trials, the event served no qualifying function. Since closing roads for the purpose of running motor racing events was perfectly feasible in Ulster, the Ulster Automobile Club was able to employ this fast and flowing climb, measuring 1.3 miles, which had been used briefly back in the days before 'The Troubles', and for a local event in 1925. Since Craigantlet is only 8 miles to the East of Belfast, off the A20 Belfast to Dundonald road, and Ulster was already catching 'TT fever', a large crowd was not unexpected for a free view. No racing cars were permitted and the event was dominated by the visiting Earl Howe. He set Best Time of Day in his massive 36/220 Mercedes (the 6.8-litre 'S' Model, not the car he was to drive at Shelsley the following month) in 98.8s, just 0.2s faster than his second BTD performance at the wheel of the Bugatti T43 which he was to drive in the TT.

Although of particular interest, this was not the only British hill climb of the year away from Shelsley. Back in June the Oxford University Automobile Club had organised a little event on Ewelme Down, in the Chiltern Hills. Oxford University authorities were always less favourably disposed towards the use of cars by their students than were their counterparts at Cambridge, so Oxford tended to be the poor relation and the OUAC was in fact a newly-formed club. Small event it might have been, but there was some 'class' present with BTD falling to Brian Lewis's supercharged Bugatti T35B and with Doctor Benjafield's Alfa Romeo also competing. Over in Ulster, the active UAC had also run an event at Ballybannon, again near Belfast, where the fastest time on the 1.2 mile course had been set by a 4½-litre Bentley.

Although not strictly within the terms of reference of this work, popular speed trials were held on a straight and not perfectly flat course on the Race Hill at Lewes, in Sussex, between 1925 and 1939. These ¼-mile dashes were held three or four times a year, organised by the Brighton & Hove MC (who revived the famous Brighton Speed Trials on a larger scale in 1932), Kent & Sussex LCC, and later the Bugatti Owners Club and the Vintage Sports Car Club. Many of the Shelsley regulars ran there including Dick Nash who set a 19.06s record in 1936, driving his sohc Anzani-engined Frazer Nash special 'The Terror'. Geoffrey Taylor smashed this record in 1937, clocking 18.75s in his 2-litre Alta, a time which was further reduced in 1938 to 18.27s, by Peter Monkhouse, director of the Monaco Motor Co., having a drive in Ian Connell's ERA R6B.

Similarly popular sprint events were held in Yorkshire from 1934 in the grounds of Wetherby Grange, the home of the enthusiastic Sir Ronald Gunter, who shared a Lagonda with Doctor Benjafield at Le Mans in 1935. These Northern speed trials, held in a pleasant parkland setting conveniently close to the A1 Great North Road, attracted excellent entries. For example, in July 1938, BTD fell to Ian Craig in the beautiful 3.3-litre Bugatti T59 which he had bought from Noel Rees, beating the 'Freikaiserwagen' and further Bugattis driven by Jack Lemon Burton and Arthur Baron. A year earlier the Wetherby entry had included 5 Shelsley Specials, 7 Bugattis, 5 Frazer Nashes, 4 Lea-Francis and no fewer than 10 MGs.

But returning to hill climbing and to 1929, prospects were fairly bleak. Even Shelsley was not the subject of universal approval. Although 5,000 spectators attended the May meeting and *The Autocar*'s editorial line was highly enthusiastic, there were conflicting opinions, well summarised by a letter in the corespondence columns over the pseudonym 'Amateur':

> ...(The public) does not expect to stand, or sit if lucky, through two solid hours watching some 80 standard cars touring slowly up the hill. Any decent main road hill on a Saturday or Sunday afternoon would provide almost as much excitement as the first five classes at Shelsley on Saturday last.
> I submit again that the good old sporting days of this climb have gone and it is now run almost solely as a profit-making venture.

This rather jaundiced onlooker was wrong of course, but this lukewarm enthusiasm towards the slower cars did affect the MAC's policy in later years towards the sports car classes. The following September, they instituted a new Trophy, on formula, for people who had actually competed in the recent Tourist Trophy, with their TT cars.

Le pur sang and Prescott

During the earlier Vintage years comparatively few foreign sports and racing cars were run in British events. After all, the British sports car was an excellent proposition and the additional expense and mechanical complications attendant on running one of the Continentals were strong disincentives. But, there were exceptions, and the foreign make with a particular following, even in the early nineteen-twenties, was the Bugatti, the aristocrat of the contemporary light cars. The off-the-shelf availability of the superb sohc straight eight T35 racers, the similarly engined T43 sports cars and the more economical four-cylinder T37 Grand Prix lookalike, coupled to effective British technical back-up via Colonel Sorel made the Molsheim cars an attractive proposition for the wealthier clubman who had no comparable British alternatives.

In view of this strong interest in a make which had figured prominently in British hill climbs since the early days of Mays, Cushman and Hall, three keen *Bugattistes* got together and formed the Bugatti Owners Club in 1929. They were D. B. Madeley (the one-time owner of a Crossley-built Brescia model who had initiated the idea of a club in the motoring press), Colonel G. M. Giles and Ambrose Varley (who later disappeared in mysterious circumstances).

By 1931, the club had found somewhere to stage hill climbs, albeit on an unsealed surface (at least until concreting was carried out just before the venue's demise as a competition venue in 1935), on the unfinished estate roads of a private housing development in Chalfont St Peter, in Buckinghamshire. Only a few miles from Uxbridge, this course offered around 1,000 yards on a reasonable gradient, and with some right-angle bends. The estate was owned by the builders at the time and it was to be some five years before the houses were built alongside the roadways. Not in the same class as Shelsley, the meetings nevertheless attracted good support from Bugatti owners and other clubmen, including many of the people who congregated at Shelsley such as Bugatti drivers, Aubrey Esson-Scott (with an immaculate T39), 'TASO' Mathieson and Jack Lemon Burton, whose T37 was fitted with the skimpiest mud wings in 1931 to class as a sports car. People like the Evans family, the Bolsters, Dick Nash and

An unfinished housing development at Chalfont St Peter provided Bugatti Owners' Club members with a hill climbing alternative to Shelsley from 1931 to 1935. This is Aubrey Esson-Scott's smart black and silver Bugatti T51C.
RIVERS FLETCHER

the Skinners just enjoyed a sporting day out in a very informal atmosphere. Later on, the BOC also ran a similar meeting at Joel Park.

Actually pre-dating the first meeting at Chalfont St Peter, was the inaugural Berkhamstead & District MC hill climb at the delightfully named Dancer's End, near Tring in Hertfordshire. Although shorter than Chalfont St Peter, this course was broadly similar in character. The course was used first in 1930 but from 1933 regular meetings were held, attended by many of the hill climb regulars. John Appleton scored a notable BTD in 1938 while the last meeting of all, held in May 1939, went to the rapid Frazer Nash of Gordon Claridge, in 27.8s.

Ever since 1925 Scotland had been starved of hill climbing activity but in 1934 the Scottish Sporting Car Club gained the use of ½ mile of the Hamilton Drive, on the Kinneil Estate of the Duke of Hamilton at Bo'Ness, near Linlithgow. By 1937 an 'Open' permit was received and good sport was enjoyed, although the entry was mainly of sports cars and fairly parochial in character. T. W. Meikle's Frazer Nash-BMW set BTD in May 1937, clocking 38.5s to the 39.2s of A. J. Cormack's Alta. The unofficial pre-war record was actually set on a 'demonstration' run in May 1939 when Harry Soutar's wailing, twin rear-wheeled, Bugatti T35B, recorded 33.4s to the official BTD time of 33.6s, set by G. J. W. Moncrieff in a little supercharged Riley.

Far to the South West, another group of keen clubmen in the Bristol area, the Bristol Motor Cycle and Light Car Club, were able to hold hill climbs at Backwell, near Bristol, where the Bolsters and the Frys were leading contenders.

Over in Ireland, the Craigantlet events continued although they rarely attracted the English hill climb regulars. When the TT ceased to be held over the Ards circuit after the 1936 event, there was a sharp falling off in interest, but there were notable performances from Bert Hadley in 1936 and 1937 when he drove one of the superb little twin-cam Austin racers. He set a new course record in 1936 and then broke it again in 1937, despite clouting a bank on his first climb.

In the last two years before hostilities in 1939, there was almost a flood of new venues with Prescott, Great Auclum and Trengwainton hosting their first meetings: while in Scotland, the old Rest-and-Be-Thankful road cut out of Glen Croe, a testing hill since the early days of long-distance road trials, was by-passed and would become available for competition use once again. Great Auclum, a specially constructed 440 yards course with a downhill start and a banked first bend was on the Burghfield Common estate (near Reading) of Neil Gardiner, and Trengwainton, another short course, was on Colonel Bolitho's land two miles North West of Penzance. Both came into use in 1939. The Frazer Nash & BMW CC and the West Cornwall Car Club, respectively, ran the first, modest, meetings.

Prescott was very different, for it rapidly became an institution second only to Shelsley. This, the long-desired permanent base of competitive operations for the Bugatti Owners Club, came about in unusual and typically sporting circumstances. As befits a club catering for the owners of some of the worlds's most glamorous and expensive machinery, the BOC had considerable financial resources at its disposal and had for some time considered trying to buy its own hill climb venue. Dancer's End was considered at one stage but problems over noise nuisance ruled that out. In 1937, the Prescott House Estate, picturesquely situated just outside the village of Gotherington, five miles North East of

Cheltenham, and not far from Cleeve Hill, a notable Cotswold landmark, came on the market and was bought by a development company. Formerly the home of the Earl of Ellenborough, the Cotswold Stone house and its rough and winding drive were in need of attention but it had great potential as a hill climb course, complete with club headquarters and a second residence (Pardon Hill Farm) in the woods which shaded the middle part of the drive. The sale was spotted by the noted historian of Victorian engineering, Tom Rolt, who was also a VSCC member and who had previously visited Prescott House. The Vintage Sports Car Club, founded in 1934 to keep going the traditions of the (by then inexpensive to buy) vintage sports car, was rich in enthusiasm but not in financial resources, and could not consider making an offer to the new owners. Fortunately, another VSCC member and the owner of the old 1908 Itala 'Floretta', 'Sam' Clutton, was also a BOC member and as a member of the Cluttons estate agency business was able to come up with a solution which was satisfactory to all parties. The upshot was that Prescott was offered to the BOC, and was bought by Colonel Giles for £2,500 on the understanding that members were to be asked to subscribe to debentures totalling £4,500, enough to buy the hill for the Club and to pay for the extensive work needed to make it fit to use for hill climbs. The debenture issue was totally successful, Prescott became a reality and in return the VSCC was given the unique privilege of holding its own meeting there in addition to the BOC programme.

At 880 yards, the course was shorter than Shelsley but, with four really severe bends, including Pardon hairpin which was constructed especially to bypass an even tighter existing hairpin, it was much slower. Before events could be held, much work had to be carried out. Apart from the alterations at Pardon, the whole track was widened (to a uniform 15 feet with 20 feet on the sharper corners), given a smooth tarred surface (smoother than Shelsley which still had the notorious bump before the first 'S' bend which had caused Raymond Mays, for one, to become airborne at one meeting), and the surrounding trees and undergrowth trimmed and cut back. Full 'office' accommodation was built at the start to house officials and the timing apparatus. A return road was also provided to bring cars back down to the delightful Orchard Paddock.

Shelsley Special at Prescott. Joe Fry's fearsome Freikaiserwagen set an unofficial – the VSCC did not employ RAC timekeepers – record at the new Prescott hill of 47.62s in August 1938.
LOUIS KLEMANTASKI
via RIVERS FLETCHER

The BOC began modestly enough with an opening rally in April, from the *Queen's Hotel* in Cheltenham to the hill in April. The procession was led by the old chain-drive 'Black Bess', once the hill climb mount of Ivy Cummings, and the Mercedes of Earl Howe. Once arrived at Prescott, runs were timed and the fastest three at this rather momentous occasion were Ian Craig's massive 4.9-litre Bugatti T54 hybrid (55.58s), Ronnie Symondson's T57SC (57.83s) and, fittingly, Cecil Clutton's remarkably fast old Itala (59.03s). Craig, incidentally, was the owner of the well-known Bugatti specialist, CIC Ltd, a company which had recently taken over the firm of L. G. Bachelier and Sons, Leslie Bachelier's company.[1] Symondson and Clutton, remarkably, were still competing with the same cars at Prescott in the nineteen-eighties although the Bugatti then passed to Neil Corner.

After this enjoyable preamble a 'Closed' hill climb was run on 15 May, with 54 entries in classes catering for pre-1914 racers, touring cars, sports cars, and racing machinery. Naturally, Bugattis were numerous (there were 15 of them), but the varied field included a number of Shelsley Specials. A good crowd of 2,000 to 3,000 spectators watched Arthur Baron set BTD, flinging his twin rear-wheeled (as fitted to most of the really fast racing cars by this time) '2.3' GP Bugatti, up in 50.7s to win from Lemon Burton's similar T51 by only 0.04s, and Bobby Sumner in the Sumner-JAP (51.28s). The latter won the 1½-litre racing class from more Shelsley Specials: the old Becke Powerplus, now owned by Peter Vaughan, and the Morgan-based 'Tiger Cat' of Clive Lones. Outside the racing classes the best sports car time, beating Symondson and the T55s of Shakspeare and Craig and rather spoiling the Bugatti party, came from the South London garage owner and trials special builder, Sydney Allard, driving his friend and customer Ken Hutchison's 4.4-litre Lincoln V12-engined, four-seater, Allard Special trials car. The winning time was 54.35s. Interestingly, on this tighter course the battle of the Edwardians went decisively to Clutton (58.4s) and not to Heal's Fiat which was dominant at Shelsley.

Despite some rain later in the day the event was most successful, and after another 'rally' visit, the BOC went ahead with an 'Open' meeting in July. Despite some showers, the short-lived course record was obliterated with Baron facing formidable opposition in the form of circuit racer George Abecassis

Best Vintage performance at the August 1938 VSCC Prescott meeting was put up by Leeds haulage contractor, Tom Grimshaw, in his Bugatti T35C, in 50.74s.
LOUIS KLEMANTASKI
via TOM GRIMSHAW

---

1   It was Bachelier who had fitted the chassis and engine of a Grand Prix T54 with an elegant reproduction of a T55 body to concoct a most exciting road car. This splendid machine, long out of Bachelier family ownership, was sold for a staggering £507,000 at Christie's Monte Carlo auction in 1987 – to the chagrin of Leon Bachelier, Leslie's son and latterday hill climber in a rapid Caterham Seven.

with the 1½-litre Alta, and Fane's Frazer Nash. The Surrey driver who had gained some notable successes with the Alta showed his all-too-rarely-employed hill climbing talent with an inspired second climb on a slippery track to record 47.85s to win from Baron (48.77s), while the small racing cars were headed by a 50.86s climb from 'Grasshopper' Austin Seven trials driver Dennis Buckley in one of the twin-cam Austins. The tightness of the hill obviously suited the trials drivers for Ken Hutchison this time took the wheel of his Allard Special and lopped over a second off Allard's May time (53.32s) but Fane's FN-BMW 328 was even faster. With the course exceptionally slippery there were numerous incidents, with Clutton, Allard and Lones among those to explore the surrounding landscape. On this occasion Sydney Allard was driving his Ford V8-engined two-seater (FGP 750), with its shapely tail that had once graced a T35 Bugatti (that must have *really* nettled the BOC), and his departure through the hedge on the outside of the top corner, the Semicircle, was but the first of a number of excursions at this point which was officially christened in later years with the name Allard Gap.

Prescott was already becoming a busy speed venue and on 27 August the VSCC took over. Unfortunately, there was no RAC-recognised timekeeper present so times could not be accepted for record purposes. This was a great shame for despite a crash in practice and a singular absence of brakes, Joe Fry was timed at 47.62s in the 'Freikaiserwagen', 0.23s under the official record, to beat Ian Craig who made a very wild ascent in his T59 Bugatti. Another spectacular performance came from Anthony Heal who somehow got the old Fiat to the top in a phenomenal 55.91s, firmly putting the Itala's times in perspective. At this early stage in the Club's career, the VSCC did not place an age limit on their competing cars.

Although the sun shone for the closing September 'Open' meeting, the course was wet and the record remained intact. Rather surprisingly, a fine drive by Bob Ansell had the white ERA through the finish area in just 48.91s, to beat Abecassis (49.12s) and Fane (49.43s) for BTD. Buckley shone with the little Austin and the Bugattis were again beaten for sports car honours, as was Fane's FN-BMW, by G. Bagratouni's imposing 2.6-litre Alfa Romeo with a commendable 53.92s. Again, there were a

Peter Vaughan set the final BTD at Prescott, virtually on the eve of war, before the long hiatus. Here Vaughan rounds Orchard in the effective Becke Powerplus Special.
LOGAN *via* RIVERS FLETCHER

A memory to cherish through difficult times. Raymond Mays set a 37.37s hill record at Shelsley in June 1939, with ERA R4D. The record was to stand for ten years.
MIDLAND AUTOMOBILE CLUB

lot of mishaps, with Fry wrecking the 'Freikaiserwagen' in practice, Sumner hurting himself after his car hit a bank, and George Symonds and Peter Vaughan also running out of road, Symonds overturning his rapid MG.

There was naturally keen anticipation before the opening meeting in 1939, an 'Open' event on 14 May. In the meantime, the BOC had received a remarkable gift. In appreciation of the Club's efforts in the interests of the Bugatti marque, Ettore and Jean Bugatti presented the BOC with a twin-camshaft T51 Grand Prix car for the use of Club members. Unfortunately, although the car had reached Britain in time for the May meeting the BOC were not faced with the tricky job of deciding who would drive it. The car was held in customs by officials who frankly could not believe that a motor manufacturer would actually give away such a car! The course was wet again too, so the record stayed intact. Ansell again went well (52.3s), Abecassis's car suffered from oiling plugs and was out of contention, Fane made a polished climb in 52.67s, and Buckley clocked a superb 53.69s, but top honours went to a newcomer to the hill, Percy Maclure. This great Riley driver brought his 1½-litre supercharged model to Prescott for the first time and shot up in 51.65s. Maclure was celebrated for the success he had with unblown Riley engines, but the power for this car came from an ERA engine which had been the spare unit for Reggie Tongue's R11B.

There was another Bugatti BTD in June when the BOC ran a 'Closed' meeting in real garden party atmosphere. Unusually, this resulted in a 1-2 for that supremely elegant but technically rather outdated GP car, the T59, with Arthur Baron's ex-Charles Martin/Duke of Grafton car (48.71s) beating Lemon Burton's 3.8-litre-engined car which he and bought from Eccles (49.86s). Times were generally fast. Bagratouni officially lowered Fane's 52.11s sports car record with 52.02s, and Major Vaughan did exceptionally well to persuade the stumpy little Becke Powerplus up in 50s.

But then came the most ambitious fixture yet, an International meeting on 30 July, which garnered a superb entry and stamped Prescott's claim to having become a first-line venue in little more than a year. The magnificent entry was headed by Raymond Mays, making his first appearance on the Gloucestershire hill with his ERA R4D, and no less than Jean-Pierre Wimille with a works Bugatti. The Bugatti family had done the BOC proud on their big day by sending their number one driver with the 4.7-litre car whose bulbous, if flowing, contours concealed what was still basically a T59 chassis beneath. This time the weather held and the records fell. Before the main battle, Heal took the 10-litre Fiat to a 54.82s record, while Gerry Crozier reduced the 1½-litre sports car time to 53.07s. Bagratouni was as rapid as ever (52.11s), but the new outright sports car record now belonged to Sydney Allard who exuberantly flung his now 4.4-lite-engined Allard Special to the top in just 51.33s. Hadley and Buckley were phenomenal in the little Austins, recording 47.76s and 49.39s respectively, but after a spin on his first run, Fane beat Hadley with 47.72s to win the 1½-litre class from David Hampshire's Maserati 6CM, Maclure, and the astonishing Vaughan – who all bettered 50s.Then there was Mays. His two climbs were completed in 46.25s and 46.14s for BTD and a new course record, thereby asserting his mastery over one more course. A. H. Beadle, driving his powerful 2.litre Alta, was not far behind, and his splendid 47.37s was good enough for third BTD: not as fast as Wimille, though. Despite having a rather unsuitable car for such a tight hill, the French ace put in a dazzling performance to record 46.69s for second BTD and easily beat Kenneth Evans's Monoposto Alfa for the class.

Truly, Prescott had 'arrived' so it was doubly sad that the war intervened so soon afterwards. The VSCC just got their meeting in as the shadows of the impending conflict added to the gloom of a thoroughly wet 26 August. Even so, justice was done when Peter Vaughan set a final BTD with the little Becke in 56.07s.

After that, hill climbing – like every other form of motor sport – ceased for the duration. The last flickerings of activity being a poorly-supported event on an unsealed track at Horndeam, near Portsmouth, which is mainly remembered for the mishap when Sydney Allard overturned his Allard Special, flinging out fledgling motoring journalist Bill Boddy, who was a passenger in the car; and a meeting at Ballinascorney, near Dublin, which took place on 23 September, after the outbreak of war. Eire was neutral of course, so this meeting went ahead with a record-breaking win for MacArthur's MG Magnette.

Although this photograph was taken in 1946 at Shelsley Walsh, the people depicted represented the 'establishment' of the late nineteen-thirties and nineteen-forties. They are (left to right): Sir Malcolm Campbell, Raymond Mays, Leslie Wilson, Stanley Barnes and Earl Howe.
T. BARNES

CHAPTER FOUR

RENAISSANCE
(1946-1950)

ALL over Europe, 8 May 1945 was a day to remember. It was VE Day – 'Victory in Europe' – and the Second World War was over, at least in Europe. Whether you exhuberantly celebrated a great victory, soberly reflected on the cost of it all, or picked your way through the ruins of one of Germany's cities looking for food, it was the formal conclusion of almost six years of suspended normality. Even then, the war with Japan went on, to be brought to a close only after atomic bombs had laid waste the cities of Hiroshima and Nagasaki. Faced with the mammoth task of rebuilding economies and cities alike, amid widespread rationing of most things in most countries, few people, let alone motor manufacturers, could seriously consider motor racing as a high priority.

However, motor racing enthusiasts are a determined breed – they have to be not to lose patience with their usually temperamental and always expensive cars – and even during the war some found time to keep hopes alive for the future. Former ERA (and future BRM) Public Relations man A. F. Rivers Fletcher organised a series of a dozen or so get-togethers in London, mainly at the Rembrandt Hotel in Kensington. Much appreciated by those who were able to attend, and even by those who were not but had heard or read all about them, these impromptu 'club night'-type gatherings did much to keep the spirit of motor racing alive in Britain. Although these meetings were attended by many enthusiasts for all types of motor sport, many hill climb enthusiasts were among the regulars including John Bolster, Dick Caesar, 'Eric' Findon, Ron Godfrey, Anthony Heal, Raymond Mays and Kay Petre. Even after the return of a far from untroubled peace, Rivers was prevailed upon to hold an occasional 'Rembrandt' during the off season months, so popular had these affairs become. Although it may seem hard to believe today that such apparently minor happenings should occupy such an important role in enthusiasts' lives, in harsh and dangerous times such as those, they were rare lightenings in the otherwise all-pervasive gloom.

In Britain in 1945, the situation was most frustrating for the would-be motorist. There was no end in sight to hardships, shortages and above all rationing (especially of petrol and steel, while tyres of any sort were virtually unobtainable). A newly elected Labour Government had objectives which were fundamentally ideological rather than in the realms of practical economic revival, and that only aggravated the position. The RAC took a very cautious line, fearful of attracting official displeasure at encouraging activities as frivolous as motor racing. The basic petrol ration, which permitted around 200 miles per month of private motoring – if you were running something as economical as an Austin Seven, and some surprising people did just that – hardly encouraged anything ambitious.

The RAC in fact consented to grant permits for Closed Invitation events in June, but for some time most events were short-distance trials. So popular before the war, they were about to have a big revival which was ended only by the growing specialisation of machinery suitable for 'mud-plugging', and the arranging of ever-more-freakish hills to defeat the new trials specials.

This was all very well, but it just was not motor racing, and prospects for the purists were pretty grim. None of the three permanent British racing circuits – Brooklands, Donington Park and Crystal Palace – was likely to be released for renewed racing in the near future. Hopes were initially high (but soon to be totally dashed) for a resumption of racing at Brooklands, now occupied by greatly extended Vickers factory premises.

Fortunately, the same did not apply to the hill climb venues. Committee members of the Midland Automobile Club, in some trepidation, made their way to Shelsley Walsh for a tour of inspection, and Leslie Wilson was able to report that apart from the vigorous encroachment of vegetation the place was in surprisingly good order. The hill would be ready for use again in 1946. A similarly cheerful note was struck at the AGM of the Bugatti Owners Club on 31 May 1945. Prescott could be made ready for use at two months' notice with the expenditure of around £1,000 needed in repairing potholes and making up the return road. Compensation for wartime depreciations had already been received from the Army. On a lesser scale, it soon emerged that Bo'ness, Trengwainton and Great Auclum would also be available again before very long.

This simple fact of availability made a tremendous difference to the stature and prominence of hill climbing in the immediate post-1945 seasons. There were plans made almost immediately to utilise some of the many wartime airfields for speed events – sprints initially and then full-scale circuit racing, but until racing experiments at Silverstone and Westhampnett (Goodwood) in 1948 proved successful enough to plan full programmes for the following year, the hill climbs held sway. Without the expense and difficulties of competing away from the British mainland, and the problems such as foreign currency restrictions, deplorable road conditions on the devastated Continent, lack of spare parts and an almost total absence of new racing tyres, there was no better alternative to the timeless charm of Britain's short, sharp, hill climbs. The short competitive distances were in any case desirable when virtually all the competing cars were pre-war, and when the spares situation was so fraught.

The result was that by 1946 there was what amounted to a full programme of around eighteen hill climb events staged in the British Isles. Major meetings attracted extremely large crowds and entry lists which included virtually everyone who could find a racing car with which to compete. Drivers who were more normally associated with circuit racing – Prince 'Bira', Bob Gerard, David Hampshire, Reg Parnell, Peter Walker and Peter Whitehead, for example – became regulars on the hills for a time and the sport became a focus of motor sporting attention which was at least a match for those hectic days in the early nineteen-twenties.

The success of the 1946 season encouraged the RAC to institute a National Hill Climb Championship, for the first time, in 1947. At a time when championships were almost unknown in Britain, and three years before there was a World Drivers' Championship, this innovation served to stimulate further interest in the hill climb scene.

A plateau of popularity was soon reached. The number of hill climb events did not grow substantially. By 1950 there were still only around twenty events of markedly diverse stature. There were few new venues to add to the familiar ones, with only the full-scale revival of the ancient climb of Rest and be Thankful, out of Glen Croe in Argyllshire, plus Bouley Bay on Jersey, providing courses of the premier class, although Lydstep Haven, near Tenby, was certainly of great scenic attraction. By 1949 there were signs of movement among clubmen towards circuit racing which was now coming within

Hill climbing enjoyed a boom for a few years in the nineteen-forties, until circuit racing re-established itself. Many older Grand Prix and Voiturette cars starred on the hills and the era was typified by Dennis Poore's exploits with his seemingly cumbersome ex-Ruesch Alfa Romeo 8C-35. He is seen here at Prescott in his 1950 Championship-winning year. He retained this wonderful old car until his death. This truly 'period' racer then sold at auction for a staggering £1.5 million in 1988.
AUTOSPORT via MIKE KETTLEWELL

their reach at Silverstone and Goodwood. The following year, entry lists were sharply depleted all too often and the crowds were smaller. The support of the clubmen was essential of course as there was a general lack of manufacturer interest in hill climbing by now, not that many established British manufacturers were in any position to support much motor sport of any description for the first few years of peace. In fact, 1950 was a highly significant year for it was the last when a representative of the prewar order of adapted 'thoroughbred' racing cars, a much-modified 750 kilogram Formula Grand Prix Alfa Romeo 8C-35, staved off the new breed of ultra-light hill climb cars for the RAC Championship.

All this was far in the future when the energetic Rivers Fletcher contrived to lay on a demonstration and general get-together on 14 July 1945 on the made up estate roads of an unfinished private housing development, the Bevan Park Estate, Cockfosters, New Barnet. It was not a race, nor a sprint, nor a hill climb, for there were no permits yet available for any of these. Rivers and his willing helpers managed to lay out a 0.6 mile 'circuit' and attracted a surprising number of long-laid-up competition cars, and their well-remembered drivers, to give demonstration runs before a crowd of around 1,000 people, and with the proceeds going to Hospital funds. A great deal of determination was needed to bring to fruition this remarkable event. Rivers Fletcher was assisted by the enthusiastic efforts of many, including journalists Laurence Pomeroy and 'Bunny' Tubbs, John Bolster, Cecil Clutton, Anthony Heal, Eric Giles and a young John Wyer.

After Earl Howe had opened proceedings in his beautiful blue and black Bugatti T57SC there was much to gladden the hearts of nostalgic hill climb enthusiasts. All concerned were run singly, officially untimed, and accompanied by exhortations to be very careful and not to risk accidents which might prejudice future racing.

Albeit unofficially, 'competitors' were timed, though, and it was the effervescent John Bolster, right arm cocked skyward in the once-familiar manner, who slithered his way round the fastest in the old twin JAP-engined 'Bloody Mary'. 'The old Queen', as he was wont to refer to her on occasions, had been laid to one side in 1937 while the Bolsters concentrated on yet more ambitious specials, but now it was dusted off and was to prove as effective as ever.

Major Tony Rolt, recently released from Colditz prison camp, brought his ex-'Bira' ERA 'Remus' (R5B), while pre-war Riley diver Bob Gerard made his ERA début with R4A, the ex-Pat Fairfield/Norman Wilson car which had been retrieved from the Parnell 'collection' and rebuilt by this bespectacled, unflambuoyant, but highly enthusiastic heavy vehicle distributor from Leicester. Partnered by his wife Joan (primarily in the Joan Hall role of team organiser but also a successful driver in her own right), Gerard rapidly became a major force in post-1945 motor sport, not least because he quickly built up a significant reservoir of ERA knowledge and spares relating to the older Bourne cars.

Although hill climbs were not his forte, cars with Reg Parnell connections were to be prominent in hill climbs. Parnell was well-known before the war for his slightly wild racing exploits. This good-natured but unequivocally blunt farmer and transport business operator from Derby had offended a few socially elevated sensibilities before the war with his wheeler dealing and apparently mercenary approach to racing, but unlike his critics Reg was not a rich man and had to make his racing activities pay. Incidentally, John Bolster was another who tended to rail against the pomposity which occasionally intruded among the 'right crowd and no crowding' set at Brooklands. Parnell's exploits with a single-seater MG Magnette and the fearsome BHW (Bugatti-Hassan-Wilkins, a large single-seater powered by a 4,840cc Bugatti T50 engine and weighing all of a ton) were not sufficient to give him top rank status, but he was in the box seat for the post-war revival when it happened. He had used assets of access to farm buildings, and other assorted sheds and garages around Derby, and his own transport (often returning 'empty' from official tasks) to buy up and store redundant racing cars during the war years – all at very low prices! By 1945 Reg owned, scattered around the environs of Derby, some 30 competition cars, and although many were in pieces they were definitely recoverable. This cache, which was particularly rich in ERAs, Delages, Maseratis and Rileys was gradually sold off, and so helped Reg to pay for his post-war racing. It is remarkable how few racing cars had been destroyed during the war, but then many were hidden away in some unlikely places. For example, the Princes 'Bira' and 'Chula', unable to return to occupied Thailand, spent the war on their Cornish property, with the ERA 'Romulus' (R2B) and the ex-Straight Maserati 8CM safely berthed in a nearby shed. Their other ERA, 'Hanuman' (R12B) had stayed in its London garage and had been fortunate to escape the effects of a bomb explosion very close by.

Among the gathering at Cockfosters were George Symonds with his R-type MG single-seater, Gordon Claridge (Frazer Nash-BMW 328), Anthony Heal (1919 5-litre Ballot once hill climbed by Count Zborowski), George Dowson and Alec Issigonis (Lightweight Special) and Peter Monkhouse, with the Bugatti T51 which had been presented to the BOC in 1939. Monkhouse, another pre-war MG driver, was the Managing Director of the Monaco Motor & Engineering Co Ltd, of Watford, a leading competition car preparation company of the time, and he had bought the Bugatti in 1943 from the BOC who, while generally appreciative of the gift, could see no imminent use for it, and were also concerned about the means of deciding who should drive it. Monkhouse, on the other hand, wanted to have a good car ready for the resumption of racing, and this strong-minded, even maverick, character, a declared enemy of all formality and unnecessary regulation, was one of the first who were rarin' to go in 1945.

Relief and jubilation were comon emotions at Cockfosters, but the inevitable nostalgia was also tinged with deep sadness. Most of the cars would race again but not all the personalities would return. Fane, Johnny Wakefield, Dick Shuttleworth, Richard and Barbara Bolster, Percy Maclure, Norman Wilson, and the guiding force behind MG, Cecil Kimber, were among those who had gone.

Before the war, the Bristol area had become a real hot-bed of motor sporting activity which had its nucleus among the members of the Bristol Motor Cycle & Light Car Club and the Bristol Aeroplane Co MC, and outlets at Backwell and in what amounted to grass-track racing for the impecunious. The Frys and Dick Caesar were prominent among this group, and it was the Bristol MC and LCC who actually earned the honour of holding the first post-war hill climb, at Naish House, Clapton-in-Gordano, near Portishead, on 18 August 1945. With a timed distance just under half a mile, the W-shaped course rose some 200 feet, and the first and third bends were particularly tight. The snag was that the course was rough, partly over grass, and certainly a far cry from Shelsley or Prescott. About 30 cars and 24 motorcycles competed and Bob Gerard actually persuaded ERA R4A to run on six cylinders long enough to score an unofficial BTD for cars (0.4s slower than Falconer's Triumph motorcycle) over what was a close relative of a trials hill. In an event which boasted a class for 'wartime hacks', Walter Watkins actually scored the official BTD for cars (Gerard made R4A run properly only on a third, unofficial run) in his fierce Watkins-Nash, which featured the old recipe of JAP V-twin engine in a GN-based chassis. A future hill climb champion, Dennis Poore, made his début with the ex-

Peter Monkhouse took delivery of the ex-Bugatti Owners' Club Bugatti T51 in time for the first post-war events.
RIVERS FLETCHER

Douglas Briault/Clive Edwardes MG R-type (and was sixth fastest car competitor behind Northway in the old Dick Nash car, 'Spook'), while Len Parker actually fitted snow chains to his Jaguar SS100 in an attempt to find some grip, but was still beaten in class by Baillie-Hill's more suitable Meadows-engined HRG.

The older motor clubs were only stuttering back into life, and it was truly the Bristol people who were in the vanguard for the Bristol Aeroplane Co MC achieved another first – the first use of an aerodrome venue – when they ran a half-mile sprint event on part of Filton's perimeter track on a cold and wet day in October. This time there was no argument about Gerard's BTD, with John Bolster a whole 3.3s slower than the white ERA. Alec Issigonis bettered Watkins and Poore for a well contested class win; Sydney Allard appeared with his pre-war, 4-seater, Allard-Mercury Special; and sports car class wins were taken by Gerard, in the smart Riley Sprite which was more often used by his wife, and Parker's rapid Jaguar.

After these tantalising preliminaries to the full-scale return of speed events everyone could only suppress their impatience while waiting for something a little less makeshift in 1946. Secure in the knowledge that both Shelsley and Prescott would be ready for resumption, hill climbers saw much of the attention turning towards their activities in 1946, at least partly by default. The seemingly insuperable problem of recovering the British racing circuits received another twist when the final decision to sell out Brooklands was made at a shareholders' meeting of Brooklands (Weybridge) Ltd in January 1946. Most enthusiasts were very bitter about the sale – for £330,000 – and were highly critical of Sir Malcolm Campbell, who was one of the directors who recommended it. Sadly, and despite the track's central role in British pre-war motor racing, it was probably the right decision. If it were not sold to Vickers, who needed the land, it would have been up to three years before the old track could have been released for racing use. The track surface was in poor condition (it had been bad enough in 1939), and track racing had little relevance to post-war motor sport, at least on this side of the Atlantic.

A lack of new cars would also serve to discourage all but the most mechanically able, and determined, from contesting longer-distance events. Two of the 1939 Maserati 4CLs had come to Britain, to be raced by Reggie Tongue and Johnny Wakefield, and these were the most modern racing cars available apart from the untried E-type ERA. Reg Parnell had secured the successful Wakefield car, while the Ansell family now had the Tongue car. Unfortunately, the latter had a cracked block and was to remain out of action for most of 1946, awaiting a new block from Italy. When the car did appear it bore the legend 'This is Ansell's Best Mild' on the body. This was 22 years before advertising was permitted on racing cars in Britain and it thoroughly upset the purists. Otherwise, apart from the many specials which were generally suitable only for sprint events anyway, there were a few Alfa Romeos, Maseratis and Bugattis dating from the 750 kilogramme Formula of 1934/37, all bar one of the A, B and B/C/D-type ERAs and a few assorted Altas of which George Abecassis's 1937 car had been the most successful, plus a few highly-developed Rileys of sports car origin.

ERA Ltd, which had set up camp at Donington Park in 1939 after it and Raymond Mays had parted company, had now moved to Dunstable, and announced that they would continue to develop the ambitiously-conceived, troublesome and under-developed 1939 E-type, although privateers would have to find the resources to race the cars. Down at Tolworth, Surrey, Geoffrey Taylor laid plans for a twin ohc, Roots-blown, four-cylinder car with modern independent front suspension and de Dion rear end, to be offered to privateers at just £1,850. Taylor too lacked development resources and this car was not to appear until 1948. As ambitious and charmingly persuasive as ever, Raymond Mays made it known that he was seeking the financial backing for a national team of possibly V16 racing cars, to be designed by Peter Berthon. These were all brave plans, but for the moment, for most people, the essentially amateur sprint events contested by the existing cars had to suffice. And notwithstanding the ever-present shortages of supplies and bureaucratic obstruction at every opportunity, preparations were intense.

A number of specialist competition car preparation companies were getting back into business, concentrated in the Surrey environs of old Brooklands in many cases, and from them was to arise the beginnings of Britain's successful post-war racing car industry. Early in the field were Bugatti specialists Continental Cars Ltd (Rodney Clarke and Len Potter), near Ripley; the Lightwater-based Bob and Diana Cowell, and Pat Whittet partnership; Raymond Mays and Partners Ltd (Mays, Berthon, Ken Richardson, Harry Lester and Anthony Crook); Monaco at Watford (Peter Monkhouse and Ian Connell); Blakes of Liverpool (the Reece cousins); John Grosscurth at Maidenhead; Leslie Ballamy's LMB firm of split-axle independent front suspension fame (and with Marcus Chambers in day-to-day charge); the old Brooklands firm Thomson & Taylor; Alan Southon's Phoenix Green Garage at Hartley Wintney (specialists in Vintage and Edwardian cars); and James Boothby Motors Ltd, near Crawley.

Down in the West Country a group of ardent, if financially ill-equipped, racing devotees were devising tiny 500cc motorcycle-engined racing cars, with Dick Caesar and the Frys prominent among them. Both the Vintage Sports Car Club and the Bristol Aeroplane CMC announced that they would organise a class for 500cc racing cars in sprint events in 1946. Significantly, the latter club recommended that this class should prohibit cars with more than two cylinders or with superchargers, in the interests of reducing costs. The idea of this cut-price way of entering the racing fray had been advocated in *Motor Sport* as early as 1941 by technical journalist Joseph Lowrey and VSCC stalwart Kenneth Neve, but even by May 1946 there was no agreement on the regulations which would govern the cars. Some advocated any type of engine as long as it was unsupercharged, while four wheel brakes and a 500 lb minimum weight limit were further suggestions. Nevertheless, this nascent category received a major boost when both the BOC and the MAC announced that they would cater for the tiny cars in their events, although the BOC were likely to admit supercharged entries. Despite the uncertainties over regulations – there were also two schools of thought about the advisability or otherwise of specifying 'pump' petrol or methyl-alcohol fuel – the interest was intense and new cars were anticipated before the 1946 season was very old, thus opening the way to a new breed of sprint/hill climb specials.

Although the Darlington & DMC ran what it chose to call a 'Hill-Storm' at Summer Lodge early in April (again more trials hill than speed hill climb as far as surface was concerned), won by Richmond's HRG, the first major hill climb was not until 19 May, when the BOC promoted the first Open Hill Climb at Prescott since the war. In the meantime, the VSCC had managed to organise an airfield on which to run a ¼-mile speed trial on Easter Monday. This was at Elstree and a big crowd turned up to watch a large and varied 98 car entry contest no fewer than 35 classes for virtually anything which would run on four wheels. Most of the starts were present and it was Peter Monkhouse's howling Bugatti T51 which snatched a 15.2s victory from Reg Parnell's nephew Roy, driving a 1926/7-type Grand Prix Delage, incorporating modifications carried out by Prince 'Chula' in 1937 but actually made up from spare parts from the job lot of Delage machinery acquired by uncle Reg. The latter, driving his Maserati 4CL, tied for third place with John Bolster.

Sadly, it was very wet for Prescott, but it was still marvellous to be back competing at one of the old familiar venues. The entry list was limited to 80 as all concerned felt a bit rusty and a larger field might have over-taxed the organisation. Only 72 actually ran, though, as not everyone's preparations were well advanced. Perhaps best of all Raymond Mays was back. Despite a growing preoccupation with getting the new BRM project off the ground, Mays was still developing old R4D which appeared in post-war form with long rear radius arms to cut out judder and tramp, and with softened front torsion bars on the Porsche ifs. Despite the differential case splitting during practice, the car was repaired and Mays took a 51.7s BTD. It was a great day for ERA for next up were Peter Whitehead in R10B and Bob Gerard in R4A, although both lacked the power of Mays's 2-litre-engined R4D. Peter Monkhouse upheld Bugatti honour with a 53.5s fourth BTD, half a second clear of Northway in the 'Spook', which was now endowed with a 4-litre Mercury V8 engine, and a further 0.3s faster than BOC member number 6, Ken Bear, a 40-year old Bugattiste in the insurance business who was already pretty rapid in another T51. At this time Bear was competing in three Bugattis, the T51, one of the 1931 Le Mans T50 sports cars, and a Special incorporating mainly T44 and T49 parts. New records were out of the question in the prevailing conditions, and on the slippery and twisty slopes of Prescott it was significant that the fastest sports car time, 55.3s, was set by Jack Newton, director of Birmingham-based Newton Oils (their Notwen brand was much favoured by racing people), who had bought the rapid red HRG from Baillie-Hill, primarily for trials events! Among those defeated were Bear's big T50 and George Abecassis in his supercharged 2-litre Alta competition sports car. Northway took the unsupercharged award overall, while Mrs Gerard lifted the Ladies' Prize. Among the class winners, George Dowson, beginning a long string of 750cc and 1100cc class victories with the scientific Lightweight, said to weigh a mere 587 lbs despite the fairly heavy Zöller-supercharged side-valve Austin engine, and the 500cc Strang of the rather incongruously tall Colin Strang.

Strang was one of two competitors to complete their new 500cc specials in time for the meeting, and despite totally different design approaches they achieved closely matched and meritorious times. Strang employed a Fiat 500 chassis, complete with ifs, but much modified to accommodate a rear-mounted Vincent-HRD motorcycle engine driving through a Norton gearbox and with only a modest nose-cowling to disguise his ingenuity. In contrast, the one-time Morgan racer, Clive Lones, now turned 50 but as keen as ever, employed the chassis of an Ulster-type Austin 7 to produce a more conventional-looking front-engined racer but with an Austin gearbox taking the power from a rather old TT JAP 'single'. The result showed Strang climbing in 59.05s to the 59.10s of the St Mellons, Cardiff driver. Although the focus of considerable attention at Prescott, these two little cars were not the first 500s to be seen, for a device call 'Stromboli', built by Adrian Butler and Bruce Mardon, who were two of the pre-war Bristol CAPA grass track racing group, had appeared without much effect at Naish. A rather primitive device, this amounted to most of a Douglas motorcycle grafted into a tubular chassis to the Iota design which Dick Caesar had made available for keen types to build up themselves. The Iota name was also adopted for the name of the 500 Club's magazine and was chosen as the Greek letter 'I', appropriate as the 500s fitted into international Class I record category (351 to 500cc).

Colin Strang's Vincent-HRD-powered Strang was the successful precursor of a whole generation of 500cc racing cars. Initially, the bodywork was even more abbreviated than in the Prescott picture taken c. 1947. Note the typically informal racing attire of the period.
RIVERS FLETCHER

There was not long to wait before the battle was rejoined at Shelsley Walsh on 1 June 1946, but there were also some lesser, local climbs, in the early part of the year, a pattern which was to prove enduring. Despite a deterioration in the course surface which made the event more social than competitive, the Bristol club returned to Naish House in May, victory falling to Len Parker's Lincoln V12-engined Allard Special which had replaced the SS100. Another course well-suited to the pre-war Allard Specials was that at Fordingbridge where the Southampton MC ran their event over a loose and dusty course over the downs. This time Parker was beaten by Sydney Allard himself and by Ken Hutchison. The results were decided on aggregate but Hutchison was actually the fastest in the original, Bugatti-tailed car, CLK 5. The day before, the Scottish Sporting Car Club resumed operations on the Hamilton Drive, at Bo'ness. Again, it was small-time stuff but meant that speed events were possible again in Scotland. Bean's SS100 took top honours from a 3.6-litre Ford-engined car, the Alexander Special, which was shared by Leslie Thorne and dentist Roy Clarkson.

It is grimly ironic that perhaps the most eagerly awaited Shelsley meeting of all time, that of 1 June 1946, was also the wettest ever! Most of the huge crowd who queued to gain admittance on that Saturday were soaked before the meeting even started. The event came at the end of an exceptionally wet week when 3½ inches of rainfall was recorded in the valley, while ¾ inch fell during the actual event. Despite the discomfort the sport-starved crowd stood for hours in the sodden conditons, until the last car ascended the hill, very late, around 8 pm. It was 10 pm before the last of the well-bogged cars was extracted from the mire which had been the car park.

Naturally, there was a big entry – 117 cars – and the MAC instituted morning qualifying, insisting on a 50 seconds minimum time before a driver could go on to the afternoon runs. Only the 500s and Edwardian cars were excused what, in the prevailing conditions, was a stiff target. Despite a strong entry among the 750s, for example, only the Lightweight Special qualified. In the end just 65 ran in the afternoon, of whom a mere 38 cracked the 50s bogey time in the worsening conditions.

Despite the discomfort, it was a superb gathering which greeted the hardy crowd. Mays headed the entry with R4D but lurking in a corner of the Paddock was none other than 'Spyder'. For the first time since 1931 Basil Davenport was competing at Shelsley in the old GN. There were ERAs, Altas, Bugattis and Maseratis in profusion and a splendid gathering of Shelsley Specials, old and new. The little Strang joined the Lightweight, Appleton, Carlmark, and Skinner Specials. The latter Mercury-engined device was now owned by Ted Lloyd-Jones and was re-christened the 'Triangle Special'. The 'Martyr', the GN-based machine powered by a Zöller-blown JAP engine emitting an ear-rending din, re-emerged to maintain the Instone tradition, for this was the mount of Rupert Instone, son of Shelsley's first ever BTD man, Ernest Instone. New sights included Frank Norris's Norris Special, a Frazer Nash chassis fitted with a Roots-blown, four-cylinder, front-wheel-drive Alvis engine; and the rather terrifying 'Mephistophelgatti' of the pseudonymous Tom Norton. With a V12 Lincoln Zephyr engine shoe-horned into a shortened Bugatti T30 chassis the handling took some sorting out. The single-seater Frazer Nash which Fane had made famous and Maclure's supercharged Riley were both there, now in the hands of Lloyd-Jones and Leo Davenport respectively, while Noel Carr made a welcome comeback, driving two single-seater Altas, the 1½-litre ex-Cormack car, and the 2-litre ex-Beadle version. Leslie Johnson had one of the few sports cars – there were still no sports car classes at Shelsley – in the formidable shape of the ex-Ian Connell/Lace Darracq.

But at the end of the day the maestro, Raymond Mays, was still on top, his 42.79s BTD well outside the record and challenged closest by Surrey garage proprietor George Abecassis who recorded a resounding 43.17s in his old 1½-litre Alta. David Hampshire's Maserati 6CM – another car from the Parnell stable – led a gaggle of cars in the 44s bracket despite less than ideal gearing, and was pursued by Whitehead's ERA (with ZF differential), Bob Cowell's independently suspended, 2-litre Alta of 1939 vintage, and Ansell's ERA R9B which sprang a surprise because it was driven very well indeed, not by Bob Ansell, but by Brian Shawe-Taylor, a recently de-mobbed Major who was acting as a mechanic. Another exceptional performance came from Peter Vaughan who rocketed the stubby old Becke Special to the summit in 45.25s, faster than Monkhouse, Carr, Parnell and Gerard. That time deservedly won the Shelsley Special award, but just as remarkable after the long lay-off was the 45.65s time recorded by Basil Davenport, which gave him the unsupercharged award and was actually fifteenth fastest overall.

Despite a surprisingly small membership at this stage – a mere 200 – the Bugatti Owners Club were determined to promote a full programme of events in 1946 and their second Prescott climb, a Closed meeting, came only three weeks after Shelsley. The weather was kinder, and despite the absence of Mays, but helped by the defection of Cowell's potent Alta with a cracked cylinder head, the ERAs were dominant. The gentleman farmer from Chalfont St Giles, Peter Whitehead, scored a rare hill climb win in 47.75s, beating Ansell and Gerard, and with Ken Bear's Bugatti T51 only five-hundredths slower than the Leicester driver. Among the sports cars, both Bear's big T50 and Johnson's Darracq were beaten by a newcomer, George Abecassis's business partner John Heath, in the blown Alta sports.

Already hill climbs were coming thick and fast with Len Parker bumping his way to another Naish success in July, and with yet another BOC Prescott meeting on the last weekend of the month. By this time added interest was lent to the hill climb scene by an announcement from the RAC that they would be instituting a National Hill Climb Championship in 1947, although the details had still to be worked out.

Although it rained again at Prescott, the British weather, which really did its worst during the 1946 season, didn't turn nasty until later in the day, by which time new class records had fallen to Gordon Claridge (lightweight Frazer Nash, 53.45s), Joe James (2.3 Alfa Romeo, 51.60s), Bear (T50, 52.30s), Dowson (50.60s) and Strang (53.70s). This time it was Bob Ansell's turn to head the list overall and his 47.86s BTD was safely clear of the Bugattis of Ken Bear and Peter Monkhouse. A month later, the latter pair took their French thoroughbreds over to Ireland for the revival of the Craigantlet climb. Naturally, it rained, but the locals had no answer to the Bugattis with Bear taking best time in his 3-litre special, 1.2s faster than Monkhouse's T51, and then lifting third place as well in the T50.

Another of the new 500s had appeared at the July Prescott meeting but its untried condition kept it well away from the times of Strang and Lones. There was nothing to suggest that the neat little Cooper Special, shared by two former schoolfriends from Surbiton, John Cooper and Eric Brandon, was anything more than one more ingenious low budget special. Nevertheless, assisted by John's motor engineer father Charles, a one-time riding mechanic to Kaye Don, the Cooper interpretation of the 500cc theme was an interesting one. Like Colin Strang, but working completely independently, the Coopers had chosen a Fiat 500 for their basis, but differed in employing two 'Topolino' front ends which gave them all-independent suspension. A Speedway JAP engine was obtained and drove through a Triumph motorcycle gearbox.

Far more attention was focused on the increasingly effective little car of Colin Strang which scored a major coup by snatching overall Best Time of Day, the first time ever by a 500, when the VSCC returned to Prescott on 31 August. Strang's 54.88s was too fast even for John Bolster's Vintage category-winning 'Bloody Mary' (55.32s) and former Alta mechanic Paul Emery, who was at the wheel of the ex-Fitt Hudson Special (55.4s). With Bear and Monkhouse in Ireland, the fastest Bugatti was the T35B of a newcomer, Peter Stubberfield.

Hill climbs were now cropping up again in some fairly far-flung places, not least in the Channel Islands where the motor sporting tradition tended towards racing on sand. Notwithstanding the Channel Islands' recent occupation by German forces during the war, both the Guernsey and Jersey clubs were keen to promote events of wider appeal. The Guernsey people were able to use a short and twisty hill, half a mile from St Peter Port, called Le Val des Terres, while over in Jersey the Jersey MC & LCC were able to employ a new hill, measuring some 1200 yards, which ran down from the radio station to the harbour at Bouley Bay, a well-surfaced climb in beautiful surroundings which was actually a legacy of the Occupation.

Le Val des Terres was run in August and brought victory to ERA R9B, with yet another driver, George Bainbridge, at the wheel. A partner in Davis Motors, of Shipston-on-Stour, where the car was prepared, he had little comparable opposition and easily saw off Yates' old two-seater Maserati 8C and Jersey auctioneer Frank le Gallais whose latest special was an ohc Wolseley-engined MG TA.

Down in Cornwall, Phil Uglow had a local win at Trengwainton in his rapid HRG while Leslie Johnson took the big Darracq up to a rainy Bo'ness and had three seconds in hand over the fastest of the Scottish specials. Early in September there was another important revival when the Brighton & Hove MC ran the Brighton Speed Trials along the Madeira Drive for the first time since 1938, although with the slightly curving course now extended to a full kilometre. Naturally it was an all-star

entry with many memories of pre-war battles stirred when Mays managed to defeat a determined challenge by 'Bira' in the big Maserati 8CM. Third fastest was Dennis Poore who, after gaining valuable experience and a modicum of success with the R-type MG, had bought a truly formidable machine, the ex-Hans Ruesch Alfa Romeo 8C-35. This powerful, 3.8-litre machine was ideal for Brighton but it was to be some time before Poore mastered it on the hills.

The final meeting at Prescott, the September International, was yet again 'graced' by rain for the second runs, while a greater sensation was caused when Jack Lemon Burton arrived with the gigantic Park Ward-bodied Bugatti T41 'Royale' which now resides in the Musée National de L'Automobile · Collection Schlumpf in Mulhouse, France. The meeting was another ERA benefit with Mays (47.92s) heading Ansell (48.28s) and Whitehead (49.24s), with 'Bira', competing at Prescott for the first time, fourth overall despite a certain amount of indecision about using single or twin rear wheels on the Maserati. John Bolster climbed in a commendable 50.10s with 'Bloody Mary' but he was edged out of fifth place by Ian Connell in yet another ERA, R5B 'Remus'. Former Ford 8 Special racer pre-war, Sheffield Ford dealer Cuthbert Harrison had been making a good impression during the year with an ex-Freddie Dixon 2-litre Riley, sometimes running as a racing car and sometimes as a sports entry and at Prescott he was fastest sports car driver with a record-breaking 52.49s. His closest opponent was Sydney Allard in his latest Ford/Mercury V8-engined Allard sprint car, HLF 601, which narrowly defeated Leslie Johnson's Darracq.

During the war, Allard's business had prospered, becoming a major operation reconditioning military vehicles, with the accent on Ford machinery. With the successful Special-building experience behind him, Allard rapidly got down to manufacturing and marketing rather more refined developments of the basic theme of simple, relatively light British chassis allied to big lazy American-type V8 engines. Although chronic materials shortages and the impossibility of importing the better American V8 engines were major handicaps, the lack of other new sports cars tended to flatter the still rather crude Allards and the new venture was highly successful. The new Allard Sprint Car was basically a stripped version of the new road car fitted with a mildly-modified 4-litre Mercury engine and good torque and excellent traction stood it in good stead.

There was another new 500cc record when Colin Strang, his car benefitting from a new megaphone exhaust said to produce a whole 8 extra bhp, recorded 52.98s.

With the rough Horndean course, run in slightly different form from that of 1939, providing a similar event to that at Fordingbridge, it was no surprise to see the Southsea MC handing their premier award to Sydney Allard who was 0.6s faster than Len Parker in the old V12-engined Allard Special which had been Ken Hutchison's car before the war.

There was more innovation when the MAC ran their second Shelsley meeting as an invitation event in October 1946. The car entry was therefore most select and for the first time since 1912 a class for motorcycles was run. The Shelsley regulars received a nasty shock too when the relatively unfancied Ernie Lyons, riding a 498cc Triumph set the day's best time in 39.54s! Shelsley was becoming pretty bumpy by this stage and with rain towards the end of the day, the car drivers did not have an easy time. Apart from that fast and very steady Triumph, the situation was pretty much as normal with all-but-invincible Mays heading the list in 39.57s, over a second faster than George Abecassis driving his recently purchased Bugatti T59, the car formerly driven by Charles Martin, the Duke of Grafton and Arthur Baron, rather than his Alta which was still in France after a circuit race. Bob Gerard was third on 40.76s but Kenneth Evans (Monoposto Tipo B Alfa Romeo) interrupted the stream of ERAs by beating Ian Connell (R5B) and Brian Shawe-Taylor (R9B). John Bolster rounded off a good season by persuading the fierce old 'Mary' to the top in 41.82s for fastest unsupercharged time and an unofficial class record, although even this was but 0.32s faster than the incredible Lightweight of Dowson.

The year's most sensational Best Time of Day came right at the end of the season when the Jersey club attracted a number of mainland drivers, including George Bainbridge, Bear, Allard, Dowson and Monkhouse, over for the first Bouley Bay climb. Inexperience showed in the rather odd practice of giving everyone a flying start and, more seriously, in positioning the finish just before a sharp bend. So, although Bainbridge blasted over the line in 55.90s in R9B, the ERA went out of control, rolled over and back onto its wheels, catching fire briefly as it did so. Thus the hapless Bainbridge netted BTD and four broken ribs! BOC Victor Ludorum Trophy winner Ken Bear was less dramatic but his T51 was only 0.3s slower and well clear of Jerseyman John Gordon Bennett whose 3.7 Bennett Special inflicted a defeat on the similarly-inspired sprint Allard of Sydney himself. The Channel Islanders had to be taken seriously for the amazing Jamieson-blown Wolseley-engined MG of St Helier resident Le Gallais managed to climb Bouley 0.1s faster than both Monkhouse and Dowson.

First Hill Climb Champion
Although by early 1947 plans were well advanced to hold another race meeting on the airfield at Gransden Lodge, near Royston, regular circuit racing on the British mainland remained a distant prospect. So, the focus of attention remained firmly on the hill climb and sprint events with spice added to the existing mixture when the RAC confirmed in December that there would indeed be a National Hill Climb Championship in 1947.

The Championship was to be decided at five geographically diverse events: Bo'ness on 17 May; Shelsley on 24 May (later sensibly put back to 21 June); Bouley Bay on 24 July; Craigantlet on 30 August; and Prescott on 14 September. Competitors would be able to score marks in any four events but would have to register for the Championship at least 30 days before the first event which would count towards the total. Without a convenient precedent on which to draw, the marking system was rather curious. Based on performances on the faster of the normal two timed runs, no marks would be gained by the BTD winner, assuming he was a registered Championship contender, and the ten fastest registered drivers would be debited marks at the rate of one for every 0.2s they were slower than BTD. Thus the Champion would be the driver with the *least* marks at the end of the season!

Preparations for what promised to be an exciting season were rapidly advanced. The Scottish SCC was lengthening the timed distance at Bo'ness, widening the track by 4 feet at 'The Snake', and moving the Paddock to the bottom of the hill. With £245 in prize money on offer, including £100 for BTD, a fine entry was anticipated for May.

Several new car/driver combinations were expected. Former Allard Special trials expert Ken Hutchison had enjoyed his recent forays into hill climbing with the original Allard Special CLK 5 and was now eager to learn the sport's disciplines more seriously with the ex-Scuderia Ferrari / A. F. Ashby Alfa Romeo Monoposto Tipo B, which now featured independent front suspension, a cast-iron block

FINISH

BO'NESS
880 yards

START

permitting higher supercharger boost pressure (12 psi), and hydraulic brakes. Any lack of experience on Hutchison's part would be offset by the mechanical expertise of Robin Jackson, to whom preparation was entrusted. He was also looking after the slightly newer Alfa of Dennis Poore. Sydney Allard too was turning his attention more to pure speed events and far from allowing his growing stature as a motor manufacturer to deflect him from his competition activity, insisted that a major aim of his business was to help him and his friends (and customers) with their competition plans. Nevertheless, his latest sprint car for 1947, his first single-seater, was very much an 'after hours' project and in character a pure special. Basis of the car was a narrowed version of the production Allard chassis, but the engine was an unusual one for hill climbing. Sydney had been able to obtain an ex-military vehicle power unit with apparent potential. This was an Austrian Steyr, a 3,600cc ohv V8 which was very light as it was air-cooled (the cooling fan was dispensed with for this sprint application), could operate with a high compression ratio and was fitted with an imposing battery of eight motorcycle carburettors. Mounted well back in the chassis for optimum weight distribution and good traction, this unconventional unit drove through the familiar and far from ideal 3-speed Ford transmission and with the effective if ungainly looking 'clap hands' split-axle independent front suspension. Stark single-seater bodywork rounded off an inexpensive, even homely, one-off which looked ideal for the twistier hills, such as Prescott, where a lack of top end power could be offset. John Bolster was also known to be experimenting with larger engines and was working on a rear-engined chassis with Mercury power, although he sold off the bits before the project came to fruition.

Clive Lones' Austin Seven-based, JAP-engined, 'Tiger Kitten' was archaic in concept, but remained Colin Strang's toughest 500cc opponent, until the Coopers began to dominate.
RIVERS FLETCHER

At a more humble level, the 500 movement was growing fast and by the Spring the 500 Club had been formed and a National 500cc Formula agreed with the minimum of restrictions: no superchargers, no more than one gallon fuel capacity, 500 lbs minimum unladen net weight, 3 ft minimum wheel track, minimum outside tyre diameter of 21 inches, and efficient four wheel braking. Another Cooper Special was now nearing completion so that John Cooper and London electrical business director Eric Brandon would no longer have to share a car; the moustachioed Wing-Commander Frank Aikens was preparing another Fiat based machine, this time with Triumph Vertical Twin power; Frank Bacon was inserting a Rudge Ulster unit in an Austin Seven chassis; Jim Bosisto was following the Iota formula but with a variety of BSA (car) and Morgan parts and with a Douglas (later JAP) engine; and 500 pioneer Kenneth Neve was managing to employ the hitherto ubiquitous GN parts in a simple Douglas Flat Twin-engined device which was said to have cost not much over £100. Even that was thought to be about three times the outlay of Bosisto!

After preliminary skirmishes at Trengwainton and Naish, the 'dress rehearsal' for the new Championship season took place at Prescott on 11 May, although Mays and Gerard were missing from the line-up. The weather was good, class records fell and the establishment was well shaken up by the remarkable performance from Sydney Allard in his brand-new special. Despite obvious 'new car' problems the absolutely fearless Sydney flung his torquey Steyr-Allard at the hill and recorded an astonishing 47.25s (only 1.09s outside Mays' record) on his first run. Next time up he shot off the road at Pardon and damaged the car against a parked Riley! His first run was still enough to give him BTD from George Abecassis (47.72s) who was embarking on a full hill climb season with the '3.3' Bugatti and Peter Monkhouse (47.78s). The Monaco Director, with mechanic Jack Jaguard, had geared up the blower on the T51 for extra boost and had fitted a Wilson pre-selector gearbox. Ken Hutchison, treading carefully with the lofty Alfa, also showed well and beat John Bolster and Ken Bear (in his T51) for fourth overall. The new records were mainly in the sports classes but Colin Strang further reduced the 500cc figures to 52.49s. Anthony Heal's old Edwardian record went when Peter Clark's superb 1914 Grand Prix Mercedes clocked 54.71s, while the fiery John Heath, notwithstanding a 'spare' engine in his Alta, was fastest sports car driver with a class record-breaking 50.82s. More records fell to Jack Newton's stark red HRG-Meadows, fitted with the skimpiest of road equipment (51.29s), and Continental Cars Director Rodney Clarke who was only 0.06s faster than Newton with no less than the ex-Ian Craig Grand Prix Bugatti T59, fitted with (just) two seats and road equipment to make it into a truly fantastic sports car.

One week later Scottish enthusiasts gathered along the Hamilton Drive for the first of the Championship events. The one disappointment was the absence of Mays, for R4D's sorely tried frame had picked up serious cracks during the recent Jersey International Road Race and could not be repaired in time. This left an open event with an added ingredient provided by Bob Gerard. Conscious of the extra power of the seemingly unobtainable 2-litre ERA engine, the Leicester driver who had by now bought two other ERAs – R14B for circuit racing and R6B mainly for spares – used his growing expertise in matters ERA to incorporate a special Riley crankshaft to achieve a 1,943cc engine capacity. But 'Mr Bob's' 39.9s best time was good enough only for fourth place. George Abecassis's long-legged Bugatti was well-suited to the fairly fast course and his 38.2s climb stood as the new record, 0.7s clear of an impressive 'Hutch' with the big Alfa. It was a good day for the thoroughbreds for Ken Bear's Bugatti T51 was third on 39.0s. With his Alta running as a racing car, John Heath blasted up in 40.7s, faster than the ex-Maclure Riley which Sheila Darbishire was driving impressively rapidly and Sydney Allard (hampered by unsuitable gearing) who tied on 40.8s. The astounding Newton/HRG combination soundly defeated Liverpudlian Gillie Tyrer's fast BMW 328 and Bean's SS100 for sports car honours.

Before battle was rejoined at Shelsley, Lionel Leonard's seemingly innocuous but beautifully prepared 1,408cc MG N-type Magnette showed that the Allards could be beaten at Horndean, and the BOC ran their Closed Prescott meeting. It was one of those days when a certain giddiness seemed to prevail. Two competitors were excluded after rushing about on the public road in a rather irresponsible manner with unlicensed racing cars, and there were spins galore on a dry but slippery surface. Allard departed through the Semicircle hedge in practice at the point which was earning the name Allard's Gap. Gerard, Strang, Aikens, and Edward Pool (2.0 GP Bugatti) all left the road in varying degrees and Ken Bear, not noted for wild driving, did it twice. The final order read Gerard (48.03s), Ansell,

Allard – and Eric Brandon's little Cooper broke the Strang domination by managing 52.09s. Unfortunately, there was no 500cc class as such at this meeting and Colin's record remained officially intact.

The one venue which did not need Championship status to give it stature was Shelsley. This meeting's importance on the calendar at this time can be gauged from the remarkable coincidence of Shelsley's largest crowd to date and yet another wet day. This time Mays was back in his accustomed position and the black ERA bucked and twisted its way to yet another BTD in 41.50s. Despite being 1.71s slower than the incomparable Mays, Ken Hutchison did really well to beat 'Bira' in the Maserati 8CM, Gerard, and John Bolster who recorded 43.80s in 'Mary' and also 44.78s in ERA R5B 'Remus' which he was driving for Peter Bell, a construction company director from Ellesmere Port. Allard's car was not very well suited to this 'power' hill and was even less suited when the valves bent. Abecassis too was unusually low down after a half spin, skilfully corrected, on one run. Mrs Darbishire took the not-very-hotly-contested Ladies' Award, while many memories were evoked by the appearance in the Paddock of the old Vauxhall Villiers, now owned by Harrogate driver Anthony Brooke who was starting a long struggle to make the temperamental old car run well. This time it was bodyless and expired with water in the cylinders. Rather more effective was a 'new' Spyder from Basil Davenport. Although it looked very little different from the old car at a glance the latest version on the old theme employed a narrowed-down HRG chassis fitted with a remarkable 2-litre V-twin GN-based engine which Davenport had built up himself.

Sydney Allard's rather erratic progress continued at the BOC Summer Open Prescott when he crashed near the Bridge, damaging the rear axle. Meanwhile, in practice, John Rowley's 2-litre GP Bugatti, a class winner at Shelsley, went end over end. Bob Gerard snatched another fastest time in 47.35s from another driver with building industry connections, Ken McAlpine, who was really getting the hang of his wide chassis Maserati 8C, once the property of Earl Howe. Colin Strang put the 500cc record out of reach of his challengers again (51.78s) and another clutch of sports car records by Frank Kennington (supercharged MG K3), Tyrer, Heath and Johnson were rather eclipsed when Rodney Clarke broke 50s in a sports car for the first time (49.86s) with the Bugatti.

By this time, sadly, one of the leading hill climb cars was no more. Peter Monkhouse wrote off his well-developed Bugatti T51 in a road accident (Rodney Clarke was by no means the only person to use a GP Bugatti on the road) when the car lost a head-on argument with a lorry. Fortunately, Monkhouse was unhurt.

The big-engined hybrids were still doing well in the lesser (and rougher) events with wins going to Dr Mirrlees Chassels at Bo'ness in his Riley-engined Frazer Nash, Leslie Onslow-Bartlett's Mercury Special at Great Auclum, Trengwainton, and again (on aggregate) at Fordingbridge where Sydney Allard's brother Leslie actually set fastest time in HLF 601, the 1946 sprint car. Competitors could have been forgiven for a feeling of insecurity at the latter event, which was likely to be the last at this venue as the track was to revert to public use when the RAF cleared unexploded bombs from adjoining land!

There was clear evidence that the Jersey MC & LCC had learnt from the 1946 experience at Bouley Bay when a select field of top drivers found that the finish line had been repositioned and standing starts had been instituted. A very contemporary touch was lent to the meeting when Ken Hutchison

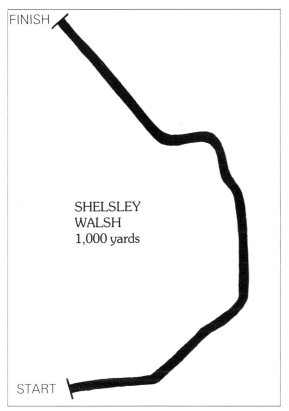

FINISH

SHELSLEY
WALSH
1,000 yards

START

BOULEY BAY
1,011 yards

FINISH

START

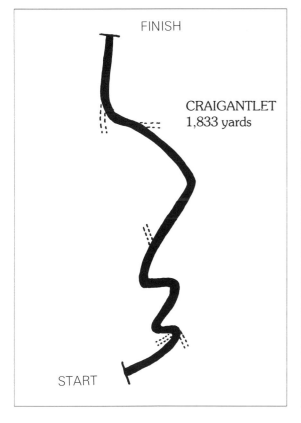

FINISH

CRAIGANTLET
1,833 yards

START

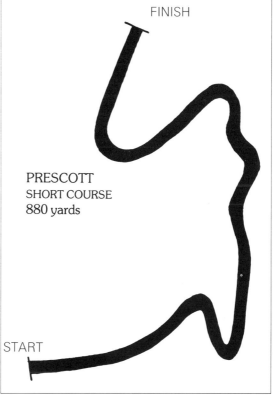

FINISH

PRESCOTT
SHORT COURSE
880 yards

START

and Ladies winner 'Bill' Wisdom (SS100) arrived in Jersey by air, taking their cars in a Miles Aerovan. This time Hutchison had to be content with tying for fourth place with Sydney Allard (62.5s), for Ray Mays was on top again with 60.80s to the 61.30s of Abecassis and a highly encouraging 61.5s from the improving Dennis Poore.

English hill climbers rarely worry about catching sunstroke but there really was a risk at Craigantlet where the UAC were subjected to intense heat. The tar on the hill melted and it was exceptionally slippery, so Bert Hadley's old 81.4s record remained intact. One of the most exciting duels of the year was settled, rather surprisingly, in Sydney Allard's favour, by just 0.2s from the usually unbeatable Mays. The latter was ahead on the first runs, but a superb second climb from the South Londoner spurred on Ray to overdo it on his second climb, spinning off in an almost unheard of manoeuvre for him. Abecassis was over 2 seconds slower but well clear of Peter Monkhouse (now driving an MG K3) and a cautious 'Hutch' in the Alfa Romeo. Poor Ken Bear spun at the start on his first run and then crashed badly near the finish on what would otherwise have been a fast climb. He was thrown out and the car then proceeded to run over him, doing little to mitigate painful facial injuries and concussion.

On the same day the VSCC held their traditional Prescott meeting, and with the big names over in Ireland, the way was left open for a success by Richard Habershon's 'spare parts' Grand Prix Delage from Peter Stubberfield's Bugatti T35B, once the car of George Eyston and also raced by George Duller. Significantly, and showing conclusively that the Cooper-JAP was now a match for the Strang, Eric Brandon further reduced the 500cc record to 51.43s.

Once back from Ireland, and with a higher final drive ratio in R4D, Raymond Mays set another majestic BTD at Brighton, his 92.17 mph speed for the curving kilometre comparing favourably with his two-way International Kilometre record at 89.70 mph.

There was really no doubt that Mays would be the first RAC National Hill Climb Champion for after missing Bo'ness he could count Prescott in September to add to his virtually unassailable advantage. Large crowds again braved another damp day and this time Mays had over a second's advantage over his strongest opponent, Gerard. Using twin rear wheels on a course which seemed singularly unsuited to the very large Alfa Romeo, Poore impressed again with third BTD while Rodney Clarke, in setting the 51.49s sports car best, was actually faster than Abecassis's T59 in full Grand Prix trim, and both of them had the edge over Allard who was best of the unblown runners. So, most fittingly, a delighted Raymond Mays became the RAC Champion with a debit of just one mark. Abecassis was the runner up (28 marks lost) with the irrepressible Allard third with 34.5 marks.

There were some very *wet meetings at Shelsley just after the war. This is Rivers Fletcher – kitted out in stylish 'ace' Continental racing drivers gear – in his ex-John Dugdale MG N-type Magnette.*
via RIVERS FLETCHER

A week later the South Londoner was off to Scotland with the Steyr-Allard, and a pleasing minor BTD ensued, with 41.7s as against the 42.0s from Mirrlees Chassels in the fastest of the Scottish specials, the Riley-engined Frazer Nash.

Astonishingly, it was dry for the September Shelsley meeting and despite the late time of the year there were new things to see. London car dealer Roy Salvadori arrived with the ex-Kenneth Evans Monoposto Alfa, Rupert Instone had fitted a new body, independent front suspension and disc wheels to the ear-splitting 'Martyr'; Basil Davenport had altered the camshaft drive arrangements on the new 'Spyder', and Joe Fry re-entered the fray with a completely rebuilt 'Freikaiserwagen'. After Walter Watkins had died in a motorcycling accident his successful Watkins-JAP was bought to use in the re-build of the 'Freik' which had been crashed badly at Prescott in 1939. The chassis frame and the front end of the Watkins-JAP were employed while the old Robin Jackson-tuned Blackburne engine was more powerful than ever. Wrestling with the enormous steering wheel, Joe Fry shot up in 40.61s and took the 'Shelsley Special' Award despite marginal transmission and distinctly dicey directional (in)stability. There was more excitement when Eric Brandon (44.11s) and John Cooper inflicted a re-sounding defeat on Colin Strang. The new sponsor of the post-war ERA project, Leslie Johnson, was warmly applauded when he forced the Darracq up Shelsley in 42.21s, faster than Ian Connell's pre-war sports car best. But above all it was Mays's *tour d'honneur*, and his 37.69s at last got within strik-ing distance of his own 1939 record of 37.37s. This time Bob Gerard was on top form and his 38.55s was enough to beat Dennis Poore, Hutchison, 'Bira', and the smaller-engined ERA of Bob Ansell. Sydney Allard went the wrong way on gear ratios and was right out of the picture.

The news that the Government were withdrawing even the meagre basic pleasure petrol ration, thereby threatening to halt motor sport once again, did little to improve the end-of-season mood. When Rivers Fletcher – by now a regular competitor in the Monaco-prepared N-type MG Magnette with K3 engine originally built by Wilkie Wilkinson/Bellevue Garage for John Dugdale – set about or-ganising another 'Rembrandt' meeting for February 1948, it really did seem as if the wartime spirit would need to return.

The methyl-alcohol-based fuels which were then almost universal for the pure racing machinery were not affected by the measure, which owed more to political expediency than to a genuine shortage of petroleum, but conveying the cars to events, and getting officials and spectators there was another matter. Nevertheless, everyone pressed on with preparations for 1948 on the assumption that the re-striction would be short-lived. Fortunately it was, and before the new season was many months old a limited ration of petrol for restricted use was made available again.

Despite the gloom there was no shortage of activity. Ken Bear had bought the Bugatti T59 from George Abecassis who was expecting to be circuit racing his new Grand Prix Alta in major events. Bear, in turn, sold his 3.3-litre hybrid (shortened T44 chassis with T49 engine and T35-ish bodywork) to Peter Clark. Bob Cowell sold his 1939 Alta to Gordon Watson, while a 'Winged Horse' symbol was to unite the Robin Jackson-tended efforts of Ken Hutchison and Dennis Poore. A development programme was under way with both Alfas, with radical changes to 'Hutch's' old Tipo B including the fitting of Lockheed 2LS brakes, new alloy cylinder blocks, and a Wilson pre-selector gearbox. Peter Vaughan was shortening the wheelbase of the ex-Fane Frazer Nash single-seater with which he had appeared the previous year; Ken McAlpine replaced his existing Maserati with the slightly newer 8CM which had had such a distinguished career in the hands of Straight and Prince 'Bira'; enthusiast engineer Geoff Richardson now had the ERA-engined Riley which Sheila Darbishire had run in 1947; Geoffrey Ansell purchased the ERA R9B from his cousin Bob; Mays's R4D was rebuilt around a much-needed new chassis frame, and another ERA rebuild was under way in Cheshire where George Boyle was overhauling R5B for John Bolster to drive on behalf of Sir Alfred McAlpine Director, Peter Bell.

Most of the wheeler-dealing still involved shuffling around with ageing cars and there were few new racing machines outside the growing ranks of the 500 movement, although there were a few raised eyebrows when it was learnt that Archie Butterworth was intending to wheel out a four-wheel-drive car owing much to the familiar military Jeep, and powered by a Steyr engine of the same type as that employed by Sydney Allard.

As for the 500s, the National Formula was amended to insist on cars having some kind of bodywork "even if only of canvas", unlimited fuel capacity (a function of the organisation of the first circuit

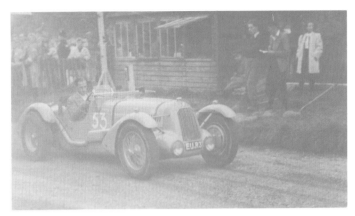

Leslie Johnson's ex-Connell/Lace Darracq was about the most formidable sports car in 1946-47 events.
C. D. PEARCE

Although he preferred long distance racing, the perennially underestimated Bob Gerard was a formidable hill climber. He leaves a muddy startline here at Prescott. Normally, Gerard kept his ERA R4A for hill climbs, whereas he used R14B for circuit racing and kept R6B as reserve.
C. D. PEARCE

races for these cars), and the independent operation of front and rear brakes. Most significantly, the success of the two Cooper Specials had led to a number of people asking about replicas, and the Coopers decided to go into limited production with a slightly modified car with a longer wheelbase, larger diameter brake drums integral with new alloy wheels, and a number of minor changes to suspension and bodywork in the light of the experience with the prototypes.

During February 1948 the RAC confirmed that the National Hill Climb Championship would be promoted again, with the same five meetings to count although Bo'ness would now take place on 26 June, after Shelsley Walsh. The big change was in the marking system which abandoned the rather eccentric method employed in 1947. Now, competitors would have to nominate in advance which four events they wished to count for scoring purposes while the fastest ten registered contenders would be marked at the rate of 10 points for BTD, 9 for second BTD and so on down to 1 point for tenth BTD. The whole thing was made "subject to petrol rationing".

Raymond Mays dominated hill climbing after the Second World War, until the BRM project demanded his exclusive attention. ERA R4D was the most highly developed of all 'old style' ERAs and was a major factor in Mays' winning two RAC titles.
C. D. PEARCE

John Bolster resurrected 'Bloody Mary' after the war and with the car in two, JAP-engined form, was highly successful. Note JVB's right arm cocked in characteristic manner in order to clear the rear mudguard.
C. D. PEARCE

As the ban on the use of petrol for pleasure remained in force thoughout April and May, the season got off to a slow and rather bizarre start. The Vintage Sports Car Club chanced their arm by organising a speed trial in Luton Hoo Park, Bedfordshire, where a remarkably large assembly of vehicles gathered bearing probably the largest display of trade registration plates in living memory. Unfortunately, there were also many policemen in evidence too, checking up on the legitimate or otherwise use of these coveted plates. A number of prosecutions followed but once again the motor sporting world contrived to overcome yet one more obstacle in those difficult years. Bob Gerard scored first blood for ERA at Luton Hoo, and then went on to the traditional Spring Open Prescott on 9 May where he sprang two surprises. Firstly, he appeared with ERA R6B rebuilt and fitted with his special 1943cc engine, and then he rocketed up Prescott's twists and turns in the Team Event at the end of the day to stop the clocks at 45.67s. At last Mays's 1939 record had fallen. Ironically, Gerard was not expecting to do many hill climbs during the year as he preferred long distance circuit racing and in this, the year of the first Silverstone and Goodwood meetings, he was anticipating more opportunities for serious racing. Because of this he did not even enter the RAC Championship. Some indication of form to come was demonstrated by the finishing order behind him: Poore (46.41s) – Carr (in the 2-litre Alta which he was now sharing with Ray Merrick) – McAlpine – Allard (fastest unsupercharged although the Steyr-Allard was not on its best form despite a winter rebuild) – Hutchison-Gillie Tyrer (the Bugatti T51 which had been Ken Bear's car). Despite a shortage of competing sports cars because of the lack of petrol there was much interest in the classes. The 500cc record fell yet again, but not to Strang or a Cooper. It was Clive Lones in 'Tiger Kitten' who chipped the time down to 49.98s against the 50.04s of Strang, for a popular success.

The smartest turnout among the 500s was to be seen in the equipage of the Moss family from Tring, in Hertfordshire. Parked next to Allard in the Paddock was a cream Rolls-Royce towing a matching horse-box which disgorged one of the new 3-inches-longer wheelbase production Cooper-JAPs, also finished in cream. Alfred and Aileen Moss had been well-known competition drivers before the war and now they were introducing their 18-year old son Stirling to the sport. Fourth in class (from nine), 0.38s slower than Eric Brandon in the original Cooper was a good start. A rare failure by the Lightweight Special brought Ken Wharton's Wharton Special into the limelight. This talented and versatile driver from Smethwick had been consistently fast for the last couple of seasons with an Austin Seven-based car fitted with a supercharged MG J4 engine, but all too often he had to run against either the Lightweight or the Appleton Special. Some of the more exotic sports cars ran on methyl-alcohol fuels, while a few had somehow managed to save or 'obtain' petrol. Fastest in 50.55s was another of the 'converted' Bugatti Grand Prix cars, 'Twink' Whincop's T51, although he was only 0.07s faster than the class record-breaking MG of Lionel Leonard.

Before the RAC Championship got underway at Shelsley there was a new event on the calendar, although it was really more sprint than hill climb. The Brighton & Hove MC had laid out a 0.8 mile course in Stanmer Park, Falmer, between Brighton and Lewes. The course wound its way across the attractive parkland, close to the elegant Stanmer House and turning sharp left in front of the Stanmer church before curving right between farm buildings. Despite the Club's long experience with the Brighton Speed Trials the organisation was a mite chaotic and there were many delays. Far worse, the top Paddock was much too close to the finishing line with minimal braking area for the faster cars.

It was Bob Gerard, the safest of racing drivers, who suffered most. His 50.87s climb was the fastest of all but he lost the lot after the finish and wrecked his recently rebuilt R6B, ricocheting from car to car in the Paddock. Fortunately, no injuries were suffered but apart from the badly damaged ERA, Crampton's ex-Birkin Maserati and Bathgate's AC-Nash were also bent, and amid apologies from an embarrassed Gerard and recriminations against the organisers the balance of the meeting was called off. Before all the drama Dennis Poore and Ken McAlpine had run Gerard the closest but an outstanding fourth overall was John Cooper with a further 'stretched' Cooper chassis powered by a 996cc V-twin JAP engine. The idea for a bigger-engined Cooper had come from customer Alvin 'Spike' Rhiando, for the new Formula B circuit racing category, but the Cooper's agility and light weight, to-

Brighton & Hove Motor Club held just one hill climb in Stanmer Park, near Brighton, and it was nothing if not dramatic. Here, Peter Stubberfield's ex-Eyston/ Duller Bugatti T35B – already using twin rear wheels, but not yet in more familiar single-seater form – is eased out of the straw bales whence it had strayed. The owner, crouching in front of the car, checks to see if all is well, while Lord Howe is nearest to the fence. Record breaker Goldie Gardner stands on the inside of the bend.
W. E. AVORY

gether with a rear-mounted big twin engine, immediately looked most promising for sprint events. Young Stirling Moss was most impressive too – smooth and very fast – and his first class win resulted.

The Brighton club and the local council, who owned Stanmer Park, had been mulling over the possibilities of creating a permanent motor racing circuit in this large park, but the idea was soon abandoned. By the early 1960s the new University of Sussex was taking shape on the East side of Stanmer Park although the area near Stanmer House remains virtually unchanged.

Notwithstanding his accident, Bob Gerard presented himself in the Paddock at Shelsley just one week later with his 1943cc engine back in R4A. Raymond Mays reappeared with the re-chassised R4D, determined to defend his Championship even though he was finding it more and more difficult to spare the time away from the burdens of the BRM project. As a 'spare time' project, Mays had a brand-new tubular chassis ERA-powered sprint car on the stocks, but as this could not be allowed to interfere with BRM matters it kept being put back. The car was never completed but it says much for Mays's unquenchable optimism and ambition that he even tried to develop such a car at the same time as he was leading the BRM team. The Frys, Dick Caesar and Robin Jackson had not been idle either for the 'Freikasiserwagen', already the car with the highest power-to-weight ratio in hill climbing, had been rebuilt yet again. A lightened version of the Iota chassis design was now employed with an ingenious swing-axle rear suspension fitted. The Marshall-blown Blackburne engine had been turned round to have its crankshaft axis across the frame with the exhaust from the rear cylinder curving up in a manner which would have done credit to a snake charmer. On this occasion a clutch pin sheared in practice but much could be expected from this, the most powerful twin-cylinder car on the hills.

There was wet tar at the start to slow getaways fractionally and even Mays was not as inch perfect as was his norm, hitting the infamous drain on the second corner of the 'S' on his first run and running wide at Kennel on his second climb. He was still on top, though, even if his 37.89s best was still outside that elusive 37.37s record. On a course which was fairly well-suited to the big Alfa Romeo, Dennis Poore roared up in 39.16s, fast enough to beat Gerard (39.41s) and Hutchison (39.82s). Sydney Allard, always the practical man and the bane of the purists, had fitted the Steyr-Allard with a de Dion rear axle – designed by Tom Lush from what happened to be around in the Allard workshops – and this was a big improvement over the Ford axle used previously. On this occasion, on a course which never suited the car, Sydney selected reverse gear at the wrong moment and he was right out of the picture. Very much in the picture, however, was John Cooper in the intriguing Cooper 1000. John had agreed to build such a car for the Canadian Speedway exponent 'Spike' Rhiando on condition that he sold him one of the two pre-war JAP engines which he had tucked away. This unit was now in the 'works' car and with a power-to-weight-ratio of 5 lbs per bhp John had a car which was in the same league as the 'Freik'. At Shelsley, Cooper had his first run disallowed because a mechanic had inadvertently laid a hand on the car after it had left the line, but on the second ascent there was no mistake and with excellent acceleration John was over the finish line in 40.77s which broke the 1,100cc and unsupercharged class records and was good enough for fifth overall ahead of John Bolster's on-form 'Mary'.

Leslie Allard at Bo'ness in 1948, driving the lightweight J1-based sprint sports Allard which his brother Sydney had run in 1947.
BILL HENDERSON

Most of the field then departed *en masse* for the Closed Prescott meeting the next day, although there were rather a lot of non-starters, 21 in all. With no Mays to steal his thunder, Gerard set another Prescott BTD in 46.24s but John Cooper was finding that the Cooper 1000 handled as well as it accelerated and he now set second BTD in another class record-breaking climb (47.06s). This was faster even than Allard, Carr, Hutchison, Fry, and Peter Monkhouse (who was making a return to Bugatti motoring in Mancunian coachbuilder Allan Arnold's modified T51). Whincop was another record breaker (50.15s) in his sports T51 and Eric Brandon did it again with the original Cooper 500. He went faster than ever (49.22s) but once more he was in the 750cc class so the record was unofficial.

With a modicum of petrol around, the season was now well under way although there were few of the sports cars-only-type minor events being run. Mays again missed Bo'ness where the prize for winning had now been doubled to £200. Rain rather spoiled the second runs but Gerard was not deterred. His 36.3s first climb was a new hill record and he must have been regretting not entering the RAC series. His winning margin over Dennis Poore – rapidly becoming something of an 'eternal bridesmaid' – was only 0.4s while Ken Bear, now acclimatised to the Type 59 Bugatti, clocked an even 37s. Although rarely competing in hill climbs now, Reg Parnell and his team-mate David Hampshire brought a couple of ERAs to the meeting.

Reg had built up another Riley-derived 2-litre engine for R11B which he shared with Sheila Darbishire, while Hampshire had the original R1A. All three drove well with times of 37.3s, 38.9s, and 37.6s respectively, Hampshire for fifth place with Hutchison and the flambuoyant 'Spike' Rhiando having a run in his gold-painted Cooper 1000. The sports car category was another Allard success, this time with Leslie at the wheel of JGP 473, the lightweight J1-based sprint sports car which Sydney had run in 1947 and which now boasted a Marshall-blown Mercury engine.

Raymond Mays was beaten down into third place at Bouley Bay, but with good reason for he lost the use of bottom gear. He was still only 0.2s off the new record! Unusually, the new figure was set by two competitors, Dennis Poore and Joe Fry whose awesome machine fairly rocketed away from Bouley's hairpins. Allard was a second slower for fourth but ahead of Parnell and the fastest of the Channel Islanders, Frank le Gallais. Dennis Poore's consistency in the green Alfa Romeo now put him at the top of the Championship table, five points ahead of his team-mate Ken Hutchison.

Poore was now really on form and although the Alfa seemed positively huge on Prescott's twists, he put one over Bob Gerard to set BTD at the Summer Open meeting with 46.14s to 'Mr Bob's' 46.18s. It was all very close, for Joe Fry was third on 46.21s and Allard fourth with 46.44s (fastest unsupercharged). Raymond Mays took in this meeting but he was in trouble again with more gearbox problems and spark plug electrodes falling into the cylinders, which caused his withdrawal. Stirling Moss was by now winning almost every time out and his cream Cooper brought the 500cc record down to 49.51s (still slower than Brandon's most recent unofficial figure). Despite enormous wheelspin from the Bugatti, 'Twink' Whincop achieved a stunning 49.56s to break the outright sports car record, confirming that this 'Blue Riband' of sports car hill climbing was now firmly the province of converted racing machinery.

Great Auclum, now lengthened very slightly to give a full 440 yards, and the VSCC Prescott gave rare opportunities (in 1948) for the lesser lights to shine before the serious business recommenced at Craigantlet. Ken Wharton's agile little MG-engined Austin Seven Special just managed to beat Stirling Moss overall at Great Auclum with 23.34s to 23.46s and with Frank Norris's old-style Frazer Nash/Alvis hybrid a good third on 23.86s. Norris repeated that position at the VSCC Prescott which was now restricted to pre-1931 machinery, although a fairly liberal line was taken on exactly how much of the car had to be Vintage. A splendid 46.87s climb in 'Bloody Mary' gave John Bolster the top award ahead of Bugatti driver Peter Stubberfield.

The Ulster AC had shortened Craigantlet by 50 yards so there was a new record guaranteed. With R4D back on form, Mays gained his revenge on Sydney Allard for his 1947 defeat with a 75.8s climb which was 2.6s faster than the unsupercharged Steyr-Allard recorded, with Ken Hutchison a further 0.4s down in third place. Mays was into a winning streak at the right time for the run up to the Championship decider at Prescott saw R4D further reduce the Brighton Speed Trials record to 23.86s.

Whereas the previous year Mays had sewn up the title even before the last round, this year the position was different. Mays had to beat Dennis Poore to secure a Championship double, and when a halfshaft key broke on R4D in practice things did not look too promising. Fortunately it was repaired

Eighteen-years-old Stirling Moss contests his first hill climb at Prescott in May 1948, driving his smart new Cooper-JAP. He finished a commendable fourth in class. Soon afterwards the winning started.
via MIKE KETTLEWELL

in time but as far as the Championship was concerned the meeting was an anti-climax. It rained hard, Mays could only manage seventh place (behind both John Cooper's Cooper 1000 and Brandon's class-winning 500cc version) but he was still the Champion as the unhappy Poore had a dreadful day, a chapter of mishaps culminating in an off-course excursion on one run and a gearbox problem on the other. In the streaming wet conditions the day belonged to an outsider. Ever since the mid-1930s the fast and tremendously spectacular Peter Walker had shared Peter Whitehead's cars and he was entered at Prescott in the ERA R10B. Dressed in sports jacket and totally unperturbed by the streaming wet course, Walker put in a devastating drive where sheer bravado resulted in a 49.46s time which was almost 2 seconds faster than his nearest challenger, Sydney Allard. Gerard was third from Joe Fry with the tricky little 'Freik'. Leslie Allard broke the Bugatti stranglehold on the sports car category, winning in the wet with JGP 473.

After this most unrepresentative event the final Championship positions were seen to be very close. Mays won by just one point, 38 to Poore's 37, and with Allard on 35 and Hutchison on 32. The latter had found that there was not a lot more to come from his old, if well-developed, Alfa Romeo, but after Prescott he took it up to Bo'ness for the SSCC's club meeting and set Best Time of Day in a creditable 37.4s, although his strongest challenger, Rhiando, put himself out of contention when he rolled at the Chicane.

It had been noticeable for some time that the crowds at the bigger hill climbs were not as large as they had been in 1946 and 1947 and this was particularly noticeable at Shelsley on 25 September. This was a great pity for the sun shone, records fell and it was a superb finale to the season's big hill climbs. An unwanted tail-slide probably cost Mays another Shelsley record, for his 37.52s climb was

Former trials driver Ken Hutchison was a serious contender by 1948 in his much-modified, Robin Jackson-prepared, Alfa Romeo Tipo B Monoposto.
MIDLAND AUTOMOBILE CLUB

Dennis Poore's 33.09s hill record at Bo'ness, 1949, in his splendid Alfa Romeo 8C-35 was one of that year's finest performances.
BILL HENDERSON

tantalisingly close to the all-time best, but even this fine climb was overshadowed by an absolutely ten-tenths effort from John Bolster. Peter Bell had now added R11B, complete with Parnell/Riley 2-litre engine to his stable, but a halfshaft sheared on the starting line on the first run. Then in a splendid example of good sportsmanship the whole of the Bell, Mays and Gerard teams pitched into stripping and repairing the rear axle of the stricken ERA. The work was completed in the nick of time for the second runs and Bolster, well wound up by this time, put in a superb 38.16s time which owed more to bravery than finesse. That was just 0.03s less than Dennis Poore, and in spite of having only the 1,500cc R10B, the impressive Peter Walker clocked a magnificent 38.30s for fourth overall, beating David Fry (having a run in the 'Freik' which the lighter Joe normally drove) and Bob Gerard, although both were under 39s. The records? David Fry's time was the best ever by a supercharged Shelsley Special; John Bolster also took time out to break the equivalent unsupercharged time with 'Bloody Mary' (40.37s); the outright unblown record was taken by Sydney Allard at 39.56s although the Steyr-Allard was still out of the overall honours on this course; Stirling Moss set a new 500cc time at 43.84s; and there was a new Ladies' record at long last. Driving the rebuilt R6B, Joan Gerard emphasised that she was a very fair driver in her own right by clocking 43.18s.

Apart from another Southsea MC climb at Horndean, won by Lionel Leonard's basically N-type MG Magnette, Shelsley virtually rounded off what had been a superb season for the racing classes, despite the worries and petrol shortages with which the year began. Nevertheless, there were signs that hill climbing might be losing its appeal to spectators in the face of more circuit racing, and drivers of the calibre of Gerard, Abecassis and Parnell never made any secret of their priorities away from the hills. There was unrest too among the sports car competitors for mildly tuned sports machines had little chance against methanol-burning converted Grand Prix cars or the stark and highly developed sports-racing devices such as the Allard JGP 473, Newton's phenomenal HRG-Meadows and Leonard's MG. The arguments over what constituted a sports car for competition purposes were to rumble for years yet, but at least nobody complained at the lack of spectacle when Messrs. Clarke, Whincop, Allard, Newton and Leonard were on the course.

Sydney Allard's Steyr V8-engined Allard single-seater was a potent if slightly erratic contender from its first appearance in 1947. Sydney's enormous enthusiasm was rewarded with the RAC Championship in 1949.
MIDLAND AUTOMOBILE CLUB

Changing Times

With the benefit of hindsight, the 1948 season represented something of a peak for hill climbing, although as plans were made and announced for 1949 there was little to suggest that a zenith had been passed. The RAC Championship was to continue without change to the regulations, new venues were due to be used at Lydstep, Blandford Camp and Rest-and-Be-Thankful and leading cars were being further developed, although there were still few wholly new machines on the horizon.

Of the established front runners, Sydney Allard was fitting larger cylinder barrels and borrowed JAP cylinder head technology in an effort to boost the power of the Steyr engine, and was experimenting with an electrically-operated gearbox designed by Surrey inventor, Robert Clerk. The latter was also commissioned by Allard to design a far more radical, four-wheel-drive, sprint car, employing a 4.5-litre V8 Steyr-based engine which would develop around 250 bhp as opposed to the 165 bhp which the existing Steyr provided by 1949. Unfortunately, this ambitious project never came to fruition. The Fry team were also seeking more power still for the 'Freik' and Robin Jackson was working on a two-stage Wade supercharger set up for the car. The Gatwick-based Wade concern was enjoying considerable success in the sale of their superchargers at this point as the 4-lobe rotors gave a smoother compressed charge than the long-established Roots-type installations while the Wade unit was noticeably light and reliable. Dennis Poore too was having his Alfa Romeo fitted with a two-stage Wade installation.

Naturally, the possibilities with the 996cc JAP-engined Cooper chassis were much discussed and one who took the plunge and opted for a Cooper 1000 was the Managing Director of the Alexander Engineering concern, Michael Christie, who had formerly run the AC-Nash. Expected to supply an even more serious challenge to the bigger cars was another Cooper-JAP 1000 which Stirling Moss, still a teenager but already a formidable contender, was to drive. Stirling's 1948 500 Cooper passed to another former trials exponent, Austen 'CAN' May. Although a few people were still building 'new' specials along more traditional lines, such as Richmond, Yorkshire, driver Fred Harrison's Marshall Nordec-supercharged Ford Ten-engined GN chassis and the 3.8-litre straight 8 Buick-powered Neale Special fitted with the supercharger from a Sherman tank, the Coopers were the only new cars which looked like upsetting the hill climb status quo.

Thanks to the continued availability of vital engine parts, to which Raymond Mays had made a major contribution by organising the production of some new cylinder blocks, the opposition from the ERA drivers looked to be stronger than ever, despite the age of the cars. Mays himself was determined to carry on with R4D; Bob Gerard was substituting proper ERA crankshaft and connecting rods to his 'bitza' engine, bringing the capacity up to 1,980cc and permitting the revs to rise from 5,500 to 6,500 with safety; George Boyle was doing the same with the engine of R11B for John Bolster; Peter Whitehead's mechanic Charles White was fitting yet another 2-litre unit, this time Wade supercharged to 24 psi, to R10B for the mercurial Peter Walker; Geoff Ansell was another to convert an ERA (R9B) to Wade supercharging and Ken Hutchison had bought R7B from Leslie Brooke to replace his Alfa Romeo. This too was to be fitted with a 2-litre engine. Unfortunately, 'Hutch' found that he did not like the ERA one little bit, finding it crudely engineered after the tool-room standards of the old Alfa. Losing his enthusiasm, he competed little in 1949.

Hutchison's defection was but one of a number of occurences which produced a significant debit side to the balance sheet for the season. Entry lists and spectator attendances tended to reduce slightly and the MAC received a blow when the BBC decided against broadcasting from the the June Shelsley meeting. There was sadness too when leading Bugatti driver Ken Bear, a former BOC Victor Ludorum holder, was killed practising for the Jersey International Road Race when his Bugatti T59, running unsupercharged, suffered brake failure. Although, happily without fatal results, John Bolster broke his neck racing Peter Bell's other ERA, R5B, in the British Grand Prix at Silverstone, which ended his competition career although his prominence as a broadcaster, commentator and motoring journalist lay ahead. Gerard competed less and less in sprint-type events and Mays was finding it very difficult to maintain either himself or R4D in the state of 'race readiness' which was needed.

It is worth noting that while entries were not large, hill climbs on specially closed public roads were becoming increasingly popular in Ireland. Although only Craigantlet attracted English support, climbs such as Enniskerry and Knockagh tended to be slightly longer than the average British hill. By 1949, the majority of the 30 or 40 competing cars still tended to be production models or production-based specials, with Chris Lindsay's remarkably fast, unsupercharged, Ford Ten Special usually turning out to be the fastest of a new breed of Irish Fords, although BTD was just as likely to go to Hector Graham's old supercharged MG K3.

As usual, the BOC's Spring Open meeting at Prescott was the first major get-together for the most serious British hill climbers and much interest surrounded the experimental Clerk gearbox on the Steyr-Allard, the new Wade blowers on Poore's Alfa, a neat Monoposto body fitted to Stubberfield's Bugatti T35B, and one of the new BMW 328-based Veritas sports cars from Ernst Loof's little German concern, in the hands of Ken Hutchison. The new Clerk 'box was not trouble-free but the now 3.7-litre Steyr-Allard gave Sydney a 46.12s BTD to kick off his season, with Poore only 0.28s slower and a very on-form Ray Merrick on 46.54s for third place in the 2-litre Alta, faster even than the experienced Carr. Apart from Allard's unsupercharged time, there was a new sports car record when the third of the racing Frys, Jeremy, howled round the Semicircle to stop the clocks at 49.14s: minimal road accoutrements also reduced his class time (50.96s) and Eric Brandon – definitely the man to beat in the 500cc class in 1949 – took his latest, long-chassis Cooper to a 48.80s record. Chromed suspension parts made this car a particularly smart addition to the ever-growing 500cc ranks.

Six days after Prescott there was something new when the West Hants & Dorset CC held their inaugral event at Blandford Camp in Dorset. The 1-kilometre course actually formed part of the yet-to-be-utilised Blandford racing circuit for which the Club had big plans. Set amid the landscape of an Army camp and featuring a downhill start, three fastish bends, a wide (21 feet) road and a maximum gradient of only 1 in 11, this was rather out of the mainstream of British hill climb courses, one where the distinctions between 'Sprint' and 'Hill climb' merge into a rather grey area. Nevertheless, the entry was good and the top bend, in particular, caught out a lot of people. The almost frighteningly powerful, two-stage Wade-blown 'Freikaiserwagen', now boasting a neat front cowl emblazoned with a stylish 'FRY' emblem, accelerated away to a 31.13s BTD with Poore, using only single rear wheels on this occasion, running Joe Fry very close with 31.27s. Ray Merrick was again third, 0.83s clear of Sydney Allard who was running his sprint sports car, JGP 473, in the place of the Steyr-Allard which was being converted back to conventional transmission format.

The exceedingly potent Freikaiserwagen gained some new modifications almost every time out. Its finest hour came in June 1949 when Joe Fry clipped 0.2s off Mays' long-standing Shelsley record, leaving it at 37.35s.
MIDLAND AUTOMOBILE CLUB

11 June 1949 was a momentous day at Shelsley, notwithstanding the smaller crowd, the absence of the BBC, and several notable non-starters including Hutchison, Peter Walker (dropped valve on the Friday) and St John Horsfall who was to have driven Peter Bell's ERA R11B. ERA supporters really hadn't too much to smile about for Mays had to sort out Zöller supercharger problems before he could run. But all this was forgotten when at long last the Shelsley record of 37.37s, figures virtually engraved on every hill climber's mind by now, was bettered. Joe Fry's day began inauspiciously when he clouted a bank on his first climb, but after shattering acceleration away from the line he wrestled with the 'Freik's' monstrous steering wheel to persuade this ultimate Shelsley Special across the finishing line in 37.35s. The record was his although a determined effort by Raymond Mays also succeeded in cracking his old time, by the smallest possible margin, in 37.36s. Dennis Poore was down to 38.02s for third place and at least had the satisfaction of beating Moss (unsupercharged record breaking 38.57s) in the fastest of the three Cooper 1000s to feature in the top eight, for both John Cooper and Michael Christie both broke the psychological barrier of 40s, although slower than Ken McAlpine's well-driven Maserati 8CM and Carr's Alta. Even Brandon's class winning 42.78s and a splendid 42.33s from Basil Davenport were rather overshadowed by Fry's achievement.

It was a momentous weekend, for the very next day the BOC ran their Closed Prescott meeting and another course record fell on a day which belonged to Sydney Allard. He arrived with both the Steyr-Allard, now refitted with 'crash' gearbox, and his stark J1-based sports car, JYK 498, with alloy wheels and Edelbrock cylinder heads. The Steyr-Allard was still not really suited to Shelsley but Prescott was another matter. Sydney brought the record down to 45.04s after achieving an unofficial 44.93s in practice despite (or because of?) brake failure. Not content with this he also smashed the sports car record with 48.92s, defeating no fewer than three Bugatti T51s – Fry's, Whincop's and Blackburn's ex-Staniland car – and Goff Imhof's experimental supercharged 4.4-litre Mercury-engined Allard, JUC 5. A successful London dealer in electrical goods with a rare talent for promotion and graphic design, Imhof was a close friend and unofficial 'consultant' to Allard, and JUC 5 was something of a mobile test bed for the forthcoming J2 competition model. Peter Walker picked up the crumbs from the Allard table with a fine second BTD (45.33s) in the repaired ERA, beating Joe Fry and John Cooper, while Raymond Mays, after hectic but unavailing efforts, could do not better than seventh.

Use of the testing former military road from Arrochar out of Glen Croe, universally known as Rest-and-be-Thankful, had long been promised and on 9 July the RSAC attracted an excellent entry from South of the Border to contest a climb which in its bleak grandeur and longer-than-average length – over a mile – bore a closer resemblance to some of the Continental climbs than the rather arcadian British archetype. Despite spending £2,000 on the course, the RSAC still received complaints about how bumpy it was, and Basil Davenport was an early casualty when he damaged 'Spyder' in practice. However, this was the sort of challenge which Raymond Mays relished and he forced the bucking R4D to the top in 68.0s to take the £100 first prize and defeat Dennis Poore (68.6s) and Peter Walker (69.4s). Sydney Allard, not a man to give up easily, contrived to run the Steyr-Allard with two cylinders blocked off after breaking a couple of connecting rods in practice. His 71.9s time was still good enough for fourth place. It was a significant month for new hills for on 23 July the Tenby MC brought hill climbing back to Wales when they organised the first event on the attractive ½-mile climb from Lydstep Haven, rising 120 feet through five fast bends. Ken Delingpole (HRG) had the honour of setting the first record at 38s although virtually everything else was lifted by the well-developed Ford Ten-engined Buckler of chassis designer Derek Buckler. The old custom of allowing drivers to contest numerous classes still prevailed in some of the small events and Buckler's 39.4s climb won him three classes.

The RSAC had benefitted from holding their climb at 'The Rest' just a week before the Championship Bo'ness climb, so some leading hill climbers took in both events. Sydney Allard broke the unsupercharged record at Bo'ness but even his efforts were eclipsed by a simply superb, even amazing, climb from Dennis Poore. It was one of those rare climbs when everything seemed to click into place as far as placing the car was concerned and judging the split second to brake or accelerate to perfection. His time of 33.9s lopped no less than 2.4 seconds from Gerard's record and remained one of the year's truly outstanding performances.

It rained for the BOC's Summer Open Prescott where Sydney Allard débuted his exciting new sports car, KCX 170. This was the prototype J2, destined to be a most successful competition sports car, with 90 sold and many exported to the United States for use with Chrysler and Cadillac engines which were virtually unobtainable in Britain. Although the car followed many of the now-established Allard principles, a de Dion back end, coil sprung front suspension and a bored out 4,375cc Mercury engine helped it to become the most potent sports car then available on the British market where the Jaguar XK120 remained unavailable. The tricky conditions at Prescott were tailor-made for the agility and moderate power of the Cooper 1000 and Michael Christie scored an impressive first BTD for the car in 46.76s with Dennis Poore a magnificent runner-up, beating even Allard, with the over-large and embarrassingly powerful (for the conditions) Alfa Romeo. Eric Brandon was actually sixth overall and set yet another 500cc record in 48.67s when conditions were probably at their best and a significant fourth overall was the home-brewed four-wheel-drive AJB of Archie Butterworth. This Jeep-derived car, fitted with a rather ungainly single-seater body which was offset to clear the Jeep-based transmission components, and a 4.5-litre Steyr V8 engine was now working well and suited to the wet conditions.

It went even better, rather more surprisingly, at Great Auclum where it was bettered only by two Cooper 1000s, with Eric Brandon now running a 996cc JAP unit setting a 22.20s course record to leave a 0.76s margin over Michael Christie.

As was becoming a tradition, the RAC Championship contenders now tackled the Bouley Bay climb in Jersey, where local garage owner and motorcycle racer Syd Logan looked like putting up a strong 'home' defence with a new Cooper 1000. It wasn't to be, though, and the meeting was another triumph for Sydney Allard who was clearly making a strong challenge for the Championship. Even Joe Fry was beaten by the Steyr-Allard, while Stirling Moss and Dennis Poore tied for third place, and Mays had to be content with fifth. There was less opposition for Allard at Craigantlet for the UAC were disappointed to find that only Allard and Peter Walker brought front line contenders from Britain. Sydney rose to the occasion, though, and his 73.4s BTD was a new course record and decisively defeated Walker who managed 77.4s

Bugatti BTDs at Prescott were few and far between nowadays so there was joy in BOC hearts when T35Bs in the hands of Peter Stubberfield and Peter Reece were fastest at the VSCC meeting, Stubberfield in a good 48.64s, beating C.W.A. Heyward who had bought the original 1,496cc Alvis-engined Norris Special.

Allard, Fry and Poore were all in with a chance of the RAC Championship and it all boiled up to a major confrontation at Prescott in September where Sydney Allard climaxed a fine season with what can only be described as total domination. Watched by the spectators, who included both Mays and Hutchison, he smashed the outright record once again in 44.42s, then broke the sports car record with a 47.96s climb in the prototype J2, KXC 170 and rounded off the day by teaming up with his wife Eleanor in the J2 and Guy Warburton in the old 1946 sprint car HLF 601, to win the Team Award as well while further reducing the outright record to 44.26s. He thus clinched a richly deserved RAC Hill Climb Championship by five points from Dennis Poore who recorded 45.54s. Poore was beaten to second place on the day by Stirling Moss who closely challenged Allard with 44.77s. Poore did keep ahead of Brandon's Cooper 1000, while the formidable AJB, winner of the recent Brighton Speed Trials, was fifth, ahead of Stubberfield who did extremely well to take a T35B, albeit well modified, up Prescott in 47.6s. And Joe Fry? With the Championship seemingly in his grasp, he had a day of disasters which matched that of Poore the year before. A sheared flywheel key, carburettor flooding and magneto failure successively hammered his chances. On a day of records there were more sports car targets set by Jack Newton's Frazer Nash Le Mans Replica (50.74s), and Jeremy Fry (48.72s). Newton had by now sold his famous HRG to John Martin-Lewis. The Liverpudlian Jackie Reece, cousin of Bugatti driver Peter, sprang a surprise by becoming the new 500cc record holder in 48.18s. So, the final positions in a hard-fought Championship gave victory to Allard on 39 points, from Poore on 34, with young Stirling Moss on 30 and the luckless Joe Fry demoted to fourth place with 28. Former Champion Mays was a lowly seventh, with seven fewer points than Peter Walker and the ingenious Archie Butterworth on 22.

Apart from major sprints at Weston-Super-Mare (won by Joe Fry), Luton Hoo (Peter Walker) and Gosport (Eric Brandon), the season was rounded off by a second event at Lydstep, to which 500cc racing cars were now permitted to enter, and the traditional Shelsley finale. One of hill climbing's real

Scotland's thriving scene threw up many successful Specials in the nineteen-forties. This is Alex Reid's BMW-based 'Omega'.
BILL HENDERSON

One of the most successful Scottish Specials was the Chassels Special of Dr Mirrlees Chassels, using a Mercury V8 engine in a Frazer Nash chassis.
BILL HENDERSON

veterans, Jack Moor, broke the Lydstep record with 34.17s in the latest car to bear the 'Wasp' name and stripey bodywork, an Iota-chassised 500 with a 'square head' Manx Norton engine.

The motorcyclists administered another jolt to the car drivers' pride at Shelsley with George Brown shattering the outright course record with a superb 37.13s climb on his 998cc Vincent 'Black Lightning'. Ironically, now that it didn't matter as far as the Championship was concerned, Joe Fry's fortunes improved and although he couldn't quite match his June time, 37.40s was good enough for the car BTD. Dennis Poore was faster than ever at 37.47s snatching second BTD from Raymond Mays on 37.56s while Peter Walker also broke into the 37 seconds bracket with 37.89s and Stirling Moss edged the new champion out of a new unsupercharged record by a mere 0.01s in 38.19s

Many of the trends which were becoming apparent during 1949 – the growing popularity of circuit racing in Britain, the smaller hill climb crowds, fewer thoroughbred road racing cars on the hills but slightly more events at an essentially club level – gathered momentum in 1950. Sydney Allard, the man who had once fitted a Bugatti tail to a Ford Special and who must have relished winning the BOC's coveted Victor Ludorum Trophy almost as much as the RAC Championship, was riding the crest of a wave. His Allard production cars were at the height of their popularity and he planned to concentrate on major sports car races in 1950, with the J2 model. Although the Clerk-designed lightweight sprint car with duralumin chassis frame was as far away as ever, he even went so far as to offer the Steyr-Allard for sale, inviting offers around £1,000. Happily, when it was clear that the Clerk car would never be completed, he changed his mind and entered the Steyr-Allard in the RAC Championship once again.

For 1950 the RAC added Rest-and-be-Thankful to the Championship schedule, one week after Bo'ness, although drivers could still nominate only four events to count for Championship points.

Over in Jersey, Frank le Gallais had contrived to obtain one of the new Jaguar XK120 engines and was fitting it to a radical new car which had first appeared the previous year employing a pushrod Jaguar Mk V engine as a stopgap. Like the pre-war Auto Union Grand Prix cars, the LGS-Jaguar employed its engine amidships, behind the forward placed driver. The strong twin tubular frame was suspended on Citroen components at the front and mainly Riley parts at the rear although a swing axle, derived from the Lightweight Special's design, was fitted. Neatly formed bodywork cowling ensured a professional appearance and made the car resemble a very large Cooper apart from the air intake for the front-mounted radiator. This was the most technically interesting of the newcomers while more Cooper 1000s were sold to former special-builder Ken Wharton, Walsall engineer Bertie Bradnack (definitely the largest man to take the Cooper route) and experienced sports car driver Betty Haig. With the tendency towards cars designed more for sprint events rather than adapted circuit racers, the BOC instituted a new award, the Staniland Trophy, which was to be contested over the season by Grand Prix-type cars with four or more cylinders, in order to encourage the drivers of the spectacular thoroughbreds. A further sign of the times was the admission of A-type ERAs into the VSCC's Historic Racing Car category since the four cars concerned were now fifteen years old.

Denied the Championship the previous year, the Fry stable had ideas of extracting yet more power from the 'Freik' by the drastic expedient of adding a third cylinder to the Blackburne engine, and giving the driver more time to concentrate on guiding the projectile in the right direction by fitting a self-change gearbox. Like the projected Mays Sprint Car and the Clerk-designed Allard, these intriguing possibilities remained unrealised. Returning to the realms of the feasible, the long-established firm of J. A. Prestwich were much impressed with what had been achieved in Cooper chassis with their old, pre-war design of 996cc vee-twin, and decided to make available to Cooper the much-refined 1098cc JAP engine. This was a current design developing 95 bhp and it was hoped that the latest Coopers would be suitable both for sprint events and for the new Formula B (or Formula 2 as it rapidly became known) racing.

Although it was not unusual for hill climbs to be held early in March, or even in February, and well into October during the pre-1925 era, the season was shorter by the later 1940s. The major meetings kicked off with Prescott in May and it was all over by the end of September. In 1950 the leading hill climb contenders had to wait until 20 May for the Spring Open at the BOC venue, but there was enjoyable sport in a lower key down in the West over Easter. Jack Moor repeated the previous Autumn's success at Lydstep where the much vaunted, JAP-powered, Arengo 500 was rather disappointing. Moor's 'Wasp' was slower this time but was possibly the first car to take a BTD after overturning on its first climb! In this, the first year when the new 500cc Formula 3 was recognised internationally, there was enormous interest in the fast developing little cars and Lydstep also witnessed the rather unremarkable début of the channel-framed, double-wishbone-suspended Kieft-JAP. Promoted as a future 'production' car, this new make was the brainchild of South Wales hardware manufacturers Cyril and Denzil Kieft who took over the assets of the defunct Marwyn concern, and later transferred manufacture to Wolverhampton. Two days after Lydstep, the now traditional Easter Monday climb at Trengwainton remained a sports car province and was dominated by that latterday evocation of the GN/Frazer Nash tradition: the HRG. Honours were shared with both John Martin-Lewis's ex-Newton car and Dennis Scobey's Singer-engined version both recording 27.2s, a whole second faster than Ashley Cleave, not in the remarkably rapid Morris Special which he normally ran, but in Phil Uglow's Riley-powered HRG.

Times were affected by the weather at the opening Prescott meeting where Sydney Allard defeated the growing Cooper challenge in 48.36s with the old Steyr-Allard. The excellent traction and 'long' second gear, allied to the torque of their big lazy V8 engines, ensured that all Allards were well-suited to Prescott's twisty character and this meeting was another where the marque enjoyed a double success. Guy Warburton, still driving the modified 1946 car, HLF 601, was the fastest sports car driver with 52.78s. Eric Brandon (49.61s) led the Cooper pursuit from Michael Christie and John Cooper, although the latter craftily listed an 1102cc JAP engine. This put him into the now rather weekly contested 1,500cc class, which he won. Clive Lones in the red 'Tiger Kitten' beat the other 500s but this famous name was no longer adorning the old Austin Seven-based car. Clive had bought the prototype of the production Iota chassis from Dick Caesar, a car which Joe Fry had run a few times, and a good season appeared in prospect.

Unusually, the RAC Championship opened with the Craigantlet round, brought forward from August to 3 June. Sadly, only Allard went over from England and his 75s BTD was a virtual walkover, with Chris Lindsay's remarkably effective Ford Ten Special and Ernie Robb's Mercury Special leading the 'home' side but a poor match for the reigning Champion. This rather lacklustre start to the season was also tinged with sadness when Peter Monkhouse was killed in the Mille Miglia sports car race, and ironically while he was riding as a passenger.

Despite a really hot day a lamentably small crowd made their way to Shelsley Walsh on 10 June. Although the record was out of reach on the melting surface, Raymond Mays demonstrated that R4D was still a worthy contender with a 38.61s run which defeated Dennis Poore's 330 plus bhp Alfa Romeo (38.86s) and the sharply contrasting Cooper 1000 of Smethwick driver Ken Wharton (39.89s) for BTD. In fact it was to be Mays's last Shelsley BTD, the final triumph in an amazing record of 21 outright wins (including one shared success and one car BTD which was bettered by a motorcycle) stretching right back to 1923. As was often the case, Ken McAlpine was only just slower than the accepted aces, heaving the big Maserati up in 39.95s, over a second and a half faster than Peter Stubberfield's modified Bugatti T35B. And Joe Fry? The 'Freik' got away from him just after the start, hitting the bank and rolling over, although the driver escaped lightly with only a cut hand. The overall standard of the entry was not up to the class of a few years earlier, yet enterprise was far from dead. If Archie Butterworth's four-wheel-drive AJB had raised a few eyebrows, his efforts paled in comparison with the device fielded by Swandean, near Brighton, garage proprietor Ted Lloyd-Jones. Successful exploits with the old Triangle-Skinner Special (now driven by Alick Pitts) paved the way for the Triangle Flying Saucer. This awesome machine boasted no less than a 21,250cc Rolls-Royce Kestrel aero engine in the back of a four-wheel-drive special which owed it provenance to a Daimler Scout Car. In the circumstances 46.63s was more than creditable. For the first time for some years there was a real battle for the Ladies' Award, with Betty Haig's new Cooper recording 43.31s, just 0.13s outside Joan Gerard's record, to beat Joy Cooke (44.15s) who was driving Ken Wharton's Cooper. Despite the theoretically liberating experience of the Second World War, there were rather fewer women competitors than in the 1930s and those that there were actually found it harder to gain entries in circuit racing well into the 1950s than their predecessors had done at Brooklands.

Dennis Poore, whose much modified Alfa Romeo actually had two gearboxes, a Jackson-fitted ENV pre-selector 'box and the original, non-functional, Alfa component left in the tail of the car, looked set for a good season and emphasised the fact at the BOC Members' Prescott on the following day. His 45.74s stood as BTD on a day when times were fast but not record breaking – with one exception. Peter Collins, the teenage son of a Kidderminster garage owner, was beginning to make his mark on the 500cc class with a Cooper, but had fitted the car with a very rare 749cc twin-cylinder JAP engine. With this he scuttled up the hill in 47.52s to break Bert Hadley's long held 750cc record.

The scene now shifted to Scotland where the visitors mingled with the unfamiliar – and generally most effective – array of Scottish specials bearing such exotic names as 'Girastro', 'Axis', 'Omega' and 'Staponak'. With two Championship rounds bringing the Scots firmly into the mainstream of British hill climbing, local interest was high. At Bo'ness there was only one new record, that secured in 42.53s by the supercharged Ford-engined Buckler of Derek Buckler, although Guy Warburton took top sports car honours in 41.40s, fast enough to be fifth overall. Ken Wharton, who had consistently impressed in the rather unlikely J4-engined Wharton Special, really came into his own and he shot to a

Guy Warburton had many class wins in HLF 601, the ex-Sydney Allard 1946 sprint Allard. This fine picture shows Warburton, arms flailing, hard at work at Bo'ness.
BILL HENDERSON

major BTD with the unblown Cooper in 38.41s, an almost imperceptivle six-hundredths of a second faster than Dennis Poore. Peter Collins's unique 750 Cooper did well to record 40.13s, which put him ahead of the fastest Scot, Edinburgh's David Murray in ERA R12B.

Poore gained his revenge one week later on 'The Rest'. Competing over a shortened course of 1,425 yards, Dennis turned the tables on Wharton, although this time there were only four-hundredths of a second in it, with Poore's time being 57.60s. Old hands Mays and Allard had to be content with third and fourth places.

Now on peak form, Dennis Poore returned South to score a second Prescott win at the BOC Open meeting, but only by the smallest possible margin of 0.01s from Eric Brandon's Cooper 1000, with 45.61s to 45.62s. Another formidable addition to the 500cc ranks was Mancunian Alan Rogers and he brought the record below 48s with a rousing 47.94s. There was a new Ladies' Record too, when Betty Haig demolished another pre-war Prescott figure, chopping the time down to 49.64s.

Before the Championship resumed at Bouley Bay, the highly distinctive Great Auclum and Blandford meetings took place, and both resulted in outright wins for the much improved AJB of the bearded Archie Butterworth. Another successful special, Gordon Parker's Jaguette, was the fastest sports car at the Burghfield Common venue with the steeply banked first corner. Parker, from Shorne, in Kent, had fitted an N-type MG Magnette chassis with a 1939 2,664cc pushrod Jaguar engine in 1946. Originally weighing in around the ton mark, the car was now much more competitive after losing around 400 lbs excess weight and gaining a supercharger for its modestly powerful engine.

Most of the leading drivers returned to Blandford so in defeating both Poore and Wharton with a fastest-yet time of 30.36s, Butterworth's well-merited success was considerable. Tragically, it was totally overshadowed by the grievous blow inflicted by the death of Joe Fry. Once again the difficult 'Freikaiserwagen' went out of control just after the start, this time with fatal results. Deeply felt by fellow competitors, this was almost certainly the first-ever fatal accident to a car driver in a British speed hill climb. Although she could have gained little joy by it, Betty Haig also broke the Ladies' Record in 36.55s. Further fatalities at a later circuit racing meeting discouraged all concerned from using the venue again for some time.

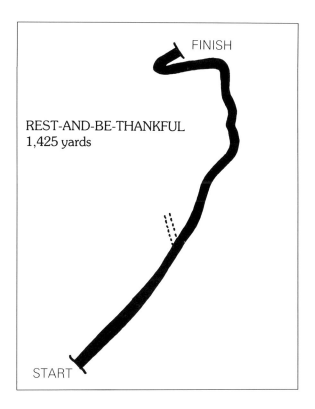

FINISH

REST-AND-BE-THANKFUL
1,425 yards

START

Although Dennis Poore won on the shorter Val des Terres climb, the Alfa Romeo driver was beaten by Ken Wharton at Bouley Bay. The little Cooper 1000 fairly flew up the Jersey hill's 1.011 twisting yards, leaving the new record at 55.4s. Poore was 0.4s slower but still second from the improved Jerseyman, Syd Logan in his Cooper (56.4s), Allard (56.6s) and a tie between Frank le Gallais's LGS-Jaguar and Peter Collins's 750 Cooper.

There were no major surprises at the VSCC Prescott, won by Stubberfield's Bugatti, or at Brighton where Raymond Mays set another BTD, and the International Prescott meeting was also rather an anticlimax. The entry list was not inspiring, the crowd was not particularly large, there was but one Bugatti in the Members' car park, and even the Championship had already been clinched – by the consistent and hard-driving Dennis Poore. He and Robin Jackson had come a long way with the 1935 Alfa Romeo since a none too confident Poore had overturned his then recent acquisition at Bo'ness in 1947. His Championship win was richly deserved for few could understand how he achieved such times on Britain's narrow and sinuous climbs with such a large and heavy, albeit very powerful car. He emphasised his success in the best possible way by winning at Prescott with 45.39s to the 45.44s of Sydney Allard and 46.67s of Raymond Mays. Ken Wharton, who had certainly put a marker down for the future, clocked 46.87s and headed Michael Christie (47.02s) and Peter Collins (47.29s). Christie did particularly well for he was driving the latest 1,100cc version of the Kieft, which certainly looked less agile than the Cooper, while Collins snatched another Prescott record, that for 1,500cc cars. He had located another odd-sized JAP engine, this time of 1,260cc. Sydney Allard had been favourite to win the sports car category with his latest 5.4-litre Cadillac-engined J2 but it was off form and his class-winning 50.78s was bettered by the 50.48s recorded by Ron Willis's much lightened BMW 328. The new Champion, Poore, also won the newly instituted Staniland Trophy, while the runner-up position in the RAC title was a tie between Wharton and Allard, with Mays fourth.

In fact, the season ended on a high note with Gordon Parker's Jaguette scoring an initial 31.4s best at the Bentley Drivers' Club's new hill at Firle on the Sussex Downs, Dr Mirrlees Chassels taking his Mercury-engined Frazer Nash-based Chassels Special to a win at the well-supported SSCC Bo'ness finale, and a really first-class Shelsley meeting.

The MAC had not really catered for the sports car drivers for many years but well remembered drawing a distinguished sports car entry by tying in their regulations with those of the Tourist Trophy. Since the war most organisers had taken a very liberal line where sports machinery was concerned. As long as it had wings and was road-registered it was eligible! But with the Tourist Trophy revived at Dundrod in Ulster in September 1950, and with the entry restricted to fairly strictly production models, the MAC decided to link the September Shelsley with this race once again and arranged classes for Production Sports Cars. The Club was rewarded with an excellent entry, including many of the cars which actually competed in the TT. Despite rain later in the day, and an accident during practice which sidelined Butterworth's AJB, the meeting was quite an occasion. It was opened by a demonstration climb by Ian and Pat Appleyard in their Alpine Rally-winning Jaguar XK120 and there was another 'sideshow' when Lt. Col. Goldie Gardner handed over the newly presented Austin Mobile Workshop to Denis Flather, Chairman of the British Motor Racing Research Trust, otherwise the 'committee' behind the BRM project. Perhaps a little uncharitably, the Editor of *Motor Sport* declared that 'Without its lettering, we thought it looked a bit like a piece of undertaker's equipment.'

Dennis Poore finished the year in fine style with another BTD, in 37.74s, while Sydney Allard, after a season which had seen his attention often diverted away from hill climbs, put up his best-ever Shelsley performance with 38.05s, a new unsupercharged record. Ken Wharton was sixth in his Cooper, beaten by Mays and Collins's 1,260cc Cooper, but he was also having a drive in Peter Bell's 2-litre ERA R11B. Despite his lack of experience in an ERA, Wharton did a superb job, taking just 38.83s to snatch third BTD, although even this was slower than Bolster's inspired 1948 climb in the same car. Basil Davenport was now down to 41.56s – faster than he had ever gone before – which was a mere 0.1s clear of Rupert Instone's latest special, the 'Djinn'. Fitted with a rear mounted JAP engine, this workmanlike special looked pretty modern but was 'still a bit GN' under the skin, hence the name. Joan Gerard's Ladies' Record fell, if only by 0.02s when Joy Cooke managed 43.16s in Christie's Kieft 1100.

Power-to-weight ratios were all-important at Shelsley, so the Jaguar XK120s which had proved victorious at Dundrod were well beaten by the BMW-derived, Bristol-engined Frazer Nash Le Mans Re-

plicas. Donald Pitt, driving Anthony Baring's car, was fastest of all with a sizzling 43.91s (only 0.15s outside the pre-war sports car record set by Connell's 4-litre Darracq) and with the similar Frazer Nashes of Anthony Crook and Jack Newton making it a clean sweep. Peter Walker's works-blessed XK120 was the best of the bigger cars (44.61s) and defeated the Allards, but the relatively underpowered works Aston Martin DB2s were right out of the picture. Even George Abecassis, making a brief return to the hills, could not better 47.73s, although he was well clear of team-mates Reg Parnell and Charles Brackenbury. Other competitors included Allard, Warburton and Ken Watkins in TT Allard J2s, Hay's famous Embiricos Bentley saloon and one which was definitely not a TT competitor, Ken Wharton's yellow Ford Pilot rally car!

Despite this end of season filip, there was no disguising that an era of hill climbs fiercely contested by mainly road-racing-derived thoroughbreds and highly-developed one-off specials was ending. Mays decided at the end of the year that he really could no longer devote the time necessary for success to his own competition programme and regretfully retired. Allard was becoming more involved with sports car racing, Joe Fry, sadly, was dead, and Gerard had completely abandoned sprint events. The relatively cheap and uncomplicated Coopers had proven that even 95 bhp was enough if it was allied to light weight, good traction and sheer agility. Taken as a whole, the years since the war had been dominated by Raymond Mays, although in 1949 and 1950 he could not match the sustained success of Allard, Poore and Wharton in particular. Nevertheless, in the four years of the RAC Championship, which ignores the 1946 season when the Mays/R4D combination was unbeatable, the Linolnshire veteran still scored the highest number of Championship BTDs with six. Allard scored five, and Poore four (one of which was shared with Joe Fry).

CHAPTER FIVE

THE COOPER-JAP
(1951-1961)

THE bare statistic that the winner of the RAC National Hill Climb Championship in every year from 1951 to 1961, inclusive, drove a 1,000 or 1,100cc JAP-powered Cooper is indicative of the near-total domination of this remarkably simple little car for more than a decade. The only partial exception to this supremacy came in 1954 when Ken Wharton bought the old ERA R4D and scored his Championship points both in this car and in his highly developed Cooper 1000.

Even this is significant, for although R4D had been much modified over the years and boasted a post-war chassis, it was fundamentally a 'thirties design. But it had been developed in later years as a sprint/hill climb car. Hill climbing had become a very specialised motor sporting activity and the Cooper-JAP was just perfect for the job. Although the power output of a basic unsupercharged 1,098cc JAP was not world shattering at 95 bhp, the engine's characteristics gave it tremendous torque and it was light. Located in the back of a modified Cooper 500 chassis the all-up weight was less than 5 cwt, plus that of the driver, so the acceleration – vital in these short sprint events – was phenomenal. Since the resulting car was extemely small and agile, the result was domination. It is amusing to note that the elements which went together to achieve this success really came together only accidentally in the first place, as a bye-product of a wish to devise a cheap and wieldy Formula B car. Ironically, reliability was never good enough to make the car a serious proposition for the longer circuit races, especially with the drip-feed lubrication of the original 996cc engines. The later dry-sumped, pressure-lubricated 1100s did enjoy some success in short distance circuit races.

Although the driver sat in front of the engine – and the true worth of that positioning was not appreciated in a wider context until the late nineteen-fifties – the Cooper-JAP was really the culmination of a tradition of light, modestly powerful hill climb cars, eschewing complexity and expense, dating right back to the GNs and especially to Archie Frazer Nash's 'Kim', via the 'Freikaiserwagen' (although this device became much more complex as time went on), and a whole succession of Shelsley Specials of which Basil Davenport's 'Spider' was the most famous and successful. While not appealing overmuch to the purist brought up on Bugattis, Alfa Romeos and ERAs, the Cooper-JAP also had the estimable advantage of being cheap to buy new at around the £700 to £800 mark in the early 'fifties, and inexpensive to run. With prize money at hill climbs tending to remain in the range of £50 to £200 for a BTD, it was possible to complete a successful hill climb season without any additional net outlay. One driver, Brian Eccles, who was scoring some successes towards the end of the period covered in this Chapter, once assured the author that he actually made money out of his hill climbing. That would certainly not be feasible today.

The attraction and success of the Cooper-JAP, although it made for a rather uninteresting era in terms of technical advances and variety, was timely. Circuit racing was burgeoning throughout the nineteen-fifties and few of the big names bothered to compete on the hills. The backbone of the sport was now a group of enthusiasts who rarely, if ever, competed in circuit races although it is significant that the three drivers who stand head and shoulders above their contemporaries in hill climbing stature all had a successful circuit racing background.

All too often the spectators too preferred to patronise the now freely available circuit racing and even the most efficient and eminent of hill climb organisers went through some tricky periods, financially, during the period. The Bugatti Owners Club went through a financial crisis in 1951, so did the Midland Automobile Club in 1957/58. The Royal Scottish Automobile Club found that Rest-and-be-Thankful's remote location and often dour weather made it a constant drain on Club funds, while even the more conveniently situated Bo'ness went into abeyance for a few years.

Yet overall, the period witnessed growth for the sport, even if it was never spectacular. In 1951 there were 35 hill climbs of widely varying stature held in these islands, including 9 in Ireland on roads closed for the occasion once a year. By 1961 the total had risen in small increments to around the 60 mark, but without any increase in numbers of Irish events. Entry lists too were rising, indeed more sharply, in the last few years of the period, with more single-seaters, including the latest Formula Junior cars, and many more small sports, Grand Touring, and modified saloon cars. Hitherto the bigger meetings had not catered for any but racing and the more potent sports and sports-racing cars, while for many years Shelsley and Rest-and-be-Thankful did not even include separate sports car classes on their programmes at RAC Championship meetings. By 1958/59 this was changing. The BOC instituted a class for Grand Touring cars in 1957 and Great Auclum, which was included on the RAC Championship schedule in 1959 (along with Westbrook Hay and Stapleford) actually included a class for saloon cars. Spectators who did come to hill climbs could now see in action a very wide range of machinery.

Although contested seriously by only a handful of competitors each year, the RAC National Championship had rapidly become a significant part of the hill climb scene, and provided the élite drivers with something to aim at over the whole season. Up until 1957, Championship points were awarded on times achieved during the normal two class runs, but the series was given added prominence that year by slotting in two extra runs for a Championship class, solely for the purpose of scoring title points which were no longer to be awarded on the strength of class ascents. Conversely, times which broke class records during the Championship runs did not count for official records. The only official record which could be broken in this way was the outright course record. At first, these extra runs

The old order. Rivers Fletcher on his way to a Bugatti handicap win and a new record for unsupercharged Bugattis at Prescott in 1951, in his T35.
THE MOTOR now AUTOCAR & MOTOR *via* RIVERS FLETCHER

The new.
Ken Wharton ushers in a new era of Cooper-JAP domination with his lightweight 996cc Cooper MkIV.
via MIKE KETTLEWELL

were held between the first and second class climbs, not at the end of the day as became later practice. The scope of the Championship was broadened in 1959 when three new venues – Great Auclum, Westbrook Hay and Stapleford – were added to the series, making 10 counting events.

Two further championships were instigated during the period. Wishing to encourage newcomers to the sport, the MAC instigated a Junior Hill Climb and Sprint Championship in 1956 for which eligible drivers were those who had not achieved class or outright wins at any race or speed event of higher than closed-to-club status.

Growing interest in the non-racing machinery encouraged two motoring journals, *Motor Racing* and *Sports Car and Lotus Owner* to sponsor a third championship, this time purely for sports cars, in 1959. Points for this were scored in up to and over 1,600cc classes, during the normal class runs, at the RAC Championship meetings. The MAC's Junior series was different in this respect for points were awarded at a number of restricted meetings which were outside the RAC Championship schedule.

From 1958 onwards there were signs of new challenges to the Cooper-JAP supremacy, initially with four-cylinder, 1,460cc sohc and 1,475cc dohc Coventry-Climax-engined Formula 2 cars from Cooper and Lotus, but the breakthrough did not come until 1961 when Tony Marsh arrived at Shelsley with an Inter-Continental Formula (and formerly Formula 1), 2½-litre, rear-engined BRM P48 and shattered the outright record.

The sports car scene had changed too with the domination of the converted GP Bugattis, the Allards and other American- or Jaguar-engined cars coming under fire from a whole new generation of light-weight, small-engined sports racers from Cooper (seemingly inevitably) and Lotus, where the now familiar combination of low weight, modest power, good acceleration and excellent handling at least matched the far greater power of the bigger cars.

The period was not one of spectacular innovation or dramatic change but there can be no doubt that hill climbing was a far healthier sport in 1961 that it had been in 1951. The prospects for the future were intriguing, there were new technical avenues beckoning, and hill climbing could now draw on an increasing number of enthusiastic clubmen who saw hill climbing as a sport in itself rather than just something to do when there was no circuit race to enter. The days of manufacturer interest and professional involvement were largely gone, but the appeal to the amateur clubman had never been higher.

While many other competitors had their days of glory it would be fair to say that three drivers dominated the era of the Cooper-JAP: Ken Wharton, who won the RAC Championship in 1951, 1952,

Ken Wharton: the supreme all-rounder.
via MIKE KETTLEWELL

1953 and 1954; Tony Marsh, who was Champion in 1955, 1956 and 1957; and David Boshier-Jones, who succeeded him in 1958, 1959 and 1960. Although all three were prominent in 1955/56 they were never to compete all together on truly equal terms, so their relative brilliance cannot be compared directly, although their pre-eminence is unquestioned.

The nineteen-fifties were years when versatility in motor sport was the norm. These were the years when racing drivers took part in rallies, when drivers such as Stirling Moss and Roy Salvadori might compete in three or four different cars at the same race meeting, where it was not considered strange to compete in a World Championship Grand Prix one weekend, a sports car race the next, and then take in a club meeting when the less-crowded international calendar allowed a weekend off. This versatility is epitomised by Ken Wharton. This talented garage proprietor from Smethwick was already a leading hill climber in 1951, but he was much more. At 34 he was already a triple RAC Trials Champion, an International rally winner (Lisbon and Tulip), and was breaking into circuit racing in a serious way with a 500cc Cooper. Moreover, he was an able engineer having built succesful specials for both trials and hill climbs and succeeded where many had failed in supercharging the V-twin engine. As the early nineteen-fifties progressed, Wharton's circuit racing career encompassed factory drives for Frazer Nash, BRM, Jaguar, Vanwall, and even Ferrari. He was one of the select group who succeeded in winning races in the original V16 BRM Type 15, albeit minor ones, and was truly one of the sport's great all rounders. His consistency and precision on the hills, allied to perfectly prepared cars, made him all-but unbeatable and his ability to hop out of one car with which he had achieved record times and then jump into another with widely differing characteristics and then repeat a record-breaking performance was quite astonishing. It is undeniable that Wharton's opposition for BTD was not always very strong by past standards, but he didn't seem to need close competition to spur him on to record-breaking times. His death in a sports car race at Ardmore, New Zealand, in January 1957, at the age of 40 was a terrible blow and the institution of a memorial fund to build a new timing pavilion at Prescott and the naming of the country's premier driving tests meeting after him perhaps gives some impression of the impact he had on motor sport.

Racing commitments and a bad accident at Silverstone probably cost Wharton the 1955 Championship, but the man who took that honour was a worthy successor, Tony Marsh. Another Midlander, Marsh's background was rather different from Wharton's for his family were principals of the Marsh & Baxter pork products concern and Tony was a bailiff on the company's farm at Kinver, near Stourbridge. Looking even younger than his 22 years, Marsh came into motor sport in 1952, via sporting trials and then hill climbs in a Dellow (one of the well-made, Ford-engined, dual-purpose trials and sports cars built in Alvechurch, Birmingham, by Ken Delingpole and Ron Lowe). Marsh rapidly graduated to the 'big banger' Coopers and became a very difficult man to beat. In his early days it was all too easy to overlook this reserved, rather shy, young driver as his driving style was as unflamboyant as his demeanour outside the car. Although he did have an engineering background, Marsh was above all a meticulous observer. He may not have said very much but he would take in a great deal about the mechanical make-up of the opposition and the precise line needed to set the best times on a given hill. 'Precise' is indeed the word to summarise the Marsh style, for his record-breaking ascents rarely stirred crowds into tumultuous applause. His ascents were just too neat and unspectacular. But they were very fast.

A triple Champion, Marsh also competed on the circuits with growing success, and although he never attained the eminence of Wharton in terms of securing factory drives in Grand Prix and sports car racing, he was racing in Formula 1 with distinction as a privateer in 1961, although after 1957 the increasing circuit racing commitments rather detracted from his hill climbing success.

This was a pity, for it made an all-out fight between him and David Boshier-Jones rather rare. 'Bosh', a wiry Welshman with a garage business in Newport, Monmouthshire, enjoyed a career which spanned only from 1952 to 1960, but in three short years, from 1958 to 1960, he carried all before him to become another triple Champion. At the end of that season he retired from regular competition, although he did occasionally share his younger brother Peter's car in 1961. Not one to alternate between different kinds of car, Boshier-Jones was the great specialist. He began with a new 500cc Kieft, switching to a Cooper after a couple of seasons, and attained a formidable record in his class before putting an R. R. Jackson-prepared JAP V-twin in the same Cooper for 1957. Until then he had also raced regularly and successfully with the Cooper, but henceforward he concentrated solely on the

David Boshier-Jones: the great specialist.
via MIKE KETTLEWELL

hills. This was beneficial when Marsh's attentions were split and 'Bosh's' single-mindedness certainly played an important part in his three-year domination. He *looked* faster than Marsh, closer to the limit (which he rarely overstepped), and was superbly consistent. Although the extra RAC Championship rounds held from 1958 onwards rather distort the picture statistically, it was Boshier-Jones who achieved the greatest number of BTDs at Championship meetings in this period, with 22, and with all except one recorded in that amazing three-year period. Wharton was only one behind with 21, despite the fewer Championship rounds each year for him, and Marsh's total stood at 13, although with many more to come in later years. It is a measure of the superiority of these three that no other driver could boast more than four Championship BTDs.

Those four outright successes fell to the driver who so often found himself runner-up to all three of the Champions, Michael Christie. This tall and sporting engineer from Haddenham, Buckinghamshire, always strikingly attired with black overalls and a red crash helmet, was consistently capable of giving any of the Champions a hard fight and, like Wharton, was just as good in Cooper-JAP or ERA. Yet this relaxed, pipe-smoking, sportsman who had cut his competition teeth on the old AC-Nash and had been one of the first to switch to the Cooper-JAP formula in 1949, never managed to win the

The lighter side of hill climbing. Master Nicholas Moor 'blasts' away from Prescott's startline in the 'Wasp Grub', a fine 150cc replica of 'Wasp', built for him by his father, Jack.
MURRAY HARDY
via RIVERS FLETCHER

There was a thriving Scottish scene in the early nineteen-fifties. Ian Hopper's highly professional Hopper Special is watched by a large and appreciative crowd in Bo'ness sunshine.
via MIKE KETTLEWELL

Championship. He withdrew from the Championship class after the 1958 season, by which time his Alexander Engineering company had become one of the leading concerns in the fast-growing production car tuning business.

The Wharton years

Returning to 1951, the year began fairly inauspiciously. It was rare now for the sport to receive the attention of leader writers, even in the specialist motoring press, and what concern there was only reflected criticism of the trend of hill climbing voiced in the correspondence columns. In *Autosport*'s editorial for 5 January there appeared the following:

> In the correspondence columns, Mr. P. A. Collins criticizes the British Hill-Climb Championship and gives it as his opinion that the series should be organized on a classes basis. Admittedly the present competition is tending to become uninteresting owing to the paucity of entries. This is no doubt explained by the system of marking which makes it almost imperative that the eventual winner must be capable of putting up best time of the day at each of the nominated events.
>
> Mr. Collins's suggestion is well worth studying. However, AUTOSPORT feels that each year there should be one, and only one, British Hill-Climb Champion. A possible solution, and one that would certainly provoke a great number of entries, would be the adoption of a hill-climb formula, on the lines of the 'Index of Performance' at Le Mans. Standard times could be set according to engine capacity, and marks awarded to drivers making the best improvement on these standard times. This would still produce the incentive to make best time of the day, in addition to promoting fierce 'class' warfare.

For the time being these suggestions went unheeded, but in essence the *Autosport* proposals are those which were finally adopted by the BARC in 1968 for their successful club series which was sponsored for many years by Castrol and then by Guyson.

Apart from the limited scope of the Championship, there were more immediate problems to be faced. The Bugatti Owners Club was going through a difficult financial phase, one where the costs of running Prescott in a professional manner, in the face of reduced popular and competitor support, and with a small club membership, had become prohibitive. Drastic measures were taken to return the running of the Club to purely honorary officials and a membership recruitment drive aimed at the non-Bugatti owner was put in hand. Under the Chairmanship of Roy Taylor, and with invaluable backing from the Treasurer Ken Nightingale and Secretary John Newton, among others, the BOC fought back. During 1951 Prescott, the Club's greatest potential asset yet in 1950 something of a financial liability, hung in the balance as a hill climb venue.

There was a sad loss too before the season began when Geoffrey Ansell, not a BTD man but a regular 1,500cc racing class winner in ERA R9B, died after a short illness.

More positively, the 'coming man' of 1950, Ken Wharton, had bought another Cooper, the rather special lightweight chassis which had been destined for Frenchman Raymond Sommer in 1950, to which Wharton was fitting a 996cc JAP engine with his own design of supercharger set-up. Michael Christie, on the other hand, had temporarily deserted the Cooper fold and was to run a twin-cylinder version of Cyril Kieft's little car. Another intriguing variation on the V-twin theme was under preparation by Robin Jackson for former Alta driver, Ray Merrick. This was a new Cooper Mk 5 chassis fitted with an 1132cc engine which combined both Norton and JAP parts. In sharp contrast, Sydney Allard, who had now all but abandoned the Clerk project, was intent on running the old Steyr-Allard with a simple four-wheel-drive system which was to be engaged only for the all-important start. In fact, the benefit from this typically homely Allard 'mod' was doubtful for although the car was very rapid off the line it became decidedly tricky in the tighter bends.

On the sports car front, the so-desirable Jaguar XK120 was at last becoming a little easier to obtain on the home market and during the year those of Macclesfield industrialist Phil Scragg, Cyril Brough, Cecil Heath (who also ran a Cooper 1000) and Geoffrey Mansell, in particular, became familiar sights on the hills, although the weight of the XK did it no favours in this sort of competition.

The now traditional curtain-raiser for the major climbs, the BOC's May National at Prescott was not too auspicious for the hard-pressed club as it rained and the Best Time of the Day was actually set by

Peter Stubberfield's twin rear-wheeled, single-seater Bugatti T35B in 46.84s, in the Handicap class for Bugattis! This 'extra' climb was not allowed to count for the official BTD awards, so the premier trophy fell to Michael Christie, thus giving a rare BTD to the 'big banger' Kieft. Guy Warburton managed to break 50s in the old Allard and was the fastest sports car driver.

This was pretty unrepresentative and the June Shelsley, held in the MAC's Golden Jubilee year, was eagerly awaited. It was quite an occasion with a commemorative cavalcade of men and machines long associated with the hill, a demonstration by Alan Hess of the 'Round the World' Austin A40 Sports, and a very different demonstration by Master Nicholas Moor, Jack Moor's young son, in the beautifully made 150cc replica of 'Wasp' which his father had built for him. Dubbed the 'Wasp Grub', this delightful and most effective little miniature was run at a number of other events to the evident delight of all concerned.

When it came to the serious stuff, Ken Wharton made it clear that he was out to relieve Dennis Poore of his Championship title. Already a winner and record breaker (29.87s) with the new blown Cooper-JAP at Lydstep, Wharton smashed the Shelsley record with a 37.27s climb, although Poore, driving the big green Alfa beautifully, was very close to the old figure at 37.38s. The Smethwick driver was also fourth overall in Peter Bell's ERA but his 39.58s time was bettered by the remarkably effective four-wheel-drive Jeep-based, Steyr-engined AJB of Archie Butterworth.

There was no respite, for after Shelsley the two Scottish Championship rounds at Bo'ness and 'The Rest' followed on successive weekends. Dennis Poore's meteoric ascent of Bo'ness in 1949 made him a great favourite over the border, but this time his luck was out on the Hamilton Drive. The old Alfa broke its flywheel, which in turn damaged the gearbox mainshaft. With his strongest opponent out of the running Wharton had a field day although Poore's 33.9s record remained inviolate for another year. BTD in the Cooper (34.60s), 2nd BTD in Bell's ERA (34.97s) and a new 500cc racing car record (38.38s) in a Cooper borrowed from Scotsman Pat Prosser, was the sort of virtuoso performance which was to become associated with him. Sydney Allard came closest with 36.04s, while a trip down an escape road did not deter Guy Warburton from celebrating a new sports car record at 38.31s.

Dennis Poore had his revenge at Rest-and-be-Thankful where the timed distance had been increased slightly to 1,425 yards, thus creating a whole new set of records. There was only 0.03s in it but Poore's 56.32s enhanced his Scottish reputation and Wharton had to be content with second and third places, well clear of Peter Collins's 1,260cc Cooper-JAP and a young engineer from Edinburgh, Ron Flockhart, who was attracting favourable attention with a 1,000cc Vincent-engined JP, one of the Cooper-ish chassis built by Joe Potts at Bellshill. Flockhart was only one of a number of Scots who were making a considerable impact on the expanding Scottish racing and hill climb scene, others including Bob Haddow (Cooper 1000), Edinburgh businessman David Murray (ERA and Maserati), Riley driver Archie Calder, the highly successful Healey Silverstone exponent Jimmy Stewart (elder brother of future World Champion Jackie), and the builder of some highly professional specials, Ian Hopper.

The interruption to the Wharton domination was only temporary. He returned to Bouley Bay at the end of July and lopped a whole 1.2s off his own record with the highly effective Cooper, defeating Poore by two full seconds, and with the speedy Jerseyman Syd Logan (Cooper 1000, winner of the earlier 'club' Bouley climb in May) and Allard next up. Locally-owned Jaguar XK120s in the hands of Bob Sangan and Arthur Owen dominated the sports car category.

The 1949 Champion, Sydney Allard, did at least score one Championship 'first', at Craigantlet in Ulster, where his Steyr-Allard faced only local opposition. The time, 73s, was a record, though, and one of Ireland's best-known Ford Special exponents, Chris Lindsay ran him fairly close with 74.6s. Lindsay was not driving the deceptively mundane-looking Nufor on this occasion, though, but the ex-Ansell ERA R9B which had now passed to Irishman Ernest Wilkinson. The Ulster Automobile Club was badly hit by withdrawals before the meeting, losing Wharton, Collins, Anthony Brooke (Vauxhall Villiers) and Redmond Gallagher's self-built 998cc Leprechaun-JAP, an effective Irish evocation of the Cooper theme.

After another win at Lydstep augmented by a new 500cc record in the latest type of Ray Martin and John 'Autocar' Cooper-designed Kieft (Stirling Moss's regular car), Wharton set the seal to his first RAC Championship with another outright hill record, this time at Prescott in September when just 43.81s sufficed to edge out Dennis Poore (a highly creditable 43.98s) and Allard. One of the day's best performances, though, came from Chipping Norton, Oxfordshire, driver Clive Lones. This acknowledged veteran flung his Iota 'Tiger Kitten' round Prescott's tight corners to clock 45.66s, a new class record and fourth fastest overall, better even than Brian Shawe-Taylor who was competing in the ex-Earl Howe/Cuth Harrison ERA R8B/C with which he had been doing great things on the circuits. This meeting did much to put new heart into the BOC and also drew a first-class sports car entry with most of the year's top two-seaters pitted against each other for once. Sydney Allard's Cadillac-engined J2 came out on top although his 48.16s time was outside the record, and Gordon Parker's Jaguette managed to beat Guy Warburton who had had an excellent season, and Gillie Tyrer who did break his class record in his very special 1940 'Gran Premio Brescia' BMW.

This, Wharton's fourth Championship win, gave him a maximum possible points total of 40, with Poore's best four performances giving him 37, and Allard third on 33. Wharton also scored 24 points with the ERA, 10 more than Peter Stubberfield.

Although it still did not count for the Championship, the September Shelsley meeting remained one of the year's highlights – especially for Wharton. He broke the course record for the second time in 1951 with an amazing 36.62s in the Cooper twin, and then bettered the old record for second BTD with R11B (37.01s), thereby relieving R4D of the honour of being the fastest ERA up Shelsley. As usual Poore was next in line but a 38.45s unsupercharged record demonstrated that Sydney Allard was making the Steyr-Allard work at Shelsley. Sydney also set a 41.60s Production Sports class record in the J2 but he was not the fastest of all the sports cars for Anthony Crook's beautifully-turned-out Frazer Nash Le Mans Replica – ideally suited to hill climbing – reduced that particular record down to 41.46s. Regretably, the day was marred by a dreadful accident to Archie Butterworth at the Crossing, where the AJB overturned. Archie was badly injured, but although he happily recovered to produce ingenious flat-four Formula 2 and 'swing valve' sports car engines in the future, his driving career was ended just a few weeks after he had won the coveted BTD at the Brighton Speed Trials.

Away from the big meetings there were a number of innovations during the year. Most notably, the successor to the old Junior Car Club, a major hill climb promoter pre-1925, returned to hill climb organisation in a small way. The South Western Centre of the BARC obtained the use of a farm service road at Brunton, near the delightful-sounding village of Collingbourne Ducis, in Wiltshire. The timed distance was only a third of a mile, the road was narrow and climbed round one long bend between high banks, but the hill had a reasonable gradient and provided good entertainment for the sports car drivers. No racing cars were allowed at this stage.

In July two new hills were used for the first time and both were in the North of England where hill climbing had been virtually extinct for many years. The Lancashire Automobile Club's first meeting at Clerk Hill, a short 250 yards climb up a twisting loose-surfaced incline near Whalley was more reminiscent of a pre-1925 event than a modern speed hill climb with BTD going to Jack Clegg's trials special. Great fun, and well supported but not really in the mainstream of speed hill climbing. On the other hand, Jim Lafone and his associates in the Westmorland Motor Club had found a first-class hill in the road leading up to Barbon Manor, on the Shuttleworth Estate near Kirkby Lonsdale in the Lune Valley. Climbing up through most attractive parkland over a timed distance of 0.6 mile, and with an average gradient of 1 in 9, the hill offered two contrasting left-hand bends and a right-hand hairpin and with a decent straight before anchoring up for the right-hander. Originally scheduled for April, the first public meeting had to be postponed until July because of lambing on the estate. The narrowness of the course made it prudent to limit entries to cars with no more than 2-litres capacity and the honour of holding the first official record went to Kendal garage proprietor Bryan Crabtree who stopped the watches at 37.2s in his supercharged MG TC.

Anxious to make the fullest use of Prescott, the BOC invited the North Staffordshire Motor Club (of which Roy Taylor was also a senior official) to run a closed meeting the day after the May National. This was the first time that any 'outside' club – apart from the VSCC – had been able to run at Prescott and BTD was secured by Cecil Heath, a successful sprint driver, in his Cooper 1000. The June Members' meeting at the hill gave Peter Stubberfield the official BTD which he had missed the previous month, and he did it again at the August VSCC meeting. The latter club was able to run a second climb that year, in September, and this time the weather turned sour and with times in the 52/53s bracket at best, the consistent Stubberfield was beaten by "an armchair preceded by a smokescreen", otherwise the Caesar Special of Dr W. A. 'Tony' Taylor, more usually referred to simply as 'Doc'. Fitted with but two gears this was one 'Shelsley Special' which did not actually compete at Shelsley! It had been built in 1937 by Dick Caesar, employing a 1929 AC 'Six' engine, an early GN chassis frame, primitive independent front suspension and the inevitable chain drive, but nothing meaningful in the way of bodywork. Before the war the car had been bought for £30 by Joe Fry, who had later sold shares in it to Taylor and R. D. Price. A fairly undistinguished pre-war career ended with a connecting rod through the side of the old engine at Backwell, but after the conflict 'Doc' Taylor had laboriously restored the car to life and it had now become surprisingly reliable. In later years it even contrived to run in the Formula 1 class at Prescott!

Most of the lesser hills which were now springing up round the country had a strong localised following, and none more so than the Cornish hill, Trengwainton. In 1951 the familiar group of HRGs, plus Ashley Cleave's deceptively innocent looking Morris 8/10 Special, were unable to match the prototype Allard J2, with which John Broad won in April. He then sold the car to Jack Bassett who repeated the performance in August when his 25.94s climb of this tight and twisty hill constituted a new outright record.

Ken Wharton's 1951 season had also included some notable performances in Continental hill climbs, with third BTD at Susa/Mont Cenis, fourth BTD at Aosta/Grand Saint Bernard and second in the 500cc class to Stirling Moss at Freiburg, but in 1952 he exceeded even that level of success. He entered all six of the qualifying rounds of the RAC Championship and won the lot! Since the Smethwick all-rounder held a virtually unbreakable grip on British hill climbing for the next three seasons these three years can be considered together as having a single theme, at the top at least.

The second half of 1951 and a successful September International put new heart into the BOC and an innovative 1952 programme opened with an excellent May National where good weather and an encouragingly large crowd set the season off in the right way. Wharton gave this meeting a miss, and a worthy BTD in 45.43s fell to Dennis Poore's veteran Alfa Romeo with Michael Christie, now Cooper-JAP mounted once more, runner-up. The RAC Championship should actually have started by this time for the MAC broke with tradition and announced that their first meeting of the year would run in April. The object of the exercise was to hold a Shelsley Walsh meeting in the school holidays for once, but the idea misfired. At the time when a decision had to be made very few entries had been received, and the meeting was cancelled. This unheard of phenomenon at Shelsley came about purely because many competitors had not registered the early date and had simply forgotten to get their entries in on time.

Although Wharton, Christie and Poore would be following the Championship trail again, Sydney Allard would be concentrating on circuit racing and the Steyr-Allard was sold to Jack Bassett, although he was not to keep this difficult car for long. During the previous year Bertie Bradnack had had his JAP-twin supercharged. The car was instantly recognisable by the bulbous extension on the rear cowling and as 1952 progressed, the combination's competitiveness improved. A distinguished

Although not yet an RAC Championship venue, Great Auclum presented a unique short, sharp, challenge. This is Rivers Fletcher's Bugatti T35 which later passed to Hugh Conway.
JAMES BRYMER *via* RIVERS FLETCHER

As effective in ERA as in Cooper-JAP, Ken Wharton finished second at Shelsley in August 1952 in Peter Bell's ERA R11B – to himself in the Cooper-JAP.
FRANCIS PENN *via* MIKE KETTLEWELL

newcomer to the Cooper ranks arrived in the form of Air Vice-Marshal Donald 'Pathfinder' Bennett, famous for his wartime exploits with the Mosquito Pathfinder aircraft, and also a noted rally driver with a Jaguar XK120. Unusually, he fitted a Vincent-HRD engine in the back of his Cooper. Meanwhile up in Scotland, the promising Ron Flockhart was to share the original ERA R1A with motor trader Alastair Birrell, although they did not contest the whole of the Championship.

It was the Scottish rounds which opened the series, and Dennis Poore was always at his most dangerous North of the Border. This time Wharton managed to beat him by just fifteen-hundredths at Bo'ness although the winning Cooper-JAP time of 34.50s still left Poore's near-legendary record intact. Ken was only half a second slower in Peter Bell's ERA than in the Cooper, and over 2 seconds up on Ron Flockhart in the rather more 'basic' 1½-litre ERA. Sadly, a pall was cast over proceedings when Scottish clubman Ian Struthers, a regular Bentley competitor but driving an Allard J2 on this occasion, crashed at the Snake. The Allard overturned and pinned Struthers beneath it, inflicting fatal injuries.

Glen Croe is not noted for sunshine – at least not with hill climb competitors – but this time the weather was gorgeous and Wharton's winning margin with the supercharged Cooper-JAP was 1.91s. Ken's 54.23s climb was a new hill record and the man he beat was himself driving the ERA! Poore was only 0.07s down on that time and Bertie Bradnack had an excellent day to record 58.94s for fourth place, ending out the fastest Scots: Flockhart and the class-record breaking 500cc Cooper-JAP of Ninian Sanderson.

For the third year in succession Wharton set BTD at Bouley Bay even though he completed only one competitive climb because the gearbox broke on the Cooper second time up. Nevertheless, the first climb in 55.4s was still 0.8s faster than that of Le Gallais who had sorted the powerful LGS-Jaguar to the extent that he was able to climb his local hill 0.4s faster than Denis Poore.

As usual, the full Championship entry did not venture across the Irish Sea to Craigantlet. But Wharton did and, undaunted by a wet Ulster hill, recorded 80.2s to defeat some unusual opposition from the wealthy proprietor of the *Belfast Telegraph* newspaper, Bobby Baird. The Ulsterman was second overall in his new four-cylinder Tipo 500 Ferrari Formula 2 car (82.8s) and fourth in his glamorous Tipo 225S sports car. Splitting the two Ferraris was another Ulsterman, Desmond Titterington, who was beginning to make a big impression on local climbs with an immaculate maroon Allard J2.

Following the cancellation of the April meeting, the August promotion at Shelsley now counted for the RAC series. Michael Christie, who had not made a great impact so far after his initial BTD at Prescott, broke the unsupercharged record in 38.08s but it was to no avail against Wharton. The Championship was already his for a second year but 36.97s in the Cooper and 37.27s in R11B produced another 1-2 result. Since he also lifted the 500cc class in the works Kieft, even an encouraging 39.92s fourth BTD from Donald Bennett tended to be rather overlooked. On the other hand, Wharton's success did nothing to detract from Peter Walker's exuberant destruction of the sports car record in the Production classes. The 1951 Le Mans co-winner was provided with a factory Jaguar

And again. Shelsley Walsh opened the 1953 RAC Championship in June and Ken Wharton took another second BTD in ERA R11B to himself in the Cooper-JAP. He also won the team prize all on his own.
FRANCIS PENN *via* MIKE KETTLEWELL

Ron Flockhart shot to prominence in 1953 with this 33.83s record-breaking climb at Bo'ness in his ex-Mays ERA R4D.
BILL HENDERSON

XK120C and his spectacular 41.14s ascent finally defeated the Frazer Nashes which were headed by, yes, that man again, Ken Wharton. In fact, the Isleworth car stopped the clocks a mere 0.02s up on George Abecassis who put in an inspired performance in the relatively underpowered works Aston Martin DB2. The Production Sports class was certainly pulling in some high-grade entries, even though the Tourist Trophy, to which it had been linked, was not run in 1952.

After this excellent meeting, and with the Championship settled, the September Prescott could so easily have been an anti-climax. It was not and a marvellous entry was received. Even the hitherto hard-pressed Club Treasurer was smiling. This time Christie, again setting a new unsupercharged record (43.84s), ran Wharton very close but the older Mk4 Cooper fairly shot round Prescott's tight bends to clock an outright hill record in 43.70s. Wharton's second entry, the ERA, claimed third place in 44.47s but a refreshing fourth, and Staniland Trophy winner, was circuit racer Ken Downing driving his own Formula 2 Connaught A-type, the brainchild of the same Rodney Clarke (with Mike Oliver and with the financial backing of former Maserati driver Kenneth McAlpine) who had once been a leading Bugatti driver. Peter Walker was out again in the C-type Jaguar and two blistering climbs in 47.66s and 47.53s gave him and Jaguar both the premier sports car hill records.

Wharton's two-pronged main offensive remained unchanged for 1953 while Christie's Mk 6 Cooper now had its JAP engine listed at 1,107cc, taking it into the often rather weak 1½-litre class. Growing business commitments and the Alfa's advancing years meant that Dennis Poore was tending to run the car mainly in VSCC events rather than on the hills now[1]. Another old favourite, the Steyr-Alllard had changed hands once again. 'Doc' Pinkerton had taken over the car, which gradually underwent modification, including the use of a 4.5-litre engine, as in Butterworth's AJB. Brewing magnate, the Hon. Edward Greenall, who had raised a few eyebrows by fitting, out of necessity, a Ford V8 engine in a Grand Prix Bugatti, now joined the ever-growing Cooper twin band with a new chassis, and familiar cars in new ownership were the ex-Merrick Cooper-NorJAP bought by Australian-born Bill Sleeman, and the ex-Collins long chassis 1,260cc Cooper-JAP which the youthful-looking Tony Marsh had acquired. Another former Bugatti driver to switch to a 'big banger' Cooper was the extrovert publican C. S. 'Dick' Henderson. Up in Scotland the really exciting news was that Ron Flockhart had bought no less than R4D from Raymond Mays.

By this time, Ken Wharton was carrying out a tremendously busy racing schedule and he returned to the May Prescott meeting overnight after finishing runner-up to Mike Hawthorn's works Ferrari in the International Ulster Trophy in his Cooper-Bristol. Any fatigue certainly didn't hinder this exceptionally veratile driver who again competed in four cars. The score was BTD in the Cooper-JAP (44.66s), runner-up- in R11B, a Formula 1 class win in Bill Goodman's ERA R2B, and an unplaced outing in Lt. Col. Guy Arengo's Arengo 500. At this non-Championship meeting Michael Christie drove a couple of Kiefts, finishing fifth overall in the JAP twin-engined version and third in class in the rather fearsome experimental Formula 2 edition of the now Wolverhampton-built marque, fitted with the flat four AJB engine. With the Haddenham driver otherwise occupied, former Bugatti drivers Greenall and Liverpudlian Peter Reece ran Wharton closest in their Cooper-JAPs. The erstwhile Downing Connaught had now passed to R. R. C. 'Rob' Walker and was just starting an even more successful season of home events, usually in the hands of Tony Rolt. For Prescott, the unrelated Peter Walker shared the drive and, true to hill climb form, it was the latter who took the Formula 2 class with 46.70s to Rolt's 46.84s.

For the first time both the big Shelsley meetings counted towards the Championship and on 6 June Wharton turned in another totally demoralising performance. He arrived looking very much the worse for wear, as the previous Sunday he had escaped luckily with only minor injuries when his BRM had overturned at well over 100 mph at Albi in France. Shrugging off any stiffness and painful bruises he proceeded to smash the course record once more in his Cooper-JAP (36.60s), took second BTD in R11B (37.68s), was a relatively lowly fourth in a 500cc class won by the increasingly formidable David Boshier-Jones (Kieft-Norton), and then rounded off the day by winning the team prize, the Fray Challenge Trophy. Since hill climbing is essentially an individual sport the team award at Shelsley seldom received a lot of attention, but on this occasion it was different for the winning team of Cooper-JAP 1000, ERA and Arengo 500 were all driven by Ken Wharton himself! His visit to Worcestershire

---

1 Poore retired from competition in 1955 but he never sold the old Alfa. After a distinguished career as an industrialist where he played a major role in efforts to salvage the British motorcycle industry, he died in 1987. The following year the once familiar Alfa Romeo 8C-35, together with its old transporter, was auctioned for a whopping £1.5 million! One of motor sport's true gentlemen, Dennis Poore also made a financial contribution to Gregor Grant's fledgling *Autosport* magazine in 1950 – few people knew this and he was at pains to ensure that he received no undue editorial coverage.

was in every sense a flying one for he arrived on Friday from Zandvoort practice, and departed immediately after the meeting to compete in the Dutch Grand Prix the following day. What a man! The now familiar clutch of Coopers, in the order: Christie, Sleeman, Bradnack, took the minor honours but even Christie was over a second slower than the ERA. It was a fine meeting and records fell among the sports cars too. After the early Alta days John Heath and George Abecassis of H. W. Motors had developed their Alta-engined HWMs into celebrated British flag wavers in Formula 2, but by 1953 limited resources on their part and strengthening Italian, French and even British opposition caused them to turn their attention towards sports car racing. So, George Abecassis returned to Shelsley in a car of his own team's manufacture, the XK Jaguar-engined HWM two-seater. Based on a widened version of the de Dion rear-suspended single-seater, the new car, registered HWM 1, went well but the 40.64s time was beaten by Cyril Wick in the special lightened J2 which Sydney Allard had built for his own use, in the new record time of 40.45s. Earlier, Gerry Ruddock, one of the season's most consistently successful sports car drivers, in one of the Monkey Stable's Harry Lester-built Lester-MGs broke the 1,500cc class record in 43.99s. This was the first time that sports car classes had been run in June in recent years, and the regulations were more liberal than they had been in previous August/September meetings.

The leading contenders then trecked North for Bo'ness and Rest-and-be-Thankful with the added incentive for select English and Scottish teams of an additional event at Bo'ness on the Monday evening after the Championship meeting, run specially for the benefit of BBC Television. There were surprises in store. On 27 June Dennis Poore's long-lived Bo'ness record was at last beaten – but not by Wharton, who missed it by 0.01s in the Cooper and 0.29s in the ERA. Man of the day was Ron Flockhart who handled R4D in a manner which would have done credit to Raymond Mays. The young Edinburgh driver became the toast of Scottish motor sport with a resounding 33.82s. The competition was close with Peter Reece on 34.82s, Greenall on 35.12s and Christie on 35.23s, but the day belonged to Flockhart. Bo'ness regular Jack Walton (37.80s) was fastest sports car driver in his quasi-racing Cooper-Bristol from the impressive visiting Ulsterman, Desmond Titterington, in the Allard J2.

The ingredients for the television meeting therefore could harldly be bettered and the excitement was palpable. Both Wharton and Flockhart went faster still, although times were unofficial and could not count for records. The Edinburgh driver flung the howling ERA through the Snake and up the final straight to clock 33.74s, but this time it was not enough. With the blown Cooper on top form, Wharton was faster still at 33.61s. It had been a highly significant weekend which left Wharton pondering over what *he* could do with R4D, even after so many years, and was a contributory factor to Mays's invitation to Flockhart to come South to join the BRM team in 1954.

After this, 'the Rest' was a total anti-climax. It rained heavily producing conditions which Flockhart found too bad to remain competitive in the twitching ERA and Wharton was even worse off. The Cooper's JAP engine broke a connecting rod and R11B also failed with transmission trouble. So it was

By 1953 Bouley Bay was almost a private preserve for Ken Wharton. Here he wrestles the Cooper-JAP to a 52.8s hill record.
via MIKE KETTLEWELL

Michael Christie's 1,107cc Cooper which emerged on top in 55.81s, two full seconds less than runner-up, Bill Sleeman. The promising Titterington, who achieved factory Jaguar, Vanwall, and even Mercedes-Benz drives during his brief career, secured a class win.

Ken Wharton had made Bouley Bay something of a private preserve and his Cooper-JAP was back on form to reduce his own record to 52.8s on 23 July, beating Christie by a second, and with Frank le Gallais heaving the big LGS-Jaguar through Bouley's many hairpins in 55.2s, faster than either Greenall or Sleeman. Yet another record fell to Wharton at Craigantlet where he faced no comparable opposition (Titterington was runner-up in the Sports Allard in 80.6s) and took just one run in his Cooper. It was enough to leave him a 10s margin with a 70.6s hill record.

The eager enthusiasts who made their way to Shelsley in August had an intriguing prospect before them. Ken Wharton was to do some 'demonstration' runs in the V16 BRM. In practice this shrieking, near-500 bhp machine left long black swathes of rubber on every getaway. Despite the lack of torque by hill climb standards, the phenomenal acceleration once the revs rose enabled the skilful Wharton to clock 37.97s despite the car's unfamiliarity with the course. Then, frustratingly, raceday was wet and it was like a rerun of the Stuck/Auto Union struggle of 1936, one of Shelsley's 'might-have-beens'. Records were out of the question on the soaking course but Wharton went as well as ever with his performance in R11B earning BTD for the ERA for once in 41.82s to the 42.56s which he recorded in the Cooper. 'Dick' Henderson showed that he was certainly not afraid of the wet conditions by beating Christie and an increasingly confident Tony Marsh for third place, while the winner of the 500cc class, Austen May, in his ex-Eric Brandon JAP-engined Cooper Mk 6 took full advantage of the conditions to finish sixth, little more than half a second slower than Marsh. Abecassis went one better than in June and his 45.01s climb was the best by a sports car.

A simply superb entry was received for the Prescott International meeting which turned into a nine-hour marathon. The Cooper works sent along a Cooper-JAP which was certainly the hardest-used car, being driven by Stirling Moss, Nancy Mitchell, John Cooper and Rivers Fletcher. Les Leston also

Wharton/Cooper/hill record. The familiar combination of factors was repeated at Craigantlet.
J. R. BAINBRIDGE
via MIKE KETTLEWELL

Prescott International 1953. Peter Stubberfield's much modified Bugatti T35B may not have been competitive with the top runners any longer, but this member of the team could be relied upon to give a dogged performance, with the benefit of four-paw-drive.
E. J. COOK

Peter Hughes, an Edinburgh-based Englishman, had a lot of success in 1954-55 in the Tojeiro-JAP sports car. This is at Bo'ness.
BILL HENDERSON

brought his Cooper twin; Moss, making a rare return to the hills, produced his hastily-built production chassis Cooper-Alta F2 car; Le Gallais brought the LGS over from Jersey; Peter Walker had both the R. R. C. Walker Connaught and a works Jaguar XK120C; former hill climb Champion Dennis Poore a works Aston Martin DB3S; and the International permit was justified by the presence of American-in-Europe Bob Said (OSCA Sports) and Frenchman Georges Trouis (DB–Panhard). But there was no Wharton. Ken was ill and the meeting was a triumph for Michael Christie who recorded 44.39s in his 1,107cc Cooper-JAP. Despite little recent practice at this sort of thing, Moss was runner-up in the works Cooper-JAP and third in his Cooper-Alta, running on potent nitro-methane fuel. It was close behind Christie for Moss's times of 46.35s and 46.48s only just bettered the 46.49s of an impressive le Gallais, 46.57s by Leston and 46.68s by Bill Sleeman. The 500 Perpetual Challenge Trophy, awarded on aggregate performances from the May and September meetings, was won by Austen May even though Boshier-Jones won the class, and a battle royal among the sports cars left Peter Walker on top with 49.69s but a splendid 50.06s by Shorne clubman Bill Coleman (ex-Parker Jaguette) bettered the times of even Dennis Poore and George Abecassis.

Rally driver Nancy Mitchell handled the Cooper-JAP with respect but her cautious 51.78s climb was enough to secure the Ladies' Award.

But absent or not, Ken Wharton was the Champion again and he had every intention of doing it again in 1954, and with this in mind he retained his faithful old Cooper of 1950 vintage but created great interest by buying R4D from Flockhart. Since both were to drive for BRM in 1954 Formule Libre races, the old ERA remained very much 'in the family', and careful preparation was put in hand. With this programme in view, Wharton relinquished his seat in Peter Bell's ERA. Bell added a new supercharged Cooper-JAP to his private stable and brought in Michael Christie to drive his cars in addition to his own unsupercharged Cooper-JAP. Rather surprisingly the Championship rounds remained unchanged. Surprisingly, because there had been fears the previous year that Rest-and-be-Thankful would be abandond by the RSAC when the existing lease ran out. However, despite the hill's doubtful economic viability, it remained on the calendar for 1954. It was the Silver Jubilee Year for the Bugatti Owners Club, and their fortunes had indeed improved since 1951. They were in a sound financial position and a successful debenture issue permitted the club to buy the freehold of Prescott.

It was a rather unusual year, very much a case of Wharton versus Christie, and with both drivers hopping from one car to another, with the potential on occasion of filling the top five palces between them. Wharton did not actually appear with the revitalised R4D until Shelsley in June. By then Christie had already struck a telling blow with a new course record for unsupercharged cars at the May Prescott National in 43.75s in his own Cooper-JAP, then 'doing a Wharton' and finishing runner-up to himself in Peter Bell's ERA. Tony Marsh, now with 1,100cc JAP engine, managed 45.17s for third, but only narrowly defeated Les Leston's record-breaking Cooper 500 (45.26s) and 'The Spirit of Prescott', the wonderful old Bugatti T35B of Peter Stubberfield (45.33s).

The week before Shelsley, in June, most of the leading runners competed at the BOC members meeting at Prescott, where conditions were very muddy. Dick Henderson again showed how good he was in the wet with a 49.13s BTD to beat Greenall, Marsh and Christie, with all four Coopers covered by less than a second. But Ken Wharton's return to the fray put everything firmly into perspective. Watched by a delighted Raymond Mays, who later had a run in his old car *sans* crash hat, the Champion guided R4D up the slopes of its spiritual home in a magnificent 36.58s, and the old ERA was once again the Shelsley Walsh record holder. Not to be outdone, the skilful Michael Christie snatched second BTD with a 37.50s climb in R11B, just 0.21s faster than an impressive Tony Marsh. The Kinver farmer was now running a conventional 1,100cc JAP in his old Cooper and did extremely well to beat both Wharton and Christie when they were Cooper-mounted.

But absent or not, Ken Wharton was the Champion again and he had every intention of doing it again in 1954, and with this in mind he retained his faithful old Cooper of 1950 vintage but created great interest by buying R4D from Flockhart. Since both were to drive for BRM in 1954 Formule Libre races, the old ERA remained very much 'in the family', and careful preparation was put in hand. With this programme in view, Wharton relinquished his seat in Peter Bell's ERA. Bell added a new supercharged Cooper-JAP to his private stable and brought in Michael Christie to drive his cars in addition to his own unsupercharged Cooper-JAP. Rather surprisingly the Championship rounds remained unchanged. Surprisingly, because there had been fears the previous year that Rest-and-be-Thankful would be abandond by the RSAC when the existing lease ran out. However, despite the hill's doubtful economic viability, it remained on the calendar for 1954. It was the Silver Jubilee Year for the Bugatti Owners Club, and their fortunes had indeed improved since 1951. They were in a sound financial position and a successful debenture issue permitted the club to buy the freehold of Prescott.

It was a rather unusual year, very much a case of Wharton versus Christie, and with both drivers hopping from one car to another, with the potential on occasion of filling the top five palces between them. Wharton did not actually appear with the revitalised R4D until Shelsley in June. By then Christie had already struck a telling blow with a new course record for unsupercharged cars at the May Prescott National in 43.75s in his own Cooper-JAP, then 'doing a Wharton' and finishing runner-up to himself in Peter Bell's ERA. Tony Marsh, now with 1,100cc JAP engine, managed 45.17s for third, but only narrowly defeated Les Leston's record-breaking Cooper 500 (45.26s) and 'The Spirit of Prescott', the wonderful old Bugatti T35B of Peter Stubberfield (45.33s).

The week before Shelsley, in June, most of the leading runners competed at the BOC members meeting at Prescott, where conditions were very muddy. Dick Henderson again showed how good he was in the wet with a 49.13s BTD to beat Greenall, Marsh and Christie, with all four Coopers covered by less than a second. But Ken Wharton's return to the fray put everything firmly into perspective. Watched by a delighted Raymond Mays, who later had a run in his old car *sans* crash hat, the Champion guided R4D up the slopes of its spiritual home in a magnificent 36.58s, and the old ERA was once again the Shelsley Walsh record holder. Not to be outdone, the skilful Michael Christie snatched second BTD with a 37.50s climb in R11B, just 0.21s faster than an impressive Tony Marsh. The Kinver farmer was now running a conventional 1,100cc JAP in his old Cooper and did extremely well to beat both Wharton and Christie when they were Cooper-mounted.

Ken Wharton was again in control at Bo'ness, although he was driving his Cooper when he reduced Flockhart's record down to 33.76s, and managed only 34.02s in R4D. Marsh again did well, beating Christie (R11B) and Greenall for third BTD. For the second year running, Rest-and-be-Thankful was rather a disappointment after the competition on the Kinneil Estate. The rain once again pelted down on the exposed slopes of Argyllshire, and Wharton was absent, racing at Rheims, in France. This left the field clear for Christie who was on top form and 'did a Wharton', lifting the top three places in his own Cooper (63.87s), Peter Bell's blown Cooper, and the ERA. Bil Sleeman was fastest of the opposition, heading the '500s' of Ninian Sanderson and Les Leston who, for the second successive meeting, was quicker with his Formula 3 Cooper than he was in his 1,100 twin.

With the remarkable exception of the two pre-war ERAs, hill climbing was truly the province of the cars from Surbiton, and the necessarily select entry at Bouley Bay, where Paddock space is at a premium and the road can be closed for only a limited period, included no fewer than 13 Coopers. Christie was there with his full complement of three cars whereas Wharton brought only his personally developed Cooper. It was enough, and a climb in 53.6s gave him his fifth successive BTD at Bouley. Christie was fastest in the ERA (54.0s) and tied for third place with Les Leston's well-driven Cooper 500.

Craigantlet had one of its better entries, totalling 57, and including both Wharton and Christie with two cars apiece. The day brought another hill record for Wharton and R4D in 70.1s, a second faster than Ken managed in his Cooper. Christie, on the other hand, had a poor day, non-starting the Bell Cooper after clouting a bank in practice and having to be content with third in his own car.

It is fairly rare for Shelsley to have two record-breaking days in one year but it certainly happened in 1954. Ken Wharton succeeded in bettering even the June mark in R4D, leaving the hill record at 35.80s. The Wharton/Christie domination monopolised the first five places overall, with the Haddenham engineer this time having a works Cooper twin at his disposal. He recorded 36.98s in this for second BTD, ahead of his ERA efforts. Bertie Bradnack was the next best driver, in 6th place! Records really tumbled for little Don Parker, driving his familiar maroon Kieft-Norton, lowered the 500cc time to 39.79s; Nancy Mitchell, now more confident in the Cooper-JAP twin, took the Ladies' Record in 41.07s; and the sports car best came down below 40s for the first time. Cyril Wick flung the Allard J2 through the Esses and up the finishing straight to clock a splendid 39.94s, but even this was not enough to ward off Anthony Crook in his supercharged Cooper-Bristol, a car which also ran in racing car events and was really more F2 than sports in spirit although it was a two-seater, which shattered the record in 39.06s. The 1,500cc sports car target was also lowered when Glasgow-based English journalist Peter Hughes did a 40.99s in the Tojeiro-JAP. Peter was having a tremendously successful season in the JAP twin-engined car which John Tojeiro had designed and built for Brian Lister and his protégé Archie Scott-Brown. The roughness and vibration of 'the big thumper' makes it hardly ideal for sports car use, but this lightweight machine was perfect to beat the predominantly MG-engined opposition of the time.

By the mid-nineteen-fifties the September International at Prescott was regarded as *the* hill climb of the year by many people, but the weather made a mess of the 1954 running; allowing the 500cc racing cars to have a dry run, and then the heavens opened before the more powerful cars ran. The supercharger broke on R4D, but even the Wharton/ERA combination would not have been enough to overcome the 500s' advantage. So it was a suprise BTD in 45.22s (a new class record), for Solihull's Austen May, who narrowly defeated his arch rivals Don Parker, Ivor Bueb (both on 45.66s) and the now Cooper-mounted David Boshier-Jones. A noted chronicler of the sport as well as a successful

David Boshier-Jones began his distinguished career with this 500cc Kieft, before switching to a Cooper in 1954.
via MIKE KETTLEWELL

competitor, C. A. N. May was always thoughtful about his sport which was conducted on a strictly limited budget. He remained faithful to well-prepared JAP engines (at less of an disadvantage in sprints than in circuit racing against the dohc Nortons), which in 1954 were prepared by Don Parker, and ran them in good secondhand Cooper chassis tended by Fred Fletcher, a Dellow employee.

Naturally, Wharton was Champion again, with 40 points to Christie's 36. Then there was a 14 point gap back to Les Leston, then Sleeman, Marsh and Greenall who had sold his Cooper to former N-type MG Magnette single-seater and Bugatti driver Rivers Fletcher before the end of the season.

Then as now it is all too easy to think of hill climbing in terms of the RAC National Championship, but of course this affected only a small number of competitors and six hills, even though this was the pinnacle of the sport. During the years of Wharton domination, new local hills appeared on the calendar and if interesting new single-seaters were thin on the ground, there was plenty of development in the sports car classes. Non-championship hills such as Trengwainton, Lydstep, Naish, Brunton and Barbon had a character all their own, even though only Lydstep attracted the big names during these years. It was at Lydstep in April 1952 that David Boshier-Jones, armed with a new green Kieft 500, made a highly spectacular début. On one climb he lost the lot near the finish and neatly snapped one of the poles holding the 'Finish' banner. Notwithstanding this, he achieved 3rd BTD on his other climb, bettered only by Guy Arengo and Jack Moor. In August, he set BTD and the 'Bosh' career was under way.

Some hills, including Trengwainton, Brunton and Barbon, were not licensed for racing cars, or else the organising clubs simply restricted their events to sports and touring machinery. Of late, Allards had done well on Trengwainton but in August 1952, the ever youthful Ashley Cleave set a splendid 26.28s BTD in CCV 952, his remarkable 1937-based Morris Special. He did it again too with a 26.02s BTD a year later and was rarely out of the top three on the Cornish hill, and a regular award winner elsewhere. There was nothing revolutionary about the mundane-looking Morris and its success was due to the owner's intimate knowledge of the car, and his meticulous preparation, enabling him to run with an astronomically high compression ratio, and to change up only when valve-bounce set in!

There was very little to cater for North-of-England hill climb enthusiasts at this time, but then nor had there been since the heady days of the early nineteen-twenties. Nevertheless, the Westmorland Motor Club gradually built up their once a year promotion at Barbon Manor (a motorcycle climb was also held each July) which, as the only speed event for cars in the locality, was quite a local occasion, with lively goings-on perpetrated before and after at the nearby Barbon Arms hotel which was very much 'hill climb HQ'. Barbon stories are legion but one of the best dates from the later nineteen-fifties when two well-known competitors were reported to be fighting in the adjacent churchyard in the early hours of the morning. Apparently someone's wife had been entertained by a gentleman who was not her husband and it was a case of 'gravestones at dawn'! On the hill itself, the local man Bryan Crabtree was consistently successful, beaten into third place in 1952 by Gillie Tyrer (35.8s) and Eric Lister's HRG, he bounced back to take another BTD in 1953 and was runner-up in 1954 to Ian Davidson's Cooper-MG which lowered the record to 34.07s. The WMC had the hill widened in parts that year and were able to accommodate 500cc racing cars for the first time. The class and third BTD fell to Cliff Allison, the son of a Brough, Westmorland garage propreitor, who was to go on to become a works Lotus and Ferrari Formula 1 driver.

Down in Wiltshire, the South Western Centre of the BARC ran meetings twice a year at Brunton, again limited to sports cars, and with Sessions' Healey, Wood's XK120 and the Cripps brothers – 'W.L.' and 'J.A.F.' – particularly successful in the early days. The Cripps campaigned a 5.3-litre Chrysler-engined Special which was very much in the Allard Special vein. Still down in the South West, the Bristol MC & LCC continued to run their regular events at Naish which by now at least had corners concreted. Few racing car drivers competed there but one who did and made a habit of winning BTD awards was Bristolian Wally Cuff, with a 500cc device known as 'Hell's Hammers V'. This started life as 'Buzzie II', an Iota-chassis car built by Jim Bosisto for the first big 500cc race at Silverstone in 1948.

Apart from the once a year Craigantlet and 'The Rest', the other Championship hills hosted club meetings during the year. The BOC made 1952 a year of innovation at Prescott and in July ran a major climb for 500cc cars only. This, the first such event anywhere, demonstrated the popularity of the little car and drew a good entry. To the surprise of some, BTD and a new 500cc record went to Les

Leston, a circuit racer who had not been a hill climb regular although he became one after this successful baptism. In fact, the extrovert Londoner who was to become a highly successful dealer in car accessories took the meeting very seriously. He was driving a specially lightened Cooper-Norton owned by Derek Wybourn and adopted a rather frighteningly high revving technique which rewarded him with a 45.27s record, almost a second faster than Stirling Moss who had been lent Derek Annable's Kieft at short notice after his own had been damaged the day before at Fairwood in Wales. Clive Lones had to have fifteen stitches in his head after an accident in 'Tiger Kitten' at the Semicircle during practice. The meeting went off well but there were complaints that the crackle of the 500s did become more than a trifle monotonous and, of course, there was no scope for an entry of the normal Prescott proportions, so the experiment was not repeated. Instead, the Perpetual Challenge Trophy won by Leston was in future awarded to the 500cc driver who put up the best aggregate time at the major May and September meetings, being won by Austen May and Ivor Bueb in the next two years.

More 'clubbie' in character, the Inter-Club meeting was instigated in the same year and run for the first time on 10 August. The idea was for clubs to enter three car teams who would be given handicap 'bogey' times on the strength of individual runs in the morning for class awards. Then, during the team runs the timing would start as the first car in the team got away and stopped only when the third car finished. Best improvement on 'bogey' time to win. Human nature being what it is there was a fair amount of 'sandbagging' in the morning runs in order to obtain a favourable handicap. Disqualification was not unknown in extreme cases! The first winners were the Nottingham Sports Car Club, led by the impeccably-turned-out Bugatti-Ford V8 of Edward Greenall and backed up by Ryder's Cooper-MG and Kenyon's Frazer Nash-BMW. Individual Best Time was set up by Peter Stubberfield.

The MAC were entitled to use Shelsley on three weekends during the year and they opted for something altogether more informal than their big meetings for the third promotion, which was deliberately aimed at the people who would not normally be catered for at the other climbs. In 1952 a hill climb was combined with a gymkhana, although the former attracted the most attention and was won by rally driver Denis O'Mara Taylor (Jaguar XK120). One journalist who should have known better totally misunderstood the purpose of the meeting and thought that it was indicative of the sad decline in the popularity of hill climbing.

Each year there were a couple of 'local' meetings at Bouley Bay where the entry of road cars and sand-racing specials tended to be trounced by Syd Logan, and then by Frank le Gallais with their Championship class cars. Similarly, the SSCC ran two club meetings at Bo'ness towards the beginning and at the end of the season where Jack Walton, first in Frazer Nash Le Mans Replica and then in

The innovative 500s only meeting at Prescott in 1952 tempted Stirling Moss to a hill climb in a Kieft, which he had borrowed from Derek Annable.
MURRAY HARDY
via RIVERS FLETCHER

Cooper-Bristol was difficult to beat. Scotland being rich in engineering skills it comes as no surprise that many well-made 'one-offs' did well in the Scottish events at a time when Scottish motor sport was going through something of a boom. There were the two Alexander Specials, one with a substantial 'Forth Bridge'-type chassis and twin Shorrocks-blown Ford V8 engine, and the other a light supercharged Ford 8-engined machine; Alex Reid's 100 bhp, 12½ cwt Omega, based on a Type 55 BMW; Peter Hughes's Axis with BMW chassis and Lancia Aprilia engine; Ian Hopper's three well-made if rather heavy Hopper Specials culminating in a scaled-up JP tubular chassis with wishbone/leaf spring independent suspension and fitted with a 1,496cc 'dirt track' Lea Francis engine and most attractive bodywork; John McCubbin's amalgam of BMW Type 55 and 328 parts christened 'Jackal'; Jamie Gibbon's 'Girastro' and Rover Special utilisations of mainly Rover P3 and Land Rover parts; Jack Fisher's Riley Sprite-engined Fiat 500-based Fisher Special; and Nigel Kennedy's 'Burdmonk' – Buckler chassis and Buckler-modified Ford suspension and gearbox with linered down Morris 10 engine – to name but the most successful. Special building was certainly not dead, even though few were building single-seater specials for hill climbing.

Over in Ireland there were usually about ten hill climbs per year although only Craigantlet in Ulster impinged on the mainstream of British hill climbing. All the hills were public roads closed once a year for the occasion and entry lists rarely totalled more than 40 to 50. The wide variety of competing cars meant that handicap classes were at least as numerous as the scratch categories and although fast single-seaters and sports cars were not unknown in Ireland few events seemed able to attract them all at the same time. On the other hand hills such as Corkscrew Hill, Lisdoonvarna; Syonfin (Omagh); Spelga (Newry); Knockagh (Ulster) and the 1.7 mile Dungarvan (Tipperary) in particular were longer than most of the British climbs and were challenging courses. In 1952 Hector Graham's 1098 Cooper-JAP (the only one of its type in Ireland) and the Cooper-ish Leprechaun of Redmond Gallagher shared much of the honour although Chris Lindsay's amazing Nufor, an MG TC-eingined Ford Special; Geoff McCrea's old R-type MG; and Noel Hillis's ex-Joe Kelly Maserati 6C were prominent. The following year Bobby Baird came to the fore, first with his Baird-Gryphon (or Griffin, or Griffen – even the owner couldn't make up his mind about the spelling!) which was based on an ex-Parnell Maserati 4CLT, and then his up-to-the-minute Ferrari 225S, and Desmond Titterington began to make his name with the Allard. The latter went from strength to strength in 1953 when only Gallagher provided effective regular opposition. With entries tending to be fairly inconsistent, such widely contrasting cars as Charles Eyre-Maunsell's single-seater HRG Special, Dickie Lovell-Butt's old supercharged MG K3 and Dickie Odlum's single-seater Formula 2 Frazer Nash featured among the principal award winners. By 1954, Syd Durbridge had taken over the Gryphon (Baird was killed in an accident at Snetterton in July 1953) but the most dramatic cars on the Irish hills were the two 500cc Norton-engined Mc-Candless Specials of Belfast engineers Rex and Cromie McCandless and Lawrie McGladery, which featured four-wheel-drive, all-enveloping bodywork and, in the case of the first car which the

Rest-and-be-Thankful could be very bleak. Jimmy Gibbon approaches the finish in his Rover Special (minus rear bodywork on this occasion), which utilised mainly Rover P3 and Land-Rover components.
BILL HENDERSON

A late flowering of 'the flying bedstead school of chassis design', the Farley Special was a formidable competitor in Chris Summers' hands – whilst all the drive-chains stayed attached.
via RIVERS FLETCHER

No South Western meeting seemed complete without Ashley Cleave's deceptively mundane-looking Morris Special. This remarkable car was capable of class wins into the nineteen-sixties. This picture was taken at Prescott in 1959.
CHARLES DUNN *via* RIVERS FLETCHER

Ken Wharton had a new Cooper for 1956, but the title went to Marsh again.
via MIKE KETTLEWELL

By 1955 former MG and Bugatti driver, Rivers Fletcher, was a BTD contender with a smart Cooper-JAP. Here he takes his characteristic high line round Great Auclum's celebrated banking.
ANTHONY HOLLISTER *via* RIVERS FLETCHER

McCandless's brought over to Goodwood, handlebar steering. These highly original machines secured many successes.

Back in England, the popular Great Auclum event, still regarded by some as a sprint rather than a hill climb, had to be cancelled in 1952 because of a foot-and-mouth disease outbreak in the area, but was back with renewed support the following year. The Home Counties were rich in competitors, actual or potential, but being populous and not very hilly, rather short on venues, so when the Herts County Auto and Aero Club (formerly organisers at Aston Hill) announced their intention of promoting an event at Westbrook Hay, off the A41 road between Berkhamstead and Hemel Hempstead, on 3 October 1953, interest was considerable. By comparison with the 'classic' hills this 500 yards dash, only slightly uphill and with but one corner – a long left hander – was nothing special. Nevertheless, the entry was excellent and Michael Christie set the initial target in 20.76s, to beat Jerseyman Bill Knight and Peter Stubberfield.

There were four additions of significance to the venues in use in 1954: Castel Farm; Stapleford; Catterick and Leighton Hall. The South Wale Automobile Club began running three sports cars only meetings per year at Castel Farm, Llangynydd, near Bridgend. Basically, a farm track and both narrow and rough, Castel Farm Hill was neither long nor steep but provided good sport with a misty inaugural meeting ending with BTD to Jack Williamson's Vintage Bentley in 24.5s. Stapleford was another marginal case between a sprint and a hill climb and was West Essex Car Club territory,

although the Romford Enthusiasts Car Club soon began to run small meetings there in addition. The 'hill' was in fact part of the perimeter track of Stapleford Tawney airfield, near Abridge in Essex, and boasted a maximum gradient (briefly) of 1 in 10. The road was wide, the timed distance a respectable 1,320 yards and the corners fast. Best of all Stapleford was only 14 miles from Central London and a big entry was received for the first meeting, especially from the circuit racers who found the nature of the track very familiar. And it was primarily a *racing* driver who set BTD for that honour fell to Les Leston (driving Freddie Sowrey's Cooper-JAP Mk 6) in 46.52s, from Rivers Fletcher in the ex-Greenall Cooper and Roy Salvadori in Sidney Greene's Gilby Engineering Maserati A6GCS sports car.

The two new Northern venues were different again. The Association of North Eastern Combined Car Clubs secured the use of a rather challenging half mile stretch of concrete surfaced road, with a decent gradient and enough corners to tax the sporting driver, bang in the middle of Catterick Army Camp in Yorkshire. Although the first meeting, won by Jim Blumer's Jaguar, was rather low key, the course became very popular and was to play an important role in rekindling hill climb interest in the area. Leighton Hall was not too demanding although the braking area after the finish was barely enough for the faster cars. This Morecambe Car Club event was set in attractive parkland and the course was in fact the main drive to a nineteenth-century mansion near Carnforth, Lancashire. The hill can best be summarised as a gentle, slightly uphill, right-hand curve with a bump at the crest of the gradient. Held initially in September, Leighton Hall later came forward to be held the day after nearby Barbon which guaranteed it a good entry and made for an enjoyable weekend in the North West.

Naturally, the mainstay of these increasingly numerous smaller meetings was the sports car contingent which was augmented in 1953/54 by the many Triumph TR2s, Austin Healeys, MG TDs and TFs, Jaguar XK120s and the less numerous sports cars from such as Jowett, HRG and Swallow Doretti which were now available. Then there were the small, light, competition-type cars which invariably had elements of Ford 10 or MG in their make-up: the Dellow, the tubular chassised creations of Derek Buckler, the first 1172 Ford and MG-engined Lotus Mk 6 kits from Colin Chapman's little Hornsey concern; the usually MG-engined Coopers which were closely related to the single-seaters in the chassis department, and the successful Lester-MGs among them. The descendents of the epochal BMW 328 ranging from Tyrer's very special 1940 Brescia car and Ron Willis's much stripped and lightened 328 through to the modern Frazer Nashes and Cooper-Bristols generally held sway in the medium-sized classes where sports-racing cars were permitted. Exceptions were the 1950-type dual purpose F2/Sports HWM-Altas which Oscar Moore and Scots-domiciled Englishman Ray Fielding campaigned with success. Among the large capacity sports racers, there were still plenty of Allards and American-engined hybrids such as the Cripps Special, and the Mercury-engined HRG of Birmingham builder Alec Francis, but the growing availability of the excellent Jaguar XK engine, without the heavy and poorly-braked XK120 chassis attached, did not go unheeded. Quick off the mark were: Oscar Moore, who fitted one to his HWM and later bored the engine out to 3.8-litres long before the factory got on to the idea and erstwhile XK120 driver Phillip Scragg, whose Alta-Jaguar RPG 418 was nothing more than a professional H. W. Motors rebuild of George Abecassis's 1949 Alta Grand Prix car, with Jaguar engine and attractive cycle-winged bodywork. Kentish special builder Gordon Parker sold his Jaguette to near neighbour Bill Coleman and used a Buckler chassis as the basis for a very stark, supercharged XK-engined special which he called 'Jaguara' and which, although intended primarily to attack the sports car record at Brighton (where it was eventually most successful), was regularly campaigned on the hills.

Many of the outstanding sports car achievements at the bigger meetings have been noted but 1954 brought a veritable crop of noteworthy performances which should not be forgotten such as: Maurice Wick's successive reduction of the Brunton record to 25.19s then 24.75s in the lightened Allard he shared with his brother Cyril; David Watts's new Trengwainton record (25.57s) in Tom Kyffin's ex-Bob Chase, full-width-bodied Cooper-Bristol; Phil Scragg's reduction of the Prescott class record in May to 47.63s in the Alta-Jaguar which he had sold and then bought back again; Mike Anthony's 49.42s time at the same meeting in his Lotus-MG Mk 6; Peter Hughes's fabulous 47.83s climb in the Tojeiro-MG at Prescott in September; and one 'might-have-been'. Masten Gregory, from Kansas City, decided to take in the Prescott International on a European tour with his brutally powerful 4.5-litre V12 Ferrari 375. Despite total unfamiliarity with the course, this future Grand Prix driver whose

'Les Bugaires', Mike Hattson and Peter Gaskell chat to Jim Berry and Ted Robbins at Shelsley.
via PETER GASKELL

Phil Chapman's rather handsome Chapman-Mercury Mk3 on Stone Bridge at Rest-and-be-Thankful.
BILL HENDERSON

One of the nineteen-fifties' great enthusiasts, Peter Stubberfield, makes a point to David Vickers-Jones (left) and an apparently less attentive Peter Gaskell.
via PETER GASKELL

A routine BTD for Tony Marsh on 'The Rest' in 1957.
BILL HENDERSON

slight build and mild-mannered appearance belied his skill and raw courage, was into the 46s bracket in practice despite diving through Allard's Gap on one run. Alas, the rains came and the slithering, wheel-spinning Ferrari had to give best in its class to the positively agricultural HRG-Mercury of Alec Francis, with 53.11s to 52.77s.

Tony Marsh emerges

Although Ken Wharton's extensive racing comitments were tending to impinge on his hill climbing activities, there was little to suggest a fundamental change in the pattern of the previous few years as the 1955 season approached. True, the 23 year old Marsh, distinctive in his rather old-fashioned look-ing motorcycle-pattern crash helmet, and already setting Best Times at minor meetings (including both Lydstep climbs) in 1954, looked an increasingly formidable proposition with his new, unblown, 1098cc Cooper-JAP Mk 8 to augment his old ex-Collins chassis which had been running with a super-charged motor, but there seemed a long way to go to unseat the Champion. The Christie/Bell opposi-tion was to be strengthened by a weight-saving campaign by George Boyle on the old ERA R11B, while off-season movements among the 'Co-operators' included new 500s for Boshier-Jones (a brand new Mk 9 with Robin Jackson twin plug head-equipped Norton engine) and Austen May (a second-hand Mk 8); an ex-Greenall Cooper-JAP for Dick Henderson, who sold his older car to Ray Adcock; and an ex-Guy Arengo Cooper passing to Reg Phillips of Sheffield. 'Smiling' Reg Phillips was (and happily still is) one of hill climbing's most cheerful and truly sporting competitors. Like several of his generation, he had discovered hill climbing after years of successful trials competition, where he reckons to have been one of the first, if not the very first, to hit on the idea of using the Ford 8/10 sidevalve engine in a really light chassis circa 1940. A director of Fairley Steels, from which the name of his creations derived – and not because they were 'fairly fast' as witty commentators were apt to suggest – Reg had obtained a lot of fun from a Ford V8-engined special which he reckoned to have knocked together in 10 days for the princely sum of £80. He even kept smiling when this crude device shed a wheel at Prescott on one occasion. Despite the purchase of the Cooper, the Fairley Special was developed (if that is the correct word in the context!) and was fitted with a more powerful Mercury engine.

Meanwhile Dr John Farley proposed to take on the Coopers at their own game with a rear-mounted

996cc JAP-engined device which was very much in the old Shelsley Special tradition. The addition of two chain-driven superchargers suggested no lack of power but the chassis, which was adorned with negligible bodywork, was unashamedly of the 'flying bedstead' school. The intrepid driver, in hill climbs at least, was to be the rather incongruously burly Midlander Chris Summers, who soon began to produce some good results whenever the Farley could be restrained from casting one or more of its plethora of drive chains around the landscape.

But the year, which was also the Golden Jubilee Year for Shelsley Walsh, did not go according to plan. Ken Wharton was quite badly burned when his Grand Prix Vanwall crashed and caught fire at Silverstone in May, so was absent until Bouley Bay. The serious part of the season began over 21-22 May with Westbrook Hay and Prescott forming a double-header. The former course had been lengthened by 150 yards the previous year, to bring in a tight, blind right-hander just before the finish, and Marsh had beaten Christie to a 25.59s record. This time, Rivers Fletcher ran Marsh the closest although the Kinver driver was slower than in 1954 at 26.01s. The following day there was a surprise when the Barnet enthusiast managed to put together one of those runs which *just* stayed the right side of disaster for a 45.08s BTD, a mere four-hundredths faster than Christie in the revamped R11B (the blown Bell Cooper was sidlined with a timing defect), with Marsh a close third. Tony Everard was officially the fastest sports car driver with a 48.66s time in the Vermin Stable's ex-works Aston Martin DB3S/3, but a major talking point was the amazing 48.04s 'demonstration' run by Cooper factory driver Ivor Bueb in the latest central-seater sports Cooper, with rear-mounted 1100cc Coventry-Climax FWA engine. A new generation of small, lightweight sports-racers, derived from pure racing practice, had arrived and on the tight confines of British hills were an instant match for the most powerful sports machinery.

Poor weather blighted the MAC's opening Shelsley promotion which gave first blood to Marsh from Christie (R11B) and Henderson, while a last minute cancellation removed Bo'ness from the Championship. As in April 1952 at Shelsley, the problem was too few entries at the closing date, with a flood of competitors a few days later, although sadly, Bo'ness was to disappear from the calendar for several years. So, the only Scottish Championship climb was 'The Rest' and it was very much a Marsh-versus-Christie occasion. The record stayed intact but it was the former's day, winning with the older supercharged Cooper (56.12s) from his newer car (56.90s), and with Christie taking the next two places.

Despite still having his arms swathed in bandages, Wharton returned at Bouley Bay, and kept his incredible unbeaten run at the Jersey hill intact with a 53.0s climb in his old Cooper to deafeat the on-form Marsh by 0.4s, and le Gallais by another second. Tying with Christie (blown Cooper) for fourth place was Wharton again, but this time in Bell's ERA R11B once more. Christie had lost this particular drive because R11B had been in dire need of an apparently impossible-to-obtain ZF differential. Whereupon, Wharton had come forard with the essential part from R4D which he was prepared to lend to Peter Bell as long as he drove the car, since Wharton had not had the chance to re-prepare R4D! Michael Christie took this very sportingly, although one feels that Bouley Bay was not one of his happier meetings. Unfortunately, it was unhappy for an infinitely more serious reason. After missing his first climb because of mechanical trouble, Bill Sleeman, 4th in the 1954 Championship, overturned before Les Platons corner and was killed. The balance of the meeting was abandoned, although one record which did fall in in 59.0s was the sports car time, secured by Edward Greenall who was now at the wheel of a Cooper-Bristol (a converted ex-Ecurie Ecosse F2 car).

Marsh decided to go to Great Auclum (where he broke the course record in 20.94s to beat Rivers Fletcher) rather than Craigantlet, where Wharton had to withdraw his old Cooper with engine problems but had no difficulty in beating Rex McCandless's ingenious '500' with R11B.

The MAC had better luck for their Golden Jubilee Climb and drew a fine entry which included Leslie Marr's new Grand Prix B-type Connaught which, running without its vulnerable all-enveloping body, won its class in 39.20s but was no match for the hill climb regulars. Times were down on 1954 but young Tony Marsh, always the epitome of neat precision on the course, recorded a splendid 36.08s which was that vital seven-hundredths of a second up on Ken Wharton, who was back at the wheel of a re-fettled R4D. The Smethwick maestro was third in his Cooper, but Michael Christie, having a rather disappointing year, was well down, beaten also by Cooper-mounted Jerseyman, Bill Knight.

This year, the Championship went right to the final round and it all hung on Prescott. Even the excellent sports car times from Phil Scragg (47.40), Peter Hughes (47.74) and Gorden Parker (47.82) were rather overlooked, when the weather played exactly the same dirty trick which it had done in 1954, and for the second successive year BTD went to a '500'. This time the winner was David Boshier-Jones in 44.45s a 500cc record which remained unbeaten in 1960. John Broad, who had been doing great things with the old ERA R5B 'Remus' which he had bought earlier in the year, was runner-up from 500 Challenge Trophy winner Bueb, and Michael Christie in Rob Walker's new B-type open-wheeled GP Connaught. It was all rather unsatisfactory with the main Championship aspirants, Marsh and Wharton, left tied on points. The RAC's Championship rules stated that a Championship tie would be resolved in the favour of what the RAC termed 'the most meritorious performance'. This invidious decision went in favour of Marsh – the youngest Champion yet – although Wharton's fight back after his Silverstone burns must have been hard to overlook.

Both Wharton and Christie invested in new Coopers for 1956, although Peter Bell had withdrawn from the scene. Wharton was employing a 1,099cc supercharged JAP engine while Christie had pinned his faith in paring the weight of his new car down to the absolute limit. Dick Henderson was now the owner of the distinctive-looking ex-Bradnack supercharged Cooper, the one with the 'power bulge', while Hay-on-Wye's George Keylock made his first appearance with an old ex-Charles Mortimer chassis and Dick James joined the ranks of the leading 500cc aspirants with a Mk9 Cooper which had been Colin Davis's circuit racing car. The amazingly competitive old ERAs still had a strong following, for apart from the cars of Wharton and Broad three more were expected to run in the hands of newcomers to the Bourne cars. Midlands-domiciled Scot, Jimmy Stuart had bought Bob Gerard's very succesful ex-Wakefield R14B, Bill Moss the original R1A, and Maidenhead dairy foods company director David Good, R1B. Despite restrictions on licenses imposed by the RAC, and some wariness by race organisers, a number of drivers achieved success during the late 'forties' and 'fifties' notwithstanding daunting physical disabilities. Archie Scott-Brown, Alan Stacey, Sidney Greene and Jim Lafone are four such, but David Good rapidly earned the respect, not to say awe, of the hill climb crowd with the way he contrived to steady the wheel of his cars with the unformed stump of his right arm while gear-changing with his left hand.

Not likely to upset the Championship standings, but very much in the old spirit of the hill climb special was a daunting contraption driven by a mysterious 'T Dryvver'. Called the De Havilland-ATN, this featured a 6½-litre De Havilland Gypsy Major aero engine shoehorned in, of all things, a Q-type MG chassis, and driving through a back-to-front Alvis Silver Eagle clutch and Ford V8 gearbox to the original MG final drive (yes the transmission was inadequate and cried 'enough' on 'The Rest'!). 'T Dryvver' turned out to be former Mephistophelgatti driver Tom Norton, who temporarily adopted this pseudonym to circumvent parental disapproval of his activities. They may have had a point!

In an intelligent effort to bring on more newcomers to the sport the MAC introduced their new Junior Hill Climb and Sprint Championship, to be contested at various restricted meetings which extended beyond the RAC Championship counters. The series was won by ERA driver Jimmy Stuart, from Coventry tobacconist Dick James and sports car driver John Rudd, who scored many successes in his ex-Tony Crook Frazer Nash Le Mans Replica.

A close battle between Marsh, Wharton and Christie seemed in prospect for the main Championship but before the 'circus' gathered at Prescott in May (still not an RAC round) there was considerable regret at the deaths of the highly successful Harrogate sports car driver, Jack Walton, after a long illness; Peter Hughes (killed in a road accident) and Duncan Hely, the man who had first 'spotted' Tony Brooks, and who also died in a road crash.

Prescott opened up intriguing prospects for Christie's new Cooper helped the Alexander Engineering boss to a new course record in 43.65s, 0.1s less than Marsh in his unblown Cooper and half a second up on Wharton's newer Cooper. Could the sporting Christie yet be Champion? Prescott is a great leveller and the fierce struggle for '500' honours, unabated on the hills even if past its peak on the circuits, had the times in the 45s bracket, and it was *very* close. The order: 'Bosh' (45.52) – Bueb (45.63) – Henry Taylor (45.74). All three were fractionally faster than the winner of the Formula 1 class, Ray Fielding from Forres in Paul Emery's 2.5 Alta-engined Emeryson. Ray's regular car at this time was the 1953 HWM-Jaguar, formerly HWM 1, but his 45.77s time on his first climb (he overdid things and went bank storming on his second climb) beat both owner Paul Emery (46.45s) and the evergreen Casear Special which 'Doc' Taylor was now coaxing up Prescott in the 48s bracket. Since the previous year, this great crowd favourite had boasted a gravity-feed fuel tank perched on a framework above the bonnet and retained its silver-painted front tyre sidewalls which the owner reckoned cut the timing beam with greater precision. This was long before anyone hit on the idea of mounting a vertical strut on the front of cars for this purpose. Ivor Bueb had issued a clear warning to the sports car brigade the previous year and this time even Gordon Parker's 47.16s in the Jaguara was not enough to match the 47.12s from the little 1100 Cooper of Tom Sopwith, son of aircraft industry pioneer and yachtsman, Sir Thomas Sopwith, and with Tony Marsh recording 47.31s in his Cooper.

Organisers would have liked to run their major meetings on Sundays when the crowd potential was greater, but in 1956 there was a lot of trouble from the Lord's Day Observance Society, so when the MAC also suffered rain for their June Saturday, the meeting made a thumping loss. Records were out of the question but Wharton slithered R4D to the top faster than anyone else (40.91s) although Christie managed to split the ERA from Ken's Cooper, with Champion Marsh down in fourth and fifth places ahead of wet-weather expert Dick Henderson. During a rather soggy day, John Broad crashed 'Remus', Pauline Brock (sharing Jackie Welton's Cooper 500 as usual) overturned, and a special class for competitors in the *Autosport* Production Sports Car Championship encouraged Ken Rudd to run with his all independently suspended Ruddspeed AC Ace and he was faster in the wet then all the sports-racers bar Tony Marsh's Cooper-Climax.

The following day, the BOC Members meeting at Prescott had the Champion back on top with a vengeance. He broke the outright course record in 43.32s (Christie also climbed under his May figure in 43.58s) and added the sports car record with a demoralising 46.49s in the Cooper-Climax, thus landing a remarkable double. Incidentally, admission to this meeting had to be free because of the activities of the LDOS. Rest-and-be-Thankful received a rather small entry but the competition was hot with Marsh emphasising his Championship form with a new 53.75s record, over a second and a half up on Christie, and with Wharton third in R4D. As was becoming a habit, Marsh also took sports car honours. His little Cooper-Climax was very much the car to beat, for a week earlier he had actually set BTD at the MAC's 'club' Shelsley (no longer combined with a gymkhana) in 38.8s – a phenomenal time.

Tony was beginning to look unbeatable, for he scored another double record at Westbrook Hay (25.05s/26.80s) before arriving for Bouley Bay the next day. But the Jersey hill was still Wharton's own private preserve and, driving his newer Cooper, Ken set his seventh successive BTD in a new record of 52.6s, but with Marsh and Christie tying for runner-up slot a mere 0.2s slower. Close. Le Gallair clocked a splendid 54.0s to keep the locals happy, which was faster than Wharton's old Cooper and Henderson, while Marsh's astounding 56.2s Cooper-Climax time was set in a racing class so the sports car honours went to Edward Greenall (58.4s) who had bought a Lotus-Climax 11.

Yet another double record (20.60s/21.62s) fell to Marsh at Great Auclum, but Craigantlet was definitely low key, and wet. Wharton arrived late and was not allowed to practice with his Cooper as he had used up both his allotted climbs familiarising himself with the tricky conditions in R4D. Amid uncustomary sourness, the Smethwick driver withdrew altogether, allowing Malcolm Templeton (Lotus 11) a hollow win for Ulster.

Conditions were not ideal at Shelsley in August either, but Marsh did it again with a 36.02s BTD and a 39.34s sports car best, and Wharton (Cooper-mounted) ascended faster than either Christie or Henderson.

Wharton set himself up for the September Prescott with his third successive win and a new 23.34s course record in the Brighton Speed Trials, although Rob Walker, enjoying his annual drive in his GP Connaught was only 0.06s slower and the same car – much to the intial disapproval of Chief Mechanic Alf Francis – was lent to Patsy Burt, a daughter of motor sporting parents (father Eric Burt was a great Frazer Nash enthusiast while Patsy's mother was a nominee director of the company, as Eric was debarred from being one because of his Directorship of the Mowlem construction company). Patsy Burt had been "horse mad" and had only got involved with motor sport in 1953, competing in all kinds of sprints and rallies for Standard-Triumph. As time went on she concentrated rather more on hill climbs, at home and abroad, and before long was to stand out from all other women competitors by her sheer competitiveness.

The gate was well down at the Saturday International Prescott and Marsh clinched his second Championship although his 44.98s time was beaten by Christie in 44.45s. The Haddenham driver did really well for he annexed third BTD in Walker's Connaught (45.20s) while Rivers Fletcher vanquished a seemingly disheartened Wharton. Marsh beat Greenall for sports car honours, and in winning the 500cc class, Austen May won the Challenge Trophy once more.

International relations once again impinged on hill climbing, and indeed on a lot of other things, over the winter of 1956/57, for this was the time of the Suez Crisis, and petrol rationing made its unwelcome return. The major British motor racing events *were* allowed to take place and the fuel embargo was dropped in May, but the MAC cancelled the June Shelsley at an early stage while meetings at Brunton, Lydstep, Trengwainton, and Castel Farm were other casualties. There was racing in the Antipodes over the winter and it was in New Zealand that one of the greatest British post-War motor sporting careers ended when Ken Wharton was killed in his sports Ferrari. During the last couple of years, conflicting commitments had perhaps tended to take the edge off Ken's car preparation and even his finely-honed driving skills, but he remained *the* great all-rounder. His stable of cars was bought by Tom Norton.

This great loss left the Championship, which the RAC declared would be held as long as four rounds were run, likely to become a straight fight between Marsh and the 'eternal bridesmaid' Christie, Nevertheless, after several years of success in the 500cc category, the wiry Welshman David Boshier-Jones looked like posing a threat since he had installed an R. R. Jackson-built 1,098cc JAP in his existing Cooper. David Good too had joined the ranks of the 'big bangers' with the ex-works/Arthur Owen/Bill Knight Cooper, while earlier Coopers had been bought by Peter 'Taffy' Cottrell and the erstwhile Bugatti drivers ('Les Bugaires') Peter Gaskell and Mike Hatton. Cheltenham health visitor Pauline Brock looked like scoring well for the ladies in Jackie Welton's Cooper 500, but she would face strong opposition from Patsy Burt who had bought the ex-Les Leston Cooper-Climax sports, which was to be turned out in the now customary smart pale blue Burt colours. On the special building front, Reg Phillips sprang a surprise when his old Cooper re-emerged with a 1,460cc sohc Coventry Climax FWB engine mounted transversely in the back and driving via chains to the rear wheels. This latest Fairley Special was rapidly dubbed 'the mobile generating station', and ran without a radiator. Very different was a new and stark sports car from another inveterate special builder from Sheffield, Phil Chapman. This, the Chapman-Mercury Mk3, comprised a tubular frame, MG TD front suspension, home brewed de Dion rear end, a 4.2-litre Mercury V8 engine nestling under an imposing array of eight Amal carburettors, and a smart all-enveloping body. Although not a match for Phil Scragg's latest HWM-Jaguar, which had débuted the previous year, the Chapman-Mercury was destined for a long and successful career. Scragg's HWM, registered SPC 982, was purpose-built at the HWM works and was the last of the HWM-Jaguar sports cars. Rather advanced wishbone suspension geometry at the front, extra wide 6½-inch Borrani wheels, a dry-sumped D-type Jaguar engine, and Scragg's favourite cycle-winged-type bodywork – easier to 'place' on the hills than the more aerodynamic all-enveloping type – all featured on this car which was a real step forward from the similarly conceived RPG 418.

With no June Shelsley, the May Prescott meeting was to count for the RAC Championship for the first time, but a greater innovation was the introduction of separate runs for competitors entered in the Championship. These were to take place between the normal first and second class runs and all Championship points would be scored only on these separate climbs. Conversely, class records beaten during these 'extra' runs for the competitors concerned would not count as official. The objective was not to provide a Championship climax to the meeting, as is the case today, but to ensure that all Championship contenders were faced with as nearly similar track conditions as possible, thus ruling out the sort of anomaly which occurred at Prescott in 1954 and 1955.

It was on on of the extra Championship runs at Prescott that Tony Marsh, the defending Champion, smashed the hill record by almost a whole second, leaving it at a resounding 42.33s. Michael Christie also beat the previous record, not in the familiar lightweight Cooper-JAP, but in Rob Walker's early 1,460cc Coventry-Climax FWB-engined Formula 2 Cooper. This, one of the first cars built to conform with the new 1500cc Formula 2 category which came into effect in 1957, was clearly on a par with the well-tried Cooper-JAPs. But it was a car designed primarily for longer-distance circuit races and although an essentially simple design when compared to Ferrari and Porsche opposition, it was

nevertheless far more expensive to buy than a Cooper-JAP, and was only at the very beginning of its development. David Boshier-Jones – already making a favourable impression with the twin-cylinder engine – and Dick Henderson took the minor places while Pauline Brock began a highly successful season by breaking the Ladies' record in 46.77s. The nimble sports cars of the new generation showed well with a remarkable 46.46s record to Michael Andrew's Coventry-Climax-engined Lotus Mk6, a 46.90s climb from Edward Lewis, purveyor of Westover driving shoes, in a Lotus-Climax 11 and a 46.84s class record to Bill Bradley's Lister-Bristol. Phil Scragg's powerful HWM-Jaguar also left with a new class record but his 46.70s climb was not enough to beat Andrew.

The next major meeting (as there was no June Shelsley) was up in Scotland at 'The Rest' on 29 June, but in the meantime most of the leading runners had paid a return visit to Prescott for the BOC Members' meeting where Christie, now back in his immaculate Cooper-JAP, put one over on Marsh, George Keylock and Jimmy Stuart (now in the ex-Gerard Cooper-Bristol) for a 43.70s BTD. At this time the BOC were taking a hard look at the banking on the inside of the Esses, for a fatality had marred the May meeting – Lord Ebury, in his recently-purchased C-type Jaguar, lost it and overturned when the banking acted as a launching ramp. This sad loss led to the bank being cut away for safety's sake and the edge of the course delineated by marker cones. Dick James, despite his inexperience in a Cooper, won the 500cc class in June but in coming second Pauline Brock again broke her Ladies' Record, leaving it at 46.48s.

It was damp on Rest-and-be-Thankful and a fairly unremarkable meeting saw Marsh on top (56.31s) from Christie and Boshier-Jones. By this time Marsh had bought a Formula 2 Cooper for racing although this was one of the 1957 cars with more powerful double-overhead camshaft Coventry-Climax FPF engine, but also with more weight. He brought this to 'The Rest' as a second string and won his class in 59.68s, although well off the Cooper-JAP pace. An all Scottish battle for sports car honours saw Perth garage owner Tom Dickson just beat Ray Fielding's big HWM with his Lotus 11.

Another Marsh victory at Bouley Bay, where his 53.3s best left Ken Wharton's record intact, made him odds-on favourite for a third title and a satisfactory day for him was rounded off with a 54.3s third BTD in the F2 Cooper, beating Christie. However, making his best performance yet, Frank le Gallais persuaded the LGS-Jaguar to the top in a splendid 53.7s. Bill Knight, who normally shared Coopers with fellow Jerseyman Arthur Owen, setting International Class speed records together, and who maintained close links with the Cooper factory, broke the sports car record (and even Marsh's 'racing' time with a sports Cooper) in a very quick 55.6s.

A rather paltry 35 entries turned up for Craigantlet at a time when Irish interest in hill climbs seemed to be on the decline. Two Englishmen, Dick Henderson and Rochdale building and civil engineering company director Jim Berry, made the crossing and the tail-sliding Henderson was rewarded with a 68.26s record, while Berry's 74.42s was over four seconds faster than the fastest of the Irishmen, Malcolm Templeton (Lotus 11). Jim Berry was the archetypal enthusiastic clubman. Supported by his equally keen family, wife Vera and sons Jim and Peter, he had started hill climbing in

1950 with an ex-Embiricos Bugatti T55 which was fitted with an attractive if non-original two-seater body. This car remained a treasured favourite although later essays with T51 and T51A Bugattis were less successful. Always ready to try something different and interesting, Jim had bought a one-off tubular chassis F2 project which had been initiated by Bertie Bradnack and designed by Horace Richards and had installed an ex-Cuth Harrison 1½-litre ERA engine. He ran this in 1954 before replacing the engine with a full 2-litre ERA unit and it was in this form that the car was run in 1957.

Shenstone, Staffordshire publican Henderson, had, with all due respect to Jim Berry, not had much opposition at Craigantlet, but he did at Shelsley, where he won again in an excellent 35.84s, although Marsh scored 10 points in the RAC runs. Acknowledged to be an outstanding driver in the wet, Henderson and his spectacularly driven blown Cooper-JAP, were now clearly formidable opposition in any conditions. Although not as fast as Marsh or Boshier-Jones, let alone Henderson, Chris Summers and John Farley were now finding ways of ensuring that the fearsome little Farley Special stayed attached to its assorted chains for a little longer. The Shelsley Special Award was secured in 37.15s. It wasn't a record day in outright terms but the intense sports car competition brought new records for Tom Sopwith in the American Lupton Rainwater's 1500 Cooper-Climax (39.09s). Henderson's BTD was not the only surprise. The Ladies' Award, and a new record, went to the long blonde-haired occupant of Paul Emery's F1 Emeryson in 40.14s. The person in question was listed as Miss Roberta Cowell who turned out to be the same individual who used to be Bob Cowell, former fighter pilot and partner in the Cowell and Whittet preparation business. In the fifties such transformations were rare, to put it mildly. Many thought it was all a huge joke, although Patsy Burt (40.73s) was not particularly amused! Nevertheless, the record stood and as late as the mid-1970s the remarkable Miss Cowell occasionally turned out in club races with a Formula 5000 McLaren.

Rob Walker, the proprietor of Pipbrook Garage, Dorking, frequently enlivened the major Prescott meetings with his circuit racing cars. In September he brought along his latest, basically F2 Cooper, fitted with the new 1,960cc version of the FPF engine, destined for that epoch-making Argentine Grand Prix victory in January 1958. With around 175 bhp to play with, Michael Christie clocked 43.51s to win the RAC class, but victory again went to the forceful Henderson in 43.32s to complete a fine hat trick. Boshier-Jones was third on 43.63s, but what of Marsh? He arrived late, with the intention of competing even though he had already clinched the Championship, be was not allowed to run without practice as he had not competed on the hill for more than a month. Naturally, all concerned regretted this but rules are rules and Tony had to be content with taking a *tour d'honneur* wearing the Champion's laurel wreath. This should not detract from Henderson's performance for after a practice engine blow-up, necessitating a hurried change to a spare unit, there was time for only one timed run, and that's when he set BTD! Pauline Brock capped a splendid year by winning the 500cc class and bringing her Ladies' record down to 45.80s, just 0.05s slower than the new sports car record by Tom Sopwith in the delightfully named Mr Rainwater's Cooper.

The format of international sports car racing was changing at the time and there was increasing interest in the Grand Touring category for the more practical road-going machinery. Always ready to institute a class to match prevailing trends, the BOC instigated a Grand Touring Class which was won by Bugatti owner T. A. 'Bob' Roberts – the future principal of the Midland Motor Museum – in a Mercedes 300SL in 52.74s, from Mrs Jean Bloxam's Aston Martin.

Tony Marsh had achieved his Championship hat trick, scoring 41 points to the 38 of Michael Christie and the 35 of the much-improved Dick Henderson. For the first time since 1933 no ERA figured prominently in the top placings, but the promising Bill Moss was really sorting out R5B 'Remus' and ended the season as winner of the MAC's Junior Championship, beating Sheila Park in the Tojeiro and AC-Bristol which she shared with her husband Alistair.

These three years of Marsh pre-eminence, if not complete domination, may not have seen hill climbing make any great advances at the highest level, at least in Britain, but the steady expansion and growing popularity at 'grass roots' level continued as part of the broader growth in participation in, and popularity for, motor sport. There were no significant new hills brought into use in 1955, but there were some outstanding performances at established venues. Cornish motor trader Gerry Scali had bought the original HWM-Jaguar, Oscar Moore's old car, and ran it with modified front bodywork. He ran it to good effect, too, for in April he broke the Trengwainton record in 25.49s. Further North, the Catterick course rapidly gained popularity, despite some poor weather at early meetings and before

Reg Phillips made BTD there virtually his own private property there was a rare tie for BTD in April, in 38.8s, between Jock McBain (Cooper-Bristol) and Keith Hall (Cooper 500), with both entered by Jock's Border Reivers team. Much later in the year Gordon Parker, who had taken some time to sort out the Jaguara, established a winning streak. The day after he had won his class at Brighton, the Shorne driver set BTD at the BDC's attractive if rather dicey Bo Peep Hill, Firle, near Lewes, and followed that up with a new course record at the BARC's Brunton venue in 24.56s. At the very end of the season, many circuit racers again took in the WECC promotion at Stapleford where Paul Emery extended the F1 Emeryson-Alta to a 45.87s course record.

Aided by some track surface improvements, Tom Cunane was the next Trengwainton record holder, attaining a time of 25.19s in his aerodynamic Lotus-MG Mk 8 in April 1956. The same month, the London Motor Club held their first meeting at a new course, another 'uphill sprint' at Harleyford Manor, near Marlow. This parkland course, hard by the Thames, made up in surroundings what it lacked in length or driver interest. Rally driver and Allard devotee of many years standing, Goff Imhoff set the initial record at 21.8s in a J2. Although the Allards were now becoming rather outmoded there were still several in active and successful competition, Sydney Allard himself having competed in a few meetings in 1955 in the late model J2R of Rupert de Larrinaga.

Despite the introduction of 500cc cars to Barbon in 1954, it was not until 1956 that the little Coopers beat the sports cars at the increasingly-well-supported Westmorland event. That year Solihull's Austen May journeyed North to show the Northerners how to do it with a 32.18s record which was to stand until 1960, and had Bradford's Peter Procter and Brough's Cliff Allison well beaten. Still in the North, Catterick was now drawing 60 or more competitors and crowds of around 3,000 to see the ever cheerful Reg Phillips overcome seemingly inevitable practice problems to set regular BTDs. By July 1956 he had reduced the record to 37.65s. When Trengwainton, benefiting from the track improvements, was thrown open to racing cars that August, Reg undertook the long trip through the summer traffic for a Cornish 'holiday'. The result was a BTD and a new hill record in 24.60s.

A new departure was introduced at Brunton in June when the BARC ran an Inter-Club meeting – along the lines of the Prescott fixture – won by a 750 Motor Club team comprising Jack French, Vic Hood, and M. J. Concannon. BTD went to Tom Sopwith who was actually unbeaten at Brunton all season, getting down to 24.91s in September when Patsy Burt, driving the borrowed Virmin Stable Aston Martin DB3S (another Pipbrook Garage-prepared car) set a new Ladies' record in 25.92s. Right at the end of the season Rivers Fletcher was fastest at the principal Stapleford meeting, although he was down on Emery's 1955 time, and the Hastings, St Leonards and East Sussex CC arranged to enjoy hill climbing among the hops! They had arranged to use a service road at New House Farm, Bodiam, on the Guiness hop farm estate. Since the course was close to Frank Nicholls's little works at Bexhill, he entered the talented Stuart Lewis-Evans in one of his Elva-Climax cars and the slim 500cc Cooper expert cleaned up the event to set a precedent for the Elva concern.

Before switching to a Cooper-JAP, Peter Gaskell (in car) and Mike Hatton did well with this Bugatti T37. Partly visible in the right background is the Lemon Burton Bugatti Royale, the Park Ward-bodied T41 – which has resided for many years in the Musée Nationale (née Schlumpf Collection) at Mulhouse.
PHOTOGRAPHIC CRAFTSMEN
via PETER GASKELL

Sydney Allard's 1958 Steyr V8-engined sports car, a stark, light machine with no frills in true Allard tradition.
via MIKE KETTLEWELL

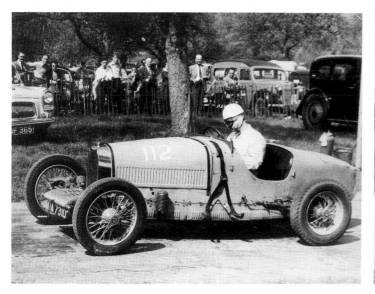

The side-effects of the Suez affair cut a swathe through the lesser meetings in the early part of 1957, but one meeting which was 'on' was the April Harleyford opener when Maurice Wick brought the record down to 23.2s in the Cadillac-Allard. The smaller meetings also gave the 'second rank' Cooper-JAP drivers a chance to shine, with George Keylock winning at a wet Brunton, David Good setting BTD at Westbrook Hat and 'T Dryvver' securing a Lydstep win in the newer of what had been Ken Wharton's Coopers. Tom Sopwith rounded off a very successful year with another Brunton course record in September, his impeccable handling of the American-owned sports Cooper leading to a 23.4s time. Bill Moss evoked nolstalgic memories with a win at Stapleford, a rare success now for an ERA outside VSCC events, and there was more nostalgia at Bodiam when the latest sports Elva arrived to be shared by Stuart Lewis-Evans and *Autosport*'s Technical Editor, John Bolster. The former again set BTD but Bolster showed that he still remembered what hill climbing was all about with 3rd BTD.

The Welsh Wizard

According to the records, the three years from 1958 to 1960 must be seen as almost completely dominated by David Boshier-Jones and his always beautifully-prepared pale green Cooper-JAP. Yet, although he was a significant force in 1957, his supremacy the following year was difficult to foresee. A combination of circumstances contributed to his apparent dominance. Both Marsh and Christie felt that the new breed of Formula 2 cars with their greater chassis sophistication and more engine power, say 140 bhp, might be the way to go, even though the new cars were heavier than the trusty Cooper-JAPs. Tony Marsh decided to split his efforts between both types of car, while at the same time his racing commitments grew. Even the great Ken Wharton's hill climbing began to suffer slightly in 1956 under the strain of this kind of multiple commitment, and Marsh was not to be immune to a slight falling off in performance due to lack of absolute concentration on the job in hand. Michael Christie, on the other hand, just started the year wrong-footed. He decided to go the whole hog and actually sold his Cooper-JAP to Phil Scragg and bought one of the new front-engined Lotus 12 F2 cars. This was lighter than the F2 Cooper yet with the same engine, so it looked promising. Unfortunately, its basic understeer handling characteristics were not suited to hill climbing and Christie hurriedly bought back his old Cooper to try to regain lost ground. As for Dick Henderson, he suffered a nasty crash at Orchard Corner, Prescott, early in the year, and incurred painful rib injuries and a strained back. Although he soon returned to the fray he never seemed to recover quite the form of 1957. On the other hand, 'Bosh' stuck to his well-tried Cooper, Welsh dragon worn proudly on the side, and concentrated solely on this car and hill climbing for he had given up circuit racing at the end of 1956. Specialisation was to pay off handsomely.

Among the opposition, both George Keylock and Reg Phillips added superchargers to their cars, and another to choose the Formula 2 way was Patsy Burt with a 1957 pattern Cooper fitted with a single-cam engine. The original intention was to do circuit races as well – as in the past with her

Jaguar XK120, Aston Martins and ex-Ray Thackwell Cooper Sports – but she decided that finishing fifth or sixth, which was the best she could hope for without a major additional financial outlay, was not enough, so she too decided to concentrate on the hills where the atmosphere ("and the parties") were congenial and success was more feasible. Big news on the sports car front was that Sydney Allard, no longer making more than the occasional Allard road car, was building a news sports-racing car. In typical practical Allard style this used up some bits and pieces from the abortive Clerk project, a spare Steyr V8 engine, de Dion rear end and front suspension derived from Ford Consul parts. The result was stark, a pure racing car apart from the light, all-enveloping, two seater body.

After successes for the early Cooper of Mike Hatton at Castel Farm (28.5s record), where racing cars were now admitted, and the later model of David Good at Brunton the acid test came at Prescott, after Fred Wharton, Ken's father, had opened the newly-completed Ken Wharton Memorial Timing Pavilion in a moving ceremony. The serious business of the season got under way with a splendid battle for BTD between Boshier-Jones and Marsh, with the Welshman clipping just six-hundredths of a second off Marsh's time to beat the Kinver driver's Cooper-JAP for supremacy. The latter could not match 'Bosh's' 42.27s, but his 43s dead was enough to drop Christie to third in his old Cooper-JAP (43.44s), with David Good only another 0.18s slower. The 'Bosh' time was set in the RAC Championship runs which were now held at the end of the meeting in the modern manner, and with only the fastest ten RAC registered competitors running. Unfortunately, Marsh had elected to nominate his F2 Cooper for the Championship climbs and although he beat Christie's Lotus, 44.28s to 45.17s for the class award, his engine then went sick and he was down in the 47s bracket. Pauline Brock, now Mrs Jackie Welton and living actually at Prescott at Pardon Hill House, again reduced her Ladies' record, but her 45.08s climb was only 0.02s better than Dick James's rival Cooper 500. Swedish driver Jon Fast, who had competed at Prescott the previous year, managed a fine 47.37s with his little 950cc Osca sports, but did even better with his black Mercedes 300SL in the GT category, where his 49.29s record fairly obliterated Bob Roberts' 1957 time. Overall, there was a 46.81s tie for the fastest sports car between Scragg, back in his trusty HWM, and Edward Lewis in a very special Lotus 7, one of the small batch which featured Coventry-Climax FWA engine, de Dion rear suspension, coil and wishbone front end and disc brakes. With the cycle front wings of the Lotus 7 but most of the running gear more familiar in a Lotus 11, this was ideal for hill climbing.

After Prescott, Shelsley seemed rather depressing. Leslie Wilson was retiring after magnificent service to the MAC – to be succeeded by Gerry Flewitt – and a well-deserved presentation to mark the event was spoilt by bad weather, a poor gate, and the knowledge that Shelsley Walsh was hitting financial problems. This time Marsh's precise driving in very tricky conditions perhaps gave him a slight edge over Boshier-Jones (37.97s to 38.55s), while burly Chris Summers, perched on the twitching, snaking, Farley Special put in a superb 38.06s for third BTD as well as a now habitual Shelsley Specials award. Reg Phillips also struck a blow for the special builders by coming sixth behind Christie and Good. The following day most people adjourned to Prescott for the Members' Day and another terrific Marsh/Boshier-Jones battle had them both in a record 41s bracket. Running with different sparking plugs and a weaker mixture than hitherto, Marsh again just had the edge with 41.87s to the Welshman's 41.93s. Dick James was also in determined mood, and his 44.64s 500cc time was the fastest since Boshier-Jones' 1955 record.

For once the weather was delightful for Rest-and-be-Thankful and, with Marsh racing at Rheims, Boshier-Jones absolutely slaughtered the opposition, shattering the record in 52.93s and beating even Christie by 2.34s, while Summers was again third and Phillips sixth. Tom Dickson (Lotus 11) was again the fastest sports car driver on 'The Rest' but the Porsche 1600S and Triumph TR3 which came first and second in one class were both driven by a rather shy young farmer from Duns, Berwickshire, who was already showing raw versatility. His name was Jim Clark.

After a winning interlude at Westbrook Hay, where David Good ran him closest, Boshier-Jones turned on an even more devastating performance at an otherwise rather lacklustre Bouley Bay which was given a miss by Marsh, Christie and Henderson and which also lacked the habitual fine performances of Frank le Gallais who had now retired. Boshier-Jones not only broke Ken Wharton's 52.6s hill record, he did it on all four runs. His final best of 51.2s he did twice while his 'slower' climbs were in 51.8s and 52.2s. Jerseyman Mac Daghorn, driving a very early Cooper was second BTD on 54.0s but it was really no contest. The 500cc class winner was another locally-based driver, Renato

'Tico' Martini, one day to become France's leading production racing car manufacturer.

Craigantlet, where the entry plumbed a new low by totalling only 33, was even easier for Boshier-Jones with 69.99s to the 73.97s of the game Jim Berry (ERA Special), but then the Newport driver finally went over his limit. He clipped the inside bank on a left-hander, the Cooper was deflected and overturned twice. Although taken to hospital for observation, he was soon released, and the damage to the Cooper was not enough to keep it away from Shelsley the following week.

For the first time, both major Shelsley meetings and the May and September Prescott climbs counted towards the Championship, making seven rounds in all. Perhaps a little shaken after Craigantlet, Boshier-Jones had to be content with 36.29s, whereas Marsh, despite ramming the VIP enclosure at the Esses in his F2 car, took his familiar dark green Cooper-JAP, with the white flash, over the finish line in 35.25s. This was surely the most *un*spectacular Shelsley record of all time! Chris Summers was third yet again, this time with a superb 36.63s Shelsley Special record, while Patsy Burt was one of the day's real stars. Her results in the F2 Cooper had been gathering momentum for some time and included a BTD at a Thames Estuary Automobile Club climb at Stapleford. Now she became the first woman to crack 40s at Shelsley and did it in a big way, getting down to a remarkable 38.25s in the Top Ten runs. Ray Fielding, now in one of the manx-tailed sports Coopers, was fastest sports car but a seemingly effortless class win was secured by Sydney Allard in his fierce new Steyr-engined car.

Both Marsh and Christie had their F2 cars into the 43s bracket at the September Prescott Championship finals, but this was well off the pace with Boshier-Jones and Marsh (Cooper-JAP) each under the record three times. This was a real showdown even though Marsh could not win the Championship after missing several meetings. Fittingly, then, it was Boshier-Jones who pulled out that final fraction to win in 41.00s exactly, with Marsh on 41.08s. Nobody else was really in the same class. Patsy Burt set another Ladies' best (44.86s), and Ray Fielding (46.35s) again had an advantage over the larger sports cars of 'Taffy' Cottrell (ex-Cliff Davis Lotus-Bristol Mk 10) and Sydney Allard, who were also slower than Jack Richards' 1100 Lotus 11.

Although it did not attract very much attention during the year, the MAC again ran their Junior Hill Climb and Sprint Championship. Peter Cottrell tied for this award with 500cc Cooper-Norton driver Eric Willmott, and with another Cooper exponent, Brian Eccles, in third place.

Financially, 1958 had been a critical year for Shelsley Walsh, and it hadn't come out of it too well. At the Midland Automobile Club's Annual Dinner in February 1959, Club President, Sammy Newsome, made a strong speech, calling for the active support of the 700 or so members. He declared: "Shelsley must not be allowed to die. It has to go on. It is a wonderful training ground for future

Tony Marsh (standing next to Peter Gaskell's wife-to-be Arlette) checks up on his old Cooper, now in the capable hands of Mike Hatton (standing) and Peter Gaskell (sat on wheel) in the Prescott Paddock.
via PETER GASKELL

drivers..." Happily, the tide was turning and he was able to announce that meetings would be held on Sundays in future – an important factor affecting gate receipts – the Orchard to the right of the Start would be available for spectator parking, there would be improved pathways to encourage spectators in the long slog up to the Esses, some tree felling to assist visibility, and improvements to the track surface. As at Prescott in 1951, it seems that it took a crisis to make everybody realise what an asset it was that was in danger of being lost.

Hill climbing was definitely gaining momentum again, albeit firmly at club level, and there were big championship changes for 1959. The RAC announced an extended ten-event schedule for the premier title, bringing in three well-supported Home Counties events: Westbrook Hay in July, Great Auclum in August, and Stapleford in October. None of these courses could compare in intrinsic interest with the classic venues. In fact, they compared unfavourably with Lydstep, Barbon and even Trengwainton, although Great Auclum definitely posed a challenge to split second concentration and precise placing of a car which was most worthwhile. Nevertheless, all three courses were handy for London and they were always well supported. One cannot help feeling, however, that it was a pity to end the Championship on an airfield where much of the entry tended to come from circuit racers rather than the specialist hill climbers. Competitors' best seven performances in the Top Ten runs were now to count for marks and the scoring system was also changed. BTD still scored 10, second 9, and so down to 5 for sixth, but the last four in the Top Ten scored no marks. On the other hand, anyone who broke the record which had stood at the beginning of the meeting was to be awarded a bonus mark.

In recent seasons interest in the sports car category had increased considerably, with may close contests – irrespective of class placings – between the efficient lightweights, epitomised by the various Lotus and Cooper models, the usually Bristol-engined 'middleweights' and the powerful and spectacular bigger machinery with Jaguar and Allard variants predominating. Until now, they had no title to aim for but in 1959 two magazines, the BRSCC's *Motor Racing*, and *Sports Car and Lotus Owner* joined together to promote a Sports Car Championship with points to be scored in two classes, up to and over 1,500cc, by drivers running in their normal class runs at the RAC Championship meetings.

In the battle for RAC Championship honours, Michael Christie decided to retire from serious hill climbing, selling his lightweight Cooper-JAP to Mike Hatton. Although more than ever preoccupied with circuit racing matters Tony Marsh had not given up the idea of making a Formula 2 car truly competitive with the Cooper-JAPs. To this end, he bought Christie's Lotus 12 and modified it considerably, moving the engine well back in the chassis in an effor to improve the weight distribution for hill climbs. He called the modified car the Motus and annoyed more than a few people by entering it as a Shelsley Special at the Worcestershire hill, winning the award for such machines. It seems that some folk took the entry rather more seriously than Tony had intended! A significant new challenge came from Arthur Owen who obtained a new Formula 1 Cooper (actually very closely related to the F2 car) fitted with a 1,960cc Coventry-Climax FPF engine. In fact, bigger cars were making something of a comeback, for Jim Berry now had his ERA engine in a 1953 front-engined F2 Cooper chassis, and Rivers Fletcher had exchanged his Cooper-JAP (sold to Dick James) for one of the later HWM

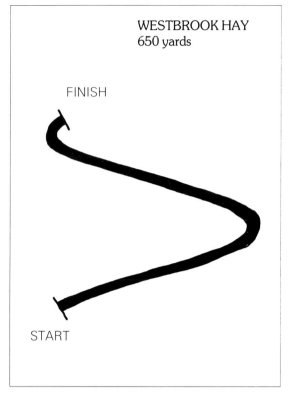

WESTBROOK HAY
650 yards

FINISH

START

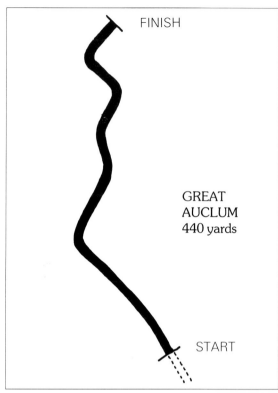

FINISH

GREAT
AUCLUM
440 yards

START

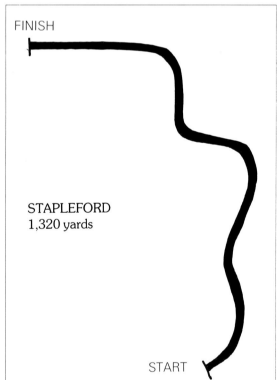

FINISH

STAPLEFORD
1,320 yards

START

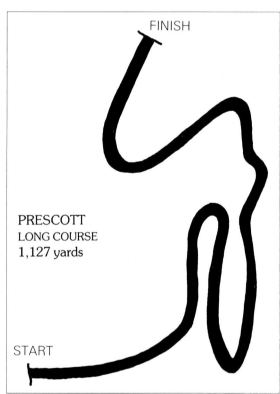

FINISH

PRESCOTT
LONG COURSE
1,127 yards

START

single-seaters, now fitted with a Jaguar XK engine and formerly the property of Australian Tony Gaze.

But it was all in vain: David Boshier-Jones was just unbeatable. This well-matched combination won nine Championship rounds on the trot. He didn't win at Stapleford because he didn't enter. He did come for a demonstration run, however, and promptly showed that he was fallible after all by spinning. Matching the performance of Ken Wharton at his best, 'Bosh's' remarkable year ran like this. He actually began by being beaten twice running by Marsh (in the Cooper-JAP) at Lydstep and a special inter-regional team competition run at Prescott specially for television. Then the Welshman really got into gear. At Prescott in May he beat Marsh (Motus) in heavy rain; at Shelsley in June, watched by an encouragingly larger crowd but slowed by the new surface of flint chippings, it was David Good (37.70s) and Marsh (Motus, 37.74s) who ran his 36.96s closest, while Owen was temporarily sidelined by a Prescott crash in which he broke his collar bone. 'The Rest', Westbrook Hay (25.46s to David Good's 25.74s) and Bouley Bay followed in rapid succession. Bouley Bay saw him break his 1958 course record in 51.0s while the other talking point was the fine second BTD, and new 'local' record for Jerseyman Mac Daghorn (53.0s), driving Peter Wakeham's ancient Cooper-JAP Mk 4, vanquishing even Good and Owen. Great Auclum brought another record, in 20.56s with Good (always effective on the shorter hills) and a very on-form Patsy Burt filling the minor places. As usual, the opposition was not too strong at Craigantlet but David's 68.74s BTD was yet another record, and with Bangor driver John Pringle in his ex-Rob Walker 2.0 Cooper-Climax (not an RAC Championship entrant) beating Jim Berry. The record breaking continued at Shelsley (35.47s to the 35.70s of Marsh's Cooper-JAP and 36.63s of the remarkable Chris Summers), where Patsy Burt also lowered her Ladies' record to 37.63s. It was 'only' BTD at Prescott in September – the meeting now downgraded to a National permit – but 41.18s was more than enough to defeat Dick James (43.06s) and David Good (43.34s). The brave and determined David Good had had a first-class season so it was fitting that he should win the one round where Boshier-Jones was not entered, at a misty Stapleford, although his 46.79s was still outside Paul Emery's long-standing course record.

That was the Championship year in a nutshell, although it perhaps does less than full justice to Patsy Burt who had just about the most successful year ever for a woman hill climber. Apart from the achievements already mentioned, and her regular appearances in the Top Ten runs, she and her powder blue Cooper scored a third BTD at the televised Prescott meeting, was fourth at the new Ragley Park venue, took BTD and the course record twice (26.57s and 25.40s) at the now BARC-leased Firle climb, reduced her Shelsley Ladies' record in June as well as in August, set a 55.4s Ladies' record at Bouley Bay, and reduced her Prescott record to 44.55s in September.

The new Sports Car Championship was most successful, attracting a regular following by the leading runners who, at least in the case of Ray Fielding, Jack Richards and Phil Scragg, even took in Craigantlet. At the end of the year it was very close but victory went to Macclesfield's Phil Scragg, enjoying his last season with his HWM-Jaguar, and underlining this enthusiastic textile engineer's consistent success over many seasons. Runner-up was the Director of the Morayshire motor engineers P. S. Nicholson (Forres) Ltd, Ray Fielding, with his 1,460cc Cooper-Climax which was often the fastest sports car of all, irrespective of class. This car could easily be mistaken for one of the new Cooper Monacos as it featured conventional seating and a full-width windscreen rather than the normal centre driving seat of the manx-tailed Coopers. Third and fourth men were equally frequent class winners: Peter Cottrell (Lotus-Bristol Mk 10) and the 1100 Lotus 11 of Jack Richards.

The variety of cars catered for at the bigger hill climbs was definitely increasing, and some notable drivers were taking to Grand Touring cars, and especially the Lotus Elite. This was one more instance of small size, chassis sophistication and agility making up for relatively modest power output, for the Cheshunt-built cars took over from the Mercedes 300SLs as the cars to beat and attracted drivers of the calibre of Tony Marsh, the semi-retired Michael Christie, Scotsman Jim Clark and Edward Lewis, and it was the latter who scored the year's premier GT achievement by reducing the Prescott record down to 48.99s in September. Great Auclum even catered for saloons and paved the way for one of the year's most amusing wins. The business of 'hotting up' ordinary saloons as opposed to running sports cars in competition was gaining ground fast – the Mini and the Ford Anglia 105E were announced that August and September respectively – but the modern concept of the 'Special Saloon' was in its infancy. One who was already achieving amazing things with apparently unpromising material was Leslie Ballamy of LMB, who had once been involved with the Allard split axle front suspension system. Taking time off from hustling the big HWM-Jaguar up the hills, Rivers Fletcher was prevailed upon to drive Ballamy's amazing LMB Ford Popular E93A. Stripped of all non-essential fittings and finishings, fitted with a well-tuned and supercharged, 1,172cc engine, and equipped with LMB split axle front suspension, lowered rear and oversize wheels, the car was distinctly radical for 1959, and Rivers, taking his habitual high line round Great Auclum's banked first corner, won the class outright in an astonishing 24.63s

Rather less noticeable was a win in the MAC's Junior Championship by Peter Hughes from Sutton Coldfield (not to be confused with the late Peter S. Hughes of Glasgow), in a Cooper-Norton, a type of car which was becoming far less popular on the hills and had virtually disappeared from all but the smaller circuit races by the end of the year. The MAC allowed their Junior series to lapse in 1960, although this eminently justifiable championship was to be revived in 1961.

Bugatti Owners Club Chairman, Roy Taylor, made the first piece of big news for 1960 when, at the Club's annual Prize-Giving Luncheon on 6 March, he announced that the course at Prescott was to be extended. Instead of curving round, uphill, to the right at Orchard corner, the track now was to turn left, run along the little valley for just over one hundred yards and then return to the steep approach to Pardon via a long hairpin and a slightly downhill, almost parallel section. The new hairpin was to be called Ettore's – after Ettore Bugatti of course – and the extension was to add 300 yards to the existing 1200 yards climb. The downhill stretch was a bit novel, although by no means unique in British hill climbing. After the first meeting on the new course, on 1 June, the general opinion about the change was favourable, and it certainly enhanced Prescott's already strong spectator appeal. The general character of the hill was not really changed, and it remained a tight and twisty climb, "like a demented piece of string" according to one unenthusiastic competitor who preferred the much faster Shelsley Walsh.

More grand touring cars were appearing in hill climbs by the late nineteen-fifties. S. Perry (Jaguar XK140) accelerates towards the Shelsley finish.
PHOTOGRAPHIC CRAFTSMEN
via MIKE KETTLEWELL

David Good gets a 'thumbs up' to commence operations at Westbrook Hay in his gleaming Cooper-JAP, with which he was third in the 1960 RAC Championship and won in 1961.
via MIKE KETTLEWELL

A further BOC innovation was the decision to cater for the increasingly popular Formula Junior class of racing cars. Inspired by Count Giovanni Lurani in Italy, this category was intended to provide the sort of training ground for future Grand Prix drivers which the old 500cc Formula 3 had done in England, but not very successfully elsewhere. The new Juniors had a maximum engine size of 1,100cc (to suit the Fiat 1100 engine, as power units had to be basically proprietary production car engines) or not exceeding 1,000cc capacity with a lower minimum weight. When the Formula got under way in 1958, it was dominated by Italian makes, such as Stanguellini, Taraschi, de Sanctis and Wainer but in 1960, the first year of large-scale British support, the balance of power shifted towards these islands, with the rear-engined Lotus and Cooper, and to a lesser extent, the front-engined Lola, Elva and Gemini models winning everything in sight with 'undersize' 1,000cc Ford, BMC and DKW engines. The BOC decided to award their Staniland Trophy, together with a useful £50 for the best Junior time at Prescott, although there was not a lot of support for the category, initially, on the hills. There was certainly nothing like the early upsurge of interest in the old 500s, for it was apparent, even by 1960, that these sophisticated little 'production' racers would not be particularly cheap to buy and run. A few people built rather more homely cars for the new category – the original Alexis of Birmingham builder Alec Francis (formerly successful with the HRG-Mercury) and the F3 Cooper-based Venom-Austin of

Downton, Wiltshire, tuning expert Daniel Richmond, spring to mind – but there was certainly no big outburst of special building for Formula Junior.

There was nothing very dramatic in the way of new cars for the season, at least at RAC Championship level, although Jim Berry bought ERA R4D from Tom Norton to add to his stable and Reg Phillips reclothed the Fairley Special in new bodywork which gave the car a strong physical resemblance to the contemporary Porsche Formula 2 car. Among the sports cars contesting the *Motor Racing/Sports Car and Lotus Owner* series, the most formidable newcomer was another cycle-winged, Jaguar-engined car for Phil Scragg. He had bought a Lister-Jaguar from Ecurie Ecosse patron David Murray and this turned out to be the special offset single-seater-bodied car which had run in the 1958 'Two Worlds' track race at Monza and which had afterwards been re-bodied for sports car racing. Now, the Monza body was reinstated as Scragg always preferred the 'slipper'-type bodywork for hill climbing. Former Lister-Bristol driver Josh Randles opted for one of the latest 2.0 Coventry Climax FPF-engined Cooper Monacos, while the potent and nimble Climax-engined, de Dion-axled Lotus 7 theme was adopted by Dick James (ex-Eric Pantlin, who was killed in a road accident) and the experienced all-round driver, Betty Haig (1,460cc FWB-engined former Chequered Flag stable car). The RAC Champion's brother, Peter, was all ready for a full season with a Lotus 11, and while there was no rush to switch to Formula Junior cars, the Weltons, Jackie and Pauline, bought a DKW two-stroke-engined Elva (very successful in 1959 circuit races) and sold their familiar ex-Ivor Bueb Cooper 500 to Birmingham coach operator Ian McLaughlin, a former rally driver.

Before the major climbs began there was near tragedy at the Prescott practice weekend when Rivers Fletcher lost his HWM-Jaguar, overturned, and suffered a fractured skull. Happily, after a short convalescence, he fully recovered and was competing again by August.

In the major events there was still no answer to the prowess of David Boshier-Jones. Although he won 'only' seven of the ten RAC rounds this time his domination was actually just as total as it had been in 1959, with a heavy programme which took in several non-championship successes. Baldly, the year ran thus: BTD by almost two seconds from Dick James (still in his ex-Cottrell Cooper twin) at Lydstep; BTD at Ragley Park by 0.4s from Mike Hatton; BTD at Castel Farm, 1.2s clear of George Keylock's supercharged Formula 2 Cooper; victory at the opening RAC round on a very dusty Prescott, the last event on the old course and with the construction work causing all the dust; a 35.76s BTD at the June Shelsley, 0.33s up on Arthur Owen's F1 Cooper; the inaugral record on the lengthened Prescott course (52.48s); a 32.66s record on the resuscitated Bo'ness course; a new 52.05s course record at Rest-and-be-Thankful where he had 2½ seconds advantage over David Good; another record at Westbrook Hay (24.06s) before the rains came; yet another hill record at Bouley Bay (50.84s) before rain caused the abandonment of the meeting ahead of the Top Ten runs and led to RAC points being allocated on class performances; a second Castel Farm BTD; BTD once again at Great Auclum; BTD but *not* the top RAC points at Shelsley, where an even more cheerful than usual Reg Phillips got in a rapid 37.35s first class climb before the rain came down for the umpteenth time that season; a new 50.96s hill record at September Prescott, 0.41s faster than the now most formidable

Bo'ness was revived in 1958 and in 1960, in his last full year of competition, David Boshier-Jones broke the course record. Here he lifts a wheel through the Courtyard.
BILL HENDERSON

Conveniently close to Edinburgh, Bo'ness invariably drew in a large crowd. Bill Turnbull's Mowog Special heads for a class win in 1960.
BILL HENDERSON

David Good; and a season closing BTD at Castel Farm. What a record! He did not enter either the Craigantlet or Stapleford RAC Championship events, but ended the year a triple Champion with 92 points to the 71 of Arthur Owen and 66 of David Good, with Owen and Good usually proving to be most spectacular but never having the edge over the little Welshman.

Behind this rather one-sided battle for outright supremacy, there was rather more interest at the major meetings, although it should be noted that the Jerseyman, Owen, who had now fitted a slightly more powerful 2.2-litre Climax engine to his F1 Cooper, was at last showing that the Cooper twins *could* be beaten – as long as 'Bosh' was not driving. Back at Prescott in May, a new sports car record in 45.19s (0.8s faster than the next fastest sports car, Peter Boshier-Jones's well-driven Lotus 11) demonstrated that Phil Scragg had certainly chosen well in his latest big sports racer. Since this meeting was the last to be held on the old course for many years, except for the traditional VSCC meeting which has continued on the 1,200 yards course right up to the present day, the records then standing remained in virtual perpetuity. The outright best was 41.00s by 'Bosh' while class honours stood to Jack Richards (Lotus Climax 7, 45.94s, set in 1959); Tom Sopwith (45.75s, 1957); Bill Bradley (Lister-Bristol, 46.84s, 1957); Scragg; Michael Christie (F2 Cooper, 42.82s, 1957); Boshier-Jones, (500 Cooper, 44.45s, 1955); Reg Phillips (43.33s, 1960); Boshier-Jones (1100 Cooper, 41.00s, 1958); and Edward Lewis (Lotus Elite, 48.99s, 1959).

The accompaniment of thunder and lightning to the opening meeting on the extended Prescott was an accurate augury for a rain marred season but it did nothing to deter Phil Scragg for the Macclesfield driver left the hill with new sports (60.41s) and Grand Touring (62.36s, in his Jaguar XK150S) records to his credit. His excellent season continued with a 39.29s sports car record at Shelsley where Betty Haig took the Ladies' Award in the absence of Patsy Burt, and where Reg Phillips beat David Good for third BTD.

Amid the stark grandeur of Glen Croe Jim Berry showed that old R4D was still a useful hill climb car by climbing in 57.94s, for fifth in the RAC Top Ten, just ahead of the very effective Cooper-Climax sports of Ray Fielding. Back in the Home Counties, at Westbrook Hay, the weather turned sour for the RAC runs and behind the inevitable 'Bosh', Berry and Fielding really excelled by taking second and third places, beating Patsy Burt. Daniel Richmond (Weber-carburettored Lotus-BMC 7), Peter Boshier-Jones and Fielding all set sports car records on their first climbs but Scragg's luck was out. He spun on his first climb and it was wet for his second.

Despite Arthur Owen's good 1960 form, he still had to give best to Mac Daghorn at Bouley Bay (53.75s to 53.83s for second and third BTD), where Peter Gatehouse's little 1100cc Cooper rather surprisingly vanquished the Lotus 11s of Peter Bailey and Peter Boshier-Jones with a 56.21s sports car record.

Craigantlet was unrepresentative to say the least. The Ulster Automobile Club sportingly allowed the visitors to run early in the programme so as to allow them to catch a ferry back to Heysham before an impending shipping strike took effect. The weather was less accommodating, and after a handful of climbs, on one of which Arthur Owen set the 72.41s BTD, the skies opened. Owen could not maintain his advantage in the RAC runs when Ray Fielding, for the first time, took the honours with a sports car. Owen was second and Jim Berry, driving Scotsman Alan Bateman's B-type Grand Prix Connaught in place of R4D (which was suffering from a blower problem), was third.

As was becoming something of a tradition, the September Prescott was *the* meeting of the year although it took place without Owen (who had damaged his car in the Italian Grand Prix the previous week) and the event was spoilt by the death of John Forbes-Clark, the former Jaguar driver, who had been campaigning a well-prepared supercharged Formula 2 Cooper. The throttle may have stuck open as the Cooper came out of the new loop and he crashed with sickening force in full view of many spectators. On a happier note Phil Scragg again beat Boshier-Jones, Fielding and Randles for the hotly contested overall sports car honours, and Tony Marsh made a welcome return to the hills with his latest, brand-new Formula 2 Lotus 18 and his Lotus Elite. Two new class records in 53.27s and 58.95s showed he had not lost the specialist hill climbing skills. After a season of indifferent entries in the Formula Junior class, the incentive of winning the prestigious Staniland Trophy drew a good field of 11 Juniors, from which future Mini-Cooper S racing star John Rhodes emerged on top with 54.04s in his Cooper-BMC.

Fittingly, if rather unsatisfactorily, it was wet for the Stapleford Championship finale where Phil

Scragg actually set BTD in 48.20s, although the RAC Top Ten class was won by Owen by a mere 0.03s from Patsy Burt who always went well at Stapleford, and with Good edging Mike Hatton (who had had a consistent if unspectacularly successful year in his Cooper-JAP) out of third place.

It had been a superb year of intense competition among the leading sports car drivers and this showed up in the secondary Championship, divided now into up to and over 1,600cc classes, although on most hills the division was rather superfluous. Ray Fielding took the title with 69 points, by just one point from the 1959 Champion, Scragg, and with Peter Boshier-Jones also on 68 marks and Josh Randles on 67. Fielding also entered the RAC Championship and his speed and the relatively few real top-liners contesting the series in racing cars, combined to place him fourth overall, ahead of those two great sportsmen, Reg Phillips and Jim Berry.

Transition

The pace definitely quickened in 1961, a year of new beginnings in motor racing generally. This was the year when the controversial but ultimately successful 1,500cc unsupercharged/450 kilogramme Grand Prix formula came into effect, when the British-inspired Intercontinental Formula never really got off the ground, and at a lesser level, the year when the Grand Touring car supplanted the sports racer from many major race programmes, and when an American V8 saloon, courtesy of Dan Gurney, briefly hinted at the end of Jaguar domination of saloon car races. Hill climbing was gaining an ever-increasing grass roots support, while at the pinnacle of the sport the old order was indeed changing at last. After winning his third successive RAC title, David Boshier-Jones decided to retire although allowing himself the odd outing in younger brother Peter's ex-Edward Greenall Lola-Climax sports car which Peter had bought to replace his successful Lotus 11. The courageous and forceful David Good now headed the Cooper-JAP ranks although Mike Hatton, after a good 1960 season, could not be underestimated with his ex-Christie car. Jerseyman Peter Wakeham bought the Champion's car for the talented Mac Daghorn to drive, while Doug Haigh fitted an 1132cc supercharged Norton-JAP composite engine to the 500 Cooper which Wells driver Eric Willmott had campaigned, Willmott joining the increasingly numerous Formula Junior fraternity with an Elva-DKW.

Although Tony Marsh intended to give top priority to his Formula 1 commitments he was keen to enter his well-sorted, rear-engined Lotus Climax 18 in as many hill climbs as possible, although he did not enter the RAC Championship until after the season had started. Oddly, there was actually some criticism that he should enter a contemporary Grand Prix car in hill climbs, as this was felt to represent unfair competition. Clearly there were some who had short memories concerning the type of car which contested hill climbing in former days, and one suspects that a healthy respect for Marsh's ability as a driver had something to do with the anguish! However, as Marsh pointed out, the Lotus was powered by a relatively modest Coventry-Climax FPF engine, delivering probably little over 150 bhp, which gave the car a less dramatic power-to-weight ratio than the best of the Cooper twins.

Arthur Owen, Patsy Burt and George Keylock continued with their 'modern' Coopers, although the

Tony Marsh at Wiscombe Park in his Lotus-Climax 18 during 1961. Representing contemporary Formula 1 chassis design, the car was a major contender in Marsh's hands despite an unremarkable power-to-weight ratio for hill climbing.
ANTHONY HOLLISTER
via MIKE KETTLEWELL

powder blue Burt colours were also to be seen on a brand new Porsche RSK sports car, complete with rugged twin ohc flat four engine. This, the only car of its type in British ownership, had been bought primarily to contest the European Mountain Championship, revived in 1957 for 2-litre, then 1½-litre sports cars, but would run in British events as well. In fact, the car had a fairly undistinguished season, for Patsy Burt found it difficult to readjust to not having open wheels to help place the car, while the Porsche, designed primarily to survive tough long-distance events and alp-storming, was a little heavy and over-engineered for British sprint events.

Another approach to the old power-to-weight-ratio problem was taken by Tom Norton who had disposed of his ex-Wharton Cooper-JAP to Bristolian Wally Cuff. Norton bought a Formula Junior Lotus and fitted it with a supercharged version of the 1,220cc (Lotus Elite-sized) Coventry-Climax sohc engine.

Apart from the Boshier-Jones Lola, there were other new sports car challengers, headed by an interesting one-off for Ray Fielding. He had commissioned Paul Emery to provide one of the new Emeryson Formula 1 chassis, adapted to take a neat two-seater body bearing a close resemblance to the Cooper Monaco design. After several successful seasons and many class wins with the ex-Cliff Davis Lotus-Bristol Mk 10, a 1955 car, 'Taffy' Cottrell, now concentrating firmly on the sports car classes, added an ex-Mike Taylor/Taylor & Crawley Lotus-Climax 15 to his armoury.

The outright records stayed intact at the first Prescott and Shelsley climbs of 1961, but Marsh topped the list on both occasions. At Prescott his 52.70s was not matched by David Good (53.16s) or Peter Gaskell (53.64s) on the fastest of the RAC runs which the Kinver farmer did not contest. The big shock came when Peter Boshier-Jones 'did a Fielding' and an astonishing 54.38s for third best Top Ten climb. Although it could not count as a sports car class record, this was faster than Scragg's just-established 54.78s best in the Lister-Jaguar, but then the Lola's agility had been amply demonstrated on the circuits since Eric Broadley's Lotus-beater appeared for hte first time in 1958. All the sports car records fell, with Boshier-Jones (55.26s), Fielding (55.22s) and Randles (56.70s) as the other beneficiaries, while Austen Nurse, carrying a very definite personal weight penalty, sprang a surprise by

Patsy Burt, seen talking to Ron Smith, bought an exotic Porsche RSK for Continental hill climbing in 1961. It proved rather heavy and over-engineered for British sprint events. Registration number 200 EMA related to a tender car. The Porsche was not road registered.
via MIKE KETTLEWELL

winning the Grand Touring class from the similar Elite of Marsh and Phil Scragg's latest mount, an Aston Martin DB4GT.

At Shelsley, Tony Marsh and George Keylock forced Good down to third in the RAC runs. Although Marsh was now registered in the RAC Championship, his 35.86s BTD was set on a class run, but even this was a mere 1.64s faster than an incredible new 37.50s sports car record by Peter Boshier-Jones with just 1100cc of Lola Climax. Perfect judgement, excellent traction and Lola's impeccable handling made up for sheer bhp on this acknowledged 'power' course, leaving even Phil Scragg behind on 37.72s.

Two years earlier, the Lothian Car Club had revived hill climbing on the well-liked Bo'ness course, the 1959 event being won by Jim Clark in the Border Reivers Lister-Jaguar. For 1961, the Kinneil Estate course was reinstated in the RAC series and so the old Scottish fortnight was back on the calendar. Marsh missed Bo'ness and David Good's 33.07s BTD was outside David Boshier-Jones 1960 record and a hairsbreadth faster than Arthur Owen's 33.08s with the big Cooper. The tables were turned in the RAC climbs when, after a day-long battle, Owen recorded 33.09s to the 33.51s of Good and 34.14s of the consistent Mike Hatton. Phil Scragg was actually third fastest overall in 33.95s. A week later and Marsh was back at the Rest-and-be-Thankful meeting where changeable weather failed to stop him landing a 54.40s BTD, and going on to beat Good, Owen and Hatton in the RAC runs. Fielding got his revenge on Scragg with a 56.94s sports car best although it was Boshier-Jones who ran him closest on 57.00s

Isobel Robinson (later Mrs Willis) was a major contender for 500cc honours around 1960 in this late model Cooper.
PATRICK BENJAFIELD
via RIVERS FLETCHER

Marsh let everybody off and gave Westbrook Hay a miss, and on this short parkland course the Cooper-JAPs were back in charge. Good (24.18s) heading Hatton, Owen, Keylock, Reg Phillips and Jim Berry. The latter was now driving yet one more imposing but not totally competitive machine, the ex-Rob Walker B-type Connaught with which Michael Christie had done well at Prescott five years earlier.

Thanks to an inadvertent but rather devastating bout of oil spraying from Tom Norton's Lotus-Climax, there was only one Top Ten run at Bouley Bay, but Tony Marsh certainly did not use this as an excuse to justify being beaten for Best Time of Day by an inspired Mac Daghorn in the ex-Boshier-Jones Cooper which climbed in 51.75s to Marsh's 52.93s. After many years of hard effort by Syd Logan, Frank le Gallais, Bill Knight, Arthur Owen and Daghorn, a Channel Islander had at last won Jersey's premier motor sporting event.

David Boshier-Jones may have retired but the family name was little less prominent as Peter went from success to success. The climax (in both senses) came at Great Auclum where, on a tricky little course tailor-made for the agile Lola and Peter's precise skills, 21.57s was fast enough for BTD. Not content with this on the class climbs, Boshier-Jones did it again in the Top Ten climbs, ascending in 21.66s to the 21.72s of David Good, the 21.79s of Ray Fielding, and a 21.90s from Mike Hatton. What a day for the sports cars! Sadly, Arthur Owen went off in a big way, shooting over the banking on the first corner, and hurting his back in the process.

Although Scragg (third BTD in 70.28s), Fielding (winner of the Top Ten class in 72.47s), Berry and Daniel Richmond (Venom-Austin) took in Craigantlet, it was definitely a day for the Irish, with the Craigantlet record falling in 67.24s to John Pringle, from Bangor. After starting to race in 1957, in an MGA, Pringle had competed with a succession of F2 and F1 Coopers (including the ex-Moss/Walker 1958 Argentine GP winning car). By 1961 he was winning just about everything there was to win in Irish events with a 1959-type Formula 1 Cooper, powered by the full 2,495cc Coventry-Climax FPF engine, and the Craigantlet record was not unexpected. Ulsterman Brian Bleakley did well to break 70s for the second BTD in his much-campaigned Kieft 1000.

The return to Shelsley in August was keenly anticipated by all, despite the continuing convalescence of the injured Arthur Owen. The BRM organisation were about to pension off their 1960/61 P48 cars as their latest 1½-litre V8 engine was nearing race readiness, but as a final flourish prepared an Intercontinental specification car, complete with 2½-litre engine running on nitro-methane fuel for Marsh, who was intending to race a private BRM in 1962 Formula 1 races. With Chief Mechanic 'Wilkie' Wilkinson, once of the Evans family's Bellevue Garage and more recently of Ecurie Ecosse, in charge, this was going to be no mere demonstration. Added interest was lent by the appearance of veteran engineer Geoff Richardson with his latest Cooper-RRA, a rear-engined F1 car with a Connaught B-type engine crammed in the engine bay, and which showed its effectiveness with a 35.43s time. Fortunately, the fickle Worcestershire weather was impeccable and the MAC put on one of those real milestone Shelsleys. First, Marsh broke the course record, narrowly, in the familiar Lotus 18, a performance which was overshadowed by a superb 35.08s climb from Reg Phillips in "the mobile generating station". But then came the BRM. In a manner truly worthy of Raymond Mays himself, Marsh drove the powerful Bourne car up the course four times, including his two RAC runs. He broke the outright hill record every time, and became the only man to climb Shelsley in under 35s – four times! At the beginning of the meeting the record had stood to David Boshier-Jones, with 35.47s, set in 1959. At the end of the day the BRM driver had reduced that by over a whole second, leaving it at 34.41s. Interestingly, it was the 'specialists', Summers (36.15s) and Phillips (36.77s) who came closest to Marsh in the Top Ten, but it was really no contest. Marsh and BRM had brought a new dimension to hill climbing. Almost overlooked by all this, Peter Boshier-Jones again beat Scragg by 37.57s to 37.59s, and Daniel Richmond, enjoying a most successful season with the Cooper-based Venom-Austin Junior, brought the FJ record down to 39.04s at the expense of Geoffrey Wilson's previous best in a Lotus 18.

Even without the rather mixed weather which afflicted the BOC, even the September Prescott seemed a bit anti-climactic after Shelsley. Marsh had no BRM this time but he still set a new course record in the F1 Lotus in 50.70s, one of 10 records to fall, a crop which was at least partly attributable to the replacement of the marker cones at the Esses by a bevelled kerb which could be 'straight lined' with beneficial effects on the times. Among the new record-holders were John Rhodes (51.82s to retain the Staniland Trophy for another year), Boshier-Jones (53.45s), Fielding (53.36s), Randles (55.72s), Scragg (53.32s), Austen Nurse (58.34s), Gordon Chapman (ERA R2A in the newly introduced Historic class, 56.70s), Peter Hughes (500cc Cooper, 53.33s), Phillips (51.72s), Gordon Parker (single-seater HK-Jaguar, 54.38s), and Mac Daghorn who came over from Jersey to clock a superb 50.76s. Sadly, the rain then put a stop to what was developing into a re-run of the Bouley Bay battle, and the times in the RAC runs were some 7 or more seconds slower. Marsh was still on top but a splendid effort by Jim Berry, back in the veteran ERA R4D for the occasion, was second, beating even David Good.

This rather momentous season was rounded off, as far as Championship hill climbing was concerned, by Stapleford, where Patsy Burt, who had not enjoyed the best of seasons, but who was always thoroughly at home on the fast open sweeps of this airfield course, was the first to break Paul Emery's 1955 record, but she was still a second slower than Arthur Owen who followed and who set BTD. David Good had a brake lock and shot off the course, demolishing a post en route. Fortunately, he could not be cauht for the RAC title which he richly deserved, even though his total of 2 Championship meeting BTDs pales against the 5 of Marsh. The Cooper-JAP was still the Champion car but 8 out of 11 Championship events had fallen to more modern, essentially circuit-racing machinery. The final points total was: Good, 63; Owen, 50; Hatton, 49; Marsh, 49; Berry, 42; Fielding, 35. Consistency and total superiority in the over 1,600cc division gave Phil Scragg a one-hundred per cent 70 points for his second Sports Car Championship, with Fielding on 68 and Randles on 66, while Coventry driver Gordon March, who drove the ingenious little 500cc Mezzolitre and Instone's difficult old Djinn won the revived Junior title.

The later nineteen-fifties were years of sharply growing enthusiasm for motor sport as a whole in Britain, encouraged by growing national prosperity after the difficult immediate post-war years, and more specifically inspired by Britain's far stronger role in international motor racing. Success in the Le Mans 24 Hours sports car race and in International rallies was no novelty, but between 1958 and 1960 the assorted World Championship successes of marques Vanwall, Cooper–Coventry Climax and Aston Martin, and drivers Mike Hawthorn and Jack Brabham made major contributions to establishing Britain, for the first time, as the premier motor racing power. The boom was reflected in the growing support for hill cimbing among competitors in an unprecedented variety of cars. Only in the Championship-aspiring racing car classes was this boost not readily apparent. The breakthrough there really gathered momentum only in 1961.

Ever since the heady days before 1925, one of hill climbings's most serious limiting factors had been the shortage of first class venues, but in 1958 there were several significant additions. By far the best of these, and a hill worthy of bracketing with the classic hills included in the RAC Championship, was Wiscombe Park. Set in a secluded, tree-lined valley, six miles from Honiton in Devon, this originally 730 yard course actually forms the main drive to the home of Major Richard Chichester, himself a keen enthusiast and, in later years, co-driver with his friend and business partner Major Charles Lambton in the ex-Rivers Fletcher HWM-Jaguar single-seater. Beginning with a slightly downhill run to the tight left-hander at Wis, the course climbs up across open parkland before diving right into a

Second BTD at the June 1961 Prescott meeting fell to Peter Gaskell's Cooper-JAP.
via PETER GASKELL

particularly tricky succession of fast curves in thick woods. The sudden contrast between bright sunlight and the deep shade at this point presents an added problem. A tight and steep right-handed hairpin at Sawbench then brings competitors onto a straight which in the hill's pre-1961 form had the finish line on it. Apart from the host West Hants & Dorset Car Club, the hill rapidly became popular with other clubs such as Yeovil CC, the Taunton, West of England and Plymouth clubs, Southleigh MC, and the 750 Motor Club who switched to Wiscombe after running modest club events for a few years at the old Blandford Camp venue. The challenging nature of the course and a beautiful setting, set off to perfection by the Paddock laid out in the parkland in front of Gothic-styled Wiscombe House, soon recommended the hill whose only real disadvantage was its distance from the main centres of population. AC Ace-Bristol driver Alistair Park had the honour of setting the first BTD, in 44.78s, in August 1958.

Very different, but conveniently situated geographically was Mancetter, promoted by the Coventry & Warwickshire MC. This course was laid out in the quarry workings at the Man-Abell quarry near Atherstone, and presented a rather grim and forbidding appearance, not to say a daunting one as competitors at the top gazed down over the precipitous 'cliffs' to the start far below. This was one more course with a downhill start before climbing up out of the workings. The first meeting was held on 21 September, and the relatively local Coventry driver Dick James (Cooper 500) turned in a 39.91s run to defeat the Lister-Bristol of Josh Randles (40.11s).

Most of the regularly-used venues were now able to run racing cars, including Castel Farm, Trengwainton and Brunton, and Mike Hatton, benefitting from an ex-Ken Wharton JAP twin in his Cooper, opened the year most satisfactorily with a 28.5s course record at Castel Farm. There was another course record at Firle in June with the BARC (South East Centre) joining the BDC as promoters at the latter's hill, which the BARC was actually to take over from the Bentley Drivers Club for 1959. This time it was the supercharged Cooper-JAP of David Roscoe (26.71s) who came out on top from Rivers Fletcher (27.01s), who had recently enjoyed a BTD with his Cooper-JAP at the frequently-used Harleyford course, near Marlow. Josh Randles reasserted sports car supremacy at Barbon, taking his Lister-Bristol to a 34.31s BTD, but Austen May's course record remained out of reach. Tony Marsh took his Cooper-JAP to Firle for a demonstration climb at the BDC's traditional September meeting the day after the Brighton Speed Trials (won that year by Jim Berry's ERA Special from Patsy Burt's Cooper), and firmly placed Roscoe's record into context with an unofficial ascent in 25.31s. By 1958, the Surrey horsewoman turned sporting motorist, Patsy Burt, was really becoming a force in hill climbs and her 46.16s BTD at Stapleford in October demonstrated this most emphatically.

There were more new courses available in 1959, with Ragley Park and Castle Howard appearing on the calendar for the first time, courtesy of owners the Marquis of Hertford and Mr George Howard, and promoting clubs SUNBAC and the Yorkshire Sports Car Club respectively. Both hills enjoyed the ambience of notable English stately homes, although both the courses were fairly short and not very steep. Ragley Park, near Alcester, was a half-mile climb and its lack of really tight bends made it very fast, so much so that accommodation of spectators anywhere near the action was rather a problem. On the other hand a profusion of mushrooms growing in the Paddock was a great incentive to arrive early! The old established SUNBAC club held a damp and muddy opener in April, won by Brian Eccles in the so-successful 1950-chassised 998cc, supercharged Cooper which had formerly been Ken Wharton's car, but when the club returned in June, David Boshier-Jones set a truer target with a 24.00s record.

Unlike Ragley Park, located in the Midlands heartland of speed hill climbing, Castle Howard did not immediately attract the big names. With fairly sharp left- and right-hand bends, the latter fairly steep and blind because of rising ground on the inside, leading onto a straight blast past the magnificent Vanbrugh-designed Castle Howard house, this narrow and fairly short 600-yards climb was not in the premier league. But the setting, between the house and Castle Howard lake was second to none and two meetings were held in June and September. Unfortunately, the June meeting was brought forward in later years so as not to interfere with the house opening season, and the September meeting was put back to the very end of the speed season for the same reason, so Castle Howard events were rarely to enjoy good weather. The success of Barbon and especially Catterick was fostering a big upsurge of interest in hill climbing in the North, and especially in the North East. Although events tended to be rather parochial in the scope of entry lists, the numbers and enthusiasm were most encouraging. Both the initial meetings at Castle Howard were won by Catterick regular (he set BTD in April) Alan Ensoll with 26.03s and then 24.20s records in what appeared superficially to be one of the rare XKSS Jaguars, but which was actually TKF 9, the ex-Murkett Brothers, ex-Border Reivers D-type with which Henry Taylor and then Jim Clark had enjoyed considerable success before Alan bought it and fitted it with additional road equipment.

Perhaps *the* outstanding feature of the smaller meetings in a season which saw a hill climb BTD for Jim Clark (Border Reivers Lister-Jaguar) when the Lothian Car Club revived Bo'ness, were the two outright course records at Firle to the credit of Patsy Burt. The BARC had put in hand some minor improvements to the Sussex course since taking over responsibility for it and held two meetings in May and October. Always a staunch BARC supporter, the keenly competitive Miss Burt successively reduced the course record to 26.57s then to 25.40s. Mike Barker, later to become a partner in the Midland Motor Museum project with Bob Roberts, won the September BDC climb in his workmanlike Alton-Jaguar, a 3.8 Jaguar-engined, tubular-chassised creation with glassfibre body, but his 28.39s time was well outside the record. The BARC's South West Centre was busy in 1959 too, for the Brunton course was lenghtened in time for the September meeting where David Good set the new target in 23.85s. Added interest was provided by simply bringing the start back alongside the Paddock, which added a left-hand bend to the course's simple format.

Similar treatment was meted out to Catterick for 1960, increasing the approach speed for the first bend, but the changes didn't stop Alan Ensoll winning again, as had become quite a habit at the North Eastern meetings. However, he had to be content with second BTD at Barbon in May where Josh Randles produced his new Cooper Monaco and powered up this fast hill in 31.47s, at last breaking C.A.N. May's long-standing course record. There were records too down at Wiscombe where racing cars were now permitted and Arthur Owen set the new target in 38.02s. Certainly the closest meeting of the year was that at Ragley Park in September where a run-off was needed to separate David Good and Reg Phillips. The latter came to the line with the Fairley not properly warmed up and the car came to a halt just a few yards into the climb. In a characteristic act of sportsmanship, David Good insisted that 'smiling Reg' had another go, but it was the Maidenhead driver who came out on top with a 23.9s

course record to the 24.0s of Phillips, a time which was matched by Mike Hatton.

One important new course came into use during the year, Loton Park, in parkland at Alberbury, 8½ miles West of Shrewsbury. The Severn Valley Motor Club came to an agreement with Sir Michael Leighton to use 770 yards of his 600-acre game park which was well endowed with service roads and hard standings after wartime use as an RAOC bomb store. In its original form the course was neither particularly long nor steep but it was not an easy climb: the sharp left-hander at Fallow, coming at the brow of the steepest part of the course, in particular, needed care. SVMC committee member Tom Leake secured an early BTD here with his Aston Martin DB4. This was most appropriate as although Bryan Cooper had carried out much of the vital negotiation to gain use of the course, Tom played a major role in the climb's early years. As a member of the family which owned the local *Wellington Journal* and *Shrewsbury News* newspapers, he was able to obtain some valuable sponsorship and publicity for Loton, as well as taking on the task of commentating. Characterised by the potentially car-swallowing bracken which bounds the course, Loton rapidly became a popular venue. Unofficial 'gamekeeper' in the early days was Shrewsbury Town Clerk Ronald Loxton, a keen competitor with Invicta and later, Sunbeam Tiger, cars. Since he lived just across the road from the course he was always the first to practise and it was his habitual task to provide audible early warning to any still straying deer that it would be a good idea to depart to a more peaceful part of the estate!

The rather inadequate saftey aspects of Harleyford led to the abandonment of this venue for 1961 but in this, the busiest year since 1924, the loss was not too serious. After its early success, Wiscombe had been treated to a facelift over the winter, with resurfacing carried out, and the course lengthened by carrying on after the original finish line before heavy braking was demanded by a new, very tight and steep, left-hand hairpin, to be called Martini. This brought the length up to 1,000 yards and no less a personality than the still competing Basil Davenport opened the new course in April, when test pilot 'Dizzy' Addicott (Lotus 11) climbed in 49.30s in wet conditions to beat even David Good. Unfortunately, a differential failure sidelined Arthur Owen.

Mike Hatton, who scored BTDs in rapid succession at Ragley Park, Loton Park and Mancetter, left the Loton record at 35.68s when the SVMC catered for racing machinery for the first time and garnered a fine entry. Nevertheless, the amazing Peter Boshier-Jones was not far behind in his little Lola sports on a day when brother David briefly emerged from retirement to have a go with Patsy Burt's Porsche RSK (38.0s against Peter's 35.92s in the Lola).

Josh Randles scored a hat-trick of Barbon wins with a 30.81s record, and a highly successful weekend was rounded off by BTD the next day at Leighton Hall. Unfortunately, the Morecambe CC-organised course left rather marginal braking distance after the finish line before hard objects, not to mention the T-junction with the public road, were encountered. On his third run Josh 'did a Bob Gerard' and lost it after the finish, hitting parked cars, and suffering cuts and bruises himself.

In June Arthur Owen returned to Wiscombe Park when the WH & DCC obtained a National permit for their biggest meeting yet – although still with a predominantly West Country entry – and made amends for his earlier mishap by clocking a record 47.08s BTD. That record didn't last long either for David Good reduced it to to 46.98s in August, and then when the 750 Motor Club ran their climb in October, Tony Marsh brought his Formula 1 Lotus to the hill for the first time. After a long and strenuous season there were a lot of non-starters, Good joining their number with a broken crankshaft, but Marsh was undeterred and his 45.80s BTD lopped over a second off the record.

If Wiscombe was rapidly gaining stature the same was true of Loton Park where Mike Hatton bettered his earlier time in August with 33.95s, although with Peter Boshier-Jones still running him very close at 34.40s. Towards the end of the year Arthur Owen broke Patsy Burt's Firle record at a BARC/MGCC co-promotion (25.21s) and Reg Phillips took over Alan Ensoll's mantle at Castle Howard (25.14s), although Ensoll's record remained unbroken.

August actually saw two new hills used for the first time: Baitings Dam, on Blackstone Edge, near Ripponden; and Dyrham Park, 3 miles outside Old Sodbury, off the Bath-to-Stroud Road. Knowldale Car Club was the first of a number of clubs to use Baitings Dam which, as its name implies, employed a service road running up in the shadow of the dam wall. The presence of three tight hairpins in its short length meant that many competitors never got out of second gear but this safe climb, which also offers excellent vantage points for spectators from the dam wall or from the central spectator area, gained lasting popularity as a club venue without ever aspiring to Championship status. Dyrham Park was rather different and its 800 yards climb was far more in the mainstream of British hill cimbs, although a moderate gradient and only two real corners meant that it wasn't quite in the Wiscombe class. The promoters were the former Naish organisers, the long-established Bristol MC & LCC. Cheltenham car dealer Jack Browning won the first premier award with a genuine Jaguar XKSS while the second meeting left the record at 35.96s in the hands of the Cooper 1000 driver George Fisher, and a clear impression that the West Country had another important and well-received venue.

The BARC was becoming a significant hill climb club and the next Centre to join the lists was the Yorkshire Centre, headed by a real organisational heavyweight (in both senses), Mike Wilson. The Yorkshire Centre had been running very successful (slightly uphill) sprint meetings within the Hudson Road, Leeds, mill complex of the Burton tailoring concern, made available through Centre member and noted rally driver Arnold Burton. Now they had been able to arrange a hill climb on Oliver's Mount, at Scarborough. For the previous couple of years the Jaguar Drivers Club had concluded a semi-social weekend on this spectacular, municipally owned motor cycle racing (and occasionally 500cc car racing) circuit just a mile from the centre of Yorkshire's premier seaside resort. The BARC, in conjunction with the East Yorkshire CC took over the JDC's date to hold a full scale hill climb on a 1,600 yards section of the circuit which made it the longest hill on the British mainland. The combination of tight Mere hairpin, steep climb, sharp left- amd right-hand bends at the summit, a really fast final stretch to the finish and a generous (by hill climb standards) width of 15 ft, opened up a superb prospect. Word soon got around and there were 120 starters for the inaugural meeting, with another 80 regretfully refused. Circuit racer Jimmy Blumer (Cooper Monaco) was fastest in 49.24s, well clear of Sheffield's Phil Chapman in the Chapman-Mercury, and Olivers Mount was well and truly launched as a hill climb, albeit only available once per year at the end of the season.

It had been a really vintage year for hill climbing with more and more competitors eager to compete with modified saloons, GTs, and all manner of sports cars, together with the traditional single-seaters and specials, and a smattering of the new Formula Juniors (including experienced special-builder Arthur Mallock who took a third place at Prescott in his boxy little front-engined U2 creation). One established event which appeared in new guise was the Inter-Club climb, hitherto run at Prescott, but now transfered to the Shelsley 'club' date. The venue may have changed but the attempts to 'fox' the handicappers remained just as ingenious!

Following on from the Lotus Mk6, Buckler, Dellow and numerous Ford-based low-cost sports cars of the earlier nineteen fifties, the Lotus 7 became one of the commonest sights on the hills with specifications varying from BMC 'A' Series and Ford side-valve-engined models up to the potent Coventry Climax-powered, disc-braked, de Dion-axled machines of people like Edward Lewis, Jack Richards and Betty Haig. Especially sucessful in the later years of the 'Cooper-JAP era' were Daniel Richmond who later sold his first BMC-powered '7' to Austen May and then produced an even more potent Weber-carburettored version; May, Graeme Austin, Richard Blacklidge, Michael Sumner,

Harry Epps and Horace Appleby, while Jon Derisley did great things with his 1172 Formula racing Lotus 7, especially at Great Auclum.

The new generation of small saloons such as the Triumph Herald, Ford Anglia 105E, and above all the Austin Seven/Morris Mini-Minor fostered great interest in tuning and competing in a type of car which until the mid-nineteen fifties would have been totally rejected by competitors brought up with saloons which were singularly unsporting. By 1961 the Mini was already becoming one of the most numerous types of car to compete. Drivers of the calibre of Ralph 'Broadspeed' Broad, Daniel 'Downton' Richmond, Yorkshire mechanic Peter Kaye, Leeds journalist Allan Staniforth, and North Easterner Nicky Porter were already chalking up successes which had many drivers of traditional production sports cars scratching their heads in amazement at what could be achieved with the clever and inexpensive Mini, brainchild of Alec Issigonis.

Even in Ireland, where hill climbing had gone through a rather uninspiring phase in the mid-fifties, although there were still around ten events held during the year, the arrival of John Pringle and his powerful Coopers, Dan MacAlister with a Formula 2 Cooper and Hector Graham, former Cooper driver but now with the ex-Christie/Marsh Lotus 12 injected new interest.

Hill climbing was entering a new era of great popularity as a club sport laying to rest the idea that it was a secondary substitute for circuit racing with only limited support for its own merits.

CHAPTER SIX

GETTING THE POWER DOWN
(1962-1968)

IF the Cooper-JAP met its match in 1961, in succeeding seasons it was simply eclipsed. During the next three years hill climbing advanced by leaps and bounds with more competitors, more top-class venues and a degree of technical innovation unseen for many years.

For RAC Championship aspirants there was no longer only one rational approach. The advances in competition car chassis and suspension design by British constructors – Lotus, Cooper, BRM and Lola in particular – meant that more power could be transmitted, more efficiently, to the road. A new factor intruded when a streaming wet Aintree '200' Formula 1 race in April 1961 gave Dunlop the opportunity to try out publicly a new soft compound, 'high hysterisis' racing tyre designed primarily to increase grip in wet conditions, albeit at the expense of dry weather durability.

This was the Dunlop R5 D12 and cars fitted with these tyres dominated the race. The well-tried Dunlop R5 D9 – hitherto a constant factor which drivers and team managers could virtually take for granted – was no longer the automatic choice for all conditions, and thus was ushered in the modern era where tyre choice and tyre technology loom larger than most other factors in racing at its higher levels. One by-product of the availability of the 'high hysterisis', soft compound tyres (also referred to as 'low bounce' or simply 'highly hysterical' by the irreverent) was that leading hill climb contenders – unworried by rapid tyre wear and overheating in such short distances – were able to avail themselves of a really grippy tyre which permitted then to take full advantage of the enhanced roadholding potential of the newer circuit racing cars.

At first, the D12s, which were outwardly identical to the all-purpose D9s, were available only to suit the latest 1.5-litre Grand Prix cars, such as Tony Marsh's Lotus 18, but the range was soon extended to other circuit racing chassis. Although there were still many adherents to the Cooper-JAP ormula in 1962/3, including Ian McLaughlin, Mac Daghorn, Mike Hatton, Peter Gaskell, Tom Elton (his ex-David Good car soon being passed on to his son Spencer) and Wally Cuff, the old Cooper's combination of light weight, agility and good torque, was no longer a match for the new generation of more sophisticated circuit racing cars with their ability to offset greater weight with excellent roadholding, and more power.

Nevertheless the choice of approach was a difficult and potentially expensive one. Some competitors simply opted for a Formula 1 or Intercontinental Formula circuit racing car, while others followed Tom Norton's lead by taking a small and light Formula Junior chassis and adapting it to take a larger, and often supercharged, engine. Seekers after even more power took a larger F1 (or older F2) chassis and shoehorned a big torquey V8 engine into it. The 1961 Champion, David Good even had the idea of putting a JAP in a Cooper Formula Junior chassis. The options were many, and the new technical interest helped to generate more competition and greater interest in the sport than at any time since the nineteen-forties.

One more ingredient was added to a fascinating mixture in 1963 when Ferguson Research lent the unique four-wheel-drive Ferguson P99 to the Rob Walker team for Jo Bonnier to drive at Ollon-Villars in Switzerland, and then to Surrey engineer Peter Westbury to 'demonstrate' at Wiscombe Park. Four-wheel-drive was not new in hill climbing – witness the efforts of Jean Bugatti, Robert Waddy, Archie Butterworth and Sydney Allard – but the well developed Ferguson system, with centre differential and permanent 4WD opened up new possibilities.

Perhaps the momentum faltered slightly in 1965 when a new period of Tony Marsh domination began, while a couple of summers when atrocious weather seemed to be the norm did little to raise the spirits, yet by 1968 there was a further upsurge of interest, fed by an influx of new driving talent – such as Peter Lawson, Sir Nicholas Williamson, Martin Brain, David Hepworth, Roy Lane and Jimmy Johnstone – and major boosts to hill climbing in Yorkshire and Scotland.

In a sense 1968 was the end of an era too, for after contesting just three Championship rounds, Tony Marsh, six times Champion and winner of a record 43 BTDs at RAC Championship meetings, decided to retire and move on to powerboat racing. Although he won the RAC title in 1965, 1966 and 1967, developed his own ingenious and highly successful four-wheel-drive system, and remained the yardstick by which other drivers were judged, it would be an exaggeration to say that he totally dominated the 1962-68 period. On the other hand, one always felt that there had to be a valid reason why he did not always win! For 1969 there would also be a further important option on the mechanical side – the Formula 5000 car.

One of the factors which, in the face of increasing business commitments, caused Marsh to decide to withdraw was the proliferation of RAC Championship meetings which made following the Championship a major undertaking. Marsh began competing when there were only 6 or 7 top-class events on the calender, yet by 1962 there were 11, in 1963 there were 13, rising to 14 the following year and 15 in 1965. Although that record total fell back to 12 in 1967, there were 13 in 1968.

This 'problem' was simply a reflection of the sport's popularity. There were many more hill climb venues worthy of holding top-class events in the nineteen-sixties than there had been a decade earlier, reaching a peak in 1965. Wiscombe Park, Loton Park, Dyrham Park, Harewood, Longleat, Tholt-y-Will, Doune, Gurston Down, Fintray and Pontypool Park all either joined the RAC Championship schedule, or staged their first climbs during this period. There were other additions too, if not with high aspirations towards Championship status. For the first time competitors ascended the slopes of Valence School (1962), St Audries Bay (1962), Woburn Park (1963), Hemerdon Quarry (1963), Oddicombe (1963), Hurstwood (1964), Nettleton (1963), Lulworth Gunnery Ranges (1964), Furnace Grange Farm (1966), Ditcham (1968) and Scammonden Dam (1965). The changes were not all gains, though. The demands of housing development finally overtook Bo'ness, the National Trust declined to extend the Bristol MC & LCC's lease at Dyrham Park, Longleat both came and went during the period (a lion park and racing cars were definitely not compatible), and so did St Audries Bay. Gurston Down – a much more interesting hill – replaced Brunton; Mancetter, Lydstep and Catterick became unavailable; Stapleford came and went again and no more meeting were held at Westbrook Hay. The biggest net gains were in Yorkshire where the eventual loss of Catterick was offset by the arrival and rapid rise in stature of Harewood, and the growing popularity of Castle Howard and Oliver's Mount, where the size and calibre of the entry were increasingly high. Smaller meetings were being held regularly at Baitings Dam towards the end of the period. In Scotland too the loss of Bo'ness was more than compensated for by the development of the fine course at Doune – in delightful surroundings – and the debut of Fintray, near Aberdeen.

Ever since the BOC had responded to a demand to provide a separate class for Grand Touring cars

The 'Swinging Sixties' was a good time for hill climbing. Minis were becoming popular and films starring Peter Sellers were legion. R. Barrett leaves the line with a sideways glance, as well he might, with the celebrated film star, who was also a great car enthusiast, wielding the 'hockey stick'.
via MIKE KETTLEWELL

in 1957, the straightforward division of entries into racing and unrestricted sports car classes had seemed less relevant when the demand grew for classes to suit the new breed of modified touring cars (especially from 1960), and the wide variety of road-going sports cars encompassing Ford 100E and 105E, and BMC 'A' Series-engined Lotus Sevens at one end of the spectrum and Aston Martin, Jaguar E-type, and even the odd Ferrari 250GT at the other. As the nineteen-sixties progressed fewer competitors chose to campaign pure sports-racing cars – the Sports Car Championship itself was abandoned – but organisers responded differently to the changing make-up of their entry lists. The BOC, traditionally the most sensitive of leading organisers to such demands, changed their class structure in 1962, whereas the MAC were less ready to accommodate the road car competitors. Perhaps long memories of criticism of nineteen-twenties 'closed' meetings for tediously slow climbs by near standard cars lingered on. Further North, the Yorkshire Centre of the British Automobile Racing Club took the problem of ensuring fair class divisions very seriously. The Centre was headed by lifelong motoring enthusiast Mike Wilson, a second-generation Centre Chairman who was inspired by his father's dedicated furtherance of motor sport in the region, who devised a lengthy list of classes for BARC (and Yorkshire Sports Car Club) events. These, split standard and mildly modified saloons from the more highly developed Special Saloons. The same was done with the sports cars, separating the 'traditional' road sports cars (christened Marque 'Y' – for Yorkshire), from the limited production and Grand Touring machines (the new breed of racing GTs), which were further separated from the pure sports-racers. The classes worked well and large entries were secured from people who might not have bothered otherwise because they would have found themselves outclassed. Although critics of the BARC system felt that there were just too many classes, often with very few entries in some of them at the less well supported meetings, there was considerable progress by the end of the nineteen-sixties in bringing about some standardisation of classes throughout the country. Nevertheless, progress was by no means uniform, The MAC, not unexpectedly, insisted on going their own way, and, in fact, so did most of those involved in the older established Championship rounds.

Quite apart from the growing variety of machinery to be seen on the hills, the sporting and colourful atmosphere of hill climb paddocks was enhanced by seemingly ever-improving standards of car preparation and presentation. This was noticeable throughout motor sport, and had been apparent even in the early nineteen-fifties. In hill climbing the day of the deceptively effective but decidedly tatty looking special was definitely over. Even in the hayday of the Cooper-JAP the immaculate presentation of some cars – notably those of Michael Christie, David Boshier-Jones and David Good – did much to enhance the image of the sport. In the nineteen-sixties that standard became the norm, a reminder that for the vast majority of hill climbers the car was the weekend 'pride and joy' – not the tool for commercial or industrial betterment.

While the RAC Championship went from strength to strength during the nineteen-sixties, the Sports Car Championship and the rather low-key MAC Junior series fell by the wayside. In 1968 a major and enduring new Championship was introduced by the BARC to fulfil the long-felt need to provide a season-long target for the competitors who either could not or did not wish to embark on the big single-seater trail. The old Junior Car Club had been a major force in hill climbing until 1926, but it was not until the nineteen-fifties when the succeeding British Automobile Racing Club began staging regular club climbs at Brunton and Firle, that the BARC again became associated with hill climbs. Oddly enough, the initiative was coming from the regional centres rather than the Club Headquarters which was, and remains, race orientated. While the South West and South East Centres set the ball rolling, it was Mike Wilson and his colleagues in the Yorkshire Centre who really generated the impetus in the nineteen-sixties, building on the success of the sprint meetings held on the Burton clothes factory roads in Leeds. Oliver's Mount, in Scarborough, provided a first class hill but one with very restricted usage, so the key factor was the purchase from the Harewood Estate of Stockton Farm, Harewood, only seven and a half miles from Leeds, off the Harrogate road, by club stalwart Arnold Burton, purely for the Centre to have a permanent hill venue. Further South the arrangement of the South West Centre with the enthusiastic Hitchings brothers to use their much up-graded farm road at Gurston Down in 1967 and, in the same year, an agreement between the Club's South Wales Centre and the Pontypool local authority to run hill climbs in Pontypool Park, gave the BARC a number of really challenging venues in various parts of the country. These were linked together to form a new and different sort of national Championship.

This was promoted for the first time in 1968 – in a fairly low-key way, to see how it progressed – with Championship marks based on performances in classes rather than the battle for BTD. Competitors scored points, and fractions of points, by reason of achieving times under the bogey time for the class, set at eight seconds over the class record. So, if you climbed in 35.50 seconds and your class record was 35.60s, you scored 8.10 marks whereas your 'rival' with a more potent car in a racing class who climbed in 32.50s in a class where the record was 31.50s, scored only 7.00 marks. The idea was ingenious and, with minor adjustments, proved to be very successful, although gamesmanship among the more determined had seen much research over the winter months trying to find a hitherto 'slow' class and therefore with a favourable bogey time, in which to introduce a super-competitive car!

Cooper topples Cooper

Over the close season in 1961/2 there was keen anticipation for the season ahead, with memories of Tony Marsh's devastating Shelsley Walsh performances in the BRM fuelling much speculation. The well-liked, if rather remote, Wiscombe Park hill, owned by Majors Richard Chichester and Charles Lambton – enthusiastic Alta and later HWM-Jaguar (the ex-Rivers Fletcher car) drivers both – was added to the RAC Championship schedule for 20 May. The Bugatti Owners Club completely re-jigged their class structure, grouping what they called Sports Touring cars (MGs, Triumph TRs, Austin Healeys and the like), with GTs and modified saloons and splitting racing cars into four classes. One, two and three-cylinder 'Formule Libre' machinery, that is the Cooper-JAPs and the old 500s, were lumped together in one class. Racing cars with four or more cylinders were just divided at 1500cc, but a separate class was provided for the Formula Junior brigade.

Although splitting his efforts between circuit racing and hill climbing probably cost Marsh the 1961 Championship, he intended to cover both spheres again in 1962. The first man to race a BRM outside

The ex-Tony Gaze, Jaguar-engined, HWM was associated with Wiscombe Park like no other car. It was driven at the hill for many years by the Majors, Richard Chichester and Charles Lambton, after they had bought it in 1964. However, the car's previous owner, Rivers Fletcher, was still at the wheel when this picture was taken.
ANTHONY HOLLISTER
via RIVERS FLETCHER

the factory or factory-blessed British Racing Partnership team, Marsh had bought his 1960 P48 model in 1961 with both the 2.5-litre BRM engine (as run at Shelsley) and a 1.5-litre Coventry-Climax F1 unit, and it was with the latter engine in place that he won the Lewis-Evans Trophy at Brands Hatch in October 1961. For the new year, and with technical assistance from the Owen Organisation, he intended to race a 1961 P48/57 model which had a carburettor version of the new BRM V8 grafted into it. Unfortunately, this wasn't successful as the works were unable to spare time and resources to develop this hybrid. For hill climbs and sprints, instead of running the P48 with 2.5-litre engine, he put that unit in a new BRM-inspired Marsh sprint car chassis, and ran the P48 with the alternative 1.5. His old Lotus 18 was sold to Gerry Ashmore for circuit racing.

Over-dissipation of effort looked likely to be Marsh's biggest problem, but the opposition was becoming stronger too. The Champion, David Good, made the rather curious choice of fitting a JAP twin into a 1961 Formula Junior Cooper, but Arthur Owen looked a strong challenger with his third big Cooper, an Intercontinental Formula car raced in 1961 by the Tommy Atkins/Bruce McLaren partnership.

Marsh was not the only hill climber to buy an obsolete BRM, for long time sports car contender Ray Fielding bought a sister car to Marsh's P48, the car normally raced by Dan Gurney in 1960, and used for Intercontinental races the following year. Ian McLaughlin's yellow Cooper-JAP headed the traditionalists with their Cooper twins, while two new 'specials' were under development and were to have a significant influence in the fullness of time. The burly conductor of the remarkable Farley Special, and successful circuit racer, Chris Summers, had for some time run an old 1958 leaf sprung Formula 2 Cooper in circuit events. But down at Jack Newton's Thornton Heath workshops John Farley and mechanic Jim Thornton were fitting the car with a 4.4-litre V8 engine out of a Chevrolet Bel Air, mildly modified and developing around 255 bhp at 5000 rpm, and driving through the 1958 Cooper 4-speed gearbox. This £75 engine was further modified as the season progressed, being bored out to over 4.6-litres, and eventually churning out some 320 bhp at 6000 rpm.

The same theme of obtaining power and torque on the cheap occupied the fertile mind of a Surrey engineer called Peter Westbury. He was bent on improving an equally 'different' concoction which had first appeared – without much success – the previous year. The bearded Westbury, from the delightfully named village of Holmbury St Mary, near Dorking, had taken up hill climbing as his wife wasn't keen on him racing, and in 1960 had competed with an early, 1957 leaf sprung F2 Cooper which had already had an arduous career at the hands of Brian Naylor and John Campbell-Jones. Westbury showed himself to be an innovator by deciding that the Edward Turner-designed 2,548cc Daimler SP250 engine was ideal. For its size the engine was not heavy and 160 bhp was developed at 5800 rpm without sacrificing flexibility and low speed punch. The substitution of some ex-Rob Walker suspension parts of the coil and wishbone variety helped to sort out the suspension but in early 1962 few looked to this car for any big surprises.

That true sportsman and enthusiast for 'different' cars. Jim Berry, sold his Connaught and bought the Cooper-ish JBW with 2.8-litre, 4-cylinder Maserati engine from Brian Naylor. Although the cheerful Lancastrian had no Championship aspirations, his recent performances in R4D and the B-Type Connaught were not to be sneezed at, so his prospects with this Intercontinental Formula car looked bright. Tragically, it was not to be for Jim crashed and was killed testing the car at Oulton Park in March. The accident happened on his Silver Wedding Anniversary, the final bitter irony for a man devoted to his family and his sport. The JBW was repaired and passed to Haslingden Formula Junior Elva driver, Jack Cordingley, who scored several successes with it including setting BTD in the new record time of 30.46s at Barbon.

There was no real dress rehearsal for the RAC series in 1962 although there were early successes for Patsy Burt's impeccably turned-out, Ron Smith managed F2 Cooper at Wiscombe Park, a 40.95s record for Josh Randles' Cooper Monaco at Catterick, a win for Wally Cuff's Cooper-JAP over David Good's temperamental new JAP-engined FJ Cooper at Brunton, and a fine record breaking 23.5s climb at Ragley Park by Ian McLaughlin to see off Reg Phillips and Doug Haigh at a meeting where 'CAN' May lifted a 25.00s Formula Junior win in his Lotus 18. Probably the most daunting (to the opposition) early season performance came when Tony Marsh took his new BRM-based Marsh Special to Wellesbourne for a demonstration run at a sprint meeting. He was 10 full seconds faster than any of the competitors!

Tony Marsh fielded two challengers for 1962. This is the BRM P48, spinning its wheels as it leaves the Prescott startline.
MICHAEL WARE
via MIKE KETTLEWELL

Prelude to disaster. Tony Marsh accelerates away from the Rest-and-be-Thankful startline, as low cloud makes Glen Croe look particularly menacing. Seconds later he crashed, wrecking the 2.5 Marsh-BRM.
BILL HENDERSON

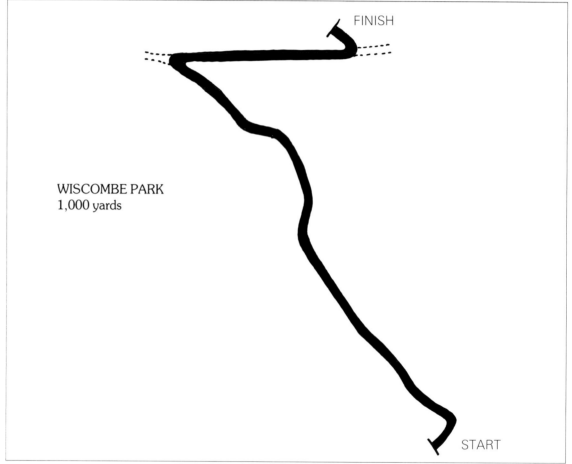

FINISH

WISCOMBE PARK
1,000 yards

START

The RAC series began predictably enough at Prescott where Marsh blasted the Marsh-BRM to a new hill record in 48.84s and set the second BTD with the 1.5 BRM-Climax in 51.00s. Raymond Mays should have been doubly proud for Ray Fielding immediately impressed with his car and finished runner-up to Marsh in the Top Ten runs in 51.58s, well clear of Reg Phillips in the old Fairley. Ian McLaughlin beat David Good in the Formule Libre class but it is perhaps significant that Bill Bradley's Formula Junior Cooper-Ford, a Midland Racing Partnership car normally raced rather than hill climbed, scuttled up in 51.57s to the 53.20s of McLaughlin's class winning time.

It was almost the same story at Wiscombe Park when West Hants & Dorset CC made a big occasion out of their first Championship meeting. Marsh set a 45.49s hill record on the class run, but then it started to rain and the Top Ten was another matter with the impressive Ray Fielding guiding the powerful BRM round Martini and over the line in 51.65s, almost a second up on Josh Randles' sports Cooper, and with Arthur Owen also beating Marsh. Ray took another 10 points at Shelsley where his 34.65s was also the official BTD. Although he was competing mainly in circuit races, Chris Summers brought along his crowd pleasing Cooper-Chevrolet and ended up only 0.15s slower than Fielding's thoroughbred and ahead of Phillips, McLaughlin and Randles. Marsh? He had intended to go to the Monaco Grand Prix but problems with his BRM V8 caused him to withdraw and although he had not put in an entry in time for Shelsley he came along to do a 'demonstration' run. His time of 33.91s was under the hill record, although it could not count, of course. However, since the scoring system did not demand attendance at every round there was no reason to suppose that his chances were seriously affected. This was emphasised when he went up to Bo'ness for the first time since 1954 and came away with a new course record in 30.99s, and maximum points, and with Arthur Owen also beating the 'local' man, Ray Fielding, whose early season form later seemed to lose some impetus.

It was at Rest-and-be-Thankful where the Marsh campaign suffered a serious reverse. After setting a 52.52s BTD, Tony set off to improve on this in his first RAC climb. The Marsh-BRM landed badly after the notorious Hump, shooting to the left and then veering off to the right where it bounced off a bank, shot back across the road and landed upside down on a wall before toppling thirty feet into the bracken below. Fortunately the driver was virtually unscathed after a very nasty accident but the Marsh was wrecked and was not rebuilt. This left the Championship points to the increasingly consistent Arthur Owen (52.63s), with Mac Daghorn's ex-Boshier-Jones' Cooper-JAP coming over from Jersey to make it a Channel Island benefit ahead of Fielding.

Suddenly, Arthur Owen looked as though he could mount a really strong challenge, and with Marsh absent, he broke the Westbrook Hay record in 22.85s, with Bryan Eccles' Cooper-JAP and Fielding filling the minor places. (Eccles now seemed to prefer his christian name spelt with a 'y' instead of an 'i').

There were more shocks at Bouley Bay, though, where victory fell to a Channel Islander, but not to Owen (who was RAC runner-up on 51.02s) or Daghorn, but to the Italian-born former 500cc Cooper driver Tico Martini who shattered the course record in 50.63s, driving a self-built 650cc device which was a very close relative of a Kart. The astonishing 650 Triumph Tiger 110 vertical twin-engined Martini Special had already won the Jersey's Club's spring event at Bouley, but now it was 2 seconds faster and caused consternation. While everyone had been concentrating on larger and more powerful machinery, Martini had gone in the opposite direction and his beautifully finished device had a wheelbase of only four feet six inches and weighed but 365 lbs. The mild steel tubular chassis boasted Norton motorcycle transmission, independent suspension by swing axles, Lambretta scooter front brakes, motorcycle brakes at the rear, tiny 8-inch-diameter wheels and direct steering controlled by two stirrup-type controls. At first Martini was excluded from the results because of doubts over his eligibility as an Italian national. Some time after the meeting, the wrangle was resolved in Tico's favour and he retained his BTD and RAC points, although his remarkable Special caused the RAC to add a regulation demanding that cars had to have a minimum wheelbase of six feet in later years. Nobody relished the prospect of the RAC Championship being dominated by overgrown Karts, however ingenious. During the class runs Mac Daghorn (surely the most naturally talented driver never to be able to tackle a full RAC season), came very close to Martini with 50.74s on his first run, then damaged the Cooper's suspension at Les Platons second time up. Very sportingly, Peter Westbury, who had just repaired the Cooper-Daimler after an accident at Brunton and found the car much improved for the experience, lent it to Daghorn for the RAC runs. Mac really excelled himself and his 51.80s was beaten only by Owen and McLaughlin (51.75s), and was 0.36s faster than Westbury himself. Unfortunately, he was not allowed to count his points because he had not practiced in the car. This was the beginning of a fruitful association between the Jersey mechanic and Westbury which eventually led to Mac driving in International Formula 3 races for Westbury's FIRST team in later years.

Several of the leading contenders took in Craigantlet and the newly sorted Cooper-Daimler of Westbury succeeded in edging out both Owen and Fielding, but none could match the local man, John Pringle, who smashed his 1961 record in the class runs in 65.97s, and while the 1959-type 2.5 Cooper-Climax slowed slightly to 66.42s in the RAC runs it was still good enough for maximum points.

There is no sharper contrast than that between the lengthy Craigantlet hill and the short sharp quarter-mile dash at Great Auclum and, now confirmed as a *bona fide* RAC Championship contender, Tico Martini brought over the tiny Martini Special to contest an event which seemed tailor made for it. The result was another record, in 20.14s, to deal another telling blow at the hill climb establishment. In fact, it was another Jersey Benefit for Arthur Owen did well to record 20.62s in the big Cooper, just 0.01s up on Mac Daghorn who tied for third place with Peter Boshier-Jones who had swopped his Lola for the latest in Lotus-Ford 23 sports racers and was setting class records in his accustomed style.

In this season of surprises, it was the weather which dealt the next one, at Shelsley, where it stayed dry just long enough for the sports cars to get in a fast time, but the rain spoilt the efforts of the single-seaters. Fastest of all was actually George Brown's Vincent Special motorcycle 'Nero', but among the cars it was a 37.24s tie between Phil Scragg's powerful Lister and the nippy rear-engined Lotus 23 of 'Bosh', with Josh Randles just 0.32s down in the Cooper Monaco. Tony Marsh, his Championship chances blunted, returned to the fray with the 2.5 BRM engine, taken from the wreck of the Marsh, back in the BRM P48. It was a day for the bigger cars on this power hill, with Tony back on top in the RAC climbs with a 38.48s, almost half a second faster than Summers' mighty Cooper-Chevvy and with Westbury's Cooper-Daimler defeating Owen, Fielding and David Good. The latter had despaired of his new style Cooper-JAP and was having an outing in Marsh's BRM. Marsh too was to be seen in an unfamiliar cockpit. He recorded a commendable 46.03s in Ian Sievwright's historic Ferrari 625, the car with which Maurice Trintignant won the 1955 Monaco Grand Prix.

So it was all down to Prescott, where this traditionally fine meeting was opened by Bob Gerard in an ERA once more. Although 'Mr Bob' had competed in three of the Bourne cars this was not one of them for he was driving Dudley Gahagan's red R7B, the ex-Arthur Dobson/Leslie Brooke car. However, when the serious business was over, Arthur Owen emerged as the 1962 Hill Climb Champion. His 50.50s Top Ten best was good enough for third place and the Championship was his after a consistent season although he had actually only set BTD at one RAC round. Although he did not crack his own record, Tony Marsh made a point by setting BTD and winning the Top Ten competition and a revitalised David Good, now with a 1.5 Coventry-Climax engine in his FJ Cooper, broke 50s for runner-up spot. His engine, incidentally, had originally come out of Marsh's Lotus 18.

An unexpected challenge in 1962 came from Peter Westbury, using the Daimler SP250 V8 engine in an old Formula 2 Cooper chassis.
via MIKE KETTLEWELL

In the final points table Ray Fielding's excellent start to the season helped him to 68 points (to the 73 of Owen), while the most regular upholder of Cooper-JAP honours, Birmingham's Ian McLaughlin, scored 51 points after a most determined season in the little yellow car. The unlucky Marsh scored 48, Josh Randles totted up 33 with his formidable sports Cooper and Westbury's late run in the smartly prepared Cooper-Daimler – now boasting an opened-out and shortened 'Monaco' nose – rounded out the top six.

Outside the rarified atmosphere of the RAC Rounds, the old Cooper-JAP formula was still capable of winning performances, witness the BTDs at the May Dyrham Park (Cuff in a record 34.75s), May Ragley Park (McLaughlin in a record 23.4s), June Ragley Park (McLaughlin with his third record in a row in 23.31s), the July Inter-Club Shelsley (McLaughlin in his familiar yellow Mk XI Cooper once more), the July Members' Prescott (Doug Haigh's gold-painted supercharged Cooper-NorJAP), the July Dyrham Park (Freddie Floyd in a record 34.20s), the 'Four Clubs' Wiscombe Park (Cuff), the final Castel Farm climb (Fred Jones), and the October meeting at St Audries Bay (Cuff in 42.91s). Peter Westbury may not have scored highly in his earlier academic engineering training, but he was certainly a fine empirical engineer for in a late run with the Cooper-Daimler, he broke the Dyrham Park record in 32.08s, set another record breaking BTD at Brunton (22.71s) and then shared BTD with David Good at the BRSCC (South Western Centre) promotion at Wiscombe. Good was planning to have Westbury install a Daimler V8 in the back of his FJ Cooper and these friendly rivals waived the offer of a tie decider and toured up the hill together with their mechanics perched on the tails of their cars before an appreciative audience.

The most successful hill climber of his era: Tony Marsh.
via MIKE KETTLEWELL

Gone were the days when the hill climb season was virtually all over after the September Prescott meeting, for although the RAC series was over, there remained major climbs at Dyrham Park, Wiscombe Park, the brand-new Harewood course, Castle Howard and Oliver's Mount. There were no fewer than 150 entries for the latter northern finale where Jack Cordingley powered the 2.8 JBW-Maserati to a record-breaking 47.32s, twice!

Overall, the level of entries up and down the country was unprecedented, and fine performances were being achieved every week in many types of car. The Formula Juniors were still not all that numerous, but Austin May was outstanding with his Lotus 18, while Eric Wilmott was a regular winner in his red front-engined Elva. Apart from Scragg's mighty Lister-Jaguar, Randles and Boshier-Jones, the sports car honours were well shared. Keighley driver Tommy Clapham, in the same Lotus-Climax 7 which he was still competing in almost thirty years later defeated a superb field at Prescott in September with a record-breaking 53.88s, capping a fine year, and vanquishing the likes of Jack Richards' similar car, John Macklin's 7, Gerry Tyack's ex-Fielding Emeryson, Welshman Tony van Moyland's ex-Fielding Cooper, and Jerseyman Peter Meldrum's Lotus 7. In northern events, Phil Chapman's big Chapman-Mercury, distinctive with its cutaway bonnet top revealing a formidable array of Amal carburettors, Graeme Austin's deceptively rapid BMC 'A' Series-engined Lotus 7A of the Wirral Racing Team, Jill Hutchinson's Terrier Mk II (an early Len Terry design for 1172 Formula

Peter Westbury.
via MIKE KETTLEWELL

racing), and yet more Lotus 7s in the hands of 'Fast Fred' Smith, John Brierly and John Butterworth, took a lot of beating. Down in Wales, and especially at Castel Farm, 'Taffy' Cottrell reigned supreme in his Lotus 15.

The growing numbers of GT and modified saloon cars provided plenty of entertainment with Phil Scragg a difficult man to beat in his glorious Jaguar E-type. Down in the West Country, Bath garage owner Ron Fry brought a touch of real glamour by entering the fray with a superb red Ferrari 250GT Berlinetta. Ron was around 40 before he began competing, but his successes in the next few years belied the fact. Midlander Bob Rose lifted many prizes with his fast Lotus Elite, but at the May Prescott Meeting the similar car of Altrincham jeweller John Lepp had to accept defeat at the hands of the amazing Ashley Cleave and his even more amazing 1937-based Morris Special, still changing up only when valve-bounce set in! It was delightful to see, among all the new blood taking to the sport, lifelong enthusiasts like Basil Davenport, Cleave and his arch rival Tommy Pascoe in his Porsche Carrera, still competing with undimmed vigour. Among the saloons, apart from another Westcountryman, Amie Lefevre with his Sunbeam Rapier, and sundry big Jaguars, most of the attention focused on the increasingly radically modified Minis, and especially on those of Rod Embley, Nicky Porter, and a strong Yorkshire contingent including Leeds *Daily Mirror* journalist Allan Staniforth, Ken Lee and Peter Kaye. Blackpool driver Richard Blacklidge was usually in the running too.

The year witnessed the first climbs held at Valence School, Harewood and St Audries Bay. Alister Crawford's Lotus Elite (33.28s) was the fastest of 83 competitors at Valence School, near Westerham in Kent, when the Sevenoaks & DMC (co-promoting with the Austin-Healey Club, the London MC and the VSCC) arranged with the Governors of Valence School for Backward Children to hold a hill climb over 706 yards of the School grounds, with proceeds going to the School. With a downhill start, two hairpins, a blind right-hander onto the straight and an ess bend, the hill was interesting and this first charity meeting set a successful precedent for what became an annual event attracting a good entry for a rare type of meeting in that part of the country.

September 16 was a great day for the BARC's Yorkshire Centre, when over 100 entries were received for the first climb up the 1200 loose and bumpy yards of Stockton Farm, Harewood. Although the hill clearly needed resurfacing, the potential was obvious on a hill which rose some 250 feet, offered a good variety of medium speed corners, a short straight between the rather daunting walls of the farmyard, a long, climbing wide radius hairpin at Farmhouse, a slightly curving 'straight' and a final tightening and blind right virtual hairpin at Quarry just before the finish. Another feature which was appreciated by competitors was that since the Paddock, unusually, was at the top of the hill, and commanded views over most of it, it was possible for drivers to have a good look at how everybody else was doing before making their way down to the start. Fastest at this first rather experimental meeting was a young Bradford confectioner who was beginning to make a name for himself in circuit racing with an Elva-Climax Mk6. That was Tony Lanfranchi and his 51.61s time was 1.27s better than Derek Scott's Cooper-JAP. Interestingly, a number of that day's successful drivers were still competing 25 years later, including local heating and insulation engineer Jim Johnstone (class winner in his Team Speedwell Yorkshire Sprite), and Mini drivers Staniforth and Kaye.

If hill climbing was thriving in Yorkshire, the same could be said of the sport in the West Country where, inspired by Bill Cawset of the Taunton Motoring Club, and with the assistance of the Yeovil CC and the Burnham-on-Sea MC, the first two meetings were held up an 880 yards climb at St Audries Bay. This climb had some similarities with Harewood in that the gradient was much steeper on the higher slopes, and that the road ran between farm buildings, but this fairly fast climb was particularly tricky as it was bounded in places by high banks, quite apart from the farm buildings, was narrow, and generally left little margin for error. Wally Cuff ended the year on top with his rather untidy Cooper-JAP and there were some pained expressions when Ron Fry slightly modified the bodywork of his scintillating Ferrari in trying (unsuccessfully) to match the class-winning time of Tom Cunane's successful Ford Zephyr-engined AC Ace.

An engineer's approach

Tony Marsh had set BTD at no less than six of the 1962 RAC rounds yet the title had fallen to the consistent Owen, whose sights were now turning towards the challenge of European hill climbs. Owen did not in fact complete another full hill climb season. Once again Marsh looked to be favourite for top honours, and there were many who thought that he would be invincible with the P48 BRM. However, once again Marsh had his own ideas and although he retained the BRM he intended to build his main offensive round a new Marsh Special. Enough power allied to agility was the objective, and the Marsh-Climax was notably small and weighed in at a mere 8 cwt with fuel and water. The basis was a modern spaceframe chassis, coil and wishbone suspension with radius arms at the rear, and the latest in Dunlop racing rubber to get the power down. The latter commodity was to be supplied by a 1.5-litre Coventry Climax FPF Mk1 engine, Shorrock supercharged at 6 psi with a view to producing 170 bhp. Various Cooper parts such as steering and wheels were incorporated and this tiny six foot four inch wheelbase machine was clothed in a body built by Shapecraft of Egham. It was no mean achievement for Tony and Ted Jeffs to build the car in three months flat, but events showed that Marsh *might* have been better off to stick to the BRM. The Marsh was very tricky to drive, the short wheelbase making it all too easy to spin, while the blown Climax engine was disappointing – it never developed more than around 140 bhp – and was replaced by a 2-litre FPF in May.

Peter Westbury, the revelation of the later stages of the 1962 season, also presented a purpose built special for 1963. This was the Felday-Daimler, named after Peter's new Felday Engineering business which in turn took the name from the medieval predecessor of Westbury's home village, Holmbury St Mary. Less ambitious than the Marsh, the Felday was basically a much-reworked Lotus 20 prototype, with the rear end adapted to take the Daimler V8 engine which was now supercharged at a theoretical 8 psi (it turned out to be nearer 4!). The resulting output was not enormous at around probably 165 bhp (220 bhp was quoted!) but the low and mid range punch certainly was. Westbury's technique was more or less to scrabble round the corners and then step off smartly up the straights, a procedure to which the metallic blue car was ideally suited.

It was almost a case of all change in the close season after the lessons of 1962. Superchargers were in vogue with several more adherents. Peter Boshier-Jones made his début in the single-seater category with a yellow Lotus 22 FJ chassis fitted with a Shorrock-blown 1.2 sohc Climax engine, while Tom Norton had bought the ex-Marsh Lotus 18, which also boasted a compressor. After trying his hand at single-seaters with his self-built HK-Jaguar, Kentish enthusiast Gordon Parker bought the supercharged F2 Cooper-Climax of George Keylock, who substituted a Geoff Richardson-built machine inspired by the Summers Cooper-Chevrolet. This was a Cooper Junior fitted with the light and compact 3.5 Buick V8.

George was not the only man to see the potential in this alloy engine which in developed form was to become very familiar in the Rover SD1, Range Rover and Morgan Plus Eight. Seven Fifty MC stalwart Mike Eyre fitted another Buick to an older F2 Cooper chassis, whereas Bryan Eccles was building up an even more powerful car, an ex-Yeoman Credit/Roy Salvadori Cooper allied to a 4.7 Chevrolet V8. Then again there were those who tried to strike a compromise over power, like Patsy Burt who pensioned off her old F2 Cooper and emerged with a 1962 FJ Cooper propelled by a 2-litre Climax, the cars immaculate turn-out once more the responsibility of Ron Smith and his assistants, who had been preparing her cars for some years. David Good started the season with a supercharged 1.5 Climax in his FJ Cooper, but this soon gave way to a Felday Engineering Daimler V8.

Also expected to figure prominently was Ray Fielding who now boasted an ex-Jim Clark/Team Lotus 21 with 2.2 Climax engine, and the Glasgow husband and wife team, Gray and Agnes Mickel who, after many years of more modest competition in Scotland, took over no less a car than the reigning Champion's Cooper-Climax. One surprise addition to the single-seater ranks was Phil Scragg, who always preferred to compete with a sports car which could be driven on the public roads when necessary. He had sold the Lister-Jaguar (advertised at £1850) to north eastern Bentley racer Keith Schellenberg, and had actually ordered an exotic 5.3 Chaparral-Chevrolet, one of the front-engined 1963 cars, from Jim Hall's Texas team. Since there was no prospect of the car arriving for some time, he bought Ray Fielding's BRM as a stopgap.

Over in Ireland, the Craigantlet record holder, John Pringle had a brand-new Intercontinental/ Tasman Cooper with 2.5 Climax engine although his garage business still kept him at home and ruled out a serious attack on the RAC Championship. His earlier 1959-type Cooper went to double Sexton Trophy winner Dan McAlister, who fitted his 1.5-litre engine out of his previous year's car which had been written off in a crash.

All these and many more changes made the season ahead a fascinating prospect, and although Peter

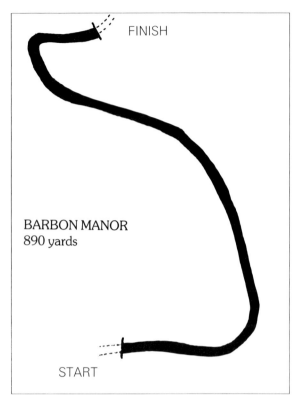

BARBON MANOR
890 yards

FINISH

START

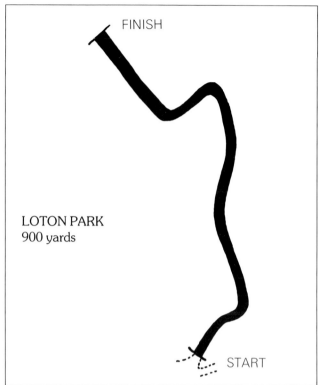

LOTON PARK
900 yards

FINISH

START

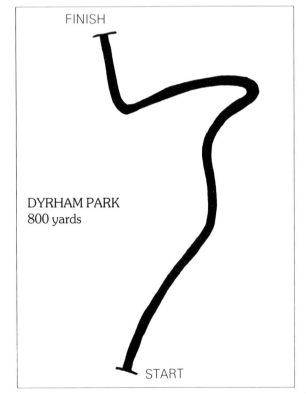

DYRHAM PARK
800 yards

FINISH

START

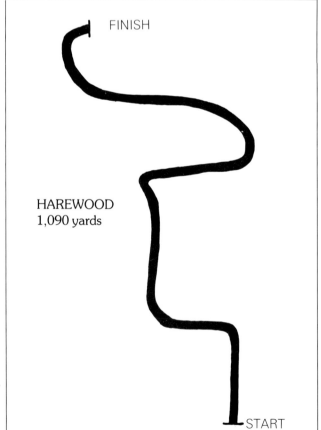

HAREWOOD
1,090 yards

FINISH

START

Peter Westbury's 1963 RAC Championship-winning Felday-Daimler was effective, if rather inelegant. The chassis owed much to the prototype Lotus 20.
PATRICK BENJAFIELD *via* MIKE KETTLEWELL

Tony Marsh's 1963/64 Marsh-Climax was both underpowered and skittish to handle. The back end is sliding out here at Craigantlet.
BRIAN FOLEY *via* MIKE KETTLEWELL

Westbury drew first blood with the Felday at the Aston Martin Owners Club Wiscombe meeting early in April, many of the new cars were troublesome, so all attention was focused on Loton Park on the 28 April. The SVMC had deservedly won RAC Championship status for the first time and opened the series on a course which had been lengthened to 900 yards, the extension coming at the top of the hill.

After his disappointing 1962 season and the fast-growing cost and complexity of front line Grand Prix machinery, Tony Marsh had decided to concentrate wholly on hill climbs and sprints. His campaign began well with a 37.03s best at Loton in the Marsh Special although the closeness of the competition can be gauged by the cluster of five other competitors in the 37s bracket. Despite his inexperience with the BRM, Phil Scragg ran him closest on 37.25s, with Westbury's Felday, Boshier-Jones' nimble Lotus 22, Good and Ian McLaughlin's game Cooper-JAP also in contention.

After 12 years as Chairman of the BOC, Roy Taylor handed over the office to long-time Bugatti driver Ronnie Symondson for the new season. His first Prescott in this new capacity saw something of a turnaround as a rain shower slowed times later in the afternoon. Marsh smashed the course record in 48.68s before the track became damp but that was in the BRM and he had nominated his Marsh Special for the RAC runs where he could only tie with 'Bosh' on 50.90s for second place, 10 points going, rather surprisingly, to a determined Bryan Eccles with his brutish Cooper-Chevrolet. It really did look as though nothing would deny the Kinver farmer (and garage owner by this time) 1963 honours, though, for he set a 44.23s BTD on the RAC runs at Wiscombe, the third Championship round. He *was* in the BRM this time as he had gone straight on at the Gateway in the Marsh on his second class run. Westbury was only 0.14s slower this time and Ian McLaughlin drove superbly well to record 45.00s.

The position was similar at Barbon, with Marsh competing at the Westmorland Motor Club's fairly short but fast climb for the first time. The reason for his appearance was that the Westmorland Motor Club had at last secured an RAC round for the North-West, although some competitors felt that the hill was a little narrow and bumpy for the most powerful machinery. Although the meeting got off to a bad start – commencing an hour late – because Murray's pre-War Spikins Special had dropped a sumpful of oil all over the road, the day ended with Marsh on top and a new hill record of 28.779s (note times to a thousandth of a second) to the credit of the tiny green Marsh Special. Westbury was again runner-up (28.805s), and Scragg held off an impressive Gray Mickel for third place.

Although the June Shelsley gave Marsh yet another record, ascending in 33.54s in the BRM, it wasn't really a classic meeting because there were many non-starters, delays and disappointments, such as Westbury's Felday breaking its cwp and 'Bosh's' superbly handled Lotus dropping oil after running Marsh very close on the RAC climbs. As Marsh set yet another BTD at Bo'ness, there was more trouble for Westbury when a broken hub-carrier sidelined the Felday. Straightaway, David Good offered the Cooper-Daimler for Peter to share and the Surrey engineer managed sixth place points behind Ray Fielding (31.33s), Gray Mickel, Good himself and the increasingly formidable Agnes Mickel, who had set a fine 36.30s Ladies' best at Shelsley. At this stage Marsh had 61 points, 21 ahead of Scragg and 22 ahead of Westbury.

Then the tide turned. The bearded Westbury set a 51.33s record on 'The Rest', half a second ahead of Marsh, while Gray Mickel's good results were interrupted when he cleared a gully after an 'off' and bent the front end of the red Cooper, and Good also damaged his Cooper at Cobbler. With the Championship leader absent, Westbury topped the list with a 47.97s record at Bouley Bay, beating Daghorn on 48.50s. Marsh also missed Great Auclum where Westbury broke the course record in the class runs in 19.33s, but had to give best to Boshier-Jones in the Top Ten with 19.90s to the Welshman's 19.57s. Fourth here was Guernseyman Peter Wilson, now the owner of the Martini Special which had created such a sensation twelve months earlier. Although he competed in most of the mainland rounds he was never able to match Martini's own form with the car. Also in the points at Great Auclum was the 1962 Champion Arthur Owen who was now running a Lotus 23 which had been bought with a view to tackling the European Championship.

Suddenly, the Felday-Daimler, with its outstanding acceleration, was going really well and Westbury shattered John Pringle's Craigantlet record in 64.44s, with Pringle's new Cooper also bettered by Ray Fielding. But there was no Felday at a wet August Shelsley where both Chris Summers and Arthur Owen were non-starters after running out of road *after* the finish in practice. The March Special was notably tail-happy and Tony may well have been regretting selling the BRM to Welsh sprint contender Ken Wilson. The man of the moment was Boshier-Jones who rocketed up in 39.16s in a fine exhibition of car control and judgement which left even Good and Marsh in his wake. This was the meeting where Phil Scragg débuted the as-yet-bodyless Chaparral and found that it was a real handful. He had sold his BRM to Kidderminster garage owner and Territorial Army Officer Tony Griffiths who had impressed by winning the Junior Championship in an E-type Jaguar and then achieving regular class honours in the ex-Geoffrey Wilson Lotus 18.

Yet arguably the most significant happening that August was Joe Bonnier's BTD at Ollon-Villars in Switzerland in the borrowed Ferguson P99 4WD. That set both Marsh and Westbury thinking. Back at home the scene shifted to Prescott where Westbury snatched another BTD, only to be eased out of an extra RAC point by the on-form Boshier-Jones, but it was enough for him to take the lead in the title chase by 1 point with Marsh down in ninth place with a very sick car.

The scene was set for a real cliff-hanger of a finish at Dyrham Park for the final round, with Westbury, Marsh and Boshier-Jones all in with a chance. The tension mounted even more when Westbury had another cwp go at the crucial moment. However, Tony Griffiths instantly came up with a spare, there was a frantic effort by all concerned to ready the Felday for the RAC runs and the sporting Marsh readily agreed to delay things while the rather angular Felday was re-fettled. A duly inspired Westbury shot up in 31.60s, the record was his, the meeting was his, and he was RAC Champion. 'Bosh' edged Marsh's woolly-sounding Special out of second place, but still had to give best to Tony in the Championship. It was a superb, dramatic and very sporting day, and the drama was heightened when Christchurch driver John Macklin – successful hitherto in a Lotus 7 and then a Formula Junior Lotus 20 – wedged his ex-Keylock Cooper-Buick on its side at Neptune corner, with no harm to himself and remarkably little to his recently purchased mount.

Behind the top three, Fielding scored 64 points (to the 83 of Westbury, 79 of Marsh and 73 of Boshier-Jones), Good scored 57, Scragg 40 (all in the first part of the season); and McLaughlin in the best of the Cooper-JAPs 31.

There were still some major meetings to take place however, and although Westbury set a 43.54s BTD at the 750MC Wiscombe National meeting, the climb which set all the tongues wagging came when he 'demonstrated' the Ferguson P99, and had the Walker blue 4WD test bed over the finish line in a sub-record 43.30s. The Felday team, including Mac Daghorn and Rupert Kosmala stayed on for some more testing the next day when Peter recorded a fantastic 41.98s!

The following week the Severn Valley club held another National meeting at Loton Park where Boshier-Jones's impeccably-handled Lotus 22 smashed the course record in 36.10s, and circuit racer Jack Pearce, driving a 1.6-litre Lotus/Ford Twin Cam-engined Lotus 22 put one over Westbury for second place. Regrettably after a splendidly sporting season, Marsh was protested out of the results for taking his runs consecutively after arriving late because of low cloud interfering with his flying arrangements. Even sadder was the accident which befell Basil Davenport, who had set his best ever Shelsley time in 41.08s earlier in the year. The Macclesfield veteran suffered painful facial, shoulder and rib injuries and it was feared that the post-War 'Spider' might be a write-off. Happily, this was not so and car and driver were in action again during 1964.

Formula Junior, highly successful in circuit racing, but never attracting more than a modest following on the hills, was to be replaced by International Formulae 2 and 3 in 1964 and in this final year of international status the category carried on much as before in hill climbing with the class rarely attracting more than about half a dozen competitors. Having said that, there were notable performances from Griffiths and Macklin before switching to bigger machinery, from veteran Austen May with his ex-Midland Racing Partnership/Bill Bradley Cooper; Yorkshireman Geoff Gartside in the Garford built by father Gordon, Howard Bennett's Merlyn, Midlander Malcolm Eaves' Lotus 20 and Bristolian Ted Williams' front-engined Elva.

After so many years of success with Jaguar-powered machinery, Phil Scragg had a most disappointing time with the Chaparral, and the Sports Car Championship fell to Josh Randles for the second time, his Cooper Monaco now radically modified with the Maserati 2.8 engine and with a rather unhandsome cycle-winged body, complete with bulbous centre section to clear the Cooper's wide chassis, fitted to assist in placing the car on the narrow hill climb roads. There was a definite falling away in support for the out-and-out sports-racer, although much was expected for 1964 from the 2.0 BMW-engined Elva Mk7 of John Barnes while Scragg was also planning something new and exciting in the form of one of the very latest 4.7 Ford V8-engined Lotus 30s. Among the rest, Graeme Austin continued the successful career of the one-off Emeryson, and Lotus 7 drivers Tom Clapham, Ray Terry and, in the West Country in particular, John Grafton were well to the fore. Terry, son of one of the MAC's regular Shelsley Walsh course marshals, beat Tom Jones (FJ Envoy) to win the MAC's Junior Championship in his 1460cc Climax-engined Seven which boasted a number of Lotus 20 suspension components. In the Northern meetings Keith Schellenberg had several wins in the ex-Scragg Lister but did not run the car for long.

If there had ever been a 'Spirit of Hill Climbing Award' it would surely have gone to John Bolster in 1963. *Autosport's* Technical Editor was persuaded to extract his splendid old 'Bloody Mary' from the (then) Montagu Motor Museum, blow off the cobwebs, and 'demonstrate' the old favourite at Shelsley in June. Much encouraged by ascending those hallowed slopes only 2 seconds slower than his best time of close on 20 years earlier, and determined 'to grow old disgracefully', JVB entered the car for the VSCC meeting on the old course at Prescott. Arms flailing in the accustomed manner, Bolster urged 'Mary' to the finish in a resounding 47.90s, second to Doc Taylor's much-campaigned Caesar Special (47.42s) in his class, and comparing well with Gordon Chapman's 45.08s BTD in ERA R2A.

The dramatic impact on the sport of Tico Martini's crypto-Kart the previous year had encouraged at least some people to explore the possibilities of really tiny machines, although the later restrictions on minimum wheelbase did not really encourage this avenue of development. Apart from Peter Wilson in the Martini itself, there was Peter le Gallais (son of Frank) with the supercharged 500cc LGS II; Sir Jon Samuel's chain-throwing 500cc Tiger Shrike, particularly Kart-like in concept; the Ford 105E-engined Rudeani of Jack Heaton-Rudd and Frank Dean which ran on ten inch Mini wheels and was distinctly twitchy; and the really tiny 250 Villiers-engined BB Special 'worn' by an ever-youthful Rivers Fletcher. In the sharpest possible contrast to Rivers' old HWM-Jaguar and Jaguar Special cars, the BB was designed by Leslie Ballamy – he of the Ballamy split axle and LMB Popular fame – and Mike Luff, and was built at Buckler Engineering. Some of these ingenious machines, and especially the Martini and the Rudeani achieved a fair degree of success, but all added to the variety and technical interest in the sport at the time.

Smooth lines of the Lotus 23 are apparent here as Betty Haig climbs towards a Ladies' Record at Prescott in May 1963.
PHOTOGRAPHIC CRAFTSMEN
via MIKE KETTLEWELL

Miniature racing cars were sometimes successful in the mid-nineteen-sixties and few more so than the Ford 105E-engined Rudeani of Jack Heaton-Rudd and Frank Dean.
via MIKE KETTLEWELL

Although the Westbrook Hay and Mancetter venues were lost to the scene during the year, there were new hills in use. The Duke of Bedford put part of Woburn Park at the disposal of the Sporting Owner Drivers Club, who ran their first climb there in April. The course was only around 440 yards long but rose 70 feet and included three bends and some adverse camber within that modest distance. Bob Bodle's Bodle-Bristol Special set the first target at 21.56s, and although this was not really a classic hill, it rapidly became popular with the regular meetings attracting good entries to this scenically attractive and conveniently located course. There were no fewer than three new courses down in the South West. The Riley MC (Cornwall and Devon Centre) and the Plymouth MC obtained the use of Hemerdon Quarry, near Plymouth, for a South Western version of Mancetter. The course used was mainly concrete surfaced and was both steep and winding. The initial climb in June saw Amie Lefevre set BTD in 25.34s in his fast MG Midget, although the hill soon became a happy hunting ground for John Grafton's successful Lotus 7. The same could be said of Torbay MC's 750 yards Oddicombe climb. Still in regular, twice-yearly, use today, Oddicombe abounds in tight hairpins and runs up through wooded slopes from the seafront overlooking Babbacombe Bay, Oddicombe Beach is one of Torquay's popular attractions). With no aspirations to more than regional status, Oddicombe is picturesque, council-owned, and has the distinction of having a nearby cliff lift as an alternative mode of getting to the top!

Rather more ambitious possibilities were evident at Longleat, the vast parkland surrounding Longleat House, in Wiltshire, owned by the Marquis of Bath. This latest 'stately home' hill was first used by the Burnham-on-Sea MC on 30 June when 44.76s was the time taken by John Ford to take his ex-Freddie Floyd Cooper-JAP to a narrow win over John Macklin's Lotus 20. Using 1200 yards of the main drive, the course ran through both open parkland and rather sombre woodland, necessitating the fairly unusual adjunct of a travelling marshal – on horseback!

For the rest, Castle Howard was lengthened at the start to take in a short sprint to a really tight right-hand hairpin – some people tended to stay in bottom gear until after this hazard – which added interest, although to most, the best feature of the hill was the magnificent blast past the front of the House towards the Obelisk. Keith Schellenberg set a 27.38s target for the revised course. Both Bouley Bay and Harewood benefited from resurfacing and while the latter hill hosted a full programme of meetings, Boshier-Jones, lowering the record to 46.72s at the best yet September meeting, there was a notable innovation later that month when the BARC(Y) held a Novices' Meeting. Designed to encourage the newcomers and 'hard triers', this excluded anyone who had won an award in hill climbing since 1959. Winner was Gary Whitehead in Tony Lanfranchi's Elva Mk7 in 53.52s. Lanfranchi himself was hill climbing a fortnight later, when ABC Television featured the same club's superb seasonal finals at Oliver's Mount, Scarborough. A huge entry, many of whom shared the organisers' belief that this hill was a *must* for the RAC Championship, was rather held up by the intrusive demands of television but at the end of the day 'Big Tone' set a 48.74s BTD, edging out Schellenberg and Brian Waddilove who had obtained yet another of the BRM P48s.

As thoughts turned more and more towards 1964, many were saddened to learn of the death, at the early age of 52, of Tom Norton, after a heart attack, while during the winter Derek Buckler and Eric Findon too departed from this sphere. Happily still very much with us was Reg Phillips, although he decided to retire from active participation after 21 years competing, and had sold the Porsche-like Fairley to Keith Moore some time before. Events were to show that 'Smiling' Reg just couldn't keep away.

All-wheel-drive

In a remarkably short time Peter Westbury had established a fine reputation both as an engineer and a driver, and his little Felday Engineering concern was attracting serious attention from the likes of Alf Francis – who supplied the bits to update the old Cooper-Daimler chassis – Ferguson Research, and the Owen Organisation, who agreed to assist with the BRM V8-engined 4WD sports car project aimed at the European Mountain Championship. As expected, the extrovert Surrey driver was able to obtain the Ferguson P99 to tackle the Hill Climb Championship and, for once, Tony Marsh did not start the season as favourite for the RAC title. Elsewhere, there was not as much chopping and changing of machinery as during the previous year, although the success on a strictly limited budget of Peter Boshier-Jones had encouraged several to follow a similar route. Jerseyman Peter Meldrum's Pinner

Racing team put an Allard Dragon (Shorrock supercharged 1650cc Ford pushrod) engine in a maroon Lotus 22, Malcolm Eaves swopped his FJ Lotus 22 for a Lotus 22 with 1.6 Lotus/Ford Twin Cam power, while Bryan Brown took over the ex-Peter Gaskell 1650 Kieft-Ford, which won at Prescott in July when the BOC ran a 'Special' meeting for people who had not won there previously, *a la* Harewood. Ian McLaughlin sold his successful Cooper-JAP to Colin Watts and bravely built up a Kieft FJ-based device with 4.7-litres of Chevrolet power, called the Clewer-Chevrolet. Yorkshireman David Harrison was another to go for American V8 bhp, putting a Buick unit in the back of an F2/F1 Cooper chassis. The formidable Felday passed to Welsh veteran 'Taffy' Cottrell for a return to single-seater competition after several successful years with the Lotus 15, and David Good's Cooper-Daimler went to Wally Cuff who was soon winning West Country events with it. The 1961 Champion, however, decided to have a season away from the pressures of the RAC series and was to share a light-weight competition Lotus Elan 26R with another former racing car driver, George Keylock.

The notorious Hump at Rest-and-be-Thankful produced some spectacular pictures. Agnes Mickel aviates the ex-Owen Cooper.
BILL HENDERSON

Peter Boshier-Jones, seen at Craigantlet, never managed to win the RAC title with his supercharged yellow Lotus-Climax 22.
BRIAN FOLEY *via* MIKE KETTLEWELL

With Harewood added to the RAC schedule for the first time, there were 14 rounds in 1964, and although the competition was generally pretty close, only two drivers actually set a BTD at a Championship meeting. Westbury set 9 with the fascinating Ferguson which well suited Westbury's 'scrabble round the corners and squirt up the straights' style, while the other 5 fell to Boshier-Jones who had a superb season with the little yellow Lotus. When the points were added up at the end of the year, and taking the best 8 performances by each, Westbury's winning margin over 'Bosh' was only 3 points (87 to 84) with Marsh's underpowered Special third on 78, then a big gap to Tony Griffiths and John Macklin who had been very evenly matched all season and ended up tying on 56 points. Both were capable of taking BTD at lesser meetings (Griffiths in particular had been very successful, winning at Castle Howard, Loton Park, Ragley Park and Longleat) but tended to be not quite fast enough to beat the 'big three'. Both the dark green and white BRM, which had a Bourne-rebuilt engine at the beginning of the year, and the strikingly liveried black and yellow Cooper-Buick were immaculately turned out, while Griffiths' starts, shrouded in Dunlop tyre smoke, were well worth seeing! Ray Fielding scored 36 points with his Lotus 21 and two women were in the top seven. Agnes Mickel piled up 26 points in the family Cooper, and only Peter Meldrum separated her from Patsy Burt's less powerful Cooper on 17 after an excellent season which included BTDs at Brunton and the first meeting to be held at Stapleford for a couple of years.

Peter Westbury rapidly established a narrow but psychologically important advantage with a 36.56s hill record at Loton and a 50.348s BTD at Prescott where a new timing set up permitted two cars on the course at the same time. The same was now the case at Loton where the safety aspect was emphasised with extra marshals and closed circuit television. There was another course record for the Ferguson driver at Wiscombe, in 42.53s (slower than in testing the previous autumn), but on the RAC

Tension subsides as the leading drivers relax after climbing 'The Rest' in 1964. Tony Griffiths clearly amuses (left to right) John Macklin, Peter Boshier-Jones, Tony Marsh and Peter Meldrum.
BILL HENDERSON

Alan Ensoll was successful in Northern events, especially with the ex-Henry Taylor/Jim Clark Jaguar D-type, TKF 9. This novel cornering method with his later E-type-engined XK120 didn't work!
BILL HENDERSON

runs a particularly determined Marsh beat him by just one hundredth of a second to take 10 points. Marsh was runner-up for the third time in four RAC run-offs at Barbon where Westbury reduced the hill record to 27.174s in the class runs. The WMC gave considerable thought to spectator interest at this climb. The previous year they had installed a large 'clock' on the inside of the hairpin, clearly visible from the main spectator point, so that onlookers could see how everyone was doing at any point on the climb. For 1964, there was the addition of a speed trap towards the end of the main 'straight'. The closeness of the 1964 competition was emphasised with fastest speeds recorded by Westbury (96.4 mph), Marsh (95.2 mph), Griffiths (94.6 mph) and Boshier-Jones (94.6 mph). Unhappily, a cloud was cast over the entire meeting when Marske-by-Sea driver Mike Gray, who had graduated from an old Jaguar XK120 to the original ex-Summers Cooper-Chevrolet, lost adhesion on the bump exiting the second left-hander (the author saw an unidentified fluid escaping in the vicinity of the rear tyres at the start) after getting on the grass after the first bend, went off, and overturned after 'tripping' over a tree stump. Gray was killed instantly after the rollover bar bent almost double although the car was hardly damaged. This was a tragic reminder that even hill climbing can be dangerous.

Westbury was absent from Shelsley, for he was competing at Mont Ventoux in France, campaigning his interim 1.8-litre BRM V8-engined Lotus 23 sports car in the European series. After Basil Davenport, who appeared with his original 1924 'Spider', had been presented with a scroll marking 40 years in the sport, Peter Boshier-Jones took charge. He had been particularly impressive at Shelsley during the previous year with the Lotus, but this time he really excelled, clipping 0.01s from the record in 33.35s to beat Marsh and a very on-form Ray Fielding. Westbury was back on top for a 29.87s hill record at Bo'ness but he was absent once more for 'The Rest', where 'Bosh' ignored the depredations of wandering spectators to rocket the bright yellow Lotus to a superb 50.09s record, almost a second and a half faster than the nearest challenger, Fielding.

There was a new top surface awaiting competitors at Bouley Bay, although melting tar later on tended to slow times. Westbury made it six BTDs out of six by just clipping 0.07s off Marsh's best. But the Ferguson/Westbury combination was not unbeatable – not quite. Although his blower drive-belt broke earlier on, 'Bosh' recovered his composure with an inspired 19.18s dash which gave him the Great Auclum record and 11 points, for Westbury was only on 19.65s and Marsh on 19.81s. Fourth-best was Patsy Burt, after a fine display of judgement on a course which she always found to be rather deceptively challenging. The 1964 Championship was not destined to be a cliff-hanger for Westbury actually clinched it at Craigantlet with four rounds yet to come. His 61.99s was yet another record, and this time the margin was a hair over 2 whole seconds better than Boshier-Jones.

Westbury again missed Shelsley, preferring to go to the Swiss Mountain GP, and Boshier-Jones headed the awards as in June, although his hill record remained unbeaten. As usual the September Prescott meeting was superb, with 'Bosh' well and truly defeating Westbury on a tight course which was perfect for the Lotus' excellent handling and not so ideal for the Ferguson. Peter's 48.180s BTD was yet one more record in this year of records. whereas Westbury was close on 48.231s but not close enough. On a day graced by fine weather and especially by the presence for the one and only time of European Mountain Champion Edgar Barth in a factory Porsche Flat 8 Spyder, record after record fell. New holders included: Agnes Mickel (Ladies at 52.093s); Nicky Porter (970cc Mini-Cooper S,

57.840s); Geoff Breakell (Lotus-Ford 23B, 52.160s); David Good (Lotus Elan, 53.557s); Len Woodcock (FJ Lotus 20, 52.917s), Westbury in his Lotus-BRM in 51.253s to beat a fine 51.973s effort from Barth on his first visit to the hill; and Westbury again with the Ferguson with 48.754s in his class. The newly instigated Prescott Gold Cup Competition, awarded on the basis of the greatest improvement on a class record standing at the beginning of the year, and achieved at one of the major meetings, was presented by Edgar Barth at the close of the proceedings to Phil Scragg[1]. The Gold Cup, to which the BOC gave premier status and considerable prestige went on the strength of Phil's performances with his new factory Lightweight Jaguar E-type GT car. He had also campaigned the Felday-rebuilt Summers Cooper Monaco-Chevrolet after aborting the Lotus 30 project when the early development of the car proved so troublesome.

When The RAC 'circus' arrived for the first time at Harewood one could have been forgiven for expecting something of an anti-climax after Prescott, and especially as the destination of the title was settled. Not a bit of it. This meeting really emphasised that the BARC Yorkshire Centre and Harewood had well and truly arrived in the forefront of hill climbing with another superb meeting, during which 14 records fell. Despite a rush to ready the Ferguson after a piston had cracked during testing, Westbury set the new outright record in 44.454s, but with former holder 'Bosh' close on 44.583s. After a most successful season, Kingswinford's Len Woodcock had the misfortune to overturn his Lotus 20 at Farmhouse in practice, breaking a leg.

There was a real end-of-term-type atmosphere at Dyrham Park on 19 September for the final round. In fact, it all got a bit too spectacular, with a remarkably large number of off-course excursions. Even 'Bosh' ended up in the straw bales, and so did John Barnes who had replaced his 997cc BMC engine in his Elva Mk7, not with the BMW originally planned, but with a blown 1500cc Ford unit, with beneficial results. More seriously, Tom Elton broke several ribs when he overturned. Among all the alarms Westbury ended the season where he started it – on top – with a 30.32s course record, beating 'Bosh' (before he departed from the course), Marsh, Macklin and Griffiths in a result which was an apt summary of the season as a whole.

It had been a really vintage year with many interesting aspects. Even in the 1100cc racing class the old Cooper-JAPs were having to look to their laurels, with the rapid Lotus 20s of Woodcock and Leeds driver Les Hinchcliffe, and especially the ex-Ken Tyrrell Cooper-BMC Mk3A of Birmingham newcomer, Mike Hawley providing close competition. Tom Adair, a Cooper-JAP driver from Port William, also ran a 600cc Norton-powered, Kart-like device with handlebar steering, called the Klystlis, but this was not notably successful; nor was Sir Jon Samuel's latest JAP twin-engined Japperwock which threw drive chains with an abandon unseen since the heyday of the Farley Special. Conversely, after several years of steady diminution of the ranks of the 500cc brigade, there was a sharp rise in interest in the old Cooper-Nortons and their contemporaries, at least in part due to the campaigning efforts of Shrewsbury enthusiast Peter Williams, who ran one with great success. However, even his efforts were eclipsed by those of John Horrex who contrived to qualify his Cooper-Norton Mk9 for the RAC runs at both Bo'ness and 'The Rest' only to have the engine fail on him on both occasions, which was heartbreaking. Happily, at Shelsley the car made amends and John broke Dick James' long standing '500' record in 38.54s. The MAC's Junior Championship also fell to a single-seater driver again, this time to Bryan Brown with the Kieft-Ford in his first season of hill climbing.

Simple and workmanlike cockpit of the Marsh Special.
via MIKE KETTLEWELL

Shorrock supercharger installation on the 1,220cc Coventry-Climax engine in Peter Boshier-Jones's Lotus 22.
BRIAN FOLEY *via* MIKE KETTLEWELL

---

1 *Prescott Hill Climb 1938-1988* Peter Hull, published by the Bugatti Owners Club, lists the first four Gold Cup winners, from 1964-67 as Doc Taylor, Geoffrey St John and Bernard Kain (twice) – all VSCC racers. During the four years, as the BOC's Geoff Ward explained to the author, there were effectively two Gold Cups. The Cup which Grover Williams won at the Monaco Grand Prix was awarded for performances at Prescott at the VSCC meeting for a time, before it became the highly appropriate reward for winning the VSCC's annual race at Cadwell Park for two-seater Grand Prix cars. Both Gold Cup awards **should** have been listed in the Prescott book of 1964-67 but a Gloucestershire gremlin saw otherwise!

Although the Sports Car Championship had been allowed to lapse, there were several interesting new sports-racers on the hills. The glorious rich engine note of Peter Westbury's red Lotus-BRM enlivened a number of meetings once the car had been sorted, which unfortunately came too late for European success. There were wins at Barbon, Harewood, Prescott and Dyrham, and then late in the season the car netted a couple of BTDs at the 750MC Wiscombe Park national where David Good had a go in the car and beat the rain-afflicted single-seaters, and then at Castle Howard where Westbury's 33.9s BTD was a record and saw off the challenges of Agnes Mickel and Brighouse domestic appliance refurbisher David Hepworth in another Chevrolet-engined F2 Cooper. Arthur Owen too had eyes on the European events but he obtained delivery of his 2.0 Brabham-Climax BT8 only when the season was well under way, although he did make the Top Ten at Great Auclum. Phil Scragg had rather an unsettled year trying to obtain an effective large-capacity British sports-racer. The rebuilt Cooper-Chevrolet was not the most refined of cars and before the end of the year it had gone back to Chris Summers and Scragg had bought another former circuit car, John Coundley's 2.7 Lotus-Climax 19. Ray Terry had an excellent year with his much modified Lotus-Climax 7, now fitted with a Hartlin bodyshell and re-named the Terry Aero-Climax. In the North of England, there were several 'old stagers' who were an integral part of the sports car scene, even if they rarely hit the headlines. There was Phil Chapman with the big Chapman-Mercury, Malton trout farmer George Tatham with the very first Lister-Jaguar built (the rather DB3S-like private venture car commissioned by Edgware jeweller Norman Hillwood before Brian Lister built Jaguar-powered Listers and bought by George from a trombone player in Mantovani's orchestra), and the smart if rather dated, and formerly Riley-engined, Walton-Bristol of Roy Walton.

In fact, the out-and-out sports racers were matched on times in some events by a few of the latest generation of competition-orientated Grand Touring cars, such as Phil Scragg's Prescott Gold Cup winning Lightweight Jaguar E-type and the Lotus Elan 26R of Keylock and Good. David Good was normally the faster of the two in the Elan and ran Scragg close for the Gold Cup. Down in Bath, Ron Fry had replaced his original Ferrari 250GT with an ex-Maranello Concessionaires 250GTO for 1963 (the 1962 Earls Court Motor Show Exhibit), while towards the end of the 1964 season an immensely powerful but harder-to-handle, rear-engined, 250LM was obtained. Because of his business commitments Fry found it difficult to get away for any length of time so most of his competition activities were restricted to the South West still, although he certainly made the most of his time. He competed in hill climbs, sprints and circuit races according to what was on in the area, usually switching from Ferrari to equally successful Mini-Cooper S, which was most instructive and demonstrated Ron's versatility. Tough competition to the Ferraris sometimes came from a hard-trying Ian Swift with a very rapid Morgan Plus Four. Further North the BARC(Y) class structure encouraged the owners of the less specialised cars. Future Chairman of the BARC's Yorkshire Centre, Derek Clark (Jaguar E), rhubarb grower Peter Smith (Speedwell GT), and Sprite driver Richard Sutherland were among the most frequent award winners. Not surprisingly, the safe and handleable MGB was often favoured with York novice driver Mike Nickell-Lean (who actually broke a class record at the Harewood 'Novices' meeting) and Roy Ashford doing particularly well in their own areas, as did Amie Lefevre with his MG Midget.

Rather more specialised was Arthur Rusling's de Dion axled Reliant Sabre Six, normally driven by rallyman Bobby Parkes, but occasionally by Tony Marsh. Another former single-seater driver to move to a sports car for 1964 was Doug Haigh, who ran a Frazer-Nash Le Mans Replica until his untimely death in a road accident.

Among the saloons it was very much the era of the Mini, although Ford Cortina GTs and Lotus-Cortinas were gaining in popularity, and Colin Wild scored many northern wins with a Volvo 122S. Nicky Porter, working down in Worcester at the time and an acknowledged Mini expert, was also to be seen in an Alfa Romeo Giulia entered by Steels of Hereford.

In this peak period for the sport, new courses seemed relatively easy to come by, even if they were not all of total suitability for anything more than minor club meetings. The Lincoln & DMC & LCC had been running small meetings since the previous year at Nettleton, near Caistor, in the Lincolnshire Wolds, where a steep (rising 300 feet) course of 660 yards was used. All the hoary old jokes about the frozen north sprang to mind when the Lancashire AC held their first climb at Hurstwood in March 1964. The course was on Calder Water Board land in the Pennine foothills, and its not particularly in-

The era of the Mini.
J. Featherstone lifts a wheel at
Trengwainton watched by a
large (and rather close) Bank
Holiday crowd.
PENWITH PHOTO PRESS
via MIKE KETTLEWELL

spiring format comprised a near straight 700 yard ascent with one left-hander just before the finish. Moreover, the bleakness of this first climb was due largely to the fact that it was run in a minor blizzard! Not surprisingly a number of would be competitors non-started when they saw the conditions, but 45 near-frozen souls persevered with good humour. One wit actually blamed a slow time on his having to take avoiding action in order to miss a polar bear! J. R. Latham's Austin-Healey made best time in 26.619s, and a class winner with a Mini-Cooper was a young Lancastrian enthusiast called Brian Redman. The weather was almost as bad when the Darlington & DMC held their April meeting on a revised course at Catterick. Now measuring 1100 yards, the hill was extended to include two extra fast bends at the top, although the start was moved up nearer to the first hairpin once again. The meeting attracted Peter Boshier-Jones up from South Wales and his impeccably handled Lotus 22 recorded 44.6s, a whopping 2.4s faster than his nearest competitor, Tom Clapham, now running a 1.2 Cooper-Climax single-seater.

Hill climbers are not unused to dealing with off-beat hazards, not least the hornets nest discovered in the gents' toilets at one Wiscombe meeting, but when the Vickers-Armstrongs (Hurn) CC restricted the entry for their first event on the Lulworth Gunnery Ranges to closed cars only, there was a slightly sinister reason. The 1400 yards course was bounded by barbed wire – at head height – and even if you ploughed through this obstacle with your secure closed car you would land in areas where there just *might* be unexploded ammunition. A good incentive to stay on the track!

Hill climbing was booming as never before, but the one ingredient which was still sadly missing was a hill which was long enough to be considered for the European Mountain Championship which had attained a status at least on a par with the great years of *Bergmeister* Han Stuck. The London Motor Club tried to secure the use of the four mile Porlock toll road, in Somerset, which had been used on both the RAC and Bournemouth Rallies, but this came to nothing. On the other hand, the Lancashire AC were having better luck in their negotiations with the Isle of Man authorities, and with the Manx Tourist Board, for the motor sport minded Manxmen were keen on the idea of using part of the celebrated Isle of Man TT motorcycle racing course for a hill climb. Towards the end of January the Lancastrians were able to announce that a trial event would definitely be held on 30 May, with financial support from the Manx Tourist Board. The stretch of closed public road to be used was 3.6 miles between Sulby and The Bungalow, where the road was approximately 16 feet wide and the maximum gradient was 1 in 5. This was an intriguing prospect and the meeting was sure to be over-subscribed as ferry restrictions would limit the entry to 60 cars.

Marsh's second hat-trick
But for the present there was just one addition to the RAC Championship for 1965 and that was Longleat which had enjoyed a successful 1964 season, but where the promotion had been taken over by circuit racing-orientated British Racing and Sports Car Club. Tony Marsh had at last admitted

defeat with his Marsh Special and rebuilt it to take a 4,160cc General Motors V8 driving through a Hewland HD4, 4-speed gearbox. At first thought to be an Oldsmobile unit, it actually turned out to have Buick origins. Relatively mildly tuned and breathing through twin choke Rochester carburettors, this delivered around 220 bhp and sufficient torque to necessitate the use of only two gears most of the time. The existing Marsh chassis had to be lengthened by eight inches in the wheelbase to take the new set-up and this had the desirable side effect of improving the car's previously very nervous handling. It didn't cost a fortune – Marsh reckoned it cost about £2500 in this form – but it was good enough to bring Marsh another two RAC Championships after a ten-year gap.

Peter Westbury's Forest Green, Dorking-based Felday Engineering Company was now involved in a number of significant projects, not least a 4WD BRM V8-engined Felday sports car, while Felday were also agents for Colotti gearboxes by this time. Peter's links with BRM and his Ferguson experience led to the idea of using the under-developed Ferguson 4WD Formula 1 BRM 670P which Richard Attwood had practised but not raced at the 1964 British GP. Westbury ran the car at a wet AMOC *Daily Mirror* Trophy meeting at Wiscombe in April, beating Marsh in 45.16s to 49.60s, and a third Championship for the Surrey driver looked most likely. Unfortunately, it was not to be for the head of the Owen Organisation, Sir Alfred Owen, a sincerely religious man, did not wish the car to run in Sunday events. In any case, the BRM team had their hands full with the 1965 Grand Prix cars, the Rover-BRM gas turbine car project, their 1000cc F2 engine and the early development of new engines for the 3-litre Grand Prix Formula which was to come into effect in 1966, so did not have the spare capacity to devote to the 4WD car. Westbury 'demonstrated' the 670P at Shelsley in June but announced, with regret, that he would not be able to defend his Championship as the Ferguson had been returned to Ferguson Research. Westbury's considerable energies now turned more and more towards circuit racing, initially with the 4WD Felday sports cars, and later with Formula 3 and Formula 2 single-seaters of proprietary Brabham manufacture, with which his FIRST team had many successes.

Of the other leading runners, Boshier-Jones, Meldrum, Griffiths and Macklin all retained their

existing machinery. Macklin's Cooper-Buick benefited from a rebuild by Ecurie Ecosse. Beginning to make a real impact, especially on Northern events, was the bluff and burly Yorkshireman David Hepworth who was alternating between his Cooper-Chevrolet single-seater and a fairly fearsome but perhaps surprisingly successful Chevrolet-engined Austin-Healey sports car. David was not averse to taking a relatively unwieldy car 'by the scruff of the neck', and the same applied to Ian Swift who had forsaken his Morgan for a 4.7 Ford V8-engined ex-Camoradi International/Masten Gregory F1 Cooper with which Bill Liddell had achieved some success the previous year. Right from the start, Swift's spectacular style reaped results. He turned out for the first big hill climb of the year, at Longleat on 4 April, and recorded 39.93s to the BTD 39.84s of John Macklin's refurbished Cooper-Buick. Both of them defeated the brand new Marsh-GM combination, although the latter was afflicted by a broken wishbone.

Not everyone was intending to use the big V8s though. The ready availability of 'off the shelf' F2/F3-type cars from Brabham and Lotus, good handling and relatively easy-to-maintain production cars which could be fitted with the highly effective Ford pushrod or Ford-based Lotus Twin Cam 4-cylinder engines, was an attractive proposition. Bryan Brown followed the Meldrum example and used an Allard-blown pushrod engine in a Lotus 22, while the Brabham BT14 chassis was favoured by former Lotus 7 driver from Forton, Preston, 'Fast' Fred Smith, and by another Lancastrian, the taciturn John Butterworth, who had been consistently successful with both Lotus 7 and 23 sports cars. His Brabham employed a blown pushrod engine as opposed to the Twin Cam of Smith's. Bob Ashcroft, for whom Chevron designer/builder/driver Derek Bennett drove, was another Brabham user. Tom Clapham, on the other hand, favoured a Lotus 22 chassis.

Daimler engines had not been forgotten either. Wally Cuff, who tended to stay down in the South West for his sport, took the radical step of fitting the 4.5-litre Majestic version of Edward Turner's V8 into his ex-Good Cooper, while the original Westbury car now reappeared, immaculately rebuilt, in the hands of a bespectacled oil 'magnate' from Sutton Coldfield, Martin Brain. Martin, the proprietor of Golden Knight Oils of West Bromwich, had dabbled with Austin-Healey and Jaguar E-type sports cars for some time, but was beginning to take his hill climbing rather more seriously. Yorkshireman Geoff Gartside (and sometimes younger brother Vic) was another to run a Cooper-Daimler with some success.

Drizzly conditions and a wet track greeted the 'circus' for the first Championship round at Loton Park, and although Marsh took 10 points from 'Bosh', Mike Hawley's well-suited little Cooper Mk3A, Griffiths, Cuff and Patsy Burt, none of them set BTD. That fell to a surprised Tom Clapham, who climbed in 39.36s on the second run of the day in his old Lotus 7 – just before it started to rain. Modest commercial sponsorship of the major meetings was noticeable that year, and Cutty Sark

Patsy Burt was a regular Top Ten runner again in 1965 with her 2.0 Climax-engined Formula Junior Cooper. This unusual shot emphasises the high standard of preparation, characteristic of her cars, masterminded by Ron Smith (who is partly visible at the extreme right of the picture).
via MIKE KETTLEWELL

The experienced Bryan Eccles and a 4.5 Traco/Oldsmobile-powered Brabham BT14, seen here at Harewood, proved to be a highly successful combination.
HAYDN SPEDDING

whisky were the benefactors at Prescott in May. This time Marsh took BTD *and* 10 points, by 0.444s from 'Bosh' and, with the increasingly formidable Meldrum beating Macklin and Griffiths in the old BRM, the pattern was set. The first two places stayed the same at the Whitbread and Martini-supported Wiscombe round.

There was a slight setback for Marsh at Barbon when a lack of power turned out to be caused by the GM V8 running on only 7 cylinders, which initially went unnoticed because the engine was relatively quiet and had an uneven exhaust note anyway! In fact, Marsh later fitted a Porsche-like two-into-one tail pipe, the better to judge the revs by ear. Marsh's problems helped Meldrum take a 28.552s BTD, although he was beaten by Boshier-Jones in the Top Ten. Marsh, Macklin and Griffiths filled the next places, while David Hepworth scored points for the first time with sixth place in the Cooper-Chevvy. Up until now hill records had been rather elusive, but Marsh really excelled at the MAC's Diamond Jubilee Shelsley meeting, twice breaking 'Bosh's' previous best and leaving it at 32.94s. Unfortunately, Boshier-Jones suffered transmission failure and was out of the reckoning, and it was Meldrum's Pinner Racing Lotus which was runner-up.

There was another Marsh BTD at Bo'ness, in 30.07s, but Tony, an outspoken critic of the apparently ever-increasing number of Championship rounds, gave the rough and bumpy Rest-and-be-Thankful a miss, preferring to check over his car. True to form, the final battle was between Meldrum and Boshier-Jones, and it was the former who had the edge with 56.63s to 57.81s. Guards cigarettes were the sponsors at Bouley Bay, for which Marsh arrived with his car strapped to the deck of his father's ketch! Once again the Marsh Special had a clear advantage, climbing in 45.13s, and defeating Boshier-Jones and Meldrum.

Longleat on 1 August promised well but the meeting was marred by long delays and a surprising lack of organisational finesse. In fact it was to be the one and only Championship meeting there for at the end of the season, the Marquis of Bath made his momentous decision to go ahead with his plans for a Lion Park, and as racing cars and lions don't mix too well, the hill climbing had to go. Marsh had already scored several non-Championship wins at Longleat and it was no surprise to see him leave with a new 36.76s course record, a second and a half faster on the RAC runs than 'Bosh', with Macklin and the brave Ian Swift the next fastest. Two interesting newcomers to score points were Tony Johnson's Forward-Daimler and David Good's latest acquisition, a 4.7 Ford V8-engined Lola T70, one of the new generation of Group 7/CanAm sports racers with American V8 engines. This white example was not brand new, having been bought from circuit racer David Cunningham, and clearly met the need for something a bit more challenging than an ex-Ian Walker Racing Lotus Elan 26R which David had been running that season. The Forward-Daimler was actually a 1961 Cooper Mk2 from the Gerard Racing team into which had been fitted another 4.5 Daimler V8.

Boshier-Jones always excelled at Great Auclum, and even if Marsh had not decided to miss this event he might have been pushed to match Peter's 19.099s course record. A poor entry at Craigantlet, missing even John Pringle who was awaiting a new crankshaft and bearings from the USA for the Oldsmobile engine which he had fitted to his Intercontinental Cooper for 1965, gave Meldrum a fairly easy win over Tony Griffiths. Marsh had already won the Championship at this stage as only the best 8 results from 15 would count. Because of a timing problem in his engine he non-started at Dyrham Park and did not run in any of the last three rounds after winning again at Shelsley. Boshier-Jones won at Prescott (meeting sponsored by W. D. & H. O. Wills cigarettes), although only by 0.05s from a spectacular Ian Swift, while Harewood, which clashed with the traditional Brighton Speed Trials and was marred by rain, went to Meldrum, from John Butterworth, Macklin and Les Hinchcliffe's Lotus 20. This was Peter Meldrum's fourth win of the year at the Yorkshire course, and he was in the middle of a tremendous run of seven successive BTD awards there which certainly made him the unofficial 'King of Harewood'.

The last act at Dyrham Park, where there was talk – and nothing more – of constructing a Prescott-type loop in the course, was anti-climactic. Apart from Marsh's problems, there was an appalling practice crash when Ian Swift lost control on a muddy surface and rolled into a tree after the finish. He was hospitalised with fortunately not too serious injuries but the Cooper was wrecked and RAC Steward Bryan Corser insisted on the course being shortened to allow more braking area after the finish. The event which followed brought a welcome and deserved 27.74s BTD to John Macklin, from Boshier-Jones and Meldrum.

So the year ended with Marsh winning his fourth RAC title with 83 points to the 76 of Boshier-Jones who had finished as runner-up in no fewer than nine rounds, and the 72 of Meldrum. Macklin and Griffiths were again fourth and fifth, this time with 9 points separating them, and the unlucky Ian Swift, Bryan Brown, Gray Mickel, Patsy Burt and the talented Solihull driver Mike Hawley, with his tremendously successful Cooper-BMC, rounded out the Top Ten.

Not helped by a fair amount of rain, 1965 was not considered to be a vintage season and there was some unrest about the number of RAC rounds in the series when only 8 could be counted for the title. For the following year, Longleat was not replaced and the best 10 performances from the remaining 14 rounds would count. A further change was to award points right down to tenth (instead of sixth) place in the RAC Top Ten runs. This did nothing however, to satisfy people like Marsh who just felt that there were too many rounds, although everybody had a good reason for not wanting any specific climb to be dropped from the schedule!

The Champion was already thinking seriously about a 'different' four-wheel-drive system, one which would give him the prodigious acceleration of the Ferguson system but which would eliminate the understeer on tight corners, but for 1966 he was content to stay with the successful Marsh-GM. Peter Boshier-Jones too stayed with his faithful Lotus 22 but planned to fit a 1460cc long-stroke Climax engine. Both Meldrum and Brown were upping the engine sizes of their supercharged Ford units, too, to 1650cc and 1800cc respectively. John Macklin stuck to the same formula as before but he sold his Cooper chassis to John McCartney-Filgate and fitted the Buick V8 to one of the 1964/5 Cooper F1 chassis. John's sparring partner Tony Griffiths was also ready for a change since he felt that the BRM was at the limit of it development. He planned to have a new Brabham chassis but the prospect of not having a car until the middle of the season decided him to commission a spaceframe, two-wheel-drive, chassis from Felday Engineering. This rather ungainly looking car, the Felday 6, with its distinctive high-set driving position was equipped with a Ford V8 engine of 4.7-litres.

Still among the big V8s, Patsy Burt had a spaceframe chassised car on order from the newly-established firm set up by New Zealand Grand Prix driver, Bruce McLaren, while David Hepworth was set to drop a Chevrolet Corvette engine in the original Brabham BT3 F1 chassis, formerly raced by 'Black Jack' himself and, later, by privateer Ian Raby. After a couple of years away from the sport, Bryan Eccles was back in the running with a 4.5 Traco/Oldsmobile-powered Brabham BT14 (the chassis formerly John Bridges's circuit racer), which turned out to be a most successful combination.

With all these new developments in the offing, the season looked promising, although there was regret at the passing of Sydney Allard, aged 55, after a long illness. In fact it was not to be a classic season for the simple reason that the weather, dismal enough the previous year, was simply atrocious, although it was dry enough for the RAC opener at Loton Park on 24 April.

Among the new cars to be seen was the two-speed Felday 6; Patsy Burt's stunningly impressive-looking, if rather massive, McLaren M3A, fitted with a 350 bhp Traco/Oldsmobile engine (she hit a bank and damaged a wheel and the rear suspension on her first class run); a brand new Twin Cam engined Brabham BT16 for Mike Hawley; and, after trying both Lotus 19 and a Lister-Chevrolet without real satisfaction the previous year, Phil Scragg arrived with a new 4.7 Lola-Ford T70 MkII. Scragg (who, in his capacity as Chairman and Managing Director of Ernest Scragg & Sons Ltd, had received a CBE for services to export in the New Years Honours List), had at last found a big sports car with real potential and went straight into the Top Ten. But there was no beating Marsh, and his 35.81s, set on new low-profile Goodyear tyres, was just too good for a spectacular Bryan Eccles (36.09s), an impressive Hawley (36.26s), Brown and Tony van Moyland, who had been campaigning an ex-UDT/Laystall/Innes Ireland 1.5 Lotus Climax 18/21 for over a year.

It was raining hard at Prescott, where the field was without John Macklin after the Christchurch driver had written off his new Cooper when the throttle jammed open at Harewood. On the other hand, Ian Swift was back with the rather homely Swift-Ford V8, built out of the remains of his old Cooper, around a spaceframe chassis. Marsh was over a second up on everyone else and Scragg showed that the big Lola was surprisingly nimble in the wet by beating Eccles, Griffiths and Geoff Rollason's tiny F3 Lotus 41 (the actual car exhibited at that year's Racing Car Show).

Although the Felday 6 was not really fully sorted and both Griffiths and a 'guesting' Peter Westbury had wild moments with it at Wiscombe, Tony was runner-up to the inevitable Marsh and ahead of Eccles at this, the first Championship climb on the Devon hill since Wiscombe Ltd (principals Majors Charles Lambton and Richard Chichester) had handed over the running of the hill to the West Hants &

After running his Lola T70 with standard full width bodywork during 1966, Phil Scragg commissioned Williams & Pritchard to build this skimpy, cycle-winged bodywork for 1967, to make it easier for him to place the car more precisely on the road. Phil was immensely successful with this configuration, dubbed 'the beach buggy' by the irreverent.
HAYDN SPEDDING

Despite competing with no problems for several seasons with the Lola T70L, Phil Scragg had scrutineering problems latterly and, after selling and buying the car back once, re-converted it to full-width body specification. This is at Harewood.
HAYDN SPEDDING

Dorset CC – long-time organisers of individual events there. Peter Boshier-Jones only joined the battle at Barbon, and on a very wet and miserable Westmorland hillside managed 32.568s for fourth place behind Marsh (31.373s), Eccles and Meldrum.

It did start to dry out later on at Shelsley, where 'Bosh' arrived with his new long-stroke engine and the latest Dunlop R7 tyres on the back wheels. His 37.08s had the edge over Meldrum, Scragg (who was second fastest in the wet class runs) and Eccles, but that man Marsh was still uncatchable (36.22s).

Tony van Moyland had become increasingly competitive with his Lotus 18/21 but at Bo'ness he overturned in practice, suffering severe injuries, including a fractured skull. Happily, he did eventually recover but he did not compete again. This time Bryan Eccles had his potent Brabham really wound up and recorded 31.13s, the fastest of the class runs and BTD. Then, seemingly inevitably, the rain started and it was Meldrum who snatched the 10 points from Marsh and Yorkshire heating engineer Jimmy Johnstone with the supercharged Lotus 18 with which he had been scoring many 1100cc class successes over the previous season and a half, and with the unlucky Eccles down in sixth place. Still in Scotland, a mere 48 runners turned out on the rough, bumpy and mountain-stream-eroded Rest-and-be-Thankful, minus Marsh who could be forgiven for not being wild about the hill after his 1962 experience there. Meldrum, Eccles and Hawley were all in the hunt, but it was 'Bosh' who really excelled, climbing in 50.88s for BTD.

There were fewer cars still – just 36 plus motorcycles and combinations – at Bouley Bay but the wet track was still all-too-present. This time 50.21s was enough to keep Marsh, well on target for Championship number 5, on top, and with Mike Hawley, always neat, precise and very fast, edging out yet one more Channel Island challenger from second place. This was Brian de Gruchy, who had bought the Forward-Daimler from Tony Johnson.

Peter Meldrum set a 22.14s BTD at Great Auclum but there were no points for him or anyone else. It had been wet all too often up until then but this time the rain came in torrents and the meeting had to be abandoned midway through the second runs with the RAC round declared null and void – an unprecedented occurrence. It was *still* wet at Craigantlet although a good entry – but minus Marsh – was

On the basis of Peter Westbury's previous technical achievements, there were high hopes for Tony Griffiths's Felday-Ford 6 V8. In the event the car was rather a disappointment, and certainly looks a little wayward here in the wet at Prescott.
RIVERS FLETCHER

attracted over to the Ulster hill which most people agree to be one of the very best *courses* in the whole series, albeit an inconvenient and expensive round to attend for non-Irish drivers. Practice dramas eliminated Martin Brain, who was beginning to make an impression with the old Cooper-Daimler (he tore off a front wheel on the first bend on his first climb, and thereafter shared Norman Ludlow's road-going Jaguar E-type) and 'home' favourite Richie Heeley's Allard Dragon-engined Lotus 22. Peter Meldrum also had an adventurous time in both practice and the meeting proper and was shunted down to third by Hawley and Phil Scragg, whose Lola really went well and which set a notable 73.24s for a sports car BTD.

Shelsley Walsh had been treated to a new surface in the braking area after the finish but this confidence-inspiring improvement was to no avail as the rain came down in torrents yet again, the deluge delaying the meeting for an hour at one point. 'Bosh', normally particularly formidable at Shelsley, was afflicted by a faulty fuel pump and (separately) a loose battery lead. Using his old 1.2-litre engine once more, and despite the problems, he climbed in 40.36s to beat Marsh (40.42s) and Scragg (40.55s); but the deceptively fast Hawley was faster yet and recorded 40.17s for a closely-contested BTD.

After this a patchily damp course at Prescott was positive luxury, and it was the yellow Lotus, in 1.5-litre form, which excelled in *the* meeting of the year. Boshier-Jones clocked 48.72s, whereas both Marsh and Meldrum were in the 49s and only Eccles in the 50s bracket. Phil Scragg climaxed his best season for some time with his second Gold Cup, in which the meteoric Mini of Roger Hickman and Ray Terry's Elva-BMW Mk7 were runners-up.

After six successive BTDs at Harewood one could be forgiven for making Peter Meldrum the favourite for the Yorkshire climb, and sure enough as the track dried out after early rain, he made it with a hectic 45.99s which ended with a spin *after* the finish – not unusual as the acute Quarry Corner is only a few yards from the finish line. The big surprises came, firstly, when Phil Chapman was fastest on the wet first runs in his latest home-built four-wheel-drive creation, the Mercury-Olds-mobile. With 'gearboxes all over the place' this nose-less device was stark in the extreme, but after appearing in a very untried state at Shelsley, was clearly becoming sorted. Perhaps even more surprising was that as the track dried out, the likes of 'Bosh', Hawley and Eccles were all beaten by a young fair-haired lad in his early twenties, from nearby Knaresborough, who was driving a new Twin Cam-engined Brabham BT16 in only its fourth event. This was Peter Lawson, who worked in his father's plant hire business, and who bought the Brabham after very limited experience in a Lotus Cortina, back in 1964, and an MGB. His 1966 efforts had been severely curtailed by a bad attack of mumps and a damaged arm but his obvious flair marked him out for a serious challenge in 1967.

Although the Championship was not in doubt, there was a fine, close battle at Dyrham Park where it was dry and a course record fell for the first time in the 1966 Championship. It took just 30.05s for Bryan Eccles to exert his superiority (would a drier year have given him a real chance of beating Marsh with the effective Brabham-Olds combination?) although Meldrum (30.32s), Boshier-Jones (30.33s), Swift, Marsh, Hawley and Griffiths were all in the 30s bracket. Regrettably, the meeting was rather soured by the knowledge that this would be the last held at this attractive hill. The Bristol club had made the unpleasant discovery that after they had developed the course from a tractor path, surfacing it and maintaining it on a six year lease, the National Trust simply declined to give them a new lease.

This time the ubiquitous Marsh had totted up 6 BTDs at Championship meetings and his unassailable points total of 93 was well up on Meldrum (78), the rather unlucky Eccles (77), Hawley (74), Boshier-Jones (69 after starting the season late), Scragg (50) and Griffiths (46).

The four-wheel-drive vogue now really took off. Ever since being impressed by the Ferguson P99 in 1963, Tony Marsh had been thinking hard about a 4WD system for his own car. The fruits of his deliberations appeared in 1967, incorporated in a new Marsh Special, typically workmanlike in the Marsh manner, and incorporating as many parts as possible from the earlier car, including the 4.2 GM engine, albeit 'stretched' to 4.5-litres. The new 96 inch wheelbase chassis was built up from square-section tubing and was revolutionary only in the drive system. The power to the front wheels was transmitted through the rear-mounted Hewland HD4 gearbox via a gear train to a drive shaft running the length of the car to a Lotus Elite differential. A cockpit-mounted switch on a mysterious-looking 'black box' – the subject of much intrigued speculation not exactly discouraged by Tony – operated a simple mechanical overrun clutch which enabled the driver to cut off the power to the front wheels in the corners while enjoying the extra traction of 4WD away from the start and under acceleration away from the corners. The system was designed in association with Hewland and was not actually operational until June Shelsley because of the late arrival of components. Initially, the car was run in 2WD form when it was already up against another 4WD challenger. This was none other than the BRM 670P which David Good had bought from the Owen Organisation. After three seasons with GT and sports cars, the 1961 Champion from Maidenhead was back with a vengeance although there were misgivings about the complexity of this still only partially developed car – misgivings which were heightened when it needed a new propshaft from Bourne after the April practice weekend at Prescott.

There were also plenty of changes among the other Championship aspirants. Windway Service Station, Cardiff proprietor Peter Boshier-Jones was staying faithful to his old supercharged Lotus 22, its yellow finish enlivened for some time by red 'flames' at appropriate places, for a fifth season, but fellow Lotus exponent Peter Meldrum was working on a home-brewed 4WD creation of his own – one which, alas never gave him anything like the success of the Lotus. Bryan Eccles was keeping to his successful Brabham GM V8 formula but had disposed of his BT14 to Merseyside circuit-racer John Scott-Davies and obtained a newer BT18 chassis with Traco/Oldsmobile engine. Big V8s were in vogue but Birmingham baker Mike Hawley had shown how competitive a 4-cylinder car could be in 1966, without benefit of supercharger, and for the new season he switched to a brand-new Brabham BT23B, basically an F2 chassis but fitted with a 2.0 Climax FPF from Racing Services (who were looking after the parts and development of these engines now that Coventry Climax had withdrawn from racing). Up in Scotland, the Mickels (Gray had had a poor year after suffering from eye trouble) sold their old Cooper, and obtained Ray Fielding's Lotus 21, to be run with a Buick V8 engine. The practice weekend at Prescott produced another talking point when Phil Scragg presented his Lola with cycle-winged bodywork after undergoing a transformation rather like that carried out by Josh Randles on his Cooper Monaco. Felday Engineering had carried out modifications to the suspension to adapt the car for hill climbing while Williams & Pritchard produced the superbly executed if not very elegant bodywork. After a fine season with his Elva-BMW Mk7, Ray Terry had sold this to Georgina Baillie-Hill, the daughter of one-time HRG driver Ken Ballie-Hill, and who had put in some pretty impressive drives in the still-effective ex-Fielding/Tyack/Austin/McCartney Emeryson-Climax. Ray was replacing the Mk7 with a new Elva Mk8 with Buick V8 engine and looked likely to challenge Scragg for the honour of being fastest sports car.

The Aston Martin Owners' Club's *Daily Mirror* Trophy fixture in April at Wiscombe could be regarded as a dress rehearsal for the Championship season ahead, and Marsh, without 4WD but with a distinct misfire was down in fourth place behind an on-form Bryan Eccles (43.77s), Good's already most purposeful BRM with its gorgeous wailing exhaust note, and Ian Swift's now absolutely immaculate metallic dark red and yellow Swift-Ford. When it was 'for real' at Loton Park a fortnight later, Good was more than a mite hairy. The torque transfer device wasn't working as it should and the courageous Maidenhead driver was down in eighth place. Taking full advantage of a basically simple and well-proven type of car, Bryan Eccles blasted the Brabham up in a record 35.37s, just 0.24s faster than Marsh, and with Mike Hawley an astonishing third on 35.97s. It was astonishing as his new Brabham was not ready and he was having a run in Griffiths, Felday 6 which was not always regarded as the best thing to have come out of Felday's Forest Green workshops! Northerners John Butterworth

By the end of 1967 Les Hinchcliffe was campaigning this ex-Peter Sadler monocoque Lotus 27/32 with twin-cam engine.
HAYDN SPEDDING

Leeds-based journalist Allan Staniforth pioneered a new approach for the small capacity racing classes. He and Richard Blackmore used Mini components in a simple spaceframe chassis with great success, and then made detailed plans available to other special builders. This is Staniforth on Oliver's Mount.
HAYDN SPEDDING

(still with his successful blown Brabham BT14) and Peter Lawson both managed to push Boshier-Jones down another place.

The intervening weekend had seen Eccles beating local man Lawson at Harewood so the Alcester driver came to Prescott on the crest of a wave. A spin at Ettore's on his first class run and a noiseless halt with water in the fuel next time up soon put paid to that in a meeting which suffered intermittent rain. True to form, Phil Scragg and the Lola were in their element and 52.41s sufficed for BTD, while on the RAC climbs 55.14s gave him fourth place, bare fractions behind 'Bosh' (55.07s) and Marsh (55.13s), but way down on Good who really gained the 'unfair advantage' with the BRM in a demoralising 52.73s.

It was wet and wintery at Wiscombe for the third round although Eccles got in a 44.36s BTD climb before conditions really deteriorated for the RAC runs, when David Good again demonstrated the Ferguson 4WD system's effectiveness when traction was at a premium. This time he was over 2 seconds up on 'Bosh' and the fast-maturing Lawson.

According to official times at Barbon, Phil Scragg was the new course record holder in a fantastic 25.340s, but although it was a fine run Scragg was the first to deny that it was possible, and that someone must have sneezed or something in the timing box! Phil was still third in the RAC runs, though, beaten only by Eccles and the very suddenly confident David Good who lifted another 10 points with 27.375s, although it should be noted that this was still slightly slower than Westbury's 1964 record at 27.174s with the Ferguson.

For once Shelsley Walsh was bathed in sunshine and one of the best meetings for some time graced the famous Worcestershire hill. No fewer than 62 climbs were made under standing records during the day and the closeness of the competition can be appreciated by noting that the Top Ten began their Championship ascents with a single second covering them. Once the excitement caused by David Harrison (literally) flying off the road in his Crosslé-Buick sports car had died down, the serious stuff really developed in the run-off. First time out with 4WD and Tony Marsh was back on top with a new hill record in 31.23s, only 0.32s clear of Eccles and with Patsy Burt a superb third on her favourite hill in the big McLaren. Her time of 31.92s was naturally a Ladies' record. Mike Hawley at last had his new Brabham but he was narrowly edged out of fourth place by 'Bosh' and the top six was rounded off by the fast-rising Baronet from Mortimer, Sir Nicholas Williamson (in another Twin Cam Brabham), and Butterworth. Poor David Good, after a fine run of success, was down in seventh spot after a hesitant start on one run and a swipe at a bank on the other.

For some time now Bo'ness had been threatened by a housing scheme which was to be built on the Kinneil Estate and now the end had come. Fortunately, the Lothian CC had matters in hand with a more than adequate replacement at Doune in Perthshire, but this, one of the original RAC Championship rounds, had gone and for 1967 'The Rest' was the only Scottish qualifier. Although the bottom third of the hill had been resurfaced, the Hump had been ironed out, and there was less 'low flying' at The Bump, only 42 entries were tempted out. It was a close thing but Marsh (51.55s) beat Good (51.86s) and Eccles (51.91s), and the Championship was clearly going to go to one of these three.

That impression was strengthened at Bouley Bay where Marsh took the Championship lead with a 45.26s record, beating Good and Eccles, and the cheerful 'Sir Nick' – still smiling after taking to the escape road on Radio corner – heading the 4-cylinder brigade in fourth place. Unfortunately, tragedy intervened when local builder Lee Olver (1276 Cooper-JAP) dived down the steep bank after Les Platons and suffered head injuries to which he succumbed.

David Good and mechanic Malcolm Angood had coped remarkably well with the sophisticated BRM, but the car had to be withdrawn at Great Auclum after a promising practice run when the first gear failed. With Marsh – as usual – missing this round it looked like a good opportunity for the 4-cylinder contingent, and so it was with Hawley winning (19.38s) from 'Bosh' (despite a gear jumping out and the car proving reluctant to fire up), Eccles and Patsy Burt.

Poor Martin Brain again damaged his car in practice for Craigantlet but this time the Stewards would not let him run in Ray Terry's Elva which was sportingly put at his disposal. Neither Marsh nor Good went over and it was no surprise to see Bryan Eccles on top with 62.84s although Hawley ran him close. Bryan had lowered the Shelsley record to 30.83s at the non-Championship July meeting, and despite finding his engine 300 rpm down after a top end overhaul, nearly did it again in August with a 30.98s which was good enough to defeat Marsh and Hawley, with Good and Patsy Burt absent as they were competing in Switzerland. After the poor conditions experienced in recent seasons the MAC prudently took out insurance against rain in 1967. Naturally, it was dry for all three meetings!

In contrast, the BOC had a wet road to contend with at Prescott and accidents befell Boshier-Jones (in practice) and Eccles (on his first Championship run). Marsh's subsequent win over Hawley, Good and Williamson was one of his easier ones. From there the leading contenders went on to Harewood where Marsh clinched his sixth Championship at a fine finale, where the course record was broken no less than nine times by Hepworth, Marsh and Lawson, with Marsh setting it at 42.94s. Lawson was runner-up in the RAC climbs with a no-longer-surprising 43.27s, beating Eccles who recorded 43.71s before spinning at Quarry in a last desperate attempt. During the meeting, Peter Lawson, initially rather shy but a real joker once the ice was broken, really fired up the partisan Yorkshire enthusiasts by announcing that he was buying the BRM from David Good for 1968. So Marsh had won again, this time with 79 points to the 75 of Eccles who came so close for a second successive year, the 64 of Hawley, the 63 of Good, whose season had tailed off slightly, and the 58 of Peter Boshier-Jones, whose Lotus 22 really was becoming a little outmoded in this company (although Peter's finances would not run to anything more sophisticated and his own exceptional skill made up for a lot). The newcomers, Lawson and Williamson were next up after impressive seasons. Williamson, whose car was maintained under Ron Smith management, as was Patsy Burt's and David Good's, is the nephew of Major Charles Lambton and this slightly larger than life character, with his characteristic and tremendously endearing stammer, brought a new flash of *joie de vivre* to the sport, on and off the track. In fact, Peter Lawson rapidly sold off his Brabham BT18 to Wolverhampton garage proprietor Peter Blankstone, and ran the BRM 670P at the YSCC's traditional end-of-season Gunter Trophy meeting at Castle Howard. Despite the failure of a driveshaft as he crossed the finish line, he set a new course

record in 31.21s – 0.79s up on David Hepworth – so there was no doubting his challenge for 1968.

During the nineteen-sixties the importance of the RAC Championship in the minds of hill climbers, and to the British motor sport scene generally, increased sharply. The close competition, the technical innovations and the sheer spectacle of the much more powerful cars competing on the same narrow and sinuous hills saw to that. However, hill climbing had great strength in depth too during this period, with great variety and competition outside the still relatively restricted ranks of those who wished, or could afford, to compete with the larger single-seaters and the odd sports-racer capable of matching them.

During the three years of Tony Marsh's stranglehold on the Championship, there was a particularly close-fought situation among the smaller racing cars, normally with an 1100cc class limit, where the old guard of Cooper-JAPs, as still campaigned by the Eltons and Colin Watts with particular distinction, and the Formula Junior, and 1000cc F2 and F3-based cars predominated. In 1963 Yorkshireman Jim Johnstone, already with a string of success behind him with an Austin-Healey Sprite, started to make a considerable impact on Northern events with a Lotus 18, while a significant entry at Prescott in May was circuit racer – but regular Prescott competitor – Bill Bradley. He was competing in international F2 races that year with a David Prophet-entered Brabham BT16 with the single overhead-cam Cosworth SCA engine. Despite a restricted rev band necessitating full use of the Hewland five-speed gearbox, this approximately 120 bhp 1.0-litre 'screamer', loosely based on the Ford 105E block, could be successful on the hills in the right hands. Bradley's 51.123s class record, shattering the old 52.917s record and defeating the very successful Cooper-BMC of Mike Hawley (51.50s), proved that

Like Phil Scragg, Ray Terry was capable of beating most single-seater drivers in his Elva-Buick Mk8S sports racer.
HAYDN SPEDDING

Jim Thomson's rather special road-going 4.2 E-type Jaguar was probably the fastest of a healthy contingent of E-types which provided much spectacle on the northern hills.
HAYDN SPEDDING

point although the SCA was then an expensive front-line F2 unit and it was to be some time before it became regular wear on the hills. Lotus-Ford 20 or 22 drivers Les Hinchcliffe, Colin Priddey and Derry Nicklin were conspicuously successful although Hinchcliffe moved on to an ex-Peter Sadler Lotus 27/32 with Bill Crosland-built 1.6 Twin-Cam engine before the end of the year.

A radically different challenge came from Leeds-based *Daily Mirror* journalist Allan Staniforth who wanted to move into the single-seater category at low cost after several highly successful seasons campaigning a Mini. He and Richard Blackmore, from Tadcaster, set to work to design and build a single-seater using the transverse Mini engine/gearbox power pack at the rear of a simple spaceframe racing car employing Mini 10 inch wheels. The intention was to build a car for each of them and initial efforts were concentrated on finishing Allan's car which duly appeared with 1071cc Mini-Cooper S power in 1965. This distinctive looking device was dubbed Terrapin and was an immediate success, gaining a supercharger for 1966. The sequel to this was that Staniforth wrote an equally successful book entitled *High Speed – Low Cost*, published by Patrick Stephens, which encouraged many to build their own Terrapins in some remarkably far-flung corners of the world aided by large-scale working drawings prepared by the Yorkshire driver. After many award-laden seasons, spent constantly developing and up-dating the basic theme, Allan Staniforth was still campaigning a Terrapin – the Mk7C with Talbot Imp-based engine – well into the nineteen-eighties.

In 1966 Staniforth was joined in the increasingly competitive class by a young engineer from Warwick, Roy Lane with a fairly old but immaculately turned out 1100cc Cooper-Ford and another member of the Blankstone family, David from Stourbridge, who had bought the Racing Car Show F3 Lotus 41, complete with 1000cc Cosworth MAE 'screamer' engine. A novice, Sir Nicholas Williamson, had an old FJ Cooper-BMC with which he made a good impression and at the September Prescott 'big spender' Rollason turned out with a monocoque F2 Lotus 35 with SCA engine, although confusingly fitted with a Lotus 41 nose. Nevertheless, Jim Johnstone, now running his Lotus 18 supercharged, and contesting more Southerly meetings, tended to be at least a match for the opposition.

The following year, Roy Lane had substituted a Roots-blown Twin-Cam engine for his 1100cc unit and moved up a class. Rollason's Lotus-SCA 35 looked pretty dominant but he was soon joined by Chris Court, from Sedgley, with an SCA unit in an F3 Lotus 31, David McDougall in a 1964 F3 Cooper-BMC T72, and the Terrapin-ish supercharged Mamba of John Thornton. Despite splitting his attention between the 1.0 Lotus and a Tecalemit Jackson fuel-injected Twin-Cam-engined Lotus 41, Rollason was very much the man to beat.

The leading 1600cc racing class contenders were heavily involved with the RAC Championship contest although there were less sophisticated machines competing, such as the ingenious Rudeani (a rear-mounted Ford Cortina-engined device with chain drive) of Bill Heaton-Rudd and Frank Dean and the Cooper-based DMF Mk3 of former Autotest exponent Don Harris, from Cambridge. While not in the front rank of Championship aspirants, both scored many successes at smaller meetings.

After a period of relative decline, 1965 to 1967 brought a number a significant additions to the sports car ranks. Phil Scragg and Ray Terry were perfectly capable of Top Ten performances and so, occasionally, was John Barnes whose Elva Mk7 was transformed with a 1650cc supercharged Ford pushrod engine, but was still occasionally run on the road. In particular, John enjoyed a run of BTDs at Woburn with this car. In 1965 the experienced Brian Field, rally driver as well as sprint/hill climber was well in the running with a Lotus 23B, but Ray Terry with his Elva-BMW Mk7 was definately the man in form until David Good arrived on the scene with his Lola T70. Ilkley Cooper-Buick single-seater driver David Harrison debuted an Irish-built Crosslé, with Buick power, in 1966 although this was never a real match for Terry's Elva-Buick Mk8S. Another to follow the Buick V8 path was westcountryman John Grafton who, after several notably good seasons with a Lotus 7, took to a Cooper Monaco-Buick, a notably 'hairy' car. After impressing with the little Emeryson, Georgina Baillie-Hill really became a major force when she took over the Terry Elva-BMW.

By 1967 there were two 4WD sports cars running regularly – Phil Chapman's daunting but fairly effective Mercury MkIII, and the superb BRM V8-engined Felday 4 which was eventually sold off to Horwich enthusiast John McCartney. An unassuming purist who hill climbs purely for the pleasure of driving interesting cars in period specification. John had already campaigned the ex-everybody Emeryson and an E-type Jaguar with success and the Felday was to lead on to a variety of Formula 1 BRMs, the unique Parnell-BRM sports-racer, an ex-McLaren Racing/John Love Tasman Cooper-Climax and several FJ/F3 cars. He did fit the Felday 4 with an ungainly 'Randalised' cycle-winged body at one stage but his cars are normally completely faithful to their original specification.

Among the devotees of the big sports-racer, Don Farrell (6.0 Farrellac) and Maurice Starbuck (6.0 Chrysler Special) were regulars while George Tatham competed with a ''knobbly' Lister-Chevrolet for a while. At the other end of the spectrum, there were still a lot of Lotus 7s about, notably the very potent example with a Twin-Cam engine and a Lotus Elan rear end of the now retired Austen May's son Tony which he campaigned before graduating to a 1500cc Holbay-engined F3 Cooper T72 single-seater, in 1967. Ever since Arthur Mallock had raised a few eyebrows at Prescott with his boxy U2 Formula Junior, the Roade-sourced, front-engined Mallock U2s, similar in concept to the Lotus 7 but designed purely for racing and remarkably cheap to build, had been regular sights on the hills. The examples of Brian Moyse, young Bournemouth solicitor Jeremy Lord and Malcolm Smith (in Northern events) were regular class winners by 1966. However, the real potential for hill climbing of these cycle-winged, front-engined Clubman's Sports chassis was forcibly demonstrated in 1967 when Dennis Firkins and Robin Skelcher fitted a Mk5 version with a 1.6 Twin Cam engine. Then the class records really began to fall and the way was prepared for the U2 to become about the most popular type of chassis, irrespective of category, on the hills in the later nineteen-seventies and nineteen-eighties.

The new breed of Special GT/Group 4 Sports Cars tended to be fairly expensive choices for hill climbing but in 1967, Paul Ridgway scored some decisive wins in the Worcestershire Racing Association Ginetta-SCA G12, while the previous year a Ford GT40 appeared to rival Ron Fry's Ferraris for the title of most glamorous car on the hills. After the disastrous end to his second Cooper-Buick, John Macklin returned to competition with a blue E-type Jaguar before the ex-F English Ford GT40.

Closer in concept to roadgoing sports/GT machinery, the agile Lotus Elan was naturally a popular mount: the competition lightweight Elans of George Keylock and David Good being notably success-ful. Prominent further north in 1966/67 were John Cussins (son of Manny Cussins, the Chairman of the Waring & Gillow furniture company, who was even better known for his Chairmanship of Leeds United Football Club) and one 'Spotty Muldoon', revealed to be the almost equally unlikely-sounding 'Stanislas Smith' or just plain 'S. M. Smith'. These aliases were favoured by Yorkshireman Tony Bancroft who faced parental disapproval for his weekend exploits. This scion of the Yorkshire textile industry managed to keep 'the cat in the bag' for several years before his family discovered what he was up to and became reconciled to Tony's other innocent, non-drinking, pursuit! While hill climbing at the top was definitely serious, albeit generally most sporting, there were happily many who supplied sheer *fun* to the proceedings, including the supposedly retired Reg Phillips. Aided and abetted by BMC executive and BBC broadcaster Raymond Baxter (who had shared the driving of the original Fairley V8 back in the nineteen-fifties, which was still extant as the Fairley-Mercury in the hands of the intrepid Peter Bevis), 'smiling' Reg had concocted a contraption known as the Fairley Poke. This was based on the terribly fashionable Mini-Moke 'fun car', fitted with a 1400cc engine of considerable potency. Despite diversions such as the attempt by Messrs Marsh and Eccles to load the thing with straw bales on the start line at Shelsley, the Fairley Poke certainly did not disgrace itself.

Returning to the conventional, Midlands sprint exponent Bob Rose had garnered an impressive total of awards with a Lotus Elite before buying one of the then new and exceptionally good-looking Dennis Adams-designed Marcos-Volvo GTs in 1964. Although Bob tended to stay in the Midlands, he won a tremendous number of class wins with this car before selling it in 1967 for something really powerful, the ex-Keith St John 4.7 McLaren Elva-Ford M1B sports-racer. Every region had its favourites among the sports/GT classes, such as those with the spectacular yet predictable Jaguar E-type. Apart from Phil Scragg's Lightweight and later 4.2 model, the ex-Protheroe car of Mike Wright and the generally rather tatty-looking but very fast example of Michael Miles, there was a positive battalion of the Coventry cars competing in the big Marque (Y) sports class on the Northern hills by 1967. One of the most consistently successful was Jim Thomson, from Timble. Jim, a director of a (then) modest family industrial blast-cleaning-equipment company in Otley – Guyson – had begun with a Jaguar XK150S before starting to win his class regularly in 1966. His opposition often came from York motorcycle dealer Alan Mountain and his Sales Manager John Lambert; from Henry Crowther; David Stead; future Yorkshire Centre Chairman, Derek Clark; Sheriff Hutton farmer, Bill Wood; and later on, from Yorkshire-based Mancunian car dealer Fred Cliffe. And in later years there was always a cheer for property men John and his cousin David Walker. with a rough-looking but fast white XK120 which they ran until themselves switching to an E-type Jaguar.

Among the saloons this was the golden age of the hot Mini, ranging from Colin Rogers' amazing 850cc Mini Estate, through all the myriad Mini-Cooper S permutations (including Irishman Dickie Barrett's 1390cc Ford-engined car which, in a splendid example of Irish logic, was sometimes forced to run in the racing car class in Irish events because 'it was too fast to be a saloon') right through to the bizarre Mini-Buick. For many years the workshops at Littleborough, near Rochdale, of pipe-smoking Harry Ratcliffe had turned out successful saloon racers, from Harry's original Morris Minor to a variety of Minis which successively appeared under Vitafoam, Team Vita D, BRT Developments and BVRT banners. One of the most successful northern tuning concerns (John Handley won the European Touring Car series with one of their Minis), they produced a dark green Mini in 1965/6 which looked fairly normal at a glance, apart from the sinister-looking duct behind one door. However, closer inspection revealed no rear seat and a 3.5 alloy V8 from Buick occupying the area where the rear seat once resided. The handling of the thing was rather terrifying and Ratcliffe soon put this one down to experience and the car passed to Jaguar E-type driver Piers Martin, from Claughton. Even at a simple uphill sprint like Leighton Hall, the car looked alarming. It turned a few heads on the streets of Lancaster too, as the author remembers!

Of course there were scores of successful Minis up and down the country during this period but the most notable included those of Scotsman Tom Christie; Mike Evans' Downton car; Barry Pearson's Broadspeed version; David Gould's Westune model; Roger Hickman's 1.0 version which ran Phil Scragg close for the 1966 Prescott Gold Cup, John Francis' ultra-rapid yellow 1300, Jeff Goodliff's Vitafoam 970S, and the astonishing red and black 1300 'S' of a bearded red-haired character called Peter Kaye, who was already becoming one of the most respected racing mechanics in the North. Even non-Championship meetings at places like Harewood, Castle Howard and Oliver's Mount now ended the day with a Top Ten run-off as a climax, and by 1966/67 Peter Kaye's little Mini was usually well within the fastest ten.

It was a time of expansion and optimism. After all this was 'The Swinging Sixties' and although major hills – Longleat, Westbrook Hay, Dyrham Park, Bo'ness and Catterick – ceased to be available there were always new ones to take their places, thus regularly imparting novelty to the hill climb scene. The big excitement in 1965 was the first use by the LAC of the fascinating Tholt-y-Will climb in the Isle of Man on 30 May. The mainly Northern competitors who went over were enthralled by this European-style hill, with 3.6 miles of wide (by hill climb standards), sweeping bends. Only Tony Griffiths (BRM) of the leading single-seater contenders competed and he duly took BTD at 170.725s, just over five seconds up on Phil Scragg's E-type, and with Ken Aitchison's TVR Griffith and John Cuff's E-type taking the next places overall to emphasise that this course really allowed the drivers of the big powerful cars to extend their mounts.

With the SWAC deeply involved in running Llandow circuit, Castel Farm had become rather neglected until the Swansea MC took over the running of meetings there in 1965, although their first meeting was marred when the surface started to break up near the new chicane on the straight, necessitating a shortened course for the event proper. In hill climbing's West Midlands heartland, the MAC changed the format of their non-Championship July date from an Inter-Club meeting to a straightforward 'clubbie', while up in Scotland the Aberdeen & DMC held their first meeting in September at Fintray House. It had been a long time since Scotland had gained a significant new hill but the 650-

yard climb at Fintray, close to Aberdeen, soon gained good local support although rather far North for English competitors. Picturesquely set among the rhododendron bushes and with the River Don in the background, Fintray provided a starting straight, sweeping right up to the 90 degree Crombie Bend, another short straight, then a U-turn before the sprint to the finish.

Innovations during the following year included a 'Special' meeting at Prescott in April for competitors who had not won an award there during the last three years. This was a similar concept to the Harewood Novices meeting which was now firmly established on the calender. There were two meetings at Tholt-y-Will, both won by Fred Smith's rapid Brabham BT14 although Griffiths' record remained intact. However, despite the erection of additional crash barriers for the September meeting – Jack Cordingley had written off his JBW in a high speed accident in May – the RAC were not that keen on upgrading the hill to Championship status for, apart from the safety aspect, an additional round outside the mainland would add to the commitment needed from the already rather stretched hill climb 'circus'. Unfortunately, the Isle of Man authorities were not prepared to continue with their invaluable financial assistance beyond 1967 unless RAC status was achieved as the tourist-drawing power of the existing club meetings was not great. Fortunately, RAC status was eventually awarded although there was always some concern expressed at the speeds attained by the fastest cars, as there was on the finishing straight at Oliver's Mount.

There were two notable occurrences outside the top-line events in August, 1966. There was the final destruction of Douglas Hull's VSCC record on the old course at Prescott, which had stood to ERA R11B since 1959 at 44.17s. Alan Cottam steered his less powerful but better-handling Connaught A-type F2 car to a fine 43.46s record. Secondly, a woman other than Patsy Burt set an outright BTD, the honour falling to Agnes Mickel in 31.4s at Fintray. Another Midlands climb, at the 650-yards Furnace Grange Farm, under the aegis of the Dudley & DCC briefly graced the scene. Malcolm Eaves won the inaugural climb at this slightly dicey hill at Truscott, near Wolverhampton. Further North, Fred Smith at last broke Jack Cordingley's 1962 record at Oliver's Mount (so named after the Cromwell Memorial at the Summit) with a resounding 45.49s time which defeated Meldrum, Lawson and Bryan Eccles (who had fitted his Brabham with the Buick V8 out of John Macklin's wrecked Cooper). 'Fast Fred' from Forton, near Preston, never took the RAC Championship seriously but he was a very difficult man to beat on the Northern hills in his yellow and black Brabham BT14.

The BARC's Yorkshire Centre were keen innovators but one good idea which didn't really come off was the holding of a hill climb specially for ITV's World of Sport television programme at Harewood, in November. A varied field of 55 was garnered for this out-of-season affair although the promised appearance of Jim Clark in his RAC Rally Lotus-Cortina came to nothing after the ex-World Champion crashed on that rally. Sadly, it was very muddy and visibility – crucial for television – was terrible. By the time a halt was called everyone had had three runs and in these distinctly gripless conditions it was no surprise to see Peter Westbury, driving the 4WD 7.0 Felday-Ford 5 sports car winning from Phil Chapman's own 4WD creation. The gap, a mere 0.1s, reflected very well on the Sheffield amateur.

Notwithstanding this climatic misfortune, the BARC emphasised once again their growing stature as a hill climb promoting club. Seventeen years of operations at Brunton, many events at Firle, now an RAC round at Harewood – widely acknowledged to be on a par with even Shelsley and Prescott for slick organisation and, at this stage, probably ahead of then in terms of promotional flair – as centrepiece of a full Yorkshire programme, a superb end-of-season finale at Scarborough, and a hefty contribution by Mike Wilson and his Yorkshire Centre colleagues in the YSCC's events at Castle Howard, all added up to a most substantial contribution to the hill climb scene.

And there was more to come, for in 1967 there were two new BARC hills in use, and both of them were of Championship potential. The South Western Centre capitalised on its long experience of running meetings at the popular if less than classic hill at Brunton with their first two meetings at the Hitchings Brothers' farm at Gurston Down, near Broadchalke in Wiltshire, and just a few miles from Salisbury. Set in generally open, sweeping downland, the 1100 yards course begins just beyond the farmyard Paddock and drivers are faced with a steep and exhilarating – not to say daunting in some cars – downhill sweep to the left before the climb starts with a fast approach to the difficult and rather steep Karousel complex. Once this is successfully sorted out competitors accelerate up a short straight before turning hard left and up the final slopes. This fast hill, resurfaced and incorporating the newly built Karousel loop, had had the benefit of some 'consultancy' advice from Tony Marsh. The opening 'practice' meeting on 25 June was won, appropriately in view of her regular support and success at Brunton and Firle, by Patsy Burt in the powder blue McLaren in 39.90s. Just a month later a rather more ambitious meeting attracted Marsh himself and his 35.50s record with the 4WD Marsh Special was more than a match for the supercharged Brabham of John Butterworth (37.82s) and Don Harris' DMF (38.28s).

On the same day as the inaugural meeting at Gurston, the Club's South Wales Centre realised the fruits of long negotiation with the Pontypool local authority and ran the first climb in Pontypool Park, within the town boundary of Pontypool. Starting off almost on the flat and curving away between the celebrated Pontypool Park benches, the course then turned sharply to the right round a most substantial tree and in deep shade before starting to climb more steeply away through the Esses and up through a long double-apex left-hander to the finish. With a maximum gradient of 1 in 7, a half-mile length, good amenities and the attractive surroundings of a former deep park, this was by far the best Welsh hill since the demise of the lamented Lydstep. The South Wales Centre, and in particular R. G. Phillips and V. H. Hesketh, worked extremely hard in their negotiations with Pontypool Urban District Council (to become Torfaen Borough Council after Local Government Reorganisation), and in the construction and surfacing work on the course itself, so it was a pity that it rained for the first meeting when 'local boy' Peter Boshier-Jones slithered up to a 37.38s BTD. Conditions were much better in August, when Mike Hawley set a more meaningful target at 30.63s, scoring over even 'Bosh' who had to be content with 31.18s.

Up in Yorkshire, and close to the major West Riding population centre, Harewood was attracting just about the largest hill climb crowds of all, and although the 10,000 to 16,000 'gates' claimed were almost certainly over optimistic, the Yorkshire Centre's attractive programmes and good viewing facilities certainly drew in many thousands. At the June meeting for several years a charity occasion was laid on too, a meeting held in conjunction with the Variety Club of Great Britain. Since the programme included such diversions as parachute displays, glider aerobatics, Vintage cars, and the appearance of 'Batman' complete with Ford Galaxie 500 'Batmobile', this event invariably pulled in the families.

Longer courses were earnestly desired by many and after the October 1967 meeting on the 900-yard long course at Loton Park, the SVMC commenced work on a programme to lengthen the already-extended Shropshire hill. The longest and most testing hill of all, Tholt-y-Will, had a poor year, afflicted with miserable weather. In September, with thick mist swirling about Snaefell, the LAC even had to lop the last mile off the wet and slippery course in the interests of safety. The burly David Hepworth with his powerful Brabham-Traco/Oldsmobile BT11 set a brave BTD but it was significant that third BTD fell to Harry Ratcliffe's rapid Mini-Cooper S. Fortunately, with the future rather doubtful, the LAC gained new heart when they learned that the RAC had agreed to include the Isle of Man hill in the Championship for 1968.

Spencer Elton won a final event at St Audries Bay in September, for after some fourteen meetings, the Taunton MC had to admit defeat with a hill which was deemed too bumpy and rough for future use.

Just as 1966 had ended with an unseasonal one-off at Harewood, so 1967 had a rather bizarre postscript. This time the meeting was on 23 December and it was again for the benefit of a television audience, although this time it was for the BBC and a shortened (1000 yards) Gurston Down was used. The weather behaved, there was an interesting entry but the great foot-and-mouth-disease outbreak which had already wiped out the RAC Rally almost killed this event too. However, after helpful discussions between BARC (SW), the Ministry of Agriculture and the National Farmers' Union, the meeting was allowed to continue although Hawley and Griffiths were unable to come as they lived in an infected area, no spectators were allowed and all vehicles were disinfected on arrival. Surprisingly, the hill was in good condition and Tony Marsh set a rapid 30.6s BTD, with exciting TV footage coming from John Barnes who had a camera fitted to his Elva, from Ian Swift who performed a spectacular if harmless spin, and from circuit racer John Fenning in Sir Nick Williamson's Brabham BT21A. Fenning declared hill climbing to be more dangerous than circuit racing!

Apart from the annual excursions to Craigantlet in Ulster by the RAC Championship contenders, the Irish hill climb scene had virtually no point of contact with the British mainland sport, although the annual outings to the familiar closed public road hills continued as before with very mixed entries. The

Eire Hills counted towards the premier RIAC's award, the Walter Sexton Memorial Trophy, as did sprints and circuit races but there was no all-Ireland series to pull together a rather fragmented season. The outstanding (and mechanically best-equipped) John Pringle never took in anything like all the hill climbs and in 1962 Dan McAlister's elderly F2 Cooper-Climax took the Sexton Trophy – on handicap – for the second successive year, with Frank Keane winning the following year in an FJ Lotus 18 which later, in 1964, appeared with an Alfa Romeo twin overhead cam unit. In Ireland, just as in the rest of the UK, the well-modified saloon was becoming ever more popular and formidable. Ever since 1960 the Sexton Trophy had had a Saloon Car Section, won in 1962 by Johny du Moulin's near-legendary 1650cc Ford Anglia, and in 1963 by the Mini-Cooper S of Michael Ivis, who was the Service Controller for Eire Austin assemblers, Lincoln & Nolan Ltd. The following year, he went one better and won the Saloon Car Section and the Sexton Trophy outright!

For 1965 the Sexton Trophy regulations were changed in favour of awarding the Trophy on Scratch – and it was still won by a Mini. This time Ivis and Keane's Lotus-Alfa Romeo had to give best to the 1304cc Mini of Robin Rennicks – who confessed to hating hill climbs! If this did not exactly enhance the stature of hill climbing in Ireland, the following year did something to restore the situation when regular BTD man Richie Heeley, a garage proprietor from Malahide, Co Dublin, lifted the Trophy in his Shorrock/Allard blown Lotus-Ford 22, while Eddie Regan's Mini won the Saloon Section. Heeley, this time with an upgraded Lotus 31 chassis won again in 1967 but although Terry Power (Mini) won the Saloon Section his success was rather less meaningful as the men who were really enlivening the Irish Saloon category – Alec Poole (with his fabulous Wolseley Hornet), Robin Rennicks, and Steve Griffin – tended to steer well clear of the hills. Then again, two of the best single-seater racers in Ireland, Belfast's Tommy Reid and Malcolm Templeton, were Ulstermen and therefore ineligible for the Sexton Trophy. One has to admit that with more circuit racing available in the Emerald Isle during the nineteen-sixties, interest in hill climbing was definitely declining during the period.

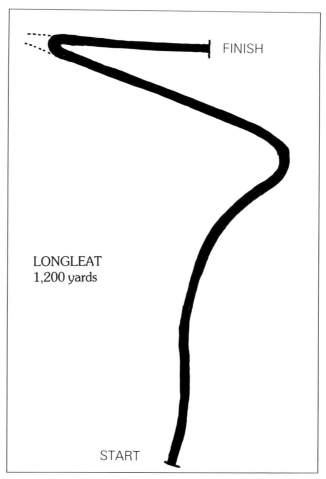

FINISH

LONGLEAT
1,200 yards

START

A Yorkshireman on Top

David Good had firmly demonstrated the potential of the melodious-sounding 4WD BRM in 1967 but it remained to be seen whether the relatively inexperienced, if undoubtedly talented, Peter Lawson could extract the full potential of the car in 1968.

In fact, the 1968 season looked a particularly open one as Tony Marsh made it known that conflicting calls on his time would probably prevent him from contesting a full season. The formidable Bryan Eccles had sold his BT18 to circuit racer Chris Cox and was working on his own variation on the disconnectable Marsh 4WD system to fit in a newer Brabham BT21A chassis to be 4.2 Oldsmobile-powered. As it transpired, Eccles was unable to compete, but both Ray Terry and David Hepworth were working on 4WD projects, the former having Chas Beattie convert his Elva-Buick and the latter using Brabham F1 components in his own Hepworth single-seater.

But not everyone was taking the tempting but technically difficult and potentially expensive 4WD route, and those who did were not all successful. It fell to Peter Meldrum to demonstrate that all-wheel-drive was not an automatic short cut to success when he began campaigning his PR2 at Harewood – scene of so many Meldrum triumphs – in April. This rather ungainly contrivance used the now Centric-blown, methanol-burning 1650cc Ford engine out of the old Pinner Racing Lotus 22, driving all four wheels via a Rover 2000 gearbox. A gear selector problem on its début was only the first of many disappointments with this clever, old-style hill climb special.

Among the other established experts, Tony Griffiths had sold the Felday 6 to Vintage Bentley racer Johnty (John T as opposed to father Jack) Williamson and was running a 1.6 Vegantune twin cam-powered Brabham BT21A and Sir Nick Williamson was also sticking to this straightforward formula with a Vegantune-prepared unit in a new BT21C (F3 as opposed to the slightly heavier American Formula B/Formule Libre BT21A chassis). Lotus user Geoff Rollason had sold both his Twin-Cam 41C (to Malcolm Eaves) and his 41-SCA (to David Blankstone) and planned to try the powerful, if 'peaky' 1.6 F2 Cosworth FVA engine, buying the unique ex-Jack Oliver 41C Formula 2 car. The wealthy Martin Brain, now taking his hill climbing very seriously and working on the 'horses for courses' theory had commissioned a new Formula 2/3-based Cooper T87 chassis, specially built to take the 2.5 Daimler V8 engine for the tighter hills, and had got Coopers to rebuild the ex-Jochen Rindt 1967 F1 T81B chassis with a monstrous but only mildly-tuned 7.2 Chrysler V8 engine for the faster courses.

One notable absentee was Peter Boshier-Jones, He had decided that he did not have the financial resources to develop a fully competitive new car and would therefore retire. His withdrawal ensured that he would remain probably the best driver *not* to win the RAC title, and was a reminder that hill climbing at the top level was now a far more expensive – if more competitive and technically absorbing – than it had been when brother David was Champion. Ironically, 1968 was the first year when the RAC rules regarding advertising on racing cars were relaxed, thus making commercial sponsorship more appealing to the sponsor, although it would be some time before the move had much effect on the essentially amateur sport of hill climbing.

There were to be 13 counters in the RAC series, with Tholt-y-Will coming in on 23 June and there was every prospect of a further Scottish round in future years, for Lothian CC and Ray Fielding were well advanced with a fine new course in Doune Park, only 7 miles from Stirling on the road to Callender.

Oddly enough, several of the new contenders appeared for the first time at a circuit race, for the MAC organised their first-ever race meeting at Silverstone in March, where the aimiable Warwick engineer Roy Lane showed his emerging talent by winning with his new acquisition, a gleaming orange Brabham BT14 with 3.5 Traco/Buick engine. The top six in this well-contested Formule Libre race was rounded off by Griffiths' new BT21A and Martin Brain in the equally resplendent, works-liveried Cooper-Chrysler. Built up by Frank Boyles at Coopers, this massive car boasted 428 bhp, a formidable 488 lbs/ft of torque but a somewhat daunting 1700 lbs dry weight.

The season may have seemed open but it didn't really turn out that way. The fair haired 23-year-old from Knaresborough, Peter Lawson, simply dominated the year after rapidly mastering the BRM with its high revving engine and six-speed gearbox, but with the well-developed Ferguson Formula Ferguson Formula 4WD system. He actually set BTD in no fewer than 11 of the 13 Championship rounds. With extension work still in progress at Loton Park, Prescott hosted the first round. With a Harewood win already under his belt, the debonair Yorkshireman immediately staked his claim with a 47.34s BTD to the 48.12s of Marsh and the 49.39s of the rapid but precise Sir Nick Williamson. The promised 4WD Hepworth was still under preparation at the Brighouse base of Hepworth Domestic Appliances and David was now driving the latest of his Brabham chassis, the F1 BT19 of 1965/66 vintage (F1-3-65), with the usual Oldsmobile V8 power. He manhandled this big car round Prescott's twists and turns fast enough to beat Brain (in the theoretically more nimble T87 although he had actually qualified both cars), Ian Swift's Swift-Ford, Rollason, Scragg, Peter Blankstone in the ex-Lawson BT18, and David Blankstone.

Despite the rare sight of Marsh actually getting it sideways, the 41.52s time recorded by Tony at Wiscombe was still not quite enough to stop Lawson winning again at Wiscombe where his 41.40s time was also a record. Sir Nick Williamson was third again but this time Martin Brain, now armed with the thundering Cooper-Chrysler, beat Hepworth, Tony Griffiths, and Roy Lane, with Howard Bennett (ex-Williamson, ex-Stockbridge Racing BT21A) making it into the Top Ten. A pattern was already emerging. There was no sign of Marsh at Barbon and after Lawson had set a near-record 27.32s class time and Geoff Rollason an outstanding 28.50s, the Westmorland weather did its worst and Lawson launched forth in the wet for the first time with the BRM. He won by over two whole

Sir Nicholas Williamson's 1968 Brabham-Vegantune twin-cam BT23C at Barbon. The car was no match for the Peter Lawson/ BRM 670P 4WD combination, but was always spectacularly driven.
HAYDN SPEDDING

Many meetings incorporated an Historic element. Vintage Sports Car Club stalwart Kenneth Neve was a Barbon regular with his Bugatti T35B, normally towed to an event by his imposing Rolls-Royce Phantom II.
MARGARET DUFF

seconds with Brain a surprising second in the deceptively tractable Cooper-Chrysler and Phil Scragg a less surprising third in the stripped Lola which always went well in the wet. A resounding eighth was Jim Johnstone, who was still using a supercharged 1100cc Ford pushrod engine but now in a Brabham BT15 chassis.

Marsh was back at Shelsley, but the Marsh Special's Rochester carburation was not right and he was again runncr-up to Lawson who climbed those hallowed slopes in 31.02s. The expected challenge from Martin Brain did not fully materialise as the mightly Cooper-Chrysler went straight on at the Esses on his second climb, and the rest of the field was headed by the four- cylinder cars of Williamson and Rollason, although the less powerful Twin Cam-engined Brabham had a tiny 0.07s advantage on this power course which said a lot for the Baronet's driving. Pleasingly, Johnty Williamson also made the Top Ten in the Felday 6. Nothing was said at the time, but this turned out to be the last time that everyone had the salutary experience of admiring the neat and economical style of Tony Marsh in action in his unobtrusive-looking mid-green Marsh Special. Tony did not run again and announced at Harewood at the end of the season that he was retiring after a long, highly successful and exceptionally full motor sporting career. Marsh's record of 6 RAC Championships had never been remotely approached, his influence on hill climbing was immense, yet even if he had never competed in a single hill climb his motor sporting career would still have been notable with many trials and 500cc Formula 3, sports car, Formula 2, Grand Touring and even Formula 1 racing successes while remaining a privateer.

The long awaited RAC climb at Tholt-y-Will came as rather an anti-climax. It was misty and drizzly, and the Championship regulars found that Paddock, spectator and communications facilities were not very good. By no means all the top runners went over but Tony Griffiths' old record fell despite the less-than-ideal conditions with Lawson clocking 164.40s, Brain running him very close on 164.95s with room to exercise all those Chrysler horses and Hepworth the only other driver to crack the old figure at 167.35s. Jimmy Johnstone was a resounding sixth, spurred on by having to run in the 1600cc racing class because of his supercharger.

The course between Stone Bridge and Cobbler Bend at 'The Rest' had been resurfaced, but with Marsh, Hepworth and both Williamsons absent, this round looked like a straight fight between Lawson and Brain. Not for the first time the bleak Scottish hill caught out a champion-class driver. Peter Lawson was over Stone Bridge in under 27s on his class ascent – very fast indeed – but then the BRM slewed and shot off the road for around 100 yards, damaging the cigar-like body and putting Peter out for the rest of the day. True to form, this left Martin Brain with a relatively easy 50.52s BTD with John Butterworth and Jim Johnstone in the 53s bracket on their RAC climbs, while fourth was Griffiths, sharing the Cooper-Chrysler as a gearbox bearing had failed in his Brabham.

Before the 'circus' reassembled in earnest at Bouley Bay – less the still sidelined BRM of Lawson – Martin Brain had set a BTD at Shelsley Walsh with his Chrysler engine churning out another 40 bhp thanks to a new 4-barrel Carter carburettor on an Edelbrock manifold. But he didn't win in Jersey, where he spun on Radio Corner on his second RAC climb leaving the 10 points to the superbly-on-form Sir Nicholas Williamson in 45.82s. Poor Peter Meldrum, on his home hill, had the galling experience of having his recalcitrant PR2 beaten by his old Lotus 22 in the hands of Peter le Druillenec.

Lawson and the BRM were back in fine fettle at Great Auclum and Peter's 19.34s best was enough to beat Williamson's agile Brabham (19.60s) and the BRM's former driver David Good who was

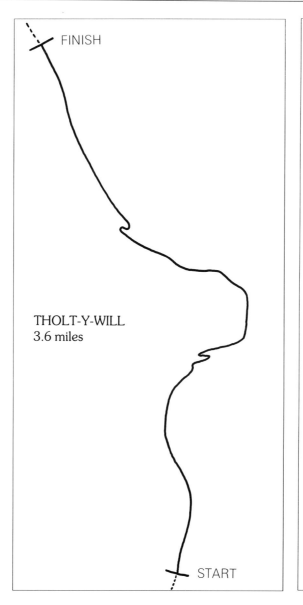

FINISH

THOLT-Y-WILL
3.6 miles

START

FINISH

LOTON PARK
1,475 yards

START

*John Cussins's Ford GT40, one
of 1968's most glamorous
contenders, at Castle Howard.*
HAYDN SPEDDING

spending the season setting new class targets in two of Derek Bennett's smart and effective new Bolton-built Chevron-BMW GT models. The day before the August Shelsley, Martin Brain sold the rather disappointing T87 to (the unexpectedly agile T81B handled better) to Kinver's 'other' hill climber, Clive Oakley, and promptly crashed the T81B in practice when the suspension broke at the Crossing! Tony Griffiths immediately returned the Rest-and-be-Thankful favour and lent Martin his Brabham. But with Williamson away in Switzerland. there was no stopping Lawson who had just beaten Brain to a 57.98s Craigantlet course record on the widened and eased Irish hill. It rained later on at Shelsley for the RAC climbs and Lawson's 4WD helped him to an advantage of over 2 seconds over his nearest conventionally-driven rivals, Griffiths and Roy Lane, who were themselves beaten by the 4WD sports car of Ray Terry. And this demoralising performance gave the RAC Championship to Peter Lawson, the youngest Champion so far after only one full season in single-seaters. It was to take another Yorkshireman to better that in 13 years time. It was a fine achievement too for Bill Crosland who had prepared the car at Mirfield and restored it to health, with different rear body and higher roll-over bar, after 'The Rest'. David Good had used the 1.9-litre engine out of the Felday 4 in 1967 but this had been back to Bourne and for 1968 Peter Lawson had the full 2070cc later-type Tasman specification, delivering 260 bhp at 9000 rpm in a car weighing a by-no-means-light 14 cwt.

The Championship was settled but it was not over, and next on the programme was a re-scheduled and 573-yards-longer Loton Park. A new loop after the start, taking in Hall, the Ess, Loggerheads and a downhill swoop to the right-handed Triangle before rejoining the established course. made the hill the longest mainland climb on the RAC schedule. Since it rained again Lawson's 2 seconds plus winning margin (58.31s) was almost a forgone conclusion, while David Good's flying yellow Chevron GT actually wound up second ahead of Rollason and Brain's repaired Cooper. The tempo was restored at a fine Newton Oils (one time HRG virtuoso Jack Newton's company) Trophy Prescott meeting where the big news for the BOC appeared to be David Good winning the Gold Cup competition. The course was in fine condition and three drivers smashed the old hill record, with Lawson (46.01s) heading the fast starting Roy Lane (46.87s) and Martin Brain (46.99s – and that proved conclusively what a tractable car the Cooper-Chrysler had turned out to be). Sir Nick's performance on the track was a little subdued but then the undeterred Baronet had returned from a French climb at Beaujolais with the bad news/good news tale of having crashed at 90 mph – into a vineyard! The way he told the story was priceless.

With David Hepworth's new 4WD car still not ready, and the rather incident-prone Martin Brain damaging the Cooper at Farmhouse, Harewood was another easy win for Lawson, setting a 41.43s record on his home patch and with the increasingly formidable Roy Lane running him closest. Amidst a eulogising home crowd it was definitely Peter Lawson's big day but he was already planning to try something else in 1969, and quickly sold the BRM to John Cussins who had been competing in a glorious green Ford GT40 during 1968. Lawson took the GT40 but eventually bought a Chevron-BMW although he found international Group 4 Sports Car racing both very expensive and highly competitive. He scored a few minor successes but soon retired from active racing altogether. He does pop along to Harewood from time to time to endure regular urgings to come out of retirement, as his brief yet meteoric career remains vivid in the memories of all who enjoyed it. His final points total was 86, to the 71 of Brain, 63 of Williamson, 51 of both Rollason and Lane, 47 of Griffiths and 46 of Hepworth.

The latter finally débuted his new special at Doune in September, and set a 53.04s BTD first time out. This ochre-hued machine was built around a Racing Frames spaceframe chassis with Brabham F1 suspension hung on it. The dry sump, Webered 4.5 Traco/Oldsmobile V8 drove through a 4-speed gearbox to the Ferguson 4WD system and the whole lot was deceptively masked by a spare Brabham bodyshell. It was workmanlike and without frills and it delivered the goods – the perfect foil for David himself.

Earlier the same month, a new 'technical' development which was to become completely universal in hill climbing appeared for the first time at the Brighton Speed Trials affixed to the shapely nose of Patsy Burt's McLaren. This was the Burt Strut (other less tactful names were bandied around) and was a vertical metal strip standing proud of the bodywork to ensure that the timing beam was cut cleanly and reliably, which had not always happened hitherto.

The growing prominence of the RAC Championship during the 'sixties was accompanied by growing support for most classes of car outside the rarified realm of the powerful and increasingly expensive bigger single-seaters. Yet there was no season-long challenge to inspire the majority in their widely contrasting cars. There was no national championship which would reward the outstanding driver irrespective of the type of car used. Up till then there had been the now-discontinued Sports Car Championship which had been restricted, in reality, to the owners of potent sports-racing machinery; the MAC's Junior Hill Climb and Sprint Championship which had been set up primarily to encourage the novice driver; and the Prescott Gold Cup which was awarded on the basis of performances relative to existing *class* records but which of course was restricted only to some meetings at Prescott.

This long-felt need was at least partially satisfied when the BARC – the Yorkshire Centre was the guiding force and organised the Championship – linked eleven of their 1968 meetings into a series where the winner would be decided on his or her performances in relation to a bogey time set at the class record plus eight seconds. This first running of the BARC Championship was held without a great deal of publicity or promotion, as an experiment, but it was successful from the start and was to continue with only minor alterations in future years, most notably in the introduction of a subsidiary Fastest Time of Day Awards series (the BARC have always insisted on 'Fastest' rather than 'Best' even though, strictly speaking, time can be neither fast nor slow!) to encourage the faster and more promotable single-seaters to enter for non-RAC BARC meetings. Appropriately enough the series began at Harewood, in April, where of those who had registered for the Championship, the slight Peter Voigt impressed most with his little 998cc Hillman Imp-engined DRW Mk 6 rear-engined sports-racing car. Apart from earning some fame as almost certainly the only violin maker in motor sport, Peter had come up from Haywards Heath in Sussex accompanied by a growing reputation in Southern events, formerly in a Lotus Seven. When the season-long chase ended at Scarborough in October, Voigt was still in contention, but a mishap at the tight and steep Mere Hairpin put an end to his hopes and his 45.17 points (from 6 best performances) was enough only for runner-up place to Lancastrian and BRT Developments engineer Jeff Goodliff who had scored 48.65 points in a tremendously successful season with a Formula Libre 'Touring' Mini-Cooper S, running supercharged. After Voigt, the next three places fell to Mini drivers: Scotsman Tom Christie; a shy and methodical Anglo-German architect from Stroud named Chris Cramer; and Welshman John Pascoe. Peter Richardson, from Braintree, rounded off the top six in his 1.0 Ginetta-SCA G12.

While this new series had gained its own enthusiastic following, there was much interest in the still far-from-uniformly-divided classes (the BARC naturally used its own pretty fair class structure) which made up the bulk of the entry list. A highlight was often the shrill tear-up between the closely-matched 1100cc racing cars where Jim Johnstone, then living in Collingham, the next village up the road to Harewood, took on and often vanquished newer cars with his blown Brabham BT15, but was always hotly contested by Chris Court's gleaming red Brabham-SCA BT21B, Roger Hickman's similar BT21B-SCA, the well-developed Terrapin of Allan Staniforth, and, until he bought the Cooper-Daimler T87, Clive Oakley's Lotus-SCA 31.

Scragg and Ray Terry in the Chas Beattie rebuilt Elva-Buick 4WD remained the top sports-racing contenders despite the efforts of David Harrison and John McCartney with their equally unaesthetically-rebodied Crosslé and Felday 4. Bob Rose could have been a regular challenger with the big McLaren M1B, but soon switched to the Brabham-Climax BT23B with which Mike Hawley had not been too thrilled. Georgina Baillie-Hill, an increasingly rapid contender, unfortunately lost her Elva-BMW in a return road fire at Loton in July, although she was unscathed herself and the car was eventually rebuilt. David Good had begun the year with a Chevron-BMW B6 GT, then sold it to Ian Skailes and bought one of Derek Bennett's latest B8s and caused the odd mutter, and indeed a rare protest at Shelsley, by stripping it of 'GT' equipment and running it as a sports-racer so as to be eligible for RAC points. The exercise was most successful at Great Auclum in particular. Peter Voigt's skilfully driven little DRW was not really in this league but his and the car's mettle were well highlighted by the BARC Championship and if Peter missed that one, he did win the one-hill Corona Championship at Gurston Down, over Chris Cramer's 999cc Mini-Cooper S and Jeff Goodliff's BRT Mini.

It was a fine year for those who admired the bigger Grand Touring cars for there was great spectacle with cars such as John Macklin's ex-John Woolfe 7.0 Cobra 427. Puttenham's cheery Bob Jennings and Coombs of Guildford Sales Manager (later Director), Mike MacDowel sharing one of the rare

Patsy Burt returns down the hill at Great Auclum in 1968 in her ultimate racing car, the superb McLaren M3A.
PATSY BURT/RON SMITH

Lightweight Jaguar E-types, John Cussins's Ford GT40, the Cobra 289s of Vic Hassall and Brian Wilson, Michael Miles's E-type, Peter Wynn-Jones's Brian Lister-built 1964 Le Mans Sunbeam Tiger, and the Northern band of E-type drivers led by Messrs. Thomson, Mountain and Lambert, but now challenged by Sheffield's Malcolm Dungworth with a TVR Griffith and the newer Tuscan V8 of the still pseudonymous 'S. Smith', all regular competitors. A bonus was the Ferrari Handicap class introduced at Prescott. The BOC had traditionally included a Handicap class at their meetings for Bugattis, and now added a similar category for Ferraris since the Club had formed an allied Ferrari Owners Club, feeling that the Maranello cars were the post-war equivalent of the immortal Bugatti. Some fabulous machinery turned out as a result with Jack le Fort setting a 58.51s record in May with his 1964 250 GTO.

In the middle of the season the Jennings/MacDowel partnership replaced the E-type with a new F2 Chevron-FVA B10 single-seater which was immediately a significant contender, especially when the pipe-smoking MacDowel was at the wheel. Another to adjust well to single-seaters was Johnty Williamson, who lifted several minor BTDs during the year and was generally recording times faster than Tony Griffiths had done with the Felday 6.

Minis were usually still the stars of the saloon classes and apart from those which figured prominently in the BARC Championship, the yellow example of John Francis was the car to beat in the South, while Peter Kaye's phenomenal red-and-black machine remained a regular Top Ten runner in the North.

Although there were plans for new hills at Ditcham, near Petersfield; at Bridgend; and at Litton Slack, in the Peak District (one BARC idea which did *not* happen), these were overshadowed by the opening of a superb new course in Doune Park, Perthshire. The eagerly-awaited Lothian CC course on Carse Hill, a mile and a half from the attractive and historic Doune village, had a cold, wet and windy baptism in May when Andrew Fletcher's Twin-Cam Brabham BT18 climbed the 1,564 yards course in 60.93s. Conditions were much better on 16 June when the first National status meeting there was opened by Raymond Mays and gave the record to Sir Nick Williamson in a more realistic 48.84s. With Ray Fielding (also closely involved with Lord Doune in the Doune Collection of historic cars which was to be an added attraction at the hill), acting as consultant, what had been just a farm road

for the Carse of Cambus Farm was converted into one of the best hills in the country with the addition of a new loop. From the start the course climbed left-handed through Carse bend to a blind right-angle corner at Garden Gate. From there the course became steeper, rising between trees and a high bank along the Dovecot Straight before cresting a rise, bursting out into open country and taking a right-hand junction onto the new loop. This took drivers along the side of a valley, swinging right to the steep, 1 in 4 East Brae before taking a sharp right turn back into the woods, followed by a left turn into the open again to the finish. With people like Williamson, David Hepworth (BTD in September) and Mike MacDowel enthusing about this major addition to the Scottish motor-sporting scene, it would clearly not be long before Doune joined the RAC Championship venues.

With Loton Park gaining a major extension, there was certainly a vogue for longer hills and Scotland's other 'new' course, at Fintray, gained a lengthened starting straight. Aberdeen circuit racer Willie Forbes (Lotus-BMW 35) set a 30.95s hill record in June when a class win was secured by a young Formula Ford Lotus 51 driver, Tom Walkinshaw, then at the beginning of a rewarding career as a driver, team manager and entrepreneur.

The BOC too sought to devise a way of extending Prescott by a further 20 per cent, without building out beyond the existing course perimeter. Plans were published which involved two crossover bridges and three banked corners in a most complicated layout which made the old jokes about Prescott resembling a 'demented piece of string' seem rather understated. If they had been realised these plans would have certainly presented a 'different' problem to drivers, not least to their sense of orientation, but the character of this charming setting would have been much altered and the plans, which were costed at £60,000, were allowed to lapse.

Overall, it had been probably the most exciting year since at least 1964, although the debit column included the likely demise of Woburn Park (Record: Martin Brain in 27.62s) as the Duke of Bedford was contemplating proceeding with a new game park which would rule out hill climbs. Among the drivers, one who was sorely missed from Southern events was Bournemouth motor trader Amie Lefevre, a competitor since 1948, and highly successful in Hartwell-tuned Sunbeam Rapier, Sprite, MG Midget and Morgan 4/4, who died after a serious illness at the comparatively early age of 60. Riper in years though he was – he was 81 – many mourned the passing of Ron Godfrey.

CHAPTER SEVEN

FOURS, EIGHTS AND MORE EXOTIC STILL
(1969-1974)

TAKING the nineteen-sixties as a whole, hill climbing had boomed. At the top of the scale the interest in the RAC Championship and the fascinating machinery which contested it had never been higher. The competition was intense yet the level of sportsmanship and camaraderie among the leading drivers remained high. More first-class courses had been found and developed, and the level of competition and sheer volume of entries in the many classes for which the sport catered continued to increase. What's more the institution of the Prescott Gold Cup, and particularly the BARC Championship in 1968, ensured that a little more of the limelight was cast on the many first-class drivers who either could not afford a top-class single-seater, or simply did not wish to take on the sort of commitment which was involved at the sport's pinnacle.

During the next few years, well into the nineteen-seventies, the position did not change fundamentally. In fact, the battle for the Championship BTDs became even fiercer and the competing cars ever more exotic and expensive. Although a few people adhered to the combination of a nimble Formula 2/3-type car powered by an engine of between 1.6 and 2.0 litres capacity, the first of a new generation of road racing Formula 5000 cars in 1969, and the advent of the pure racing Cosworth DFV Formula 1 engine in hill climbing in 1973 ensured that sheer power – and that meant something in the order of 400 to 500 bhp by 1973/74 – tended to have the edge more often than not. Yet contrary to expectations the four-wheel-drive layout never actually took over completely and was a receding influence by the mid-seventies. All-wheel drive was undoubtedly superior in the wet when traction was at a premium, but problems of understeer on the tighter corners, extra weight, the complexities and expense incurred in transmitting power to four wheels all, or even part, of the time were daunting. The growing efficiency of 'conventional' chassis design, and the availability of ever wider and grippier tyres served to close the gap, while the failure of the Grand Prix teams to make 4WD work effectively in Formula 1 discouraged the concept further. Although others persevered, only David Hepworth won the RAC title, twice, during the period 1969 to 1974 with a 4WD car. The Hepworth with its 5.0 General Motors V8 engine, although eligible for the stock-block Formula 5000 in which it ran briefly and unsuccessfully, was effective rather than exotic. Apart from the fairly-well-tried Ferguson 4WD system, the car owed most of its technical specification to a combination of rather dated Brabham F1 technology and simple, practical Yorkshire 'nous' on the part of its designer/constructor/driver. David Hepworth knew the car absolutely inside out, ran it almost throughout the period and was able to wring all the performance from the car with a hefty dose of forcefulness which made up for the lack of the finesse of a Marsh or a Wharton.

Away from the preoccupation with 'The Top Ten', the introduction of another class-based Championship by the RAC in 1970, the Class Leaders series, which was to run parallel to the the RAC's premier title at the same meetings, provided another worthwhile target for the competitor outside the big single-seater division. This Championship, sponsored initially by Shell and later by Woking Motors, and the BARC series which gained valuable Castrol support in 1969 and kept it for six seasons, attracted their own Championship 'circus' who took in virtually all the major meetings and ensured a greater uniform quality right down the programme at the bigger events.

In other respects hill climbing had attained a plateau from which it was to be difficult to climb higher. By 1974 a number of the leading contenders for Championship honours, even those who had been pacemakers in the introduction of exotic machinery to the scene, were finding the going expensive and with too much aggravation for a purely sporting activity. So much so that at the end of the 1974 season there was a positive spate of retirement from top-class events, not all of them permanent, but certainly indicating that perhaps technically things were getting a little out of hand.

From the organisational point of view the period was not an easy one, either. New hills were becoming increasingly difficult to find and retain. For one thing, the fashion among stately-home owners for establishing assorted wild life boded ill at a number of venues! Elsewhere the growing concern about safety which was running through motor sport as a whole, coupled with the increasingly lethal potential of modern 400 to 500 bhp cars, meant that the suitability of several well-established courses was questioned by the RAC. The feasibility and the cost of additional safety improvements and especially the demand for costly and unsightly Armco barriers wrinkled many a brow. Oliver's Mount was lost in this way and Doune came within an ace of disappearing too.

Overall, the scene remained healthy but the expansionist era of the nineteen-sixties was over, a comment which held good in far wider spheres than hill climbing. There was no decline but the problems certainly seemed to be more numerous and more difficult to overcome. It was harder to pull in the paying spectators who had so many rival attractions, both motoring and non-motoring, competing for their weekend attention. Costs were rising. It was even becoming harder to maintain an efficient and delay-free programme. Why? Well, the physically large and immensely powerful F5000 and F1-type machinery were not the easiest vehicles to manoeuvre from (often muddy) paddocks onto starting lines, where huge tyres needed lengthy if spectacular 'burn outs' to bring them up to the sort of temp-

David Hepworth's effective four-wheel-drive Hepworth with General Motors V8 engine won the RAC Hill Climb Championship twice. Here he manhandles this Brabham-derived Special round the Castle Howard hairpin in 1971.
HAYDN SPEDDING

erature where optimum grip could be achieved. It took spot-on organisation and complete co-operation from competitors if the Top Ten Runs – properly a superb climax to most days' Championship sport – were not to degenerate into long-drawn-out tedium at a time when most people needed little encouragement to depart in search of home and an evening meal. Happily, this sort of anti-climax did not happen very often: nail-biting finishes were the rule rather than the exception, but the odd lapse reminded everyone that while hill climbing remained an enthralling and almost wholly amateur sport, despite the modest and most welcome advent of more overt commercial sponsorship, it had become a highly demanding activity for all concerned.

Hill climbing is truly the sport for the perfectionist and in the unceasing effort to find a more effective way of reducing times, within whatever budget was available, there was a great deal of chopping and changing in machinery over the 1968/69 close season. The RAC Champion, Peter Lawson, finally decided to go circuit racing and bought David Good's Chevron B8 to do so. Meanwhile, the Maidenhead dairy-food manufacturer and 1961 Champion elected to stay with sports cars and ordered a Buick V8-engined Piper GT. Unfortunately, this did not materialise and Good reverted to his old Chevron B6, repurchased from Ian Skailes. Among the single-seaters, though, the accent was firmly on the big V8s. David Hepworth was all set for a full season with his self-built 4WD Hepworth, fitted with 5.0 cast iron Oldsmobile V8 although he intended to run in some of the newly instigated Formula 5000 races where the car was to be sponsored by Green Shield Stamps and driven by Formula 3 driver Bev Bond. This was rather an abortive venture but did little to detract from Hepworth's success on the hills. Roy Lane had sold his immaculate Brabham BT14 to Yorkshireman Jim Johnstone who dropped in another Buick V8. Meanwhile the Warwick engineer who was already gaining a fine reputation for car preparation as well as driving, was building up his own Brabham-derived car, originally intended to be 4WD, which retained Buick motivation. Four-cylinder stalwart Sir Nick Williamson toyed with a 4.5 Traco/Olds-engined Formula B Brabham BT29, but eventually reappeared with a Vegantune twin-cam-engined Brabham BT21C for the time being. Martin Brain retained the Cooper-Chrysler but was not expected to compete very often because of business commitments, and the same applied to Shropshire farmer Geoff Rollason who had taken over the 4WD Marsh. His Lotus-FVA 41B was now in the hands of David Blankstone, whose brother Peter had bought the 4.5 Oldsmobile-powered Brabham BT21 4WD (Marsh System) which Chas Beattie had built up for Bryan Brown but which the latter had not used. John Cussins had taken over the BRM 670P 4WD and David Hepworth's old Brabham BT11/19 had gone to John Butterworth who also planned to run in some F5000 races. Rather more novel in approach, the Jennings/MacDowel partnership had switched from Chevron-FVA B10 to a specially-adapted new Brabham BT29X fitted with the 'Tasman' 2.0 version of the Coventry-Climax FWMV engine, a unit which was predictably rather 'cammy' but also proved difficult to persuade to run cleanly. Another with the very latest equipment was Roger Hickman, with a new Formula 2 Brabham FVA BT30. It was all a bit like musical chairs and there were a lot of trials and tribulations in the first part of the season as many drivers struggled to master their new mounts.

The first RAC Championship round was not until the end of April, at Loton Park, although there was added interest when the series gained commercial sponsorship for the first time, from Shell.

In the meantime, Roy Lane showed off his spotless new TechCraft-Buick – Brabham BT21/28-based and with only two-wheel drive after all – with a *race* win at Silverstone, the first Harewood meeting was postponed until August because of bad weather, John Cussins scored a morale-boosting BTD at Castle Howard, and David Blankstone beat Lane and Tony Griffiths (who bought back his BT21A from the Mickels) at the SVMC Loton opener, and Ian Swift's well-maintained old Swift-Ford V8 showed the worth of a well-sorted car when the Bristolian snatched BTD at the AMOC *Daily Mirror* Trophy Meeting at Wiscombe, beating even Williamson and Cussins. Added colour was lent to proceedings by Roger Clark who demonstrated a very different type of 4WD car, one of the special rallycross Ford Capris, although there was probably more attention devoted to Peter Lawson's passenger in the course opening Aston Martin for she was the reigning Miss United Kingdom, Kathleen Winstanley.

The week before Loton, on 20 April, the 50th climb to be held by the BARC (SW) at Brunton – resurfaced and 'en fete' but soon to be completely supplanted by Gurston Down – gave Swift another narrow win over Williamson's underpowered Brabham, while the BARC's Yorkshire Centre made a delayed start to the Harewood season with David Hepworth on top but the delighted Jim Johnstone de-

Roy Lane campaigned another Brabham-derived car in 1969, the TechCraft-Buick, seen here approaching the Barbon hairpin.
HAYDN SPEDDING

The Mike MacDowel/Bob Jennings partnership experienced both limited success and some 'temperament' from the exotic 2.0 'Tasman' Coventry-Climax FWMV engine in their Brabham BT29X.
HAYDN SPEDDING

feating Roy Lane with his old car for second BTD to the tune of 0.05s. Unfortunately, John Cussins suffered a serious setback when he spun the BRM and wrecked the optimum 70/30 transfer box, necessitating tackling Loton with the inferior 60/40 box. Much had been expected of the hirsute Peter Kaye when he swopped his tremendously successful Mini for Fred Smith's Brabham BT14, but Peter lost it coming out of Farmhouse and shot up the bank in a terrifying moment which gave the driver a fright that served to put him off single-seaters for some time.

The eager anticipation which normally preceded the first round of the premier series was tinged with sadness, and not a little bitterness, on this occasion as it looked likely that this would be the last-ever meeting at Loton Park. Landowner Sir Michael Leighton had decided to rear game-birds in the Park and this would mean that the hill climb activities would be severely restricted. The Severn Valley Motor Club felt that the programme which would result would not be financially viable and so announced that unless someone else was prepared to organise meetings, that would be the end of hill climbing at Loton Park. Under this shadow, it was David Hepworth who drew first blood with a 59.41s BTD, half a second up on John Cussins – running well despite the 60/40 transfer ratio – and with the emergent Jim Johnstone again defeating Roy Lane, not to mention Nick Williamson, Tony Griffiths and Geoff Rollason, for third in the Shell/RAC runs. The 'musical chairs' continued too. Geoff Rollason had a driveshaft break on the troublesome Marsh and promptly bought back his Lotus-FVA from David Blankstone. Chris Court had damaged his SCA engine at Harewood and was sharing Tony Griffiths's Twin-Cam Brabham. In fact, he liked it so much that he bought it, leaving the TA commander and garage proprietor to come to an arrangement with Martin Brain to share a drive for the remainder of the season.

A week later at Prescott John Cussins reversed the placings with David Hepworth on a day when the Waring & Gillow Director must have felt that the fates were against him. First he was mistakenly left out of the Top Ten runs, then on a drying track and still a little flustered from sorting out the administrative error, he spun on his first Championship climb. Happily, he pulled it all together next time up to record 49.46s, the merest 0.01s less than Hepworth, and with Williamson, Lane, Phil Scragg's Lola T70L 'beach buggy', and Jim Johnstone filling the minor places. Incredibly, David Blankstone was back in the Lotus-FVA as Rollason had changed his mind again about running it because of business commitments!

After Chris Court in the ex-Griffiths BT21A and Roger Hickman had taken the honours at Woburn (which had been reprieved for the time being), the Championship contenders reformed at Wiscombe Park: all except John Cussins that is, who had to miss the meeting because of his impending marriage. This left David Hepworth in charge and even 'Sir Nick', on the hill part-owned by his uncle Charles Lambton and where the amiable baronet had first been seen selling hot dogs before he ever set foot in a hill climb car, could not close a 1.40 second gap to Hepworth during the Top Ten runs. The day was marred by a nasty accident to Roger Hickman, who went off just after Bunny's Leap and had to be cut out of the wreckage of his Brabham suffering a broken arm. Meanwhile, David Good exchanged his stopgap Chevron B6 with a brand new orange B8, with which he was but half a second slower than a misfiring BT30X in the hands of the talented Mike MacDowel.

The Shell/RAC rounds were really coming thick and fast now and at Barbon, before the rain came down in torrents to halt proceedings after but one Shell/RAC climb each, the 4WD contingent were very much in charge. Before the course was wetted Hepworth had smashed the course record with a 26.78s to the (also record-breaking) 26.97s of John Cussins, while Phil Scragg retained fourth BTD despite hitting the very hard Lakeland stone wall on the outside of the hairpin on his second climb. The Top Ten runs were slower, but with the tough campaigner from Brighouse over 2s clear of Cussins with the seemingly inevitable Williamson at least matching the time of Peter Blankstone's 4WD Brabham, and taking third place points on a tie-decider.

Five drivers ended in the thirty-one second bracket at Shelsley where Martin Brain re-appeared with a Formula 1 Cooper-BRM T86B – the last of the F1 Coopers – and where the unlucky John Cussins was sidelined with cylinder-head-sealing bothers. By now, David Hepworth was looking every inch a potential Champion, and this time it was Jim Johnstone – another Yorkshireman – who ran him closest, and who had a further 0.28s ahead of his usual sparring partner Roy Lane in the gleaming orange TechCraft.

There were improved amenities at Doune ready in good time for the first-ever RAC round on Lord Doune's Carse Hill on 15 June 1969. The Paddock, administrative offices, toilets and spectators' standing areas had all received attention and a record-breaking climb ensued. The tall, bespectacled Roy Lane at last made the breakthrough with the TechCraft and his 48.31s was the new record, edging out Mike MacDowel who was now going much better since fitting a softer type of plug in the Climax V8 engine of the shrill-sounding BT30X, and another sub-record time of 48.64s from Hepworth. John Cussins was sixth after one run but on his final attempt he got off line at Tunnel, wiped off the offside front wheel on a wall and dived into the trees. He was shaken but unhurt, although the celebrated BRM was well mangled.

One week after this the hectic schedule took the 'circus' to the Isle of Man, to the challenge of Tholt-y-Will where the meeting was much better run than the previous year. However, the long climb claimed many casualties: Peter Blankstone (sump, oil pick-up); MacDowel/Jennings (clogged fuel filter and broken exhaust); Johnstone (driveshaft) and Brain (driveshaft). David Hepworth set a record 162.16s BTD on the class climbs and then surpassed everyone by having an accident which began when he got off line at Tholt-y-Will Hotel and ended when he finally crashed at Creggan 2, a full mile

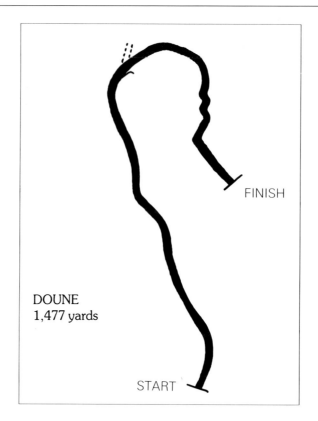

DOUNE
1,477 yards

FINISH

START

further on, where he tore off a wheel and suspension components. All this left Williamson with his first 10 points of the year in the underpowered Brabham, just over 0.5s clear of Martin Brain with the T86B before the driveshaft went.

Although Rest-and-be-Thankful had been resurfaced after complaints about its roughness, many chose to give this round a miss. Not Hepworth, though: his 53.07s gave him another high score from the increasingly formidable MacDowel and Brain. In this year of accidents, Roy Lane was this week's unlucky one, smiting Stone Bridge in the hitherto immaculate TechCraft. The day after this event many of the competitors, including Hepworth and Martin Brain, went on to Fintray, where they were roundly defeated by local Aberdonian Willie Forbes with his full Formula 5000 circuit car, a Lola-Chevrolet T142 – a portentous result.

John Cussins had had the BRM repaired in time for Bouley Bay but, worried by front differential malfunctions and problems with the fuel injection set-up, he was not really in the running. Hepworth was competing on the Jersey hill for the first time but his understeering Hepworth-Olds was beaten into third place by an on-form Mike MacDowel (45.61s), and also by Martin Brain who had recently broken the Pontypool Park course record, having found life rather dull in the first part of the season when he was away from the hills.

The course record at Great Auclum, that tight little dash with a character all its own, had remained inviolate at 19.10s since Peter Boshier-Jones set the time in 1965. It didn't survive 1969 though, for it took Roy Lane a mere 18.58s to set one of the year's most outstanding times, almost half a second better than even Hepworth could manage on his Shell/RAC climbs although he did clock 18.84s earlier on. Cussins was in more trouble, this time with a stripped thread on a plug. His season, which had started so well, had collapsed into a succession of difficulties. Peter Blankstone was this week's accident victim, climbing out unhurt after the Brabham Quattro – a name adopted many years before Audi used the name for a rather-better-known 4WD creation – broke a suspension upright and shot off the road, ripping off a wheel as it went.

Craigantlet attracted only a few of the English contingent, but Martin Brain was back in the Cooper-Chrysler which had been out of action for some time awaiting engine parts after a blow-up at Silverstone. Yet again he had a first corner 'off' during practice at the Ulster hill but this time there was no serious damage and the enthusiastic Midlander went on to score a 60.78s BTD, winning from Mac-Dowel and Martin's co-driver, Tony Griffiths. With just one week to go before Shelsley Walsh, many of the leading runners took in the Harewood Meeting, and it was disastrous for David Hepworth who hit the hedge backwards at Willow and damaged the rear-end of his car badly enough to put him out for the following week. Jim Johnstone's 42.20s climb at Harewood had given him BTD but in an unusually long-drawn-out and positively tedious Shelsley he could only manage fifth place whereas the resurgent Brain broke the course record in 30.72s in his magnificent Cooper-Chrysler, with Griffiths underlining the excellence of this big but by no means unwieldily car with third place behind Roy Lane and ahead of Cussins.

In the meantime, Sir Nick Williamson was ready to unveil his 'secret weapon' which had been built up by John Brimsted under Ron Smith's direction at Patsy Burt's PMG Garages concern at Bookham. After striving with nimble but underpowered four-cylinder cars for so long, the Mortimer market-garden owner was all set to début his superb yellow F5000 McLaren M10A. fitted with a Charles Lucas Chevrolet engine, breathing through 2 four-choke Holley carburettors, and delivering some 410 bhp for transmission through the Hewland LG600 gearbox. His first run in the car was actually at Ollon-Villars in Switzerland on the annual jaunt by the Burt/Smith partnership which in 1969 attracted no fewer than 18 British entrants.

Naturally, the beautifully-proportioned although undeniably rather large McLaren was the centre of attention at the September Prescott. Despite being governed to two-thirds throttle until he became fully used to the car, Sir Nick set a 46.67s BTD, and went on to head off Hepworth, Johnstone and Lane in the Shell/RAC runs. It had been another torrid meeting in a rather destructive year with Bob Jennings crashing the BT30X in practice (MacDowel being sportingly given a drive in the Mickels' ex-Hawley Brabham-Climax BT23B); John Cussins walking away from another big accident which saw the BRM somersault to destruction at Ettores; Martin Brain throwing away his slim Championship hopes with spins at Pardon and Orchard; and Phil Scragg suffering brake failure at Ettore s which resulted in the Lola striking course marshal John Hicks and breaking one of his legs. Naturally, Scragg was most upset about this mishap in a car which he had borrowed back from Birmingham's Tony Harrison who had bought it mid-season when Phil's business preoccupations ruled out regular competition.

And so the long Championship trail came to its final confrontation at Harewood, where the Yorkshire crowd were able to cheer another 'home' Champion, 29-year-old David Hepworth. His best climb was 42.09s but he was defeated, by the smallest possible margin of 0.01s, in the Shell/RAC runs by Williamson's McLaren, although the Baronet had earlier set a 42.00s course record and looked to be faster still on his final run until he inadvertently knocked off the ignition! Poor old Bob Jennings damaged the BT30X for the second meeting running, and for the umpteenth time the Mickels came to the rescue of a car-less driver, so Mike MacDowel again had his runs. David Hepworth ended the year with 78 points, an outstanding achievement for him and his part-time mechanics David Hurst and Peter Sykes, to the 69 of Lane and Williamson (settled in Roy's favour on a tie-decider) and with Brain (68), MacDowel (61), Johnstone (55), Cussins (43), Griffiths (34), Jennings (29) and Peter Blankstone (28) rounding out the first ten.

A fortnight later, the other major Championship, the Castrol/BARC series came to a superb finale at Oliver's Mount. At the beginning of the year Jeff Goodliff had decided that he had "too many good customers with Minis to stay in the class" and switched to a radical MiniSprint GT. With this, using the shell of one of Neville Trickett's lowered Mini-based devices, the Technical Director of British Vita Racing & Tuning came up with an excruciatingly noisy and twitchy little weapon which boasted an overall height of a mere 3ft 6in, an all-up weight of just 9-cwt and a solid back axle. Power from the 8-port headed BVRT 1275S engine was boosted to an ear-splitting 165 bhp at the flywheel with a Godfrey blower and TJ fuel injection. This tremendously spectacular machine took the intrepid Jeff to his second BARC title from the 999cc Mini (also with BVRT 8-port head) of the painstaking architect from Stroud, Chris Cramer, and the very fast 1.8 Ford-engined Morgan 4/4 of David Way. Also major contenders in their classes all season and filling out the next Championship places were the 'plastic' Midget of John Northcroft, Peter Voigt's nippy little DRW, Sandy Hutcheon's 1.0 Mini, the glorious red ex-Maranello Concessionaires/Vic Wilson/Ron Fry/David Skailes Ferrari 250LM of Newcastle hotelier Jack Maurice (which had also lifted the Prescott Gold Cup from Cramer and Bristolian Terry Smith's old 1100 Cooper-JAP Mk 10), Eric Stansfield's Mini, Fred Whittaker's Flying Wheel, Burnley-entered MG Midget and the well-campaigned Buick V8-engined TVR of Brian Alexander.

Castrol's stated decision to carry on sponsoring the Championship rounded off a fine day which had seen a white-faced Martin Brain returning to the Paddock after working out that he had been doing 172 mph on the final stretch in the Cooper-Chrysler! Undeterred, he went on to set a new course record at 41.27s, 0.31s faster than David Hepworth, who was able to claim a 4WD win for the BARC had instituted a separate class for the four-wheel-drive brigade during the year. Earlier on, Mike Slinn's U2 had come unstuck on the entrance to Mere hairpin and had come to rest with the front of the car overhanging the Paddock below. The incident was a minor one but the RAC took rather a dim view of the risk of someone toppling into the Paddock and the area at risk was subsequently cordoned off.

It had been an exciting year with hill climbing at the top becoming a pretty serious and ever-more-expensive business, but the sport continued to have great depth and many, many competitors who were just enjoying their motor sport, like those perennial rivals Ash Cleave and Tommy Pascoe. Ash celebrated 50 years in motor sport by scoring several award-winning performances with CCV 952, his amazing 32-year-old Morris Special. Tommy showed how impressed he was by slipping Cleave's number on his Porsche at Shelsley and touring up the hill at remarkably low speed! Even the Shell/RAC contenders could still find time for lighter entertainment during these years, such as when Nick Williamson reduced many to helpless mirth at Barbon by proceeding to run over his own crash helmet in the Paddock. There was quite an upsurge of interest too in the old Cooper 500 and 1100 models thanks to the energetic promotion of the 500 Owners' Association headed by Peter Kendall. The Association ran its own season-long Championship for the old 'one-lungers' and 'big bangers' and Kendall deservedly won this from Geoff Inglis, with veteran Tom Elton winning the 1100cc division. The awards were received, most appropriately, from the hands of Austen May.

Perhaps the worst feature of the year was the threat to several notable hills. Loton has already been mentioned but it was known that the West Hants and Dorset Car Club were looking for someone to take over the financial burden of running meetings at Wiscombe, although they later confirmed that they would carry on. Woburn Park still looked to have an uncertain future and on 1 June the pleasant

Exotic road car. Long established Porsche dealer Jim Parker and his son Colin shared this Porsche 904 GTS. Reputed to be the ex-Böhringer Monte Carlo Rally car, this road-equipped 904 was regularly used on the public road.
HAYDN SPEDDING

little uphill sprint at Leighton Hall, once the home of the Gillow family of furniture manufacturers, was used for the last time as the house owners had had a certain amount of aggravation from the local villagers who objected to this once-a-year activity. This final meeting, held the day after Barbon as usual, was won by Kendal VW/Porsche dealer Jim Parker in his exciting road car, the road-equipped Porsche 904 GTS which had originally been the SMART/Innes Ireland car and was reputed to have been the car which Eugen Böhringer took to an astonishing second place on the Monte Carlo Rally.

With the 1970 season fast approaching, great interest focused on the likelihood of several of the new generation of powerful F5000 cars taking to the hills, cars of far greater sophistication than Chris Summer's old Cooper-Chevvy and the Lotus-Chevrolet 24 which succeeded it and which demonstrated for the first time what could be done by allying a light Formula racing chassis with an American 'stock block' V8 engine. Shell/RAC Champion David Hepworth would be continuing to campaign his quasi F5000 Hepworth 4WD, although he still hankered after taking circuit racing seriously, while down at PMB Garages John Brimsted was updating Sir Nick Williamson's McLaren M10A to M10B specification with new suspension parts and wheels. Since David Good's plan to run a Buick V8-engined Piper GTR sports car had fallen through, and he had tried the ex-Sid Taylor/Frank Gardner Lola T142 towards the end of 1969 with some success, the Eden Vale Director opted to buy a new McLaren M10B which was modified to feature a lowered cockpit surround and a left-hand gearchange so that Good could drive with his customary exuberance notwithstanding the disability which it was so easy to forget. The engine was the 5.5-litre Alan Smith-tuned Chevvy out of the Lola which, since it developed in the region of 500 bhp, was just about the most powerful engine in the sport. Even so, Phil Scragg, returning after a short semi-retirement, ran him close. He too had opted for one of Bruce McLaren's cars but, true to form, his was a sports car, a CanAm M12, fitted with the narrower M6B bodywork and sporting a 480 bhp alloy block Chevvy. Opposition was likely to come from former Lister-Jaguar and Lister-Chevrolet driver George Tatham who had mastered the 5.3 Chevrolet-engined Brabham BT17 – 'Black Jack's' unique 1966 Group 7/CanAm car – during the previous season, and John McCartney who had refitted the Felday 4 with bodywork of the original shape but moulded from glassfibre.

Skipton driver John Bosomworth was another to order a McLaren M10B after competing with the Trojan-built, lengthened McLaren-Rover M4B V8 the previous year. The strong Yorkshire contingent was, going to be without Jimmy Johnstone who was finding that he could not spend enough time away from his business to continue on a regular basis. His beautifully-prepared dark blue BT14-Buick was sold to novice Peter Scott-Walter who, frankly, struggled with it, although Jimmy did share it on occasion. Just to confuse matters, however, another dark blue Brabham-Buick was to appear in Yorkshire hands. This was the slightly newer ex-Bryan Eccles BT18 of Richard Thwaites, from Dewsbury, previously distinguished by some rapid drives in a Mini-Cooper S and the splendour of his 'mutton chop' whiskers.

Both Geoff Rollason and a recovered Roger Hickman decided to call it a day, Rollason's Marsh Special eventually went up to Newcastle-upon-Tyne for Ferrari driver Jack Maurice while the remains of Hickman's BT30 were rebuilt and fitted with a rare Winkelman twin cam unit of just 1.5-litres capacity for Brian Pickering and Nigel Woodisse. This interesting combination never really worked out as the engine was rather down on power to take on the leading contenders. In fact, four-cylinder honours were largely in the hands of Tony Griffiths (who had bought a Formula B Brabham BT29 chassis and, aided by the Service Manager of Kidderminster Motors, Roy Pallett, opted for a 240 bhp 1.8-litre Cosworth FVC sports car engine) and those of the Elton family. By this time, the Westbury Vegantune agents has a positive fleet of Brabham Twin Cams at their disposal, although the ex-Lawson BT18 was sold off to Rod Pickering, mainly for circuit racing. This left Spencer Elton with the ex-Williamson BT21C and father Tom with the ex-Hawley/Fenwick BT18.

Another centre of activity was the Warwick workshop of the increasingly respected engineer/driver Roy Lane. The tall, generally sun-tanned Midlander whose wife Betty is always present to lend enthusiastic support, had been rather conscious of being beaten on several occasions by Jim Johnstone in his old car and had sold the TechCraft-Buick to John Cussins and had taken the remains of the 4WD BRM in part exchange. From this he took the now 280 bhp engine, wheels, steering, and rear uprights and incorporated them in a new TechCraft, assisted by Brian Simmonds and Ken Nicholls, with further aid in the transmission department from former Ferguson men Ossie Webb and Stan Paskin.

The scene was set for a fascinating season with the added ingredient of a further Shell-sponsored Championship running concurrently with the main Shell/RAC title chase. This was to be called the Shell Leaders' Championship and, like the Castrol/BARC series, was to be settled on the basis of class successes at the 12 Championship rounds. However, the scoring system was simpler than in the BARC Championship, 10 points being awarded to first in class down to 1 point for tenth, with the best 8 rounds to count and no points scored in Handicap, Historic, Vintage or Veteran classes. Concocted by Freddie Brown of Shell, David Hepworth, David Good, Mike MacDowel, Ron Smith, Gerry Flewitt (MAC) and Mike Wilson (BARC), the Leaders Championship was to be co-ordinated by Brown but while the scoring system was simpler to understand than the BARC method, it had to be admitted that it would be possible for the winner to be someone with a very fast car in a relatively weak class who was yet well outside the class records. Freddie Brown had worked out that had the Championship been run in 1969 then it would have been won by Jack Maurice, and certainly nobody would have argued with that!

There were to be only 12 rounds in the Shell/RAC Championship because there would be no rounds at either Loton Park or Tholt-y-Will. The Hagley and District Light Car Club had agreed to take over an abbreviated Loton season from the SVMC, thus saving the Shropshire venue from oblivion, but there would be no Shell/RAC centrepiece at this challenging course. As for Tholt-y-Will, the Isle of Man authorities had found that the event had little tourist drawing potential without big international names and with relatively poor spectator facilities so regretfully withdrew their financial support. It was not to be the end of hill climbing in the Isle of Man, thanks to the enterprise of the Longton & DMC, successors to the LAC sprint/hill climb tradition, but to date there has not been another RAC round on the island. A strong case had been made to include Oliver's Mount in the Shell/RAC series, only for the RAC to turn down the application on the ostensible and fatuous ground that there were too many northern rounds. Since only Harewood and Barbon staged rounds in the North of England this did not really hold water but it was known that the RAC were uneasy about safety at the Scarborough course, although it was apparently the possibility of a car crashing down into the Paddock before Mere Hairpin which worried them rather than the very high speeds attained on the finishing straight.

The Shell Leaders Championship was not the only innovation in 1970. Burmah/Castrol were to promote the first ever Scottish Hill Climb Championship, with events on the established Scottish hills plus one on the 0.6 mile caravan site access road at Kinkel Braes, near St Andrews, and what was certainly Britain's most northerly speed event, held on the access road to the Rumster ITA mast near Wick, and organised by the Caithness Car Club. Over in Northern Ireland, too, there was to be a four-round Championship promoted by the Ulster Automobile Club which promised to re-invigorate a flagging sport in the province. Club events were also promised by the Truro & DMC at Tregrehan in Cornwall and by the hyper-active BARC(Y), co-promoting with the YSCC on a new course in Shibden Park, just a few miles to the East of Halifax.

The customary preamble to the season's major meetings gave Martin Brain success at the traditional Wharfedale Trophy Meeting at Castle Howard where Richard Thwaites showed good form for second BTD; David Good a narrow 0.29s victory over Sir Nick Williamson and a rather wider margin over Spencer Elton at Brunton where the surface had deteriorated badly; and a popular BTD to Reg Phillips, now domiciled in Tewkesbury, in the ex-Good/Lawson Chevron B8 at the Prescott opener. Most of the leading lights were at Wiscombe Park for the AMOC *Daily Mirror* Meeting although Roy Lane was still awaiting driveshafts for the new TechCraft and Tony Griffiths non-started after he had damaged his Brabham at Silverstone. The course was very muddy, producing many hectic moments while more raised eyebrows were caused when, after so many years of success in the hands of Phil Scragg, Tony Harrison's Lola T70L was judged not to be a sports car by the Scrutineers! In the prevailing conditions it was not surprising that David Hepworth set a 47.76s BTD although Williamson ran him pretty close on 48.21s despite a lurid slide at Martini – often the scene of Sir Nick's more dramatic moments.

In contrast to the previous year Harewood opened on a high note and a superb new record – rare at the April Meeting when the track normally bore the marks of the winter passage of much bovine activ-

Peter Voigt's pretty and very successful Ginetta G17 taking second BTD and a class win at Pontypool, 1970.
via PETER VOIGT

ity, and of rally cars – in 40.25s to the yellow Williamson McLaren, and with Hepworth and Brain beaten down into the minor places by an on-form Peter Blankstone in the Brabham-Olds. BT21 which had been third at Wiscombe and which the following week scored an easy BTD at the Castrol/RAC Championship opener at Loton Park. In allotting a Championship round to the revived Loton course, the BARC did the H & D LCC a power of good in that this, their first meeting in this make-or-break year was given some stature. Although he was 4.8s slower than the big Brabham, Peter Voigt snatched a commendable second BTD in the 'Pink Mouse', the Formula 4 Ginetta G17 which had appeared at the London Motor Show and which was powered with the 1.0 Imp engine out of Peter's successful DRW sports racer.

Competitors had to wait until the first Sunday in May to score Shell/RAC points, at Prescott, where many people seemed a little rusty, judging by the number of missed gears and generally untidy ascents. Unfortunately, David Hepworth was missing for the Champion was busy fitting a new full 5-litre Chevrolet V8 to the Hepworth, and Martin Brain was another non-starter. The chassis of the Cooper-Chrysler had been badly kinked in a Paddock unloading mishap, made all the more serious as the chassis jigs from the now disbanded Cooper works were now on the wrong side of the Atlantic. Many people were not totally surprised when they heard of this calamity as, despite the exotic nature of the cars he owned, Martin persisted in bringing them to meetings on the back of an ordinary truck, loading and unloading being effected in a rather precarious manner with the aid of two stout baulks of timber. Tony Griffiths was back in action, though, for he had bought a new Brabham BT30Y chassis to replace the written-off BT29X. His 48.57s best was good enough for sixth-place points, behind a string of big V8s. These were headed by Williamson's McLaren (46.23s) and the cheery Peter Blankstone's Quattro (46.28s). David Good's red Ski-McLaren (one of the first major contenders to

The original Quattro. Peter Blankstone's Chas. Beattie-built Brabham BT21-based Quattro-Oldsmobile; a four-wheel-drive car which achieved only limited success.
HAYDN SPEDDING

David Good put on some electrifying performances in his Ski McLaren M10B in 1970. He is seen here in the wet at Doune. The modified cockpit featured a left-hand gearchange to accommodate David's disability.
BILL HENDERSON

carry overt commercial sponsorship, Ski being an Eden Vale yoghurt brand) was in the 47s bracket and held off Mike MacDowel's Coventry Climax V8-engined Brabham and Midland sprint exponent Bob ('King of Curborough') Rose, who, after competing with a Group 7 McLaren M1B, was now spreading his wings a little with another new McLaren M10B. This one boasted a 4.7-litre V8 which actually came out of a 1956 Chevrolet sedan! A less than wholly satisfactory day was rendered rather sombre when in one of hill climbing's rare fatal accidents, Stuart MacQuarrie rolled his Cooper-Ford T72 at Semi-Circle and was killed when the rollover bar collapsed.

Roy Lane had actually recorded fourth BTD at Prescott on his first class run but first gear broke next time up so the new TechCraft-BRM was out of the Top Ten. Roy made amends at Wiscombe, where a resounding 41.79s bettered all except the seemingly inevitable Baronet in the yellow McLaren – who clipped another 0.09s off that time after over-shooting Martini yet again earlier on. MacDowel was a good third and finding that the BT30X was a much more tractable proposition with a flat-plane crankshaft and revised exhaust arrangements on the Climax V8. A chastened Martin Brain, who had ordered a McLaren M10B to replace the Cooper-Chrysler, scraped a single point with the over-geared circuit racing T86B.

Tragically, this was to be 36-year-old Brain's last hill climb, for the following weekend he was killed in a horrific flat-out accident in the Cooper-BRM at Silverstone. His death shocked hill climbing's tight-knit world and robbed the sport of a colourful if occasionally slightly erratic driver and his charismatic cars. Happily, the Cooper-Chrysler was rebuilt and was to reappear in the hands of Johnty Williamson who took it to victory in the 1971 RAC Sprint Championship.

Not unexpectedly there was a saddened air of reflection at Barbon, but some scintillating climbs soon cheered things up. The star turn was undoubtedly a simply terrifyingly fast and spectacular 26.00s BTD in a class run by David Good. It was a fabulous if alarming climb on the absolute limit and even David could not match it on the RAC runs where his 26.66s best was beaten into third place by Hepworth's 26.02s, using his new dry-sumped Chevrolet engine, and a 26.35s ascent from Williamson.

A newly resurfaced Paddock and much-needed extra braking area after the finish were welcome improvements which awaited everyone at Shelsley. Hepworth's revitalised 4WD special shot up in 30.80s to lead on the class runs but he never had the chance to score Shell/RAC points. He was sharing the car with Peter Blankstone, who had had the misfortune to have a camshaft break on the Brabham, and after making the Top Ten, Peter suffered a broken differential dog-clutch on his first Championship climb, putting the car out for the rest of the day. That left the way open to a McLaren 1-2 with Sir Nick Williamson equalling the course record in 30.72s, and Good's 30.87s keeping MAC Committee member Tony Griffiths down to third.

Mike MacDowel had been showing good form for some time now and the breakthrough came on a hill where he often shone, Doune. His record-breaking 47.35s beat Williamson and Hepworth fair and square, while lurking in fifth place behind Griffiths was Roy Lane who went well in Williamson's McLaren after the TechCraft had another first gear strip. Good had the accident which he looked to be on the verge of for several meetings, although fortunately the consequences were not serious.

Since a dock strike forced the Jersey MC & LCC to postpone their Championship meeting until October, there was a long gap before the next round on 1 August at Great Auclum, a period which marked by Hepworth equalling the 40.25s Harewood record at a meeting where Peter Lawson came along to renew old acquaintances and in a demonstration run in Sir Nick Williamson's McLaren recorded a 44s without any practice whatsoever. Truly Peter was a natural driver. Peter Blankstone took another Loton BTD, Good was on top at a club Prescott, Lane at last overcame his TechCraft 4WD problems and set a 30.87s Shelsley BTD with the aid of extra wide first gear teeth to cope with the torque, and Williamson took the laurels at Gurston.

So honours were pretty even on the run-up to what turned out to be a pretty torrid Great Auclum on a very hot day on the now rather bumpy course. Spencer Elton was lucky to have a stout rollover bar on his Brabham, saving him from serious injury or worse when his Brabham toppled over the celebrated banking. Williamson was in the wars too for the big McLaren hit a tree and ripped off its offside rear suspension on his first Shell/RAC climb. The crash was attributed to the switch from Goodyear WG14 tyres to 'dry' DG14s. Meanwhile, Roy Lane was in blistering form, setting an astonishing 18.44s course record on the class runs. His first Championship ascent was slightly slower at 18.54s (although still under the old record), but next time up he had the rotten luck to have a front suspension-link break, putting him into a tree. He was still the winner of a goodly complement of points, though, for only the persevering Good managed to beat him, forcing the very large red McLaren up in 18.50s. Both Hepworth and Griffiths also climbed under the previous record.

After this, Craigantlet could be expected to be a little less hectic although a fine entry of 16 drivers went over from England. Hepworth (58.32s) topped the points, narrowly, from Blankstone (58.35s), Good, MacDowel, Griffiths and a subdued Williamson whose M10A/B was handling badly on too-hard tyres, but all the regulars were soundly put in their place by Irish racing driver Brian Nelson who rocketed to a 56.41s course record in his 1.6 Crosslé-FVA 18F Formula 2 car – the first big win of the year for a four-cylinder car.

David Good had another accident at Shelsley, rolling the M10B at the Esses, while the course was well lubricated when the ancient engine in Bob Rose's McLaren blew up in protest at the treatment meted out to it! David Hepworth was striving to overcome his early disadvantage in the Championship and his 30.49s BTD was a record. That was on a class run but his RAC best of 30.53s was still under the record and was enough to beat Williamson by over half a second.

What's more David did it again at Prescott with a 46.07s BTD and then a 47.12s to pick up another 10 points by the tiny margin of 0.01s from MacDowel. Williamson was well down, suffering from clutch trouble, while poor old Roy Lane had the TechCraft break once more and was eighth in another M10B – this time Bob Rose's car which now had a slightly less ancient Chevrolet engine behind the driver. It was the usual 'classic' September Prescott, with David Good setting a 48.06s Sports Car record in Tony Harrison's ex-Scragg McLaren M12/6B which the Macclesfield industrialist had found not really to his liking. Phil was in fact back at the wheel of his favourite Lola T70, now refitted with its original body. The BOC's prestigious Gold Cup was settled at this meeting, too, with the winner proving to be Chris Cramer, whose lightweight Mini now had a 1330cc engine, although still with BVRT 8-port head. Mike MacDowel was runner-up and 1969 winner Jack Maurice was third after another immensely satisfying season with the howling red Ferrari 250LM.

Tony Harrison took over Phil Scragg's McLaren M12/6B mid-season, Scragg reverting to his old Lola T70 which he preferred.
HAYDN SPEDDING

Rain spoilt the Championship runs at Harewood although it made no difference to Hepworth whose late-season charge looked as though it might yet bring him his second consecutive Championship.

Earlier in the year the RSAC had decided that the safety measures which would now be needed at Rest-and-be-Thankful would be too expensive to implement, so they cancelled the RAC meeting, transferring the event to Doune in September, which thus joined Shelsley and Prescott in having two Shell/RAC rounds. The last climb of all at 'The Rest' was a Scottish Sporting Car Club meeting on 12 September, held in poor weather but with a large crowd who saw an historic BTD fall to Jim Dickson in the ex-Tom Christie dark blue BVRT Mini-Cooper S. Although ending on rather a minor key, the day must have evoked memories for former RSAC Secretary A. K. Stevenson who had timed events amid the stark grandeur of Glen Croe since 1905.

It was wet again the following weekend at Doune where the Williamson/Hepworth Championship battle was only for second place as Mike MacDowel again showed all his skill on the Scottish hill for a 51.72s BTD, and since Williamson just beat Hepworth, the two went to Bouley Bay dead level with 68 points each from their best 7 performances. Hepworth also had the pre-Bouley morale booster of a 41.04s course record at Oliver's Mount to spur him on, but alas it all ended in anti-climax. David had hurt his foot just before the meeting and took Peter Lawson along as reserve driver. Peter would not have been needed but when the clutch failed on the Hepworth it was all over for the charger from Brighouse, after setting a 45.37s BTD on the class runs. Sir Nick Williamson then took the McLaren to a 45.47s Top Ten best, defeating MacDowel and Griffiths, to take a richly deserved Shell/RAC title after several years of unavailing efforts with underpowered machinery, even though he was a bit lucky at the finish. As sporting as ever, he immediately paid tribute to Hepworth who, he asserted 'should have won again'. Not entirely unnoticed amid this drama was the appearance of a new co-driver for Peter Blankstone: none other than Tony Marsh who showed some of his old skill with eighth BTD on this one-off outing.

It is ironic that David Hepworth was able to take another course record, at Castle Howard in 29.23s just three days later, but his 76 Shell/RAC points left him two adrift of Williamson. The ever-more-formidable MacDowel was third on 69 after scoring in every round like the consistent Griffiths, Good fourth on 66 after a spectacular if rather incident-prone year; and with Tony Griffiths, Peter Blankstone, the troubled Roy Lane, a most promising Richard Thwaites (who was invariably just behind the 'stars' in a very consistent year), Bob Rose and a surprisingly uninspired John Cussins (who retired from the fray mid-season) filling out the Top Ten places.

Bouley Bay was also the scene of the final Leaders' round and at the end of the season there was only one point in it. With the inspiring, if slightly nebulous, information that he would have been the 1969 Leaders' Champion if there had been one, Jack Maurice mounted a strong attack in 1970 with the Ferrari, but although he amassed 82 points and led right up to the final round at Bouley, he was beaten, by a solitary point, by Chris Cramer. The methodical and intensely competitive architect had a superb season with his very light Mini, which also brought him the Prescott Gold Cup and a slightly fortunate runner-up spot in the Castrol/BARC Championship. With his smile as broad as ever, Reg Phillips was enjoying his motor sport as much as in earlier years and he finished a resounding third in

Jeff Goodliff made it a Castrol/BARC Championship hat trick in 1970 with this well-developed BVRT Lotus Elan.
HAYDN SPEDDING

Richard Thwaites had impressed in 1970 with his ex-Bryan Eccles Brabham-Oldsmobile BT18 and for 1971 he bought David Good's McLaren M10B. Seen here at Barbon, Richard continued to do well, employing a self-prepared Chevrolet engine.
HAYDN SPEDDING

the Shell/Leaders, on 79 points, four more than Midlander Tony Lambert's ex-John Burton Twin-Cam- engined Ginetta G4. In fact, Ginetta drivers did rather well for the rear-engined, but still Twin-Cam powered, G12s of the third of the hill climbing Blankstones, Peter's wife Maggie, and the sporting Peter Varley, from Ambergate, were fifth and seventh, bracketing George Tatham's throaty Brabham BT17. Others to figure prominently were John McCartney, the still pseudonymous 'Spotty Smith', now posing as a tripe dresser from Jump, near Barnsley, in his exceedingly fierce roadgoing TVR Tuscan V8, and a saturnine-looking (in the nicest possible way) young advertising agency director from Kidderminster, Martyn Griffiths, with a Mallock U2 Mk6/8 with Holbay power.

If the Shell/Leaders title chase had been close, there was no doubting who the Castrol/BARC winner was going to be long before the final round at Oliver's Mount. That shrieking, but shatteringly fast MiniSprint of Jeff Goodliff had been replaced by a superbly prepared Lotus Elan, built to the very limit of the class regulations, and Jeff ended up over 10 marks clear of Chris Cramer and with a rather disgruntled Mervyn Bartram (Moss Tyres-sponsored Chevron B2 Clubman's Sports car) in third place. Mervyn, a haulage contractor (and later, engine builder) from York with several years experience with a Lotus 7 before an "aberration" with a Triumph Spitfire, had had a successful year but was robbed of second place in the series because an incorrect class bogey time at Scarborough was not spotted until it was too late. Peter Voigt was fourth in the 'Pink Mouse' Ginetta G17, ahead of 'Spotty's' Tuscan, Mike Benn's Marcos GT, the hard used Mini of Nicky Porter (now permanently back in the North East), Sheffield photographer Chris Seaman's ex-Fred Whittaker MG Midget, and further Minis in the hands of John – son of Tommy – Pascoe and Brian Preston who had actually set several BTDs at places like Oddicombe and Tregrehan in the South East.

In this year of many Championships, Formula Ford Lotus 51 driver Ted Clark became the first Burmah/Scottish title holder after a successful first season for the Scottish series which featured a separate road car classification won by Ricky Gould's Lotus Elan. In years to come this road car category became accepted as one of the Championship's best features, encouraging a wider spectrum of competitor support than most other Championships. Brian Preston clinched the South West Championship at Trengwainton in August, and Maggie Blankstone secured the Shell/British Women Racing Drivers' series.

Overall though the honours truly belonged to the 33-year-old Baronet from Mortimer, Sir Nick Williamson, whose stylish and courageous driving had matured rapidly after his early forays at Wiscombe Park from around 1962, initially with an ex-Joe Potts 500, a true old-style hill climb special in the form of the GN Ariel (an ancient GN chassis into which Kenneth Neve had dropped two Ariel 'square four' motorcycle engines), an ex-Dick Stoop F2 Cooper, and the Cooper-BMC T72 with which he began to take things a little more seriously.

It had been a good year with Loton Park saved, albeit at a reduced level of activity, Tregrehan providing extra competition down in Cornwall, and at the other extremity of the country, not far from John O'Groats, hill climbing at Rumster attracting around 50 entries to this remote ITA mast access-road which measured 850 yards and which was lined by rather daunting ditches.

Far more daunting were the repeated thuds heard in the Paddock at Shibden Park, near Halifax in August, as car after car went out of control and made contact with solid objects lining this attractively-situated but unacceptably hazardous new Yorkshire venue. Starting beside a picturesque lake, the Shibden course wound its way between bale-protected trees until the competitors crossed the finish line at 75 mph plus to be confronted by a braking area which featured such diversions as a hump, a dip, trees and a solid building. Even moving the finish back 30 yards proved to be no more than a palliative and the co-promoting BARC/YSCC never used it again. BTD for the Gannex Trophy (Sir Harold Wilson's favourite raincoat manufacturer had its headquarters not so far away) fell to Terrapin pioneer Richard Blackmore, but by the end of the day, John Bosomworth had broken both legs and a Vitesse-engined Triumph Spitfire had been written off.

Power versus Agility

While 1970 had undoubtedly been the 'year of the McLaren', the Champion for one was not entirely convinced of the large F5000 car's ultimate suitability for the tight confines of the British hills. His choice of car to defend his newly-won title was a new F3 chassised Brabham BT35, using one of the 1.8 Cosworth FVC, four-cylinder sports car racing engines as employed by Griffiths the previous season. After a hectic season with his M10B, David Good decided on a sabbatical year and sold the chassis to the 'find' of 1970, Richard Thwaites, who dropped a less powerful, self-prepared. 5.0 Chevvy into the car. Good's mighty 460 plus bhp 5.5 litre engine was bought by Roy Lane who, after two unreliable seasons abandoned his troublesome TechCraft creations and bought an unused circuit racing M10B. John McCartney bought the second TechCraft and had the capacity of the ex-Felday BRM V8 reduced to a 210 bhp-generating 1600cc in order to spare the overtaxed transmission, thus providing him with an excellent weapon for the 1600cc class. Most interestingly, Mike MacDowel and John Cussins (who did not intend to drive) had joined forces to form Team Cusmac and had gone off in a new technical direction. The Len Wimhurst-designed Palliser chassis had been putting up some dominating performances in Formula Ford racing and Hugh Dibley's company was now building some Formula Atlantic cars. A new FAt-based WDH1 chassis was now built up to take one of Jack Brabham's very successful twin-cam Repco 740 series Formula 1 engines which, although delivering only a comparatively modest 330 bhp had the advantages of low weight and favourable torque characteristics.

Tony Griffiths, however, was thinking along the same lines for his new Brabham BT36, only in his case the Repco unit chosen was a full 5.0-litre sports car-intended version churning out a healthy 460 bhp on fuel injection and with even more torque. Mike MacDowel's erstwhile partner, Bob Jennings, stuck with the Brabham BT29X but got Roy Lane to exchange the difficult Climax V8 engine for the altogether more tractable and less temperamental 3.5 Buick. A similarly powered Brabham BT21C was chosen by Malcolm Eaves for a comeback season, while seemingly only David Hepworth left well alone. He arrived at Castle Howard early in April with his 400 bhp Weber-carburetted Hepworth and cheerily affirmed that his work over the winter had amounted to "just a two-hour service".

Apart from David Good, the Shell/RAC title chase would also lack Peter Blankstone who decided to have some fun with the ex-John Cussins Ford GT40, and Patsy Burt who had decided to retire from active competition after ending a long career on a high note by winning the RAC's new National Sprint Championship in 1970 with her glorious blue McLaren M3A. Although Patsy had competed in a wide variety of motor sport in the last few years with the McLaren, contesting European hill climbs, sprints and taking part in speed record attempts with the PMB-prepared McLaren 'wearing' whichever of three alternative sets of bodywork suited the job in hand, she had found time to run in a few RAC hill climb events right up until 1970 and was a consistent Top Ten runner. Without a doubt the most successful British woman competitor in speed events since the war, it was most fitting that BP should give a dinner in her honour to mark her retirement. Happily, she would still be very much in evidence in 1970 for she took over the co-ordination of the Shell Leaders' Championship.

After all the chopping and changing over the close season it was hardly surprising that David Hepworth began the year with a run of success in his thoroughly well-sorted car, even though its relatively skinny tyres and high driving position made it look rather dated. He won easily at Castle Howard, Loton Park (with the promising Richard Thwaites runner-up on each occasion) and Wiscombe Park, where his record-breaking 40.88s climb put him 0.7s ahead of the red and yellow Brabham of Sir Nick Williamson, and where David also lent the Hepworth to David Good. Nevertheless, it looked likely to be a close year once everyone got sorted out, for although David won again at the opening Harewood climb, this time the winning margin was a mere 0.19s from Roy Lane's lovely orange McLaren, and with Mike MacDowel's Palliser only a further 0.27s down.

Naturally all eyes focused on the Championship opener at Prescott where a driveshaft failure promptly removed Williamson from contention. Roy Lane, on a hill where he often excels, forgot to switch on his fuel pumps on his second Top Ten run but it didn't matter for his first climb in 45.21s was good enough for BTD. Had Williamson been wrong to abandon his McLaren? Despite severe understeer and an evident lack of rigidity in the Palliser chassis, Mike MacDowel was pretty close on 45.55s, beating Hepworth by 0.12s and with Griffiths next ahead of Bob Rose, a happy Malcolm Eaves, Thwaites, Tony Harrison's massive CanAm McLaren, Johnty Williamson in the rebuilt Cooper-Chrysler and Frank Aston with the little 1.3 BVRT Cooper S-engined Landar R7 'mini CanAm' sports-racer which had made quite an impression towards the end of the previous season, not least at Scarborough when the flywheel sheared and a piece of bell housing fired up through the bodywork in a highly diverting manner! Also in excellent form was Sulhamstead doctor, Roger Willoughby whose class-winning time in his shrieking supercharged 1100cc Brabham BT15 was faster than two of the Top Ten runners. Originally the Liane Engeman/Radio London F3 chassis, this was the car with which Jimmy Johnstone had so much success after fitting an 1100cc version of the Shorrock-supercharged set-up favoured by Peter Meldrum, had subsequently enjoyed further success in the hands of Chris Tipping and was now embarking on yet another trail in the ownership of 'Doc' Willoughby.

Although he was worried about his Rotoflex inboard driveshaft coupling spyders to the extent of taking only one class run, Nick Williamson fairly flew on what can best be described as his adopted home hill, Wiscombe Park, setting a new course record in 40.57s. On a day when a lot of people seemed to be having trouble negotiating the tight Sawbench hairpin, it was MacDowel who got closest to Sir Nicholas, albeit over half a second to the bad, with Hepworth, Lane and Tony Harrison taking the minor places, and with Jack Maurice snatching a point in his recently-purchased Marsh.

Because he had to attend a wedding, Nick Williamson had to miss Barbon where Johnty Williamson was sidelined with a dropped valve and MacDowel with a bent wishbone. Although he was running with an engine-mounting held together by a couple of Jubilee clips, there was no stopping David Hepworth who, in fine conditions, shattered the course record by around 1 second, leaving it at 24.55s and with Tony Griffiths – who had suffered a sheared camshaft drive at Wiscombe – also under the old figure at 25.44s for a most encouraging nine points from Lane and Thwaites' Packmail-sponsored McLaren. Former TVR Griffith driver Malcolm Dungworth took his first Championship point in his ex-Lane/Johnstone/Scott-Walter Brabham-Buick.

There were more driveshaft problems for Williamson, Sir N. and a practice accident for Williamson, J. at Shelsley, where the day belonged to Hepworth who made history by becoming the first man to climb those famous 1000 yards in under 30s. It was an awesome, scrabbling, over-revving climb with David Hepworth appearing simply to bully the protesting Hepworth to the top in just 29.92s. Less spectacular, but again demonstrating the potential of the Repco engine, Tony Griffiths almost cracked the 30s barrier with 30.08s, to defeat Nick Williamson (who was able to run only thanks to help from David Hepworth), Lane and MacDowel, who were all in the 30s bracket.

Despite drizzly conditions and a series of fantastic starts by the Hepworth, the Brighouse charger who was looking odds-on favourite to recover his Championship could not better third place on the first visit to Doune where course expert Mike MacDowel made it three BTDs in a row there with a 50.52s climb which had Sir Nicholas Williamson and Hepworth well beaten.

Everyone now had time to take stock before Bouley Bay on 22 July. Roy Lane took the opportunity to try out the Tom Wheatcroft-owned 4WD Cosworth Grand Prix test bed car at Silverstone but although the car seemed to have possibilities for hill climbing, it would have needed extensive modifications to be really useful. There were some excellent entries for events during this Shell/RAC hiatus, with Sir Nick Williamson winning at Gurston; Hepworth coming out on top at a Guyson Sandblasting-sponsored Harewood meeting where 11,000 spectators were pulled in by a successful local television advertising campaign; Mike Hawley returning to the hills with a new Brabham BT35 Twin-Cam to set BTD at a revised 'Inter Club' Prescott; Hepworth and Griffiths seeing off Willie Forbes at the best-yet meeting at Fintray House; Malcolm Dungworth replacing his Brabham with the ex-Brian Tarrant F5000 Harris-Chevrolet; and an excellent 'double-header' meeting at Shelsley, where Neville Hay opened a new commentary box given by him in his father's memory, and where Phil Scragg evoked many happy memories at the wheel of his old HWM-Jaguar, now owned by Tony Harrison. On the Saturday, Tony Griffiths took a well-merited BTD from Mike Hawley, although the emphasis was on the pre-war classes in which David Kergon climbed his ERA R12B in 39.58s. The following day, and despite a rather crossed-up moment early on, Roy Lane clipped 0.14s off Griffiths' 30.44s to prevent the MAC Committee man from lifting two BTDs in two days.

Indifferent weather and a delayed start (which meant that it was a close-run thing to run off the Top Ten runs before the road closing order ran out) rather detracted from Bouley Bay where Hepworth was really in a class of his own, recording a terrific 44.06s. This finally shattered Tony Marsh's 1967 course record of 45.26s which not even Nick Williamson could match. Circuit racer and engine-tuner Ian Richardson brought over a massive 6.2-litre McLaren-Ford M8 CanAm car and caused everyone to hold their breath, for his fastest sports car time of 52.75s seemed to be achieved with the massive car totally out of control!

Since Gurston Down was to be included in the Shell/RAC Championship schedule the following month, David Hepworth went down to Wiltshire to have a recce on 24 July and came away with a 32.32s course record, before proceeding on to Great Auclum where the normally sporting world of hill climbing was slightly ruffled by an unsuccessful protest of the frequently class-winning 'Production Sports' Lotus Seven Twin-Cam of Simon Riley. This was one hill where the agile little Brabham BT35 could be expected to shine and Williamson duly delivered the goods with a superb 18.36s course record, but won by the merest 100th of a second from the Hepworth.

Although Mike MacDowel had been pretty competitive he clearly needed more Repco horses and for Shelsley his John Judd-prepared engine had been fitted with new crankshaft and connecting rods from the 5.0 version, giving him a really punchy 4.2-litre unit. The result was a splendid 30.03s second BTD, beating Lane, Griffiths and Nick Williamson. But there was no stopping Hepworth, and for the second time in 1971 he lowered the Shelsley record, this time to 29.64s. Other happenings included the not entirely surprising news that Jack Maurice had decided to give up with the Marsh and ordered a Palliser similar to MacDowel's Team Cusmac car, and some jubilation from John McCartney who at last got his TechCraft-BRM to run cleanly.

In contrast to the impeccably-run Shelsley meeting, Craigantlet was definitely rather sloppy but the Irishmen were not too concerned after Brian Nelson asserted his right to defend his course record on the Shell/RAC runs even though he was not entered in the Championship, and promptly broke it again in 56.16s, 0.22s faster than the climb which earned Tony Griffiths maximum points while climbing under Brian's old record. Only eight days later, the 'circus' was at Gurston Down, where the South West Centre of the BARC were afflicted by a showery day for their most important meeting yet. David Hepworth's car now rejoiced in the name Guyson Shotblast Special as he was receiving sponsorship from Jim Thomson's increasingly prominent Otley blast cleaning equipment manufacturing firm, and he set another 'routine' BTD. The meeting was notable for the first appearance of a new Chevron B19 sports racer for Reg Phillips. Earlier in the season he had been conducting what was called the Fairley-BMW, which was actually his ex-Lawson B8, lightened and fitted with an open body.

The day before defending his Championship lead at Gurston, Hepworth had been setting a 48.01s BTD at a rather unusual new addition to the calender, organised by the Sheffield & Hallamshire MC. This, rather ingeniously, employed part of the hilly Cadwell Park racing circuit, deep in the Lincoln-

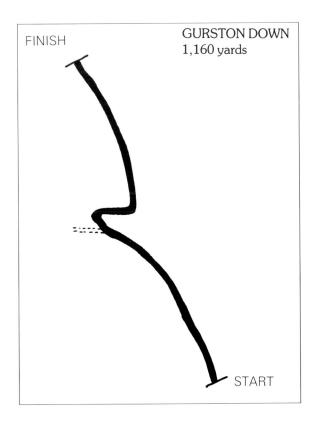

FINISH

GURSTON DOWN
1,160 yards

START

shire Wolds, as a hill climb course with a fair degree of satisfaction all round. The following weekend everyone gathered at Prescott once more for a superb meeting marred only when John Corbyn's Merlyn ran amok and broke one of *Autosport* reporter/photographer Robin Rew's ankles. It was a day for records and although Hepworth (44.64s) and Williamson, Sir N. (44.89s) dealt the existing figures telling blows, it was Roy Lane, shining at Prescott as usual despite the length of the McLaren, who pulled out something a bit extra for a 44.61s record. Interest was high among the sports cars too, with Reg Phillips coming out on top despite the presence of Phil Scragg who was trying to sort a 4.5 Traco/Oldsmobile powered Lola T212, and no fewer than three of the glamorous Ford GT40s in the hands of 'Spotty Smith' (ex-Nick Cuthbert/Eric Liddell), Peter Blankstone (ex-John Cussins) and former E-type man Mike Wright (ex-Ron Fry).

With a Castrol/BARC round on the Saturday to replace a cancelled meeting at the new Scammonden Dam course, the September Harewood was a big occasion, and one which produced a new course record after Roy Lane again demonstrated his mastery of the McLaren with a superb 39.57s climb which defeated even sub-record attempts from MacDowel, Hepworth (who had now clinched the Championship) and Williamson. After this the final round at Doune was something of a formality although it was rather a lively one after a rather sheepish-looking and very stiff David Hepworth appeared on race day after a late night celebration had ended with David taking a tumble from the roof of his transporter during some rather hazy goings on round the locality! The Champion's woes were then compounded when he went off at the first corner in the class runs. Since Nick Williamson was troubled by a misfire, it was hardly surprising that Mike MacDowel again topped the lists with a 45.36s course record, 0.3s faster than the similarly record-breaking Williamson, troubled or not.

Hepworth ended the year with a 5 point margin over Williamson, but then it became rather tight with Mike MacDowel on 76 points, to the 78 of the Berkshire driver, and the 74 of Roy Lane, who had driven better than ever. Tony Griffiths had also excelled with the potent Brabham-Repco combination – always one of the most immaculate cars around – and his 69 point total was no less than 21 more than that of Richard Thwaites who had nevertheless continued to impress, and who had beaten the still rather sprint-orientated Bob Rose, returnees Mike Hawley and Malcolm Eaves, and Tony Harrison.

The change from the immensely powerful and fierce TVR Tuscan to the rather more refined Ford GT40 didn't do 'Spotty Smith' any harm and his 44 point total gave him the Shell/Leaders' Championship by 2 points from Chris Cramer who had enjoyed another highly successful, if slightly controversial and definitely rather hairy, season in a Cramer/Staniforth/BVRT concoction which was a slightly-widened 'sports' Terrapin fitted with the familiar BVRT Mini-Cooper S engine. Veteran Reg Phillips was third, ahead of Doc Willoughby and the Mini-Cooper S of John Davies.

This was the *annus mirabilis* for those who had decided that Yorkshire had become hill climbing's second 'home' after the West Midlands, for at Oliver's Mount, where Hepworth beat Lane on a slippery course, the main attention was devoted to the final throes of a fiercely fought Castrol/BARC Championship made a lot more open when three times winner and ace spotter of potentially favourable bogey times, Jeff Goodliff decided to rest on his laurels. At the last, there was only 0.16 of a mark in

Before moving on to a Ford GT40 the pseudonymous 'Spotty Smith', later to be revealed as Tony Bancroft, enjoyed great success with a TVR Tuscan, becoming the scourge of Northern E-type Jaguar drivers.
HAYDN SPEDDING

Jeff Goodliff's Castrol/BARC Championship domination was succeeded by a victory for Jim Thomson's Blydenstein Vauxhall Viva GT in 1971.
via JIM THOMSON

it with victory going to yet another Yorkshireman, Jim Thomson who had had a splendid season with a full Blydenstein Vauxhall Viva GT, a twin to Gerry Marshall's car, and just managed to head off the Skipper Group Ford Escort GT of Blackburn car dealer Robert Speak. Jim's Championship success came after spending a couple of seasons with such machinery as a TVR Tuscan and a Chevron-BMW B8 (which he also ran in 1971) after graduating from his successful Jaguar E-type. Bob Speak was also an experienced driver in a variety of cars, notably several Lotus Elans, but rarely seemed to hang on to a car long enough to achieve success consistent with his driving ability. Despite the annoyance of having his entry turned down at Gurston on one occasion, Sheffield's most extrovert photographer, Chris Seaman was a worthy third with the Townmaster Towing Equipment-backed MG Midget, to head the rapid Birmingham-based engineer Richard Jones (Clubmans Mallock U2), and the Ford Escort Mexico of the deceptively reserved, pipe smoking Richard White from Colne. Although not a championship chaser by nature, Richard had set record after record for several seasons with an impeccably prepared and exceptionally well driven grey Ford Cortina GT (which later suffered the ignominy of becoming Richard's tow car when fitted with a milder engine) before switching briefly and not too happily to a Special Saloon Mini, Clearly rear-wheel-drive Fords were far more to his liking.

Even after Oliver's Mount, there was the Burmah/Scottish Championship to settle on Kinkel Braes, this one falling to Ian McLaren in an ex-Goodwin Racing/Cyd Williams Chevron B15, and with Tom Sleigh securing the road car award in his Jaguar E-type V12. The final fling for many was the Gunter Trophy Meeting at Castle Howard where David Hepworth took one more course record in 28.36s despite the now very rough track, from Jack Maurice's new Palliser-Repco and where Sherburn-in-Elmet dealer and Jaguar specialist Fred Cliffe packed more than most into around 35 seconds. First he all but wiped out the motoring press with an off-course excursion at the Hairpin, then he threw out most of his engine oil, and completed a grand slam by having his E-type catch fire at the Obelisk!

The season had been fiercely contested in most classes: even the old 500s were as many as 15 strong on occasions. Quite apart from machinery of the calibre of Scragg's Lola T212. Tatham's BT17, Harrison's big McLaren and Brian Alexander's 3.5 Oldsmobile-engined Ginetta G16, plus the Chevrons of Reg Phillips, Jim Thomson and 'Chippy' Stross, the sports-racing classes took on new interest with a proliferation of nimble Clubmans chassis Mallock U2s with their potential increased with the substitution of Twin-Cam engines. Notable among them were the fairly old Mk5 chassis of Temple Meads Motors, Bristol driver Jeff Hill, that of Haverfordwest brothers David and Billy Morris, and the ultra rapid Mk8 version of Stourbridge's John Stuart.

Competition was ever more fierce in the 1100cc racing class, too, where the old SCA-engined F3 chassis had tended to give way to a splendid assortment of 'Harewood Specials' (Terrapins, Gryphons and Mambas all inspired by the original Staniforth/Blackmore Mini-based concept), Formula 3-based cars like Roger Willoughby's noisy little Brabham, Mike Allan's Ecosse-Imp, and several Coopers, Formula 4 Vixens and the two Ginetta G17s of Peter Voigt (who shared much of the honours with Willoughby) and Scotsmen Alex Brown and David Fyfe, and even a few old 1100 Cooper-JAPs.

Unfortunately, all the close competition had one rather regrettable side effect. The success of the now well established class-based or 'handicap' championships had not unnaturally encouraged some of the keener types to become rather close students of what you could or could not get away with in the various classes. The objective was to find a class with relatively weak opposition, and/or a car which would be technically more advanced than anything which had contested this class before. Jeff Goodliff had shown what could be done in this direction, especially when allied to great engineering and driving skill. In 1971 there were rumblings of discontent about Chris Cramer's hairy supercharged Terrapin Mk5 sports racer and injured protestations from Stanley, County Durham driver Trevor Smith who was most unhappy when he was told that his FVA-engined Lotus 47 was *not* a GT but a sports-racer. Having lost that battle, Trevor reappeared with a Daren Mk2 sports car to attach his FVA to! Then there were some who felt that the addition of superchargers should result in cars running in the next capacity class up, more in line with the way circuit racing tended to treat such adjuncts to higher performance. This argument was promptly countered by the blower's supporters who avowed that the compressor was just one more aid to greater engine output and a rather cheaper one than many of the alternatives.

It was all rather outside the spirit of hill climbing but it was a true reflection of the fascinating technical variety to be seen in the sport and the number of people who were fighting hard to win one competition or another. Nevertheless, promoters were keen to sort things out as fairly as possible, and a panel was set up to try to remove any anomalies in the class structure of the Leaders' series, while Castrol/BARC instigator Mike Wilson announced new speed event classes at the end of the year to maintain fair competition in the face of changing trends in competition cars, and with a view to further standardisation of classes between events. Saloons were to become either 'Touring' or 'Special' with the intermediate and rather indeterminate 'Special Series' category dropped. The pushrod-engined Clubmans class was emphasised – a lead which it was to take Midlands organisers a decade to follow in the face of tremendous popularity for these cars – and a Limited Production GT class was instigated to sort out the Group 4 GT-type cars from the open sports-racers. Supercharging could remain without penalty, as per RAC Vehicle Regulations.

Repco Supremacy

One of the Major talking points of the 1971 season had been the potential of the light and exceptionally torquey Repco V8 engine, especially when it was taken out to 4.2 or 5.0 litres. Tony Griffiths had certainly had his best season for many years with his Brabham-Repco BT35X, a car which boasted specially lightened front end and rear aerofoil. Not surprisingly he retained this car for 1972, while a broadly similar Brabham BT36X (basically F2 as opposed to F3 chassis), complete with 5.0 Repco (new pistons and liners took the engine out to 4.2 litres, while a new crankshaft brought the capacity up to the full 5.0 litres) was destined for Team Cusmac's Mike MacDowel. This certainly looked a formidable combination after Mike's success with the Palliser which was certainly a cheap chassis to buy but lacked rigidity and was a brute to handle, especially on bump and rebound. The immensely talented Peter Voigt took over the ex-MacDowel chassis, into which was fitted the Repco engine out of the Le Mans Healey, but now 'stretched' to 4.2 litres. The slightly built violin maker hoped to have a fairly economical season with this combination but he was to be sadly disillusioned in that respect. Jack Maurice, who had bought the other Palliser WDH chassis was also to fade away with his own financial problems, while the Palliser organisation was itself wound up before any really useful development could be put into the cars.

But what of the two men who had dominated the last three years of Championship hill climbing between them? David Hepworth actually gave the Guyson Shotblast Special its first proper rebuild for the new season, although it was likely that his interest in circuit racing, now centred on running the CanAm BRM P154s in the Interserie Championship, would tend to interfere with his hill climbing. Meanwhile, Sir Nicholas Williamson was adamant that whatever the shortcomings of his 1971 BT35, the optimum machine for the hills was a light and nimble F3/F2-type car with a powerful four cylinder engine of around the 2.0 litre mark. After much consultation with Robin Herd of March Engineering, the new large-scale racing car manufacturer which had fairly exploded onto the scene in so many categories during 1969/70, and with engine builder Brian Hart, Sir Nick came up with something rather special. The chassis was a modified 1971 F2-type March 712 and the motive power was a prototype 2.0 alloy block engine still related to the Ford BDA, and itself the ancestor of the Hart 420R units which were to achieve so much success both in Formula 2 and in hill climbing in years to come. The March chassis was a monocoque although some assumed that it was a spaceframe until told otherwise because during 1971 March offered Formula 3 cars in 713S (spaceframe) and 713M (monocoque) versions, whereas the 'S' in 712S stood for 'Special'. All rather confusing.

Tony Griffiths had had an excellent first season with his Repco V8-engined Brabham BT35X, so he retained the impeccably turned-out machine for 1972. This is at Loton Park in April.
BOB COOPER

Roy Lane had had a good season in 1971 and his new mount took the large capacity V8 theme one step further, he sold the M10B to Yorkshire car accessory dealer and long-distance sports car racer Richard Shardlow, who had adapted well to the very different discipline of hill climbing with ease in exciting Porsche 906 and Chevron-BMW Group 4 machinery. Roy's new weapon was nothing less than the ex-Denis Hulme/Andrea de Adamich Formula 1 McLaren M14D – a lighter car than the M10B – but with the F1 power plant replaced with a 530 bhp, 5.7 Chevrolet engine, running on Lucas fuel injection and with a fairly impressive power-to-weight ratio as the whole ensemble weighed only 11 cwt. Richard Thwaites kept his McLaren M10B, soon to be sponsored by Eastern Carpet Stores, thus giving rise to tireless repetitions of the view that his performances were 'full of Eastern promise'.

Among the 'second division', the Bristolian pair Ian Swift and Terry Smith, as keen on sprints as on hill climbs, armed themselves with both the TechCraft-Buick *and* the ex-Brain/Johnty Williamson Cooper-Chrysler; the Jennings Brabham-Buick went up to Scotland for Alex Brown and David Fyfe to share, and Mike Hawley, after enjoying his return to active hill climbing, upped the output of his BT35 with the aid of a full F2 FVA engine. Geoff Rollason, too, decided to make a comeback with a new Lotus-FVA 69, the last of this model to be built. Best of all, Peter Boshier-Jones decided to come out of retirement and bought the ex-Malcolm Eaves Brabham-Buick BT21C, a straightforward car which was likely to provide him with a lot of enjoyment even if it was no longer sophisticated enough to offer a real threat for the Shell/RAC Championship.

There was plenty of activity among the sports car drivers too, with David Good opting for another season outside the Top Ten pressures with one of Romford (and later Huddersfield) racing car builder/driver Brian Martin's effective Martin-FVC BM8 creations. Phil Scragg had not got along too well with the Traco-engined Lola T212, so put an FVC back into this ex-Bonnier chassis. A glorious addition to the sports car ranks appeared in July, in the hands of one Tony Bancroft. Tony, erstwhile the notorious 'Spotty Smith' had had his illicit weekend motor sport 'rumbled' and had made peace with his family, and so felt able to compete with a non-road car, and under his rightful name, for the first time. The car was a superb white and blue Chevron B19, with a lengthened wheelbase 7 inches longer than standard to accommodate a six-cylinder 3.0 Alpina BMW engine. The car had been built for European hill climbs but had not been delivered, and with its only mildly-tuned and glorious sounding engine, was to prove a tractable and thoroughly effective hill climb car. However, all the owners of the more exotic sports-racers were being challenged more and more by the adaptable U2s – everything from Formula 1200 to front-engined Formula 2 chassis, despite such homely components as BMC live axles and cwps off 1947 Post Office vans – had shown themselves capable of impressive results when fitted with engines far more powerful than mere Clubmans Sports Car units. Then, of course, like the Lotus Seven from which a certain amount of inspiration was derived, the cars had exposed front wheels which made placing them on the hills very easy. Star performers in 1972 were to include the Morris brothers with their FVA-engined Mk8/11 version, the new Twin Cam engined Mk11 version of Tony Southall, and the older Mk4/6 Twin Cam shared by Ian James and the son of a successful Midlands motor trader. The newcomer's name was Alister Douglas-Osborn, and his raw talent was soon noted by many.

One driver who was raring to go at the start of the season with a well-sorted car was Richard Thwaites. The Dewsbury driver kicked off with a fairly easy win at Castle Howard over Alex Brown; and then repeated the treatment at the Castrol/BARC Championship opener at Prescott where the defeated opposition included Williamson's new March (overheating due to lack of radiator), Griffiths and MacDowel who had the wrong piston rings in his Repco. Engine problems also kept both Hepworth and Lane away but the many competitors who did attend found that the BOC had spent over £2,000 on Armco barriers, safety sleepers and resurfacing over the Winter, and that Whitbreads had honoured the BOC and its famous venue by renaming the local Gretton Inn, *The Bugatti*.

Thwaites' fine run of success continued at the Loton Park Castrol/BARC round, despite a misfire which restricted his advantage over Tony Griffiths to just 0.03s, and at Pontypool Park, where the margin over Jack Maurice was over 3 seconds but where the meeting nearly didn't happen at all because a lone and exceedingly irate local resident staged a protest against such noisy goings-on 'mid the peace of a Pontypool Sunday by depositing himself in the middle of the track. Considerable persuasion mixed with tact and diplomacy were needed before he could be persuaded to allow events to proceed.

In fact, Richard Thwaites met his match at Harewood the following week where Roy Lane un-

Jim Thomson was one of several drivers to campaign the Chevron-BMW B8 on the hills. Here he locks up at Castle Howard in October 1970, preparatory to understeering off and coming to a halt a little too close for comfort to some stately stonework.
HAYDN SPEDDING

leashed the mighty McLaren M14D on one of his favourite courses to clock 40.57s to Richard's 40.81s and David Hepworth's 40.87s.

One week later, the Shell/RAC battle opened with the first round taking place at Loton Park once more, where it was again possible to pursue a full Championship season thanks to the co-operation of Sir Michael Leighton and the energetic organisation of the Hagley Club. David Hepworth began his title defence in the best possible way by (Shot) blasting his way up through the woods to emerge into the open and over the finish line in a record 55.69s, breaking Peter Lawson's 1968 best, and leaving Williamson's little March and Lane's decidedly large McLaren trailing on 56.58s and 56.64s respectively. This innocently demonstrated the fascination of the sport where two totally different technical approaches could produce almost identical times. Tony Griffiths, an impressive Mike Hawley, and Mike MacDowel were all in the 57s bracket, and the first Shell/RAC Top Ten of the year was rounded out by Shardlow, Voigt, a surprisingly subdued Richard Thwaites, and cheerful Peter Varley in his Brabham BT21C Twin Cam, the ex-Williamson/Elton car.

Showers and a great deal of mud on the course completely ruined the May Prescott meeting, although Repco engine users were even more afflicted when it was discovered that they were using totally inadequate timing chains which were wearing out after less than two meetings. MacDowel had a spare which would serve until the proper materials could be obtained and promptly offered his car for Griffiths to share while the generally so sporting atmosphere of even top-class hill climbing ensured that Peter Voigt soon found a drive with Mike Hawley. However, after Hepworth had slithered his way to a 53.00s BTD, two full seconds faster than Lane, the course was deemed too slippery for the Championship runs which were postponed until the 'Inter-Club' Meeting in June, and thereby echoed an old Shelsley Walsh precedent.

The next Championship meeting was at Wiscombe Park on 14 May, by which time Hepworth and

Sir Nicholas Williamson remained convinced that an agile 'small' car remained the best bet for Championship honours and opted for a March 712S chassis with a 2.0 Hart engine (which was the ancestor of the immensely successful alloy block 420R Formula 2 and hill climb engine).
BOB COOPER

Williamson had already had a head-to-head encounter at the Devon hill at the AMOC Meeting. The Yorkshireman came away with a superb 40.31s course record but the Berkshire driver was only a fractional 0.04s adrift. Unfortunately, the Shell/RAC meeting was another to be afflicted by rain, and the generally sober mood was deepened by the knowledge that the hill really needed resurfacing and Wiscombe's rather shaky financial viability threatened its long term future. One man who was anything but sobered, though, was Ambergate's Peter Varley. Peter was (and is) a driver who competes purely for the fun of it and asks little in return, so who better to set a sprightly 1600cc racing-class time just seconds before the rain pelted down to set a 45.00s target which looked likely to give him 10 points. But David Hepworth was yet to run and the canny lad hung about in the vicinity of the start line, wasting as much time as possible and so allowing the course to dry. Then he gunned the 5.0 Hepworth 'Shotblaster' away and using 4WD traction to the ultimate, set a fantastic 40.07s course record to win by almost 5 clear seconds.

He came down to earth with a bump at Barbon, though, for after flying in late for practise after practising at Silverstone in his Interserie BRM, he jumped into his car and promptly went off on the first left-hander, breaking a wheel on the Armco and rendering him a non-starter. Mike MacDowel was given a highly suspect 23.40s time which Mike was the first to disavow, and as the thunder rolled preparatory to a Lakeland downpour, Sir Nick Williamson shot up in 24.69s, 0.09s up on MacDowel's best 'proper' time, and another 0.02s faster than Tony Griffiths. The little March was really showing its worth on what is normally regarded as a 'power' hill, while the Repco engines, with their exceptional flexibility in evidence at the hairpin, were also looking good. Fastest of all through the Westmorland MC's usual speed trap was Roy Lane with a record 111.94 mph, but he was having to be a little circumspect as his oil pressure was low after a piston had digested a circlip, so his 25.29s was good enough only for fifth between Thwaites and Voigt's still rough-sounding Palliser-Repco.

With his engine sorted out, Roy Lane returned to Prescott for the 'Inter-Club' Meeting and put in one of his real Prescott virtuoso performances. Despite having a driveshaft coupling part as he crossed the line, his winning time was a record breaking 44.28s, just 0.12s better than Williamson, whose March was theoretically better suited to Prescott's sinuousness, and with Thwaites third on 45.31s, ahead of MacDowel, Shardlow and Hepworth who was in trouble again. Once again he arrived for the meeting at the last minute and he was forced to qualify for the Championship runs with his car stuck firmly in second gear, although this was one course where this was serious but not disastrous.

At Doune it was poor Peter Voigt who was in the wars, removing two wheels from the Palliser along with a barrier in practice. The Williamson/Hepworth battle was renewed with Sir Nick taking the premier award with 47.20s against David's 47.30s, and with Roy Lane also edging out Mike MacDowel. Williamson's old Brabham BT35X had gone to Broxburn driver Iain McLaren, and the reigning Scottish Champion showed well on home ground by taking sixth place in 48.57s on a rather showery day. A long break before the first ever Welsh Shell/RAC round at Pontypool Park allowed Lane to take time out to beat Hepworth on home ground again at Harewood, Thwaites to take a win at Loton, Griffiths and Hawley to lift BTDs at Shelsley where Lane kinked his car's chassis slightly after a hair-raising 'wall-of-death' act, and for Hepworth to journey up to Aberdeen to set a new Fintray

Basil Davenport in 1972.
BOB COOPER

Still competing regularly with his post-war 'Spyder', Basil Davenport tackles Barbon.
HAYDN SPEDDING

House record where Richard Shardlow's perennially smoky McLaren and Tony Griffiths' Brabham also cracked 30s.

The BARC South Wales Centre were rewarded with a superb meeting at Pontypool Park as reward for their hard work in sustaining top class hill climbing in this municipal park, despite the absence of Hepworth who was racing at Hockenheim and Lane's damaged McLaren. In fact, Roy borrowed Johnty Williamson's ex-Williamson N. M10A/B and was a worthy sixth. Any thoughts that Sir Nick might have an easy day were soon dispelled when it became clear that Tony Griffiths was on tremendous form. In the end Nick Williamson did prevail with a record breaking 29.66s, but Griffiths clocked 29.67s, and Geoff Rollason, who was fastest of all on his first Top Ten run finished a surprise third on 30.28s.

For neither the first nor the last time the annual trip to the Channel Islands for Bouley Bay was complicated by a shipping strike, and this was especially disappointing for the Guernsey Club who had pulled in an excellent entry for their Val des Terres meeting two days after Bouley Bay, which was seen as a try out for possible inclusion in the RAC schedule the following year. David Hepworth was particularly hard hit by the strike for his car was stuck in Portsmouth. Nick Williamson set a 43.15s mark at Bouley Bay which was not beaten on the final runs. This was just as well as he overstepped the limit next time up and rolled just before the Café. The driver was fortunately unhurt but there then ensued a panic to get the damaged car back to England to be repaired in time for Great Auclum, ten days hence. Behind Williamson it was all very close with a mere 0.45s covering Thwaites, Mac-Dowel, Griffiths, Voigt and Lane's repaired M14D. With most of the mainlanders fearful of becoming strike-bound, there were a lot of star non-starters in Guernsey where only Richard Shardlow and Peter Varley stayed on to share the latter's Brabham, and it was Shardlow who set the 36.29s BTD through

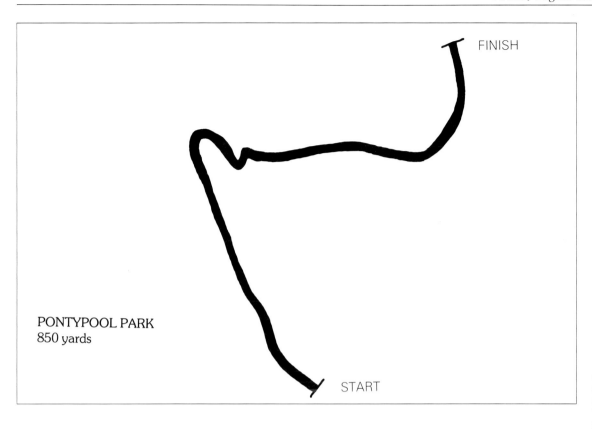

PONTYPOOL PARK
850 yards

FINISH

START

A fine study of Mike MacDowel heading towards a 39.14s Harewood course record in the Team Cusmac Brabham-Repco BT36X.
HAYDN SPEDDING

the succession of sweeping bends bordered by unyielding walls up from St Peter Port.

Thwaites, Shardlow, Voigt, Varley and John Stuart failed to make it to Great Auclum where Sir Nick Williamson earned some ribald remarks when his hurriedly rebuilt March arrived sporting body panels declaring the driver to be one Jean-Pierre Jaussaud. He could do no better than fourth on 18.76s, one place ahead of Hepworth, on a day which belonged to Tony Griffiths, who took the record at 18.34s to lead a Repco 1-2, for MacDowel clocked 18.39s, with Lane third in 18.42s, on a course where a small car might have seemed a better bet. Griffiths' win was actually his first ever BTD at an RAC Championship meeting after almost a decade of consistent endeavour.

The state of unrest in Northern Ireland, mounting in its intensity since 1968, made it seem prudent to delete Craigantlet from the Championship schedule and therefore not risk any danger to English competitors. With hill climbing hardly booming in the Emerald Isle, this was hard luck on Irish enthusiasts although understandable in the circumstances. Notwithstanding, the absence of English runners, Brian Nelson made history, becoming the first three-time winner with a sizzling 55.72s record in the Desmond Mack Crosslé-Hart 22F which was well over 2 seconds faster than veteran Tommy Reid's best in the Cosworth Vega-engined Brabham BT38.

That left a breather before the August Meeting at Shelsley where a vintage, record-breaking day, was marred only slightly when it started to drizzle during the final Shell/RAC climbs. Fortunately, this came after an awe-inspiring climb from Mike MacDowel which began with the Brabham-Repco getting distinctly out of shape at the Triangle, and ending with a blistering 29.29s course record to affirm that the MacDowel/Brabham/Repco combination was now fully sorted. Roy Lane was on good form, too, but his 29.77s was good enough only for second place, from Richard Thwaites (29.88s), and with Williamson, Hepworth and Griffiths well beaten.

On to Gurston Down, another 'power' hill but then the Brabham-Repco was one car which had both considerable top end bhp and exceptional flexibility and torque. In a nutshell, the deceptively easygoing, pipe-smoking Sales Director of Coombs of Guildford pulled out another '10/10ths' effort, swirling through the Karousel to bring the Wiltshire hill's record down to 30.94s, to the 31.10s of Hepworth, 31.37s from Thwaites, who was regaining his early season form, and 31.52s from Lane. Griffiths and a rather under-powered Williamson rounded out the fastest six, while another record to go was that for sports cars, falling to Tony Harrison who was now right back with the big McLaren M12. His figures were 33.83s.

Mike MacDowel was equipped with the very latest in Firestone tyres for Prescott but on a fast day which also saw Tony Bancroft set a sports car record in the Chevron B19 that he was sharing with Robert Sunderland, in 46.24s, the outright record did not fall to MacDowel. After all, this was Prescott and Roy Lane was on top form. 43.07s was the result, and Roy finished 0.63s ahead of Williamson, with Hepworth – now the only man able to beat Williamson for the title despite his rather erratic season – clocking 43.83s and MacDowel not too content with 43.89s.

Before Harewood the following week it was made known that Shell would not be continuing to back the RAC title the following year, a move which was regretted by all parties, although Shell were to continue with lower key support of hill climbing for many years to come, especially at Harewood. Harewood was another drama-laden meeting, even though a few of the younger spectators were probably more interested in the presence of Jon 'Dr Who' Pertwee than in any hill climb stars. Practice was enlivened when Richard Shardlow rolled his McLaren at the tricky, blind Quarry Corner, thus removing the now celebrated Shardlow smokescreen from the proceedings. The Chevrolet engine actually had a scored cylinder bore, hence the smoke, but for some time the car bore the legend: 'HM Government Warning – Smoking can damage your health'! At the end of a hectic day, Nick Williamson clinched his second RAC title but was not too pleased to do it with a mere sixth place, but then this was one title which owed a lot to consistency as well as to five BTDs. For the rest, Roy Lane was down to 39.50s, David Hepworth, striving to keep his Championship hopes alive, lowered that to 39.38s, but even they had no answer to the devastating MacDowel. His 39.14s brought him one more course record. It was a real day for records and much attention was focused on a really well-supported Sports-Racing category which, in addition to the regular runners, boasted such well-known sports car racing names as Pete Smith (Chevron B19) and Trevor Twaites (Chevron B21). But despite this being on 'Spotty's' home ground, it was Tony Harrison who set the best times, bundling the mighty McLaren over the finish line in 41.96s.

That only left Doune to complete the series and nobody would take high odds against MacDowel on this hill. Yet it was not to be another Team Cusmac triumph, for a puncture caused Mike to crash at the first corner, happily without injury. Hepworth was a non-starter in the RAC runs because of clutch failure, and the rebuilt Palliser to be shared by Peter Voigt and a carless Richard Shardlow was another non-runner with a broken differential. All this left Sir Nick with a clear run to a new course record in 45.08s to round off his Championship in the best of styles, over 1 second faster than Thwaites. There was more drama in the battle for the Shell/Leaders' Championship where David Good's Martin BM8 held a narrow advantage over Chris Cramer who had been enjoying yet another successful season, this time with the same 8 port Cooper S-type engine as before, but this time mounted less controversially, but just as effectively, in a new Mallock U2 Mk11. Unfortunately, David crashed heavily on his first climb, thus handing the Championship to Chris, by 1 point. The places went to the very fast and extensively lightened Sprite of Robin Leathart, John Stuart's Twin-Cam-engined U2 Mk8B, Colin Myles' little 500cc Cooper Mk9 (the Leaders' series incorporated a 500cc category in a simple but not always terribly fair class structure), and the balding proprietor of Bristol's Huntsman Garage, David Franklin. David had earned a lot of success with a Hillman Imp before graduating to a little Formula 4 Vixen-Imp single-seater with great success.

In the premier Championship, Williamson was well clear on 83 points, but MacDowel's devastating late run brought him level with David Hepworth on 75, and with Roy Lane just 1 point adrift on 74. Griffiths had 66, two more than Thwaites who had promised more as he had begun the season with a well-tried car, although his self-prepared Chevrolet engine was by no means as powerful as some. Mike Hawley totted up 41 points, both Shardlow and the rather troubled Voigt 32, and the Top Ten was completed by Rollason ahead of Varley and Boshier-Jones who had been as neat and purposeful as ever but was definitely outclassed in the technology stakes.

Same day, same place, and Roy Lane had to settle for third position in his beautiful orange, Formula 1 chassis, McLaren M14D. As the nineteen-seventies progressed Roy made Harewood his own, with no less than 20 BTDs at the Yorkshire hill.

Oddly enough, Richard Thwaites ended the season rather as he had begun it, being given a meteoric 38.47s time at the final Harewood meeting which was most certainly a very rapid run, although there were many who doubted whether it was actually that fast. Nevertheless, the record stood, and Richard then proceeded to the much-postponed first Huddersfield Motor Club meeting at Scammonden Dam where his 23.54s BTD was 0.09s faster than the more agile circuit racing Brabham-FVA BT30 which was owned and raced by haulage contractor Ken Walker, and prepared by Peter Kaye who drove it here and at Harewood and was finding that he rather liked single-seaters after all despite his unhappy experience with Fred Smith's old BT14. A service road to the pump house at the base of Scammonden Dam, which was built to hold back water in the Scammonden reservoir and with the M62 running across it, this new hill was steep, short and with four tight corners. High up on the Yorkshire side of the Pennines, and with the dam wall towering over the start, Scammonden is not the most cheerful place on a grey day, and although it is not as tortuous as Baitings Dam a few miles away, this new addition to the northern hill climb scene could not be regarded as more than a 'club' venue. A surprise entry for this first meeting was Jeff Goodliff, who dusted down the fabulous BVRT MiniSprint which howled up the bare hillside to a third place.

A generally dramatic and exciting year was typified by the battle for the now well established Castrol/BARC Championship, with most of the headlines being made by three Sheffield based contenders who just happened to include two of the most unquenchable extroverts around. Chris Seaman, whose sense of fun belied his driving skill and his tremendous determination, transferred the engine of his successful Towmaster MG Midget into the much lighter Modified Sports racer which had been Pat Bryant's circuit car. On the other hand Brian Kenyon and his fiancée Pat Hopkinson (they were married at the end of the season, the day before Castle Howard), stayed with their blue and orange Marque Sports Sprite which they had shared with great success for several seasons. Unfortunately, Brian lost his road licence for twelve months in 1970/71, but during this period Pat more than upheld 'family' honour, and when Brian returned to the wheel it was to find that he really had to shift to beat her. Right from the start these three looked likely to be in with a chance if Chris Cramer's Mallock U2 could be kept at bay. If anything, Chris Seaman looked to be the favourite but he then suffered the most appalling piece of bad luck in July.

Chris Seaman achieved much success with this smart ex-Fred Whitaker MG Midget before transferring its engine into a lightweight former circuit racer. With this and a Biota kit car, Chris secured a dramatic Castrol/BARC Championship win in 1972.
HAYDN SPEDDING

Sheffield seems to breed extroverts. Seaman's greatest rival was Brian Kenyon (Austin Healey Sprite), who narrowly lost the 1972 Castrol/BARC title to Chris. Pat Hopkinson (who became Mrs Kenyon at the end of the season) was a highly competent co-driver. The picture shows Brian clapping on the brakes as he emerges from Harewood's farmyard.
HAYDN SPEDDING

While his car was 'safely' tucked away in Peter Scott-Walter's garage, a runaway lorry smashed into the building and flattened the Midget under a load of bricks! Fortunately, all was not lost for John Houghton, a former Mini driver from nearby Harworth, had masterminded a rather curious Mini/BMC 'A' Series-based GT called the Biota Mk1C and he sportingly offered it to Chris to share for the rest of the season. He derived some good publicity for his kit car, too, for Chris carried straight on winning and ended up an immensely popular Castrol/BARC Champion, despite a superb last ditch effort from Kenyon. That effort came at a late September meeting at Harewood, not on the magnificent Oliver's Mount course, for the RAC had deemed the Scarborough hill to be unsafe for hill climbing. Few of those associated with the hill agreed with the RAC's verdict and it does seem odd that a course which is unsafe for this branch of the sport should be acceptable for International motor cycle racing and for International rallying. But then, in long refusing to add this 'obvious' course to the RAC Championship schedule, the sport's governing body had seemed to have a blind spot about it in any case. That last effort of Brian Kenyon's may not have won him a Championship, but it did earn him enduring success, for his 47.16s time remained unbeaten in the class for over a decade. John Houghton wound up third with the Biota, while the seemingly inevitable Chris Cramer edged Pat Hopkinson down into fifth place.

North of the Scottish border, the year certainly belonged to Iain McLaren and his Brabham BT35X, although the Mickels in another BT35 with ex-Hawley engine, and the little F3 Ecosse-Imp of Doug Thomson, were usually in contention.

It was something of a vintage year for the Welsh, too, for apart from enjoying their long-overdue first RAC round, at Pontypool Park, and having the pleasure of welcoming back Peter Boshier-Jones, an entirely new Welsh hill had its baptism on 8 October. This was a hill in an idyllic setting at Penrice Castle, on the Gower Peninsula, and reached from Swansea via the A4118. Owned by Christopher Methuen Campbell, who provided Swansea MC with excellent facilities in his castle grounds, the hill was close to the beach, and the club were able to negotiate a seven year lease for its use. Well surfaced, the course was of a respectable 840 yards – the same as Pontypool – although when the first meeting took place the surface was already laid to take the distance up to 1,000 yards. Drivers soon discovered that after leaving the start, hard by an attractive lake, the first hairpin was the decisive corner on the hill. A large crowd watched Peter Voigt gain recompense for a difficult season with a 30.05s BTD, a comfortable 1.52s less than the fastest time recorded by David Morris' Mallock U2.

In sport's wider context there have been many claims that commercial sponsorship has detracted from the sporting activity which is thus promoted. It would be very hard to make the same claim with any justification in regard to hill climbing. It was undeniable that the support of Shell had raised the stature and wider awareness of the RAC Hill Climb Championship, without in any way lessening the fundamentally amateur sporting atmosphere within which it was contested. So Shell's withdrawal was regretted, the more so when it became clear that the RAC did not have a successor lined up. Woking Motors eventually lent their name to the RAC Leaders' Championship, but their level of promotion was nothing like that of Shell.

However, any lack of a series sponsor which might have lifted prize money levels above the 'nominal' sums such as the £60 for BTD at Harewood and Barbon – far less in real terms than the sums offered in the 1950s for comparable events – was not apparent as leading drivers revealed what they felt to be the optimum car for 1973. The Championship trail would be back up to 15 rounds. For the RAC did indeed confirm that the Guernsey hill, Le Val des Terres, would form part of the RAC Championship, being run two days after Bouley Bay.

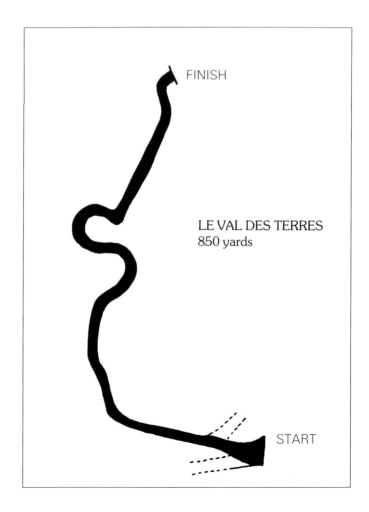

The one man everyone was looking over his shoulder towards was Mike MacDowel. His stunning run of success with the Brabham-Repco in the second half of 1972 had encouraged him to retain the car for the new season, modified only to the extent of a larger rear wing and taller fuel-injection trumpets. The combination looked the favourite to upset the 'private' dispute for the Championship between Sir Nicholas Williamson and David Hepworth. David was talking about a new 4WD car but it came to nothing and his other interests were still threatening to reduce his hill climb appearances. On the other hand, Williamson was one of three drivers who were about to introduce a new factor onto the hill climb scene – the 3.0 litre Cosworth DFV Formula 1 Grand Prix engine. Towards the end of the previous season, David Good had bought a couple of DFVs from the de Cadenet team, and these John Nicholson/McLaren maintained units were destined for a couple of interesting machines for Williamson and David himself, both built up by Martin Slater of Lyncar. Slater was an ex-March employee, so it was appropriate that he should modify Williamson's March 712S yet further to take the uprated 9-series DFV which was fitted with slightly 'milder' cams of the type used in sports car applications. For Good, there was one of Slater's own Lyncar chassis, basically a Formula Atlantic design of the type which John Nicholson himself used with great success.

The excellent 2.0 Hart engine out of the March found a deserving home in the back of a Formula 3 March 723 with which Chris Cramer was to make his début in the big single-seater class. After winning just about everything there was to win with Mini-Cooper S-engined saloon and sports cars, the meticulous and thoughtful architect from Stroud had found financial backing from long-time hill climb enthusiast Edward Greenall's Greenall Whitley brewing firm to run a single-seater in the appropriately Germanic sounding Grünhalle lager livery.

There was to be another Cosworth DFV-engined car on the hills too. Tony Griffiths, soon to become both a Territorial Army Colonel and Chairman of the MAC, rather surprisingly sold his Brabham-Repco to John Cussins for John to share with Waring & Gillow transport manager Malcolm Dungworth, the car to be run as the Saxon Hawke Special. The name came from a Leeds clothing brand in which Cussins had an interest. Griffiths replaced this excellent car with no less than the ex-Wilson Fittipaldi (and Graham Hill) Grand Prix Brabham BT33/3, complete with DFV engine, but with a BT37 nosecone. After two reasonably successful years with the 1600cc TechCraft-BRM, John McCartney was to bring yet another Grand Prix car to the hills, this time the charismatic V12 BRM P153C which had been Helmut Marko's Grand Prix mount. The engine was 'only' a 2-valves-per-cylinder unit but the sound was just as rich and the car looked superb in authentic Yardley livery, less the Yardley name.

Roy Lane was staying faithful to his McLaren M14D but was returning his engine to Weber carburettors, while Richard Thwaites, now with Eastern Carpet Stores backing, was looking forward to greater power from an uprated 5.7 Chevrolet engine. A new addition to the McLaren ranks was Tony Bancroft, who had bought the ex-Bill Wood circuit racing car after the unique Chevron-Alpina/BMW had gone to Phil Scragg in a deal which left Robert Sunderland with the Lola T212 which Scragg had never totally liked. Competition in the 1600cc racing class looked to be hotting up, too, with Geoff Rollason expecting challenges from Ken MacMaster's ex-Tetsu Ikusawa GRD-Hart/BDA 272, Tony Harrison's ex-Hawley Brabham-FVA BT35 (Hawley having retired), the Mickels' BT35-Hart, and Peter Varley.

The first major meeting of the year was the Castrol/BARC Championship opener at Loton Park on 1 April, on a hill which was benefiting from £2,000 worth of resurfacing on the lower slopes. BTD, a class record and top points in the new Castrol/BARC FTD Awards competition demonstrated that Ken MacMaster – who bears a slight physical resemblance to Sir Nick Williamson – was going to be a major force in his basically Formula 2 GRD, for he beat even Griffiths and Lane, although rain probably made the task a little easier in the Top Five runs. This new Castrol/BARC competition had been instituted to try to encourage the crowd-pleasing big single-seater drivers to enter more Castrol/BARC Championship meetings, yet without upstaging the efforts of the people for whom the series was devised.

The same series visited Prescott the following Sunday, where despite flurries of snow, Sir Nick Williamson enjoyed a morale-boosting BTD with his drastically revised car which had been renamed the Marlyn (and not Merlyn as so many people insisted on calling it at the time). Despite poor organisation, many delays and no Top Ten runs, the pace really quickened at Wiscombe Park for the traditional AMOC 'Climb of Champions' Meeting. Despite the fears of closure, Wiscombe *was* to continue and resurfacing had also been completed here too. Unfortunately, both Good (at Bunny's Leap on the Saturday), and Williamson (who hit a tree after the finish line on the Sunday) damaged their cars, but Roy Lane was on tremendous form. He had decided that the big McLaren really *ought* to go well on the Devon hill, and in this positive frame of mind, wound himself up to set a splendid course record in 39.70s.

Two minor but significant changes were instituted for the 1973 RAC series. Firstly, the tradition of awarding an additional point to anyone who broke the course record standing at the beginning of the meeting was dropped, since course changes (such as resurfacing) and weather factors could make the extra point a bit of a lottery at times. The second change was the allocation of permanent racing numbers for the year to the ten competitors who finished in the top ten places in the previous year's Championship. Apart from being a help to the less-well-informed in appreciating programme running order and in reminding commentators of previous performances, the idea lent a strong prestige factor. In fact, the battle for tenth place in the Championship was liable to become almost as intense as that for first, not for any mere prize money, but for the honour of wearing a 'permanent' number 10 during the following year!

It was wet for the first round at Loton Park, and the mood was perhaps less than festive in one or two camps for Tony Harrison was a non-starter after two engine blow-ups in two weeks, and David Hepworth was mourning the loss of his rather grand ex-Red Rose Racing transporter which had burnt out the previous day. That didn't stop David recording a 62.89s time in the dated-looking Hepworth 4WD, which was beaten only by Williamson's 62.34s in the shrill-sounding Marlyn. MacDowel and Griffiths were in the 64s bracket, Lane managed a 65.20s while Chris Cramer opened his account in fine style with his ex-Jarier March, recording a 66.05s.

The 'circus' re-assembled at Prescott a fortnight later with Richard Thwaites on a 'high' after breaking outright the Pontypool record in 29.46s the previous week, his efforts aided by the use of some new Firestone slick tyres at a time when the norm was still to use treaded tyres in hill climbing. Prescott, too, was slow after morning rain and after starting the seasons off so well, Williamson got into a lurid slide on the vital second class run and failed to make the Top Ten. Good, too, was in trouble, for Firestone had broken the news to him that he had been using tyres with a faulty compound mix. While his return to single-seaters was not proving to be straightforward, David must have been grateful that Martin Slater had persuaded him that his original intention of running a 7.0-litre Chevrolet engine in a March 711 chassis, driving through a Matra 4WD system just was not feasible! Although he looked a bit frightening at times, Richard Thwaites maintained his new form and recorded 46.18s, fairly narrowly defeating Mike MacDowel (46.37s), Hepworth (46.47s), Lane, Richard Shardlow (sharing with Hepworth), and Ken MacMaster. Perhaps the old order *was* changing.

Wiscombe Park brought Richard Thwaites another 10 points, his 39.16s climb just edging out Mike MacDowel's 39.27s, and with Roy Lane, Williamson and Tony Griffiths all in the 39s bracket. In fact, Williamson had suffered yet another spin at Martini, and his earlier class time of 38.80s was not only BTD, it was a new course record, thereby emphasising the potential of the Marlyn. The weekend was just a disaster for Hepworth and Shardlow. The 'Guyson Sandblaster' suffered a suspension failure in practice, and after an overnight rush to get parts from Brighouse to Wiscombe, the suspension broke again on the Sunday.

There was no sign of David Hepworth or Richard Shardlow at Barbon, for the old car had broken its transmission amid the previous meeting's excitements, but Williamson was right back on form, and despite a potentially disastrous tail-slide at the hairpin, the Champion smashed the 24.22s course record which had just been set by Richard Thwaites, leaving it at 24.02s. In an intensely exciting meeting, a growing challenge from MacDowel manifested itself with a 24.23s, Lane was on 24.34s, Cramer on 24.79s and Griffiths on 25.04s.

By the time the RAC Championship battle was rejoined at Shelsley, the charging Thwaites had added BTDs at Gurston and Penrice (a record 29.13s) to his laurels, and his 29.10s class run at Shelsley put him on target for more Top Ten success. Once it was established that veteran Tom Clapham's accident in his U2 Mk11 had left him with nothing worse than a dislocated collar-bone and a broken leg – although that was quite bad enough – battle was joined in a superb climax, which left Richard Thwaites as Shelsley record holder for a very brief period indeed. After starting the season less prominently than many expected with a well sorted car, Mike MacDowel was now looking dangerous and after fitting slick tyres on his Brabham, he made a superb climb which left the record at 28.82s. Williamson got down to 29.08s. Thwaites was marginally slower at 29.14s, while Lane, Cramer and Griffiths were all in the 29s bracket. Boshier-Jones did extremely well to clock 30.45s in his far less sophisticated Brabham-Buick.

At Doune, only Roy Lane was using slicks on his rear wheels as Richard Thwaites had suffered a puncture and could only manage fourth place. Being Doune, it was no surprise that MacDowel broke another record, leaving this one at 44.33s to the 44.65s of Williamson and 45.00s of Lane. It was pleasant to see Reg Phillips back in the Top Ten runs here, clocking 49.10s for ninth place with his Chevron B19 which now benefited from a 1930cc FVC engine, ex-Canon Racing.

The MacDowel success story continued in July at Bouley Bay where a fine 43.09s climb brought him another course record, and where Williamson was sidelined after clipping his car's suspension. The big surprise was the 43.61s climb from Chris Cramer which bettered all but MacDowel, although Lane and Thwaites were both in the 43s bracket. Good looked happier with the Lyncar on 44.14s, and Richard Shardlow was now going well for eighth place with his 2.0 BDG-engined Brabham BT38, ex-Tate of Leeds.

Chris Cramer had taken readily to single-seaters and after this boost he really excelled himself two days later at Le Val des Terres, St Peter Port. True, he had the benefit of a re-run but his 33.60s course record was truly outstanding and gave him his first RAC win, from terrifying-to-behold 33.97s climb from Williamson, and a 34.04s from the consistent Lane. Shardlow was an excellent fourth, from Griffiths and a surprisingly far down MacDowel. Thwaites was put out by a broken suspension wishbone, so all in all there was quite a turnaround from Thursday's meeting on Jersey.

Cramer's performance with the agile little March was no flash-in-the-pan, for he returned to the mainland, to Great Auclum, where he promptly reduced the record down to 17.56s, and helped himself to another 10 points, from a resurgent Good (18.03s) and MacDowel (18.05s). Fuel pressure

Mike MacDowel – seen all but airborne here at Gurston – achieved his second RAC title in 1974 with his well-sorted Brabham-Repco BT36X. Fourteen years later the same Repco engine won another RAC title in the back of Charles Wardle's Pilbeam.
BRUCE GRANT-BRAHAM

Chris Cramer – also pictured at Gurston – really began to make an impact mid-season in 1973, with the little 2.0 Grünhalle Lager March-Hart 723, scoring wins at Le Val des Terres and Great Auclum.
BRUCE GRANT-BRAHAM

problems kept Williamson out of action while although Lane finished fourth he frightened himself considerably by all but going over the top of the celebrated banked first corner.

The return to Shelsley in August demonstrated just how rapid the pace of development had become, for all but one of the Top Ten climbed in under 30s, a time attained for the first time only in June 1971. MacDowel survived a scary moment with a stuck-open throttle to bring the record down to 28.21s after a superb year at the Worcestershire course, scoring three wins (he also won in July), and cracking the record at two meetings. Thwaites ran him closest on 28.42s, from Williamson, Griffiths, Lane, Good and Cramer, who was struggling with a recalcitrant gearbox. Another outstanding performance was the 30.85s class record scored by Richard Jones with his 1600 Hart BDA-engined Mallock U2 Mk11B before crashing at Kennel Bend on his next climb.

Mike MacDowel, a 750 Motor Club Chapman Cup (1172 Formula) winner in the mid-1950s and one-time Cooper works driver in circuit races (he shared the seventh placed F2 car with Jack Brabham in the 1957 French Grand Prix), was beginning to look very much like the 1973 RAC Champion. The Team Cusmac driver now proceeded to reduce the Gurston record to 30.50s in the class runs. His Top Ten best was 'only' 30.77s but this was still enough to beat Thwaites, Williamson, Bancroft in the Pennine Motor Group-supported McLaren, Cramer and the game Boshier-Jones. Gurston had in fact been preceded by Craigantlet but although the Irish hill was technically reinstated in the Championship nobody crossed the Irish Sea to contest it. Brian Nelson was not defending his record either, although it remained unbroken with BTD falling to Nelson Todd in Brian's old Crosslé 22F.

Richard Thwaites arrived at Prescott for the September Meeting fresh from a 45.61s record on the unusual 1500 yard Cadwell Park hill climb course, but neither he (43.90s), Roy Lane (43.83s) nor Williamson (43.91s) could do anything about MacDowel clinching the Championship most convincingly with a 43.12s climb on a day when there were class record-breaking performances from Geoff Rollason (45.75s), Phil Scragg (45.72s), and a virtually perfect climb from 'Bosh' in 44.66s for fifth overall. Nevertheless, Peter, who had been assisted at most meetings by a third 'Bosh' brother, Anthony was talking about retiring again. There was just no substitute for expensive new machinery and there seemed little point in battling on against impossible odds. The Prescott Gold Cup was settled, as usual, at this event and David Morris secured this for the second time, the Haverfordwest Mallock U2-FVA Mk11X driver enjoying another most rewarding season.

It had been noticeable during the season that the normally impeccable organisation of the BARC (Yorkshire Centre) at Harewood had become a little stretched at times, and the RAC meeting was particularly protracted after problems with electric cables, oil on the course and a couple of accidents. Roy Lane set a 38.81s BTD but it was again MacDowel who took the 10 points in 29.10s, from Lane, the still understeering Marlyn of Williamson, Thwaites, Dungworth (sharing with John Cussins who had not driven the Saxon Hawk until now) and 'Bosh' who had actually sold the Brabham BT21C to former E-type Jaguar driver Nigel Pow, from Bristol. Another car which was for sale was 'Doc' Willoughby's splendid little Brabham BT15, and Peter Voigt, who had been out of action since deciding that he could not afford to continue with the Palliser, demonstrated what a good proposition the old supercharged car still was by taking it up in 41.76s. This not only won the usual huge 1100cc class – 25 entries at this meeting – but set a new class record while trouncing the usually dominant David

Franklin (Huntsman Vixen-Imp), Ellesmere Port estate agent and former autocrosser Don Robinson (ex-Wilson Fittipaldi Lotus-Novamotor MAE 69), the Ginetta G17Bs of Alex Brown/David Fyfe and Cheltenham former Mini-driver Sandy Hutcheon, the Cosworth MAE-engined FF Dulon LD4 of Croxdale engineer Bob Prest, and Allan Staniforth's Terrapin, which now boasted an NSU power unit.

The final round at Doune gave MacDowel his habitual Scottish BTD in 45.04s before the rain came down, although he had to give best to Williamson in the Top Ten runs. That left MacDowel with a season's total of 88 points. Williamson was on 81 after finding it hard to sort out the handling of the Marlyn, while Thwaites racked up 77 in his best year yet in the M10B to lead a consistent Lane with the Manpower-backed McLaren M14D, the highly promising Cramer (66), Griffiths (51), Good (43), an outstanding Boshier-Jones (34), Bancroft (28) and Shardlow (25) who managed the number 10 slot despite rather mixed fortunes with his BT38. David Hepworth, who stuck to circuit racing after his Wiscombe mishaps, didn't contest another Championship round.

Despite never really getting back into the groove after switching his Twin-Cam engine in favour of a BDA, and suffering a gearbox breakage at the last round, Alister Douglas-Osborn was one of the outstanding drivers of the season with an ex-Dick Mallock U2 Mk12. He lost the Woking Motors Leaders' Championship on a tie-break decision after both he and Edinburgh architect Alex Brown ('Pink Mouse' Ginetta G17B) ended up with 72 points. This was three more than Phil Scragg who enjoyed his best season since his Lola T70L days with the Chevron B19. Phil's biggest problem in the sports car category nowadays came from the phenomenal times being set by the various FVA, BDA and Twin-Cam engined Mallock U2s which were so well suited to hill climbing. Apart from Douglas-Osborn, John Stuart's Mk8B with BDA power, the Mk11X of the Morris brothers and Richard Jones' Mk11B were particularly formidable.

Although the car proved difficult to sort out, the Martin Slater-developed Marlyn (March + Lyncar) with Nicholson-built Cosworth DFV engine, added much to the 1973 score and gave Sir Nicholas Williamson plenty of excitement.
BRUCE GRANT-BRAHAM

At the end of the season Mike Wilson organised a forum for discussion in Leeds to consider whether it was desirable to make changes in the Castrol/BARC regulations for 1974. The meeting was euphemistically described as being a bit rowdy, with much argument taking place about the vexed topic of whether or not superchargers should carry a penalty. The Modified Sports regulations came in for some heated scrutiny too – with a typically vociferous Brian Kenyon at the centre of both discussions – after a year when 'plastic Sprites' had been much discussed and Mike Hanson's ex-Leathart car had been moved into the GT class at one Harewood meeting. Yet when the hullabaloo died down it was decided to keep things as they were. From this one might conclude that a supercharged Spridget had won the Castrol/BARC Championship. In fact this was not quite correct although Sheffield's Mike Flather never really looked like being beaten for the title with his supercharged Aldon Mini-Cooper S. Mike, son of that arch-enthusiast for most forms of motor sport, Denis Flather, certainly chose his class wisely, but, nevertheless, drove extremely well to win by 6.23 marks from Richard Jones, who had only 0.45 of a mark to spare over Robert Speak (Lotus Elan). Also scoring high, in order, were David Morris, Leighton Buzzard civil servant John Meredith (Mini-Cooper S), David Franklin, the Lassman Mini of Alex Boyle, Brian Kenyon, Nicky Porter (still on top form with his old Mini-Cooper S) and Robert Sunderland with the Lola T212. The Castrol/BARC FTD Awards Top Five' series had proved successful in attracting at least some of the leading single-seater drivers to more Castrol/BARC rounds and gave Richard Thwaites a well deserved Championship win.

Up in Scotland, Iain McLaren had now exchanged his BT35 for the ex-John Wingfield BT36, and another Scottish Championship resulted. As usual, hill climbing at local level had continued to thrive wherever it was possible to run meetings. In fact, this was becoming the sport's biggest problem. With so many Championship meetings now appearing on the calendar, and with organisers anxious to enhance the crowd-drawing potential of the limited number of meetings which could be held at most venues, there were comparatively few real 'clubbie' meetings other than at Baitings Dam and in the West Country. It was increasingly difficult to find new venues for hill climbing, so the problem was not readily soluble. One of the lesser meetings at the reprieved Wiscombe course injected something new onto the scene, however, for in July the Jaguar Drivers' Club promoted their first hill climb there, although the fastest of the Coventry built cars – Guy Beddington's rare Modified Sports Jaguar E-type V12 – was beaten for BTD by Brian Alexander's beefy Ginetta-Buick G16 and Brian Moyse's little Clubmans U2.

Despite the unhappy experience at Shibden Park in 1970, the Yorkshiremen tried again and managed to arrange a meeting in Norfolk Park, Sheffield, a civic park only half a mile or so from the Town Hall. Sadly, this was marred too. Ford Mustang driver Terry Stone had his throttle stick open and he hit a tree, putting him in hospital with a broken shoulder and cracked ribs. BTD went to Alan Mountain's Sales Manager in his York motorcycle business, John Lambert in Alan's F5000 Leda-Chevrolet LT22. One of the bravest drivers on the hills, John had graduated from Jaguar and TVR Tuscan to a rather evil and much 'butchered' 1963 F1 Cooper – once the 1963 RRC Walker/Jo Bonnier car – into which was dropped the healthy 4.7 Ford V8 out of the Tuscan. Despite a chassis which was *visibly* flexible, John achieved some minor successes with this in northern meetings before moving on to the marginally superior Leda.

For some time the Lancashire AC had been trying to revive hill climbing on the Isle of Man and in

1973 they succeeded, using a 2.15 mile course, initially classified as a sprint, as the final round of their Hill Climb and Sprint Championship which remained rather sprint-orientated. This series was soon to be overseen by the enthusiastic Longton & District Motor Club, based at the little Longridge circuit near Preston, and they were to develop the end-of-season Isle of Man event as a full-scale club weekend, hiring (and filling) an entire ferry and making the whole thing quite a money spinner for this enterprising club.

For once the main topic of conversation over the winter months of 1973/74 was not about who was to drive what the following year, but the future prospects for hill climbing at Doune. They didn't look too good. Ever since the mid-nineteen-sixties the motor sporting world had become increasingly aware of the need for greater safety. The problems of making safer both international racing circuits and the cars that raced on them were the first priority for the FIA, and for their 'arm' in Britain, the RAC. Yet it was not long before club events and hill climbing came under the spotlight. Armoured barriers started appearing on dangerous bends – as at Prescott the previous season – and courses which seemed unduly hazardous came under increasingly careful scrutiny. Expensive and sometimes 'politically' inexpedient modifications were demanded before track licences would be renewed. The cause was undoubtedly worthy and the price was generally justified, although the loss of Oliver's Mount had been bitterly criticised. Now, however, Doune, already well established as one of the most challenging and popular hills after such short time, was threatened.

The RAC demanded that Armco steel barriers should be erected on the left of the course from the Start to Junction, but the Lothian CC had the sad task of announcing that this was not acceptable to Lord Doune and the Directors of Doune Admissions Ltd. It looked as though there would be no more sport on Carse Hill and the LCC even went so far as to announce that they were seeking the use of a hill elsewhere. Fortunately, a good old British compromise was reached whereby the Armco was rendered unnecessary by cutting out the first 150 yards of the hill and in June the RAC Championship contenders once again journeyed North for the first of two Doune rounds.

On the sponsorship front the position remained unchanged for the premier events. The RAC Championship still lacked a series sponsor to take over Shell's mantle, Woking Motors continued to lend their name to the Leaders' Championship, and for the sixth successive year Castrol backed the popular BARC series and its FTD offshoot.

Before the season began not too many people would be prepared to bet against Mike MacDowel retaining his Championship for another year, for the Godalming driver, whose ever-courteous and easy going manner belied his skill and determination as a driver, kept the Brabham-Repco for another season. Sir Nicholas Williamson, David Good (both drivers with cars now prepared by Station Garage Taplow) and Tony Griffiths persevered with their Cosworth DFV-engined machinery and Geoff Rollason joined their ranks with an ex-works Brabham BT37. The difference was that he proposed to compete with Formula 1 cams in his engine. He did and many an exciting moment ensued!

Perhaps the most significant change was that effected by Roy Lane who wanted to stick with the big V8 engine concept but wanted something a bit less bulky than the McLaren, which was sold to sprint specialist Bob Rose. In its place, Roy bought one of the F5000 McRae GM1s designed by New Zealander Graham 'Cassius' McRae and built by Malaya Garage who had been responsible for the earlier and not wildly successful Leda cars. Roy's car had been built as a back-up to McRae's own GM2 model and was unraced. The car was more compact than the McLaren, offered better driver visibility and when allied to a 5.0-litre small pin crank Bartz/Chevrolet engine running on special Weber 51 IDA carburettors gave the Warwick engineer a power-to-weight ratio of 500 bhp/12 cwt. As with all Roy's cars it was impeccably turned out, predominantly in orange, and bore allegiance to Castrol and Goodyear.

Many of the new cars appeared for the first time at the test weekend at Loton Park in March. One such was the Formula Atlantic chassised March 74B, running with Grunhalle Lager sponsorship again for Chris Cramer. The engine was a 2.0 Hart BDG, and the potential of the new generation of very powerful F2-type engines was not lost on several competitors. Alister Douglas-Osborn took to single-seaters with a sinister black machine called the Temple Row Special, and named after a Birmingham property development company. In fact this turned out to be the ex-Richard Shardlow Brabham BT38, now powered by an ex-John Burton 2.0 BDA engine. Shardlow himself bought an ex-Jim Crawford Chevron B25 and fitted this with an 1800 BDE unit, and for the first time since 1961 Reg Phillips was

Mike Flather's supercharged Team Aldon Mini-Cooper S leaves the start at Scammonden. He was a convincing 1973 Castrol/BARC Championship winner.
HAYDN SPEDDING

Iain McLaren, pictured at Fintray, scored his third successive Scottish title in this ex-John Wingfield Formula 2 Brabham BT36.
BILL HENDERSON

to be seen in a single-seater again. Smiling Reg was planning to spend a 'restful retirement' with the ex-Peter Gethin Chevron B18, with BDA motivation.

A discernible trend back towards a smaller and more agile car was also apparent in the mounting competition in the 1600cc racing class which was fast becoming a sort of unofficial hill climbing 'Formula 2'. Ken MacMaster kept his GRD but gave it a wider nose, both David Franklin and the

Morris brothers bought ex-Formula 3 Ensigns, rapid Scotsman Doug Thomson obtained Thistle Metallics backing to run the ex-Wheatcroft/Williamson GRD, Peter Kaye was due to share the Brabham BT35 he was preparing for Robert Sunderland, and Mickel's BT35 passed to fellow Scot Jim Campbell, from Bothwell.

But they would all have to watch out in terms of overall times in the face of probably the most powerful Mallock U2 yet. Stourbridge 'old hand' John Stuart had sold his old Mk8B version to advertising man Martyn Griffiths and had tricked out a new U2 Mk15 with an 1850cc Swindon BDA engine, rear-mounted radiator and 5-speed gearbox. Griffiths in fact did not stay with the Clubmans-based cars for very much longer for in mid-season he took over the McLaren M10B from Richard Thwaites who had decided to abandon the increasingly expensive world of top-class hill climbing to try the growing enthusiasm for historic sports car racing. His departure was a loss to hill climbing but his subsequent success in historic events certainly justified his decision.

The first 'dress rehearsal' events of the season are always fascinating to see whose winter theories are proving to be correct and to see who looks bound for a season of aggravation! Prescott on 30 March saw the Castrol/BARC Championship off to a fair start, with Mike MacDowel continuing where he left off with a 45.49s BTD, but with Chris Cramer beating Roy Lane, Richard Shardlow and Ken MacMaster. However, while it is undeniable that Garstang's John Barratt had a few questions to answer with his little sports-racing Theta with SCA-headed 1300 Ford engine, the most puzzled expressions surrounded the tiny machine with which Peter Voigt was proposing to re-enter the fray. Looking like a cross between a Formula 4 car and some kind of grown-up kart, this was the Voigt-Renwick Special and used a developed Johnny Walker JW4 chassis. Its engine really had everyone baffled. The amused Voigt added to the mystification by affixing an oriental legend to the car which seemed to indicate that the power came from China! This unfamiliar engine turned out to be a two-stroke/flat-four Konig of marine extraction and neatly fitted into the 500cc category. The ingenious team had actually come up with the first 'modern' 500 which after a few exploratory outings really began to fly. With Peter's undoubted skill at the wheel, the 500cc records really began to tumble and the Leaders' Championship looked a likely result.

Before the RAC Championship began at Loton Park on 14 April, most of the leading contenders journeyed down to Wiscombe for the AMOC *Daily Mirror* Trophy meeting and this time MacDowel was beaten by 0.04s by Sir Nick in his refettled Marlyn which smashed the course record on a fine 38.75s climb. David Good was also back on form with a 39.51s, to beat Tony Griffiths (a good day for the DFVs), a most impressive David Franklin, MacMaster, Shardlow, Nigel Pow's Old Brabham BT21C, the 'all-or-nothing' Brabham BT37 of Rollason and a disappointed Roy Lane's understeering McRae.

Unfortunately, a broken driveshaft rather blunted Williamson's challenge at Loton, where Cramer was troubled by a misfire and MacMaster also suffered engine problems. There was no problem for MacDowel, though, and his 53.51s climb was a new course record, over a second faster than Roy Lane who was sorting out the handling of the McRae. Franklin was again most impressive – fifth behind Griffiths and Good – and John Cussins made a polished return in the shared Waring & Gillow Brabham-Repco BT35X.

By the time everyone arrived at Prescott for the second round the competition was really hotting up, to the extent that Griffiths, Rose, MacMaster, Bancroft, Roger Willoughby (now in the old TechCraft-Buick after selling his little Brabham BT15 to George Dowson's son Chris), and Chris Cramer all failed to make the Top Ten. The latter was a special case, though, for his usually rather fluffy-sounding engine had run its bearings. Showing real flair, Williamson had the edge and his 44.45s was enough to give him an 0.39s advantage over an uncharacteristically untidy MacDowel, with the much smoother John Cussins ahead of Good and Shardlow. Roy Lane was unusually far down at Prescott, in sixth place, but then he was driving with a one-week-old broken wrist to contend with, which couldn't have made things easy.

Peter Voigt's 1974 surprise package, the devastatingly successful 'modern' 500cc Voigt-Renwick Special, employed a two-stroke, flat-four, König motor in an adapted Johnny Walker JW4 chassis.
BRUCE GRANT-BRAHAM

The big Championship Meeting at Wiscombe Park benefited from a far more informed commentary than of late – by Robin Boucher – but there were few spectators to appreciate it at this slightly remote hill, and to see Mike MacDowel turn the tables on arch-rival Williamson with a 38.69s climb to shatter Sir Nick's so recently established course record. The sporting Baronet countered with 38.80s but it was not quite enough even though it had Lane, Cussins and Good beaten.

Rain later on in the afternoon and some rather lengthy delays marred Barbon, and by virtue of running a shared car out of class order, John Cussins took an unexpected BTD in 24.25s. Nevertheless this did emphasise that a 'new' John Cussins was apparent this year, much smoother than of yore even though perhaps some of the raw speed was not quite so apparent. Everyone was on an even footing again for the Top Ten where there was great satisfaction for Chris Cramer and his long-time helper Jeremy Speed. After suffering from persistent engine problems early in the season, his newly rebuilt Alan Smith BDA was running really well and enabled Chris to climb the fast Westmorland hill in 27.17s, beaten only by MacDowel's 26.94s, and faster than Lane, an impressive Tony Bancroft, Williamson and Cussins.

It was one of those meetings at Shelsley which the MAC insist do not happen very often: a wet one. There was nostalgia in the air as well as rain, for the Club presented special awards to Basil Davenport, who was still competing 50 years years after his debut, and to Ashley Cleave who had recently had to retire because of eye trouble, thus leaving the field open – to his great feigned regret – to Tommy Pascoe. The times were slow, naturally, but the result gave MacDowel a narrow 0.20s advantage over Williamson, with Cramer again scoring well on a 'power hill' to beat Lane and the increasingly competitive Alister Douglas-Osborn whose imposing name tended to be reduced to ADO or even just 'Big Al' by most.

MacDowel seemed to be opening out a decisive Championship lead despite the early bid by Williamson's spectacularly driven Marlyn. Before making the long trip up to Doune, most of the top contenders were attracted to the Alcoa Manufacturing Co National Meeting at Penrice Castle. The Swansea Motor Club attracted a superb entry for their biggest promotion yet on this attractive Welsh hill, and despite the showery conditions which came close to giving the £150 prize for BTD to Alan Richards with his screaming supercharged Cooper S engined Gryphon, Williamson pulled out all the stops for a 30.14s best after one of those heart-in-mouth runs which he alone seemed capable of getting away with.

Doune is MacDowel country and even the change of course length didn't stop Mike from chalking up another win. This time it was really close, though, for his 40.67s was but 0.01s faster than the little March of Cramer, and with ADO going better than ever for third place ahead of Roy Lane, Richard Shardlow and Doug Thomson, who was setting his sights on the Scottish Championship with his GRD. There was a new sports car challenger, too, to give Phil Scragg, John Stuart, Richard Brown (ex-Good Martin BM8) and the other U2 drivers something to think about. George Tatham had bought the ex-Scragg/Harrison McLaren M12/6B from a gentleman who blew up engines fairly regularly while testing the beast but appears not to have competed with the car. Perhaps this meeting was the real decider for the Championship, with MacDowel's run of success continuing and the brave Williamson ending up ignominiously in the undergrowth.

After a morale-boosting 22.67s BTD for Chris Cramer at a Castrol/BARC round on the tight and short climb beneath towering Scammonden Dam, the scene moved to Harewood. For the first time the BARC(Y) were experimenting with a July date for their premier meeting. Unfortunately, the day ended with rather an anti-climax with a long delay following the excursion of Sir Nick Williamson into the particularly unyielding hedge on the outside of Willow. Despite the early date, MacDowel virtually clinched the Championship with a 38.59s BTD – tantalisingly close to Thwaites' notorious record – although Lane was only a tenth of a second down on a hill which usually sees him at his best. Waring & Gillow Managing Director, John Cussins and Cramer also broke 40s, but the day's outstanding performance came when Doug Thomson – a descendant of Robert W. Thomson, the inventor of the pneumatic tyre – reduced the 1600cc racing car record to 40.10s.

It was now becoming headline news if Mike MacDowel did not win. It was exceptionally close at a fine Pontypool Park meeting where 0.73s covered the entire Top Ten, and with the first nine breaking Thwaites' record, but the end result was just the same. Employing the exceptional flexibility of the Repco engine to the full – Repco-powered drivers did less gear-changing than anyone else – Mac-

Dowel left the record at 28.60s. It was John Cussins in the other Brabham-Repco who ran him closest at 28.76s, beating Williamson (28.90s), ADO (29.04s), Lane (29.12s), Franklin's 1600 Holbay BDA-engined Ensign (29.14s) and another Huntsman Garage-prepared car, Nigel Pow's well driven Brabham-Buick (29.14s). Despite the arrival of another 'modern' 500 of considerable ingenuity on the scene, the dope-fed Hocus Pocus-Honda of Paul Rhys, Peter Voigt remained streets ahead of any mainly Cooper-mounted 500cc opposition, although Barry Brant, Tim Cameron (Joe Potts Special), Ron Warr and Barry Oddy were still wringing the utmost from their ancient ex-Formula 3 machinery.

Once again the Channel Islands round rather upset the form book. Still, after his previous year's performances on the home territory of his sponsor, Jersey-domiciled Edward Greenall, nobody could overlook Chris Cramer. This time it was Bouley Bay which he won outright, and with MacDowel pushed down into third place by an inspired Alister Douglas-Osborn with the black Temple Row Special. MacDowel moved up a place on Guernsey, but there was a real surprise when Richard Shardlow secured the BTD in his Chevron B25.

The RAC rounds were really coming thick and fast at this stage of the season, and with the performances of the 2-litre and even 1.6-litre machinery on the faster hills proving to be surprisingly competitive, one could have been forgiven for thinking that Great Auclum was liable to be won by a four-cylinder car, even though this, the shortest hill in the series, is by no means the slowest. Not so, for Roy Lane's throaty McRae bellowed up through the swerves to record 17.97s with MacDowel snatching the runner-up position with 18.22s to the 18.24s of Williamson, who appeared to have lost a little of his customary fire after his mid-season mishaps. In fact, the best of the 'small' cars was Cramer's March, in fifth place behind Good, Cussins' good run ended with a Brabham bending incident on his second class run which robbed both him and Malcolm Dungworth of any Top Ten runs.

The Coombs of Guildford Director was back on top at Shelsley, MacDowel's latest triumph taking just 28.61s, five-hundredths less than it took Lane to blast the orange McRae over the finish line, and only another 0.04s faster than Williamson's sweet-sounding Marlyn. Cramer had the misfortune to break a cwp on this occasion, while Chris Dowson was also in the wars with an accident in the little Brabham BT15. Richard Jones, who had embarked on a low budget single-seater programme with a 1600 Hart twin cam-engined F2 Surtees TS10, was beginning to get somewhere but he was still slower than he had been in his Mallock U2. And that, more than anything else, shows how perfectly attuned to hill climbing the relatively humble Clubmans chassis from Roade, Northamptonshire really are. Fastest sports car driver, however, was Scotsman John Cleland who had gained some success with a Chevron B8 before moving on to a B23 Spyder. His 30.21s best was getting tantalisingly close to the 30s mark.

It was a year for settling championships fairly early in the season, for by the time the 'circus' gathered for a wet September Prescott, the Scottish title had been won at Fintray by the talented Doug Thomson. Malcolm Dungworth, normally rather in John Cussins' shadow, came to Prescott fresh from a BTD at the Castrol/BARC meeting at Cadwell Park. The Lincolnshire course, which employed a fair chunk of the racing circuit, run in the opposite direction to usual, had been shortened by 250 yards because of a rather bumpy surface. Malcolm beat even Roy Lane after finding a marked improvement in the handling of the Brabham-Repco by the simple expedient of moving the battery to the front of the car. Not for the first time Phil Scragg excelled in the wet on the Gloucestershire hill and his 49.02s remained BTD as conditions worsened for the RAC runs. Here, Roy Lane toppled the new Champion with 51.66s to 52.50s, and with Chris Cramer in third place after curing his car's propensity for chewing up cwps by adopting the then current Formula 1 practice of using the FT200-based Hewland gearbox in conjunction with the heavier duty DG300 differential.

Another event to change from its established date was the Craigantlet climb in Ulster. After a two year lapse there was some 'overseas' competition. This time ADO decided to go and so did the Scottish pair Alex Brown and David Fyfe with the Palliser-Repco which they had been campaigning all year. Nevertheless, on a miserably wet day where events were very long drawn out, the home side came out on top again, with Tommy Reid's Brabham-Vega BT38/40 having over 3 seconds to spare over Douglas-Osborn. In fact, it would be fair to say that the RAC Championship rather fizzled out for the final meeting at Doune was also wet, although at least the Scots had something to cheer about for BTD on the soaking wet course went to Alex Brown.

Despite the early challenge from Williamson, MacDowel's second successive Championship victory was crushingly decisive. He finished the season with 99 points, only one short of a maximum, after winning nine Top Tens with one second place. Not since Peter Lawson's year in 1968 had we seen such domination, although this time it was less a case of burning natural talent allied to a revolutionary car, rather a skilful man of great experience and with the perfect temperament extracting the best from a well-sorted, fundamentally simple car which was fitted with the best engine for the job. Roy Lane had definitely benefitted from the change to the handier McRae, although not by any quantum leap. Consistency remained his strongest suit, although flashes of brilliance shone through at Prescott, Harewood and Great Auclum in particular. Chris Cramer brought a four-cylinder car into a more than worthy third place, but for the first time since 1967 Sir Nicholas Williamson was out of the first three, a disappointed fourth after an indifferent season by his high standards. Completing the first ten were the highly promising Douglas-Osborn, Good, Shardlow, Cussins, Tony Griffiths (who was tending to miss rounds because of his TA commitments), and Tony Bancroft who all too often just missed out on qualifying for the Top Ten.

Although he turned his main energies towards the ex-Good/Thwaites McLaren later on in the season, the rather introspective advertising agency director from Bewdley, Martyn Griffiths won the Woking Motors Leaders' title with his ex-John Stuart Mallock U2 from Peter Voigt. The Voigt-Renwick Special, a great favourite with the crowds all season, gained some higher-sided bodywork as the season progressed which made it look more like a conventional racing car. Third in this important series was a large and cheerful auto electrician from Cheltenham in a very small Sprite. Russ Ward had made a big impression the previous season in the more southerly events, but in 1974 he totted up no fewer than 23 wins and 8 class records with his yellow and blue Aldon-tuned Sprite, entered (like his brother-in-law Alan Cox's almost equally successful Mini) by John Brown Motors.

As was now customary, the 'other' Championship, the Castrol/BARC series climaxed at Harewood in September where the BARC provided a return road for the first time, from the Paddock exit slip road down to the start. Unfortunately, there was insufficient cash available to do the job properly and this very rough and dusty track was never popular. Such low slung machines as Dud Mosely's little Kart-based Motus-Ossa 250 being unable to use it at all for fear of becoming stranded on the ruts! Eventually, the return road idea was abandoned until a time when it could be properly surfaced, leaving the track to the mercy of the special stage rally competitors and hill climb support crews who needed to be on hand at the start to tend their temperamental charges. This last ever Castrol/BARC round saw Mike MacDowel take his umpteenth BTD of the season, while the title honours fell to the irrepressible Peter Voigt by a fairly comfortable margin from the 1973 winner, Mike Flather. The latter actually did very well for he was competing with the same blown Mini and was attempting to

better his already rapid times from the previous year and generally succeeding. Although he was almost nine marks down on Voigt, David Franklin took a remarkable third place with his Ensign (bogey times for the larger single-seaters were usually among the hardest to improve upon by the required margins). The remainder of the prize-winning places fell to Nicky Porter's formerly red and black Mini which had now taken on an awesome 'passionate purple' hue, Russ Ward, Jim Thomson's Guyson-sponsored Blydenstein Vauxhall Firenza, John Barratt's little Theta, Alan Cox, Lincolnshire-based RAF officer Terry Sims with the ex-Cramer Terrapin Mk5 (with less highly tuned 'A'-series engine than Chris had used), and Roy Lane.

Roy had loyally supported this series and in so doing beat Chris Cramer by a single point for the BTD Awards series where third place was taken by David Franklin.

One other 'Championship' of note was the Prescott Gold Cup, although some rather unrealistic class-record targets had tended to reduce the award's significance in recent years. However, there was no doubting the speed of the unusual Ford BDA-engined Morgan 4/4, owned by Andrew Duncan and driven by Ray Meredith which took the 1974 edition of this premier single venue competition.

The anxieties about Doune and Wiscombe had provided forceful reminders that the increasing costs involved in holding hill climbs in the face of steady (at best) revenues were not making the lot of organisers any easier, even though there was no falling-off in competitor enthusiasm at the grass roots of the sport, What's more, the always difficult task of finding new courses to use was becoming harder than ever when stringent safety precautions had to be taken in order to gain a track licence. North Cornwall MC found this to their cost when they had to abandon their plans to hold events on around 1200 to 1400 yards of a farm road at Holland Hill. The RAC's safety demands were just too expensive to contemplate in this part of the country where the chance of promoting meetings of a premier status was not high.

At least the Boro 19 Club, the Rochester MC and Tunbridge Wells MC had better luck when they banded together to hold what they freely admitted was a rather experimental event with a 1600cc limit – again for safety reasons – on an 1100 yards course at Ely Grange, Frant, in Sussex. The meeting went off pretty well in this hill climb starved part of the country with an interesting entry received. Richard Jones brought his Surtees TS10, with which he had appeared increasingly prominently, and walked off with BTD in 33.28s. Runners-up were not regular hill climbers at all but two of the country's leading Ford-backed rallycross stars: Rod Chapman (who farmed part of the land and had played a major role in making the event happen) and John Taylor. The spectacular Ford Escort drivers recorded 34.19s and 34.26s respectively.

The Longton & DMC had also repeated the previous year's experiment in bringing the sport back to the Isle of Man, where their end-of-season 'treat' was classified as a hill climb rather than a sprint this year and employed 2.15 miles of the TT course, run in the reverse direction to the motorcycle racing, from Hillberry to just beyond Kate's Cottage. Winner this year was John Briggs who recorded 76.96s with the ex-Dungworth F5000 Harris-Chevrolet.

But the end of the season also brought the unwelcome news that Swansea MC had given up the struggle to hold meetings at the delightful Penrice Castle. After paying generous compliments to Christopher Methuen Campbell in providing then with the facility, they admitted that the provision of

Roy Lane's mighty McRae was to be the car of 1975, but occasionally things did not go according to plan. The harvesting was done at Gurston Down.
BRUCE GRANT-BRAHAM

the necessary manpower to lay and remove the extensive safety barriers, and associated chores, before and after every meeting was beyond their resources. The last meeting in 1974, held on 10 October, had given David Morris BTD but a fine runner-up was another 'Bosh'. Young Anthony, who had become a regular on the hills when he accompanied brother Peter, was now out to add to the lustre of an already highly distinguished hill climb name with a Mallock U2. On the same day, David Hepworth brought the old Hepworth 4WD over to Castle Howard – his first hill climb of the season – and proceeded to smash the record for the shortened course, leaving it at 26.74s, to the 27.28s of Tony Bancroft, who let it be known that he was intending to retire after an expensive and rather unrewarding season.

He was not to be the last, for suddenly, it all began to look like the end of an era. "Last year I won nine meetings out of ten, and how the hell do you beat that? I seem to have become the victim of my own success. I think I'd like to have a go at a handicap series with a sports car". The words were those of Mike MacDowel who had begun to feel the pressure of being expected to win, and who had little incentive to carry on at this level of concentration. However, he did make it clear that he was only contemplating a year's 'sabbatical', to have a rest and then return with something a little less demanding. And before many more weeks it became apparent that Sir Nicholas Williamson, David Good, Geoff Rollason and Richard Shardlow were all calling it a day. For Williamson, whose enthusiasm, normally so infectious, had seemed on the wane from the middle of the season, the pressures had also told. "It's now terribly professional. I didn't enjoy the year as much as before. The stresses and strains were possibly the reason for not doing so well, it all seemed to become very hard work which is not what it should be". His close friend, David Good, cited the costs of competing at the top level. and his increasing family and business commitments, although both freely admitted that they themselves had probably been as instrumental as anyone in introducing exotic and expensive machinery to the sport. Geoff Rollason, another DFV user, also felt the financial draught although he needed to spend more time on his farm. However, both Williamson and Good were intending to maintain their links with Wiscombe Park so were unlikely to be totally absent from the scene.

Sadly, indeed tragically, the same could not be said for Phil Scragg. The most consistently successful sportscar hill climber since the early 1950s, and an outstandingly successful businessman, Phil died in a sprinting accident at Silverstone in November. Ironically, he was driving, not one of the big hairy sports-racing cars with which he had been associated for so long, but the latest in a long line of E-type Jaguars. The impact of his death, hard enough, was made well nigh unbearable for his family and those close to him when his son too was killed in a road accident just the very next day.

With five of the 1974 RAC Championship Top Ten 'declaring', there was no doubt that 1975 would see some big changes in the sport at the highest level, and with the perceptible resurgence of smaller-engined cars in 1974 there seemed at least a possibility that slightly less exotic cars might be in with a chance – although this hope was to prove ephemeral. The competitive spirit saw to that.

Edinburgh architect Alex Brown, 'Pink Mouse' Ginetta G17B, took the 1973 Woking Motors Leaders Championship on a tie-break decision after both he and Alistair Douglas-Osborne had finished up with 72 points.
via DAVE BAKER

'Pink Mouse'. Peter Voigt took the Imp engine out of his successful DRW sports-racer and put it in a Formula 4 Ginetta G17, one of two which appeared on the hills, with great success.
HAYDN SPEDDING

Tony Lambert won his class outright in the 1970 RAC Leaders Hill Climb Championship, driving his Twin-Cam Ginetta G4, seen here storming up Prescott in May.
via TONY LAMBERT

CHAPTER EIGHT

THE PILBEAM ERA
(1975-1983)

IT is a tribute to the lasting appeal of hill climbing and of the congenial surroundings for the major meetings that most of the rather disillusioned-sounding star drivers who announced their retirements at the end of 1974 were unable to resist having a go at some time during 1975! Once the pressures of top-class hill climbing were removed, the sporting enjoyment could still be savoured.

Nevertheless, the elimination from contention of Sir Nicholas Williamson, Mike MacDowel and David Good, in particular, opened the way for other, relatively new 'names' to steal the limelight. While Roy Lane started the new season as favourite with many as 'heir-apparent', Chris Cramer, Alister Douglas-Osborn and leading 1600cc contender David Franklin could be expected to mount major challenges. It is a mark of hill climbing's continuity that these four drivers, together with Martyn Griffiths (who was then still finding his feet with the ex-Good/Thwaites McLaren M10B), were to become something of a hill climb establishment which was not seriously challenged until the mercurial arrival of 20-year old James Thomson in 1981.

But rather than look to individual drivers as dominant features of the intervening, hotly-contested seasons, it would be more realistic to stress the influence of a chassis-designer/builder from Lincolnshire and an engine builder from Essex, both areas hardly central to hill climbing's strongholds. In 1975 the approaches to putting together the ideal hill climbing car remained diverse. Yet eight years on the Top Ten competitors at Pace/RAC Championship rounds were almost all driving purpose-built if Formula 2/3-sized chassis built to individual order by Mike Pilbeam's small operation in Bourne, Lincolnshire. What's more, the majority of the really serious people were relying on motivation from one of Brian Hart's 2.5 or 2.8-litre alloy, four-cylinder 420R-based engines which are distantly related to the Ford BDA, via the Hart alloy-blocked 420R Formula 2 engine, but again specially developed for the hill climbing application to a point where small size, abundant torque and sheer power were combined in virtually the optimum compromise.

After the diversity of the nineteen-sixties and nineteen-seventies – a diversity which, incidently, remains as strong as ever outside the highest echelon of the sport – a position was reached where the Pilbeam-Hart domination attained a supremacy unmatched since the primacy of the Cooper-JAP in the nineteen-fifties. Yet there was no sense of finality about the strength of Pilbeam or Hart, nor was success the overnight sensation of a quantum leap in technology. There was nothing revolutionary about the Pilbeam chassis, nor about the Hart engine. They were steadily and methodically developed by people who understood the special needs of a hill climb car – as opposed to a circuit racer – and who devoted the time needed to develop it away from a circuit-racing basis. It could be argued that one of the main reasons for success was the lack of attention bestowed on hill climbing by other chassis and engine builders, thereby permitting Hart and Pilbeam a unique niche in the competition car market.

In the late nineteen-sixties and nineteen-seventies, the Cooper Car Company (before it ceased to build racing cars), Ron Tauranac of Brabham and later Ralt, and especially Robin Herd of March showed an interest in the special demands of the uphill sprinters, and even found time to build adapted machinery for individual buyers. Robin Herd, in particular, worked with enthusiasm on projects for Chris Cramer, David Franklin and Roy Lane, and by the late nineteen-seventies it was the March which was the most numerous chassis choice among the top drivers. But the pressures of servicing so many competition car markets meant that the 'minor distraction' of hill climbing could not really be justified. For Mike Pilbeam, after his early work on Alister Douglas-Osborn's much-developed Brabham BT38, the position was different. A former BRM (among others) Grand Prix car designer, Pilbeam has always been rather more interested in design than in production chassis for the popular racing formulae. Although he certainly did not set off with the intention of becoming a hill climb specialist when he established his own company, the appeal of designing and developing highly individual cars as distinctive projects on commission was strong. The specialist expertise, built on the sound foundation of years of racing car design experience, had been built up over the years of concentrating primarily on the demands of hill climbers who need superb traction, good low and medium-speed handling, the reduction of the understeer which is endemic at these speeds in the modern wide-wheeled, mid-engined machinery, and the achievement of a commanding driving position so as to place the car very precisely. Although Pilbeam's East Midlands base is far from hill climbing's heartlands, Bourne was of course the home of Raymond Mays. It was here that the pre-war ERAs were built and in more recent years the BRMs too. That's how Mike Pilbeam came to establish himself in the town and since the demise of the BRM operation there have remained a number of experienced specialists who, with their combined knowledge, help to make racing cars something of a 'cottage industry' in the area. It is rather pleasing and wholly appropriate, that most successful hill climb car of the nineteen-eighties can trace its spiritual ancestry back to Raymond Mays.

As for the Hart 420R engine, that was designed by Harlow-based Brian Hart for use in international Formula 2 racing when the FIA dropped the regulation which demanded that 'stock blocks' were employed in the category. A successful racing driver up to Formula 2 level, the prematurely-bald Brian Hart remained primarily an engineer. Before it was eligible for use in F2, Hart's alloy-block, four-cylinder 2.0-litre unit appeared in Chris Cramer's hill climb March, and the impressive characteristics of the engine soon attracted the interest of other hill climbers such as Martyn Griffiths and Ken MacMaster. Although the 420R did go on to become a successful F2 unit, winning the European Formula 2 Championship in the back of Brian Henton's Toleman, Hart, commissioned by the hill climb drivers themselves, went on developing the engine for the hills. Over succeeding years successive 2.2, 2.5 and 2.8-litre versions have seen both power output and, more importantly, low and mid-range torque rise drastically while retaining the light-weight and compact dimensions of the four-cylinder base engine. Yet even so, the developed versions of the Ford/Cosworth DFV V8 remained more than a match on the faster hills, the BMW four-cylinder M12 unit was not far behind, while the 5.0 Repco V8, with scarcity its greatest disadvantage, was to power the 1988 Guyson/RAC Hill Climb Championship. So, just as with the Pilbeam chassis, the domination was not all that secure. One of the fascinations of the next few years will be to see from which direction the ultimately successful challenges will come.

Since 1975, major changes in hill climbing have, as usual, been evolutionary and rarely radical. Only Pontypool Park of the venues which staged major climbs in 1975 is no longer used. The always strong anti-motor sport element in local amenity pressure groups in the area finally overcame the BARC's determination to provide a first-class hill climb venue in Wales. In its place, the energetic and resourceful Aberdeen and District Motor Club succeeded in upgrading Fintray House to RAC Championship stature, thus giving Scotland two courses in the premier series, which eventually stabilised at 16 qualifying rounds.

Costs remained the biggest bugbear and even the loyalty of long-term sponsors such as Guyson, Waring & Gillow, the Duport Group, Newton Oils, Bradburn & Wedge, Cheltenham Cameras, Grampian Television, Shell, Burmah and many more, could not totally insulate the sport from the recession which afflicted Britain in the early nineteen-eighties. Since it is possible to compete in hill climbing for less money than it takes to compete with any hope of success in circuit racing or rallying, entry lists did not shrink in the alarming way that they did in some other spheres. But with sums well in excess of £50,000 quoted as needed to contest the then Pace Petroleum-sponsored RAC Championship with the best equipment for just one season, it was little wonder that by 1983 there was a marked reduction in the number of truly competitive entries tackling the premier Championship. Only a marked upsurge in commercial prospects on a national scale could be expected to reverse that trend.

Fortunately, there was a great increase in the prevalence and popularity of secondary class-based or 'local' Championships in the period, based on the successful precedents of the BARC series and , to a

A strengthened Waring &
Gillow team was headed in
1975 by a new Formula 5000-
derived Chevron-Chevrolet
B32 for John Cussins, seen
here at Wiscombe Park.
BRUCE GRANT-BRAHAM

Although he was not one of the
sport's most consistent
drivers, John Cussins was
undoubtedly fast. He is
photographed being
interviewed by Gurston Down
commentator Richard
Speakman.
BRUCE GRANT-BRAHAM

lesser extent, the Prescott Gold Cup. The Shelsley/Prescott/Loton-based Midland Championship and the Harewood Championship, both well-sponsored, were particularly successful in this context. As a side effect, the increasing importance of class-based championships encouraged the most competitive souls to go all out to produce cars which were designed to be ultra-competitive within a class. This trend was visible from the earliest days of the Castrol/BARC series when Jeff Goodliff chose his classes and his cars so successfully, but now there were a number of people who travelled the country like RAC Championship contenders, and who both provided great spectacle in the class runs and, sadly, made class results all too predictable. While the predictability element is a drawback it is undeniable that more drivers than ever before had a realistic chance of winning a prestigious, thoroughly worthwhile, and actually promotable, championship than was so even ten years earlier.

Returning to 1975, the now traditional H & D LCC Practice Day at Loton Park in March demonstrated that those who feared a sharp fall-off in interest in the RAC Championship had nothing to fear. Roy Lane arrived with his imposing McRae GM1 sporting a new cross-over fuel-injection system on the Alan Smith/Dave Whitehurst-prepared Chevvie engine, and the support of Castrol augmented by sponsorship from Fenny Marine, a manufacturer of canal narrow boats from Fenny Compton, Warwickshire. The car was now to be rechristened the Fenny Marine GM1 and the skilful and astute Lane was set for a fine season. Chris Cramer was another to benefit from additional financial support, this time from Shell, while his March 74B was now fitted with a 2.2-litre version of the experimental Hart engine which he had used the previous season. The extra capacity was obtained by using a rather special new crankshaft and this alloy block unit was to be the forerunner of so many successful 'oversize' Hart 420R alloy block engines. At least as significant, the West Hagley property man Alister Douglas-Osborn had had his Brabham BT38 carefully rebuilt by Mike Pilbeam over the winter and also had more power with a 2.2 iron block BDG engine. Ken MacMaster debuted a brand new 2.0 Modus-Hart M4 from Teddy Savory's rather shortlived Norfolk company, while even before Loton, a greatly strengthened Waring & Gillow team had announced plans for a two-car challenge which was sure to create a strong impression in the furniture company's striking red, green and white livery. John Cussins had commissioned a new Formula 5000-derived one-off, the B32, from Derek Bennett's successful Chevron concern in Bolton. The engine was to be an Alan Smith/Dave Whitehurst-built 5.7 Chevrolet and with an expected 500 bhp the car looked likely to be the most powerful on the hills. Although the car was resprayed to match Cussins', W & G transport manager Malcolm Dungworth retained his effective Brabham-Repco BT35X.

The new season gained another fillip with the last-minute announcement that the BARC Championship, which had seemed likely to remain unsponsored after the withdrawal of Castrol, was to gain the support of the Otley-based manufacturer of light industrial blast-cleaning equipment, Guyson International. Thanks to the successful exploits of Managing Director Jim Thomson as a competitor and support for David Hepworth, Guyson was already well known in the sport but this rather hasty arrangement was to form the basis of an eight-year partnership with the BARC.

Even rain towards the end of the programme failed to dampen excited discussion after the opening

RAC round at Loton on 30 March. Never before considered to be an *outstanding* hill climb car (or even circuit car for that mater), the Pilbeam-rebuilt BT38, guided by the talented ADO, was a revelation. 'Big Al's' class best of 54.57s remained Best Time of Day, and although he spun after the finish on his first RAC climb, knocking off the nose-cone in the process, his 56.44s climb gave him 10 points too. Although his engine sounded rough, Chris Cramer ran him closest on 57.46s. Lane actually matched this time but he missed out on aggregate times. The other shock came when Bristol garage owner David Franklin recorded an exciting 57.58s to beat Cussins, MacMaster, Tony Griffiths, Dungworth *et al* with a mere 1600cc Holbay BDA powering his Huntsman Ensign LNF3.

A week later there was more rain (much more) and further drama at Prescott where the Guyson/BARC series opened its 13-round season. Lane, Cramer and Franklin took the top honours but only after Douglas-Osborn crashed after the finish line once more. This time it happened in practice and ADO really did the job properly, wrecking the monocoque tub of the car but thankfully escaping unscathed. So, the car was sent back to Bourne for another rebuild. Of those who had 'retired' at the end of 1974, Geoff Rollason had already been out at Loton and now Mike MacDowel reappeared although, true to the word of 'the gentleman of hill climbing', Mike was at the wheel of a sports car. He had bought the splendid ex-Bancroft/Scragg Chevron-Alpina B19, and straightway the Champion was most impressive, scoring fifth BTD in the muddy conditions.

After more encouraging wins at Wiscombe Park and Harewood, Roy Lane's challenge was beginning to look unstoppable until the Guyson/BARC series moved to Pontypool Park on 27 April. In the early hours of the morning the finishing touches were being put to the now much modified Pilbeam R15, formerly Brabham BT38. Mike Pilbeam, who is a graduate mathematician and who had just left the BRM team for whom he had put together the original 4WD 670P way back in 1964, had taken the opportunity to save weight on the Brabham while at the same time increasing the suspension travel. This gave the car a softer ride and – most importantly – increasing the traction. The determined Doug-

Waring & Gillow's transport manager Malcolm Dungworth's well-proven Brabham-Repco BT35X appeared in the team's new red, green and white livery in 1975.
BRUCE GRANT-BRAHAM

Richard Brown's beautifully presented and most successful, ex-David Good, Martin BM8 rounds the Karousel at Gurston Down.
BRUCE GRANT-BRAHAM

las-Osborn rewarded all the effort with a 28.17s course record, 0.43s under MacDowel's previous best, a time which was matched by Lane.

Nevertheless, when the BARC Championship resumed at Prescott, the tall, bespectacled engineer from Warwick was back in charge with a 44.98s BTD and with ADO a 'mere' fifth. David Franklin, on a twisty course which well suited the little Ensign, was a splendid runner-up, only 0.25s down on Roy Lane. And more people succumbed to the urge to put on their crash helmets once more. David Good was sharing the wheel of his old Martin BM8 with present owner Richard Brown, Sir Nick Williamson was having an outing in Robert Cooper's Lola Mk1, and Peter Voigt was back at the wheel of the ingenious Voigt-Renwick Special, and setting a 50.41s record in the process. The meeting was remarkable, too, for ending with a woman leading a national hill climb championship for the first time. Diana MacMaster (Ken's wife) earned that honour in the Woking Motors Leaders Championship in her Clan Crusader although it was to be a rather brief lead.

Despite an inoperative clutch release, Chris Cramer benefited from a cleaner-running engine at Wiscombe where he took his first BTD of the year ahead of Lane, while at Barbon, where sponsorship from the local *Lancaster Guardian* newspaper helped to pull in a very large crowd, there was another winner. ADO broke another record at 23.76s on his faster class climb but had to be content with a 24.24s Top Ten best for fourth place just ahead of Peter Voigt who was sharing the Pilbeam. In contrast, John Cussins began by having a driveshaft break on the big Chevron. Not in the best of tempers, he jumped into Malcolm Dungworth's old BT35X and shot up this fast hill in just 23.69s to smash the record again and win the run-off! This performance did make a number of onlookers wonder whether John might not have been better to share the so effective Repco-engined Brabham than to go to the expense of commissioning the seemingly less wieldy Chevron.

1975 was an important year for the Midland Automobile Club for it marked the 70th year of

Shelsley Walsh. The anniversary found the club and the hill in excellent sporting and financial health. The Midlanders were rewarded by a closely-fought June meeting watched by an appreciative crowd which included Raymond Mays, Basil Davenport and Whitney Straight among many other former Shelsley drivers, Both Lane and Cramer clocked 28.94s on their class ascents while in the Top Ten Roy unleashed the big McRae to a 28.74s BTD, just 0.1s faster than Cramer, and with the NJR Installations-backed Pilbeam of ADO on 28.87s. And taking life easier or not, the stylish MacDowel was in the Top Ten yet again with his sports Chevron.

Shelsley also marked the beginning of a tremendous run of success for Lane. He set a 40.55s record at Doune (where Cramer was also under the existing figures); again beat Cramer and Douglas-Osborn at a hot and dusty Harewood; gave the midsummer Shelsley (where ADO scored two BTDs in two days) a miss in favour of the Guyson/BARC round at Scammonden where he won easily and set a 21.97s record despite spinning uncomfortably near his own transporter after the finish line; and defeated Cramer and ADO yet again at Pontypool Park where Richard Brown – happier in the Martin than in the ex-Good Lyncar MS4 which he soon sold – set the fastest sports car time yet in 29.19s.

And the winning streak continued on the Channel Islands. The crucial margin was only 0.02s over the seemingly inevitable Chris Cramer at Bouley Bay, but had opened out to a slightly more comfortable 0.57s at Le Val des Terres, where Richard Shardlow shared ADO's Pilbeam and actually snatched third place from Alister himself on Richard's favourite hill. Roy lifted another Guyson/BARC win at Harewood but like most of the English contingent gave Craigantlet a miss. Martyn Griffiths went, though, and wheeled the big McLaren M10B up the closed public road in 58.59s, fast enough to take second BTD behind Patsy McGarrity's Chevron B29 (57.27s) which gave the Northern Ireland Hill Climb Championship to the successful Formula Atlantic circuit racer.

Alister Douglas-Osborn had already proved himself to be particularly good at Shelsley and when the 'circus' returned in August for the Duport-sponsored meeting his 28.44s best was enough to beat Cramer. But it wasn't enough to master the inevitable Lane who blasted the charismatic orange car to a 28.03s BTD and in so doing clinched the RAC Championship in the best possible way at last after so many years of effort.

Although Chris Cramer had been encouraged by a fine win at Pontypool Park earlier in the month when he had further reduced the record to 27.96s, Lane made it nine RAC wins by maintaining an 0.63s margin over ADO at Gurston Down. At least he showed that he was still human by wiping off the nose of the McRae at the first corner of practice for the Guyson/BARC encounter at Loton on 31 August. After hurried repairs he competed but was narrowly headed by both ADO and Cramer.

The tenth RAC win – not unexpectedly on a hill where he has shone so often – came at Prescott but Roy was the first to admit that the day really belonged to the amazing Peter Voigt. He kicked off by setting a 50.22s class record in the now David Fyfe owned Voigt-Renwick Special which won him the Prescott Gold Cup no less. Not content with this he swapped over to Alister Douglas-Osborn's Pil-

Man at work. Alister Douglas-Osborn concentrates hard in his Temple Row Special, otherwise a Brabham BT38 which, after two major rebuilds, became the Pilbeam R15 and spawned a whole generation of hill climb cars.
BRUCE GRANT-BRAHAM

beam and proceeded to motor the R15 over the line in a resounding 43.76s, a mere 0.06s slower than Lane and second BTD, 0.24s up on the car's long-suffering owner who had now had two guest drivers beat him. It is one of hill climbing's minor tragedies that Voigt, a deceptively mild and slight figure, was never able to run a competitive big single-seater for long enough to have a serious crack at the premier Championship. Runner-up in the Gold Cup competition was Churchdown's effervescent Russ

John Milford was one of the South West's most successful drivers in the mid-nineteen-seventies. Here he cocks a rear wheel on his Mini-Cooper S as he sets a 33.50s Oddicombe record.
BRUCE GRANT-BRAHAM

Ward who had been having another spectacular and highly successful season in the John Brown Motors Sprite, which now boasted a Shorrock supercharger blowing through Weber carburettors.

Still the Roy Lane triumphs continued. Handling and engine bothers hampered him at Wiscombe Park where the BARC's racing-orientated Headquarters team made a rare foray into hill climbing with sponsorship from Langtonian Finance, but they didn't stop him snatching another BTD before proceeding north for the RAC win number 11 despite being afflicted by a broken driveshaft, a puncture and running out of fuel at various points in the meeting.

Roy's 90-point maximum total left him 8 points clear of Chris Cramer who had driven consistently well and whose March-Hart had been impressive once the early season roughness had been exorcised from the engine. Third, on 77 points, came the season's revelation, Alister Douglas-Osborn who was most enthusiastic about the excellent traction provided by his transformed BT38, but was anxious to obtain more power than a BDA-based engine could give him. A 16-point gap to John Cussins emphasised to what extent the season had belonged to Lane, Cramer and ADO. Although fourth place was no mean achievement, John was somehow never *really* convincing in the big Chevron and his season – as usual – was punctuated by a number of car-damaging incidents. He finished 4 marks up on Ken MacMaster who was as neat and unobtrusively fast as ever, while a resounding sixth overall came David Franklin who dominated the 1600cc division despite the increasingly effective and determined opposition which came from the immaculate Brabham BT35s of Peter Kaye (shared with Robert Sunderland) and haulage contractor Rob Turnbull, who was sponsored by B & W Motors, the Brierly Hill Scania truck dealership. Rounding out the coveted Top Ten permanent numbers for 1976 were Malcolm Dungworth, Richard Brown (who was prevented from total sports car domination only by the occasional forays of Mike MacDowel), Tony Griffiths and his unrelated namesake Martyn.

As usual, the Woking Motors Leaders' Championship omitted the RAC rounds which were held outside the Mainland, and gave a worthy win to Alan Richards who had the support of Cheltenham Cameras prominently displayed on his shrieking supercharged 1100cc Gryphon-Ford 3AR. His domination of the 1100cc racing class, despite challenges from the ex-Franklin Dinitrol Vixen of Terry Smith, Sandy Hutcheon's well-tried Ginetta G17 and the hoards of northern-based small single-seaters, was all the more striking as this was one of the best-supported classes of all, often drawing well over 20 entries. One of the comparatively few real crowd-pullers among the 'production' classes, the almost unbelievably-rapid and entertainingly oversteering Sprite of Russ Ward was runner-up while another crowd favourite was third. This was the 25-year-old Mercian Group Cooper-Triumph 500 of Barry Brant, who finished ahead of two highly enthusiastic Scotsmen who covered more miles than most to contest the Championship: Lanark wholesale butcher (and later motor trader), Norrie Galbraith (Ginetta G15) and Thurso farmer Barrogill Angus (Davrian).

With the RAC titles all wound up the scene shifted to Harewood where £500 and the Guyson Sandblast Trophy awaited the winner of the Guyson/BARC Championship, and a further £300 was destined for the FTD Awards winner. To nobody's surprise Roy Lane set BTD from John Cussins, while Mike MacDowel had a run in the big Chevron and set sixth BTD. Roy thus added the Guyson/BARC FTD Awards title to his RAC Championship, scoring 57 points to the 50 of Cramer, 43 of David Franklin and 27 of ADO and Peter Kaye. However, to Franklin went the premier award in the Guyson/BARC Championship – no mean achievement with the 1600cc racing class bogey times to overcome – so it was rather a pity that David chose to miss the meeting in favour of an RAC Championship sprint at Yeovilton. In a particularly busy season, the Bristolian also contrived to finish runner-up in this series as well, beaten only by his fellow Bristolian Dave Harris. Franklin's 56.96 Guyson/BARC marks remained 0.88 mark clear of Haverfordwest's fastest dentist, Stuart Watts who made a late charge with his Lotus Elan to beat another Elan, that of Guy Brooker. In fourth and fifth places were the fast Minis of Ford employee Colin Rogers and former motorcyclist John Meredith. Lane was sixth, from Nicky Porter who was now about to discard his remarkable 11-year-old Mini for an ex-Tour-of-Britain Mercedes 280E for some rallying exploits; Lancastrian newcomer Brian Walker (Ford Escort RS1600), the similar car of Richard White and Alan Cox's John Brown Motors Mini. The series ended with Jim Thomson promising bigger and better things for 1976, although a slightly sour note was struck by a petition circulating in the Paddock advocating a 40% cubic capacity equivalence penalty for cars which were supercharged. This vexed topic was always good for some lively controversy.

Of the regional Championships, the now well-established Scottish series was won by Alan Thomson's rapid and well-driven Holbay Twin-Cam-engined Chevron B17, while Lancastrian Bob Speak kept a Lotus Europa long enough to clean up the Longton & DMC Championship in a year when he broke 14 class records to head Croxdale, Durham veteran Bob Prest – successful in such varied machinery as Formula Junior Elva, Lotus 7, Formula Ford Dulon and, latterly, his very fast, self-prepared Mallock U2 – and the Mini-Cooper S of John Casey.

With 24 BTDs from 29 starts, the 40-year-old Roy Lane enjoyed a truly phenomenal year. His domination was even more total than that of Mike MacDowel the previous season, and his success was especially popular for this canny midlander always combined generous sportsmanship and extrovert good humour with a gritty competitiveness and a rare ability to make by no means unlimited personal financial resources stretch a very long way. His immaculate car preparation also remained a byword to the extent that at the time of his success with the McRae he was also looking after the sprint cars of Dave Harris, Bob Rose and Johnty Williamson, with all the work carried out in a 20 foot x 20 foot garage at his home in Warwick, in his 'spare' time. And all this was in addition to his everyday work as foreman in charge of the inspection of finished machines at Banford Ltd, the Warwick manufacturer of construction plant. Of course, it was all made easier and immensely enjoyable by the total support, both at home and on the hills of his family; wife Betty, son Anthony and daughter Julie who were as much a part of the hill climb scene as Roy himself.

Lane versus ADO

Far from losing the competitive edge after such a remarkable season, Roy's appetite for success and for the sport remained as strong as ever and he proposed to campaign the 'Mighty McRae' once again in 1976, although this time with additional support from Goodyear, for whom he would be testing tyres with stiffer sidewalls and different tread patterns in an effort to eliminate undesirable understeer. This support did not interfere with the continued backing of Peter Else at Fenny Marine.

Lane's triumph with a big, well-sorted F5000 car persuaded many that sheer power was again the answer. Alister Douglas-Osborn, still only 27 and now enjoying the sponsorship of his brother's company, Motosail (Jersey) had his Pilbeam R15 used as a basis for a 'stretched' R22 which was fitted with a full Cosworth DFV engine. Alister's special 'tweak' once he had become used to DFV power was to fit ex-Gulf Mirage camshafts which in terms of power and characteristics were midway between the Grand Prix tune (with which Geoff Rollason had battled so gamely) and the sports car/Le Mans components which had been used by Williamson and Good. The other member of 1975's leading trio, Chris Cramer, had also opted for more power although he had chosen quite another route with the continued backing of Grünhalle Lager and Shell. He had been attracted by the mid-range punch of the 400 plus bhp of the Ford Essex-based Cosworth GA V6 unit, descended from those in the superb Ford Capris from Cologne but now being utilised in F5000. The chassis was an F5000 March 76A, itself closely related to the contemporary F1 761, and with March's Robin Herd taking a close interest in the project to the extent that what was tried on Hans Stuck's Grand Prix car tended to be seen on Chris's car a couple of weeks later. The March-GA looked and sounded fabulous, and was rapidly dubbed 'the flagship of the hills', but there remained the niggling doubt that the car might just fall between the two extremes of power and agility.

The March concern really looked set to make a big impression for after but one year away from the Championship action Sir Nick Williamson was coming back with his old DFV engine mounted in the back of an ex-Hans Stuck F1 March 741 and Guyson/BARC Champion David Franklin moved up into the big class with the ex-Patrick Depailler F2 March-BMW after selling his successful Ensign to former Mini and Anglia circuit racer Ted Williams. David was enabled to make the move thanks to sponsorship from Wendy Wools, the brand name of Yorkshire textile company Carter & Parker Ltd, which was headed by long time enthusiast and senior BARC and RAC official Peter Griffin. Almost inevitably Franklin was dubbed 'the fastest knit', although a more favoured slogan to be found on the car at one stage was 'Baldies are best', an allusion to David's thinning locks.

It was bidding fair to be a stunning season with Ken MacMaster laying hands on one of the rare 2.2 Hart 420R engines for the Modus; Alan Richards retaining his Cheltenham Cameras support while exchanging the tiny Gryphon for the exceedingly large ex-Team Surtees/Alan McKechnie F5000 Surtees TS8; John Stuart buying Richard Brown's Martin BM8 while Brown commissioned Brian Martin to build him a short-wheelbase single-seater, the BM16, to take an ex-Tommy Reid Chevrolet Vega en-

Alister Douglas-Osborn's Pilbeam R15 was used as a basis for his 1976 mount, the Cosworth DFV-engined R22. Here he rounds Barbon's hairpin.
MARGARET DUFF

gine which Cosworth had been developing without a great deal of success; Martyn Griffiths selling his old McLaren to businessman and entrepreneur Godfrey Crompton and buying the ex-Cramer March 74B, and Tony Griffiths deciding on a limited season with the 1.8 Brabham Ford BT38 which John Hinley had campaigned. After a restricted but highly competitive season with the Chevron Mike Mac-Dowel had obtained the Ralt RT1 which Larry Perkins had used in Formula 3 but fitted with a secondhand 2.0 Hart engine. Since Mike held the old Brabham chassis in high regard it was no surprise to find him choosing a Ralt, the latest machine to be designed by Ron Tauranac after the break-up of the old MRD set up. Nevertheless, the Godalming driver was almost apologetic about the move: "It's contrary to my general belief that a big-engined car is the thing to have, but that's just not practical because of the money involved".

Also back after a much longer absence from top-class hill climbing was Bryan Eccles, who was not unnaturally all too aware of the increase in costs over the time when he could run his Cooper-JAP for a season and actually make a small profit on the strength of the prize money which he won! Bryan had bought the ex-MacDowel/Voigt/Fyfe/Brown Palliser – mainly for the Repco engine – but had discovered that the chassis was not as bad as he had been led to believe. Unhappily, his comeback was all too brief for at Wiscombe in April he had a horrifying accident when the differential may have seized, causing the car to veer off into the trees. The ensuing crash severely injured Eccles and he had to have a leg amputated.

Bryan Eccles' accident apart, 1976 fulfilled all expectations, providing a magnificently competitive season. Moreover, fierce competition in the RAC Leaders, Guyson/BARC and Longton & DMC Championships in particular ensured that it was not just the glamorous large-capacity single-seaters which were in the limelight. The exploits of Russ Ward and his howling supercharged Sprite, the newly-built Marshall & Frazer-prepared Mini-Cooper S of John Meredith, and the meteoric performances of a relative newcomer, the aimiable, pipe-smoking Charles Barter were especially notable. A watercress grower from Dorset, Charles with his brother Robert were campaigning an apparently unremarkable Hartwell-prepared Hillman Imp which was ex-David Franklin and had originally been prepared for autocrosses. The Barters, Meredith and Wood hit the headlines almost as often as the RAC front runners. Apart from fully justifying the often rather complicated class-based championships, this situation emphasised the great strength in depth in the sport.

The season was graced by truly superb weather which allowed all concerned to savour the beautiful surroundings in which most hill climbs are situated, and to put away the wet weather tyres which had now become an integral and expensive part of the sport. On weekend after weekend everyone set off to events in cloudless early morning sunshine secure in the certainty that it was going to stay that way throughout the event. It was all most un-British and it is small wonder that 1976 is still instantly recalled when sustained good weather seems to be in the offing.

As was now customary, the Guyson/BARC opener at Prescott, on 4 April that year, formed a dress rehearsal for the season. This time it was dry, the entry was first class and only Championship sponsor Jim Thomson had reason to feel frustrated. His Blydenstein Firenza, the rather special former Bill Dryden circuit car, had suffered a major blow-up at Harewood at the end of the previous year, a mishap which produced the unusual phenomenon of a V-shaped connecting rod, and the car was still not ready for competition again. In fact, Jim was to have a rather scrappy season due to preoccupations with setting up Guyson's new manufacturing plant in America, although the Championship he was sponsoring had an excellent season.

Russ Ward took an initial Championship lead with his 120 bhp (at the wheels) Sprite, the little yellow and blue car now a real crowd-puller with its distinctive engine note, phenomenal acceleration, and the flamboyant handling by the Churchdown driver. John Meredith captured his first headline of the year, too, but not in the style to which he would become accustomed. His new lightweight Mini was not yet ready so he shared his old 'Touring' model, with the new owner Terry Tattam, a cheerful cockney motor trader. Far from showing Terry how it should be done, John parked it rather neatly on its side, fortunately with minimal damage. As this was Prescott, it was only to be expected that Roy Lane would set BTD. He did on 44.79s but only after coming from behind as he found the handling rather erratic on his new Goodyears. David Franklin was most impressive in the Wendy Wools March and edged Chris Cramer out of second place after the architect had won the class but had graunched the nose of the rich-sounding March-GA on his final climb when the throttle stuck open momentarily.

Chris Cramer's Cosworth GA V6-engined March 76A looked and sounded fabulous. This is at Le Val des Terres.
BOB COOPER

Russ Ward's spectacular supercharged Austin Healey Sprite was unable to sustain an early Guyson/BARC Championship lead, but did win the 1976 RAC Leaders title.
AUTHOR

Ken MacMaster was only 0.01s slower than Cramer, beating Martyn Griffiths, while Alister Douglas-Osborn was feeling his way with the Pilbeam-DFV in sixth place, finding the handling rather unpredictable.

One week later and the RAC Championship was under way down at Wiscombe where Sir Nick Williamson made his return in the most emphatic manner. He damaged the nose of the March 741 in practice, was as hairy as ever and set a blistering 38.82s best which only Roy Lane managed to beat with a sizzling 38.57s which smashed the course record. A typically neat MacMaster was next, from Cussins, ADO and Richard Brown's new Martin-Vega but Chris Cramer was in trouble, running F2-type tyres to try to spare the driveshafts which had proved to be unequal to the strain of transmitting those 400 bhp through larger, grippier tyres.

Harewood at Easter showed that ADO was getting the Pilbeam R22 sorted out, as he was only 0.07s slower than Roy Lane on Roy's 'other' hill. Unfortunately it was rather a destructive meeting with John Cussins knocking off two corners of the big Chevron in practice when Sherburn-in-Elmet Jaguar specialist Fred Cliffe also damaged his newly, – and immaculately, – built Jaguar E-type. Then during the meeting proper Don Robinson wrecked his McLaren M10B when the F5000 car got away from him on Quarry Straight.

Not since Barbon Manor in May 1975 had Roy Lane been defeated in an RAC Championship round, but on 19 April he finally met his match at Loton Park. Roy climbed the long Shropshire hill in 53.88s but Alister Douglas-Osborn powered the Pilbeam-DFV over the finish line in just 51.82s, a narrow enough winning margin but particularly commendable in such a new car and especially so as the burly Alister had lost time at Keepers on his first climb. The taciturn advertising agency director Martyn Griffiths was on good form too, whipping the smart blue Severn Advertising March-Hart up in 53.95s, narrowly beating Franklin, MacMaster and Cramer – 0.45s covering all six. Williamson hit the barriers on his first Championship climb but was seventh next time up, beaten by... David Hepworth! The bluff Yorkshireman dusted off (literally) the positively antique looking Hepworth 4WD yet again and made everyone keep a sense of proportion by snatching sixth BTD in the class runs.

The 2.2 Hart 420R engine had made quite a difference to Ken MacMaster's performances in the Modus, although he was as neat, precise and generally unobtrusive as ever. Roy Lane gave the first Guyson/BARC round of the year at Pontypool Park a miss, but most of the other leading drivers were present, so Ken's BTD in 28.22s, ahead of ADO and the tall-sliding Franklin was a most worthy win. Nevertheless when the RAC circus reassembled at Prescott Lane was back in charge. It was the spectacular Williamson who got closest to Roy's 43.67s BTD, and with MacMaster's red Modus next up. Before the next round at Barbon, the two-meetings-in-two-days affair run by the Five Clubs at Wiscombe gave morale-boosting wins for Williamson and Chris Cramer who at least seemed to be making some headway in his search for better traction from the blaring Grünhalle Larger March. Roy Lane again made the trip to Scammonden Dam for the Guyson/BARC counter but it was to no avail for his throttle stuck open in practice and with evidence of water in one cylinder prudence dictated a regretted withdrawal, leaving the meeting to the 'spear carriers', headed by Garstang driver John Barratt who now campaigned a Cosworth FVA-engined Ensign LNF3. A fortnight later, most of the big names were chasing Guyson/BARC points at Gurston Down. Here the sheer bhp of the fastest cars was awesome to behold as they swooped away downhill from the start. Benefiting from the 'middle sports' Piper camshafts, ADO made his point and beat Lane by 0.82s, and with Cramer only another 0.02s behind the Fenny Marine GM1. Earlier in the day, Alister had the disconcerting experience of having to slow right down when a pheasant exercised its right of way in front of the Pilbeam!

There could be no doubt that the opposition had caught up with Roy Lane, and confirmation came at Barbon where the Westmorland MC were celebrating the course's 25th Anniversary with a new track surface and sponsorship from Fermanite Ltd. Lane beat ADO, 23.89s to 24.41s but Cramer also clocked 23.89s for a rare tie for BTD, a dead heat which was resolved on aggregate times to Cramer's advantage. Gurston, Barbon and Shelsley are all 'power' courses, so a similar battle was on the cards as a huge 10,000 crowd eagerly anticipated a fine Duport Group-sponsored meeting at the Worcestershire course. They were not disappointed. Alister Douglas-Osborn shattered the course record in 27.92s in the class climbs, a meteoric time which nobody could match during the RAC runs. Nevertheless, ADO was little slower and his 28.04s edged out Lane by a minuscule 0.06s and Chris Cramer by 0.5s and with Williamson and Franklin well in contention.

Roy Lane reasserted himself over ADO at the second Guyson/BARC Pontypool meeting, setting a 27.62s course record, before everyone trooped up to Scotland to compete at Doune in treacherous conditions in a meeting which was marred for everyone by a series of snags and delays, and for Martyn Griffiths by yet another in an interminable series of broken driveshafts. This time Douglas-Osborn had the edge and his 40.15s was another record, leaving Lane and Doune expert Mike MacDowel with the minor placings. Scots enthusiasts were jubilant when Allan Thomson defeated Rob Turnbull (who had taken over from David Franklin as the dominant force in the 1600cc class with the yellow and black B & W Brabham BT35) on the class climbs, although the tall Midlander turned the tables in the RAC climbs.

By the time the premier series reached Harewood, ADO had yet another record added to his growing collection (Loton Park in 53.33s) but in Yorkshire the West Hagley driver was forced down to third place in front of a disappointingly small crowd. After all, Harewood was Lane domain and the sun-tanned Roy was uncatchable on 38.72s. Harewood's preponderance of medium-speed corners and short straight rewards precise driving, which suited MacMaster. Nevertheless, he looked so neat and unflurried, nobody expected the 38.83s time which gave him second BTD. Alister Douglas-Osborn had not been entirely happy at Harewood, being unable to diagnose a new inconsistency in the Pilbeam's handling. This was finally traced to a defective shock absorber, and all was in order for the second day of the Newton Oils/Forward Lubricants July meeting at Shelsley, which incorporated a Guyson/BARC round for the first time. On the Saturday, when the emphasis was on pre-war cars, ADO set a spectacular 28.02s BTD on a day when many of the old hands paid a visit to Shelsley in the sunshine, and when Chris Dowson – who was having an excellent season with the supercharged, ex-Johnstone Brabham BT15 – delighted everyone by bringing out his father's famous Lightweight Special for a competitive airing. The following day truly belonged to 'Big Al'. With the duff shocker finally located and replaced he charged up to a fantastic 27.12s in practice. In the class climbs he was a little slower but 27.64s still set a new course record. His final Top Eight run looked faster yet, but as everyone waited with bated breath for the time there came the anti-climactic announcement that the timing had malfunctioned. Alister was clearly unsettled, for his re-run was very wild and he had to be content with the course record at a 'mere' 27.64s. In sharp contrast, poor Roy Lane crashed badly when some new tyres set up a vibration away from the start so bad that it caused Roy's vision to blur causing him to lose control and crash, fortunately without hurting himself.

Up until now the season, although particularly hard fought, had followed a fairly predictable pattern, but this changed over in the Channel Islands. At Bouley Bay Sir Nick Williamson, sporting a newly rebuilt DFV showed that he was still a major force by taking control with a 42.12s course record to head Lane, Cramer and ADO, while over on Guernsey a new and rather-to-smooth track surface caused big traction problems for the most powerful cars. David Franklin took the opportunity to snatch his first RAC win in 33.87s, while Cramer came the nearest to solving the prevailing problem by fitting hand-cut slicks to his March and recording 33.99s, which was matched exactly by Mike MacDowel. While most of the top names were making their way back to the mainland, the strength of the big single-seater class was well demonstrated by a magnificent battle at Gurston Down where 0.05s covered former AC Cobra driver Tony Brown's ex-MacDowel Brabham-Repco BT36X, Richard Jones who was consistently doing wonders with his underpowered 2.0 Hart BDA-engined Surtees TS10, and Terry Smith who had just bought Roy Lane's old 5.7 McLaren-Chevrolet M14D from Bob Rose, and was flinging it about as though he had driven it all season.

There was another RAC shock at Pontypool Park where ADO lost time on the crucial RAC runs after setting a 27.87s BTD earlier on, and found himself shunted down to third in the Top Ten runs behind Ken MacMaster (29.07s) and Mike MacDowel (28.10s) who made the most of their delicate car control on a smooth and dusty surface. Once again the Englishmen gave Craigantlet a miss, leaving Patsy McGarrity (Chevron B29) to set a 55.34s course record, although it was Derek Shortall (Vista

Chris Dowson had an excellent season with his supercharged, ex-Jim Johnstone, Brabham BT15.

BOB COOPER

Early morning paddock scene at Loton Park. The author's BMW 2002 is in the left foreground.
AUTHOR

Two cheerful characters in the Loton Park Paddock in 1976: John Meredith and Russ Ward. It was a very hot summer in 1976, hence Russ's unusual headgear.
AUTHOR

John Meredith, Mini-Cooper S, came close to winning the 1976 Guyson/BARC Championship, but did win the Prescott Gold Cup. Here he rounds Triangle at Loton Park.
AUTHOR

Chevron B27) who was dominating most of the Irish events at the time.

Shelsley Walsh was enjoying a superb season, and the undoubted star was Alister Douglas-Osborn. He had left unfinished business in July and on another record breaking day in August he broke the course record for the third successive meeting, leaving it at 27.39s – still slightly slower than his July practice best. Both Roy Lane and Chris Cramer broke the 28s barrier, while there was much praise too for Richard Jones who was fourth on 28.77s despite his formidable power disadvantage. Alister was well into a winning streak having tamed the DFV for hill climb use like nobody else. He won at Loton when the Guyson/BARC Championship returned, although he was only 0.6s up on an inspired Peter Kaye who was now having some tremendous 1600cc battles in his superbly-prepared red Brabham BT35X with Rob Turnbull. There was an unaccustomed dampness in the air when the RAC Championship visited Gurston, but Alister was still on top, from Lane.

Yet when the series returned to Prescott, the pressure was on ADO for Lane had been stacking up the points and Alister had to win to keep in the hunt for the title, a task made no easier by a swollen hand after being bitten by a dog.

In any case Prescott was not the ideal course for the Pilbeam, although Lane, too, was in trouble with gearbox problems, and also suffered a surprise defeat in the previous day's cycle-race up the hill at the hands of London builders merchant John Hart who had been turning in some fast and spectacular performances during the season with an FVA-engined Brabham BT18. It was a surprise defeat because Roy had been a very successful racing cyclist long before he had attained hill climbing stardom. On the crucial Championship climbs Roy managed 43.58s which was more than enough for him to retain the Championship since ADO could not better 44.50s, behind Richard Brown – finally getting some results from the difficult Martin BM16 – and Martyn Griffiths. But they were all eclipsed by a simply amazing climb from David Franklin, including an alarming amount of sideways motoring on the way to a remarkable 42.92s course record. The meeting also saw the significant arrival on the hill climb scene of M & H Racemaster tyres, on Peter Kaye's Brabham, and a truly worthy Prescott Gold Cup winner in John Meredith who had set the first ever sub-50s Saloon time with his Mini-Cooper S which was at last breaking the old Chris Cramer records which had stood for so long. Runners-up in this competition were Russ Ward and Barry Brant.

Although he lost the RAC Championship, ADO was in many people's eyes the man of the year and he then proceeded to clinch the Guyson/BARC FTD Awards series by setting a 38.48s course record at a desperately long-drawn-out Wiscombe meeting and then winning the RAC finale at Doune with another record – 39.62s to the 40.27s of the seemingly inevitable Mike MacDowel. Lane had been a circumspect fifth, having sold the McRae to sprinter Dave Harris but he could not be beaten for the title even though both he and Alister ended the season with 84 points apiece and Alister had set 7 Championship BTDs to Roy's 3. When the tie-deciding dropped scores came into play Lane had the advantage. After a season of much experimenting (he ran at Doune with an F1 rear wing and ground-effect-inducing clear plastic skirts), Chris Cramer was third on 70 points, with Franklin fourth (66), then MacDowel (61), Williamson (61), MacMaster (60), Griffiths (48), Cussins (40 after a rather indifferent season) and Turnbull (25, with the best 1600cc car).

Another tie-decider was needed to settle the RAC Leaders' Championship, and the series finally fell to 31-year-old electrical engineer Russ Ward with the same total of 72 points (from 8 maximum scores) as Chris Dowson who was another example of a rather large man doing exceptionally well in a very small car, – the venerable but still highly effective Penrhos Court Wine-sponsored Brabham BT15. John Meredith was six points adrift with his lightweight Mini, but well ahead of Stuart Watts' rapid Lotus Elan and the old 500cc cars of Barry Brant (Cooper-Triumph) and Tim Cameron (Joe Potts Special).

With Leeds printer John Crowson (Gunk-sponsored Terrapin) having secured a hard fought Longton Championship from Derbyshire MG Midget driver Des Richardson, there remained only the Guyson/BARC title to settle at the end of September. Before Harewood there was only 0.11 mark in it with Charles Barter leading John Meredith. The early part of the season had seen Russ Ward on top but an elusive and crippling mid-season misfire, cured with the aid of different spark plugs, was a severe setback for the jovial extrovert from Gloucestershire. All the while, John Meredith was putting up record-breaking performances in the Marshall & Frazer-prepared Mini which he was sharing with haulage contractor Bob Forth, and so was the by-no-means super-light, but extremely well-sorted Golden

Springs Watercress Imp of Charles Barter and brother Robert. The Barters were former Production-car trial exponents and were in only their second season of hill climbing with the Imp. Robert was always pretty fast by any standards but tended to be overshadowed by Charles who was a real revelation, turning in record breaking performances with absolute consistency and almost clockwork precision. According to the BARC(Y) rules he was still a novice in May but his superiority at the Novices' Harewood meeting, where he set BTD, was almost embarrassing! Despite some superb performances from Stuart Watts and Anthony Boshier-Jones (especially by the latter in the hard-fought Clubman's Sports Class at Loton Park and elsewhere) it was a fight between Barter and Meredith at the last.

With the benefit of hindsight, the crucial moment can be seen to have come at Wiscombe Park early in September when Meredith's Mini got out of phase going though the Esses and dived far off into the trees and bushes. John missed all the big ones and with the help of a band of eager bodies – including the Barters – managed to patch up the slightly damaged Mini in time for the afternoon's sport. Nevertheless, John was the first to admit that his nerves were well and truly jangled by what had been a very big 'off' in daunting surroundings and was perceptibly subdued whereas Barter was on top form, and came out with that 0.11 mark advantage. Harewood was a big anti-climax, for torrential rain in practice brought a lot of mud onto the course and although it dried out for the Sunday, the slippery track ruled out the sort of time which would have been needed to alter the position. Barter was Guyson/BARC Champion and BTD man (39.59s to Lane's 39.85s) ADO set the final seal on his richly deserved FTD Awards title. Light relief came from former Castrol/BARC Champion Chris Seaman whose photographic commitments were now making it very difficult for him seriously to contest the major championships. On one run his MG Midget shot out of Farmhouse in the accustomed rapid Seaman manner, only to start snaking all over the road before coming to an unaccountable halt. The

Charles Barter's extremely rapid and ultra-consistent driving in the Hartwell Imp, which he shared with his brother Robert, was a revelation in 1976.
BOB COOPER

Anthony Boshier-Jones was a major talent hindered by a lack of finance. He put up some superb performances in his smart Mallock U2 Mk11B.
AUTHOR

Anthony Boshier-Jones.
AUTHOR

mystery was solved when Chris's pale face appeared through the window, followed by a hand weakly waving the steering wheel!

The final Championship scoreboard, behind Charles Barter and Meredith, put Stuart Watts in third place, ahead of Russ Ward and 25-year-old Anthony Boshier-Jones who had emerged on top of a fiercely contested Clubman's category which had provided one more highlight during the year. Still using the ex-David Rudkin U2 Mk11B, with Ian Walker Racing-prepared engine, Anthony had put in some really ten-tenths drives during the year including one absolutely stunning record at Loton which had left him literally shaking. Unfortunately, money was short and he was resigned to the sheer impossibility of finding enough to run the sort of single-seater which would now be needed if he were to emulate the RAC Championship performances of his brothers. ADO was sixth in the 'handicap' Championship, just ahead of Terry Tattam who was becoming consistent as well as fast in Meredith's old Mini, the underrated Robert Barter, and U2 drivers Jeremy Hunt and Brian Moyse. With additional fierce competition from Northerners Bob Prest and Mervyn Bartram, the Clubman's category had been one of the fiercest fought, yet the RAC still declined to provide a separate Leaders class for the pushrod-engined U2s.

Alister Douglas-Osborn ended up with a 5 point margin in the FTD Awards Championship, and with Roy Lane no fewer than 22 points clear of Richard Jones – another to achieve a great deal on strictly limited finance – and Franklin, Griffiths and Turnbull rounding out the first six.

After such a magnificent year, crowded with all the best elements in the sport, 1977 promised little slackening of the pace. Although the RAC series still remained unsponsored, Guyson announced greater support for the BARC title chase. The winner would not only take a £1000 cash award, but would also have the basis of his own small business for he would also win a Guyson GBS4 Beadblaster, blast-cleaning machine. The now well respected regional series run by the enterprising Longton & DMC carried on with excellent prize money, financed by the club's own successful activities, and in Scotland the absence of Burmah Oil was compensated for by Grampian Television support for the eight-round Scottish Championship. Contested at Doune, Fintray, Kinkell Braes and Rumster, this well contested series could now look forward to greater media publicity than it had during the last couple of years.

As usual the lessons of the previous season were not lost on the leading competitors as they strove to find ways of chipping further fractions off their times, or ways of catching up with better-equipped ri-

vals. Roy Lane at last decided to go the DFV route and bought Nick Williamson's March 741, for the popular Baronet had decided to retire once more. Being Roy, he meticulously rebuilt the March, fitting Formula 5000 type wide nose and a new rear wing before turning the car out in the Fenny Marine colours. Business commitments forced John Cussins to decide to give up driving although Waring & Gillow were to continue to back a two-car team managed by Malcolm Dungworth and fettled by Dave Elliott. Malcolm was to retain the old Brabham-Repco but instead of the Chevron B32, the team took under its banner Alister Douglas-Osborn's formidable Pilbeam-DFV MP22, with both cars turned out in a new predominantly white livery, with green and red striping, to match the company's commercial vehicles. Chris Cramer had often seemed on the very brink of a breakthrough with the charismatic March-GA 76A during the previous season and over the winter the car was given a thorough rebuild by Mike Pilbeam with a view to making it more wieldy and endowing it with better traction. When the car reappeared it sported a shorter wheelbase, a Ferrari F1-type scoop nose and a re-designed rear wing which combined to make it seem a much smaller car. Of course this was the time when the motor racing world was becoming almost obsessed by the magic words 'ground effect'. Even at the comparatively low speeds achieved on the tight British hills there were benefits to be had by inducing more downforce on the cars. On the other hand the calculations needed to be fairly precise – otherwise the advantage would be totally cancelled out with the onset of the dread understeer.

Another driver to beat a path to Bourne for the Pilbeam treatment was Martyn Griffiths who reappeared with the March 74B looking superb in the dark blue, red and white Severn Advertising livery. If there was one driver who might have regretted the dry 1976 summer it was probably Ken MacMaster. When grip was at a premium and delicate control was more advantageous than sheer power and extrovert handling, the Modus had been a formidable contender. Although there were no major changes to the car, Ken had had it rebuilt by designer Jo Marquart for the new season. David Franklin, too, retained his F2 March-BMW 742 while Richard Jones was hoping for greater things by fitting a turbocharger to his McEvoy Oilfield Equipment-sponsored Surtees. Further backing from Kingswinford, Staffordshire motor dealers Bradburn & Wedge (B & W Motors) enabled Rob Turnbull to move into the over 1600cc racing class with a new Ralt RT1 fitted with a 2.0 Cosworth BDG engine, the record-breaking Brabham going to Tony Street.

Outside the top class the big news was that at long last the much-discussed 40 per cent supercharging penalty (naturally to include cars with the increasingly fashionable exhaust-driven turbochargers used to achieve forced induction) was applied for the major series. One of those most affected, Chris Dowson, managed to stay in the 1100cc racing class by the ingenious expedient of having his Cosworth/Ford engined linered down to 784cc, an operation which certainly did nothing to reduce the noise level!

Alister Douglas-Osborn, the pre-season favourite for the RAC title, had been the fastest at the pre-season get-together at Loton Park, but when the Guyson/BARC Championship opened at Prescott, ADO was not really in the running. Instead, David Franklin repeated his September win in 45.72s, although he was only 0.06s faster than Roy Lane who was making an excellent start with the March 741, beating Cramer, an on form Malcolm Dungworth in the so-torquey Brabham-Repco, and Mike MacDowel. Peter Kaye, whose Brabham BT35X had also received attention from Mike Pilbeam, made the Top Eight and looked set for a year of 1600cc racing car domination now that main rival Rob Turnbull had moved on. The main 1976 Guyson/BARC contenders were back again with the Barters

Informal course side prizegivings round off many hill climbs. Charles Barter collects the first of many championship pots; this one was for the 1976 Guyson/BARC Series. The substantial figure – in both senses – of Mike Wilson is beside him.
AUTHOR

At the same Harewood prize-giving, Alister Douglas-Osborn keeps everyone amused as he clutches the FTD Awards Trophy. Championship sponsor Jim Thomson is on the far right, while the youngster in the middle is a teenage James Thomson.
AUTHOR

The glorious red AC Cobra of Paul Channon – a feature at hill climbs for many years – leaves the Loton Park startline.
AUTHOR

remaining with the Hartwell Imp despite the prospect of having to tackle Charles' own records now. John Meredith had upped the engine capacity of his Mini to 1428cc while Russ Ward had gone so far as to fit an Arkley SS shell with his Sprite mechanicals and, since the resulting yellow and blue car bore a striking resemblance to a certain 'literary' creation of Enid Blyton, Russ had to endure many references to 'Big Ears' and 'Noddy'.

Before the first RAC counter at Loton Park, a very wet meeting at Harewood saw Roy Lane manage BTD in 46.26s (it was that wet), but the premier Championship got off to a good start with a well-promoted meeting drawing some 4,000 spectators who saw that Martyn Griffiths' money had been well spent with Mike Pilbeam. The Charles Lashford-tended March looked superb and Martyn looked like Championship material with a 53.21s course record. ADO was close on 53.36s while both Lane and Franklin were in the low 54s. Peter Kaye dropped a valve after securing eighth place in the Top Ten on a course which always seemed to suit him, but Chris Cramer was really unlucky. He scored no points after a minor 'off' had more serious consequences when a piece of loose tarmac dented the tub and pulled off an oil pipe.

There was no time to mull over the Loton results as the AMOC round at Wiscombe was only a week later. Sponsored by Aston Martin Lagonda who provided a glorious V8 Vantage model for Stirling Moss to open the course, round 2 went firmly to Douglas-Osborn in 38.66s but there was a big surprise when Richard Brown took second place with 39.25s in the hitherto rather troublesome Martin BM16. In fact, Richard had been testing at Wiscombe where he was a director and the development work had obviously paid off, as had the extra practice for the driver. Martyn Griffiths emphasised that he was going to be a major force during the year but had to be content with a 39.34s best when he suffered a puncture as he crossed the finishing line.

One of the charms of hill climbing is that within well-established national Championships, courses

Rob Turnbull moved into the over 1600cc racing car class in 1977, but never matched his previous success in the Brabham BT35. Pictured here at Prescott.
BOB COOPER

Martyn Griffiths had entrusted his March 74B to Mike Pilbeam to be revamped for 1977.
BOB COOPER

and clubs remain highly individualistic. In most cases organisers are pure amateurs and are understandably proud of the traditions and achievements of their own particular clubs and venues. The obverse of this particular coin is that a certain insularity, not to say parochialism can intrude among people who rarely look beyond their own particular 'corner'. For example, there was the rather embarrassing occasion one year at Barbon where the Westmorland MC allocated the coveted numbers 1 to 10 to mere saloon cars before someone had a quiet word. Even the longest-established and most distinguished clubs have their idiosyncrasies. One such is the Bugatti Owners Club and for many years competitors with production-based cars somehow got the impression that at Prescott if you weren't driving a racing car, a Bugatti or a Ferrari you were there rather on sufferance. The author certainly never had that impression when racing Haydn Spedding's E-type Jaguar but maybe the odd die-hard

Once his perennial rival Rob Turnbull had moved on, there was no stopping Peter Kaye in 1977 driving his Pilbeam-modified 1.6 Brabham BT35X.
BOB COOPER

Bugattiste really does think that is the case. The impression certainly gained credence when the BOC announced that, as an experiment, the May meeting would be run as a two-day affair with the saloons and sports cars running on the Saturday, leaving the Sunday for more glamorous things. In the event, virtually no spectators turned up on the Saturday, it rained on Sunday, there was an almost total lack of the usual delightful Prescott atmosphere on either day and the experiment was not repeated. David Franklin made it three in a row at the Gloucestershire hill with a 52.71s BTD, but with ADO showing much better Prescott form with 52.89s and MacDowel benefiting from the conditions with a 53.83s third place. Interestingly, there were three newcomers to the Top Ten runs. Fastest of them at 56.46s was motor trader Ted Williams, who was running an ex-Roy Baker March 752, fitted with ADO's old 2.2 Hart engine, under Ted's Redland Motor House banner, while 'Gentleman' John Stuart clocked 58.49s with his 2.2 Chevron B25, and 'Doc' Willoughby rounded out the Top Ten with his 3.5 March-Buick V8, the chassis of which was Nick Williamson's old 712S.

The problem of a small crowd the previous year caused by a clash with other nearby attractions, caused the BARC(Y) to go for a mid-May date for the RAC Harewood meeting, where Martyn Griffiths impressed with a smooth 38.82s BTD which even Lane, Franklin and ADO could not match. The day's other star performance was the 40.09s 1600cc record from local man Peter Kaye while Tony Bancroft made a class-winning return at the wheel of his old Chevron B19 which was now owned by Yorkshire bearing manufacturer David Garnett.

Martyn Griffiths' then rather fragile confidence was further boosted by a 38.88s BTD at an extra Guyson/BARC round at Wiscombe Park before trecking North to Barbon where the Westmorland MC had attracted the sponsorship of Kendal VW/Porsche dealers Parker and Parker. This one looked like a good bet for the abundant bhp of Alister Douglas-Osborn's majestic Pilbeam-DFV but his 22.82s best, fast as it was, was not quite fast enough to pip Martyn's beautifully-controlled 22.80s course record climb. ADO was actually rather lucky as his gear-lever broke on his first RAC climb and he was only able to continue thanks to the loan of a gear lever by John Hart whose BT18 had been sidelined by a practice accident. The stricken Brabham had already been denuded of a driveshaft which, when fitted to Peter Kaye's BT35X, allowed the Yorkshire Dealer Opel Team engineer to lop a whole second off Rob Turnbull's class record at 24.72s.

Better still for Martyn Griffiths, his 28.71s best at Shelsley not only beat Cramer, ADO and Mac-Dowel – whose recent engine rebuild had not cured his motor's smoke-generating tendency – but it also made him the first MAC Committee member to win at Shelsley since the days of Dick Henderson and Reg Phillips in the nineteen-fifties. 'Smiling' Reg was still competing, of course, but had now given up his Chevron single-seater for some refined sport in his Ferrari Dino road car.

Alister Douglas-Osborn managed to beat Griffiths at a sun-baked Doune where Parker Pens was added to the increasingly varied firms now sponsoring hill climbs, and where the start line was moved fractionally back level with the Paddock. But at Pontypool Park, where the climb's 10th Anniversary was being celebrated, even ADO could do nothing about a really vintage battle for supremacy between Franklin, who broke the hill record three times, and Griffiths who broke it once, the crucial time, to leave it at 27.09s to Franklin's best at 27.19s. The spectacular Franklin also had a no-time given when his final all-or-nothing effort ended at the Esses after an enormous 'moment' which had actually begun at Pool Hairpin!

By now ADO looked to have his work cut out if he was to halt the Griffiths momentum, but his morale was boosted with yet another Shelsley record in July (27.35s) before he went over to Jersey and Guernsey. This was where Griffiths' luck ran out. His Hart engine displayed worryingly low oil pressure, then the cam drive-belt stripped, causing damage to the valve gear, which put him out of the competition on Jersey. ADO made the most of the opportunity and narrowly beat Cramer, MacDowel and Lane (all in the 42s bracket) with a 42.48s best. As usual, the sporting spirit prevailed and both Roy Lane (who later damaged his own car slightly) and Mike MacDowel offered Martyn the use of their cars at Le Val des Terres. Griffiths decided to drive the Ralt but never looked really at home and the 33.22s BTD went to David Franklin before the always spectacular Bristolian had another huge excursion, this time after the finish line. In the RAC runs, despite the demise of Griffiths' and Franklin's cars it was still a March on top for Lane recorded a 33.73s to beat – just – a splendid 33.79s from Ted Williams, a 33.93s from Cramer and a fine 34.00s from a holidaying Dave Harris in the big McRae.

For some time now there had been something of a decline in the organisational standards prevailing at Harewood, a model to other organisers in the later 1960s. There seemed to be too few people trying to do too much, and personality clashes did not make things any easier. The nadir came in July when what Clerk of the Course Mike Wilson freely admitted was a shambolic meeting saw the *first* class runs finishing at 5.30 pm and the Top Eight and Guyson/BARC Top Ten runs being cancelled lest they take place in starlight. Happily, all concerned realised the depth to which matters had sunk and a gradual recovery was soon under way to the extent that by the early nineteen-eighties the BARC(Y) again became a worthy force in hill climb organisation. The prevailing mood of recrimination and general gloom detracted from a sterling performance from Roy Lane who at long last broke Richard

Thwaites' 5-year old and rather controversial course record in 38.41s.

By now ADO looked to have his work cut out if he was to halt the Griffiths momentum, but his morale was boosted with yet another Shelsley record in July (27.35s) before he went over to Jersey and Guernsey. This was where Griffiths' luck ran out. His Hart engine displayed worryingly low oil pressure, then the cam drive-belt stripped, causing damage to the valve gear, which put him out of the competition on Jersey. ADO made the most of the opportunity and narrowly beat Cramer, MacDowel and Lane (all in the 42s bracket) with a 42.48s best. As usual, the sporting spirit prevailed and both Roy Lane (who later damaged his own car slightly) and Mike MacDowel offered Martyn the use of their cars at Le Val des Terres. Griffiths decided to drive the Ralt but never looked really at home and the 33.22s BTD went to David Franklin before the always spectacular Bristolian had another huge excursion, this time after the finish line. In the RAC runs, despite the demise of Griffiths' and Franklin's cars it was still a March on top for Lane recorded a 33.73s to beat – just – a splendid 33.79s from Ted Williams, a 33.93s from Cramer and a fine 34.00s from a holidaying Dave Harris in the big McRae.

For some time now there had been something of a decline in the organisational standards prevailing at Harewood, a model to other organisers in the later 1960s. There seemed to be too few people trying to do too much, and personality clashes did not make things any easier. The nadir came in July when what Clerk of the Course Mike Wilson freely admitted was a shambolic meeting saw the *first* class runs finishing at 5.30 pm and the Top Eight and Guyson/BARC Top Ten runs being cancelled lest they take place in starlight. Happily, all concerned realised the depth to which matters had sunk and a gradual recovery was soon under way to the extent that by the early nineteen-eighties the BARC(Y) again became a worthy force in hill climb organisation. The prevailing mood of recrimination and general gloom detracted from a sterling performance from Roy Lane who at long last broke Richard Thwaites' 5-year old and rather controversial course record in 38.41s.

This year there was no question of either ADO or Griffiths missing Craigantlet, and Alister put recent Irish efforts into perspective with a searing 51.64s which set the enthusiastic Ulstermen fairly twittering as it lopped over 4s from the existing record. Martyn Griffiths could do nothing to match this on a hill which allowed Alister to extend the 450 plus horses of the Pilbeam, while Peter Kaye also took over his 1600cc Brabham and came back with a fine 54.76s – under the previous record and only 1.34s slower than Griffiths.

Chris Cramer, still not the dominating force which many knew him to be capable of becoming, and endlessly carrying out modifications to try to extract more from the March, enjoyed his first win of the year at Pontypool Park before moving on to Shelsley where the MAC had to suffer a wet meeting for the first time for quite a while. Wet course or not, ADO was unabashed and set his eighth Shelsley BTD in 31.09s, to win from Lane and Cramer. It all seemed to be slipping away from Martyn Griffiths who had a troubled weekend and never really settled down to show the form of which he was capable, although he was fifth behind David Franklin, who was now finding his Championship third place under pressure from a revitalised Roy Lane.

Run on the Sunday of the Bank Holiday weekend in order to avoid a clash with a Thruxton race meeting, Gurston favoured the DFV engines and sure enough the day ended with another Douglas-Osborn record in 29.15s, and with Lane also getting into the 29s (29.58) to further dent Griffiths' Championship hopes. Poor Chris Cramer was out with a suspected seized engine after going back to trying a longer wheelbase.

It was all going Alister's way at last and at Prescott he finally clinched the Championship even though his 42.99s best was good enough only for fourth place behind Roy Lane, who recaptured his Prescott record in the big March-DFV in 42.33s, Griffiths, whose strenuous efforts left him on 42.47s, and Ken MacMaster on 42.98s after a typically smooth drive.

Godfrey Crompton, who had been steadily improving for some time with a 5.0 F5000 Leda-Chevrolet LT25 after writing off his old McLaren M10B at Loton Park the previous year, scored his first ever points with 43.93s which was good enough for nineth place. Runner-up the previous year in the Gold Cup Competition, Russ Ward went one better by winning it despite the Arkley being *hors de combat*. He shared the bitza Porsche of Autofarm Director Josh Sadler (Josh's yellow 2.7 '911S' in fact had started life as a mundane 912), and showed his class with a 49.27s record which was 1.82s below the previous class best, to beat Meredith and ADO for the BOC's premier trophy.

Clearly on a real 'high', Douglas-Osborn set a 37.74s course record at a Wiscombe two day affair which incorporated an RAC Leaders' round as well as the usual Guyson/BARC counter, but at Doune where DAF Trucks lent financial support his season ended with a crash at Oak Tree, writing off the off-side suspension and kinking the tub. While the wreckage was cleared Roy Lane had to sit on the line for half an hour, but it didn't put him off, for his 42.70s best was 0.15s faster than a happier Chris Cramer and 0.18s up on Championship runner-up Martyn Griffiths. The final points positions left ADO on 87 with a two point margin over Griffiths, with Lane on 77, followed by Franklin (67) and Cramer (65). Completing the Top Ten were MacDowel, Dungworth, Turnbull, MacMaster (who had missed several meetings earlier in the season) and Peter Kaye who emulated Rob Turnbull by attaining Number 10 for the following season after a splendid fifth place at Doune. John Meredith, who was trying to get a Hill Climb and Sprint Association off the ground to look after the interests of the sport's drivers, secured the RAC Leaders Competition after another fine year, no fewer than 11 points ahead of the widely-travelled Norrie Galbraith, from Lanark, who had switched to a Clydesdale Retreads sponsored Mallock U2 Mk8/16 with Twin-Cam engine with such success that he also claimed the Grampian Television Scottish Championship despite the efforts of his friend, travelling companion and arch-rival Jim Campbell in the John Young Brabham-BDA BT35, and even found time to win the Scottish Sprint Championship. Newbury engineer David Gould was third in the Leaders, with his highly-developed Terrapin Mk1G which was fitted with a 1.1-litre John Robinson built Ford/Cosworth BDJ engine, four points ahead of Duncan Welch's MG Midget, and with Russ Ward and Anthony Boshier-Jones next up.

After the disasters of July it was a relief to find a more relaxed and less ambitious timetable at Harewood for the Guyson/BARC final and it was a far more enjoyable meeting, even if a cloudburst did interfere with proceedings. In fact, in contrast to the previous year, this series was afflicted particularly badly with poor weather. At one point in the season four successive meetings had to have the Top Ten runs (for class improvements as opposed to the Top Eight FTD Awards climbs) cancelled as deteriorating weather and/or delays made their running pointless or impracticable. It has to be admitted that the extra set of Top Ten runs taxed many organisers at the end of a long day and with some competitors, who knew that they could not further reduce their times, declining to take their final climbs, all too often meetings came to a late, scrappy conclusion while the 'Top 86 Run Off' as it was dubbed by the more cynical, ran its course. Even in the RAC Championship the Top Ten runs were not always the dramatic climax to the meeting that they should have been. The increasing sophistication of the modern racing car, the critical factor of maintaining the correct tyre temperature and the endemic reluctance of man to be prompt and in the right place at the right time combined to make even these climbs rather long drawn out.

As for the Guyson/BARC Championship itself, it went to Charles Barter (against expectations – for the second consecutive year) by 0.95 mark from the seemingly inevitable John Meredith amid much humorous speculation on the usefulness of a Beadblaster on a watercress farm! Despite sportingly volunteering to transfer his Porsche from Marque Sports to GT classification because of its rather mongrel modifications, Josh Sadler, who ran the Autofarm Porsche specialists with partner Steve Carr, took third place from West Country Mini driver John Milford who had long given John Meredith the strongest competition down in the South West but had only recently taken to competing rather further afield. Behind him it was simply a reshuffle of the 1976 results with Boshier-Jones, Watts, Robert Barter, Tattam, Moyse and Roy Lane taking the prize money from fifth to tenth place. Alister Douglas-Osborn made it a double by winning the FTD Awards Championship by 4 points from Roy Lane and with Peter Kaye in a commendable fourth place behind Cramer.

Outside the major events the year had been notable for the first meetings at two new venues – pretty rare by the nineteen-seventies – even though one of them was only new to hill climbing. The 750 Motor Club Scottish Centre used part of the Knockhill race circuit on a particularly bleak hillside beyond Dunfermline for a meeting in April. Run in the reverse direction to racing, the course featured six corners, a dip and one good gradient and gave Russell Paterson a 29.98s BTD in his Chevron B17. Meanwhile, down in Kent, after over 40 years of motor sport, the Maidstone & Mid Kent Motor Club prepared for their first-ever hill climb at Great Farthingloe Farm, just outside Dover. Almost a mile in length, the course featured both tight bends and sweeping curves, yet even with the erection of Armco barriers it was deemed advisable to restrict this first meeting to saloons and sports cars. Dover is not far from Lydden Hill and this is Rallycross territory so it was no surprise to find BTD on 14 July falling to John Greasley's Rallycross Porsche Carrera in 44.06s from John Taylor and Rod Chapman in Escorts. The long established Valence School event run by the Sevenoaks Club was a less happy occasion than usual though, for 28-year-old physicist Jonathan Canning, from Burgess Hill, was killed when he crashed his old U2 Mk7.

During the course of the year John Hart sold his Brabham BT18 and replaced it with a much newer BT40 to be shared with his son Greg, who was setting some pretty fast times while still an 18-year-old schoolboy, although he did have the odd big accident. John's brother Tom was a more consistent award winner for several years with a little F3 Chevron B9/15. The old BT18 was bought by Jimmy Johnstone who after an eight-year absence from competing decided to have some enjoyment at local meetings, and proceeded to set BTDs at Scammonden and at the Novices Harewood meeting for which he was now eligible!

One of the strongest appeals of hill climbing is the individual character of each course and even specific, distinctive, meetings which have held an established place on the calender for many years. A case in point is the annual Vintage Sports Car Club meeting on the original short course at Prescott. Long after they ceased to be competitive in the premier events, old favourites such as the ERAs, Frank Wall's ex-Stubberfield single-seater Bugatti T35B, Basil Davenport's GN 'Spyder', Freddie Giles' JAP-powered 'Salome', 'Doc' Taylor's Casear Special, Guy Smith's Frazer Nash-Alvis (formerly Norris Special), and Ron Footitt's AC-GN continued to entertain as star performers at this evocative annual fixture. Best time of the day seemed to become the personal prerogative of regular VSCC racer Alan Cottam and his gleaming 1953 Formula 2 Connaught AL10. The extent of this combination's domination was emphasised on 13 August 1977 when Cottam broke the VSCC course record in 50.09s. This was the fourth time he had broken the record and the *twelfth* successive BTD!

Baldies are best.
Most of the leading hill climbers concentrated on further development to their existing cars for 1978, although a notable exception was a brand new Cosworth DFV-powered Pilbeam MP31 for Waring & Gillow team leader and RAC Champion Alister Douglas-Osborn. The new chassis incorporated lessons learnt from the evolutionary MP22, but with the advantage of a lower chassis with refined ground-effect characteristics. The MP22 was totally rebuilt after the Doune mishap and was taken over by the steady and consistent Malcolm Dungworth, whose old Brabham-Repco was sold off to west-countryman Terry Smith.

After a disheartening season, Chris Cramer still maintained faith in the March-GA 76A, but had Brian Martin overhaul it and incorporate some of his own ideas. The yellow and black car now featured flat side panels and appeared altogether less bulky. Roy Lane decided to carry on with the March 741, but fitted a McLaren M23-type 'chisel' nose for better air penetration and, incidently, less vulnerability to minor mishaps than the wide nose. After such a tantalising season, Martyn Griffiths returned his March 74B to Mike Pilbeam, who further updated the car, including fitting new bodywork. The Severn Advertising entry was now so different from its original form that it was re-designated the 78P.

A more radical approach was taken by Mike MacDowel who still hankered after more power while appreciating the excellent handling of the little Ralt RT1. He commissioned Derek Gardner (formerly the Tyrrell Grand Prix car designer, but recently returned to the motor industry mainstream with Borg-Warner) to rework and 'stretch' the Ralt to take a DFV engine. Mike and John Cussins had dissolved the Team Cusmac set-up so the car was now to be entered under the Coombs of Guildford banner, and was named the Coogar, from COOmbs and GARdner.

One man with a new car lined up was David Franklin who, with continued backing from Wendy Wools, obtained a newer F2 March-BMW 772 with a notably good Rosche BMW power unit and the co-operation of Robin Herd in developing an effective hill climb car out of a successful circuit racer. The old 742-BMW went to Alan Richards who now added Minolta support to the enthusiastic backing of Ted Gilbert's Cheltenham Cameras concern. The rather ineffective and troublesome turbocharger set-up on his Surtees TS10 had not brought Richard Jones any joy so this very fast driver with strictly limited resources tried another tack. He bought the Cosworth GA-engined Chevron B30 with which David Purley had won the F5000 racing Championship. However, a good circuit car is not necessarily ideal on the hills and, without the resources available to develop it, the car was always a bit unwieldy

Mike MacDowel commissioned Derek Gardiner to revamp his Ralt RT1 to accommodate a Cosworth DFV engine. The resulting Coogar was to have a long and varied hill climb career.
BOB COOPER

despite the determination of the Stroud engineer at the wheel.

Although the rewards for successful hill climbers, in terms of prize money, remained generally minimal, there was good news on the sponsorship front. The RAC's premier championship remained bereft of a commercial sponsor but the Leaders' series gained added stature and promotion by virtue of new backing from the Haynes Publishing Group, the fast growing motor instruction manual and general motoring book business. Guyson and Grampian Television continued with their sponsorship for the BARC and Scottish series, although Jim Thomson decided to promote the Skipton-based Euroblast subsidiary of Guyson International in the Championship title, while substituting a new Blydenstein Vauxhall Chevette for the venerable, and latterly 2.6-litre, Firenza for his own hill climbing. The go-ahead Longton club, too, could boast a commercial backer for the well-endowed Sprint & Hill Climb Championship. This was the Dutton-Forshaw Group of garages, part of Jack Barclay Ltd, and they were lending their name to a 14 round Northern series which offered £3,000 in prize money, with a substantial £600 to the winner.

Unfortunately, the year got off to a bad start in Scotland for alterations in progress at the Kinkell Braes caravan site ruled out the St Andrews club's first Grampian Television counter in March, while there was a sadness at the enforced retirement, after a minor heart attack, of former Eccosse-Imp and Cymru Vixen-Imp driver Les Jones, from Stirling, who had twice won both Scottish Hill Climb and Sprint Championships.

The increasing interest of the relatively small M & H tyre company in hill climbing had obviously spurred on the opposition at Goodyear for there was much evidence of experimental tyres from the latter company at a cold and wet Loton test day, just a week before an unusually early – too early for some – March start for the RAC Championship at the same venue. Benefiting from the winter work on his 'Pilbeamed' March, Martyn Griffiths again got off to a flying start to clock 53.15s, enough to edge out an encouraged Chris Cramer, who was most enthusiastic about Brian Martin's work on the March-GA (53.26s), and David Franklin's new March-BMW (53.35s). Since both ADO and MacDowel also

Maggie Blankstone (pictured at Bouley Bay) had an excellent season with the Mallock U2 Mk20, which she shared with her husband Peter.
BOB COOPER

broke into the 53s bracket with their new (or substantially new) cars, it all augured well for another close fought season. Roy Lane, on the other hand, got off on the wrong foot, leaving the road on his second RAC climb and having to be content with a solitary point for his first climb (54.87s).

A week later a healthy 4,500 spectators turned out at Prescott to see the Euroblast/BARC Championship open, where a highlight was Richard Brown's new weapon: a Clubmans chassis Mallock U2 Mk18C but with no less than a full 270 bhp Hart 420R engine installed, with which he beat Arthur Mallock's 'works' U2 for a 52.31s class win before going even faster (51.23s) for 4th BTD in the Top Eight climbs. Overall, it was another Prescott success for David Franklin in 49.85s, although Ken MacMaster did well to vanquish Roy Lane for second place.

The season was off to a fairly hectic start, for just a week later everyone had to be down at Wiscombe chasing RAC points. Chris Cramer enjoyed a boost by winning Saturday's AMOC club meeting (39.60s), and he almost won again on the Sunday with a majestic, power sliding 38.49s. But even that was not quite enough to head a resounding 38.45s from the formidable Franklin. Despite an off-course moment at Martini, the tall, prematurely grey Rob Turnbull showed improved form with 38.92s, faster than Lane and Griffiths, the latter adversely affected by sticking throttle slides.

There was quite a break now before the next RAC round at Prescott, but with three well-supported Euroblast/BARC meetings in the meantime there was no respite for most. Finding that his March now possessed much better traction after its winter 'simplification' programme, Chris Cramer took a popular win at Harewood (38.75s), almost a second up on Griffiths, although the positions were neatly reversed at the Bank of Scotland-supported Doune meeting which now figured in the series as well as providing the Grampian Television opener. Appropriately enough the meeting saw the début of the new 2.3 Guyson Chevette, turned out in the predominantly yellow (the original livery was mainly red) team colours. Then it was back down to Wiscombe for the Five Clubs promotion, where continued suspension sorting helped Roy Lane back on top, almost a second faster than Cramer and Franklin. Other notable performances came from the 1600cc GRD-BDA 273 of the increasingly prominent Alan Clennell who had been one of the very few drivers who still regularly combined hill climbing and circuit racing until the latter became too expensive (43.27s for fifth), and from Terry Smith who was a spectacular seventh with the Brabham-Repco.

The great importance of having the right tyres was most apparent on 7 May at Prescott where mud and chalk carried onto the hill from the Paddock put grip at a premium. Under these conditions M & H tyres seemed to have a definite advantage in front-end grip especially, and a combination of M & H fronts with Goodyear rears found favour. Nevertheless, Roy Lane, who had secured new sponsorship from Northamptonshire Computer Bureaus, and who could rely on having the best that Goodyear could provide, reasserted himself with a fine 46.93s on Goodyear slicks all round. In conditions where neatness and precision counted strongly it was no surprise that Ken MacMaster was runner-up with a close 47.18s, while Cramer (47.22s) did well to beat the agile F2-based machinery of Griffiths and Franklin, using a curious but effective combination of 1977 M & H tyres on the front and 1974 Firestones on the rear!

The BARC(Y) retained a May date for their premier meeting of the year but were rewarded with wet weather. This did no favours for Roy Lane for the March-DFV was crippled with water in the electrics. Undeterred by the conditions, David Franklin was as exuberant as ever and his 42.38s best was a whole 1.6s up on Chris Cramer in the Martin-fettled March, a performance which actually put him in the lead for the RAC Championship although he had not yet won a single round. Griffiths headed Turnbull and MacDowel for third place but reckoned that he had been too neat and tidy and had lost time. Although still not in a position to do a full season again, Jimmy Johnstone clocked a superb 45.58s for seventh overall in the old BT18, his lines on the corners being well nigh perfect. Also noticeable among the more exuberant competitors was Tony Bancroft, who had now taken up running a Porsche 911. Although initiated purely for fun, Tony's Porsche exploits were to become one of the highlights of the non-racing classes in future years.

After winning the 50th meeting to be held at Gurston Down, Roy Lane looked on good form for Barbon, another hill where the DFV-engined cars would have a chance to make best use of their abundant horses. But in this season of surprises, it was David Franklin once again who fairly flung the March-BMW through the hairpin and over the finish line in 23.04s, 0.27s less than it took Chris Cramer, and with Alister Douglas-Osborn (after rebuilding the fuel system), Griffiths and Lane all mere fractions away. An unlucky Mike MacDowel had the disconcerting experience of having a suspension failure at the hairpin, although fortunately at low speed.

All the while Chris Cramer was doing rather well in the Euroblast/BARC series and he even beat ADO and Lane to a 22.67s BTD on the tight and twisty little hill in the shadow of Scammonden Dam. However, when he (and about 10,000 others) arrived at Shelsley his RAC lead had been eroded by Franklin. This was the 100th national meeting to be held at Shelsley and was quite an occasion. Yet despite his rare and avowed dislike of the hill, Franklin was unstoppable and left BTD at 27.92s with MacDowel on 28.06s and Griffiths, Cramer (whose March had been re-designated 78H), ADO and Lane (labouring under the dual handicap of tonsillitis and a sprained wrist) all under 28.50s. Mac-Dowel's effort in the Coogar, using a special 3.3-litre version of the DFV engine, was a fine reward for Ron Tauranac and Charles Lashford after an overnight rebuild on the car following a practice mishap at the Esses. Eyebrows were raised when Walsall's Ray Rowan took his 250cc Motus-Yamaha Mk7 Kart up faster than Peter Voigt had achieved with the Voigt-Renwick Special, while another landmark was to the credit of Maggie Blankstone. After selling their Ford GT40 to BBC disc jockey and car enthusiast Noel Edmonds, Maggie and husband Peter had been enjoying some evenly matched and successful motoring in a Twin-Cam-engined Mallock U2. Now, Maggie went faster than ever in their latest Mk20 version and in recording 31.85s at last broke Patsy Burt's old Ladies' record which had stood since 1967.

While the Euroblast/BARC contenders were attacking records at Loton Park, some of the RAC hopefuls took in Fintray the week before the first RAC Doune meeting. The Aberdeen club had resurfaced the startline and the return road for their big meeting where David Hepworth's 1972 record looked in grave danger. Sure enough, it went, but although both Martyn Griffiths and ADO were in the 28s bracket, it was Rob Turnbull who sprang a surprise and left the new record at 28.33s. Alas, at the Burmah Oil sponsored Doune meeting Rob crashed after Tunnel, hitting a tree, although he was unhurt. This time Franklin had to give best to Martyn Griffiths, although only by 0.27s.

July brought the sad news that there would be no more hill climbing, for the time being at least, at Pontypool Park because of growing pressure against the noise nuisance in this municipal park. On a happier note, Mike MacDowel scored his first BTD win for over 4 years, at Shelsley, with a 28.12s BTD over Cramer and ADO who was feeling rather happier after tracing a persistent handling problem to a flexing rear suspension mounting. This Euroblast/BARC counter also saw the long-awaited début of another Pilbeam-DFV MP31. Sponsored by H S & D Computer Services, this gleaming red and white twin to ADO's car was for the red haired (and bearded) Peter Kaye, and he made an auspicious start with this brand new car, climbing in 28.86s for seventh BTD. On the other hand, the Guyson Chevette had been rather more troublesome and it took some sorting from Gerry Johnstone before the Thomson car was in a position to win its class. It did so at Shelsley but after tieing with his father Jim, and going ahead on the aggregate of both climbs, the class winner was 18-year-old James Thomson. Even more spectacular was the first hill climb contested by Ray Mallock. The younger son of 'the major' broke 30s (29.93s) in the run-off with the development 'works' U2-Hart Mk18GW, to beat class winner Tony Southall's ultra rapid Mk18.

Now it was Martyn Griffiths' turn to hit top form, for after Doune, the Severn Advertising Director clearly found the Channel Islands air to his taste. It was exceptionally close at Bouley Bay with Martyn's superb 41.76s smashing the course record but only defeating Cramer by 0.03s and with Franklin, Lane and ADO all bettering 42.00s. Over on Guernsey, Martyn made it a double with another record, in 32.41s. Unfortunately, it was a rather destructive meeting, especially at the first right-hand bend. Rob Turnbull's recently repaired Ralt had a tyre deflate and the ensuing accident badly damaged the tub as well as the suspension. Then Malcolm Dungworth had the frightening experience of the throttle jamming open. He bruised himself when he hit a rockface, but the damage to Pilbeam MP22-01 was far worse.

Peter Kaye had missed Le Val des Terres and had gone to Gurston Down instead, where a 35.56s climb gave him a close win over Allan Humphries' Allwood Cars 2.1 March 762.

For several years now Jim Thomson's imposing Pace Arrow had been a feature of hill climb Paddocks – not to mention the narrow access roads which lead to some of them – but Jim's home-from-home had been quite upstaged by the Doug Eyre-liveried, red and blue ensemble of motor home and matching trailer, festooned with motorcycles and things, effected by Stourport-on-Severn entrepreneur Godfrey Crampton. This young company director then raised a few more eyebrows by replacing his old Leda with a pair of March 772s. Eventually the Hart engine out of the ex-MRE car went into the ex-Peter Bloore 772P and the other chassis was sold to Rob Turnbull to replace his written-off Ralt chassis.

Early handling problems had made ADO's title defence a not particularly happy one, but on the relatively wide and very fast Craigantlet climb, one of his favourites despite the time and expense needed to compete there, everything came right and Alister's 53.62s best was 0.62s faster than Martyn Griffiths, but with Peter Kaye an increasingly threatening third. Yet when everyone returned to Shelsley again, Alister was in more handling problems and was 0.21s down on Kaye in sixth and seventh places. David Franklin reasserted his earlier form with a blistering 27.71s – in a 2-litre car remember – whereas even Griffiths and the consistent Cramer could not break 28s. Shelsley is rarely without a catalogue of dramas, and this time they were supplied by the meteoric Ray Mallock who took his U2 over the finish line in an almost unreal 29.22s and by one of the hill's most spectacular accidents which befell the rapid Greg Hart. His Brabham BT38/40 somersaulted and burst into flames. Fortunately, extremely prompt and well-drilled action by the marshals soon had the fire dealt with and a shaken but unhurt Hart out of the wreckage.

Incredibly, just a fortnight later, Greg was back in action at Gurston Down with a re-chassised Hart-Brabham and what's more broke the 1600cc class record in 32.10s. The hirsute Peter Kaye had given notice of his serious intentions at the July climb and now the man who made the 1600cc class virtually his own the previous year really showed what he could do with the Pilbeam. His 28.92s was a devastating BTD and course record, almost half a second faster than Griffiths who had had to have his engine rebuilt after buzzing it at Shelsley.

Matters were now becoming critical in this rather open championship season. Roy Lane was fastest in the class runs at Prescott but when it came to the Top Ten he clipped a suspension upright which collapsed a few seconds later giving him a no time. On his first RAC climb Griffiths spun at the Esses, damaging the nose of the March. In the best sporting manner everyone pitched in to help ready the car for the critical final run where Martyn rewarded the efforts by setting a 42.95s BTD, pipping Franklin, Cramer and Kaye, and leaving Prescott tying on points with Franklin with one round to go and with a slight advantage when it came to 'dropped points'.

Before the crucial meeting at Doune, the final Harewood meeting gave Chris Cramer the Harewood course record in 38.39s, and sealed his Euroblast/BARC FTD Awards victory.

It is not unusual for the RAC Hill Climb Championship to be settled at the final round after immense tension and anticipation. Unfortunately, all too often the final act has been something of an anti-climax. So it was in 1978 when the wet weather rather spoilt things. Franklin and Griffiths were locked in combat certainly, but ADO beat them both for a 47.33s BTD. However, since Franklin beat

Griffiths, it was the Bristolian garage owner, whose power slides were the most lurid seen since Nick Williamson's heyday, who lifted the sport's premier award by just 1 point, 86 to 85. A much better season with the big March-GA left Chris Cramer with 77 points and a 10 point gap over a rather disappointing ADO. Roy Lane's rather expensive and none-too-consistent season gave him 63 points, three ahead of MacDowel, and with Ken MacMaster, latecomer Peter Kaye, occasional competitor Dave Harris and Rob Turnbull completing the Top Ten places. Ted Williams, driving an ex-Ricardo Zunino March 772, failed to obtain one of those coveted permanent numbers by but one point.

If the RAC title was close it was as nothing to the three-way tie at the head of the British Haynes Leaders' series where once the tie-deciders had been brought into effect victory was seen to have gone to Charles Barter who had bought a brand new Davrian Mk7 for the year. Fitted with a 1030cc Hartwell Imp engine, and immaculately turned out in the familiar yellow and white Golden Springs Watercress colours, the new car was somewhat disconcerting at first sight as there was definitely something distinctly asymmetric about the front elevation! However, the aimiable Charles was as fast and as consistent as ever in the car and another major championship was his, but with the well-engineered and developed Gould Terrapin of David Gould and the U2 Mk18 of Edgbaston engineer Martin Bolsover equal on points after excellent seasons. In a year when nobody really dominated the 1600cc racing class (Johnstone, the Harts, the Morris brothers' chopped and much reworked Ensign, Alan Clennell's ex-Kazato GRD and John Barratt's Theta 003 – another reworked Ensign – were all prominent), Scotsman Jim Campbell piled up enough points for fourth place in the John Young Brabham BT35, ahead of John Jordan's rapid Imp and John Meredith's latest variation on the Mini theme, which employed an 843cc Imp engine.

As for the Euroblast/BARC Championship, well it never really looked as though it was going to leave the Waddock, Dorchester, watercress farm. At the end of the season Charlie Barter was a whopping 8.97 marks ahead of his nearest rival: brother Robert in the same car! David Gould was third from Spondon, Derby, MG Midget driver Des Richardson, Cramer, Tom Hart, Lane, Rugby GRD driver Alan Clennell, Hampshireman John Jordan and Alan Cox who was now driving the little Harrison-Imp KH4 F4 car.

It took another tie-decider to resolve the Euroblast/BARC BTD Awards series in the favour of a well deserving Chris Cramer, for Roy Lane also totalled 58 points.

With such good prize money available, the Dutton-Forshaw Longton Championship attracted a high level of support once more with the £600 first prize won by Des Richardson's fast Midget which was nevertheless still not matching the Sprite times of Brian Kenyon, set several years before, on some hills. The hard-trying Bob Prest, from Croxdale, Co Durham, was runner-up with his self-prepared U2 Mk16, beating Terry Carthy's Mini, Brian Walker's turbocharged Ford Escort RS2000 from Longridge, John Casey's Mini and the crowd-pleasing Ford Mustang of Palmer Hewardine.

David Franklin contrived to win both the RAC Hill Climb and RAC Sprint Championships in 1978. David has his March-BMW 772 on opposite lock here on Prescott's Pardon hairpin.
BOB COOPER

Looking back over another hard fought season, there had been a new Valence hill record in 28.71s for Roger Willoughby in the March-Buick 712S, and a new Wiscombe Park hill record at the September promotion put on by the Woolbridge MC. Giving one of his best performances in a patchy season, Roy Lane reduced the Devon hill's record to 37.53s. Another happy event, which made up in a small way for the loss of Pontypool Park, was the first meeting for six years at Bodiam. The Hastings 1066 Club were able to come to terms with the land's new owner, the Reverend M.N. France, to use the former Guinness land although about 10 yards were lopped off the timed distance at the start.

One of the features of hill climbing during 1976/77 had been the smart ex-John Meredith Mini of Terry Tattam, turned out in rather unusual brown and cream colours. The likable cockney had not competed in 1978 but it was still a cause of great regret to learn of his early death in September, killed in a road accident at 29.

The Champion, David Franklin, a rather unassuming individual out of a racing car, had not competed in as many of the lesser British hill climbs as some of his main rivals, but he had had an exceptionally busy year even so for he also contrived to win the RAC Sprint Championship – the first time that this 'double' had been carried off – and had also found time to indulge in his annual pilgrimage to compete in the big Swiss hill climbs. David Franklin liked variety in his motor sport, and in 1978 that had been combined with outstanding success in a very good car which somehow few had considered as a likely bet for the RAC title at the beginning of the year. He wasn't intending to rest on his laurels either, for the Huntsman Garage proprietor would be carrying the Wendy Wools colours on yet another F2 March-BMW in 1979. March had sold him the ex-Bruno Giacomelli 782 chassis, fitted with a new tub, and again with Rosche BMW power. The updated 772 went to meat-processing machinery representative Alan Richards who, in turn, sold his earlier 742/772 to Scotsman Norrie Galbraith who was taking to single-seaters for the first time in his continuing battle for Scottish supremacy with the chain-smoking Jim Campbell.

Changing Fortunes

In earlier years when the motor sporting calendar was less crowded, most people took an active interest in most varieties of sporting activity and many competitors would take in Goodwood, Silverstone, Shelsley, Prescott, the Brighton Speed Trials, and even the RAC Rally because they were major occasions on the motor sporting fixture list, not because they were race meetings, hill climbs, sprints or rallies. In the crowded, higher pressure, and immensely more professional scene of recent years such catholic tastes are rare. Motor sport has become much more fragmented, with the affairs of one group rarely impinging on the activities of another set of people. Since hill climbing was now, healthy as it was, firmly in the realms of club sport the goings-on of the uphill racers rarely generated headlines outside this narrow sphere. But at the beginning of 1979 there was a real sensation, a real crowd-drawer, for which the indomitable Roy Lane was to be thanked. Having sold the March 741 to sprinter Simon Riley, Roy was at Bicester with a view to negotiating with Robin Herd for a 761 to carry his trusty Engine Developments prepared DFV (believed to the the engine which had powered Bruce McLaren to victory in the 1968 Belgian Grand Prix).

While he was there Roy stumbled on the unraced 761-based 2-4-0 six wheeler, built as an experiment when the Tyrrell team were enjoying limited success with their six-wheeled P34 project. Hampered by lubrication problems and a weight penalty over conventional F1 cars, the project had been quietly set on one side, but appeared to have real potential in hill climbing with its 'normal' front wheels and four small driven rear wheels on two axles (hence the railway inspired 2-4-0 designation). This layout would serve to maximise traction, like the twin rear wheels on the same axle of former days, while the over-large width of a modern racing car was reduced by well over a foot. Ever the practical engineer, Roy worked out that the source of the lubrication problem was centripetal force directing an oil feed away from the additional transmission gears. With this sensational set-up grafted onto the ex-Ian Scheckter/Rothmans 771, the former Champion was ready to go. His backing for the year was not large, but some support from Castrol and Severn Advertising was soon augmented by limited sponsorship from Guyson.

The March-versus-Pilbeam character of the sport's top echelon was most apparent. Apart from Lane, David Franklin was to run an ex-works F2 782-BMW while Chris Cramer was joining forces with Godfrey Crompton to run a pair of 2.2 Hart 420R-engined 782s, Chris opting for the lighter Hewland FT200 gearbox which some felt to be only marginally strong enough to cope with the 300 plus bhp developed by the Hart. Cramer's old 76A reappeared – mainly in sprints – in the hands of London chef Paul Edwards.

Of the Pilbeam runners, most attention focused on Martyn Griffiths, who had sold his much-modified March chassis to John Barratt. Mike Pilbeam was building a new Formula 2 chassis for circuit racing, and a basically similar 'state of the art' ground-effect chassis, the MP40, was to be turned out in the very smart blue, red and white Severn Advertising colours for Martyn. A little smaller than the MP31, the new car bore a strong resemblance to the DFV-engined cars. Exceptionally stiffly suspended, the car featured side radiators and the desirable facility to change the brake balance very rapidly. The 2.2 Hart 420R engine was retained while Griffiths preferred to accept the weight penalty of the beefier FGA gearbox. Douglas-Osborn, Dungworth and Kaye kept their DFV-engined cars, the latter using one of the 90mm bore, 465/475 bhp, 3.3-litre John Judd-built engines as used by Mike MacDowel.

The markedly crab-tracked chassis of the March 2-4-0 is evident here as Roy Lane takes Shelsley's top 'S'.
BOB COOPER

Roy Lane produced a real sensation in 1979. This was the six-wheel March 2-4-0, seen here at Loton Park.
BOB COOPER

Added interest was to be provided in the RAC MSA[1] Championship by the addition of a concurrent Award of Merit competition to be won by the highest-scoring driver who had not featured in the previous year's Top Ten Championship placings. The demise of Pontypool Park left a gap in the Championship which was filled, to the delight of the hard working Aberdeen and District Motor Club, by another Scottish counter at Fintray House.

On a broader front, the Hill Climb and Sprint Association at last got off the ground, with active competitors taking a welcome lead. Founder and Secretary, John Meredith was backed up by Chairman, Russ Ward; Vice Chairman, 'Doc' Willoughby; Treasurer and Membership Secretary, Alan Richards; and Committee Members, Charles Barter and Des Richardson. There were mutterings about a Southern bias to the Association but it was the Southerners who had got this useful representative body off the ground and, apart from Des Richardson, from Spondon, Derby, the Northerners appeared less keen to take an active part in helping to help themselves.

An eager audience far greater than the sport's normal following focused their attention on Wiscombe Park on April Fool's Day where the blue and silver March 2-4-0 was to make its first public appearance at the initial RAC round. In changeable weather conditions, which suited the car perfectly, Roy's début was sensational. With visibly better grip, Lane shot up to a 42.88s BTD, 0.74s faster than ADO and another 0.47s up on Griffiths' impressive new Pilbeam which had set a 40.83s BTD in drier conditions at the previous day's AMOC club meeting. Ted Williams' March was an excellent fourth – and an excellent start in the Award of Merit series – while more eyebrows were raised when Richard Brown, armed with a new 285 bhp 2.0 Hart 420R-engined U2 Mk20B, split Alan Richards and David Franklin in sixth place (44.96s). Among the class winners, despite both relative inexperience in single-seaters and suffering from the after-effects of being kicked by a horse, was Russ Ward, whose ex-Tom Hart 1.1 Chevron B9/15 was publicising Russ' new Cheltenham Spa Motor Company business.

It was wet again for the Guyson/BARC round at Prescott (the Guyson name being re-applied to the Championship after the Euroblast interlude) and Lane did it again with 51.52s to the 52.88s of a hard-trying Peter Kaye who was using 'softer' cams in his DFV and who bumped the bank at the Esses on his final climb. Although Jimmy Johnstone scored a deserved BTD at the Easter Harewood meeting, in his recently-purchased Brabham-FVA BT30, most of the star names went straight to Loton for the following day's RAC round where the H & DLCC were not keen on people practising on Monday morning after competing at Harewood the previous day. Lane was again fastest in practice only for him to be sidelined by stripped transmission gears – twice! That left the way clear for David Franklin's new March to produce one of David's devastating 'on the brink' climbs to leave the Loton record at 51.66s. Much happier now with the handling of his smart red March 782, Cramer was only a little slower in 51.83s, while Peter Kaye took eight points, a just reward after a hurried gearbox rebuild. Griffiths was also out of the picture after hitting a tree at Triangle.

Before the May Prescott meeting there were Guyson/BARC counters at Doune and Wiscombe with more gearbox trouble for Lane at the Scottish hill where Chris Cramer's now updated 782/79B broke the hill record in 41.76s. A week later he lifted another BTD at Wiscombe with 37.75s. The talented if inexperienced Falmouth printer Max Harvey did well to make the Top Eight here with his one-off F2 Boxer which he was sharing with Peter Kendall. It was a rather sad occasion, too, for it marked the last meeting for the old ex-Rivers Fletcher HWM-Jaguar single-seater in the hands of Majors Charles Lambton and Richard Chichester before it was sold. The old car – it was one of the few tangible assets of Wiscombe Ltd – must have hardly needed a driver to take it up Wiscombe after all these years.

As usual early in the year, Prescott was pretty dusty and slippery but despite this a tremendously determined Peter Kaye put in a 43.28s climb which beat Roy Lane's 43.90s in the charismatic 2-4-0. Almost as much attention focused on a highly incongruous saloon car duel. The latest in a series of exotic BMWs from Curfew Garages, Moreton-in-Marsh, Gloucestershire, proprietor Gerry Tyack, the Tom Walkinshaw-prepared ex-EBG Freizeit Team Group 5 320i, was taken on by 'Smiley Riley'. This was Alan Payne's dark green Riley 1.5 which had been getting faster and faster and no less twitchy over the last few seasons with a little help from a 3.5 Rover/Buick V8 engine. The duel was resolved in the favour of the bearded Birmingham driver with his true amateur creation in 53.87s

---

1   The RAC Motor Sport Division was reformed as a limited company of 1 January 1979, becoming the Royal Automobile Club Motor Sports Association Ltd (RAC MSA).

Straight after Prescott it was up to Harewood where Peter Kaye emphasised that this vastly experienced driver, although only lately able to field an RAC contending car, could well be the 1979 RAC Champion. Although the in-form Chris Cramer with his Douglas & Gavin/Centurion Helmets March matched the course record in 38.39s to edge out ADO, Griffiths and a subdued Lane (with steering problems), Kaye gritted his teeth and flung the now adequately torquey 3.3 DFV-engined car up in 38.18s for a new course record and an immensely popular home win.

It was wet at Gurston on 20 May so it was no surprise to see Roy Lane back on top with the 2-4-0, but the premier battle was renewed at Barbon, a 'DFV course' with a vengeance.

In stark contrast to the jubilation following Peter Kaye's Harewood win, there was near tragedy in Westmorland. The Yorkshireman went off after the notorious bump on the exit of the second, very fast, left-hander and the Pilbeam rolled sickeningly into a heap of wreckage. The author witnessed the accident just as he had Mike Gray's fatal crash at virtually the same point in 1964, and a feeling of deep apprehension was not alleviated by the lack of movement in the car. Peter Kaye was rushed to hospital where his injuries were found to include a fractured skull, a broken bone in his neck, a broken leg and a broken arm. Happily, he was to recover and indeed return to the wheel, but his Championship hopes were dashed. It was Alister Douglas-Osborn who set a 23.92s BTD before rain came to depress the mood further. In these conditions Lane looked a good bet for 10 points but in fact a 26.78s climb from Chris Cramer bettered Roy's 27.19s and a 27.37s climb from Alister.

For some time the old complaints about the bumpiness of Shelsley had become increasingly strident. The after-effects of a landslip in 1975 had played a part in the deterioration, and now the MAC had taken the bold step of putting in hand a £15,000 improvement programme – made possible by several really good years – which included a completely resurfaced course, a new toilet block in the Paddock, redesigned spectator pathways, an improved public address system and a new teleprinter link from the timekeepers to the Paddock. One who was not there to see the improvements was Basil Davenport who had died in the Spring. Ill health had forced him to stop competing only quite recently after a career which stretched back to 1923, interrupted only by the 15 years when he withdrew and concentrated on running the family mill in Macclesfield.

With the Pilbeam-DFV now well sorted, another Douglas-Osborn success might have been predicted but it was Martyn Griffiths who came within 0.02s of the course record with a 27.37s best, a fractional 0.04s less than ADO, while Cramer, although fourth, was afflicted with a slipping clutch.

Once confirmation was received of RAC Championship status, the Fintray organising team went all out to improve and promote the course. New Paddock and access roads, and resurfacing at the hairpin, were put in hand and Paterson Travel and Tours sponsorship secured for the RAC meeting when 4,500 spectators were attracted. Times were affected by the new surface, which lifted, but there was no disguising the emerging Cramer-versus- Griffiths struggle in this year of fluctuating fortunes. This time the honours went to Chris with 28.35s to Martyn's 28.77s, a time matched by Rob Turnbull's less exotic 2.0 March-Hart 762.

The Scottish spectators had one disappointment, for Roy Lane had returned the March six wheeler to conventional 771 specification. Although superb in the wet, the car was less competitive in 2-4-0 configuration in the dry, such as at Shelsley where it failed to make the Top Ten. The 2-4-0 system imposed a hefty 180 lbs weight penalty while the 4WD muff joint absorbed 70-80 bhp, and that was too high a price to pay in such competitive company. A further disincentive was the very short life of the special gears needed – at £250 a set!

When the 'circus' moved to Doune, Griffiths turned the tables on Cramer (41.81s to 42.44s), and began a run of success which included a new course record at Loton (50.81s), another BTD at Shelsley (27.48s) and two superb performances in the Channel Islands, locked in combat with the red March of Chris Cramer. Both broke the Bouley Bay record (41.57s for Griffiths, 41.68s for Cramer), and although the Stroud architect's Le Val des Terres time of 32.12s just missed a record, Griffiths' storming 32.04s set a new target.

Handling problems had rather blunted Roy Lane's challenge by now but he did split Cramer's winning 38.23s best from Griffiths' 38.67s at July's Guyson/BARC round at Harewood, whimsically

Hamlet without the Prince. The Top Ten cast assemble for a Shelsley prizegiving in 1979. They are (left to right) Mike MacDowel, Rob Turnbull, Ted Williams, David Franklin, Richard Brown, Alan Richards, Chris Cramer, Alister Douglas-Osborn and Dave Harris. Missing is Martyn Griffiths, who was taking the spoils of victory as this picture was taken. His Pilbeam MP40 is in the foreground.
BOB COOPER

The ingenious Murrain-FVC of Joy Rainey, an exceptionally brave and determined lady, leaves the Prescott startline in 1983.
BOB COOPER

referred to as 'The Harewood 12 Hours' after a surfeit of off-course excursions caused delays leading to an 8.30 pm finish!.

Clearly the latest 2.2 Hart engine, with its considerable mid-range punch, when fitted to an F2-sized chassis, made for a very good combination indeed on most courses, but at Craigantlet, where around 135/140 mph was attainable with a DFV (even faster than Shelsley or Gurston), there was no answer to the Waring & Gillow Pilbeam of Alister Douglas-Osborn. His winning advantage on one of his favourite hills was almost a whole second, although Griffiths did manage to beat Lane.

Cramer had given the Ulster event a miss but when he rejoined the battle at Shelsley his 27.78s was not quite good enough to match ADO's 27.58s, while Griffiths was faster yet in 27.40s, although still outside Alister's course record. Could this finally by Martyn's year? One record which did go was the Ladies' record, for the third Shelsley meeting running. The latest time was 30.08s, and the lady who was chiselling away at Maggie Blankstone's time was Joy Rainey, a very remarkable and courageous lady indeed. This tiny figure was an inspiration to anyone depressed by physical handicap. The Australian principal of a Guildford language school, Joy and her father Murray had been familiar figures for some years with pre-war Alfa Romeos, before Murray built up the Cosworth FVC-engined Murrain for Joy. Based on a Dastle chassis, this short-wheelbase sports-racing car bristling with ingenious features was most effective and was now enabling Joy to achieve remarkable success.

A most welcome sight at Shelsley, albeit looking rather drawn and by no means fully recovered, was Peter Kaye who must have found it galling not to have the chance to pursue the Championship which he had looked odds-on favourite to win.

Before the classic September Prescott, Chris Cramer further reduced the Loton Park record to 50.77s, and kept his Championship hopes alive with a resounding 43.42s victory in Gloucestershire. David Franklin was a non-starter at Prescott after an accident at St Ursanne les Rangiers, in Switzerland, where he had damaged the front of his March and hurt his wrist. A disappointed Griffiths – who had taken 10 points at Gurston in 29.78s – clipped a nose fin and rather upset his Pilbeam's handling, and had to be content with 43.59s, beaten by rare RAC hill climber, as opposed to sprinter, Dave Harris (43.44s), Ted Williams (43.49s) and Lane (43.53s). Roy had actually taken BTD at Gurston the previous week only to go off twice in the RAC runs and fail to score a point! Since this was the September meeting, the Prescott Gold Cup was settled, the trophy having fallen to Barry Brant, the leader of 16-strong group of 500cc competitors, a reminder that the old single-seater 500s were still very much a part of the hill climb scene.

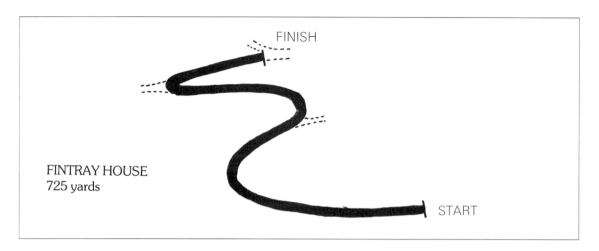

FINISH

FINTRAY HOUSE
725 yards

START

In this season of improvement at several hills, Prescott, too, had benefitted with Marlboro support enabling a new saloon car Paddock to be hard surfaced.

Now there was a wait for the final two RAC events at Wiscombe and Doune, but in the meantime Chris Cramer emphasised his late charge with a superb 38.04s Harewood record, achieved in spite of a gear jumping out. This was the Guyson/BARC Championship final and was not without drama. That man Barter had led the series yet again earlier in the season but by the last round he had slipped to third behind a fight-to-the-finish between a most impressive young James Thomson in father Jim's Vauxhall Chevette HS and Josh Sadler, who had caused a certain amount of anguish by turning out his 2.8 Autofarm Porsche 911 in a particularly awful shade of pink! Sadler ripped a tyre and actually competed with an odd-sized replacement lent by fellow Porsche driver 'Spotty' Bancroft. Not one whit discouraged, Josh still took the Championship by 0.04 point from Thomson who had had to have a lunchtime gearbox rebuild. Fourth behind Barter was the consistent Des Richardson (although his familiar MG Midget also suffered a gearbox failure on the day), and the single-seaters of Cramer and Griffiths, who naturally took the premier positions in the Guyson/BARC FTD Awards Championship.

A fine shot of Martyn Griffiths and his beautifully-prepared Pilbeam MP40 as they emerge from Doune's trees, on the way to a 41.72s hill record and the 1979 RAC Championship.
BOB COOPER

There was much publicity for the Longton Isle of Man excursion as the club arranged a 'match race' between Brian Redman – Lancashire's greatest racing driver – in the Tom Coughlan Racing 5.7 Chevron-Chevrolet B32 (John Cussins' old car) and Phil Read on a 750 Yamaha motorcycle. Unfortunately, after all the publicity the 'bike' melted a piston and the Chevron was misfiring badly, and all this rather detracted from a 61.79s record from Alister Douglas-Osborn who wound the Pilbeam up to well over 160 mph (as did Terry Smith with his Repco-engined March 761) to emphasise that this was the fastest British hill climb of all since the demise of Oliver's Mount.

The Five Clubs (from Bristol, Burnham-on-Sea, Haldon, Taunton and Plymouth) were in charge of the crucial Wiscombe meeting where Chris Cramer was in a totally determined mood. He had damaged his car's nose on his first RAC climb, and had had to carry out a frantic repair job. Nevertheless, he went back out and broke the course record for the second time that day, leaving it at 37.45s. Griffiths meanwhile was only a tiny fraction slower at 37.48s and it all rested on Doune.

For once it was not an anti-climax, and the struggle went on until the penultimate climb of the day when the sometimes-rather-tense Martyn Griffiths smashed the record in 41.72s to clinch the title. Cramer sportingly 'declared' after his 41.93s best and a splendid day was 'made' for the Scots because Norrie Galbraith (43.51s) and Jim Campbell (43.63s) took the next two places, Jim in the Modus which he had bought from the retired Ken MacMaster earlier in the year. Behind the two Hart 420R-powered title contenders, ADO and Roy Lane finished third and fourth in the Championship, while in finishing fifth Ted Williams thoroughly deserved to take the new RAC MSA Hill Climb Award of Merit. Numbers 6 to 10 in 1980 would be on the cars of Franklin (who had not competed in every round), Dungworth, MacDowel, Turnbull and Jim Campbell, who also won the Scottish Championship.

As usual the Leaders' series, now backed by Haynes Publishing Group, of course, was fiercely contested, with final victory falling to former motorcycle racer John Meredith whose thinning and greying locks had caused the title 'Old Man of the Hills' to rest on his shoulders with increasing authority despite counter-claims which some insisted should be made by Roy Lane! A new generation of circuit racing inspired 'GT' saloons – space-frame devices which did little more than borrow the name of the car they vaguely resembled – were now beginning to venture onto the hills, and John's now 985cc Imp-engined Marshall & Frazer Mini really belonged in this category, ad did Rowland Hand's Wallinger Stiletto with 1800cc BDG engine, which the South Yardley driver had débuted the previous year after nine years with a highly-modified Anglia 105E; and the Davrian Stiletto-BDG of Thurso farmer Barrogill Angus. Runner-up to the Leighton Buzzard civil servant was Edgbaston engineer Martin Bolsover who had really become a force to be reckoned with in his BDA-engined U2 Mk18 and who headed Russ Ward (now topping his 200th hill climb class win target), Norman Hutchins in the U2-like Phoenix and Redditch mechanic Alan Payne in 'Smiley Riley'.

The tense and fluctuating fortunes of a fascinating RAC Championship contest tended to divert attention from many other worthy performances in a rich variety of cars during the year. Recurring highlights had included the ongoing struggle for Ladies' supremacy between Joy Rainey and Maggie Blankstone, the seemingly-ever-increasing popularity and speed of the variously-powered Mallock U2s – Richard Jones (1600 BDA), Charles Wardle/Jim Robinson (1600 BDA), Bolsover, Ian Curtis (1600 BDA), Nick Bridge and occasional forays by the Mallock family stealing the limelight at various times – and the battles for the smaller-capacity racing classes. Among the 1100s, and apart from Russ Ward, the battles featured the well-tried Brabham-Cosworth BT28 which had been driven by Paul and Andrew Squires and Phil Kidsley for several years, Wellingborough's John Corbyn (Terrapin-BDA Mk1G), the Anson-BDJ SA1 of Londoners Eryl Davies and John Bevan, Jerry Sturman's Harrison-Imp KH4, and Ossett's John Buck who had fitted a 750cc Honda motorcycle engine to his Terrapin Mk8. In fact, Allan Staniforth's versatile design was still as popular as ever and had proved itself to be amenable to such varied power plants as Mini, Ford BDA, Imp (as currently used by Allan himself), NSU TTS, and even a Rover/Buick V8-engined version, although the latter did verge on the terrifying in the handling department. Among the 1600s, John Barratt's now 1600 BDA-engined March Pilbeam 74B/MP28 often vied with Jim Johnstone's BT30, the Harts' re-worked Brabham – now the Hart J/G 79 – Alan Newton's rare Formula Atlantic Huron and the ingenious March 722 of BL development engineers Rob Oldaker and Andy Smith from Bromsgrove. They had what was most definitely the only Austin Allegro-engined March in existence. However, the BL advertising slogan 'Vroom' emblazoned on the side of the March was for once no mere advertising hype. The 1140cc engine (still within the 1600cc class despite the turbo penalty) was fitted with Garrett AiResearch turbocharger and was churning out more than 200 bhp, endowing the car with immense acceleration in the characteristic turbo silence. A similarly unlikely application for the increasingly fashionable turbocharging trend was successfully carried out by Nic Mann, from Newbury. His turbo was attached to an MGB engine which he had fitted to his self-prepared Morris Minor. If this seemed remarkable enough it paled into insignificance when compared with what was to come for the long-suffering roadgoing Morris.

There were plenty of other novelties in what was a generally very good year. Although a paucity of entries forced the H & DLCC to cancel a mooted team event at Loton Park (a similar event had been successful the previous year), the BOC enjoyed a real club occasion at Prescott in June. This was designated as a 'Classic' meeting, catering primarily for the post-Vintage older cars and gave Tim Cameron a rare BTD for the Joe Potts Special. The meeting further featured on the International Bugatti Rally for this was the BOC's Golden Jubilee Year and a magnificent gathering of over 100 Bugattis were to be seen at the course.

Further North, the YSCC returned, rather quietly to a well-modified Shibden Park course where one more Northern success fell to Ian Curtis of the Bradford wool family. Father Laurie and brothers Simon and Martin were all regular competitors with a variety of Mallock U2s. It was something of a vintage year in Scotland too, where apart from the upgrading of Fintray, there was an entirely new course brought into use by the Coltness Car Club in September. This was the mile-long Strathclyde Country Park, just off the M8 motorway in Lanarkshire. At 1527 metres, to be precise, this was unusually long for a British course, and at 30 feet wide (except for a 5 feet wide detour at Triangle) exceptionally spacious. This excellent course had its inaugural fixture on 22 September when plant-hire company director Jimmy Jack set the record at 44.66s with his March-BMW 772, beating Scottish Champion-to-be (and reigning Champion) Jim Campbell, former Champion Norrie Galbraith and the rapid U2 of Kenny Allen. Jack, who had gained his early experience with an Imp saloon, went on to snatch second place in the Grampian Television sponsored series from Norrie Galbraith on a tie-break.

Cramer's Turn

Just as 1979 turned out to be a year characterised by a torrid battle for supremacy between Martyn Griffiths and Chris Cramer, so too did 1980, although there were plenty of people who set out to make it otherwise. The reigning RAC Champion kept his Laurie Billings-prepared Pilbeam MP40, which had benefited from running on very soft Goodyear G45 tyres, but Griffiths had a potent new weapon in his armoury. This was a newly developed 2.5-litre version of the 420R engine from Brian Hart. The new unit developed 335 bhp but, more importantly, produced a healthy 220 lbs/ft of torque and gave Martyn a wider power band to play with. It was purpose-built for hill climbing and the prodigious acceleration from low revs was a revelation at the season's earlier meetings, reminiscent of the old Brabham-Repco with which Mike MacDowel was formerly supreme. Chris Cramer had had his March updated to 782/79B specification with narrower Formula Atlantic-type sidepods. Although separately run, and still tended by Chris and his long-time friend and helper Jeremy Speed, the March remained under Godfrey Crompton's patronage with Godfrey shortly to replace his 782 with a new 802. For the time being Cramer had to be content with the 2.2 Hart and it was not until Bouley Bay in July that he had the use of a 2.5 to match Griffiths'.

Roy Lane was happy enough with the power of the DFV but sought something smaller than the March 771. His solution was to build up the March 79S, for which the old TechCraft name was revived. This was a mixture of 782 and 79B components, with a specially fabricated, John Thompson-built bulkhead to permit the installation of the trusty DFV, and with a 793 cockpit section for good measure. The car was turned out in silver and blue and bore allegiance to Roy's latest sponsor, Steel King Safety Footwear, the company run by Ferrari enthusiast Richard Colton.

Mike Pilbeam had been kept busy over the winter although Alister Douglas-Osborn was retaining his MP31 for the time being. Waring & Gillow team-mate Malcolm Dungworth had a new MP22, chassis 03 built up and fitted with a stretched 3.3 DFV which had been intended originally for a Group 6 sports car project by Italian Umberto Maglioli. Malcolm's old MP22-02 went to the almost fully-recovered Peter Kaye who had enlisted Guyson and Kingston Video support for a brave if rather underfinanced comeback. There were yet more Pilbeams in the offing though. Sutton Coldfield driver Rob Turnbull enlisted unusual sponsorship from the Recro '80 Exhibition for the one-off ex-Formula 2 (Onyx Racing/Patrick Neve) MP42 which differed from the successful MP40 mainly in having a longer wheelbase, narrower track 'circuit' chassis. There was also the first Pilbeam sports-racer, the MP43. Beautifully engineered and finished as all the Pilbeams had become, this was really a wider, two-seater version of the MP40/42 design, and was commissioned by David Garnett. The Yorkshire thermoplastic bearing manufacturer had enjoyed considerable success (and a few off-course excursions) with the old Chevron-Alpina B19, which he intended to keep for 'guest drivers', but was now aiming to set new standards with the 2.0 Hart 420R-powered machine which was the first true ground-effect sports car designed for the hills.

New standards or not, David would have his work cut out to keep up with the ever more formidable and more sophisticated Mallock U2s which looked likely to worry a few of the big single-seater contenders. Richard 'Ferret' Fry, who had successfully campaigned a variety of old U2s including the old Chris Cramer 1300cc BL-engined car, was to compete with a 2.3 Hart in his Mk20X, while Richard Jones – who had given up trying to compete with a big single-seater on an inadequate budget, was set to cause a few sensations with his 2-litre version.

One successful Mallock U2 driver who had moved on, though, was Martin Bolsover. He was tackling the 1600cc racing class with an updated March 772 where his strongest competition was liable to be the latest, and most radical, variation on the Terrapin theme. David Gould, an electrical contracts manager from Newbury, was one of the more seasoned Terrapin drivers and he and Allan Staniforth together designed a genuine ground-effect Terrapin for David to run, with a 1600 BDA power unit. The very rigid square-tube chassis was designed to split, rather neatly, at the double roll-over-bar behind the driver, to facilitate the removal of the transverse engine and gearbox.

Returning to the larger racing cars, David Franklin was intending to carry on with his Wendy Wools March-BMW although he was now finding a lot of enjoyment in circuit racing an MGB GT in MGCC races, and was gradually to run down his hill climb activities in favour of this and Historic racing. Without fuss, Mike MacDowel had decided to hang up his helmet for good and the John Judd DFV out of the Coogar was bought by the jovial Ted Williams who intended to run himself and son Mark in hill climbs and sprints in an unused Formula 1 Hesketh 308E. Roger Willoughby, too, had decided to cut back on his activities and intended to lend the old March 712S to Middleton Motor Services (Redditch) mechanic Alan Payne. The McRae GM1 which had had such an illustrious career with Roy Lane, and had then earned Dave Harris many sprint successes now went to Stephen Cuff in Frome, while one of 1979's most promising newcomers, Falmouth printer Max Harvey exchanged the old Boxer for an ex-Brian Henton 2.0 March-Hart 792, rebuilt for him by Laurie Billings.

Two days before the RAC opener at Loton Park, Roy Lane had been up to the new Strathclyde Park course which had been added to the Guyson/BARC schedule but did not find the course as much to his taste as the leading Scots, finding it "too open and featureless". Nevertheless, his new March was beaten only by Jimmy Jack, although he was only 0.28s faster than Norrie Galbraith who had had his March 742 updated to 782 standard by Robin Smith. The event was watched by a reported 35,000 spectators, a phenomenal number until one realises that entry to Strathclyde is free!

Yorkshireman David Garnett commissioned the first Pilbeam sports-racer, the MP43, for 1980. Seen here at Shelsley, David enjoyed considerable success in 1980/1981.
BOB COOPER

The story of the RAC Championship began with an almost demoralising domination by the reigning Champion. At Loton Park Martyn Griffiths kicked off with a new hill record in 50.37s, to give him an 0.63s advantage over David Franklin, who was only 0.11s faster than Harris, with Cramer fourth after a spin at Fallow and a general discontent about the tyres and handling of his March, Chris was rather happier at Wiscombe, setting a 38.42s BTD at the traditional Saturday 'warm up', and then getting down to 38.06s on the Sunday, a mere hundredth of a second up on the highly competitive Harris. But that was not enough to deal with Griffiths as the blue Pilbeam shot away from Wiscombe's hairpins to record 37.83s. Chris Cramer looked as though he might have Prescott in the bag after a superbly controlled 41.32s course record on the class runs. It was BTD but it still didn't stop Griffiths from snatching maximum RAC points. At the end of the day Martyn turned in an only fractionally slower 41.33s whereas Chris was unable to better 41.84s, and with both Franklin and Lane also in the 41s bracket. At Barbon, Griffiths' 22.34s gave him another course record, beating off the DFV-engined cars of ADO and Lane, and with Cramer and Harris lacking the advantage of Griffiths' 2.5 Hart, beaten into honourable fourth and fifth places.

The first chink in Griffiths' armour manifested itself at Harewood, or to be more precise, Chris Cramer had got the March handling to his liking on a course where he often excelled. His 37.46s best was a new course record, although Griffiths was only 0.23s slower. So far, Alister Douglas-Osborn did not seem to have found much advantage over his previous year's performances, but the Waring & Gillow Pilbeam came back into the reckoning with a vengeance at Shelsley, in the MAC's 75th year (the MAC are very proud of their long history and never miss an opportunity to boost their hill with a convenient anniversary). The shrill note of the world's most successful Grand Prix engine was heard for only 26.71s before 'Big Al' could claim another Shelsley record, and in so doing set a landmark time for the hill. Roy Lane also made the best of his Cosworth horses to leave Griffiths and Cramer in third and fourth spot although the day's other sensation came from Richard Jones who took seventh

After giving up the struggle of trying to compete in the big racing car class on a low budget, Richard Jones put up some stunning performances with his 2.0 Mallock U2 Mk15, especially at Shelsley.
BOB COOPER

place in the Top Ten with a remarkable 28.30s, the fastest time at Shelsley by a Sports car – although not a class record according to the Shelsley rules: his earlier 28.91s counted for that – and a mind-blowing time for a front-engined Mallock U2.

Back on the twistier hills and Chris Cramer's challenge began to gather momentum just as it had the previous year. At Fintray, Chris lopped a prodigious 1.19s off the record to leave it at 27.14s, and with Griffiths down in fourth place behind Lane and Turnbull on a day when both Alister Douglas-Osborn and Godfrey Crompton destroyed their cars in accidents. Crompton was quick to replace his crashed March with a new 802 chassis while ADO soon made it known that he would be aiming to début the new Pilbeam MP47 at Gurston in August. The latest Waring & Gillow/Maples car was to have a narrow tub with wider sidepods for more effective ground-effect in the absence of the now banned skirts, although the same DFV 144 would be utilised.

Chris Cramer made a clean sweep in Scotland for his 44.80s at Doune defeated Griffiths and Turnbull, although before Bouley Bay Martyn recovered some of his morale with a 49s BTD climb at Loton Park and then broke into the 26s bracket at Shelsley with a 26.99s best which was matched exactly by Roy Lane. This was only Shelsley's third-ever tie for BTD but even more remarkably, Martyn took BTD on aggregate because he recorded 26.99s on two occasions! Although not by any means a record-breaking climb, the 39.48s time put up by Peter Kaye gave him a morale boosting BTD at Harewood after a shaky first appearance with MP22-02 at the previous Harewood meeting.

The big difference when the Championship trail reached the Channel Islands was that Chris Cramer had fitted a 2.5 Hart engine in the red March. As usual Bouley Bay had the support of long-time sponsors Randall's Brewery (part of Greenall Whitley/Grünhalle Lager, Cramer's former sponsor) and Fuel Supplies (CI) Ltd (Shell) while Lombard North Central presented an award for the first driver to break 40s. It was Chris Cramer who claimed that one, and another 10 points, with a scintillating 39.88s record to which Griffiths could only reply with 40.32s, and with Rob Turnbull on 40.43s before his efforts were spoilt by oil spraying onto the Pilbeam's rear wheels.

Although he was having a rather erratic year, David Franklin put up a vintage 'Baldies are Best' type performance on his 10th Wedding anniversary to win at Le Val des Terres, where his 32.14s compared to Griffiths' 32.79s (before crashing rather heavily on the last bend of his second RAC climb) and Cramer's 32.88s. Chris Cramer had missed Craigantlet the previous year but this time he certainly could not afford to pass up the opportunity and stunned the Ulstermen with a 51.03s course record, 2.91s faster than Peter Kaye, who was lucky to miss the rain shower which ensured that Lane and Griffiths were unable to better the 55s bracket.

In formally celebrating Shelsley's 75th Anniversary, the Midland Automobile Club were rewarded with a truly vintage meeting where ten records fell, including ADO's short-lived outright figure. An exceptionally neat and precise climb from Martyn Griffiths gave the MAC Committee member the record at 26.60s, well ahead of Lane and a rather wild Cramer. With his new Pilbeam MP47 still not ready, ADO was unable to defend his record but was competing in David Garnett's superb MP43 to score 3 RAC points with a resounding 28.17s. Fastest sports car time ever? No. Richard Jones did another electrifying climb to leave that particular target at 28.05s! There were more notable records from Joy Rainey (now promoting the motor and cycle trades charity BEN) in 29.75s, Martin Bolsover's ex-Ted Williams March in 28.95s and the glorious and very rare lightweight, ex-works Porsche Carrera RSR of Roland Jones (32.40s). Shelsley never overlooks the people and the machinery which have made up its heritage. Anthony's Brooke's ex-Mays Vauxhall Villiers; MAC Secretary Mark Joseland who had moved from his usual mount, Frazer-Nash 'Patience', to 'Terror III'; Ron Sant in Basil Davenport's legendary 'Spider'; and Roger Willoughby in the ex-Dick Henderson Cooper Mk7 all took part. What a pity that Raymond Mays, who had died the previous winter, was not there to see it.

Gurston brought a pleasant surprise in that while ADO clocked an encouraging 29.30s (sixth place) on his first outing with the new MP47, it was Peter Kaye who really excelled with a 28.58s hill record to show that he was well and truly back to form, over half a second up on a three-way tie on 29.10s between Griffiths, Turnbull and Cramer. The worth of the new MP47 was demonstrated at Prescott where Alister's 40.93s was good enough for 8 points on this sinuous hill even though Dave Harris matched the time. Also going well in ninth place on 42.18s was the new, lightened March 802 with 2.3 Hart engine driven by Godfrey Crompton. Christened Aliclimber, the car bore allegiance to

Linden Alimack system scaffolding, marketed through Crompton's Freeline Plant business. But all the while these performances were overshadowed by a blistering 40.37s course record from Cramer, the critical factor being Chris's fantastic progress through the Esses. Even Griffiths could not match this, although his 40.74s was good enough for second. Not for the first time the Prescott Gold Cup went to someone rather out of the mainstream of Championship hill climbing, to Dudley Mason-Styrron. However, the Trophy was just reward for the pleasure which he and Sally Colton (now Mrs Mason-Styrron) had given everyone by campaigning the jewel-like Ferrari Dino 206S sports car, the ex-works/Tony Dean car. This hard-worked machine ran in the Ferrari Owners Club class which was still run at Prescott events even though the club had now gone its separate way from the parent Bugatti Owners Club, the feeling being that although the Ferrari was the nearest post-war equivalent to the Bugatti, the owners of the modern Ferrari tended to be rather different types of people from the present day owners of Bugattis.

When the points were totted up it could be seen that Chris had a three point margin over Martyn, although then there was an 18-point gap to Lane. Rob Turnbull was fourth after a good year with the Recro '80 Pilbeam, leading Award of Merit winner Dave Harris who had gone exceedingly well in his first really serious year of hill climbing as opposed to sprinting, although he had faded somewhat in mid-season before reset suspension and new tyres set him on his way again. The Top Ten were completed by ADO, Franklin, Godfrey Crompton (runner-up in the Award of Merit despite a bad run of mechanical problems around August), the ever-consistent Dungworth and an overjoyed Norrie Galbraith who also won the Scottish Championship – by 4 points from Jimmy Jack – for the second time.

As early as 25 August, at Gurston Down, the Haynes-sponsored Leaders' Championship had been won by Charles Barter. This was just the first of three major championships to be won by the exceptionally consistent Dorset watercress grower in a highly successful year, even by Barter standards. He had sold his immaculate Davrian to John Foran, the Group General Manager of the Elliot Group of Construction Companies who continued to gain more awards with the car, while Charles returned to the saloon class – with a difference. His 1200cc Hartwell-engined Imp was a Davrian spaceframe job and his succession of new class records gave him top Leaders' honours over that much travelled Scotsman from Caithness, Barrogill Angus and Charles Wardle with the screaming ex-Alan Jones Formula Atlantic BDA-engined Mallock U2 Mk21 which he shared with Costock's Jim Robinson, and which kept Russ Ward's little Chevron B9/15 down to fourth. Robinson had many seasons of increasing success with Mallock U2s before he joined forces with Wardle who had cut his teeth on a road-going Lotus 7, and rapidly showed himself to be very fast indeed.

Barter won the Guyson/BARC series for an unequalled fourth time, by a healthy 4.23 marks, from the rather-ordinary-seeming but always most competitive Ford Escort RS1600 of burly George Swinbourne, from Shaw, near Oldham, who rather more narrowly beat off the attentions of James Thomson in the Guyson Chevette and the amazing Richard Jones who also contrived to finished fourth, behind Norrie Galbraith, in the RAC MSA Award of Merit competition in his U2. Fifth in the BARC series was Davidson Pearce advertising account controller, and spare time hill climb reporter, Ian Crammond with the colourful Snackpot Sunbeam Talbot Lotus, prominently bearing allegiance to one of Bachelors convenience foods. Just as had happened on more than one previous occasion the Guyson/BARC FTD Awards series resulted in a 'consolation prize' for the runner-up in the RAC title. Martyn Griffiths had an 8 point margin over Roy Lane, with Rob Turnbull dropping Chris Cramer to fourth in a year when Chris understandably concentrated harder than ever on winning the RAC title.

The strength in depth of British hill climbing was emphasised by the most successful institution of yet another major Championship series. The Wolverhampton Datsun and TVR dealership of Bradburn and Wedge (well known as Rob Turnbull's B & W Motors sponsors for several seasons) backed a six-round Midland Hill Climb Championship co-ordinated by Hagley & DLCC luminary Tony Fletcher. With a substantial £2,000 prize fund and two rounds each at three of the country's finest hills: Shelsley, Loton and Prescott, this compact series could hardly fail given that every counting meeting was likely to be well supported by hill climbing's leading talent even without incorporating a new championship. Nevertheless, the new series added extra interest and gave many Midlanders an extra Championship incentive without adding a punishing schedule of distant events to their stretched budgets.

This provided Charles Barter with his third title, although this time he had only two points to spare over Richard Jones, while the Davrian of Terry Clifford beat off regular Champion pot winners Ward, Martin Bolsover, and Martyn Griffiths.

At the same regional level – although some regions are definitely more equal than others – Burnley florest Nick Bridge won the Dutton-Forshaw/Longton series for the second successive year in his U2 Mk20B, and his father Derek and brother Tony were exceeded in numbers in Northern events only by the Curtis family. Up in Scotland the always well-supported road car division of the Grampian Television series produced a tie which even the tie decider could not break, so joint winners were Alex Graham from Wishaw, in his Mini-Jem, and Invergordon Chrysler Avenger driver, Richard Martin. A little extra interest was injected into the lacklustre Irish hill climb scene with a short Pioneer Hi-Fi sponsored series with a £500 first prize which went to veteran Formula Atlantic competitor Ken Fildes, from the Formula Vees of Mick Merrigan and Shay Lawless.

Despite the ready availability and growing sophistication of factory-built racing cars, hill climbing continued to attract those who enjoyed designing and building their own cars, the spiritual descendants of those enthusiasts who enjoyed themselves in the 1920s and 1930s with remarkable concoctions incorporating assorted GN, Morgan, JAP, Ford and Austin Seven bits. There was Nic Mann's splendid and most effective Morris Minor, complete with turbocharged MGB engine; the Broadspeed Jaguar XJ 5.3C-liveried Austin A35 shaped device of Andy and Alex Williams which was built round a Lotus Elan chassis and was fitted with a Skip Brown-built Imp engine; hill climbing clergyman Barry Whitehead's Suzuki-engined RBS; and Keith Gowers' Monopin-Honda, among many more, some of which have already been mentioned.

Added interest, particularly at the Midland meetings, came from the splendid battle for Ladies supremacy between Joy Rainey and Maggie Blankstone, both of whom were perfectly capable of holding their own in open competition. This was the first time since the days of Patsy Burt and Agnes Mickel that there was a real fight for ladies' honours. New record figures were set by Joy at Prescott in

Jim Campbell, seen here on Strathclyde Park's relatively wide open spaces in his ex-MacMaster Modus M4, was one of a doughty band of Scotsmen who covered long distances to contest British championships. He won the Scottish title in 1978 and 1979 with a Brabham BT35.
BILL HENDERSON

May with the 240 bhp Murrain which boasted a compressed-air-activated clutch employing a Soda-stream bottle and concocted by the ingenious Murray Rainey; Maggie reduced the Shelsley time to 30.04s in her family U2 in July; only to have Joy retake that record in August in 29.75s. Joy dropped the Loton record to 55.17s in August, while the following month she reduced the Prescott time to a resounding 43.92s, by which time Maggie had won back the Loton record in 54.74s.

Even the odd 'celebrity' was attracted to this colourful amateur scene. Television personality John Noakes, a children's favourite with his 'Go with Noakes' programme acquitted himself honourably at Harewood in David Garnett's Chevron B19 although an even more apprehensive John Burnham, the car's regular mechanic, was almost two seconds faster. The following month Porsche endurance racing driver and Le Mans star Derek Bell – never one to lose his genuine enthusiasm for motor sport – accepted the invitation to drive Godfrey Crompton's March at Loton. Unfortunately, the car shed its drive belts but, quick as a flash, Roy Lane sportingly offered his March to Derek. After a familiarisation run in 61.06s, Bell showed his class in a strange car and in a totally unfamiliar discipline by shooting up in 53.21s, only just over 2 seconds slower than the former Champion himself in his regular car.

The problem of finding extra courses on which to run the smaller meetings remained as intractable as ever although the Plymouth MC, who had formerly run the Hemerdon climbs, now found a course at Werrington Park, near Launceston, where Nigel Bigwood struck the first blow with a 40.8s BTD in the Ensign which had been David Franklin's car. Still down West where these smaller courses seemed to proliferate over the years more than anywhere else, the Taunton and Burnham-on-Sea Clubs were holding meetings restricted to saloons and sports cars at Cricket St Thomas, near Chard.

Establishment defeat

Although the 1980 RAC Championship had been won at the wheel of a March, the chances of a repeat performance in 1981 appeared to be fairly remote. Champion Cramer and Godfrey Crompton were to have a pair of the ex-works Formula 2 Toleman TG280 chassis, designed by Rory Byrne and which had been driven to the previous year's Formula 2 Championship by Brian Henton. These cars had been designed from the beginning to make optimum use of Pirelli radial racing tyres. That was another challenge for Chris Cramer to face up to. Another change was that his car would appear in the green and white J. Jack Crane Hire colours after a fairly complicated arrangement with Jimmy Jack which gave the Scotsman Chris's Championship winning March for a serious attack on the Scottish Championship and enabled Barrogill Angus to have the BMW engine out of Jack's older March installed in his 'GT' Stiletto.

Chris Cramer indulges in a spot of kerbing, at Harewood's Orchard corner, in his 1981 contender; an ex-Formula 2 Toleman TG280.
BOB COOPER

Martin Bolsover obliterated the 1600cc racing car opposition in 1981 with a new Pilbeam MP51. Some of the records he set were still standing in the late nineteen-eighties.
BOB COOPER

With David Franklin no longer taking the hill climb championship as seriously, that left Roy Lane as the leading hope for Bicester with a Steel King-backed 802. Roy had sold the 79S to sprint specialist Ken Ayers, from Reading, and opted to try a Formula 2-type set-up after so many years of bigger cars. His 802 Hart was updated to 812 specification but in practice Roy was never really happy with it. Before the season was out he had come to a mutually acceptable deal to swap it for the older 782-Hart of Team Five Steps import/export specialist Roger Philpott, from Dyce, Aberdeen. For the rest, Tony Brown took Jack's old March, Max Harvey retained his 792 (fitted like Lane's 802 with a full 2.5 Hart); Pershore's Chris Dowson exchanged his Unidraw Engineering Design & Manufacturing-sponsored, ex-Jim Campbell Brabham BT35 for the splendid old Brabham-Repco BT36X; Nigel Bigwood took on the ex-Cramer/Edwards March 76A/781, still with the tall and heavy GA engine; and Norrie Galbraith opted for one of the last of the Bolton-built Chevrons, the F2 B48S, rebuilt in Scotland by Robin Smith.

But what of the Pilbeams? The grip on British hill climbing by Mike Pilbeam's creations was strengthening. Jim Thomson's Team Guyson was reorganised to run its own single-seater after several essays into sponsoring other people's cars. Jim had bought the superb handling MP40 from Martyn Griffiths and this, complete with 2.5 Hart, was to be campaigned by Jim's 20-year-old elder son James – a big step after barely 2 seasons in saloons – while Jim stuck to the Chevette. Peter Kaye was taken on to maintain the team cars, although Peter was still trying to find ways and means of mounting another challenge of his own. Griffiths had found the previous year's efforts a mite expensive and had not ordered a new car, but had taken over Dave Harris' former mount while the 1980 RAC Sprint Champion ordered a new MP50. Up in Yorkshire the Waring & Gillow/Maples mechanics Dave Elliot and Steve Oyibo had rebuilt their two cars which were ready for a major challenge. ADO's MP47, with 2 inches longer wheelbase and 2 inches wider track was fitted with a special new Alan Smith-developed 3.6-litre version of the DFV which had been dyno-tested to 520 bhp at 9,750 rpm, and an FGA as opposed to FG400 gearbox to cope with the additional power and torque. Malcolm Dungworth 'made do' with a 486 bhp 3.3 Alan Smith DFV in his MP22. Apart from David Garnett's sports racing MP43 (which was later written off in one of David's bigger off-course excursions), there was a glorious new red and blue MP51 for Martin Bolsover. The Edgbaston engineer had been pretty dominant in the 1600cc racing class with his March but he was about to obliterate the opposition with this BDA-engined Pilbeam, which was closely related to its 2.5 Hart-engined cousins and for which Martin had gained sponsorship from no less than Ladbrokes. With Rob Turnbull now able to run a full 2.5 Hart in his chassis, the Pilbeam hand was indeed a strong one.

That left only one other serious contender for outright honours. After finding the Hesketh hardly ideal for hill climbs, although son Mark finished runner-up to Dave Harris with it in the Sprint Championship, Ted Williams went into partnership with Richard Fry to run an F3-type Ralt RT1, but fitted with a 2.5 Hart 420R.

Before the first RAC round at Wiscombe Park on 12 April there were full-scale dress rehearsals at the first Midland Championship counters at Loton and Prescott. A 51.38s climb from Martyn Griffiths at Loton left him 0.2s up on a rather spectacular Dave Harris, but with young James Thomson a mere 0.15s further in arrears after winning the class earlier in the day, and recording a time which was that decisive 0.01s faster than ADO. The following week James went even better. Showing great speed, precision and sheer natural ability, Thomson left Prescott with a 40.68s BTD to the 40.97s of Alister Douglas-Osborn who many felt to be the best bet for the Championship now that even more mid-range torque had been added to the enormous power of the DFV.

Dave Harris always seemed to slip into top form very quickly at the beginning of the season and he made the best use of the latest F1 qualifying-type Avon tyres to strike the first blow at Wiscombe with a 38.29s climb although it was close with the Waring & Gillow Pilbeam on 38.57s and James Thomson very happy with a 38.65s best for 8 points after winning the class with 38.62s. Further down the list, behind Lane, Griffiths looked less content with his MP40/42/46 update, Franklin was sixth without sidepods on the March but with a rather special 2.3-litre BMW engine and a new sports-racing challenge figured in ninth place on 40.75s. Guernseyman Graham Priaulx had fitted a 2.0 BDX engine in a Sports 2000 Tiga SC80 chassis and to get into the Top Ten he even managed to topple Richard Jones with his 2.2 Hart 420R-engined U2.

A busy Easter weekend saw important meetings at Strathclyde Park, Harewood and Loton Park on successive days, and James Thomson arrived at Loton fresh from a 38.89s BTD at Harewood. Still in the right frame of mind, James became the youngest driver ever to win an RAC round when he ascended the Shropshire hill in a fine 49.85s, a solid 0.68s faster than Douglas-Osborn. Harris was third but an incredible fourth was Richard Jones who flung the U2 up in 51.30s. Fifth was Ted Williams – in Pilbeam MP41. The Equipe Ricardo-Eduardo had bought the car off Rob Turnbull who was finding the financial going a little tough, and the Redland Motor House proprietor and his younger partner were immediately appreciative of this notably good handling chassis.

Alister Douglas-Osborn emphasised what a good all-round car the MP47 had been developed into by taking the maximum points at Prescott in 46.80s (he had recorded 46.34s earlier in the day), while Thomson was a solid third behind Prescott expert Lane and ahead of Cramer who seemed to be making his usual painstaking progress with the difficult Toleman. Conversely, Dave Harris was dropping down the list, finding that his sticky Avon tyres were really good enough for only three or four meetings, such is the cost of state-of-the-art technology. After this performance at Prescott, ADO was pretty confident on arrival at Barbon. It wasn't misplaced, for he blasted the DFV-engined machine up Barbon Manor's front drive in a 21.75s course record. Two other drivers were awarded the rather attractive Barbon Gold Stars, presented to anyone breaking the course record at the beginning of the meeting. The amazing James Thomson clocked 21.84s and Chris Cramer really came back into the reckoning in 21.98s, running the Toleman on an interesting concoction of M & H front tyres and Goodyear rears – having decided that the Pirellis really were not the way to go in hill climbing.

Far from being able to acclimatise himself to single-seaters in his first season without Championship pressures, James Thomson now found himself being talked of as a possible Champion, especially among his well-meaning and enthusiastic fellow-Yorkshiremen. This was where his calm and undemonstrative temperament helped him enormously for 20-year-olds are not normally noted for calm calculation and ability to attain one hundred per cent concentration, which are so vital in hill climbing at this level.

Twenty-year-old James Thomson was 'only' third at Prescott in May 1981 with his ex-Griffiths Pilbeam MP40K, now tended by Peter Kaye. However, this talented youngster was already shaking the sport's establishment on his way to a remarkable clean sweep in the 1981 Championships.
BOB LIGHT

But he was human. The pressure took its toll, for the one and only occasion at Shelsley where he had failed runs through overdoing it, and ADO made it three wins in a row with a 27.30s BTD to the 28.01s of Cramer, 28.09s of Williams, Franklin, a rather subdued Griffiths and Richard Fry. James Thomson recovered his composure with a 37.65s win at Harewood before it was off to Scotland where the Championship tide turned. A seized engine in the MP47 meant that ADO had to drive the less potent MP22 at the Five Steps-sponsored Fintray meeting and his best efforts were good enough only for fourth place. James Thomson set another BTD in 27.51s but dropped to third in the RAC runs where Chris Cramer scored his first big win with the Toleman in 27.62s and where Lane also beat the Guyson car. But at Doune, at a sun-drenched meeting, Thomson was uncatchable. His 39.70s smashed the course record and give him an 0.3s margin over Chris Cramer, while ADO was still only fourth even though he was back in the MP47.

The RAC round at Harewood had now moved back to July, by which time James Thomson had joined the select band of Shelsley BTD winners with a fine 26.88s to wipe out the June memories. With two wins at Harewood already to his credit much was expected of him. And he delivered. Twice he broke the course record but with only one RAC climb yet to run he was down in third place behind Chris Cramer (36.73s) and ADO (37.05s). Calmly working out that his now warmer tyres would give him an extra three or fourth tenths without any extra effort on his part, he executed a superbly-controlled climb which stopped the watches at 36.72s. He had won by 0.01s!

Ever since the beginning of the season Martin Bolsover had been making the 1600cc class his own province and had regularly made the Top Ten runs, but there was grave doubt about the validity of the 39.00s record time he was given on a class run at Bouley Bay, especially when he was over 2 seconds slower in the Top Ten for no very good reason. Rather overshadowed by this triumph by the timekeepers, James Thomson snapped up another 10 points, this time with a whole seven-hundredths of a second to spare over Cramer.

Crossing over to a very slippery Le Val des Terres, the margin widened when James, now looking very like a possible Champion, reduced the record to 30.95s to the 31.56s of Cramer and a commendable 31.77s from David Franklin on distinctly inferior tyres.

In 1980, James had gone over to Ulster to help Peter Kaye at Craigantlet but this time the roles were reversed and it was a straight fight between Cramer, the hill record-holder, and Thomson. Chris was on good form and climbed in 50.51s but the tall, fair-haired Yorkshireman was unstoppable. His 50.39s climb added one more to his growing tally of course records, while Jimmy Jack made a very hectic weekend worth while – he was competing at a Scottish Championship round at Fintray the next day – by beating Lane and ADO (who came close to losing control of the Pilbeam) for third place.

Alister's season had rather lost momentum after the engine problems at Fintray but he bounced back at Shelsley in August where he recaptured his course record in 26.42s, although Thomson's 26.48s was the fastest-ever Hart-powered time, and Ted Williams also went notably well, dropping Chris Cramer to fourth place. With a gap now to the next round at Gurston, Alister was left to reflect on his 6 point Championship deficit over the Otley newcomer, and his reflections could not have been made any more cheerful after a stunning Thomson virtuoso performance at the August Midland round at Loton. James' four runs were timed at: 49.06s; 48.98s; 48.89s and 48.84s. That gave him a new course record on every run! He followed that up by returning to Harewood where he again came from behind to rob Chris Cramer of another BTD in 36.75s to Chris' 36.81s.

Alister Douglas-Osborn simply had to win at Gurston, and he did, leaving the course record at 28.54s, but with Thomson the only other driver to break into the 28s bracket. As the battle reached fever pitch, the Championship moved to Prescott where the course record fell five times. But at the end of the day James Thomson greatly strengthened his position with a 39.39s BTD which was just out of reach of Alister's 39.44s and Chris Cramer's 39.59s. These three were in a class of their own which even Dave Harris, an acknowledged expert at Prescott, could not quite join.

The title was finally clinched by Thomson at Wiscombe with his lowest placing of the season (apart from Shelsley in June), sixth in 38.94s! It was almost a formality really, and a harmless spin on the

A new Shelsley course record in 26.42s was a highlight of Alister Douglas-Osborn's 1981 season in the Pilbeam MP47.
BOB COOPER

damp track on his first RAC climb by the new Champion made no difference for ADO's 38.69s was good enough only for fourth place. There was rather an 'end-of-term' atmosphere, and the day really belonged to Ted Williams, the cheerful and immensely popular Bristolian. Ted had rarely been far adrift of the main Championship battle during the season but at Wiscombe the Pilbeam MP41's excellent handling characteristics were seen to good effect on a greasy track to give Ted his first ever RAC Championship win in 38.17s, beating Harris and Griffiths, who had put up one of his best performances for some time. Into the Top Ten for the first time came the unassuming Alan Payne. After his forays in Roger Willoughby's trusty March-Buick, and some outings in the ex-Mark Williams U2, Alan had campaigned the ex-Alan Humphries March-GA 761 but had now obtained the ex-Mike Mac-Dowel Coogar to which he had fitted his self-prepared Buick engine out of 'Smiley Riley' (now being driven by Scotch Egg Racing's Nick Langdon). Alan's first point was well-deserved as he always made the most of his low-budget machinery and was also gaining something of a reputation for extreme bravery in the wet. Not far off a Top Ten time was the 40.77s recorded by the old March-Buick of Roger Willoughby. But Roger was not at the wheel. The chassis' original owner, Sir Nick Williamson, was having an outing just to remind everyone how fast he was!

Before the last act at Doune, there was much celebration at Harewood where the BARC(Y) were holding their 100th meeting at Stockton Farm, and where the new Champion (by the end of the day he had racked up six assorted Championships!) came 'home' to receive the acclamation of his enthusiastic supporters. Then 'Big Al' went and spoilt it by ending James's run of Harewood BTDs by recording 39.24s on a rather muddy course after Saturday rain. Of those competing, Allan Staniforth, who was second in the 1100cc racing-division to Wellingborough crash/repair specialist John Corbyn (Saracen SF79), and Jimmy Johnstone who drove Roy Lane's superbly restored and little used ex-Martin Brain/Clive Oakley Cooper-Daimler T84, had competed at the first meeting back in 1962.

It was wet at Doune but James Thomson set the final seal on a year when he had achieved a mercurial success exceeding even that of Peter Lawson by climbing in 46.76s and beating Roy Lane who was much happier in the older March 782 even though it had a less powerful 2.3-litre Hart engine than that in the 802. BTD actually fell to Martin Bolsover again as he clocked 46.73s on a class run just before the heavens opened and ruled out further improvement from the big single-seaters.

So, James Thomson had broken the mould of top-class hill climbing where no driver had won the title without several years of big single-seater experience since Peter Lawson's time. In fact, ever since Mike MacDowel's 'sabbatical' after his 1974 title year, there had been no serious challenge to a tight group of vastly experienced competitors consisting of Lane, Douglas-Osborn, Franklin, Cramer and Griffiths who had taken the RAC title turn and turn about. The final points tally gave Thomson 98 points to the 93 of Douglas-Osborn and the 87 of Chris Cramer who had done well to bring the Toleman – very much a circuit racing car, albeit a highly successful one – to a fine pitch of competitiveness. Dave Harris totted up 74 points in a rather uneven season, ten more than Lane, and with Griffiths a lowly sixth on 60 after finding that his MP46-designated chassis was not as good as the MP40 (now known as MP40K in deference to Peter Kaye's preparation contribution). Completing the Top Ten were Ted Williams, Martin Bolsover (who had been exceptionally consistent, qualifying for the RAC runs on 13 occasions), David Franklin and Richard Fry.

The Award of Merit competition was really no contest, with James Thomson naturally taking a maximum score, from Bolsover, Williams and Max Harvey.

The Haynes RAC Leaders' Championship was a very different story with Barrogill Angus only winning the premier class-based Championship on a tie-break from John Meredith. The Leighton Buzzard driver had had a relatively quiet 1980 season with a radical Marshall & Fraser-built spaceframe Mini Traveller with Imp engine, but for 1981 he finally abandoned the Mini concept and set out to match his old friend and rival Charles Barter with a 1.2 Hartwell Imp-engined Maguire spaceframe Imp-lookalike. Charles Wardle lost a little ground after a Shelsley mishap, in the screaming BDA-engined British Racing Green (rare by the 1980s) U2 but his 66 points total was only 6 behind the other two. During the year both Charles and co-driver Jim Robinson were finally overcoming the obstacle of Martin Bolsover's 1979 class records! Josh Sadler enjoyed another good season, now running a more socially acceptable white and blue liveried Porsche 911, fitted with a rather special Autofarm 3.5-litre engine, and kept John Corbyn down to sixth. This particular Top Ten was completed by Jim Robinson, Charles Barter's 1.2 Solo Imp (charles competing in a less strenuous season as his business was demanding rather more time), Roland Jones' silver lightweight Porsche Carrera RSR, and the little Davrian Mk6 of David Watson, from Berkhamstead. Russ Ward managed tenth place with an 1100cc March 773, although his later performances were in his brother-in-law's Harrison KH4 after Russ had written off the March. John Corbyn's success with his 1100cc BDA-engined FF2000 Saracen chassis was particularly well deserved. After many seasons in this class he had actively encouraged a number of competitors to take up the sport, and in 1981 the class featured several John Corbyn Motors entries in Terrapins which had been through John's hands. His firm's bodywork specialist Graham Butcher, with his wife Helen, shared John's ex-David Gould Mk1C/B, John Beeden was entered in the original Corbyn Mk1C, and Derek Sharman had yet another Terrapin on the strength.

After a highly successful first year, the B & W Motors Midland Championship was expanded for 1981 with three counting events at each of the three venues, more prize money, and further sponsorship and promotion forthcoming from Wolverhampton independent radio station, Beacon Radio, and *The Birmingham Post* newspaper. The latter was to back another innovation: *The Birmingham Post* Top Ten Awards, to a similar format to the Guyson/BARC FTD Awards but with only five meetings to count. These excluded the RAC Championship meetings. A Clubmans Sports Car class for the popular Clubmans chassis cars which retained their Ford pushrod engines was also added to the main Championship class structure, as per Guyson/BARC.

Unfortunately, as plans for 1981 were being formulated some uncharacteristic acrimony crept into relations between the BARC's Yorkshire Centre and the Midlands series promoters. Although strong

Charles Wardle (pictured) and Jim Robinson were finally overcoming Martin Bolsover's 1979 1600cc sports-racing car records in 1981 with their shrill Mallock U2-BDA.
BOB COOPER

personalities were involved on both sides and some felt that the well-established Guyson/BARC series had little to offer the Midland clubs, the problem seemed basically to be one of communications, or rather the lack of them. The rift was eventually patched up with customary good sense but for 1981 the net result was a greatly strengthened Midland series and a weakened Guyson/BARC Championship, divided into Northern and Southern zones, but with a rather obvious gap in the middle with no rounds scheduled at Loton, Shelsley or Prescott. After six years of sponsoring the series Guyson were intending to withdraw at the end of 1980 but when things were not looking too rosy for the Championship their extended support was most gratefully received. The revised 12-round programme now featured an event at Great Farthingloe and a substantial Scottish element with rounds at Strathclyde Park, Fintray and Doune.

Moreover, after being devised, instigated and run by the Yorkshire Centre since its inception, the Championship was now to be run by the BARC's racing-orientated Thruxton Head Office. It was a rather wearing time for the Yorkshire Centre for their own racing activities at Croft had had to be curtailed for financial reasons, by edict from Thruxton, although the fortunes of Harewood were definitely rising again. For 1981 Mike Wilson and his colleagues had put together a well-endowed (£3,000 total prize money) single-venue Championship with long-term Harewood sponsors Shell. Organised in a similar fashion to the Guyson/BARC series, with a subsidiary FTD Awards 'scratch' Championship, over five rounds, the Shell Super Oil Harewood Hill Climb Championship was an immediate success.

So was an innovative scheme to provide extra revenue for this consistently financially successful venue. The 'Support the Yorkshire Centre Scheme' offered a low-cost promotional package – at £250 – to local businesses, which gave advertising and on-course promotion to subscribing parties throughout the season. It wasn't long before upwards of 30 companies – many of them run by Centre members – were taking part in this beneficial form of mutual self-help and the scheme earned an unexpected award from Castrol as the best motor club innovation of the year.

A powerful single-seater is not necessary to enjoy hill climbing. Jeremy Goodman economises on tyre wear at Loton Park in 1981 in his Ford Escort RS2000.
BILL GOODMAN

Martin Bolsover won the expanded B & W Motors/Beacon Radio Midland Championship by five points from Charles Wardle, with the next places filled by Roland Jones, Charles Barter, James Thomson and Richard Jones. A crowd-pleasing ninth overall was Nic Mann with his superbly self-engineered Morris Minor which now boasted a turbocharged Rover V8 engine and remarkably good handling and general tractability. James Thomson may not have won the main Championship but he certainly made his mark on *The Birmingham Post* Top Ten, winning this competition by 4 points from Dave Harris, with ADO and Martyn Griffiths third and fourth.

A rather low key Guyson/BARC Championship gave another win for the disguised Josh Sadler – he had now dispensed with the beard which had formerly graced his visage – in the impeccably prepared 3.5 Porsche 911, with a clear 4.81 marks to spare over John Meredith. The strong Scottish flavour to the series was emphasised by third and fourth places falling to Jim Campbell and former Ginetta G17B driver Tom MacMillan who were now sharing the Fife Fabrications Modus M4. Although Jim had campaigned this ex-Ken MacMaster car with a 2.2 Hart engine it was now fitted with a 1600cc unit. This was one Championship where Alister Douglas-Osborn actually beat James Thomson, into fifth place, while the Northern Zone and Southern Zone awards both went to Mallock U2 drivers: Alex Graham and Alex Grenfell respectively. Joy Rainey took the Ladies Award after a year when she and her father had experimented, rather disastrously at first, with a turbocharger set up on the FVC engine of the Pace Petroleum and Sodastream – (yes really) supported Murrain. Murray Rainey had raced against Ron Tauranac, no less, in 500cc racing in Australia in the 1950s, and the man behind so many Brabham, Trojan and Ralt designs had helped with the Murrain which apart from so many other unusual features employed an ignition cut-out which came into effect whenever Joy took her foot off the throttle.

Once again James Thomson won the FTD Awards section of the Championship, this time by four points from Roy Lane, while behind ADO and Chris Cramer, David Gould stacked up a worthy 30 points with the sophisticated BDA-engined Gould Terrapin in a year when he had been rather over-shadowed by Martin Bolsover.

The almost total domination of the Harewood season by the yellow and red Guyson Pilbeam naturally had its effect on the inaugural Shell Super Oil series, James won both sections! In winning the main Glen Garnett Trophy he again put one over on Alister Douglas-Osborn, with Josh Sadler and his sparring partner, drinking companion and Autofarm customer Tony Bancroft leading the rest from Burnley residents John Casey (Mini Cooper S) and Tony Bridge (Davrian-Larton/Imp). The order of the first two stayed the same in the FTD Awards for the Wilson Trophy, with Roy Lane and Malcolm Dungworth taking the minor places.

At least Thomson stopped short of winning the Scottish Championship. With Norrie Galbraith struggling with the Chevron B48S which gave him a bad fright at the opening Strathclyde Park round when the suspension broke, pitching him off the road at the first corner, and never gave him much confidence thereafter, and with Campbell and MacMillan contenting themselves with just 1600cc, it was no surprise when Jimmy Jack won the title with the ex-Cramer March 782/79B. But it was mighty close. The trouble started when Jimmy had an engine failure at Shelsley in June. After receiving assurance that a change was in order, from an official who had clearly not checked the Championship rules, Jack shared Chris Cramer's Toleman at the RAC Fintray and Doune meetings before reverting to his own car. Unfortunately, after apparently clinching the Championship he was informed that the points scored in the Toleman could not count and he had to win the Championship all over again – which he did at the last round from Norrie Galbraith.

Hill climbing is a very difficult sport to give up – witness the comebacks of Nick Williamson, Mike MacDowel, Geoff Rollason, Jim Johnstone, and David Hepworth, among many – and a welcome return was made in 1981 by Paul Tankard, from Lightcliffe, who took to the hills once more in the same rather brutal and twitchy TVR Tuscan V8 which he had campaigned in the mid-nineteen-seventies. This car had always looked a handful but it had reserved its most alarming party piece for the Harewood Paddock on one occasion when Paul had the alarming experience of having the battery explode! As this component lodged in the back of the car the force of the blast was carried away with the large TVR rear window, which was probably just as well. Paul's return was marked by a 45.49s BTD at the traditional Harewood Novices Meeting.

Although Nick Bridge had made a successful transition to Clubmans Sports Car circuit racing, the

Jimmy Jack broke the Norrie Galbraith/Jim Campbell hold on the Scottish Championship to win the 1981 title in dramatic fashion in this ex-Cramer March 782/79B.
BILL HENDERSON

family continued with its tenure of the Dutton-Forshaw/Longton Championship with brother Tony winning in his Davrian.

After a rather troubled period, the BARC's Yorkshire Centre, now headed by Chairman Derek Clark while Mike Wilson concentrated on his duties as Clerk of the Course at Harewood, had reason for satisfaction at the 100th Harewood meeting. The new Shell Championship had been well received and the hill's sponsorship scheme had also taken off spectacularly well. Yet barely a week later came a real bombshell which threatened to undo all the good work. Because of unrelated financial reasons, Arnold Burton would be putting Stockton Farm up for sale in the very near future. With no guarantee that a new owner would be as amenable to the continuation of hill climbing, the club was faced with the daunting prospect of raising at least £90,000 to buy the freehold, at a time of deep economic recession. Fortunately, while plans were drawn up and put into effect, a Centre member, Steven Smith (a former Ford GT40 owner and now running a delightful replica Jaguar D-type) agreed to buy the farm and the adjoining land as a holding operation, before selling it to a new company, Harewood Hill Ltd, which was set up specially. After great efforts by Derek Clark and his colleagues, the money was raised, with major contributions from the BARC's Head Office, Steven Smith and Guyson International, and smaller sums from some 110 members who all became shareholders in the new company. After the rather unhappy relations during the previous year, one of the most valued of those contributions came from the Midland Automobile Club.

By the beginning of the 1982 season Harewood was safe, and the Yorkshire Centre was now effectively its own master with a long-term plan to develop the hill and its facilities. The success of the project was a tribute to the positive attitude of the sport's participants in assuming the responsibility to guarantee the future of hill climbing.

Bolsover takes over

At the end the 1981 season, with the sport's premier title secured at the first attempt, the 21-year-old James Thomson decided to move on to circuit racing, a field which he soon found to be a tough proposition, at least in the highly-competitive and professional Formula Ford 2000 category. After so many seasons driving saloons, father Jim elected to drive the Guyson Pilbeam MP40K himself, although James would be having the odd 'guest drive' when other commitments allowed. The family Chevette was passed on to younger son Tim, and the old Firenza finally sold off to North Yorkshire plumber Bob Claxton.

The Thomson family Vauxhall Chevette was passed on to Tim Thomson for 1982, pictured here at Barbon where Tim's concentration is not helped by the passenger door!
BOB COOPER

Seven out of the first ten in the 1981 RAC Championship had driven Pilbeams and there was no new challenge for the Bourne-built cars on the horizon. Martyn Griffiths sold his MP42/46 to Roy Lane who had the car fitted with a 2.3 Euroracing BMW engine, ex-Norrie Galbraith, and had John Thompson shorten the moncoque. The chassis was now to MP51 specification and was designated accordingly. Griffiths went into partnership with Max Harvey to run a brand-new 2.5 Hart-engined MP53 which would carry the kingfisher logo of Chase Web Offset. After so many successful seasons in the predominantly blue Severn Advertising colours, it took some getting used to see Martyn in the Falmouth printer's yellow livery.

Both Ted Williams and David Franklin had now followed Richard Thwaites' example and switched to Historic circuit racing, but Ted's son Mark, who had driven a variety of different machinery since the mid-nineteen-seventies, was to share the MP41, now fitted with a full 2.5 Hart, with Richard Fry. The growing number of people sharing cars was testimony to the financial pressures which many were facing in running top class machinery, but an unavoidable side-effect was the tendency to delay and break-up Top Ten runs – normally the climax to any major meeting – while cars were handed over to co-drivers. Dave Harris stuck to his Haynes Publishing-backed MP50, while Martin Bolsover also retained his red MP51 but moved into the over 1600cc class with a full 2.5 Hart engine. This chassis was re-designated MP50 in later years, taking account of its modifications. Whereas James Thomson's successful attack on the hill climb establishment the previous year had been rather unexpected, everyone fully expected that Martin would be a major contender from the word go. The two previous seasons had shown his ability with a single-seater in no uncertain terms.

The Waring & Gillow team, now with Crown Furniture sharing the space on the cars, could never be overlooked and for the new year ADO was to have the benefit of an even more highly developed 3.7-litre 'DFY' engine. Malcolm Dungworth carried on with his familiar car while the surviving MP22 went to Jersey, to Noel le Tissier. Noel had previously driven the ex-Purley/Jones Chevron B30 but this now formed the basis of the BMW M1 Donington GT project of Jeff Wilson. Among all these Pilbeams – and yet another was the 1600cc MP45, a Formula 3 chassis, of Terry Clifford – only Chris Cramer of the leading runners persevered in another direction. He had re-developed the Toleman TG280H to run on Avon tyres and now the car had been uprated by Martin Slater and was running a Hewland FG gearbox instead of the less rugged FT200. Godfrey Crompton also retained his relatively little used Toleman, and was soon to be co-driven on occasion by Peter Kaye.

Older March chassis still abounded but they were only likely to challenge for BTD at second line meetings. After a fairly unhappy year with the Chevron, Norrie Galbraith returned to a 782 chassis, with 2.3 BMW engine, and to be shared with John Barrett, while John Meredith decided to try his hand at single-seaters, just for fun, with the ex-Alan Richards 772P, complete with 2.1 BMW engine and Cheltenham Cameras/Minolta backing, Chris Dowson still enjoyed the immense torque of the old Repco-engined BT36X Brabham, but leading March users were to be found in the 1600cc class. Rugged Glaswegian Brian 'Boss Hogg' Frazer had made good progress with an old Formula Atlantic Argo before switching to a hybrid March 77/8/2; former U2 driver Tony Southall was about to achieve considerable success with a BDA-engined 783/793, and Clitheroe's Alan Newton was the latest owner of the 74B-based MP28.

Really good news at the beginning of the season was the advent of a new sponsor for the RAC Championship after an uncomfortably long gap since the well-remembered Shell backing. The new sponsor was Pace Petroleum, an oil company operating through a growing South of England chain of filling stations, and headed by arch enthusiast Victor Gauntlett. This could not help but add to the stature of the sport's premier series at a time when hill climbing seemed to be far less adversely affected by the recession than most other forms of motor sport.

The Midland Championship also had a new main sponsor in Stourbridge Porsche specialists Swinford Motors (Continental) Ltd who took over from B & W Motors, and as usual it was the opening Midland round at Prescott which really began the serious stuff. As was becoming equally traditional, Dave Harris struck an early blow with a 39.51s BTD to the 39.68s of Martyn Griffiths, and with young Mark Williams up behind ADO in fourth place. Before the Pace/RAC trail began at Loton Park on 12 April, James Thomson made his first hill climbing appearance of the year and went home with another Harewood BTD in 37.51s.

Pilbeams took the first seven places at Loton Park for the Cramer Toleman was not handling at all well. Despite a run which 'didn't seem all that fast', it was the Haynes MP50 of the Bristol garage owner which snatched the first 10 points of the year in 49.48s, only twelve-hundredths faster than the ruby red MP41 of Mark Williams, who was still only 23 and looked a major threat to the more familiar names at this point, as was Bolsover who was fourth behind Griffiths. But at Wiscombe it was different. Martyn Griffiths seemed to have taken on a new lease of life with the better handling MP53 and he turned the tables on the class-winning Alister Douglas-Osborn to clock a superbly controlled 36.40s best which equalled the record and demonstrated Martyn's neat, precise and economical style at its best. Alister was a very good second on 36.73s while Bolsover – winner the previous week up at Doune – was advancing week by week and now broke 37s for third place.

That advance really became menacing at Prescott on 2 May, where Williams lost the nose of his car in the Esses, ADO brushed the nose of his car in the same complex and even Griffiths 'dropped it' at the Semi-Circle. His red MP51 now bearing allegiance to Roger Philpott's Five Steps organisation and to Holiday Inns, the 29-year-old Bolsover recorded 39.77s to vanquish ADO, Lane (happy with his stiffened chassis but definitely losing out to the Harts on power), Griffiths, Cramer and a surprisingly unimpressive Harris (tyres going off already?).

The Westmorland Motor Club really had an expensive time at Barbon where a recently resurfaced track and perfect weather conditions helped to relieve the Club of no fewer than eight 18-carat-gold Barbon Stars! With one major challenge blunted when the Chase Web Offset MP53 was sidelined with transmission bothers, Bolsover rose to the occasion with a superb performance which saw him break the record on three climbs, leaving it at 21.21s. Harris was back on form with 21.24s while ADO was on 21.26s in a desperately closely fought affair, which saw Cramer, Fry, Lane, Williams and Griffiths (before the gearbox broke) all under 22s. Most of the leading drivers crossed the Pennines to compete at Harewood the next day where a fine entry (although there were *only* 22 Mallock U2s as opposed to the 28 at Prescott!) of Pace/RAC contenders were put firmly in their places by James Thomson who reduced the hill record once more, to 36.64s against the 36.96s of the flying Bolsover.

Further encouraged by a BTD at Gurston Down, the now Chaddesley Corbett-domiciled Bolsover tackled Shelsley. His 26.75s climb was good. It beat Harris, Williams and Cramer. But the day belonged to Alister Douglas-Osborn, truly the modern master of Shelsley, who missed the course record by a mere 0.01s, recording 26.63s. Martyn Griffiths too is an acknowledged Shelsley expert and his 26.67s was truly outstanding in a less powerful car.

Five Steps sponsored the Pace/RAC MSA meeting at Fintray where a little bit of controversy entered proceedings. A certain amount of unrest among 'conventional' saloon and sports car drivers at the increasingly radical spaceframe devices in their midst had been brewing for some time. Now, when Ron Cummings' GT racing Esprit, with central 'single-seater' driving position (showing the car's ancestry) arrived on the scene the irritation boiled up into a formal protest – which was dismissed. After the class runs it really looked as though Chris Cramer might be heading for a win with the Toleman, but a gearbox failure for the former record holder ended the challenge, leaving the day to Bolsover again. Martin lopped no less than 1.15s off the existing record but he was only 0.29s up on Griffiths. Martyn got his own back at Doune with a 39.42s course record, 0.23s faster than Bolsover and with Cramer snatching third place notwithstanding a rather untidy climb.

Before the Harewood Pace/RAC meeting on 11 July, there were wins for Bolsover at Loton Park and Douglas-Osborn at Prescott, but at the Yorkshire hill Martin Bolsover was again faced by James Thomson who seemed to find no problem in adjusting back to the very specialised hill climb discipline. The Guyson driver made the first mark by winning the class in 36.87s, but then suffered a setback with a spin at Orchard on his first Championship climb. Next time up the Yorkshireman stopped the watches in a resounding 36.64s, but Bolsover had been faster still, setting a new course record in 36.42s. The triumph of the younger generation was complete when Mark Williams fairly flew up a course he did not know well in 36.77s.

Martyn Griffiths had not been quite on the ultimate pace at Harewood but before the Championship circus crossed over for its annual Channel Islands excursion, he bounced back with a 26.58s BTD at Shelsley where Cramer also impressed and Peter Kaye was back, sharing the Crompton Toleman and recording 28.44s for seventh place. Business commitments actually kept Griffiths away from Bouley Bay, where the bespectacled Bolsover suffered a severe setback. He crashed and bent the tub of his car fairly severely against a tree. He was unhurt but was helpless to affect a close battle which ended with

Brian Walker's Chevron-based Skoda-Hart was a typical example of a radical new breed of Special Saloons. He was runner-up in the 1982 RAC Leaders Series, and achieved a major championship double in 1983.
BOB LIGHT

a tie for BTD. Always a tough proposition on the Channel Islands, and now finding the revamped Toleman rather more amenable, Chris Cramer clocked 40.18s on his best class run (and took the BTD award on aggregate). At the end of the day Chris was fractionally slower at 40.26s, 0.01s faster than Bolsover's counting first Championship climb. But Dave Harris had really pulled out the stops and recorded . . . 40.18s. Jim Thomson sportingly offered Bolsover the loan of the MP40KX for Le Val des Terres, and although Martin gave Jim a small fright with a spin the exercise did net a couple of extra points. This time Chris Cramer did the job properly with BTD and 10 points with a 32.01s climb which was half a second faster than Martyn Griffiths.

This was a very busy time, for Craigantlet followed on 31 July and Shelsley on 8 August. One began to wonder at Craigantlet whether the Bouley crash had affected car or driver in the longer term for Bolsover could do no more than achieve fourth place, beaten by a scintillating hill record from Cramer in 49.80s, an almost equally rapid 49.89s from Griffiths and a splendid 50.02s from Max Harvey. Sharing the MP53 had certainly given Martyn Griffiths a new lease of life but it had also seen Max Harvey progress by leaps and bounds. When the Falmouth printer had first taken up the sport with the Netherton & Worth Boxer he had shown immediate promise, but later progress with the March 792 had seemed less marked. Now, with Martyn's vast experience and example to guide him in a first-class car, his times were tumbling.

Although hill climbing is normally conducted in a thoroughly sporting atmosphere, controversy is not totally absent and there were mutterings at Shelsley when ADO was allowed an 8 minute delay before taking his final climb in order to replace a broken driveshaft. After this, Alister was all fired up and nobody could begrudge his triumph when the mighty Pilbeam-DFY left the Shelsley record at 26.37s! Although nobody else cracked 27s, an on-form Dave Harris edged out Cramer and Bolsover for second place. At the other end of the Top Ten, Peter Kaye took three points (28.03s) despite a broken cwp on the Crompton Toleman, and Richard Jones took two points (28.08s) before a horrifying crash at the Crossing which had the U2 end-up inverted and Richard lucky to emerge with no more than a grazed arm.

With a long gap now until Gurston, the 'double header' meeting at Harewood drew a fine entry. On the Saturday the Lane family scored their 20th Harewood BTD, but although Roy had won the other 19 this time it was his son Anthony in the Pilbeam (with which he had already been entrusted in the odd sprint), and a commendable 40.85s climb brought him the Novices BTD. The following day James Thomson was back again and he reversed the results of the RAC meeting by climbing in 36.45s to defeat Bolsover. It was a notable meeting when other landmarks were set by Paul Tankard, who at last broke Josh Sadler's class record on a re-run (he had done it unofficially in practice more than once) with the brutal TVR Tuscan, and by Charles Wardle. Using the 226 bhp of screaming Phil Marks BDA power in the U2 to best effect, Charles broke 40s for the first time in an under 1600cc sports car.

Alister Douglas-Osborn still had a chance to lift the Pace/RAC title and at Gurston he closed the gap on Bolsover to just 5 points, although Griffiths was but 2 points adrift of the Championship leader. ADO's 28.51s BTD again broke the Gurston record but it was entirely necessary for Martyn was on 28.60s and Martin 28.62s. The meeting also saw a well-deserved first Championship point fall to Chris Dowson in the splendid old Brabham-Repco.

The rain intervened at Prescott, where Chris Cramer set a 39.49s BTD before the track surface became too slippery for fast times. Martyn Griffiths and the Laurie Billings prepared MP53 made the most of things and 46.71s was enough for 10 points and the Championship lead! Less troubled by lack of power, Roy Lane was a close second and Cramer and ADO both beat Bolsover. There were the first three points, too, for John Meredith who had been having an excellent introduction to single-seaters, with sprint results which were to make him runner-up in the RAC Sprint Championship to Ken Ayers, in Roy Lane's old March 79S, and rapid times on the hills which were fast enough to give him the odd BTD at secondary meetings.

There was more drama at Wiscombe in the penultimate round although the mood was subdued because of the terrible news that Norrie Galbraith, who had intended to retire after clinching his third Scottish Hill Climb Championship, had been killed instantly at a special demonstration for the TV cameras at Doune. His March had collided head-on with a tractor which had somehow got out onto the course. It was bitterly ironic that this hospitable and sporting 42-year-old butcher-turned-motor trader should die while promoting the sport, for he had been a splendid ambassador for Scotland in hill climbing for many seasons, as well as being no mean driver. Down at Wiscombe, Bolsover was back on form with a 36.37s hill record but then down came the rain again for the RAC MSA climbs. Nevertheless, Martin stayed on top in 42.07s and retook the Championship lead thanks to a storming 42.22s from Max Harvey, Martyn Griffiths' co-driver! That pushed Griffiths down to third, while Douglas-Osborn was now out of the Championship reckoning.

Bolsover kept in trim with another Harewood record – 36.28s – after yet another duel with James Thomson (36.33s) and all was ready for a real cliff-hanger at the 50th Doune meeting. For a time the event had seemed in doubt because of the repercussions of the Galbraith tragedy which had deeply upset all concerned with the hill. Happily, the Championship finale went ahead, sponsored by Guyson, and with that man James Thomson setting another BTD in 40.86s. He did not run in the RAC climbs, although father Jim was fifth at the end of a learning season with the MP40 derivative, one place ahead of the very brave Alan Payne in the old Coogar (which had actually been placed fourth at one point at Wiscombe when the track was at its most gripless). In the end it was Bolsover versus Griffiths, and it was the man from Chaddesley Corbett who settled the issue with a 46.14s after the rains came yet again to mar the Top Ten. Bolsover was Pace/RAC MSA Champion after a magnificent first year in the over 1600cc division although he must have been fairly relieved that he didn't have the extra problem of James Thomson on a regular basis!

In the final analysis Bolsover's 93 points were two up on Martyn Griffiths: runner-up yet again but a revitalised driver in the process. Another typical Douglas-Osborn season, brilliant at times but all-too-inconsistent, left him 8 points adrift of Bolsover, but 7 ahead of Dave Harris (another slightly erratic performer) and Chris Cramer who had recovered well after a difficult start to the year, and had proved the worth of a development Hart engine of 2.7-litres. Mid-year redundancy and a power disadvantage had done nothing to make it a year to remember for Roy Lane but he still took sixth place ahead of the harder, more aggressive Max Harvey, and with Mark Williams, Richard Fry and Richard Jones completing the numbers 1 to 10 for 1983. After a fine start, Mark Williams had rather lost interest in the

Championship, sidetracked by family circuit-racing pressures, after showing that he could be very good indeed even if he did occasionally fly off the road. The Award of Merit Award was won by Harvey from Williams.

A two point advantage gave the Haynes-sponsored Leaders' title to the meteoric Charles Wardle from one of the increasingly common 'GT' saloons. This was the 2.0 Hart 420R-powered sports-racing Chevron, sponsored by Dalgety Spillers, and disguised as a Skoda Coupé. It was a natural winner in Longridge driver Brian Walker's more than competent hands and headed Dave Watson's ex-John Meredith Maguire-Hartwell Imp, which Dave demolished in practice at Doune. Also figuring strongly were Andy Sim's lightweight Morgan 4/4-BDA, Tony Tewson's spaceframe Imp Californian, and Charles Barter who, like his rival Meredith, had switched to a single-seater for 1982. He had chosen to fit a Hartwell Imp engine (with which he was more than familiar) to a new Delta 824 chassis, and was straightaway a major contender for 1100cc racing-car honours.

Among the plethora of hill climb Championships the Prescott Gold Cup retained its own character with the 1982 Cup providing a triumph for the delightfully named Scotch Egg Racing for Pleasure Clubmans Sports team which had for long been a mainstay of the class in Southern events. Alan Lloyd (Mallock U2 Mk18CW), from Walton-on-Thames won it and his team-mate Chris Anderson, from Esher, was runner-up in his Phantom for most of the year although both drivers were sharing the works U2 Mk24 for the September Prescott.

The always spectacular Josh Sadler won the Swinford Motors/Beacon Radio Midland Championship from the Davrian Mk6 of Bridgnorth motor-accessory dealer Richard Nayler, and Kenilworth engineer Tony Tewson. Fifth in this series was Nic Mann whose amazing Morris Minor also took him to victory in the BARC(SW) Gurston Championship from Alan Lloyd. Fast becoming hill climbing's most-talked-about car, the Alden Performance Centre-backed 'Moggie' Minor represented a phenomenal engineering achievement for Nic Mann. To harness over 400 bhp of turbo-charged Rover V8 engine to a *real* (not 'GT' lookalike) old Minor, make it handle well, and accelerate in a truly awesome fashion (like 0–60 mph in 3.8s in its developed form) speaks volumes for Mann's abilities.

Nic Mann's turbocharged Rover V8-engined Morris Minor was perhaps the biggest spectator attraction of all on the hills in the early 'eighties.
BOB LIGHT

Perhaps the best trick of all, though, came at the end of meetings where the proud owner simply turned down the turbocharger boost, changed the tyres and drove his tractable little runabout home with a performance which would still give nightmares to Porsche 911 Turbo drivers at the traffic lights!

A single point decided *The Birmingham Post* Top Ten competition in favour of Martyn Griffiths, from Harris and Bolsover. The latter won the low-key Guyson/BARC FTD Award title, and the main Championship was won by Paul Tankard in the final year with Guyson sponsorship. Charles Wardle made it two major Championship wins after a superb season, for he also clinched the Shell series at Harewood, and although he may not have been seriously hill climbing at all during the year, James Thomson still won a Championship: the Shell FTD Awards title.

Poor Norrie Galbraith had clinched the Scottish Championship way back in August and was also eleventh overall in the Pace/RAC standings, and it was much appreciated when his widow Sheena accepted the Scottish Championship Award on his behalf over the winter. Edinburgh's Bill Lord was the runner-up in his smart red ex-ICI/de Angelis Chevron B42, from Alex Graham's really rapid U2 Mk20; Robin Gray's Lotus 7 won the Road Car Award.

Triple Scottish Champion Norrie Galbraith breasts East Brae at Doune in his March 782. His tragic death in 1982 robbed the sport of one of its finest ambassadors.
BILL HENDERSON

Norrie Galbraith (left) shares a dram with Martyn Griffiths. Engine-tuner Jim Urwin looks on disapprovingly.
BILL HENDERSON

In the motor-sporting world the economic recession which took a grip of most business activities in the late nineteen-seventies and early nineteen-eighties took considerable toll. Falling entry lists for many circuit-racing categories, and the increasing reluctance of the casual racegoer to pay spectator admission charges, took their toll. Nevertheless, and given the extent of the supposed cutback in disposable incomes, the wonder was actually how little motor sport suffered. This was especially true in hill climbing which most people find relatively inexpensive – at least when compared with the motor-sporting alternatives – and which retains a thoroughly enjoyable and sporting atmosphere. After all, if money is tight, it is only natural to spend the available cash on something which really does give pleasure and which involves the minimum of aggravation. This said, it *is* possible, and indeed almost unavoidable, to spend a lot of money if one is attempting to win a major national championship. At 1983 values something in the region of £50,000 was needed to set oneself up with a top-line Pace/RAC MSA Championship car, assuming that one was starting from scratch. This made it increasingly difficult to break into the sport's élite group even though the demand for road car, historic Clubmans sports-type classes was never greater.

Reg Phillips, as cheery and enthusiastic as ever, climbs Doune in his Ferrari 308 GTB – rather a contrast to his early Fairley devices.
BOB COOPER

For some years now the Midland clubs had catered for the increasingly popular 'Historic' cars, with special classes, often run on a handicap basis, for a wide variety of machinery which more often than not was just plain old rather than truly 'Historic' but which provided a lot of characterful motor sport for people who could not afford, or just did not wish, to run some of the latest and highly specialised racing machinery. The Bugatti Owners Club had gone so far as to instigate a special 'Classic Car' hill climb at Prescott in May, but then that club's own roots with Bugattis and its close links with the VSCC made it fully conversant with the charms of the older car. The Aston Martin Owners Club, too, had long catered for older machinery, naturally with Astons predominating, at its hill climbs at Wiscombe Park in particular. Now, in 1983 the BARC's Yorkshire Centre introduced a handicap class at all its Harewood meetings for 'Harewood Classics', a most successful innovation that attracted a large entry of exceedingly varied cars which also provided unexpectedly close-fought competition. The most successful entries were Jimmy Johnstone's superbly rebuilt, ex-Bryan Eccles Brabham-Buick BT18, Haydn Spedding's ex-Mike Franey/Ted Worswick Modified Sports Jaguar E-type (which the author had the pleasure of sharing, with modest success), Colin Elstrop's remarkably effective and well-driven Triumph GT6, Malcolm Dearnley's Morgan 4/4 and Allen and Lyn Craven's now 1100cc-engined, one-time Formula Ford Lotus 51B. That also gives some idea of the sheer variety of car catered for.

Another innovation at the Yorkshire hill, although it was a little slower to gain momentum, was a class for pre-1979 Formula Ford 1600 cars. The author played a part in bringing this class about by suggesting it in his *Autosport* column as a way of providing a low cost introduction to single-seater hill climbing. Early successes were scored by Staffordshire driver Tony Harris and Yorkshire Centre Chairman Simon Clark (Derek Clark, sadly had died suddenly the previous year after playing a vital role in safeguarding Harewood for the future), but before the end of the year some well-known saloon-car drivers – George Swinbourne and David Sturdy in particular – were considering switching to the FF1600s.

The need to generate large capital sums from within an essentially amateur sport could bring major headaches for club treasurers, not least when courses needed to be resurfaced to the standard which modern racing machinery demands. Harewood's supporters – drawn largely from the ranks of the sport's active participants – had shown what could be achieved in the way of self-help. They were not alone. During 1981/82 the Aberdeen and DMC had mounted a successful fund-raising campaign to pay for the resurfacing of Fintray, while in 1983 the often-threatened Wiscombe Park faced another financial crisis as the need for resurfacing became critical. Far from centres of population and not always particularly well promoted, Wiscombe Park is nevertheless one of the most challenging and attractively situated hills and the will has always been there to overcome its recurring financial precariousness. An appeal was launched in May, 1983 – the Silver Jubilee season – and by September the future had again been secured, thanks largely to major financial assistance from Pace Petroleum, the AMOC and Max Harvey. Hill climbing really has been pretty good at helping itself.

In view of the prevailing conditions, it can be no surprise that in 1983 there was a definite reduction in the number of competitors with the sort of car which would enable them to fight seriously for the Pace Petroleum-sponsored RAC Championship. The fight for the title was as hard fought as ever, but there were fewer runners in the over 1600cc racing class. Mark Williams had dropped out of the reckoning before the end of the previous season, but Chris Cramer, too, was without a car for 1983 with the Toleman sold to form the basis of a 'Lancia GT' car and with its 2.7-litre Hart development engine in the back of the Pilbeam MP41 which had now been bought by Tony Brown. There was talk of Cramer sharing with Dave Harris but this came to nought, with Harris himself doing a more restricted season than of late with his Pilbeam. Malcolm Dungworth, while remaining team manager for the Waring & Gillow team effort, was to amuse himself with his pre-war Riley in 'Historic' events after the Pilbeam MP22 was sold to John Meredith who retained his Cheltenham Cameras/Minolta support inherited from Alan Richards.

Although Guyson International were no longer sponsoring the BARC Championship and the Thomson family Chevette had been sold to rally driver/hill climber Richard Jackson, the proprietor of Nidd Vale Motors of Knareborough, this portended no cutback in the Guyson presence on the hills. Martin Bolsover's Championship winning MP51 was resprayed in the yellow and red Guyson livery to spearhead a three car Team Guyson challenge. Aided as he had been the previous year by the 'retired'

Rob Turnbull, Martin was to have the formidable benefit of a new, extra torquey 2.8-litre version of the superb Hart engine. Jim Thomson himself kept to the trusty MP40RX, using the 2.5 Hart unit, and gradually gaining confidence with the car after fighting many early season battles with John Meredith in the big MP22. The third car in the Team Guyson fleet did not actually appear until May. This was a new sports-racing Pilbeam MP43, virtually a replica of David Garnett's written-off car, but with a 2.5 Hart engine. This was for young Tim Thomson and was bound to provide stiff class opposition for Graham Priaulx's Tiga, Peter Blankstone's faithful Mallock U2, Joy Rainey's now 400 bhp, turbocharged Murrain and veteran George Tatham's old CanAm McLaren.

Martyn Griffiths and Max Harvey were to continue with the Chase Webb Offset MP53, but this car too was fitted with one of the latest 360 bhp 2.8 Harts. The one new single-seater Pilbeam was the MP54 for Richard 'Ferret' Fry, who was using the 2.5 Hart out of the old MP41. The MP54 didn't look much different from its predecessors but this time a honeycomb rather than sheet aluminium monocoque was used, together with the very fashionable pull-rod-type suspension all round. The car was altogether stiffer and its driver found it very different in feel from the MP41. Of those retaining their 1982 cars, Alister Douglas-Osborn was hoping for a more consistent season to prove that a derivative of the Cosworth DFV engine was still *the* power unit to have, while Roy Lane's Steel King March had received a much-needed power boost by having fitted a 2.6 Euroracing-prepared BMW engine. Later on in the season Roy also bought back his old McRae to use in sprint events.

The pattern which the season was to follow was soon revealed over a hectic Easter weekend with Strathclyde Park on the Saturday, Harewood on the Sunday, and the Pace/RAC opener at Loton on the Monday. The latter, naturally, also provided the first round of the Leaders Championship which was to be sponsored for the first time by a car manufacturer: Aston Martin. This was due to Victor Gauntlett's enthusiasm as he had important interests in the Newport Pagnell-based Aston Martin/Lagonda concern. The conspicuous absence of Jimmy Jack, Bill Lord (who was to share Jack's March 782 for the season) and the nitrous oxide-injected March of Brian Frazer left Strathclyde Park in the hands of U2 drivers Alex Graham (BDA-engined Mk20, 45.75s) and Kenny Allen (1.7 Clubmans pushrod-engined Mk21, 46.10s class record). Other centres of interest were the now 2.5 Hart-engined Skoda of Brian Walker which set a class record-smashing time of 49.38s to commence a year of almost unbeaten success, and the "frisky" new TVR Tuscan of Paul Tankard. Although this looked at first glance to be the familiar metallic blue 4.7 V8 of old, it was actually a new spaceframe 'GT' machine, shorn of a lot of weight and potentially a lot stiffer. Overnight snow(!) at Harewood filled Roy Lane and Martin Bolsover with a sense of futility and they packed their bags and drove straight down to Loton, leaving the Yorkshire meeting to the 'second division'. In fact the weather cleared up most satisfactorily, and although the very fast Mallock U2s of Charles Wardle and the Harper brothers Ray and Peter, from Sheffield, with their Chamberlain Clubman engined Mk21, put up stern opposition, the meeting brought a popular BTD for an increasingly confident Jim Thomson in 41.88s.

The Hagley club had enlisted Castrol support for Loton Park, where the honours were typically close-fought. Martyn Griffiths led going into the final climbs but a last run slide lost crucial time and he had to be content with a 50.13s time which was not enough to beat the very last run of the day by Martin Bolsover which took just 49.97s. Alister Douglas-Osborn recorded 50.90s for third place but this was over a second up on Max Harvey with Roy Lane in fifth place, finding the extra power useful but still not having the benefit of the wide power band of the latest Harts. With 6.22s spanning the Top Ten times, some indication could be gained of the relatively small number of truly competitive runners this year. The remainder of the point-scorers were Jim Thomson, Chris Dowson's Unidraw Brabham-Repco BT36X, Alan Payne's stiffened-up Coogar-Rover, a fairly cautious John Meredith and Totteridge sprint and hill-climb veteran David Render in his Formula Atlantic Lola T460. After many years of competition in a variety of cars including the charismatic John Player Special-liveried Grand Prix Lotus 76 and 77 models loaned by David's old friend Colin Chapman, this was actually his first-ever RAC Hill Climb Championship point! The classes naturally provided some pointers for the Aston Martin Leaders' title; prominent in them were: Tony Tewson's Maguire Imp; Brian Walker; the gleaming Rod Chapman-supported Caterham Super Seven of Hatfield driver Chris Knapman, who had been most impressive the previous season despite breaking a bone in his arm in a rather minor incident at Barbon; Nigel Garland, from Malvern, who had taken over the ex-Sadler 3.5 Porsche 911; Roland Jones in a 2.3 BMW-powered Chevron B8 and set to give the Porsche 911 some competition; Neil Crump's latest U2 Mk21/23 (the Malvern driver's old Mk14/18 model had gone to former Datsun driver John Istead, from Cheam); Alan Lloyd's Scotch Egg U2 Mk18CW; Jim Robinson and Charles Wardle in their familiar U2-BDA; and Charles Barter in the little Delta.

A track surface which varied from greasy to sodden wet marred the Midland Championship opener at Prescott which, happily, was also back on the BARC schedule. Despite the conditions it was a narrow win for ADO in 45.92s, from Griffiths and Bolsover, and with Alan Payne a typically brave fourth in the wet. One week later, at Wiscombe Park, the weather was still rather uncertain and there was a rather small entry. A stiffer anti-roll bar for the Chase Webb-Offset Pilbeam proved beneficial and 37.15s by Martyn Griffiths gave him BTD and 10 points, by 0.22s from ADO, with Bolsover a close third on 37.37s and a much happier Lane on 37.85s.

After taking in a winning weekend up at Doune, the reigning Champion rejoined the Pace/RAC MSA title chase at Prescott where he set another BTD in 45.97s. He didn't take any points, though, because a near-monsoon hit the Gloucestershire venue in the middle of the second runs causing the abandonment of the meeting before anyone hurt themselves. The final straw came when Jim Robinson's U2 spun on a sheet of water on the straight after Ettores in a most alarming incident. This was only the second time that an RAC round had to be scrubbed because of the weather.

Although there might have been a slight shortage of top-class Championship contenders, there were a number of interesting developments affecting other single-seater drivers. Wiscombe Director Richard Brown was going well in Southern events with an ex-Bernard Devaney Chevron B47/49 fitted with a BDA engine, Kentishman Barrie Dutnall had swapped his rather fearsome Brabham-Rover BT40 for a March 782 and Andover farmer Geoff Hunt brought yet another Pilbeam to the hills. This was the ex-HART (Hampshire Automobile Racing Team and nothing to do with Brian Hart)/Pharmacin F3 chassis MP51, now fitted with the 1.6 Twin-Cam motor out of Geoff's old March 733. Most dramatic of all, though, was David Render's decision to fit no less than a full 2.8 Hart to his formerly Abarth-powered Lola T560.

There were more rain showers at Barbon where ADO fulfilled practice form by winning the class in

the 3.7 Pilbeam in 22.67s. But then it all went wrong again for Alister when the car slewed out of line on that tricky second left-hander on the first Pace/RAC climb, wiping off the nose against a tree which also broke a front upright. That left the day to Bolsover in 22.55s, from Griffiths (22.90s) and Lane (23.20s): and Ray Rowan did exceptionally well to make the Top Ten on this power hill with his 1.6 BDA-engined Chevron B45.

More wins for Bolsover at Harewood (39.21s) and at a newly-resurfaced Gurston Down (29.30s) put Martin in the right frame of mind for Fintray, where mud on the course was something of a problem. Martin's 32.96s was good but Griffiths, now using the latest Japanese Yokohama tyres, was better still on 32.54s and so was ADO in the repaired MP47 (32.81s). Even at this early stage of the Championship it was inconceivable that it would go to anyone outside the trio of Bolsover, Griffiths and Douglas-Osborn.

After the dreadful spring weather, the sun broke through at Shelsley where Bolsover set a 26.69s class target which remained unbeaten thanks to none other than Malcolm Dungworth depositing a lot of oil on the course after an incident with his old Riley! This enabled Douglas-Osborn to win back some lost ground with a 27.06s best, beating Bolsover, Griffiths and a welcome addition to the front runners: Dave Harris. Also back in action was Chris Cramer, who won the 1600cc class in 29.71s in Richard Brown's Chevron, and Richard Fry in his new Pilbeam. A broken back axle did nothing for the Leaders' prospects of Charles Wardle and Jim Robinson but they still dominated their class when Jim won in Edinburgh driver Bill Wood's U2 Mk18 from Charles in Paul Bason's Myers Special (which Paul had lent to him before when the Mk21 was *hors de combat*). Fastest sports car of all was Guernseyman Priaulx in his very rapid Tiga-BDX with a 29.06s climb which had the edge over Peter Blankstone and Tim Thomson.

A slight gearbox problem at Harewood for Martin Bolsover at a BARC and Shell Oils round in June helped a delighted Roy Lane to score his 20th Harewood win in 37.69s before it was back up to Scotland again for Doune, where Bolsover won again (39.93s in the class runs, 40.22s in the Championship) from Griffiths and ADO but where the main talking point was the fantastic 42.85s Clubmans record achieved by Kenny Allen, one of the very few drivers who still combined circuit racing with hill climbing. The Scotsman was an incredible sixth in the run-off, beating Thomson, Meredith and Dowson with his Agra-prepared, Ford pushrod-engined U2 Mk24.

There was now a breathing space before Harewood, but with a couple of Midland rounds to contest at Loton and Prescott. Griffiths took the honours at Loton where Bolsover finished with a seized engine after a bad oil leak, while Dave Harris and Alister Douglas-Osborn tied with 33.36s at Prescott. 33.36s? This apparently unbelievable time had a simple explanation. The BOC decided to run the meeting on the old short course, used only for VSCC meetings since 1960, although there were mixed feelings about this among competitors. The times were certainly a reminder of the progress made during the last 23 years for the record had stood to David Boshier-Jones at 41.00s.

Martin Bolsover was simply superb at Harewood, reducing the course record to 36.12s, whereas even ADO could not get nearer than 36.84s. Peter Kaye made sixth place in Godfrey Crompton's infrequently-seen Toleman and the day's other outstanding drive came from the always-hard-trying Chris Seaman, who clocked 40.94s for a fine class win in the old ex-Johnstone Brabham-FVA BT30 from which he extracted the last scrap of potential. Bolsover really was getting down to opening up a Championship lead now and he followed up the Harewood win with a 39.66s BTD at Bouley Bay, an unusually lowly third to Griffiths and Lane at Le Val des Terres, a blistering 49.75s record at Craigantlet where the Chase Webb-Offset team were a little breathless after an overnight rebuild following a couple of practice excursions, and where ADO was afflicted by a broken electrical lead. Fifth overall here was Northern Ireland Championship Leader Richard Parsons with his 1.6 Chevron-BDA B34. Apart from Craigantlet, the Irish hill climb scene was still rather a low key business with few people really concentrating on the hills but there were now both Eire and Ulster titles. Winner South of the border was David Manley in a Formula Ford Van Dieman RF81.

The MAC laid on a superb meeting for their final Shelsley of the year and with the glorious summer sun shinning brightly, Alister Douglas-Osborn produced one of his superb records with a 26.08s class run which remained BTD although his 26.56s Pace/RAC MSA best still defeated Bolsover by a fractional two-hundredths of a second and with Griffiths another 0.02s down! But Al's Shelsley performance was as nothing to what he did a couple of weeks later at Gurston Down. It was a record-breaking day on the new track surface but ADO's 'wheelie' through the Deer's Leap was one of the most terrifying sights of the season. The time was a fantastic 27.77s hill record (ADO's old record stood at 28.51s), while Bolsover hung on for a fine if overshadowed 27.95s best. Then there was a 1.27s gap to Martyn Griffiths! On a day of dramas, Brian Walker lost the lead of the BARC's Championship to Paul Tankard when he bent the valves in his Hart engine.

The climax of the year really came at Prescott where Bolsover cracked 39s for the first time ever (38.81s), clinched the Pace/RAC title for the second successive year and gave Team Guyson its second RAC title in three seasons. Oil leaking from David Render's Lola rather spoilt the RAC Top Ten, but Bolsover was still fastest at 40.14s, winning from Harris after both ADO and Griffiths had spun in their desperate efforts to keep in the Championship race. Seventh in the Top Ten was the 'unemployed' Chris Cramer, this time Chris Dowson's Unidraw Brabham and perhaps wondering how a Repco would perform in a modern chassis. It was a day for sewing up Championships, for Brian Walker bounced back from his disappointment at Gurston to secure both the Aston Martin Leaders series and the Midland title (from the impressive Chris Knapman) with a 43.90s class record. Martyn Griffiths had a 2 point advantage over Dave Harris in the *Birmingham Post* Top Ten challenge and Knapman's excellent year was rewarded by the Prescott Gold Cup.

Even before the RAC titles were settled, the Grampian Television Scottish series had been won by Kenny Allen, breaking the run of wins by single-seater drivers. He clinched it at Rumster where his 25.34s BTD was an amazing record, faster even than Chris Cramer's old hill record, and leaving Jimmy Jack with second place in the Championship although even this was to be overhauled at the final round at Strathclyde Park where Jimmy was absent and Bill Lord overhauled him in the shared March. This final round also went to the astounding Kenny Allen, only 0.5s short of Jack's outright hill record. The Road Car title deservedly went to Ginetta G15 driver George Ritchie from Tommy Mackay's Ford Escort RS1600.

Now the battle was on for second place in the Pace/RAC Championship, and at Wiscombe, Griffiths came through the drizzle to win in 41.01s from Bolsover and Lane with ADO down in fourth place. A solid ninth place-winning 44.60s time from Jim Thomson gave him the RAC Award of Merit

George Ritchie powers his Ginetta G15 round the hairpin at Fintray, in August 1983: the year he clinched the title of Scottish Road Car Hill Climb Champion.
JIM MCDOWELL

Chris Knapman won the 1983 Prescott Gold Cup, was runner-up in the Midland Championship and finished third in the RAC Leaders battle with his Caterham Super Seven.
BOB LIGHT

Two more titles fell to the trusty ex-Griffiths/James Thomson Pilbeam MP40RX in 1983. Jim Thomson won both the RAC Award of Merit and BARC FTD Awards Series in an enjoyable season.
BOB LIGHT

It was difficult to escape Team Guyson livery in 1983. This is Tim Thomson at Gurston Down, enjoying a successful season with his new Pilbeam MP43 sports-racer.
BOB COOPER

after a most encouraging year and with more to come at the Championship Finals meeting at Harewood. Bolsover was firmly on top here, in 36.29s and this won Martin another title – the Shell Oils Harewood FTD Awards Championship – by five points from Roy Lane and with Jim Thomson, who had shared the lead going into the final round, another four points adrift. Nevertheless Jim hung on to his BARC FTD Awards Championship points lead to secure this title after a consistent and steadily improving year. He totted up 71 points in this, four more than Bolsover who overhauled Jim's regular sparring partner John Meredith at the last round. Also settled, of course, were the main BARC and Shell Oils Championships, otherwise the Brian and Paul Show. In the national series, that Gurston problem had cost Brian Walker dear for Paul Tankard won by 1.67 marks, with John Istead third after an excellent first season in a Clubmans car, from Tim Thomson and Mervyn Brake's Maguire Hartwell/Imp. In the Shell Oils Harewood Championship, Walker kept his advantage to win his third major title of the year, inevitably from the mighty TVR of Tankard, and with another 'GT' Skoda, the ex-Auger 1300cc BDA-engined car of former Porsche 924 driver Alastair Cobb, from Sheffield, taking third place from the more genuine saloons of Mike Kerr (Vauxhall Chevette HSR) and Richard Wood (Mini-Cooper S).

With all three RAC Championships settled before the final round, Doune was perhaps a little lacking in high drama although there was no lack of urgency from Martin Bolsover. The Pace Petroleum Champion scored his eighth Championship win of the year with a record breaking climb in 39.39s. Despite a really determined final effort, even Douglas-Osborn could not approach nearer than 39.85s. This left Bolsover with a six point Championship lead over Martyn Griffiths who was runner-up yet again, by just one point, although he had been beaten by third man ADO in the last round. Lane, Harvey and Award of Merit Champion Jim Thomson completed the first six, well spaced out ahead of Dave Harris and Richard Fry, neither of whom had contested all the rounds. John Meredith and the hard-trying Chris Dowson gained numbers 9 and 10 for 1984.

Although he pulled away later on the season, Jim Thomson still had John Meredith as his nearest Award of Merit rival. Alan Payne beat Chris Dowson for third place but the Pershore driver turned the tables in the main Championship.

Despite missing Doune (the previous day he was busy setting a remarkable BTD in the Isle of Man with the 'Surprising Skoda'), Brian Walker retained his tie-break advantage over the Nayler Road and Motorsport-sponsored, Greethan-engined, Maguire Imp of Kenilworth's Tony Tewson to win the Aston Martin Leaders' Championship, both drivers racking up 72 points. Chris Knapman took third place from John Hunt's glorious silver Porsche 911 RSR which had formerly belonged to Roland Jones. Charles Wardle and Jim Robinson took the next two places, with the former also managing to take fifth place in the Award of Merit competition in their U2. Even so, Scottish Champion Kenny Allen was faster still at Doune in his Clubmans-engined Mallock, the Scot recording a blistering 42.06s to take a phenomenal seventh place in the Top Ten, faster even than Jim Thomson and John Meredith.

These superb end-of-season performances by Bolsover and Allen at Doune, Brian Walker in the Isle of Man, and a sizzling fourth BTD and class record (beating the Walker Skoda on this occasion) at the final Gurston meeting by Nic Mann in the nitrous-oxide-injected 400 bhp Morris Minor, further emphasised the sheer variety in the sport and far from leaving the hill climbers jaded after a long season merely whetted the appetite for even greater things to come in 1984.

Although he never really mounted a sustained attack on the RAC Championship, Dave Harris was always a major contender in a series of Pilbeams, especially at Prescott where he is photographed leaving the notably grippy startline.
BOB LIGHT

CHAPTER NINE

A REMARKABLE STABILITY
(1984-1989)

THE national economic recession of the early nineteen-eighties, and the recovery which succeeded it, had remarkably little fundamental effect on British motor sport. On speed hill climbing the effects were barely perceptible.

Only at the sport's apex, among RAC Championship chasers, did economic factors visibly intrude. In an essentially amateur sport the cost and complexity of a serious Championship challenge continued to increase and few could afford to sustain the effort. To be in with a chance it was necessary to run a sophisticated 2.8 Pilbeam-Hart or to develop a competitive alternative, all the while striving to stay one step ahead of the opposition with the latest tyre (and briefly, electric tyre warmer), engine, fuel, split-ratio gearbox and aerodynamic tweaks.

Substantial business interests to sponsor this kind of campaign became ever more desirable. Perhaps it is not surprising, therefore, that the age of top class hill climbers was tending to rise during the nineteen-eighties. By 1988 the average age of the RAC Championship Top Ten drivers was around the 38/39 mark. There was certainly no shortage of talented youngsters but few could afford, or command the resources to afford, a campaign in the premier division.

There was a growing tendency to pool resources with double-driven cars. That ensured that a number of top drivers who would otherwise have had to drop out were able to carry on. This was undoubtably beneficial but greater wear and tear on double-driven cars increased the incidence of mechanical failures and driver changeovers further extended the often long-drawn-out Championship run-off at the end of the meeting.

This last, unwelcome, feature of so many of the bigger meetings became a regular bone of contention as the nineteen-eighties progressed. So much so that there were even suggestions that what *should* have been the climax of the meeting might be dispensed with altogether. By the end of 1989 that remained only a suggestion but the increasing demand for the limited entries available for other classes of car made a precious hour or more spent giving a dozen drivers (the Top Ten run-off became Top Twelve in 1984) another two runs seem ill spent.

Anguished saloon and sports car drivers who had had their entries rejected from Championship meetings (Prescott, which could take as many as 200 entries thanks to a return road and good organisation, was still having to turn down around 80 people at times) pointed out that the hour could be better spent giving thirty more clubmen two competitive climbs rather than allowing a meeting to lapse into a scrappy finale before a fast diminishing gallery of spectators. The latest generation of over 1600cc racing cars and their tensed-up drivers did not seem fitted for speeding up the action, although they were undoubtedly very spectacular when they finally got going. An early solution to the problem seemed unlikely.

For all but the minority of championship chasers, speed hill climbing remained one of motor sport's affordable branches so overall demand from competitors grew, especially after the mid-'eighties. With road rallying legislated virtually out of existence and special stage rallying becoming ever more expensive, speed hill climbing's support was set to grow even more.

The limiting factor remained the lack of major new venues and the shortage of 'clubbie' meetings at the major hills. Spectators were guaranteed a big and varied field to entertain them but that was little

consolation to the would be competitors who found that getting an entry to Shelsley or Barbon, for example, was akin to obtaining Centre Court tickets at Wimbledon for Finals Day. Some new courses were found, notably Durris in Scotland and Rotherfield Park in the South East of England, but they were never enough to satisfy demand. Thanks largely to environmental pressure groups and stringent local planning regulations on the one hand and necessarily tough RAC MSA safety restrictions on the other, finding new motor sport venues in the nineteen-eighties was far harder than it had been in the nineteen-fifties or 'sixties; and it had never been easy.

One environmental factor which became increasingly important during the nineteen-eighties was noise pollution. With growing pressure to reduce noise levels in most branches of motor sport it was only a matter of time before hill climbing was affected. Few hills actually had a major problem over noise with local residents but Prescott, for one, did, even though the complainants were few in number. Experiments with cars and noise testing equipment were carried out with often rather confusing results until all the variables were better understood. By 1986, the RAC MSA had settled on a maximum noise level of 115 dBA at 5,000 rpm, measured six feet from the car's exhaust(s), at a 45 degree angle and 0.5 metre above the road. The new regulations were made mandatory at Prescott for 1986 and for all hill climbs the following year.

Inconsistent readings with the same exhaust set-up and an arbitrary rev limit were early sources of grievance. One big single-seater recorded 113 dBA at Doune and 118 dBA at Prescott under theoretically the same condititions. There were complaints from competitors with low revving engines were being tested near to their maximum revs whereas those with high revving engines who were being tested under their normal operating range. One or two entrants did have major problems but with goodwill and a degree of flexibility all round the difficulties were largely ironed out by 1988. Revised regulations took effect in September 1988 with a 113 dBA limit at 0.5 metre from the exhaust(s), but at just two-thirds of maximum revs. By this time there were few complaints from competitors or spectators and a reduced level of noise certainly made hill climb Paddocks rather more civilised. The changes did remove one undoubted spectacle from the vicinity of start lines. For some years it had been necessary for unsilenced racing and sports-racing cars to be fitted with silencers in the Paddock at places like Harewood and Prescott. Detachable devices of varying effectiveness and ingenuity had been developed and the sight of mechanics whipping off these warmish contraptions as their charges came up to the line could be highly diverting!

Back in the mid-nineteen-seventies many hill climb and sprint competitors felt a growing need for some kind of representative body which could promote the interests of all competitors, and indeed of the sport as a whole. This was at a time when the interests of the 'Top Ten' elite were perceived, rightly or wrongly, to command disproportionate attention and when hill climbing and sprinting were often overlooked or at least given scant attention by motor sport authorities.

At an impromptu meeting in the Paddock at Shelsley in 1978 a group of competitors decided to form a Hill Climb and Sprint Association (HSA) to further the sport's interests. Initially, progress was slow but by 1985 the Association could boast 600 members and by the end of 1988 the membership was nudging the 1,000 mark. Thanks to sterling efforts by mainly active competitors including John Meredith, Russ Ward, Charles Barter, George Gilbert, Roger Willoughby, Des Richardson, Marcel Junod, Robin Boucher and Jerry Sturman, the sport has benefitted greatly.

Although by 1988 the RAC MSA was still not fully utilising the HSA as a genuinely representative body – which it had become – in forming regulations, much had been achieved. Thanks to an increasingly professional magazine, *Speedscene*, edited by Robin Boucher and later Jerry Sturman, successful initiatives to achieve television coverage (a Channel 4 'special', put together rapidly, out of season, was especially successful in fostering interest) and an HSA presence at city centre shows and demonstrations, the sport's profile was raised significantly. Meanwhile, properly run and inexpensive HSA test days and, latterly, novices' sprints, at centrally located Curborough proved most useful additions to the calendar.

Hill climbing (and sprinting) has to fight hard for attention in the media, and fair coverage – even in the motor sporting press – has normally depended on a soberingly small number of able and enthusiastic journalists. During the last twenty years Quentin Spurring, Robin Rew and Marcus Pye have done much to publicise the sport. Latterly, driver-cum-cartoonist-cum-writer Jerry Sturman has made his mark. But it is Robin Boucher who has been the most single-minded in his devotion to the sport and become almost ubiquitous as reporter, publicist, commentator, editor and competitor too! Formerly in the motor trade, working at one stage for Dave Harris, this immensely likeable and enthusiastic Westcountryman was based in Kidderminster by 1988, publishing the revitalised *Wheelbase* magazine.

With no drastic changes to regulations governing the sort of cars catered for, hill climbing remained an unusually stable part of the motor sport scene. Certainly, there were changes regarding silencing and the use of methanol fuel, actual and proposed amendments to the RAC MSA's class structure which looked increasingly outmoded for the production-based categories – but nobody faced the all-too-frequent racing or rallying dilemma of a car which could not be made eligible. Overall, the scene remained extremely healthy.

A surprise treble

After achieving back-to-back RAC Championships, Martin Bolsover opted for a quieter life in 1984, just as Mike MacDowel had done a decade earlier, and swapped cars with Tim Thomson within Team Guyson. Young Tim took over the Champion's MP50/51 single-seater while Martin looked set to break a few sports car records with the now methanol-fuelled Pilbeam MP43 TSR. Jim Thomson happily stuck with the trusty MP40 theme but a new honeycomb MP40H/03 monocoque was obtained for the car.

The season looked likely to be fairly open at the top with greatest interest surrounding the new partnership of Alister Douglas-Osborn and Blakedown businessman John Hunt. The long-standing Waring & Gillow sponsorship was reduced but Hunt's AWS/Glissade Door and Window Systems company backing enabled ADO to plan a campaign with a potent new weapon, a brand new Pilbeam designed to take a 4.2 Alan Smith Cosworth V8. John had impressed in his début season with the ex-Roland Jones Porsche RSR – which wife Sue was eventually to take over – but he was making a big step up for one so inexperienced.

After two successive years as Championship runner-up, Martyn Griffiths, together with his partner Max Harvey, redoubled their efforts with the Chase Web Offset MP53, now to be run by the Waring & Gillow mechanics. A new honeycomb monocoque was obtained to make the car stiffer and lighter. Meanwhile Roy Lane left well alone with his 2.7-litre Steel King Safety Footwear MP51 with Euroracing BMW power for his effort to score an RAC Top Ten result for the seventeenth successive year. Roy was also to embark on a new career, as a driving instructor. Successful Porsche driver Bill Goodman was the principal behind one of the best new innovations to hit the sport for many years –

Alister Douglas-Osborn was an early season favourite for honours in 1984 in John Hunt's new 4.2 Pilbeam-Cosworth V8 841. Here he sets a 26.88s BTD at Shelsley in June.
MIDLAND AUTOMOBILE CLUB

Bill Goodman and his 3.0 Porsche Turbo has been a formidable class contender for many seasons. He is the principal behind the highly successful Prescott Hill Climb Drivers' School.
BILL GOODMAN

he Prescott Hill Climb Drivers School, with Roy as Chief Instructor. There could be no one better qualified than the Warwick veteran to teach enthusiasts how best to ascend those tortuous Gloucestershire slopes in the minimum time possible, and a well-structured course soon earned much praise and oversubscribed classes. Five years on and the school is more popular than ever with students learning a great deal at reasonable cost during a thoroughly enjoyable day.

Richard Fry was another driver to have a new Pilbeam for the season, a honeycomb monocoque MP54, while perennial hard triers Alan Payne and Roger Willoughby had new mounts too. The bearded Payne sold the old Coogar to Woking's David Keer and had his John Eales Rover V8 installed in the back of an Anson SA4. Alan was always a brave driver and, initially at least, he looked as though he needed a fair bit of courage with the unwieldy Apollo Gas & Electrical Centres sponsored device. 'Doc' Willoughby had written off his trusty old ex-Nick Williamson March 712 chassis the previous year at Wiscombe, where he was now a Director. The new home for his Buick V8 was Max Harvey's old March 792S. Some fireworks could also be expected from Chris Knapman's immaculate, ex-Richard Brown Chevron B49, Richard Ames' B40, and Walsall motor engineer Ray Rowan's 1.6 Chevron-BDA B45. For those with longer memories of the torque from the rare Repco V8, there was great interest in Pershore farmer Chris Dowson's decision to take the ex-MacDowel 5.0-litre V8 out of his Brabham and combine it with ADO's former mount, the Pilbeam MP47RB. The genial Chris obtained some useful sponsorship from Unidraw Robotics of Cheltenham for the new venture.

Inevitably there would be some faces missing. Terry Smith, like Richard Thwaites, David Franklin and Ted Williams before him, was going the Historic racing route, while Chris Cramer was not expected to contest the major events either. He would be concentrating on inducting son Marc into the sport, initially with an exuberantly handled Ford Escort road car. 'The Old Man of the Hills', John Meredith, was now basing himself in the West Country, in the motor trade, and had sold his Pilbeam to Don Statton. John would be competing at a more modest level in a Clan Crusader. Saddest event though was the death of John Bolster, in January. Active as Technical Editor of *Autosport* almost until the last, despite serious heart trouble, JVB personified the specialist approach to hill climbing of an earlier era. He would be greatly missed but never forgotten.

The serious action began down at Wiscombe on 8 April, when the Pace/RAC Championship began amid predictable new car teething troubles. Engine maladies afflicted the yellow Chase Web Pilbeam, the Hunt/Douglas-Osborn combo was afflicted by fuel pressure problems, Tim Thomson suffered a spin, and Martin Bolsover had fuel pump trouble. Not unexpectedly, it was Roy Lane who was early into top form, recording a 39.24s BTD on a class ascent and then clocking 39.46s to dominate the Top Twelve. Yes, Top Twelve as for the first time the fastest twelve were to be given RAC runs in 1984, but with only the top ten scoring points as before. This was expected to benefit the rapid drivers of Clubmans chassis sports cars and would ensure that there would always be ten points scorers, notwithstanding mechanical failures and off-course excursions. Roy Lane found himself with an 0.78s winning margin over an outstanding Ray Rowan while Chris Dowson did well to overcome timing gear maladies and secondhand tyres to snatch third from Westcountryman Richard Fry's new Pilbeam-Hart. The man who had developed Allan Staniforth's Terrapin theme furthest, David Gould, returned after a two year absence with the same 1.6 Langford BDA powering a superb new, self-designed and self-built, up-to-the-minute 'ground effects' chassis. The beautifully made, aluminium honeycomb tub of the red Gould 84/1 was a work of art and David straightway took a third in class.

A week later the Castrol/Beacon Radio Midland series kicked off at Prescott and although Lane's 40.25s BTD was no surprise, Bolsover's 40.69s second BTD, a new sports car record, did raise a few eyebrows. It was a typically varied and entertaining Prescott with outstanding drives, among many others, coming from Yorkshireman Mike Kerr's fierce Vauxhall Chevette HSR, Nic Mann's whispering Morris Minor turbo V8 (which was without a doubt *the* favourite of the crowd), Sandra Tomlin in father Phil Chapman's famous Mercury sports car, and David Sewell who recalled a much earlier age with his spirited, wheel-lifting climbs in his recreated Bugatti T13 Brescia.

The RAC MSA title chase, which was again sponsored by Pace Petroleum, was rejoined at Loton Park and although Thomas Wolley's record-breaking QED Lotus 7 secured him the Beacon Radio Man of the Meeting Award, the day belonged to Bolsover. The penny dropped that Martin, still a relatively young 30-year-old, might just be a major factor in the Championship after all. His 49.53s best was enough to put the Team Guyson sports-racer at the head of the pursuing pack of Lane, Dave

Still very much a newcomer, a surprisingly relaxed Tim Thomson (Pilbeam MP50 OTJ) was a worthy runner-up at Shelsley in June 1984.
BOB LIGHT

Harris in the Unican Pilbeam and Griffiths. Unfortunately, a practise mishap by ADO badly damaged the magnificent AWS/Glissade Pilbeam, dubbed 841/01 just to be different.

There was more disaster at Prescott when Griffiths and Harvey were sidelined by a suspected camshaft breakage, Bolsover had the flywheel shear, Dowson emerged unscathed when he barrel-rolled his Pilbeam at Semi-Circle on his final climb and Roy Lane had a really dreadful weekend using up two cars before practice was over! First the gearbox broke on the Pilbeam and then he had the throttle stick open on his hastily substituted and just rebuilt McRae. After an alarming moment through Orchard, Roy shot across both legs of Ettore's Loop and took to the trees. Happily, the lovely old McRae wasn't too badly damaged, unlike the TVR of Richard Knibbs which was utterly destroyed the next day when it got away from the very shaken driver after Ettore's. Dave Harris was the lucky one with a 39.93s BTD which was achieved only after a nail-biting wait while W & G men Dave Elliott and Steve Oyibo replaced a broken driveshaft. Tim Thomson showed that he was learning fast with an excellent 40.20s, separated from his father by Dowson's pre-accident 40.45s.

McRae wasn't too badly damaged, unlike the TVR of Richard Knibbs which was utterly destroyed the next day when it got away from the very shaken driver after Ettore's. Dave Harris was the lucky one with a 39.93s BTD which was achieved only after a nail-biting wait while W & G men Dave Elliott and Steve Oyibo replaced a broken driveshaft. Tim Thomson showed that he was learning fast with an excellent 40.20s, separated from his father by Dowson's pre-accident 40.45s.

ADO was back at the Bateman Motor Works-sponsored Barbon round and became the first four-time winner in Westmorland. The big Cosworth-engined Pilbeam was well suited to the hill but Al's 22.09s was but 0.02s up on a delighted Tim Thomson with Bolsover shrugging off earlier gear selection and engine problems to put the sports car in the frame again in third place. When competitors journeyed further North still, to Fintray, they found the Aberdeen & DMC celebrating their 75th Anniversary, and despite a practice mishap for Max Harvey, Martyn Griffiths too had something to celebrate. After an indifferent start to the year, Martyn clocked 26.51s for BTD in the class runs.

Before he undertook a long-term development programme on the Toleman Formula 2 chassis, Ray Rowan achieved great success with a BDA-engined Chevron B45. Here he blasts off the Prescott startline to break Martin Bolsover's class record in 41.49s.
BOB LIGHT

Graham Priaulx's shrill-sounding Tiga-BDX SC80 was one of several sports cars to trouble the single-seaters in 1980; the Guernseyman being particularly outstanding in his native Channel Islands.
BOB LIGHT

Unfortunately, a slight mistake at the hairpin marred his Top Twelve finale and his 26.73s best was pipped by ADO on 26.68s. An otherwise auspicious day was marred when reigning Grampian Television/Scottish Champion Kenny Allen crashed his Mallock U2 heavily between Combine and the hairpin, sustaining a broken leg and facial injuries. Everyone was delighted to see him back in action before the year was out, with one of the sophisticated new Middlesbrough-built Vision Clubmans chassis, but his Championship hopes were gone for 1984.

That superb 4.2 Cosworth in the back of the big black AWS/Glissade Pilbeam was now really on song and Alister Douglas-Osborn achieved three Pace/RAC wins in a row at a dampish June, rather non-vintage Shelsley with 26.88s. Once again the surprisingly relaxed Tim Thomson – the Thomsons never seemed quite as intense about their hill climbing as some of their chief competitors – snatched a worthy second ahead of Griffiths, Harris, Lane, Fry, Bolsover and Ted Williams (who was enjoying a successful guest drive in Fry's Pilbeam). Another very happy driver was David Gould with his first major class win with the superb Gould 84/1, defeating Tony Southall's well-developed Formula Atlantic March and Andy Smith's unique March-Allegro turbo which always went well on power courses like Shelsley and Barbon.

Now looking a very likely Champion, ADO made it four wins with an 0.07s margin at Doune despite fuel pump bothers eliminating him from his final climb. Max Harvey again fell off in practice, not too disastrously, but still ended the weekend fourth behind partner Griffiths and the consistent Tim Thomson. David Gould was an outstanding seventh overall after winning his class again. Bolsover gave this round a miss as his engine was being overhauled but he returned with a vengeance for the short course Midland round at Prescott where he topped the run-off order just 0.03s up on ADO. Dave Harris, usually a major factor at Prescott, was down in fourth place after his tyres went off. However, that was after he had set a fierce record-breaking 33.21s BTD in the class runs. The latest sticky Avon tyres – close relatives of F1 qualifying tyres – were undoubtedly highly effective in warming up so rapidly but, notwithstanding the excellent on-course Avon servicing arrangements from Paul Smith's BMTR company, they were only good for three or four meetings on a top class Pilbeam.

For some time now Tim Thomson had seemed on the verge of a Pace/RAC win and on home ground, at Harewood, where he had already won at a couple of smaller meetings, his 37.04s final effort looked good enough. He had already clinched the 'Award of Merit' series and even the premier Championship was not an impossible dream. But then Martyn Griffiths was famous for his last run charges when under pressure and he did it again with a neat 36.98s climb to rob the Yorkshireman of local glory. John Hunt had been getting to grips well with his daunting Pilbeam and he really excelled on this deceptively tricky course with a 37.17s climb for third place, faster even than ADO. Another surprise came from a determined Ray Rowan. Instead of the 1.6-litre Chevron he arrived with an ex-Godfrey Crompton 2.5 Toleman-Hart TG280H, similar to Chris Cramer's former mount. Seventh place was an encouraging start.

Martin Bolsover, who had lost his engine's oil pressure before he had even practised at Harewood, was not the only sports car driver to worry the single-seaters in 1984 even if the formidable sounding twin turbo Rover V8-engined Pubs 'n Clubs Martin BM18 of Colin Cordy and Trevor Panter had been a bit of a disaster. This ex-Simon Dominey chassis went a lot better when Alan Payne's help was enlisted in the substitution of a 275 bhp, normally-aspirated John Eales Rover V8. The formidable Charles Wardle/Jim Robinson partnership was regularly in the Top Twelve with their U2 Mk21 now fitted with a 2.2 PMED-prepared Hart, ex-Richard Jones, and benefitting from Alno Kitchens sponsorship, while Guernseyman Graham Priaulx could be even faster with his shrill 2.1 Swindon BDX-engined Tiga SC80.

This sports car resurgence took off on the annual trek to the Channel Islands. At Bouley Bay there was a splendid class battle between Bolsover (41.00s sports car record) and Priaulx (41.04s Channel Islands 'native' record) before Bolsover went even faster in the Top Twelve to win another Pace/RAC MSA round with a blistering 40.18s to edge out Lane (40.36s) and Griffiths (40.50s). A good 42.33s by Terry Gorvel (2.0-litre March-Hart 772P) before he was eliminated by a dropped valve, was enough for a point and a new 'native' single-seater record, but that was still slower than Priaulx (41.18s, eighth). Graham's finest hour was yet to come, though, after the ferry trip to Le Val des Terres. A stunning 31.46s climb gave him a memorable BTD before his tyres went off. Roy Lane salvaged single-seater honours by winning the run-off in 32.38s but Bolsover (32.67s) and Priaulx were right behind.

After a straight fight between Dave Harris (50.63s) and Ray Rowan (51.14s) at the Loton Midland round, battle was rejoined in earnest in Northern Ireland, at Craigantlet where the Ulster Automobile Club had attracted a good entry. This was surely Alister Douglas-Osborn territory although the reappearance of Chris Cramer, in Chris Dowson's Pilbeam-Repco was an intriguing extra ingredient. Alister fulfilled expectations with a 50.20s BTD, beating Griffiths (50.67s), the inevitable Bolsover, Tim Thomson and Hunt. The Pilbeam-Repco was being afflicted by a tiresome recurring misfire and this rather spoilt Cramer's day after being second fastest in practice and fifth in class. Richard Parsons, who was totally dominating local events with his 1.6-litre Chevron B34, finished eighth in the run-off on 53.95s.

Graham Priaulx gave the August Shelsley a miss (he had been third to Harris and Bolsover in July) but there were even longer faces by the end of the meeting. Catastrophe befell ADO's Championship hopes when John Hunt crashed heavily at the Crossing, suffering leg injuries and writing off the car. Alister had already set yet another Shelsley BTD in 26.72s but he was out of the Top Twelve. That gave Martin Bolsover his big chance and the two-seater screamed up in 26.78s, just a vital 0.04s faster than Lane and 0.18s on Griffiths. By this time the delightfully anachronistic-sounding Shelsley Specials Record had fallen in 28.76s to David Gould in his anything-but-anachronistic Gould. There was more dismay though when Russ Ward effectively ended his Aston Martin Leaders' Championship hopes by also crashing at the Crossing, destroying the effective little FF2000-based 1.1 Sparton-BDA SF79 which he shared with Jerry Sturman.

With Richard Fry following the trend towards Historic racing, he was willing to sell his Pilbeam MP54 and it was snapped up by the AWS/Glissade team in time for ADO to bed himself into it at the August Midland counter at Loton. He was third in class but it must have seemed ominous when Bolsover snatched BTD in 49.67s to clinch the *Birmingham Post* Top Ten Challenge, beating off a 49.82s challenge from Dave Harris in the orange/white Unican Pilbeam.

A week later and the Pace/RAC MSA series really came to the boil at Prescott where six drivers were covered by 0.26s. Tim Thomson drew first blood with a 39.75s class win but a slide in the always deceptive Esses left him just fourth in the final standings on 39.87s. ADO, in a still relatively unfamiliar car did well (39.91s) to come sixth, just 0.02s down on Bolsover who also had a rather hairy ride through the Esses. Harris recorded a fine 39.71s for third and Griffiths took the Pace/RAC MSA title lead with 39.68s. But he still didn't win. Despite having only a 2.5-litre Hart in his Hardwood Timber Products Toleman, the diminutive Ray Rowan showed his amazing car control with a 39.65s climb which won him his first Pace/RAC MSA round. Although Ken Snailham now took the lead in the Aston Martin Leaders' battle after another fine drive in the QED Lotus 7, he lost the Castrol/Beacon Radio Midland title, for which this was the last round, to Bolsover by one point. One of the new breed of saloon lookalikes, Alastair Cobb's 1.3-litre BDH-engined Skoda beat talented Huddersfield Mallock U2 driver David Grace for third. Semmingly inevitably, Martin Bolsover made it a clean sweep by winning the *Birmingham Post* Top Ten, six points clear of Dave Harris who had contested the series rather more seriously than he had the Pace/RAC MSA Championship.

There was no respite for the following weekend battle was rejoined at Wiscombe Park where there was a welcome return to the driving seat for John Hunt. In order to give the Birmingham consulting engineer every chance to win the title he had not set out to contest, Team Guyson had Martin Bolsover back in the MP50 single-seater (which used to be referred to as an MP51). Again BTD was achieved on a class run, by Griffiths in 40.56s. In the Top Twelve it was a jubilant ADO who came out ahead (41.03s) from Bolsover, Tim Thomson and Griffiths, leaving Martyn just one point ahead of ADO and with Tim Thomson and Bolsover four points further adrift.

This year the big meeting at Gurston, sponsored by Wadham Stringer, was run in September and also marked the 60th birthday of veteran sprint and hill climb enthusiast David Render, still going strong in his 2.8 Lola-Hart T560. Poor Alister Douglas-Osborn suffered another blow when a suspension wishbone broke on the MP54, leaving him fortunate to avoid a crash at Karousel. The day belonged to Team Guyson and the MP50/OTJ, Bolsover beating Thomson by 0.27s, and with Jim Thomson sixth in the MP40. Although rarely in the running for BTD, Jim was actually having a very consistent season and was never far behind his younger son.

Still with no respite, it all depended on Doune a week later, and Bolsover shot up the daunting Scottish hill in 40.11s to clinch BTD from ADO, Griffiths, Harvey and an on form Jim Thomson to win his third successive RAC MSA title almost, one could say, by accident. His quite exceptional talent and calm temperament had shone through during a by-no-means troublefree year to beat the desperately unlucky Alister Douglas-Osborn by 3 points. Despite his poor start to the season, Griffiths was third from the consistent Tim Thomson. It was regrettable that Tim's efforts were too often compared with those of elder brother James' for Tim's début year in single-seaters was truly outstanding, winning him the 'Award of Merit' by 11 points from Ray Rowan and 18 from Charles Wardle. Roy Lane had won the Warecrete British Sprint Championship – sponsored by David Render's building product company (but had to be content with fifth in the premier hill climb series ahead of Dowson, Harvey, Jim Thomson, Harris and Rowan).

Russ Ward's Shelsley calamity effectively dropped him to fourth in the Aston Martin Leaders' final reckoning, although equal on points with third man Charles Barter who had been as formidable as ever in the same, very strong 1100cc racing class with a smart Delta T824, Imp-powered as usual. This category had benefited from an influx of FF2000-based chassis with major opposition coming from the McBeath brothers, Andy and Simon, in a Delta-Imp T83; Eryl Davies (ex-Sean Walker Swallow

The 1984 RAC Leaders Champion, Ken Snailham, in his well-sorted QED Lotus 7.
BOB LIGHT

What started as a 'quiet' year, ended with a surprise third RAC title for Martin Bolsover after some remarkable performances in the Guyson Pilbeam MPB43 sports car.
BOB LIGHT

Pilbeam-BDJ SP2); and Adrian Desoutter in another Sparton. The Leaders' title though fell to the remarkably fast and well-sorted white/silver Lotus 7 of Ken Snailham, although he was level on points with Alastair Cobb's Skoda clone. Fifth was David Grace in the pushrod U2 Mk14/25 which he shared so effectively with Allan Warburton, edging out a consistent Roger Gregory who ran his U2 Mk 15 with a BDA in the 1600cc sports-racing as opposed to Clubman division. With other U2 pedallers seventh (former Datsun 240Z sprinter John Istead) and ninth (Neil Crump), the continuing success of these basically simple machines was underlined. The Top Ten was rounded out by Martyn Brake's Maguire spaceframe Imp 'saloon'(eighth) and Lancastrian Brian Walker's Dalgety Agriculture-backed 2.5 Skoda-Hart (tenth).

The RAC National titles were now settled and Championship Finals Day at Harewood was a bit of an anti-climax, especially as the Pilbeam MP43 had its engine go off-song. Tim Thomson fittingly set BTD from Lane, and they took the same top places in the local Harewood FTD Awards series. A rather low-key BARC Championship fell to the impressive Chevette HSR Group B car of Mike Kerr, rather easily, from Cobb and Istead, while the latter won the BARC FTD Awards title by a solitary point from Jim Thomson. John had had an excellent year with his U2 but this last success was a sad reflection on the lack of regular competition in the series from the leading single-seater entrants. Harewood's own Guyson International-sponsored series was won by the leading contender in the hill's successful Formula Ford class, Alan Stringer, a former circuit racer from nearby Knaresborough, who was running the same Crosslé 30F with which he had scored some circuit successes in former years.

The Harewood meeting was the last to feature the entertaining historic handicap class. Unlike in the Midlands where the regulations were fairly strict, the Yorkshiremen happily let in anything (fairly) old and interesting with a minimum of fuss. It was good fun but since it was threatening to attract lots of owners of old Minis and Sprites and so on, it was abandoned before things got out of hand. BARC(Y), under the Chairmanship of Formula Ford competitor Simon Clark (son of Derek Clark) was rightly endeavoring to brush up Harewood's rather tarnished image at the time.

In the regions the smaller club meetings had been as well supported as ever with Alex Graham (U2 Mk20) winning the Scottish title although, happily, Kenny Allen was back on winning form with the smart blue Vision before the end of the year. Another U2, the white Mk21/24 of the Harpers, Peter and Ray, was very successful in the North of England events, while Richard Parsons dominated in Ulster. Dr Richard Thompson's little Saracen took some beating in the South East while over to the West, Kevitt Payne's old Ensign-Holbay TC LNF3 seemed almost unbeatable.

Hill climbers generally have a good appreciation of their sport's heritage so one of the highlights of the year had been the VSCC meeting at Shelsley on 8 July, when the occasion had marked the 50th Anniversary of the birth of the ERA. A memorial to Raymond Mays was unveiled and Rivers Fletcher, still a regular competitor with his light blue Alvis Speed 25, demonstrated the howling BRM

V16 Mk11. BTD fell to Chris Mann's 'modern' Lotus 16 in 34.89s but this was not a lot faster than the splendid 35.44s by David Black, evoking memories of Ken Hutchison, in his well developed Alfa Romeo Tipo B. Martin Morris set the best ERA time (36.26s) in the 2.0 R11B 'Humphrey', a car with much distinguished hill climb form behind it in the hands of Reggie Tongue, Reg Parnell, Sheila Darbishire, John Bolster, Ken Wharton, Michael Christie, Roy Bloxam and Douglas Hull.

A Special Triumph

There had been some rumblings of discontent during 1984 regarding the classification of cars such as Alastair Cobb's Lola-based and Brian Walker's Chenron-based Skodas as saloons, using methanol fuel outside the single-seater and unrestricted sports-racing categories, and the desirability, or otherwise, of imposing an equivalency handicap on cars utilising nitrous-oxide injection in their induction systems. Yet when the 1985 season opened no major changes were effected.

Regrettably, the RAC MSA Championship would be running without a sponsor again and it would definately run without the reigning champion, Martin Bolsover, who had decided to follow the trend towards historic circuit racing with a Guyson-sponsored CanAm McLaren, leaving the 'establishment' to try to reassert itself. David Render added the Pilbeam MPB43 to his growing collection of machinery.

Most of the sport's top names concentrated on what could be described as fine tuning their mounts rather than shooting off in dramatically different directions. AWS/Glissade were to run the 2.8 Hart in the ex-Fry MP54 on methanol and a similar conversion was slated for the Chase Web hybrid MP53/54 with pull-rod rear suspension. Both cars were to be maintained by Martin Middleton Motors of Redditch. Roy Lane had bought Max Harvey's original MP53 tub and had rebuilt his 360 bhp Pilbeam-BMW concept around it.

On the evidence of the final Prescott meeting the previous year, a major challenge could be expected from Ray Rowan's now GKN Technology-backed Toleman-Hart whenever Sprint Championship commitments allowed. Ray had begun sprinting in a Ford Anglia at Curborough in 1975 and had learnt valuable lessons in car control with a Motus-Yamaha kart before progressing to a March-BDA 742, then 2.0 March-BDA 74B with which he had been the 1981 RAC MSA Sprint Champion, and the methanol-fuelled Chevron B45 which had now passed to former Hawke driver Simon Ridge.

Without a doubt, the outstanding new car of 1984 had been the Gould, originally designed by David Gould with input from Allan Staniforth, in response to the arrival of Pilbeam technology into the 1600cc class with Martin Bolsover. Now the challenge was for outright honours for David, aided by young son Sean, had converted the chassis to take the 330 bhp 2.5-litre Hart engine. Lest anyone doubted the seriousness of the challenge, David was to share the car with former champion Chris Cramer. A further useful addition to the ranks of the big single-seater drivers appeared after the start of the year. Taciturn Lancastrian Brian Walker finally forsook Special Saloons for the ex-Tony Brown Pilbeam MP40, complete with 2.8 Hart motivation.

Outside the élite ranks of the large-capacity racing cars there were numerous intriguing developments. The much modified Phil Ducker/Martin Chittenden GRD was to gain the ex-Richard Parsons BDA. Russ Ward and Jerry Sturman had bought Richard Thompson's Saracen to replace the destroyed Sparton; there was a new Martin BM24 chassis on the way for the Pubs 'n Clubs duo; Sam Hill and Nick Carr had a sophisticated Rob Cox-developed 'Black Brick' Caterham 7 with 2.1-litre BDA engine (Leon Bachelier had a slightly less radical 'Black Brick' in the 1600cc Modified Sports class), and at last Bob Dayson had put aside his remarkably rapid 22-year-old Turner-Ford. This enthusiastic and generous veteran from Rugeley, who like Roy Lane combined hill climbing in summer with sporting trials in the winter, had bought Chris Knapman's very successful Caterham 7. With continuing support from car ramp and axle stand specialists Cougar Developments, Bob's smart new mount raised a few eyebrows when it appeared with seemingly gold plated suspension components.

For a decade Charles Barter's successes with a variety of Hartwell Imp-engined machinery had been almost monotonous. Nobody could even think of any new watercress jokes to throw at this exceptionally skillful driver! The friendly and undemonstrative Dorset businessman had also served as Chairman of the increasingly significant HSA but the demands on his time had become too much so he had decided to retire from the competitive fray, at least for the time being. He sold the Delta-Imp to Richard Homer who, in turn, sold his so-successful Ginetta G17 to Tom Yapp.

Women competitors, apart from Maggie Blankstone in the potent U2-Hart which she shared with husband Peter, and Joy Rainey had been rather out of the limelight for a while but two well-known additions were expected for the new season. Former Escort circuit racer Gillian Fortescue-Thomas was to do some events in Alan Payne's now rather more biddable Anson-Rover V8, while former downhill skier and Formula 2 racer Divina Galica would inject considerable interest into Midland Historic classes in either Terry Grainger's ex-Oscar Moore/Ray Fielding HWM-Jaguar or his Simon Hadfield-built Lotus 23B.

After the now customary testing preliminaries at Harewood, Wiscombe and Curborough there was a rather soggy start to the RAC MSA Championship trail at Loton Park. By now Chris Knapman ('Gym and Tonic' of Chiswick-sponsored, Laurie Billing-modified Chevron B47/9) and Dave Harris had joined the growing ranks of methanol users and, despite a misfire on his final climb, it was Harris who struck the first blow with a 52.32s BTD. The winning margin over Martyn Griffiths was only 0.18s, and with ADO, Lane, Rowan, Tim Thomson and Cramer in the promising Gould 84/2 next up, the scene was set for a hard struggle. A newly instituted HSA 'Man of the Meeting' Award went to Russ Ward who beat the best of his class opposition by over 3 seconds. Clearly, the Cheltenham motor engineer was going to be a formidable Leaders' contender in the neat, revamped Saracen M85.

Although the RAC MSA Championship was bereft of a sponsor, the now well-established Midland series, master-minded by Tony Fletcher, had attracted new support from Warley, Birmingham BMW dealers, Rydale BMW. As usual, April Prescott constituted the second round of the series and there were a few dramas. There were 'offs' for Dave Harris (damaging his front suspension) and Tim Thomson (who also suffered fuel injection maladies) and a misfire increasingly afflicted the AWS/Glissade Pilbeam after ADO had set a 40.12s BTD. That dropped him behind Roy Lane (40.27s) in the run-off although Roy had an engine problem on his last climb.

Spring weather in 1985 was pretty poor and rain at Wiscombe after one RAC run caused the Top Twelve to be abandoned after just one climb. Roy Lane was usually better than most in having his car well sorted at the beginning of the season and his 37.27s class best stood as BTD but then, for the second week running, he had engine trouble on his final ascent. Since there was only one RAC run before the heavens opened that was disastrous and left the maximum RAC points, at last, to Tim Thomson (37.56s), from Griffiths, Cramer and Rowan.

Before the May Prescott meeting, Team Guyson had been up to Doune for some match practice and Tim Thomson returned South regaling all concerned with tales of setting BTD amid snow showers! It all clearly stood him in good stead, for this time he set BTD *and* scored maximum points in 39.58s, although there was clearly a major challenge building from Chris Cramer (39.86s). The other man who looked likely to upset the Pilbeam supremacy, Ray Rowan, was fifth behind Griffiths and Harris despite losing 0.3s off the line to spare his marginal transmission, as recorded by the BOC's useful additional timing split. The AWS/Glissade Pilbeam was absent, undergoing an engine rebuild while poor Roy Lane had almost as bad a weekend as he had had a year earlier. *His* engine was also undergoing overhaul and he entered the mighty McRae, only to wallop the Esses bank in practice. He proceeded to share sprint exponent Ken Ayers' big Lyncar-DFL, which he prepared for the popular stockbroker, and Roy scrabbled a couple of RAC points despite overdoing it at Pardon.

John Hunt and Alister Douglas-Osborn were all present and correct for Barbon with "indestructible" pistons' in their Hart engine, and Alister topping the class list in 22.07s. Sixth, after a superb, class record-breaking 22.53s performance in the Mallock U2-Hart was Charles Wardle – a drive which deservedly netted him 'Man of the Meeting' honours after a worrying morning with high oil pressure – but Roy Lane missed the cut by 0.01s. He was still driving the lovely orange McRae but this charismatic machine could not match the new breed of hill climbs cars. Barbon is always close but this time it was just unreal. Both Dave Harris and Chris Cramer clocked 21.81s for BTD and the Bristolian took the verdict, and the extra point, by virtue of his other RAC climb, which was all of 0.02s better than Chris! Griffiths was 0.15s further back, 0.07s ahead of ADO. After his recent good form, Tim Thomson was cheerfully resigned to seventh spot after suffering gearbox trouble and a spin.

The next day several top contenders were sampling Harewood's new smooth but. initially tyre-wearing surface and Cramer went one better to score his first win in the Gould before the final-drive broke, in 36.89s, on a weekend when another second-generation hill climber, Allan Staniforth's daughter Clare, showed that she would be a worthy competitor in the Terrapin Mk7E which she was

The astounding Brabham-Lysholm BT28 extracted an excrutiatingly noisy 220 bhp from 785 supercharged cubic centimetres in 1985 form. Paul Squires is at the wheel here.
BOB LIGHT

sharing with Allan. Before the RAC MSA series resumed at an unusually early Gurston meeting, Alister Douglas-Osborn took a couple of morale-boosting BTDs on successive days at Wiscombe, where John Meredith arrived armed with Ron Datson's redoubtable ex-Auger/McErlain/Cobb Skoda-BDH.

Gurston Down did not enjoy the best of weather for its showpiece meeting but come rain or shine Martyn Griffiths, neat and smooth as ever on the hill, stayed on top, by a mere 0.01s from Gurston master Alister Douglas-Osborn who made an awesome reflex 'save' at Karousel. After his initial RAC ascent Chris Cramer was not far behind but this time bottom gear broke on the Gould as he warmed his tyres for his final effort. The Aston Martin Leaders' hampionship took a significant turn here as John Meredith, veteran of 25 previous class wins on the Wiltshire hill, beat the hitherto invincible Dave Whitehead (1.3-litre Stiletto-BDA), and that gave Russ Ward sole leadership.

There were more rain showers at Shelsley. Griffiths was as consistent as ever and led the way up to the dry final climbs when his 27.18s time was bumped down to fourth by Lane (26.95s after an earlier spin), Cramer (27.05s) and ADO (27.15s). The Leaders battle intensified when Ward was beaten by the incredible Brabham-Lysholm BT28 of 'Man of the Meeting' Paul Squires. Ever since the mid nineteen-seventies Paul and Andrew Squires, and Phil Kidsley had been developing and updating the old 'Squidgley' Brabham. Both Cosworth development engineers, Paul and Phil were now employing a 785cc (80mm bore x 38mm stroke with a very special crank) BDA derivative with a Godfrey super-charger, methanol fuel and a remarkably wide rev band of 6,000-11,000 rpm. Although the blower consumed 50 bhp, and despite the 1.4 supercharging equivalency handicap, this ear-splitting 200 bhp device was very competitive on power hills like Shelsley. In the end it was only the BOC noise tester, suffering from terminal earache, who defeated this particular configuration after nine wins.

Martyn Griffiths was clearly going to take some stopping in 1985 for his 26.55s BTD gave him maximum points at Fintray, from Lane (despite a high speed excursion at Ruin), ADO and a smooth Chris Dowson. Cramer was down in eighth place after another failure in the Gould's overstressed

transmission. Fortunes can change pretty dramatically in hill climbing, though, and Chase Web Offset's Max Harvey was in despair after crashing the MP53/54 on his first Top Twelve run the following week at Doune, seemingly blunting Griffiths' chances. Yet after a rapid repair to the offside front end of the Pilbeam all was ready for Martyn's sole RAC climb after he had already set the class-winning figure at 40.69s. At his best under pressure, he flew and his 40.45s had the edge over Tim Thomson, ADO and Lane. But not Chris Cramer. The Stroud architect rocketed up in 39.78s, a mere 0.4s outside Bolsover's record for the first RAC win by a one-off car since David Hepworth's era. Then the jubilant Gould team were brought to earth with a bang when David had another final-drive breakage, dropping him from fourth to sixth place.

The action returned to the Midlands before the next RAC encounter at Harewood, with Dave Harris' 'short' hill record taking a beating at Prescott at the hands of ADO (32.97s), Lane (33.01s) and the Bristolian himself (33.07s), and another significant record fell at the July Shelsley 'double header' weekend. Gillian Fortescue-Thomas fulfilled her and Alan Payne's hopes by flinging the daunting Anson to a 28.84s time which beat the four-year-old Ladies Record. Not to be outdone, Divina Galica won her class in Terry Grainger's Lotus 23B. In the Midland Championship round Shelsley favourite Alister Douglas-Osborn was a, for him, lowly fifth (27.06s), complaining of 'not enough steam' from the 2.7 Hart currently propelling the Glissade Pilbeam. MAC Committee member Martyn Griffiths won in 26.53s, from Lane and Tim Thomson.

Rain showers rather interfered with proceedings at Harewood's big meeting of the year, and mechanical frailty even more so. The Gould team had fitted a stronger Hewland FGB gearbox, and now the engine failed! Roy Lane's clutch broke and Jim Thomson withdrew with an engine which simply wouldn't rev. Son Tim had seemed to lose that final edge of competitiveness of late but a demon short haircut was alleged to have made a difference as he won the class in 36.88s! There was a surprise for Charles Wardle too, for he was beaten 38.25s to 38.39s by Peter Kaye in a Pilbeam MP43. Peter and local motorcycle dealer John Lambert had resurrected and totally rebuilt the remains of David Garnett's well-shunted chassis. Although they weren't doing many meetings, both car and drivers were as competitive as ever. Rain and an absense of wet weather tyres made them decide to

David Gould receives the first John Bolster Trophy from John's widow, Rosemary, at the August Shelsley, for building what was undoubtedly the 'Shelsley Special' of the year, if not the decade – the Championship-wining Gould-Hart.
AUTOSPORT JEFF BLOXHAM

A big man in a small car. Russ Ward's 1985 mount, the Saracen M85, took him to both Rydale BMW Midland and RAC Leaders Championships.
BOB LIGHT

forego the Top Twelve although the deceptively abrasive new surface had dried again for the final climbs. Tim Thomson (36.36s) kept up his challenge by beating Griffiths (36.40s) but BTD, equalling the course record, went to a very neat Ray Rowan in 36.12s. Ray was still concentrating on winning the Sprint Championship in 1985, which he succeeded in doing for the second time.

Happenings on the Channel Islands have a habit of proving highly significant to the RAC MSA Championship and Chris Cramer returned to the mainland with 20 more RAC points, despite yet another gear breakage for the car's owner at Bouley Bay. Now enjoying much-needed Unidraw support, Cramer's Bouley best of 39.89s defeated a slightly wild-looking Douglas-Osborn by 0.06s, with Griffiths third even though he stripped a gear on two occasions. Tim Thomson was in trouble too when a foreign body jammed between the cam gears and the drive belt with expensive results. This relagated him to his father's trusty MP40RXH for Le Val des Terres, where he found the other car just didn't fit him. Alister Douglas-Osborn actually set BTD in 32.90s on Guernsey but the rain came down for the Top Twelve runs and Cramer's well-controlled 37.55s had 0.19s in hand over Alister's best time.

Despite worries over the transmission breakages and the high cost generally of sustaining a Championship challenge, David Gould's design/build *tour de force* was certainly vindicated and he gained a mid-season bonus at Shelsley which was one of the year's highlights.

Autosport magazine and the MAC decided to present The John Bolster Trophy to "the competitor who, in the opinion of the judging panel, achieves the most outstanding combination of technical ingenuity, engineering ability and competitive success during the Shelsley Walsh season with a wholly or mainly self-built car, having regord for the budget available". It was a fitting memorial to JVB and took the form of a tantalus of decanters, containing Vodka and tomato juice – a Bloody Mary – of course. David Gould was the recipient of this charming award, from John Bolster's widow Rosemary, at a little ceremony at August Shelsley, also attended by 'the Tudor Queen' herself.

With only the ten best scores to count in the RAC Championship, Chris Cramer *could* overhaul ultra-consistent Martyn Griffiths and he moved up to challenge Martyn with another win at Craigantlet where the three title aspirants finished on 50.27s (Cramer), 50.29s (ADO) and 50.45s (Griffiths – never yet a winner at the Ulster hill) on another generally wet day.

Even though August Shelsley began with Sunday morning rain, this was *the* event of the year, with unaccustomed BBC2 television coverage. Quite apart from the John Bolster Trophy presentation it was a day for nostalgia as it was Shelsley's 80th Birthday Meeting. The age old contest for BTD was as sharp as ever, despite dampness and Alister Douglas-Osborn's absense through 'flu but there were many cars from earlier eras on the hill: Julian Ghosh driving the Vauxhall Villiers; Clive Richards' ex-Scragg HWM-Jaguar SPG 982: Uwe Hucke's remarkably ugly 4WD Bugatti T53 which crashed so memorably in 1932; Graham Galliers' Marsh Special back in the hands of Tony Marsh, who matched his 1965 best of 33.50s in just three practice climbs; Roy Lane in the McRae; and many others. One of his last run 'specials' gave Martyn Griffiths BTD in 27.60s, but Cramer was right there on 27.99s (and drawing ahead on points because Martyn was already dropping scores), ahead of Lane's Pilbeam-BMW best in 28.02s. There was more joy for the Cramer family when young Marc, now going really well with a Ford purshrod engine in the ex-Dave Whitehead spaceframe Reliant Kitten lookalike, was awarded the 'Man of the Meeting' honours for a 39.13s class win which did his car's former owner Dave Whitehead's Leaders' and Midland Championship aspirations no good at all.

Whereas ADO had been under the weather at Shelsley, he was back on winning form (49.70s) for the final Loton Park climb of the year where both Dave Harris and Tim Thomson were feeling unwell.

Tim was having no luck at all for he had more engine bothers at Shelsley and a practice accident at September Prescott, severely damaging the MP50, putting him back in the MP40 for the rest of the meeting, and indeed the season. However, any Thomson family gloom was dispelled when Jim announced that Guyson's Saratoga Springs, USA, operation, Guyson Corporation, would be sponsoring the 1986 RAC Championship. BTD was set on the class climbs by Douglas-Osborn in 39.04s but the Top Twelve and the crucial maximum points went Griffiths' way from Alister and Cramer, who now led the series by just one point. And 'Man of the Meeting'? That presented a slight problem of gender because Maggie Blankstone won it, most deservedly, with a 42.23s climb in the Worfield Garage 2.2 U2-Hart Mk20/25 to set a new outright Ladies Record. Much interest centred on the destination of the hard-fought Rydale BMW Midland title and a smiling Russ Ward made up for his 1984 disappointments by winning by a single point from Dave Whitehead, who needed a tie-decider to beat the indecently fast, roadgoing Morgan Plus 8 of Malvern's Peter Garland. Roy Lane may not have had an exceptionally good season but he did enough to win the *Birmingham Post* Top Ten Challenge by the seemingly inevitable one point from the equally inevitable Martyn Griffiths and ADO, who was a further point in arrears.

There were still two RAC rounds to go but the drama reached its climax at Wiscombe Park in Devon on 8 September. A more than usually determined Chris Cramer – and that's saying something – was on brilliant form and smashed the hill record to head the class times with 36.35s. ADO almost matched that with an RAC run-off best of 36.36s but Chris's final effort was stunning: 36.06s, and another hill record. David Gould had wisely stood down from the Top Twelve to give Chris the best possible chance to win the title and that marvellous climb clinched it. For the first time since 1980 (Cramer again in the March 782/792) the premier hill climb championship had *not* been won in a Pilbeam. Amid the jubilation there was sincere sympathy for Martyn Griffiths who was becoming a little tired of finishing second in major championships. After an extremely consistent season it all went wrong on his RAC climbs. First he hit the Wis curb, damaging the suspension, then ten yards into his second effort, a gear stripped.

Although the title was settled the Doune finale was eagerly awaited for the Lothian CC, headed by

Fraser Madder, had won the Norrie Galbraith Memorial Trophy for the best organised RAC round at the June meeting. But it was not to be as the effects of fourteen weeks of incessant rain caused the meeting to be abandoned before it had even started. Wellies were needed even to walk the course! Championship final scores were as at Wiscombe.

Chris Cramer routinely added the 'Award of Merit' and HSA 'Man of the Year' Awards to his trophies for making such outstanding use of the 2.5 Hart-engine Gould. David Gould (tenth overall) was no mean driver himself but his greatest achievement lay in designing and building such a sophisticated and successful car. The scale of his efforts can be gauged from the estimated 5,000 hours he spent in a single timber garage/workshop building the car. He had taught himself the riveting, bonding and filleting skills for the honeycomb monocoque and had spent three months on computer research so that he could write his own programme for the computer aided suspension design. Bob Cobb carried out the milling work needed but otherwise it was all down to David, aided by son Sean, Allan Staniforth's good advice and Chris Cramer's sorting abilities.

A disappointed Martyn Griffiths was 3 points down at the last with Alister Douglas-Osborn third, 10 points clear of Roy Lane after a season when Alister drove as well as ever but, unusually for him, had to contend with a definite power disadvantage. Tim Thomson's uneven year gave him fifth, ahead of the less-than-wholehearted RAC challenges of Rowan and Harris, with Harvey, Hunt (runner-up in the 'Award of Merit') and Gould rounding out the Top Ten.

Doune's cancellation left a three-way, 72-point tie to be resolved in the Aston Martin British Leaders' Championship. Russ Ward got the nod for a notable title double in the little Saracen, over Dave Whitehead and Bob Dayson. Bob had a splendid season with the yellow Cougar Developments Caterham 7 but occasionally had to give best to the Reverend Tony Croft's red QED 7. Ken Snailham was now running a 1.7 engine in his Lotus 7 so ran in the big modified sports division, as successfully as ever despite the presence of such formidable opposition as the Goodman and Bancroft Porsche 911 derivatives, Paul Tankard's mighty TVR Tuscan 'Bluebottle' and Scotsman Alistair Jack's potent Dutton-Rover V8, to finish fourth, ahead of John Corbyn's neat little 492cc Jedi-Suzuki 84/1. The Wellingborough driver had done much in his Terrapin days to encourage low-cost single-seater aspirants and the previous year he had helped to start a new trend. For many years the enthusiastic 500 Owners

Association had tuned out to entertain with their 30-odd-year-old Formula 3 500s to everyone's enjoyment apart from anyone waiting patiently in the assembly areas, with engine temperature rising, while the temperamental one-lungers were cajoled into firing up! Not since Peter Voigt's remarkable exploits with the Voigt/Renwick Special had anyone seriously essayed a new 500, as opposed to an adapted kart. The workmanlike Jedi, a proper racing car in miniature, thus started a new trend which gradually was to gain support. The Leaders' Top Ten was completed by a consistent Chris Johnson (2.3 Vauxhall Chevette), Chris Knapman's smart Chevron, and the Mallock U2s of Roger Gregory, Barry Groombridge and John Istead. Young Marc Cramer's highly successful second season earned him the HSA's 'Newcomer of the Year' pot while another 1600cc racing class contender to watch was Oxfordshire-domiciled optician Adrian Hopkins. Adrian was doing great things with the originally Patrick Head-designed, Hamish McLeod-developed FF2000 Sark II, which now benefited from a rather special BDA-based engine and an ongoing development programme which was making Adrian an increasingly formidable competitor.

Despite the Doune washout the season enjoyed a fine end-of-term finale at one of the best Harewood meetings for years. 'Number1' was seen for the first time in 1985, on the Gould which Martin Bolsover was sharing with talented occasional hill climber/racer and professional journalist Marcus Pye. Charles Wardle, who had little left to prove in a sports car, was enjoying sharing Chris Dowson's big Pilbeam-Repco as a prelude to a full season with it in 1986 and Gillingham motor engineer Barrie Dutnall was trying to decide whether his familiar Ralt-Langford BDA RT3 might not have better handling than his newly purchased, ex-Roy Lane Pilbeam MP50 chassis for which he had obtained a powerful, methanol-fuelled ex-Ray Rowan BDA. Rowan was there too and his growing Harewood reputation rose further with a series of phenomenal, Ronnie Peterson-style, knife edge climbs in the Toleman to set a dramatic new hill record in 35.68s (from 36.12s). Martin Bolsover showed his exceptional talent in the Gould to clock 36.51, 0.06s better than even Harewood past master Roy Lane. Conditions were perfect for records on the now well bedded-in surface and no fewer

John Corbyn rounds Prescott's Ettore's hairpin in his trend-setting Jedi-Suzuki 84/1, progenitor of a whole new generation of 500cc racing cars.
BOB LIGHT

Lotus and Caterham Sevens have become very popular hill climb mounts in recent years. Rob Welch's Seven is prominent in this Harewood Paddock gathering.
AUTHOR

than eleven class figures tumbled. Most notable was a new outright sports car best by John Lambert in 37.93s, with the beautifully rebuilt Pilbeam. The meeting incorporated the final rounds of both BARC and Harewood Championships. The former may have been a shadow of its former self but gave a worthy win for tall, bearded Graham Oates (Lotus Europa), and a consolation FTD Awards title for Alister Douglas-Osborn. David Grace was the domestic Harewood series winner after another first-class season, from John Gornall's very smart MG Midget, Peter Harper's U2 and the not so smart but very rapid Sprite of Brian Kenyon. After many seasons of threatening to return to the hills, the extrovert Sheffield driver and wife Pat had done so to good effect "as someone had to beat my old record".

Gurston Down, the BARC's other hill, saw its season-long championship fall to a real clubman, Derek Mullis (Mini Cooper S), while Kenny Allen's Vision secured another Grampian Television/ Scottish title for a Clubmans Sport chassis. Over in Ireland, the hitherto near invincible Richard Parsons had graduated to a 2.5 March-Hart 792 but was pressed hard by Robert 'Turbo Sam' McGimpsey's astonishing turbocharged BDA-engined Crosslé 26F, while Shay Lawless picked up a couple of Irish titles with his 3.5 Yoplait Special (née Chevron).

Effort Rewarded

Consolidation from a position of strength was again the keynote as the 1986 season approached. After sponsoring the British 'Award of Merit' series for the last couple of years via Guyson International, Jim Thomson's company was now stepping up to back the premier RAC MSA Championship under the Guyson USA banner. Since John Hunt's AWS Group was now to sponsor the Leaders' series and Max Harvey's Chase Web Offset concern was to back the 'Award of Merit', all three RAC MSA titles were now sponsored by the businesses of active competitors. This gave a good example of hill climbers putting something back into the sport from which they derived so much enjoyment.

Shell Oils, another of the sport's loyal sponsors, especially at Harewood, had now joined Rydale BMW to co-sponsor the prestigious and well-supported Midland series. On the other hand the BARC now, sensibly, allowed their rather redundant national championship to lapse, with Harewood and Gurston Down putting added emphasis on their thriving local titles.

Although a general undercurrent of discontent remained about the outmoded regulations governing the production-based classed at RAC meetings – 'Silhouette' saloons, methanol fuel and nitrous-oxide injection all generating opposition – much pre-season speculation centred round the imposition of fairly strict noise regulations at Prescott as a precursor of universal limits prescribed by the RAC MSA for 1987. Bad weather ruled out the first attempt at a noise test day at Prescott and there was poor support for the rescheduled date on 15 March. Nevertheless, once the season got under way there was comparatively little major drama and the 115 dBA limit proved insuperable only for the odd exceptional case such as the ear-splitting Brabham-Lysholm.

After defeat by the Gould in 1985 the Pilbeams ranks would be strengthened further. Two new MP57 chassis were destined for the Alister Douglas-Osborn/John Hunt partnership and for Jim Thomson, with air-cooled, computer-controlled anti-lock braking slated on Mike Pilbeam's latest developments. The new brakes were also down for incorporation on the Chase Web Offset MP53/04 although the car was not so fitted on its sensational début at the Wiscombe test day. Jim Thomson was intending to have elder son James and Martin Bolsover drive his car occasionally, just to keep everyone on their toes, while the damaged MP50 was now rebuilt for younger son Tim to campaign again. David Render had bought Dave Harris' MP50, with fettling in Ray Rowan's capable hands while Charles Wardle's first season with Chris Dowson's MP47-Repco was eagerly awaited.

But the opposition looked stronger than ever. The Gould was due to be fitted with a full 2.8 Hart engine and a 2.6 Phil Mark-prepared, short-stroke Hart (running on methanol) was destined for Ray Rowan's Toleman. Perhaps more important, a beefier Hewland FG gearbox replaced the 'marginal' FT200, so those relatively gentle, time-wasting starts of 1985 would be no more. Rowan's previous 2.5 Hart had now found its way into sprinter Chris Knapman's Chevron B49. Chris had now joined forces with Quorn Engine Developments' Ken Snailham for a crack at the big single-seater class with a 2.5 Ralt-Hart RT4 Formula 2 chassis. A light-hearted move into this class 'for fun' was rare, but after some successful championship chasing Russ Ward and the sport's talented 'in house' cartoonist Jerry Sturman decided to have a less demanding year with the 1976 Martin-Cosworth Vega BM16, ex-Richard Brown, Tony Brown and Russ' brother-in-law Alan Cox, despite its fairly undistinguished record.

Activity seemed highly concentrated among the exponents of Clubmans sports car chassis. Kenny Allen's success with the Vision had inspired a number of people to beat a path to Paul Gibson's Middlesbrough company for their new mount, with Kenny concentrating on his existing V84 until a new 2.0 version was ready. Former Caterham 7 and U2 driver Rob Welch bought an ex-Gibson circuit car to run in the colours of Paracide Plus (sheep dip products) manufacturer Battle, Hayward and Bower, while further Visions were destined for Peter Harper and Nichol Over. The Blankstones and Jim Robinson/David Grace had ordered new U2 Mk27s with lots of Hart horses while the talented Nick Whale intended to both hill climb and circuit race his almost new Mk27, after selling his success-ful Mk21/25 to Colin Pook. Neil Crump and Alan Lloyd, who seemed to retire (not very convinc-

Alex Graham (Mallock U2 Mk 20), seen here at Strathclyde Park was a perennial rival to Kenny Allen in Scottish events and had won the 1984 Grampian Television Scottish title.
BILL HENDERSON

ingly) at regular intervals, were expected with a BDA-engined U2 while John Istead had bought Rob Welch's Mk21, passing on his trusty Mk18 to former Lotus-Sunbeam saloon driver Hugh Trotman. It all looked highly competitive.

Unfortunately, memorably awful Spring weather marred the opening skirmishes. Easter provided the now customary hectic Strathclyde Park – Harewood – Loton Park weekend for the really dedicated, with Kenny Allen's Clubmans Vision V84A landing a telling first blow in Scotland where the centre of attention was John Gray's red, rally class-winning Lancia 037. Alex Graham had been runner-up on Strathclyde Park's wide open spaces and he occupied the same spot on Easter Sunday at Harewood behind Barrie Dutnall's 1.6 Pilbeam-BDA MP50. Barrie's 45.66s BTD gives some idea of the atrocious weather. A brave Charlie Saunders actually contrived to be third in the run-off in the E-type Jaguar he shared with fellow Mirfield car breaker John Smith. The top championship contenders concentrated on Loton of course – a superb hill which unfortunately was down to two meetings a year – where they endured blizzard conditions. The Gould was unready but Ray Rowan showed that he meant business with a 53.65s class best before he was assailed with a faulty fuel pump. Roy Lane had re-prepared his Steel King MP53-BMW without major changes and the proven combination again scored well with Roy winning the run-off in 53.06s, by 0.36s from Martin Bolsover in Team Guyson's MP57 and by 0.43s from Max Harvey who put in a sterling drive to beat ADO, a troubled Rowan and co-driver Griffiths.

The weather was not much better at April Prescott when changeable conditions and an extremely slippery track left Alister Douglas-Osborn with BTD in 46.04s in AWS Group's new MP57. Guest drivers were to the fore again in the *Birmingham Post* run-off when Dave Harris, driving the Chase Web Pilbeam, edged out Roy Lane by 0.08s, with Bolsover another three-hundredths adrift. At least Prescott was completed. Devon can be very wet and the Aston Martin Owners Club's double meeting at Wiscombe was a complete washout, being abendoned after one run of Saturday's club meeting. A popular decision was then taken to replace this lost Guyson USA RAC round with a second Harewood counter at the BARC's September Finals Day.

A slightly fortunate maximum points score at a showery Prescott in May, helped Martyn Griffiths (Pilbeam-Hart MP53/ 04) on his way to his second RAC title.
BOB LIGHT

May Prescott was merely squally, the showers turning the qualifying order inside out and efectively ruining the Top Twelve climbs of ADO, Rowan, Cramer (back with the now 2.8 Gould 84C) and Jim Robinson. ADO scored BTD (40.22s) in the class runs but a slightly fortunate Martyn Griffiths, clocking 40.33s just as the rain returned, scored a maximum, by 0.37s from Lane – free from major dramas this May – and with David Gould, Max Harvey, Alan Payne (now 4.2 Anson-Rover SA4) and Brian Walker (2.8 MP40) all scoring well. Charles Wardle was still feeling his way but a week later he took a morale boosting first win, over Tim Thomson, at Harewood, the hill where he had made his hill climb début. A very dramatic new saloon made its first rather unsorted appearance at Harewood. This was Mobil 1 Oil-backed Mike Kerr's new Skoda. Under its mock Czech bodywork, this Rover V8-engined contender was actually the ex-Graham Priaulx Tiga SC80!

Almost unbelievably, the weather was still abysmal at Barbon where the gloom was deepest round Team Guyson after the MP57 became a non-starter with a blown head gasket. It was very difficult to gauge true 1988 form at this stage but nobody could argue with ADO's 23.77s victory, his Pilbeam carrying the slogan 'AWS Serves You Right', to defeat Rowan by a large, for Barbon, margin of 0.45s. Griffiths maintained his challenge with a class third place while unanimity was easy in awarding the 'Man of the Meeting' pot to new sensation Phil Jefferies. An absolutely heart-stopping, twitchy 30.75s climb also won him the 500cc racing class in his 250 Trakstar-Yamaha ZK86, a Kart-ish device which was to cause a lot more anguish among drivers of more conventional hill climb machinery as time went on.

Eight days later and it was dry at last at Gurston Down and everyone could really get to grips with some serious hill climbing amid the rolling Wiltshire downs. Gurston was ADO country and Alister set a 28.52s BTD in his class and although he was 0.05s slower in the Top Twelve it was enough to leave an 0.36s margin over Roy Lane, whereas Roy had Rowan (28.97s) and Griffiths (29.00s) very close indeed. Ray Rowan's effort was particularly good as he was in the unfamiliar cockpit of David Render's ex-Dave Harris Pilbeam following an engine failure during testing at Bruntingthorpe with the Toleman. Unfortunately, a hub problem kept the Gould out of the Top Twelve. Good conditions encouraged outstanding performance through the classes with a 34.67s record for Dave Whitehead's familiar metallic blue Stiletto Morris Minor V8 turbo only 0.1s off Brian Walker's Skoda-Hart best – and a 31.35s record for David Grace. With the new Mallock U2 Mk27 still being sorted, David was back in Allan Warburton's Mk14/25 and he was elected 'Man of the Meeting' for this climb.

With a break now before Shelsley, it was good to see Russ Ward gaining a 42.80s BTD at the BOC's club Prescott meeting – a rare success for the Martin-Vega – with 0.19s in hand over Chris Cramer in Billy Morris' 2.0 March 78/79B. This was Chris Cramer's old Championship chassis and Chris was taking time out from the Gould to sort it with the Haverfordwest veteran.

Alister Douglas-Osborn and the AWS/Glissade MP57 were looking very strong now and he made it three RAC wins in a row at Shelsley, coming close to his 26.08s Pilbeam-DFL record with a 26.27s

Ferrari-only classes have been run at both Harewood and Shelsley in recent years. This desirable collection waits for action in the Harewood Paddock slip road.
AUTHOR

Tony Bancroft and his much-modified Porsche Turbo, one of the fastest road-going cars on the hills.
AUTHOR

best. This gave him the Championship lead over Roy Lane who had to be content with fifth. Nearest to Alister – just 0.2s away in fact – was a still Pilbeam-mounted Ray Rowan, while both Cramer and Griffiths were close. Kenny Allen, although still without his promised new Vision, was looking set to win the Scottish series again and took great pleasure in upsetting the Midland regulars by coming to Shelsley and setting a new 29.54s Clubmans record.

A good Scottish fortnight could well have put ADO on the way to his second RAC title but at Fintray, the shortest hill on the RAC schedule, a throttle linkage clip failure spoilt his final climb and his 26.7s time was good only for third as Chris Cramer came within 0.01s of Bolsover's record in 26.00s to notch up his first '86 win for the Gould. Ray Rowan was back in the Toleman and was making his first visit to the Aberdeen hill so his 26.05s for second place was pretty impressive. Now that he was concentrating on the hills his title challenge was very real although this gutsy little Midlander suffered a big setback at Doune. He was third in class, again on his first visit, but a half spin at Junction spoilt his first Top Twelve run, With all to play for even his lightning reflexes were not enough to prevent a big accident at Garden Gate on his last run, wrecking the Toleman's monocoque. ADO's best efforts were again belittled by a minor mechanical malady – a misfire – and his 39.66s time was beaten, by 0.04s, by the resurgent Chris Cramer, although clear of Griffiths, Gould and Lane. Among the Scots, Kenny Allen was jubilant after clinching the Scottish title before the end of June!

There was further cause for celebration in Scotland with the announcement that the Stonehaven and District CC had arranged the first event at Durris, South of Aberdeen, as an invitation affair on 14 September. George Ritchie – former Scottish Road Car Champion with a Ginetta G15 and now running the ex-Parsons Chevron B34 – was a prime mover in adding this exciting new hill to the Scottish scene. To be resurfaced for the opening event, this very fast 1,640-yard climb formed an Independent Broadcasting Authority access road.

At this point in the season there was much of significance outside the Guyson USA British title chase. Martyn Grifffiths set a new 'short course' Prescott record in 32.73s but on the day it was young Marc Cramer who really set the tongues wagging. His father was having another outing in the Morris March and his 34.06s time was good enough for fifth in class. Marc was making his single-seater début in the same car and proceeded to break 34s, faster than the reigning champion, before a transmission failure ended their efforts.

One of the great might-have-beens of hill climb history was the fabled 1936 return of Hans Stuck to Shelsley with the short chassis Auto Union. Fifty years later the MAC and Audi importer VAG (Audi had been part of the Auto Union) arranged to mark the anniversary and in so doing promoted the highlight of the year. Saturday, 6 July was the traditional VSCC day at Shelsley and although Rodney Felton set a resounding BTD for pre-war cars in his Alfa Romeo 'Monoposto' Tipo B in 35.48s, all eyes were on historic racing car collector/driver Neil Corner as he made three evocative ascents in his recently rebuilt 1939 Auto Union D-type. In sharp contrast, one of the World's greatest rally drivers, Hannu Mikkola, rose to Shelsley's challenge in a 530 bhp Audi Quattro S1 rally car. Powersliding Kennel, Mikkola provided an awesome spectacle with the fearsome supercar, introducing hill climbers to the strange combination of enormous power and assorted popping, banging and chattering noises which characterised the turbocharged Group B car. Left foot braking for the Esses in true rally style, Hannu broke 30s on his first climb and finally recorded 29.51s – best ever by a closed car. This could not count as a Special Saloon record as FISA categorised Group B machines as Sports Cars, although Mike Kerr's Group B specification Chevette HSR was, very reasonably, classed as a saloon in its BARC title-winning campaign. The next day, and not to be outdone by the fabulously expensive works Audi, Nic Mann clocked a superb 30.49s in the Aldon Performance Centres-backed Morris Minor to break Brian Walker's official Special Saloon record. All this rather overshadowed another Shelsley BTD for Alister Douglas-Osborn (26.44s) and a splendid return by James Thomson (26.47s) who defeated both Griffiths and brother Tim.

Championship fortunes changed again as the RAC series made its first visit to Harewood. To most people's surprise, Ray Rowan had rebuilt the Toleman-Hart, with assistance from David Render, using a new tub. Not one bit abashed by his Scottish mishap he turned in an extraordinarily neat and well-judged climb to set another new Harewood record in 35.44s, over half a second up on Chris Cramer (who was beaten by David Gould in class), and with Charlie Wardle scoring a fine third

(36.12s), ahead of Martin Bolsover. Wardle and Dowson now enjoyed valuable sponsorship from Broadshot, a Shell Chemicals herbicide. The meeting also saw Harewood's longest standing record, Bolsover's 1600cc racing car time, toppled by Barrie Dutnall (38.14s) after an intense battle with an inspired Chris Seaman and Adrian Hopkins. However, ADO's run of success was halted by a blown head gasket and Lane suffered a broken driveshaft.

The engine failure caused Alister Douglas-Osborn to miss the Channel Islands events although John Hunt was there to share Jim Thomson's MP57. That should have helped Chris Cramer but during practice for Bouley Bay he clipped a rock, breaking a magnesium upright. David Gould promptly flew off back to the Mainland to organise a repair in time for Le Val des Terres. In the meantime a new set of tyres helped Max Harvey to a superb 39.34s BTD and his first RAC win. Playing down his own considerable driving ability, Max had often said that he could never win an RAC round but a smoother, neater approach in 1986 had already seen him higher up the order in previous rounds so his victory was not a total surprise to many. Martyn Griffiths was 0.15s in arrears for a Chase Web 1-2 whereas a lack of traction kept Ray Rowan down in third place. A major oil spillage from Brian Walker's Pilbeam, and consequent delays which robbed some of a second class run because of the road-closing deadlines, rather marred the Guernsey round. The Gould was back in action with Cramer looking good on 31.17s from Griffiths on 31.31s. But Ray Rowan had the last word. After spinning on the oil, Ray put in a final climb only 0.04s off the record on the still slippery hill to take a fine 30.99s BTD.

His engine problems also kept ADO away from Craigantlet where Rowan was down in fourth place with a misfire. Cramer (50.45s) and Gould (51.05s) were well in the running but this time there was no stopping Martyn Griffiths who at last won in Ulster in 50.14s. This was his twelfth attempt at Craigantlet and came after a frustrating series of no fewer than nine second places. With ADO, Cramer and Rowan – or rather their machinery lacking his utter consistency, Martyn looked well on the way to his second RAC MSA title.

He staked his claim most forcibly at Shelsley, whatever the track conditions. His 26.54s class time stood as BTD as the rain rather spoilt the Top Twelve. In these conditions his 31.68s time left Chris Cramer a clear 0.76s in arrears with Roy Lane and David Gould the only other two to crack the 33s barrier. Ray Rowan's challenge was again blunted by a lack of traction, consigning him to seventh place. Before the precipitation started it had been a day of records. The 'tin top' record took another battering as Nic Mann triumphed over Mike Kerr's Tiga-based Skoda in 30.07s and Tony Bancroft smashed the big Modified Sports figures in 31.69s in another highly developed roadgoing turbocar, his nitrous-oxide-injected, virtually 930 spec. Porsche turbo. Gill Fortescue-Thomas's Ladies record went as well, to Joy Rainey with a splendid 28.32s in her specially adapted 2.3 Pilbeam-Hart MP53.

There was a month's gap now before September Prescott but the hill climb scene was by no means dull. Charles Wardle won his third Harewood BTD to clinch the local FTD Awards series, again beating Tim Thomson who was as cheery and as relaxed as ever in the Paddock, but perhaps too relaxed on the track. Unaccustomed ill feeling intruded at this event when Graham Oates had his now more highly developed Europa excluded for having tyres protruding very slightly beyond the bodywork, after he had driven his heart out, rather than at scrutineering. Hard things were said at the time and allegations flew, but it all appeared to boil down to genuine misunderstanding, although the incident did nothing for Graham's Harewood Championship prospects.

Chris Cramer, after a shaky start to the year, had been determined to try to retain his RAC title but it all went painfully wrong in practice for Loton's August meeting. Driving the March 78/79B, he lost control just after the start, slamming sideways into a tree with such force that he was trapped for some time and, when eventually freed, was found to have hip injuries which would put him out of action for at least the rest of the year. Next day, Martyn Griffiths cheered everyone up with one of his last run virtuoso performances to break Dave Harris' course record in 48.30s, over two whole seconds less than Roy Lane's best time. The Midland Championship's regulations now gave roadgoing cars, running on treaded road tyres, their own class within the Modified Sports division and Peter Garland's brother Nigel correctly saw an opportunity to lift the overall title with his roadgoing, ex-Josh Sadler 3.5 Porsche 911. He clinched it at Loton.

Problems with slightly more stringent noise regulations, and especially with inconsistent readings, briefly looked like excluding most of the Top Twelve at Prescott! Happily, good sense prevailed and

Martyn Griffiths (39.08s) headed another Chase Web Offet 1-2 from Harvey (39.13s), Lane (39.46s) Rowan (39.67s), Gould (39.84s) amd ADO, who was back in the AWS/Glissade Pilbeam but with mere 2.5 Hart to propel him. This last win was enough to give Martyn the *Birmingham Post* Top Ten Challenge by one point from Roy Lane's always immaculately prepared Steel King Pilbeam, whereas the final Rydale BMW/ Shell Oils Midland scores put Nigel Garland five clear points ahead of Dave Whitehead, with the astonishing Trakstar of Phil Jefferies third. Hill climbing is not all about winning titles, though, and the rich variety within the sport showed when the coveted Prescott Gold Cup was won by Dudley Mason-Stryrron's spotless Rardley Motors 2.4 Ferrari Dino 246T Tasman Formula car from John Corbyn's little spaceframe Jedi. The Ferrari Owners Club class at Prescott, and later at Shelsley and Harewood, attracted many fine cars but none finer than Dudley's two rare '60s racers. To some the jewel-like 2.0 Dino 206SP sports car (ex-works/Tony Dean) which Dudley and wife Sally had earlier campaigned was even more desirable.

Griffiths strengthened his title bid with a 40.25s win at Wiscombe, although another half-second covered Rowan and ADO. The soundness of John Corbyn's low-cost, spaceframe, wishbone suspended Jedi concept, and growing support for the new 500s, were emphasised when five out of the top six places in the class were scooped up by the little machines. On the same day, Scottish enthusiasts were agog to see how the first, rather tentative meeting at Durris would go. Kenny Allen at last had his new Lowland Tyres and Exhausts-sponsored 280 bhp, 2.0 Vision 86H and, topping 130 mph, he swept to a 39.41s inaugural record, nearly 2 seconds faster than Alex Graham's older, less sophisticated U2 Mk20.

Underpowered or not, Alister Douglas-Osborn was fastest on the daunting Doune course, his victorious 38.89s climb coming in the class runs. But there was no stopping Martyn Griffiths when the Championship points were at stake. Whereas ADO took 40.04s on the only dry RAC run, Martyn Griffiths clipped 0.12s off that to secure his long-awaited second RAC title in fine style with a round to spare. David Gould was very close too on 40.12s, with an impressive Charles Wardle getting the bettter of Ray Rowan and Tim Thomson. Ray had had an 'off' at East Brae which effectively ended

Paul Tankard rounds Harewood's final Quarry Corner in his brutish TVR Tuscan V8 'Bluebottle'.
AUTHOR

his hopes, but Martin Bolsover – a driver with very few accidents on his exceptional record – gave Team Guyson another end-of-season wreck when he crashed heavily in practice on the approach to Oak Tree. All Pilbeams are different and nobody had thought that the Guyson MP57 handled as well as the AWS/Glissade car. In fact, the rebuild revealed that the problem lay in a hitherto undetected assembly fault.

The entry for the extra Harewood Guyson USA RAC qualifier, which had already incorporated a round in the multi-disciplinary MG Maestro series, was greatly oversubscribed and a fine occasion graced the Yorkshire hill. Martyn Griffiths could finally relax a bit, the new Champion taking fourth in the run-off in 36.71s, from Tim Thomson – a former tenant of the farmhouse past which the course runs – and journalist Marcus Pye whose splendid 37.16s climb in the Gould earned him 'Man of the Meeting' honours. But being Harewood, it was no surprise when Ray Rowan flew to both BTD (35.92s) and RAC (36.11s) honours, and no surprise either to find Harewood FTD Awards and Chase Web Offset 'Award of Merit' winner Charles Wardle as runner-up, despite a harmless spin at Orchard (36.33s), from David Gould (36.44s). There were records for Dick Foden in the Trakstar he shared with Phil Jefferies and Tony Bancroft's fierce Porsche, and another new sports-racing best in 37.73s for John Lambert. His Pilbeam was now even more formidable with a 3.6 Cosworth DFL V8

Dave Whitehead won the 1986 AWS Group British Leaders title in the Stiletto-BDA, which he shared with his wife Lynne (who won the newly instituted Ladies' Section).
BOB LIGHT

engine. There were smiles too for David Grace who bettered Paul Tankard's brutish TVR after a great battle for the Harewood Championship.

Ray Rowan's Harewood win left him four points behind Griffiths' 93-point Guyson USA Championship tally, with ADO third on 80, seven more points than Roy Lane could muster. Despite early misfortune and his bad Loton crash, Chris Cramer tied on points with Roy while David Gould moved up to sixth, ahead of Harvey, the impressive Wardle, Tim Thomson and Hunt. Charlie Wardle had a 14-point 'Award of Merit' lead over Brian Walker and the now Nottingham-based computer software salesman topped off his year by winning the HSA's 'Man of the Year' award.

There was triumph too for Birmingham Stiletto-BDH driver Dave Whitehead. This year he won the AWS Group British Leaders title, by three points from Bob Dayson, while Dave's wife Lynne won the newly instituted Ladies section. This would be the last campaign with the Stiletto, which had occasionally been beaten by rapid Edinburgh driver Harry Simpson (Maguire Stiletto), as they had bought Steve Allen's 1.6 Chevron B49. Third and sixth were the McBeath brothers Andy and Simon (*not* twins, in fact six year apart in age, despite a confusingly similar appearance) with the trim Woodville-Stretton 1.1 Delta-Imp T82/4. They too would be moving on in 1987, intending to fit a 1.6 BDA to the ex-Fry/Hunt/ADO Pilbeam MP54 which had been rebuilt after a late '85 shunt. Phil Jefferies and John Corbyn separated the McBeaths, while rounding out this particular Top Ten were Bancroft, Phil Ducker (1.6 Normandale/Minwall Design GRD-BDA HS85/1), Roger Gregory and another much travelled Scot: Edinburgh's Bill Wood (Leicester Building Society U2-BDA Mk18).

It had been a typically hard fought season, not least in the South of England. Sprint specialist Rodney Eyles (2.5 Ralt-Hart RT3/4) was the man to beat at Gurston but the Wiltshire hill's increasingly well-contested local championship was won by John Meredith in his ex-Cobb Skoda, defeating David Grace who did his chances no good at all by contriving to spin on both runs at the final round in October. Dr Richard Thompson, now U2 Mk21/24 mounted, set a 22.92s record on the oft-threatened Bodiam Hill, and won again at Sevenoaks & DMC's wet Silver Jubilee Meeting at the well-supported charity Valence School fixture. This occasion was graced for the 22nd time by one of Southern hill climbing's great characters: James Augustus Tiller with his highly developed and undoubtably hairy great 7.4 Allard J2. One driver who took a rest in 1986 was Richard Parsons. This left the Northern Ireland title to 'Turbo Sam' McGimpsey although Richard's old Chevron B34 was being put to good use in Scotland by George Ritchie, who finally defeated the Scottish U2s at Fintray in August.

Since most of the leading hill climbers contested meetings at Prescott, which had imposed noise restrictions in 1986, the universal application of maximum noise levels in 1987 caused fewer headaches than might otherwise have been experienced. Even the ear-splitting Brabham-Lysholm, which had won the John Bolster Trophy in 1986 in supercharged form, was back. The Squires/Kildsey team having attained the highest specific power output of any car on the hills, settled for a quieter (literally) life with a turbocharger on the little 784cc engine, and a lot fewer decibels.

Any serious attempt to rationalise the regulations for the production-based classes at the major meetings was still 'under discussion'. The curious situation remained where Special Saloons – RAC classes A and B – had far greater scope for modifications than had the Modified Sports Cars in classes C and D. For example, a racing Hart-engined Tiga or Chevron sports-racing car was a 'Saloon' as long as it had the silhouette of a rear-engined production saloon, such as a Skoda. On the other hand, clothe the same machine with a Lotus Esprit-shaped body, as was done in GT racing, and the result was excluded (some would say very properly) from the Modified Sports division! At least the Group B rally cars – banned by FISA from international rallying – had found a home. They were now eligible for classes C and D. Machines such as the Metro 6R4, Ford RS200 and even the Audi Quattro S1 seemed technically ideal for hill climbing, but they were still pretty expensive to buy and run and there was no great rush to enter them for hill climbs. In fact it was rally driver Geoff Fielding who was about the first to enter a 6R4, followed by Cyril Bolton and then Tom Hammonds with an ex-Mikkola S1 Quattro. The impact was not great.

One other controversial issue was involved when the RAC MSA ruled that cars competing in the production-based and Clubmans sports classes must run on pump petrol and not on methanol. Generally applauded, this had the unwelcome side effect of causing Nic Mann to retire his fabulous Morris Minor, at least temporarily.

There was good news on the championship sponsorship front with Guyson USA continuing their support for the premier RAC title, while a new sponsor, vehicle rental company Bratt, was to back the British Leaders' Championship. This was another case of an active competitor becoming a sponsor for Bratt's proprietor, Roger Lewis, competed enthusiastically in the 1100cc racing class with an ex-James Hunt Brabham BT21. Now in its seventh year, the Midland series would continue to enjoy

There are all too few meetings each year in Loton Park's attractive parkland. John Elliott's smart Porsche 911 is nearest the camera.
AUTHOR

Roy Lane's immaculate new contender for 1987 honours was the 3.9 Cosworth DFL-engined Steel King Pilbeam MP58.
BOB LIGHT

Shell Oils support, now as sole sponsor for the main title although the *Birmingham Post* newspaper – for long a conscientious reporter of hill climb affairs – would continue to sponsor the Top Ten Challenge.

If there was a trend to be identified in the annual reshuffle of cars among the top contenders it was in the return to more power. The most powerful 360-380 bhp 2.8 Hart four-cylinder engine had been developed to a pitch where it provided a most effective combination of power, torque, compactness and light weight but of course the big V8s of the nineteen-seventies were more powerful and had immense torque. A number of people were now looking at the possibilities of combining lots of V8 horses with the latest tailor-made Pilbeam or adapted Toleman chassis technology.

The basically fairly old Broadshot Pilbeam-Repco had shown the way and Chris Dowson and Charles Wardle were planning an even stronger offensive with a new, stiffer, honeycomb-reinforced monocoque and a four inches-shorter wheelbase to induce more predictable on-the-limit handling. Although Roy Lane had never been far from the honours with his Pilbeam-BMW cars, he had always seemed more at home with the 'big bangers' and he was now to field a stunning new Steel King Safety Footwear-sponsored contender; a brand new Pilbeam MP58 designed for a 3.9 Cosworth DFL V8, with 550 bhp on tap. Meanwhile, in deepest Walsall Wood, Ray Rowan had a 3.0-litre DFV-engined Toleman on the stocks for himself and a more conventional 2.8 Toleman-Hart in preparation for his mentor David Render. Since his own car was not expected to be finished for some time, Ray was expecting to start the season with David's ex-Bolsover Pilbeam MP43. Yet another Cosworth V8 was to be found in the back of sprinter Paul Edwards' ex-Lane 3.9 March-DFL 79S and this was to be entered in the Midland hill climbs for the formidable Dave Harris.

Among the Hart-powered contingent, there were no big changes for the reigning Champion Chase Web Offset team under Martin Middleton's charge or for Team Guyson, apart from rebuilding the damaged MP57, but unfortunately Alister Douglas-Osborn was standing down. John Hunt would compete alone with the AWS Group MP57. With Chris Cramer still convalescent, David Gould would

Alan Payne (right) shared his trusty Anson-Rover with Stow-on-the-Wold fine arts dealer, John Davies, in 1987. Note the regulation silencers.
BOB LIGHT

There was no holding Scottish Champion Kenny Allen (Vision V86H) in 1987.
BILL HENDERSON

Kenny Allen, five-times Scottish Champion (shared with Tim Thomson in 1988).
BILL HENDERSON

be sharing his masterpeice with young son Sean, who therefore faced a pretty daunting first season of hill climbing! Yealmpton, Plymouth, driver Steve Allen, having sold his Chevron to the Whiteheads, had bought Brian Walker's Pilbeam MP40 while John Meredith was returning to single-seaters, with John Trevaskis in the ex-Roy Lane MP53-BMW. Among the 1600s, Adrian Hopkins was the man to beat with the further developed Sark while Londoner Mike Lane was fitting a 1.6 BDA to the ex-Harris/Render MP50.

There was a growing demand for an additional capacity class division among the racing cars, at 2000cc, especially in the Midlands. This idea was shelved for the time being but was to be introduced as an experiment in the Midland Championship in 1988. Competitor support was growing too for the 1100cc and 500cc racing cars although the car likely to break the most records was the latest version of the Jefferies/Foden Trakstar. The little 250cc projectile had now gained a Rotax engine and aerofoils. Since the device was now painted red and bore a striking frontal resemblance to a scale model Formula 1 Ferrari T4, it was immediately dubbed the 'Rotari' by the whimsical.

Season opening wins in the South West at Oddicombe and Werrington Park for the inevitable Kevitt

Joe Ward's self-built Clubman's cars were invariably a major threat to the U2s in Northern events. This is the Ward WD8 at Harewood in 1987.
FRANK HALL

Payne's trusty Ensign showed that everything was normal, but then so was the Spring weather. For the second year running, Wiscombe Park was waterlogged and the RAC opener had to be cancelled. Once again the BARC(Y) stepped in and Harewod Finals Day was nominated as a substitute. A complete sense of *déja vu* was avoided only when April Prescott had to be cancelled as well! The Gloucester-shire hill's steeply sloping Paddock is probably the sport's most picturesque but when it is waterlogged it can be lethal. The possibility of runaways could not be risked.

Serious championship hill climbing did start over Easter. Kenny Allen, now armed with his 2.0 Vision immediately stamped his authority in Scotland, setting a 43.74s Strathclyde Park record, a mere 2.48s under Alex Graham's second BTD time! Harewood was both good and bad for Barrie Dutnall. He set BTD for the second successive year (38.87s), but then badly damaged his MP50 at Farmhouse. Naturally it rained for the Top Ten, so John Lambert had to be content with 39.87s, well clear of Joe Ward's very professional, self-built Ward WD8 Clubmans sports car and Chris Seaman's exuberantly-driven Brabham. The Guyson USA British Hill Climb Championship at last got under way the next day at a chilly Loton Park. Chase Web dealt a sharp blow to everyone else's morale by arriving with a real 'demon tweak' – tyre warmers. These electic blankets to pre-heat the tyres were accpeted Formual 1 technology and were now spreading to other classes of professional racing. Borth drivers of the vivid yellow Pilbeam were on fine form but the tyre warmers certainly helped to upset everyone else. Max Harvey was really performing well with 49.89s and it took a really vintage last run charge from Martyn Griffiths to top that in 49.34s. Ray Rowan had to be content with a worthy third in the sports MP43 (50.56s), ahead of David Gould and the 'heavy brigade': Lane, Harris and Wardle.

By the time everyone settled in at Prescott a fortnight later the Goulds, John Hunt and Dave Harris had all invested in tyre warmers, but their appearance was to be short-lived. They were expensive at £600 a set and the safety aspect of their proliferation in often damp, grass Paddocks was worrying. Fortunately, all concerned agreed to abandon them before less financially well-endowed drivers were forced to buy them to remain competitive. By the following season the major clubs were expressly for-bidding them in their regulations.

Peter Harper was Vision-mounted in 1987, but his reputation was made in this well-developed Mallock U2.
KEN MANN

Just as controversial was a change in the meeting's running order which meant that the production-based classes had to wait for the Top Twelve to complete their lengthy proceedings before they could take their second climbs. And it rained. Martyn Griffiths' soggy 46.54s climb was good enough to win the class but like most of the Top Twelve he was unlucky later on. Another ill-timed rain shower came after the two second drivers of the double-driven cars to qualify had run. Max Harvey recorded 41.27s for BTD, 0.89s up on David Gould, with Roy Lane up to third with his new mount. Griffiths was right out of the reckoning with a faulty electical switch, while no fewer than four sports car drivers – Rowan (fourth on 42.85s), Grace, Robinson and Peter Blankstone – made the Top Twelve.

Harewood had its first RAC round as early as 10 May and, sports car or not, Ray Rowan had to win. He had forgotten to bring back the trophy he had won the previous year! It wasn't a day for records – apart from Peter Harper's remarkable 38.74s Clubmans Vision V86H time – but the Guyson USA Championship run-off was the best for a while. Martyn Griffiths had led into the Top Twelve on 36.90s but his 36.59s best was just 0.04s too slow to match a mighty Ray Rowan. David Gould (36.84s) was 0.12s up on Roy Lane, who found Wardle and Harvey hard on his heels. Fifth was actually pretty low key at Harewood for Charlie Wardle but he and Chris Dowson had found the re-vamped Broadshot Pilbeam disappointingly unforgiving in its handling, with a disturbing tendency to snap out of line in fast left-hand corners. Since his Pilbeam was still not ready after its major rebuild, Jim Thomson was having fun with his latest road car, a new style Chevrolet Corvette which was patently not at home on narrow, sinuous hills!

Max Harvey's confidence had taken a quantum leap the previous season and he was now a very serious Championship contender. Barbon opened with new records to Bob Dayson's lightened Caterham 7 (25.41s) and Jefferies (25.69s), and a splendid 23.08s climb from Sean Gould which got him into the Top Twelve. This was highly promising for such an inexperienced driver and won him the HSA 'Man of the Meeting' award. Roy Lane had never won at Barbon and his 21.88s so nearly broke his duck. But not quite. Max Harvey flew up 0.02s faster for another win, with Griffiths tying with Lane, but 0.05s slower on aggregate. That was close, even by Barbon standards and while there was then a gap of 0.32s, another 0.21s covered Rowan, Hunt and Gould D.

Roy Lane's vast car preparation experience served him well in sorting his 550 bhp MP58 and the 'power course' at Gurston Down was the perfect hill for Roy's first win with the car. Recording 122 mph through Hollow, he tripped the timing gear in 28.63s, but that man Harvey was only marginally slower in 28.66s, and faster than Griffiths (28.83s) to increase his Guyson USA points lead. Ray Rowan ("reflexes like lightening, bottle enormous" according to journalist/driver Marcus Pye, writing in *Autosport*) became the first man to break 30s in a sports car (29.58s) but was out of the main Top Twelve battle. Only 0.09s down on Lane in class, Tim Thomson put in one of his best drives for some time to finish fourth on 29.05s, ahead of an impressive Chris Knapman (2.7 Ralt-QED/Hart RT4 HCS) and Dowson.

There was a welcome return to competition at this time for Allan Staniforth. This immensely knowledgeble journalist/author/chassis designer had had a bad accident the previous year at the New Brighton sprint, in the old Gould Terrapin, seriously injuring his legs. Everyone was delighted to see the not-so-young but just as gritty and irreverant Yorkshireman bounce back into action with an FF2000 Van Dieman RF85 fitted with the 140 bhp pushrod Ford engine from the wrecked Gould Terrapin.

June Shelsley was an unusually subdued affair and poor Max Harvey lost his hard-won championship lead. The Chase Web team withdrew from the meeting when Max learnt the dreadful news that a disastrous fire at his Plymouth printing works had cost the lives of several of his employees. A damp course and the regretted absence also of Alister Douglas-Osborn from the major contenders did nothing to lift the atmosphere. Shelsley favours horsepower so Roy Lane's 26.93s BTD – taking the Championship lead – was expected. Tim Thomson maintained new-found form (27.27s), to head Wardle, Gould D, Gould S (a splendid 27.73s) and Rowan. Ray was so busy working on other people's cars that he had no time to finish his Toleman-DFV. Richard Ames now had Ray's old Toleman-Hart so the Walsall engineer proceeded to buy the ex-Onyx/Pirro F3000 March 85B, basically for the DFV engine.

'Honestly, it's legal!' Dick Foden (centre) and Phil Jefferies (right) confer with Prescott Assistant-Clerk-of-the-Course, Dave Harries, beside the tiny, controversial and devastatingly effective Trakstar ZK86.
BOB LIGHT

There were more rain showers and an oil spillage at Fintray but not so many registered RAC MSA contenders. In fact, Peter Speakman's well-driven Historic class Brabham BT18 actually made the Top Twelve! In the prevailing conditions a 29.18s time from Phil Jefferies in the 'Rotari' (faster than Kenny Allen and Alex Graham) was little short of incredible. It provided Phil with another 'Man of the Meeting' award and was also 1.05s faster than former Imp driver Tony Tewson who broke the 1100cc racing record with his ex-Eryl Davies Shire Pilbeam. Max Harvey was still an understandable absentee but Martyn Griffiths and the Pilbeam were back. Martyn's 26.61s best was good, but not good enough to beat Lane's 26.54s, which gave Roy his hat trick of wins. Charles Wardle and Chris Dowson were not far behind for their best RAC result so far, although they had no luck the following week at Doune.

On this occasion, Roy Lane found his Pilbeam-DFL a big handful and dropped to sixth place on 42.04s. A subdued Max Harvey returned to the cockpit and his 40.81s climb placed him fifth but over a second off co-driver Griffiths' winning 39.67s. Closest to the smooth-driving Bewdley star were David Gould (39.96s), Tim Thomson (40.02s) and the remarkable Sean Gould (40.64s).

Martyn Griffiths was now at his most dangerously consistent and the 'short course' Prescott fell to him in 33.66s. For some time now there had been mutterings among the small-capacity racing car brigade about the eligibility of the Kart-like Trakstar. Nobody had anything but admiration for the skill and bravery of Phil Jefferies and Dick Foden but, in a situation reminiscent of the Martini controversy of 1962, the matter came to a head at Prescott and was referred to the RAC MSA for a ruling. The little red projectile, capable of three feet high 'wheelies' off the start line, was looking set to dominate both the Leaders' and the Midland Championships and was protested again, unsuccessfully, at the July Shelsley where Phil Jefferies set another (31.02s) record. Less controversially, Peter Harper brought his Vision down from Sheffield and further lowered the Clubmans record to 29.37s, while Griffiths showed what a good 2.8 Hart could do by beating Lane 26.72s to 27.08s.

Martin Middleton's car preparation contribution to the Chase Web team should not be underestimated, for the yellow Pilbeam was as consistently reliable as its drivers in 1987. Middleton Motor Services' address had a rather nostalgic ring to it for Hill Top Garage, Beoley, Redditch was actually on Gorcott Hill, one of hill climbing's pioneer courses.

By the time that the two Channel Islands rounds of the Guyson USA series had been held, Martyn Griffiths was beginning to look unstoppable. He won at Bouley Bay, although his 40.30s BTD was only a hairsbreath 0.01s less than the time of 1986 winner Max Harvey, with Lane and Gould D both under 41s. Ray Rowan was now trying the F3000 March 85B, and finding it a real handful down in eighth place. Roy Lane found his Pilbeam-DFL surprisingly wieldy on Guernsey to record 31.27s, 0.3s up on Tim Thomson's MP50-Hart, whereas Tim, Harvey, Hunt and David Gould were all covered by 0.22s. But what of Martyn Griffiths? Driving with all his usual precision and tightly controlled aggression, Martyn flew up Le Val des Terres in 30.94s, for a new outright hill record.

With Craigantlet being held later that year, there was time to note that despite growing single-seater opposition from George Ritchie's Chevron, former GT circuit racer Ron Cumming (2.0 Ralt RT2) and former Mallock U2 pilot Bill Wood (2.0 March 782), Kenny Allen was clearly heading for his third successive Grampian Television Scottish title, his 2.0 Vision V86H being just too rapid in his capable hands for the other Scottish regulars.

Both Sean Gould and Phil Jefferies had accidents in practice for August Shelsley, but although the Gould non-started the controversial Trakstar was repaired, won its class, and this time secured *two* 'Man of the Meeting' awards (both HSA and Midland) for its intrepid 'jockey' Jefferies. A stronger challenge was anticipated from John Hunt who had now replaced his 2.7 Hart engine with an 2.8, complete with full engine management system. Hunt was fourth in class but an Esses spin and then failed electrics put him out of the points. A Griffiths versus Lane confrontation was always on the cards and so it transpired with Roy's gleaming silver car blasting out of the Esses to cross the finishing line at 132 mph, just 26.14s after leaving the start. This was only six hundredths of a second off Alister Douglas-Osborn's elusive August 1983 record in the Pilbeam MP47. Griffiths (26.49s) and Harvey (27.04s) had to be content with the minor places from Wardle, Tim Thomson, Dowson and Rowan's wilful March.

Roy Lane's efforts seemed to have found new impetus with all those Cosworth horses, and his Midland win at Loton Park was by the proverbial country mile from Chris Knapman, while 'Pop'

Render was feeling his way in his new, Rowan-built 2.8 Toleman-Hart. A midsummer lull from major title pressures emphasised the strength in depth of British hill climbing. Growing support for modern 500cc racing cars now encouraged Jedi-Honda V4 contender David Tearle to put his Phoenix Foods company backing behind an experimental hill climb and sprint championship for the 500s, to be run in 1988. In the meantime, there was a massive entry for Gurston Down's 100th meeting on 30 August, when the hill's first ever, August 1967 winner Patsy Burt graced the occasion to demonstrate the lovely blue McLaren-Oldsmobile which she still owns. Although John Meredith's Pilbeam-BMW had given Rodney Eyles' Ralt a hard time at Gurston and Wiscombe of late, the Truro *garagiste* was now hobbled by a tired engine and Eyles' Ralt won the day in 30.37s from the elderly 2.0 U2-Hart Mk15 of Richard Jones.

Over in Ulster, Craigantlet had not drawn quite such a good entry as of late with no Chase Web, Gould or AWS Group teams present. Slight alterations to start and finish still left the fast Irish hill at 1,833 yards and this looked a good bet for Roy Lane. True, he edged out Tim Thomson by 0.36s, but his 50.34s time was 0.21s short of Ray Rowan's 50.13s BTD. Despairing of the March, Ray was in the Render Toleman and with this more competitive hill climb car he straightway set a BTD. Fastest of the local drivers was journalist Ricky Young who was a splendid sixth in the old Coogar, now 3.9 Rover V8 powered. His 52.41s netted him 'Man of the Meeting' honours, but although on this occasion Jackie Harris (2.0 Ralt-BDA RT1) was almost a second slower, it was Jackie who clinched the Northern Ireland Championship.

Rain and a rather dicey, muddy, Paddock did little to make September Prescott particularly festive, despite added interest lent to the day when rally star David Llewellyn demonstrated an Audi Quattro and Chris Cramer made a most welcome competitive return in the rebuilt March. The poor weather was really bad news for Roy Lane who was even less able than might normally be the case to unleash the full potential of his Pilbeam-DFL on this twisty course, and lost his RAC title lead as a result. Before the rain intruded David Render clocked a splendid 41.93s in his Pilbeam to snatch a totally un-

The growing popularity of new 500cc racing cars did nothing to reduce the appeal of the old '500s'. Barry Brant's Cooper Mk11 rounds Shelsley's Kennel bend.
BOB LIGHT

expected but immensely popular BTD. When conditions were bad for the Top Twelve, Martyn Griffiths seized the opportunity to take the Guyson USA series lead in 45.99s. Max Harvey was again his nearest rival (46.32s) but Charles Wardle (46.54s) and Dave Harris in John Hunt's MP57 (46.65s once engine management system maladies had been cured) showed well to force the hapless Lane down to fifth.

Roy did have something to celebrate, though, as he was a clear winner from Griffiths and Wardle in the *Birmingham Post* Top Ten Challenge. As usual, the meeting incorporated the final round of the Midland series and Shell Oils Midland honours might have fallen to Peter Garland (3.9 Morgan Plus 8) except that Phil Jefferies proceeded to win everything in sight with the Trakstar to secure the Championship by three points from Peter who was forced to miss a couple of rounds because of business commitments. Regular class wins by Mike Kerr, Adrian Hopkins and Les Trafford's radical super-charged Scimparts Reliant Scimitar-Rover V8 gained them the next three places. When the yellow Scimitar first appeared in 1985 in the hands of Scimitar expert Don Pither and Trafford it had been terrifyingly wayward, but effective development had made this spectacular car, built to just about the limit of the Modified Sports regulations, a consistent winner in the Tewkesbury driver's hands, until it was written-off in a Curborough sprint accident.

Neatness and precision were essential a week later at Wiscombe when overnight rain made the always tricky West Country course particularly slippery. Spinners included Dick Foden, who bent the Trakstar at the Esses, leaving the class, for once, to the gallant John Bolster Trophy-winning Karl Schollar (Spectre-KTM). With the light fading, and in conditions which well-suited his economical style, Martyn Griffiths virtually secured his second successive RAC MSA title with a 39.94s climb. The results almost mirrored Prescott for Harvey (40.51s) and Wardle filled the minor places, although this week Lane languished in seventh place. The meeting was oversubscribed to the point where even David Gould and Jim Thomson failed to secure entries.

Doune was a bit of a disappointment, for Roy Lane decided not to go to this, his 'bogey' hill, thereby ceding the title to Griffiths although he had only the slimmest chance of taking it anyway. For once, Martyn was uncharacteristically untidy on both championship ascents, dropping him to seventh behind the amazing Kenny Allen and Chris Knapman. But Max Harvey rose to the occasion for the Chase Web team to snatch victory by a tenuous 0.03s from David Gould – so close to his first RAC MSA win – and with Sean Gould separating his father from Tim Thomson. Phil Jefferies' hopes of landing the Bratt British Leaders' Championship ended when the Trakstar suffered engine problems, leaving the series to Mike Kerr's Mobil 1-sponsored Skoda-Rover V8 which had not had to face Nic Mann's projectile that season.

For the second successive year, BARC Yorkshire Centre finished the RAC Championship series on a high note, with Harewood's 25th Anniversary being celebrated in fine style. Current Centre Chairman Jim Johnstone was regularly recalling an earlier era on the hill with forays in his spectacu-larly-driven Brabham-Rover/Buick BT18 but on this occasion he was joined by Peter Voigt, now enjoying himself with the TechCraft-Buick once campaigned by Roy Lane. Guyson USA British Champion for the second successive year, Martyn Griffiths notched up a 36.81s BTD in his class but took it easy in the Top Twelve so as not to impede Max Harvey in his efforts to wrest second place in the Championship from Roy Lane. However, Harewood is Ray Rowan territory and, driving the Render Toleman TG87, Ray's 36.84s climb just prevented immensley talented Sean Gould (36.90s) from taking a first RAC win in his debut season. Gould D and Wardle tied, only 0.12s adrift, with David winning on aggregate; and although Max Harvey's 37.30s time put him fifth to Roy Lane's 37.33s seventh place it was not enough to prevent Roy becoming runner-up in the championship. In the final analysis, Griffiths was five points up on Roy and Max, tied on 90 points, and although Max had enjoyed his best-ever season it was terribly sad that it had been marred by the Plymouth factory fire that had blighted his mid-season efforts. Although his 74 points total was 16 points less than those of Lane and Harvey, David Gould's fourth place emphasised his growing stature as a driver, adding to his pre-eminence as a car designer/builder. Tim Thomson and Charles Wardle took the next two places after slightly disappointing seasons although Charles won the Harewood FTD Awards title again. A haphazard season competing in three very different cars masked Ray Rowan's undoubted brilliance and left him seventh ahead of Dowson, Hunt and Sean Gould.

The British 'Award of Merit' scoring system actually left the precocious talent of 20-year-old Sean

Gould in fourth place for that award, behind Chris Knapman – just outside the Top Ten in the Guyson USA table – David Grace and Adrian Hopkins. Although Mike Kerr could not be beaten for the Bratt Leaders' Championship, even before Harewood, the final scoreboard actually featured four drivers with 72 points. The other three were Bob Dayson in the Cougar Developments Caterham 7, the unlucky Phil Jefferies and former Imp driver Tony Tewson in the ex-Davies Shire Pilbeam-BDJ. Consistently successful seasons in their respective classes left positions 5 to 10 to Barry Goode (U2-BDA Mk21/24), Richard Homer (ex-Barter Delta-Imp), Harry Simpson (Maguire Stiletto), Ian Fidoe's Imp clone of similar provenance, the more authentic Special Saloon VW Scirocco of Meriden's Roger Jones and yet another spaceframe Imp, that of Andrew Parffrey, which he shared with John Tuckett-Good. Lynne Whitehead again lifted the Ladies' Award while Loughborough's Tim Barrington, who shared Bob Dayson's Caterham 7 with fast-growing distinction, won the Newcomers' prize.

Harewood's own Championship, the premier North of England competition, emphasised the popularity of the local Formula Ford 1600 racing class – and perhaps a slightly less demanding class bogey time – with the little single-seaters providing the mounts for four out of the top five drivers in the Championship: Redditch visitor Tim Mason (Merlyn Mk20A), Jon Collinge (Pacer FF80), Roger

Bratt British Leaders Champion, Mike Kerr (Skoda-Rover V8).
BOB LIGHT

'Reflexes like lightning, bottle enormous'. Ray Rowan made Harewood his own in 1987 in the Toleman TG280H.
FRANK HALL

A class for Formula Ford 1600 cars was a highly successful Harewood innovation. Former circuit racer Alan Stringer (Crosslé 30F) was an early front runner.
FRANK HALL

Although actually six years apart in age, Andy and Simon (in the Pilbeam) McBeath were often mistaken for twins.
BOB LIGHT

Kilty (Sparton 81FF) and David Park (Van Diemen RF79). The only interloper, in fourth place, was the irrepressible Brian Kenyon. Further South, the Gurston Championship now occupied a similar position and fell to John Corbyn's Jedi-Yamaha from Richard Thompson's Mallock U2 Mk21/24, while Rodney Eyles won the Top Six Challenge from John Meredith. More Southern honours, this time a second successive South West ASWMC hill climb title, went to Parks of Exeter Porsche driver Jonathan Williamson whose increasingly potent Carrera was enabling him to become a major force in his class further afield.

A New Champion

Any radical changes which might have been mooted for hill climbing in 1988 amounted to very little in reality. If anything, the revised – 113 dBA at two-thirds maximum revs – noise regulations were slightly easier to meet, the supercharging/turbocharging equivalency formula would stay at 1.4 rather than going out to 1.7-litres, the production-based classes stayed the same in RAC Championship events, and a new 2.0 racing car class would be instituted only in the Midlands. Most of the major clubs explicitly banned the use of tyre warmers.

Of course there is always someone or some group of competitors with a grievance and there was a significant point of view which expressed growing concern about the validity of the British Leaders'Midland scoring systems which allowed a strong car/driver combination in a weak class to score more easily than a perhaps better car/driver combination in a more hotly contested class. Conversely, a brilliant driver in a numerically weak category would score fewer points than a more average driver with a good car in a numerically strong class! BARC devotees, in particular, extolled the vitues of the Mike Wilson-devised system of scoring points against class bogey times based on class records, even if a certain amount of mathematical dexterity was needed to keep everyone appraised of the up-to-date positions. Ironically, Mike Kerr, who won the Bratt British Leaders' title with his superbly prepared Mobil 1 Skoda had raised some controversy by winning the old BARC competition in his Chevette HSR, although that was because the 2.6-litre HSR specification was considered by some to be outside the spirit of the BARC's Touring Car regulations. Naturally, nobody said so until Mike started winning with the car! In fact, Mike was a sporting and skilful competitor who, like Jeff Goodliff in an earlier era, was better than most at deciding what was the car best suited to win titles given the existing regulations.

On the championship front, the thriving 500 Owners Association's 'modern' competitors could look forward to the newly instigated Phoenix Foods hill climb and sprint series while a late decision ensured that the British Leaders' Championship would again have a commercial sponsor. Paul Edwards' Edwards Catering Company was to take Bratt's place, while also sponsoring the equivalent

What a way to spend an anniversary! Tim Thomson shelters from the rain behind the Shelsley startline.
BOB LIGHT

sprint series and the intrepid efforts of the Trakstar duo, Phil Jefferies and Dick Foden. The Midland Championship also enjoyed a new backing from Pound Garden Buildings. Jim Thomson's Guyson company was celebrating its 50th Anniversary and the Otley-based industrial refinishing equipment manufacturer's American offshoot would again support the premier RAC title chase. The sport's longest continuously sponsored Championship, the Grampian Television-backed Scottish series, meanwhile, was entering its twelfth year.

Oversubscribed entry lists and not enough courses remained the sport's biggest problem, although this paled into insignificance compared to the difficulties over in Eire where rally-inspired public indemnity insurance problems on closed public roads had put a stop to Eirean hill climbs altogether for a time, although hopes were high for a resumption of events at the Cruagh, Knockalla, Bally Albin and Corkscrew hills at the very least. The popular Cricket St Thomas, Somerset, course, now in its tenth year of operation, could look forward to an extra 150 yards on its length, although not until 1989. Most exciting for hill climb-starved South East competitors was the annoucement of a brand new venue at Rotherfield Park, Alton, Hampshire, the home of the Lord Lieutenant of the County, Sir James Scott. To be promoted by the Farnborough DMC, the initial climb would be for saloon and sports cars only, in September, on this attractive 661-yards-long parkland course which incorporated even a modest viaduct in its length. Unfortunately, this excellent news was offset by the reluctant decision to cancel the 1988 event at Valence School. Although competition was due to be resumed in 1989, clearance work after the November 1987 hurricane damage could not be completed in time for what would have been the twenty-sixth annual running of this popular fixture.

As ever, the Winter months were enlivened by announcements about new cars, or rumours about new cars, but the most dramatic change among the ranks of the leading contenders was not unveiled until the March test day at Wiscombe Park. If the Chase Web team had left well alone a third succes-sive Guyson USA title could still have been a distinct possibility, but hill climbers tend to be restless innovators and the Chase Web Offset St Ives Group MP53/04 arrived at Wiscombe with a Brian Hart-developed, 450 bhp, Holset-turbocharged version of the 2.8 Hart engine. Sceptical queries regarding intractability and turbo lag were brushed aside by Martyn and Max who insisted that the new set-up provided a wide power band and excellent response. Problems with the Zytek engine management system afflicted the team at Wiscombe, but an intriguing new solution to the age-old power/weight/agility problem was set to enliven the scene.

After a long and frustrating effort to cure the Broadshot Pilbeam of its puzzlingly unpredictable behaviour, Charles Wardle and Chris Dowson had isolated a faulty rear shock absorber. Surely it couldn't be as simple as that? Only time would tell. Unfortunately, it looked as though John Hunt would be spending less time on the hills as he was intending to join the SuperSports Historic ranks on the circuits with a Lola. Although the Goulds would be out again and Ray Rowan was working on yet another Toleman-based chassis, the Pilbeam challenge would be as strong as ever with a pair of new MP58s on the stocks. Roy Lane's proven Steel King chassis would be joined on some hills at least by another Cosworth V8-engined car for Ken Ayres while Lincoln driver Rob Welch was transferring his Battle, Hayward & Bower sponsorship, plus further backing from TNT Tristar to a 2.0 Hart-engined MP58H, tailor-made for the new Midland class.

Rob's successful Vision was bought by Barry Goode while the sports and saloon classes certainly enjoyed their fare share of exciting new developments. Wiscombe Park directors Richard Brown and Roger Willoughby (who had sold his March to Birmingham printer and former circuit racer Jeremy Bouckley) were to share the ex-Cordy/Panter Martin-Rover BM24. Jim Robinson and David Grace now had a 2.5 Hart for their U2 Mk27 and Bob Dayson and Tim Barrington (now very evenly matched) had moved up a class by fitting the trusty Caterham 7 with a QED 1.8 engine. With Mike Kerr planning a new, Tiga-based saloon, Rob Grant would be driving the formidable Skoda but in Southern events at least a serious challenge was expected from John Meredith who had the ex-Mike Hanson Skoda Kevlar-bodied and to be fitted with the 2.7 BMW out of his Pilbeam, the whole ensemble to be emblazoned with 'The Old Man of the Hills' across the tail. Best of all, Nic Mann was expected to bring out the glorious Oselli/Aldon Morris Minor V8.

Easter fell at the beginning of April and the traditional Strathclyde Park Scottish opener saw the beginning of a new challenge to Kenny Allen's supremacy. Jim and Tim Thomson had always enjoyed their forays among the hospitable Scots and after a certain amount of post-event badinage found themselves committed to doing the Grampian Television series for a change. But wee Kenny was not going to make it easy for Team Guyson for, 2.8 Pilbeam-Hart MP50 or not, Tim Thomson was well down on Allen's record-breaking 42.51s climb. Since 1988 was Guyson's 50th Anniversary, the team's cars were now tuned out in an opulent, predominantly gold livery.

The opening Guyson USA British Championship salvos were as eagerly awaited as ever, but when the circus gathered at Loton Park for Easter Monday's first round there were notable absentees. The Goulds had not been able to ready their car in time and poor Maggie Blankstone was nursing an injured leg after a nasty testing incident at Curborough when a clutch plate exploded on the Worfield Garage U2. That left a surprise sports-racing win to Richard Jones' distinctly elderly U2 as the Robinson/Grace 2.5 U2 wasn't yet sorted either. The new 2.0 racing class was clearly going to be hard fought and Rob Welch, the favourite, had to accept second place to Chris Drewett's ex-Bill Wood March 782, although the time was over 1.5s slower than Adrian Hopkins' superb 1.6 Sark 111H in the Top Twelve. Adrian's continuous development of this car had included consultation with its original designer, Patrick Head. Grip was at a premium on a slippery course and there was vindication for both the Broadshot and Chase Web teams. A beaming Charles Wardle found that the big Pilbeam-Repco had been transformed with a full complement of functional shock absorbers and he scored his first RAC win in 51.20s, just 0.05s faster than Martyn Griffiths' outstandingly tractable turbocar. Not to be outdone, Chris Dowson was only one hundredth of a second slower to be 0.75s clear of Roy Lane who had Hunt and Harvey snapping at his heels.

There were no cancellations due to bad weather this year, and the Spring saw intensive activity. April Prescott was close, just 0.08s separating the top three with John Hunt (40.35s) taking a pleasing first-ever run-off win – ironic now that his sporting horizons were now extending beyond hill climbing – from Griffiths and Tim Thomson. A week later, at the popular Cricket St Thomas course, rally driver John Price showed what a Metro 6R4 could do on the hills by trimming Colin Pook's hill record of 36.60s by 0.08s, leaving Colin's potent Clubmans U2 Mk21/25 trailing by 0.38s.

Umbrellas are rarely far away at Wiscombe in April but this time the Aston Martin OC ran their two-day fixture with only heavy overnight rain to hinder things. Saturday's club meeting gave Yealmpton, Plymouth, driver Steve Allen a fairly easy 42.00s win in his Dragon Kitchens 2.8 Pilbeam-Hart MP40 over Barry Groombridge's turquoise Modus M4 and Rob Welch, but Sunday's Guyson USA round produced the biggest shock in years. Steve Allen had never finished higher than seventh before in an RAC title run-off. Achieving staggering speed through the Gate, he clocked 37.78s on his first Top Twelve climb – faster even than Griffiths' 37.89s. The Broadshot lads were already out of contention with a cracked rear suspension cross member, while Max Harvey had crossed the finish line with a snapped throttle cable. Tension mounted for the final attempts. Allen went

Even by July 1988, Ray Rowan's fourth variation on a Rowan Toleman theme – the Roman IVH – still looked very stark. One year later, fitted with more conven-tional bodywork, and co-driver Rob Turnbull's 2.8 Hart engine, the car was propelling Ray to a richly-deserved Guyson RAC Championship.
BOB LIGHT

straight on at Wis, the first corner. Griffiths had the wretched throttle linkage break again, and it was all over with Steve Allen an ecstatic winner from Griffiths, Roy Lane (38.34s), Ray Rowan (38.52s), Harvey and Hunt. Ray was driving his fourth variation on a Rowan Toleman theme with a startling lack of bodywork. This rather less than elegant machine was thus dubbed the Roman IVH. The new-found effectiveness of the Martin BM24 was emphasised when Richard Brown recorded the fastest sports car time (40.96s) but there was disappointment when a fuel fire postponed the début of a new 2.0 racing class contender: Andy and Simon McBeath's 2.0 Hart-powered, ex-Hunt Pilbeam MP54.

After Steve Allen's hour of glory at Wiscombe, he found himself back down in eighth place when the Guyson USA series moved to Prescott a week later, but he was still ahead of Charles Wardle who survived a hair-raising trip over the grass after Orchard. Roy Lane is not Chief Instructor at the Prescott Hill Climb Drivers School (now sponsored by Hammonds Furniture of Hinckley) for nothing and his 39.80s class BTDs on a course where his horsepower advantage was less significant than good handling and driver techniques augured well for his title porspects. Roy was slightly slower in the Top Twelve (39.92s) but it was just enough to head off Griffiths (40.98s), Rowan (using only a 2.5 Hart engine), Hunt, Dowson and Thomson. Richard Brown again beat the U2s for best sports car time (42.90s) while one of the day's highlights was a 41.40s climb from Adrian Hopkins which beat Ray Rowan's four-year-old 1600cc racing car record.

Being a once-a-year venue, and given a dry day, Barbon usually produces a clutch of new records and this time Peter Harper, Phil Jefferies, Tony Tewson and Adrian Hopkins (on his first visit) set new figures. After his winning start at Loton, Charles Wardle had suffered some setbacks but now he gunned the rich-sounding green and white Pilbeam-Repco out of the Hairpin to cross the line in 21.74s to rob Roy Lane (21.76s) yet again of that elusive first Barbon win. Griffiths (22.08s) had the edge over Hunt for third place points despite copious quantities of tank tape adorning the Pilbeam after a spectacular but remarkably damage free excursion into the tyre barriers at the second left hander.

For many, though, Barbon was not *the* event of the weekend. Prescott's Classic Car meeting

marked the BOC's 50th Anniversary at the Gloucestershire hill and sunshine showed off to best effect a cavalcade of no fewer than 60 Bugattis including the now horribly valuable ex-Bachelier T54. Quite apart from the Molsheim thoroughbreds an outstanding turnout evoked many memories. ERAs abounded and eternally youthful and spirited Rivers-Fletcher enjoyed a fling in R4D, now successfully campaigned by Anthony Mayman, while Bill Morris clocked the fastest time in a pre-war car, R12B, in 51.80s. Tony Marsh was there in the Marsh Special which he had now bought back off Graham Galliers. The old master recorded 47.20s, 0.5s faster than his 1967 BTD time. All his old enthusiasm was rekindled and he was threatening a new twin turbo-boosted March-based car for 1989! Despite his far from diminutive stature, Russ Ward had developed quite a penchant for small racing cars – he had recently acquired the famous Voigt/Homer *et al* Ginetta G17 – and he now turned in a BTD winning performance in a Twin-Cam Lotus/Ford-engined Brabham BT10, shared with circuit racer John Harper.

After this delightful meeting what should have been Gurston's highlight of the year was marred by heavy rain showers, many delays and a late 7.30 pm finish. There were more disappointments when John Meredith failed to appear with his latest Skoda after a major fire in testing at Pembrey, and then the turbocharger seized up on the Chase Web Pilbeam in practice. At that point a despondent Max Harvey was all for converting the engine back to normally aspired form, although the team decided to press on with the turbo. But at least the 2.5 'Black Adder' U2 was on-form at last, to beat Richard Brown in David Grace's hands. Despite an untidy line at Karousel, Roy Lane (33.04s) used Griffiths' misfortune to the full to open out a 9 point Championship lead, while the impressive Hunt was only 0.06s adrift. The tall, prematurely grey-haired, figure of Rob Turnbull made a welcome return to competition motoring to score a resounding sixth place in the Roman.

Charles Wardle had been a close third at Gurston but, despite a spin in the Esses on his final effort, he was back on top at Shelsley, shading Griffiths (26.86s) and Lane (26.98s) with a tuneful 26.82s climb. Tim Thomson's Scottish campaign had already landed him one 41.88s BTD at Doune and the

Sean and David Gould.
BOB LIGHT

habitually 'laid back' young Yorkshireman did it again with a 41.13s and the incredible Kenny Allen fired the Vision sports car over the line in 40.84s. Only Charles Wardle (40.64s) saved English honour. Of the other major contenders, Griffiths was fourth after (for him) an off day, stalling on the line and then being unsettled by a photographer at the start. Rowan could only manage fifth while Lane was a miserable eleventh on his far from favourite course.

Happily, Roy was back on form for the second, Fintray, leg of the Scottish double, his 26.26s best defeating Griffiths (26.40s), Wardle and Rowan but it wasn't enough for maximum points in this year of surprises. The 1988 trend towards unexpected results continued with the re-emergence of the 2.8 Gould-Hart 84/E. And what a return! Sean Gould, the 'baby' of the Championship circus, put in a superb 26.13s climb to win his first Championship victory, just 0.14s outside Martin Bolsover's six-year-old record.

Although neither Martyn Griffiths nor Max Harvey had yet won with the Pilbeam Turbocar and Max in particular had become rather disconsolate at one point, there was clearly little amiss fundamentally with the concept and suddenly the results began to flow. The car's excellent tractability was confirmed at a wet July Shelsley when Martyn and Max scored a 1-2 result from Wardle, Lane and Gould S. The Chase Web Offset Pilbeam had new sidepods when it arrived at Harewood for the hill's only Guyson USA round of the year. Here the stark Roman, although still suffering the handicap of a rather tired 2.5 Hart engine, was sure to present major opposition in Ray Rowan's hands. Ray's 36.38s time had the better of Sean Gould, Wardle, David Gould and Lane but Martyn had the final say – 35.86s and ten points.

Competition was clearly mounting and while mainland visitors to the Channel Isles could not help but be intrigued by such exotic local concoctions as Rob Romeril's Jaguar V12-engined F5000 Chevron and Ken Thomson's Wedge-Rover sandracer the main focus of attention was on the Guyson USA battle. Still using the 'small' engine, Rowan beat everybody in class at Bouley Bay with 40.62s, but an ill-timed shower of rain spoilt the Top Twelve. Max Harvey got in a superb 40.23s climb before the drizzle started which was 0.28s faster than the ever-present Wardle, 0.46s up on Lane and 0.62s clear of Griffiths. Rowan was confronted by the rain and, brave as ever, put in a breathtaking on-the-limit climb in 41.45s for a poorly rewarded sixth place. Max Harvey had won his second Bouley Bay in three years, but it was his turn to be caught by rain at Le Val des Terres, effectively excluding him from the Top Twelve. This time it was Martyn's day and a class BTD in 35.71s and a Top Twelve 37.49s ensured the continued run of success for the remarkably flexible turbocar. But with Rowan, Lane and Wardle next in line there was no respite in the title battle.

Martyn Griffiths suddenly looked as though he might be heading for a third successive title on this form and his case was strengthened when he smashed the Craigantlet hill record in 49.65s, leaving an 0.8s margin over Charles Wardle, while any potential challenge from the Goulds ended when Sean walloped a bank. But just when a decisive advantage apeared to be opening up for Griffiths, he had a poor day at Shelsley. missing a gear on his first RAC climb (27.21s) and being hobbled by yet more drizzle on the final ascent. On the other hand, something of a mid-season hiatus for Charles Wardle ended when he powered the Broadshot Pilbeam through the Crossing at 119 mph and maintained the momentum to set BTD at 26.24s – just 0.16s short of ADO's elusive hill record – to see off Lane (26.69s), co-driver Dowson (also27.21s), Griffiths and Harvey. Despite a shaky start to the season, Jim Robinson and David Grace were now getting results with the Allan Staniforth-fettled 2.5 'Black Adder' U2, 'Amazing' setting a fastest ever front-engined time of 27.67s

Before Prescott's September centrepiece meeting, the Pound Garden Buildings Midland title was actually clinched at Loton Park in favour of Adrian Hopkins, who secured third BTD in 52.39s with his beautifully prepared and driven '1600', very little slower than wily Roy Lane (52.01s) and Steve Allen (52.06s). Exactly two years after Chris Cramer's serious accident, son Marc was fortunate to escape unscathed when his March 782 left the road on Cedar Straight at around 100 mph mark.

Prescott was full of drama and ended with Martyn Griffiths and Charles Wardle tying on 92 Guyson USA points. A practice accident put out the McBeath Pilbeam for the rest of the season; Dick Foden still managed to clinch the Prescott Gold Cup despite suffering an outbreak of snapping Trakstar drivechains and nursing a (unconnected) broken toe; the Chase Web team worked up a lather changing two broken driveshafts during the day, and Sean Gould took to the arboretum in the Esses! Despite his dramas, Martyn Griffiths' 39.26s best was just too quick for Wardle (39.48s), Rowan (39.57s) and Lane (39.85s).

Whatever the outcome of the premier championship, the *Birmingham Post* Top Ten Challenge was Martyn's, for the fourth time, by 5 points from Lane. Forty-year-old Adrian Hopkins, capitalising on years of steady development on the Sark, and indeed on his own considerable driving skill, had a 4 point winning advantage in the Pound Garden Buildings Midland Championship over Tony Tewson. Barry Oddy (old-style 500 Cooper Special) was third from Bob Dayson, Michael Steele (roadgoing Lotus 7 S2) and Deryk Young's smart ice blue Icerite Shop Equipment U2 Mk24.

Griffiths and Wardle may have been tying on points but when dropped scores came into play, Charles could clinch the title at Wiscombe. The West Country hill produced a day of fast changing fortunes. Fêted at Prescott the week before, Adrian Hopkins shot off the road at Bunny's Leap and rolled into the woods, being lucky not to suffer serious injury or at least write-off the Sark, in a very nasty mishap. After a marvellous run of success, the Chase Web Offset Pilbeam had an engine management gremlin strike at the worst possible time, consigning Martyn and Max to an equal fourth best RAC time of 37.01s. During the class runs Ray Rowan really flew to set a new 35.70s hill record but then a timekeeping failure and an 'off' at Sawbench spoiled his Top Twelve runs. But there was nothing upsetting the Broadshot team. A 36.07s climb gave Charles Wardle maximum points and the Guyson USA British Championship, while 36.29s was all it took Chris Dowson to secure second place. Roy Lane was also faster than the Chase Web teamsters. Thirty-eight-year-old Charles Wardle was thus the first 'new' RAC Champion since Martin Bolsover in 1982, and had ended a nine-year run of Hart-powered Champions with that same torquey Repco V8 which had propelled Mike MacDowel

to successive RAC titles in 1973/74, in a chassis which was an update of a 1980 Pilbeam MP47.

All season-long championships were coming to their conclusions now. Five wins out of seven gave Jackie Harris (Ralt-BDG RT1) the Ulster title from Ian Johnston's Chevette HSR while the Scottish series had its final round at Durris, a week before the RAC finale at Doune. Tim Thomson broke the hill record in 39.17s but tied for the title – the first-ever shared Grampian Television Scottish Championship – with Kenny Allen, well clear of George Ritchie, Jim Thomson/Alex Graham (another tie) and road car winner Mike Connon (1.6 Westfield SE kit car). A sporting series ended on a typically lighthearted note when Tim and Kenny collected their prizes at Doune in three-legged mode!

Fourth place and a fortunately harmless excursion at often-damaging East Brae was rather anti-climactic for Wardle at Doune, his 40.98s time proving slower than Rowan and Giffiths – and David Gould. A patchy season for the Goulds ended with David's long awaited first RAC MSA win in 40.27s, to even the score with son Sean. Wardle's final advantage over Griffiths in the Guyson USA British Championship was three points after a year which served to emphasise Martyn's incredible consistency. This was his fourteenth successive first or second, every year since 1976! Martyn's re-markably neat, precise style and ability to go *just* fast enough to win yet not overdrive had brought him a record 50 RAC event wins since Loton Park in 1977, to the 40 of Tony Marsh, 37 of Roy Lane and 35 of Alister Douglas-Osborn.

Roy Lane could perhaps be forgiven for being a little disappointed with his Championship third place, on 87 points, as early season form suggested that his third RAC title might be within reach. Without quite matching Martyn's phenomenal consistency, Roy's Championship record was pretty remarkable as he had never been lower than seventh in 21 years! Ray Rowan, possibly the quickest driver of all among his contemporaries, was fourth ahead of Chris Dowson and Max Harvey. If he had completed a full season, John Hunt would certainly have been higher than seventh while Tim Thomson, and the Goulds S and D respectively, completed the Top Ten. Steve Allen never quite

Charles Wardle was an immensely popular 1988 Guyson RAC Champion, using the ex-Mike MacDowel Repco V8 in Chris Dowson's revised, ex-Alister Douglas-Osborn Pilbeam MP47RB chassis, to beat the more modern Pilbeam variants.

found his early season Wiscombe form again but at least he won the 'Award of Merit' pot, by just two points from the redoubtable Adrian Hopkins.

This year there was a three-way tie on points for the Edwards Catering British Leaders' Championship and it was definately a case of 'new wine in old bottles'! Brechin General Practitioner Simon Frost, winner of the 1987 Scottish road car honours, travelled widely and successfully with Ken Snailham's famous 'Silver Bullet' QED Lotus 7 to win the title from Tony Tewson (ex-Davies Pilbeam-BDJ SP1), Barry Goode (ex-Welch Vision V85) and, two points adrift, John Whyte (ex-Whitehead Stiletto-BDH)). Tewson's partner Shirley Knox snatched the Ladies award by two points from Lynne Whitehead, denying Lynne her hat trick.

As the Championship contenders were winding down at Doune, the curtain was rising at the promising new Rotherfield Park course with the Peugeot Lion Hill Climb. The honour of lifting the first BTD fell to Colin Pook in 22.20s, and a week later the Clubmans U2 Mk21/25 driver reclaimed his lost Cricket St Thomas record in 35.12s.

Poor weather and no Guyson USA round made Harewood's Championship Finals Day less notable than of late, but not for Sean Gould who scored another BTD, perhaps putting down a marker for a real Championship challenge for 1989. Charles Wardle still won his third successive Harewood FTD Championship, though, from Sean. Another travelling Scot, Andrew Tymkewicz, from Edinburgh, cleaned up the main Harewood Championship, in his BARC Touring category Imp (a real one rather than a spaceframe clone) from Brian Kenyon's Sprite and Jon Collinge's FF1600 Pacer FF80. Pat Kenyon, now recovered from a back injury which had kept her from driving for a while, was a popular Ladies award winner in the family Sprite.

There seem to be more titles to be won every year and a significant new one in 1988 was the Phoenix Foods Modern 500 Challenge which attracted a splendid variety of ingenious little machines headed by the numerically dominant Jedis of which around a dozen were now in service, powered by a variety of motorcycle engines. Fittingly, John Corbyn's Yamaha-powered 1/84-88 won ahead of more of the little warriors in the hands of Johnny Perkins, Chris Johnson, sponsor David Tearle and Sarah Line.

Hendy Ford Motorsport sponsored the Gurston series and despite the Prescott disaster, the McBeaths, Andy and Simon, took the top places with the 2.0 Pilbeam-Hart MP54 although Andy was beaten by Rodney Eyles and Steve Allen for the BTD Challenge. Further West, Mike Brend (1.8 Caterham 7) secured the Shell Oils ASWMC Title.

Just as in the late nineteen-forties, much of the mechanical ingenuity was to be found among the 500cc racing cars and for the second successive year *The John Bolster Trophy* was awarded in this class. Clifton-on-Teme motorcycle engineer George Bewley was the worthy recipient for his beautifully-made, all-inboard-suspended Bewley-Jawa.

A Roman Triumph

When this book was nearing completion an enthralling conclusion to the 1989 hill climb season was unfolding. Talent was rewarded when Ray Rowan clinched the premier Guyson Beadblast RAC British Hill Climb Championship at Prescott in September after a nail-biting mid-season struggle for supremacy with veteran Roy Lane.

The Toleman-derived Roman IVH now benefited from further suspension development, smooth new 'conventional' bodywork, sponsorship from Hurstminster Financial Services/Holland Anglo Leasing and, perhaps most significantly, a 2.8 Hart engine provided by co-driver Rob Turnbull. Although Rob was rapid enough to complete Roman 1-2 results at the early Wiscombe and Prescott rounds, he later stood down from driving duties to give Rowan the best possible chance in the Championship. An outstanding season gave Rowan eight RAC Championship wins, plus the *Birmingham Post* Top Ten Challenge in the Midlands, while a Toleman prepared by his team also won the Warecrete RAC British Sprint Championship in Nigel Bigwood's hands.

Roy Lane and his gleaming Steel King Pilbeam-DFL MP58-1 had the hard task of winning the last four RAC rounds if he was to take the title and although he won at Shelsley, he was beaten by Dave Harris's latest Q8/Queen Anne Pilbeam-DFL MP58-4 at Prescott, so the Championship was lost, even though Rowan was sidelined on this occasion with transmission failure. Roy actually had a splendid season (despite a nasty accident at Craigantlet), winning five RAC rounds, his long-awaited first Barbon victory (making him a winner on all the current RAC Championship courses), his twenty-first win at Harewood in September, and lopping 0.17s off Martin Bolsover's long-standing Fintray course record.

Reigning Champion Charles Wardle and co-driver Chris Dowson had a poor year, with their efforts blunted by lack of finance and an accident to Wardle at Le Val des Terres. Martyn Griffiths, keen to enjoy a less hectic season, and Max Harvey, who was doing a lot of transatlantic commuting, did not seriously contest the Championship. Instead, Team Guyson and Chase Web Offset pooled their resources with Tim Thomson normally driving the formidable Pilbeam MP53/04 turbocar. He achieved a solid third place in the Guyson Beadblast sponsored series, ahead of David and Sean Gould, and victory in the Harewood FTD title.

Audi lent its name to the RAC British Leaders' Championship, but although several Audi Quattros – and especially Tom Hammonds' ultimate 580 bhp, 5-valve per cylinder Lehman-engined S1 version – added considerable excitement to the scene, the title went to a Scotsman for the second successive year. John Whyte, from Sauchen, near Aberdeen, was virtually unbeatable in his class in his ex-Ron Hand/Dave and Lynne Whitehead Stiletto-BDH, but a tie-break was still needed to confirm his victory over John Meredith in an even more exotic Special Saloon 'clone'. John's latest in a long line of such machines was nominally a Skoda S110R. Built around the ex-Cordy/Panter/Brown Martin BM24 sports-racer, the Martek Skoda employed a near 400 bhp, 4.5 Rover/NCK V8 engine for John's twenty-second year of speed events. This formidable combination quite overwhelmed their class opposition and John was unlucky also to be beaten to the Pound Garden Buildings Midland title, again on a tie-break. Winner here was Allan Warburton who joined with Leon Bachelier for a most successful season with Leon's further, Allan Staniforth-developed Caterham Super Seven 'White Brick'. Fourth in both series was the controversial 250cc Trakstar driven by Phil Jefferies. This suspensionless, kart-like, device was out for one final season, defeating new minimum wheelbase regulations with a pair of auxiliary wheels hung on the back!

Kenny Allen's hopes of a fifth Grampian Television Scottish title evaporated with the non-availability of projected Vision and Ralt RT4 single-seaters. George Ritchie was a popular winner in his 2.0 Chevron-Hart B34 after overhauling the early lead of Alex Graham. Throughout Britain, entries and interest were high, with few major meetings taking place without some new added ingredient. Jim Robinson and David Grace put their 2.5 Hart engine in a new, stiffer Pilbeam MP43C to dominate the sports racing category, Tony Marsh ran his promised twin-turbocharged March-Rover 822, Charles Barter returned to his winning ways, at Gurston in particular, with a Team Hartwell Peugeot 205 GT1, and the year's most successful VSCC racer, Anthony Mayman, added yet more laurels to ERA R4D's astonishing hill climb career. Narrowly defeating Bruce Spollon's ERA R8C on both occasions, Mayman set new records for pre-war cars at Shelsley (35.06s) and Prescott short course (41.11s) during VSCC meetings and then returned to Shelsley in August to record a phenomenal 34.61s in the Classic Car classes.

Notwithstanding the presence of the ultra-rapid 250cc Trakstar, interest in 500cc racing cars continued to grow, with production of the Jedi marque topping twenty. The enterprising 500 Owners Association revived a 35-year-old Prescott idea by organising a successful hill climb primarily for '500s', at Wiscombe Park in May. Twenty-nine drivers turned out with twenty-two, varied, 'new' cars, together with numerous entrants with the old 'one lungers' from the nineteen-forties and fifties. Appropriately, John Corbyn set an excellent, record-breaking 41.38s BTD with his own Jedi-Yamaha/ Dyson 1/84-88. History was again repeated when Chris Johnson converted his Jedi to take a 1,000cc Yamaha Genesis engine, with great success, in best Cooper-JAP tradition.

Longton and District Motor Club did well to inaugurate a new hill in the North West. This used the long drive to Shap Wells Hotel, off the A6 in Cumbria. Two meetings were held, the first in July taking place in the superb sunshine which graced so much of 1989. Despite the unusual hazard of butterflies interfering with the timing gear, the event was most successful and left regular Ulster visitor Jackie Harris (2.5 Ralt-Hart RT4) with the inaugural 29.06s hill record. The Bugatti Owners Club experimented successfully with a third course at Prescott in June and September. This was made possible by the simple expedient of laying two short, intersecting stretches of roadway between the exit of Orchard and the return leg between Ettore's and the climb to Pardon. Using this slightly longer but, for most people, marginally faster, crossover layout, competitors approached Ettore's from the opposite direction to normal, thereby giving this difficult corner an early rather than a late apex. Martyn Griffiths set the first record with the Harris/Queen Anne Pilbeam in 40.02s, but Dave Harris himself reduced that to 39.23s in September.

During the year the sport lost three doughty competitors prematurely, from natural causes, with the untimely and deeply regretted deaths of John Tuckett-Good, Alan Payne and Chris Steel.

Off-track, the Hill Climb and Sprint Association enrolled its one thousandth member and provided a lively forum for debate on the new national hill climb class regulations for 1991 onwards, which the RAC MSA announced early in the year. Designed both to accommodate existing competitors and to suit the cars which the RAC MSA believe will predominate during the nineteen-nineties, these long-awaited and much-debated regulations received a general measure of approval – but many a vociferous special interest group continued to argue loud and long for or against the detailed terms. Apart from five single-seater classes, divided at 500cc, 1100cc, 1600cc and 2000cc, and a class for Clubmans Sports Cars to Clubmans specification regarding engines, the twelve classes would be for Modified Production Saloon and Sports cars, and two divisions – likewise divided by cubic-capacity – for Sports Libre cars. This last category will encompass the more radical (such as spaceframe 'clone') Special Saloons, Group B former rally cars, Clubmans-chassised sports cars with other than Clubmans specification engines and Sports-Racing cars.

Only time will tell whether the new regulations will prove to be successful, but most competitors felt that the new classes for other than single-seaters would be fairer than the existing classes. Naturally, the organisers of smaller events will be free to arrange their class structure to suit themselves and local conditions.

CHAPTER TEN

THE SPORT

IN order to keep the narrative within reasonable bounds much of the foregoing has concentrated on the most 'significant' happenings in the sport's long history. The people, machinery and places receiving the lion's share of the attention have been those figuring in hill climbings's premier league.

That is almost inevitable but it should never be forgotten that the sport's essential atmosphere and charm depend just as heavily on the hundreds of owner/drivers of often modest cars who seek no more than a enjoyably day's sport and who rarely hit the headlines. They are as likely to be competing in small club events at Cricket St Thomas, Valence, Oddicombe or Baitings Dam as at Shelsley or Prescott, and the occasional class award is just an unexpected bonus.

Hill climbing allows this kind of enthusiast the chance to compete with his (or her) Escort, Mini, Sprite, Morgan or whatever, without vast expenditure, as long as they are happy to run their road cars. Alternatively, they may have bought an elderly racing car for perhaps £1500 to £2000, or even less, and could expect to have several seasons amusement out of this without that nagging anxiety about breaking their everyday road car far from home when it is needed to get to work the next morning!

As long as the clubman remembers to post his/her entry form in time (many of the larger hill climbs are well over subscribed), he/she can compete at the bigger meetings too, sharing the same Paddock atmosphere, the excitement, and the usually excellent organisation with the big names. There is plenty of time during the day to wander about, natter to fellow competitors, examine and admire a remarkably varied collection of competing vehicles, and generally enjoy a day out among kindred spirits in generally scenic surroundings. What's more it is one sporting event where a real family atmosphere prevails with wives, girlfriends, sons, daughters, mothers and fathers all actively involved – there is nothing exclusive about hill climbing. Attendance at meetings, in whatever capacity, does not usually involve the sort of aggravation over passes, Paddock entry restrictions, protests, eligibility wrangles or any other assorted hassles which can make other kinds of motor sport sheer hard works at times. But lest all this begins to make hill climbing begin to sound indistinguishable from one of the milder concours or garden party type of event, there in one crucial difference. Whether the competitor is driving one of the latest Pilbeams or a perfectly standard road car, the tension mounts as the time draws near to practice or to make a timed run in the event proper. No matter how hill climbers emphasise their enjoyment of the sporting and companionable atmosphere of hill climbing, they are all competitors. When the time for their climbs is nigh a certain steeliness creeps over one and all. For the short space of time which it takes to manoeuvre a car down to the start, and for that short, frenetic burst of ten-tenths motoring before the finish line is passed, the concentration, the effort to beat the clock and the times of comparably-mounted competitors is intense. The determination to 'win', whether the target is a class win, a personal best time, the best time put to by a similar car, or whatever, is just as intense and as universal as in any Grand Prix. This sharp contrast between leisurely enjoyment of a pleasant motoring gathering and sudden bursts of knife edge driving is surely one of the keys to hill climbing's lasting appeal.

That this sport has an enduring appeal to competitors of all ages is emphasised by the number of people who have competed for twenty, thirty, or even more years still. Well known characters such as Basil Davenport, Ashley Cleave and Tommy Pascoe continued to compete well into their seventies.

Enthusiasm rather than age is
the key factor for competing in
hill climbs. This is Rivers
Fletcher, still enjoying Prescott
at a pensionable age, with his
Alvis Speed 25. Rivers
designed the body for this car,
employing a design which he
originally devised for a 1938
Tourist Trophy project that
never materialised.
RIVERS FLETCHER

There is certainly no age bar in hill climbing and the scene would be much the poorer for the loss of
the 'elder statesmen'. Typical enthusiasts of this kind spring readily to mind. Prescott meetings
seemed incomplete without the handsome Bugatti T57 of Ronnie Symondson who competed at the
very first meeting there in 1938, and without one of the exotic BMWs of Moreton-in-Marsh garage
proprietor Gerry Tyack. Many years after his serious accident with the HWM-Jaguar at Prescott,
Rivers Fletcher still enjoyed competing, just for fun, in his neat ex-works MGA Coupé, having competed in a variety of cars in the interim including his pre-War Alvis. Rivers' son Peter also maintained
the family tradition by competing with the same Cooper-JAP which his father drove in the RAC Hill
Climb Championship.

And age is not necessarily any deterrent to competitiveness either. Ron Footitt, the car restoration
specialist from Cleobury Mortimer, near Kidderminster, was well into his sixties when his speed and
skill with his remarkable AC Six-engined GN Special won him an almost endless stream of awards in
hill climbs (as well as sprints and races in an intensely active programme) after almost three decades
with the AC-GN Cognac Special. Just as successful and just as ubiquitous is the pale blue Frazer
Nash-Alvis 'Norris Special' of Matlock's Guy Smith. Eleven years Ron Footitt's junior, Guy had been
competing for a mere 20 odd years and once listed one of his main interests as "Trying to beat Ron
Fottitt in the Cognac!" Then there's the beautiful red AC Cobra of Dorchester's Paul Channon, last
'survivor' of a group of very fast Cobras which were regulars on the hill climb scene in the nineteen-
sixties and early nineteen-seventies. Always immaculate and driven with considerable élan, this is one
car which never becomes any less covetable.

Further North, Allan Staniforth, competing with his umpteenth permutation on the Terrapin theme,
was as formidable an 1100cc racing class contender as he was twenty years earlier while no meeting
was complete without the rumbling CanAm McLaren of George Tatham from Malton or those stal-
warts of the Clubmans chassis cars, Bob Prest from Croxdale in County Durham, and Joe Ward from
Pickering in one of his self-built Ward chassis.

Of course, the one thing you cannot do is to describe the average hill climber – there is just no such
person. The sheer variety of people encountered in the sport is most refreshing. Perhaps there have

been more engineers (not always motor engineers though) represented than members of any other trade or profession, but then the discipline of hill climbing is a particularly exact and exacting calling. Otherwise, it is difficult to think of a line of business or service which has not been represented in recent years. There are motor traders, journalists, advertising executives, mechanics, printers, farmers (including such specialists as a trout farmer and a watercress grower), architects, estate agents, mechanics, civil servants, teachers, manufacturers, chemists and even the one and only violin maker (Peter Voigt). About the one person conspicuously absent is the professional racing driver! There are still one or two people who are fortunate enough to be able to spend a lot of time on their hill climbing over and above the working man's free time, but nobody can make enough money out of the sport to make it become a professional occupation. Gone too are the days when motor manufacturers, many of them promoted by ambitious and enthusiastic individuals who sought to achieve success at the wheel of their own products, used hill climbing as a prominent marketing tool for their cars.

That is not to say that commercialism is absent from the sport. Far from it, for a wide variety of companies have found hill climbing a cost-effective way of promoting goods or services, via sponsorship. Many of these companies certainly have hill climb enthusiasts at their head, but the commercial involvement does prove beneficial to the company concerned in most cases, and in the competitive economic climate of today the sponsorship which is merely the Chairman's tax-deductable perk is rarely possible. Men such as Jim Thomson (Guyson), John Cussins (Waring & Gillow), Martyn Griffiths (Severn Advertising), David Garnett (Bearings (Non-Lube)), and Max Harvey (Chase Web Offset) can point to definite commercial benefits stemming from their companies' sponsorship. Nevertheless, because they are themselves hill climb enthusiasts the commercial involvement has never threatened to change the atmosphere of the sport. In the same way, the support of companies like Castrol, Shell, the Duport Group, Haynes Publishing, and Pace Petroleum has been wholly beneficial, intending to raise the sport's stature and resources to achieve additional awareness among the motoring public without in any way debasing hill climbing's sporting character.

Individual motives for competing naturally vary although a strong competitive streak is present in virtually everyone who breaks the starting beam. When the author has broached the subject over the

Guyson has made a major contribution to hill climbing. This photograph was taken on the Isle of Man in 1976 and features Jim Thomson's Guyson Jaguar E-type, with William Towns-designed body. The cheerful youth is James Thomson, soon after to achieve much success on the hills himself.
MANX TECHNICAL PUBLICATIONS via JIM THOMSON

years, responses have commonly referred to good company among motor cars while a fair number find the sport an absorbing contrast to their everyday jobs, perhaps with a touch of the popular limelight thrown in to a modest extent. Few would go so far as the Bentley Special driver who once averred that every racing driver (and he was including hill climbers in the generalisation) was an egotist who sought a little bit of glory. Nevertheless, John Meredith, for one, once declared honestly that hill climbing was a rather glamorous contrast to his not unpleasant but relatively humdrum work in public service where he then earned a crust. It is not unusual to meet business men who find that they can become absorbed in the very different problems of setting fast times and in so doing leave their business anxieties behind for the day. The same applies of course to club motor racing and one noted property man used to insist that only in a racing car could he switch his mind off from his business affairs. As the man in question was noted for his way with the ladies, the author asked the obvious follow-up by suggesting that surely the bedroom could be rather distracting too! Not so, insisted the prominent clubman, only a racing car would do!

Perhaps this absorbing and self-contained form of relaxation is therapeutic, for without in any way being exclusive or off-putting to families, the sport has bred a type of relationship which is rather redolent of a club where "one doesn't go into another chap's circumstances" outside the sport itself. This is probably less common today than it was in the 'thirties when, as Rivers Fletcher recalls, "one could know fellow competitors for many years without being at all sure what their precise business was, or what their family circumstances were, if their families did not happen to accompany them to meetings". Even today, there is a rather pleasant tendency to take people at their face value within the sport which probably reflects that basically amateur tradition.

Above all, the sport of hill climbing is and always has been about having fun. It may get deadly serious for a matter of a minute or two at a time around those crucial seconds on the track but light-

Relaxed paddock atmosphere. The centre of youthful attention is Josh Randles's very successful Cooper Monaco.

J. PARK

Jim Tiller was already a favourite with the spectators in 1962 when this picture was taken at Wiscombe Park. Since then his glorious orange 1950 Allard J2 has been developed to a point where, after thirty years ownership by Jim and Sheila Tiller, it boasts a 7.2 Chevrolet engine, churning out 560bhp, and with transmission and chassis modifications to cope. Michelin X tyres have given way to fourteen inches wide Goodyear slick racing tyres!

MICHAEL WARE *VIA* JIM TILLER

Light-hearted fun. George Eyston (left) and Eddie Hall stage Shelsley's only 'race' in July 1931, in two tiny MG Midgets. They made it fairly convincing too, virtually dead-heating across the finish line.
NATIONAL MOTOR MUSEUM

heartedness dominates much of the day – always assuming that the lunch hour is not taken up with a gearbox rebuild or in changing over to wet weather tyres only to discover that 15 minutes before the afternoon runs the rain has stopped and that the course is drying with supernatural speed!

The last living member of 'The Bristol Gang', Hugh Dunsterville, recalled days when he was the original 'Designer' of the Freikaiserwagen with the Frys and Dick Caeser saying "Even writing this brings back the great *FUN* we all had on a shoestring". Sometimes the outsider would gain an impression of solemnity from magazine reports (and in later years from broadcasting) which owed more to popular convention than to the reality of the competition. Dunsterville remembered a splendid moment at Shelsley around 1937 when Austin works driver Bert Hadley outraged the proprieties with carefree abandon. He was sitting on the starting line in one of the little Austin twin-cam racers, with the revs rising to around 9,500, when his climactic moment of departure fizzled out with a burnt-out clutch. He switched off the engine and "in the deathly quiet, in ringing tones for all to hear" volunteered the concise and expressive sentiment "Oh, fuck it". One just didn't swear publicly like that in 1937.

In those now distant days the stature of racing drivers in the public eye was probably higher than that of leading sportsmen of today. They were 'Speed Kings', and feted daredevils yet the clubby atmosphere of Shelsley Walsh found even the greatest not taking themselves too seriously. David Swann – himself later a competitor – remembers the early thirties with great affection. "Since 1928 I had been at a prep school a few miles from Shelsley. The clock tower (of the school) is visible on its hill from the outside of the S Bend. This small boy, besotted by the glamour of motor-racing, using all his pocket-money to afford (just) *The Light Car* each week, he would spend every spare minute of Shelsley weekends leaning over the school fence next to a climbing bend on the road to the hill, just where it left the village of Great Witley. Howe's road-equipped Mercedes, Bugattis, and Frazer Nashes – all enjoyed as they tackled the road hill in second gear towards Mecca. Occasionally, all too seldom, a relation could be persuaded to come down to the school and take the boy out – to park the family Wolseley Hornet or Morris Cowley in a wet orchard, squelch up the hill and sit bedraggled on a wooden bench all afternoon to watch each climb."

On one such occasion the young David Swann was accompanied by his father, a distinguished churchman and former Cambridge oarsman who rejoiced in the nickname 'Cygnet' among the Light Blues. While making their way up the hill "we heard that great shout 'Cygnet' from somewhere in the Shelsley Paddock." The shout came from one of father Swann's former college rowing charges, George Eyston, now a racing driver and record breaker of great distinction. The mightily impressed young Master Swann saw that they recognised each other and shook hands over the hedge in the pouring rain. And George Eyston's greeting I have never forgotten: "Cygnet, what on earth are you doing in *these* aquatics?"

"That summed up for one twelve-year-old, the camaraderies of the sport, for it showed that hard as those demi-god drivers tried when on the move, there was ordinary life quite close to the surface all the time and easily recalled and returned to as appropriate. Aside from your Reg Parnells, hill climbing was part of life, not life itself."

In the modern age, an era when even boyish awe seems singularly lacking and we are all far too blasé about experience and excitements which we enjoy, one is perhaps less surprised to find that the hill climber does not take everything too seriously.

The 'fun' aspects of the sport are never far from the surface and are well exemplified in stories recounted by Tom Leake and Steve Butterworth. Tom Leake is well-known as a motoring journalist and as an enthusiastic competitor, but his leading role in the establishment of Loton Park as a major hill climb venue was his most significant contribution to this particular branch of the sport. The early years at Loton were not lacking in humour: "The various corners at Loton had local names – like Keeper's Bend (near the estate keeper's lodge), while Fallow Corner is where the deer had a regular crossing. In fact the then Town Clerk of Shrewsbury, Ronald Loxton – who was an ardent sprint and hill climb man with Sunbeam Tiger and Invicta 4-litre – always presented himself first of the entry for practice (well, he lived opposite the course). Every time he came back to the Paddock after his first practice run he would say: "Do you know there are deer on the course?" Actually we tended to use him as the deer-sweeper – when they saw Ronald driving furiously they knew they were in for a disturbed weekend and usually departed deeper into the bracken. . ."

Loton was certainly not without its hazards in those days, like the six-feet-high bracken which would border the course when meetings were staged in August. It was "so high that when Peter Blankstone went off at Loggerheads on the longer course... in his Brabham Quattro, we simply couldn't find him until he waved his helmet. Actually someone suggested we left him there!"

Even the intervention of the Almighty could not be completely ruled out: "Because of its location opposite the local church, hill climbs could not be held there Sunday mornings. In fact no starting up of engines, nor tannoy in the Paddock was the order until after midday on a Sunday. It so happened

Hill climbing lost an able, determined and most sporting character with the early death in 1989 of Alan Payne. He made his name in the nineteen-seventies with 'Smiley Riley', an unlikely combination of Riley 1.5 and Rover V8 engine, and went on to achieve much on a very limited budget with his Anson-Rover V8 single-seater.
AUTHOR and BOB LIGHT

Alan Payne. Anson-Rover V8

Haydn Spedding looks pensive as he waits, and waits, for a scrutineer at Loton Park.
AUTHOR

The author at work! Chris Mason manhandles Haydn Spedding's E-type Jaguar round Quarry Corner at Harewood.
ANONYMOUS via AUTHOR

that just once as the vicar was mid-way through his sermon, someone either started an engine or made a tannoy annoucement, and *snap* went the Bible, a hurried blessing and the vicar was off across the road – to be nearly run over by Phil Scragg arriving a bit sharply in his lightweight race E-type . . ."

Typical of hundreds of regular clubmen was Steve Butterworth, who worked for Rolls-Royce at Derby for a time and later at March Engineering, and who competed from 1964 until 1972 with a mildly-tweaked Lotus 7. During this time he contested events at most of the significant mainland hills, plus Tholt-y-Will. In his own words: "Success was a long way off but I had a great time". Happily he still has the Lotus, and clearly recalls the sportsmanship which enhanced his enjoyment: "I was entered for the 1968 event at Tholt-y-Will and on the Sunday morning was driving out to the hill from Douglas in the famous police-controlled convoy. A farm dog ran out from some long grass and I could not miss it. To everyone's distress, the dog later died which was particularly sad as she had been helping her master clear the fells of sheep prior to the event. The Lotus sustained a badly damaged radiator and, in view of the length of the hill, I went to the Clerk of the Course's caravan to declare myself a non-starter.

However, my conversation was overheard by David Hepworth's mechanic who said in a North Country accent: "What's the marrer wi'it – let's 'ave a luke". He set to work and did a superb repair with liberal supplies of cow dung pushed into the core! Sir Nicholas Williamson saw the commotion and gave me a bottle of Radweld and lent me his lunch box to use as a water container. So here we had two people, both frantically concerned with the Championship, helping a nobody with his 'banger' to get a start. Eventually, the radiator would hold water for just over three minutes so I evolved a system with the startline marshals whereby I pushed the car up to the line with the bonnet off and half a gallon of water in Nick's lunch box. At the start signal the water went in, the marshals replaced the bonnet while Fangio Butterworth belted himself in. All this with a deadline when the roads had to be re-opened to the public – a great lot in Lancashire AC! Sad to relate after all this, Georgina Baillie-Hill in her Elva-BMW beat me into second place by a mile – as she always did!"

The following October, Steve was in more trouble at Castle Howard. "I did a 360 degree roll at the second corner due to gross driver error. Damage was remarkably light, so having collected what was left of my wits and the fibreglass wings I decided that the quickest way of clearing the hill was to try to drive up. This I was able to do and to my amusement the time-keeper saw fit to credit me with a time. I am told that I hold the record for a climb including a 360 degree roll!'

In recent years some people have claimed that the leading single-seater drivers are becoming rather too tense and too serious to really enjoy the funny side of things. That would be forgivable when the sobering cost of their machinery is taken into account, but anyone making the charge has clearly not seen Roy Lane winding up the opposition! Few have as great an investment in the sport as Jim Thomson, yet the Guyson MD is as bubbling over with enthusiasm after a satisfying climb as the rawest competitor in his first season. A successful sports and saloon driver for many years, Jim was slightly overawed by the accomplishments of his son James when he took over the Pilbeam MP40RX. However, after a learning season in 1982, he was really beginning to gain some confidence with the car in 1983.

At the heart of it all, there remains the speed hill climbing competition. Whatever the appeals of the good company, pleasant surroundings, interesting cars and so on, all these are only trappings of the short sharp dash up a winding country lane in the least possible time. Since the turn of the century, and even allowing for temporary setbacks, the sport of speed hill climbing has survived and thrived.

Looked at dispassionately, hill climbing could be described, not unreasonably, by the uninitiated as poor value for money for the competitor. Yet the appeal is undiminished. When car preparation costs (admittedly rather less in most cases than for 'rival' forms of motor sport), travelling time and costs, and an event entry fee around the £30 plus mark are taken into account, a competitive mileage, rarely exceeding five miles and accomplished in perhaps three to four minutes, including a couple of practice runs does not sound like very good value.

In bygone years it was easy to find explanations for its appeal in a hard-headed sort of way. In the pioneering days before 1907, the nascent motoring public needed some convincing that ordinary motor cars would actually climb significant hills at all, while until that year there were no race tracks on the British mainland where manufacturers or sportsmen could demonstrate the prowess of their machines. Right up until the removal of speed events from the public roads in 1925, the alternatives open to those wishing to pursue the quest for motoring speed in Britain remained only Brooklands track, and a few notable resort promenades. During all these years, the hill climb remained a valid contest for those wishing to advertise competition success for their cars or components, and an interesting challenge to drivers requiring more than just a flat-out speed contest.

Even though road racing became rather more accessible as the nineteen-thirties progressed, and especially after Donington Park became available in 1933, the hill climbs at Shelsley Walsh, and at Prescott (just before war intervened in 1939), remained truly significant and even international events. Their social and publicity value remained high and the much reduced number of British motor manufacturers who continued to support speed events still took an active interest in hill climbs. Austin and Riley are perhaps the prime examples.

After the Second World War there was for a time almost a reversion to pre-1925 conditions. Until the converted airfields became regularly utilised to form the basis of a new circuit racing tradition, there were a few seasons where hill climbs once again became premier features on the national competition calender. Then when circuit racing grew in popularity and availability to an unprecedented extent, a definite decline set in for hill climbing which had become an almost totally amateur *and* non-commercial activity carried on by a hard core of enthusiasts.

But then came the revival in the early nineteen-sixties and the sport has never really looked back since. This is despite the many counter-attractions from other types of motor sport, the lack of consistent publicity outside the specialist motor sporting media, the generally low levels of prize money and the sheer lack of competitive driving time. The peripheral attractions of the sport have already been mentioned more than once but surprisingly little ever seems to be said about the real challenge of driving a hill climb car to competitive times.

During the last few years, and thanks to the generosity of Barnsley estate agent Haydn Spedding, the author has been able to sample the joys of hill climbing from behind a steering wheel rather than from on the end of a reporter's pencil. A former motor sporting photographer and occasional writer, Haydn Spedding hill climbs purely for enjoyment using a powerful yet exceedingly tractable and well-mannered car. This is the now 4.4-litre-engined E-type Jaguar which once set the circuits alight in Modified Sports Car racing in the hands of Mike Franey and Ted Worswick, among others. It's a true classic car and it is a privilege to drive it. Any thoughts that hill climbing might not have a lot to it, competitively speaking, are soon dissapated when one faces the task of taking this rather large and elderly sports car to even halfway useful times. Phil Scragg (among many others, one assumes) was on record as saying that to set a fast time in the short distance of a British hill you had to drive at absolutely ten-tenths yet without even slightly misjudging any corner or gearchange. It has to be absolutely right all the way through those crowded 30, 40 or 50 seconds. There is no way to recover lost time in a hill climb. Consequently, immense concentration and self-discipline are essential, even if it is only for a short time.

Until trying it out for real, the almost eerie distortion of time experienced during this frenetic burst of activity had never occurred to me. Certainly, nobody had ever mentioned it. There seems to be a phenomenal number of conscious thoughts, actions and reactions during those seconds, yet there also seems to be ample time to direct the car to best effect. In short, time appears to slow down. The illusion is well and truly shattered when one makes a mistake. Then the opposite happens. Even before the error is rectified one seems to be 'on' the next corner and the whole climb disintegrates into a bewildering succession of mistakes! Presumably all this has something to do with adrenalin and is perfectly familiar to those who spend their time driving Grand Prix cars or flying jet fighters, but for the weekend sportsman it may not be so familiar.

The vital importance of coordination, concentration and total self-discipline cannot be over-emphasised. On one occasion I had walked the course with a vastly experienced competitor who (typically) imparted a great deal of excellent advice about getting up Harewood in the best possible way. Unfortunately, I tried to put all this advice into practice at once, approached the second corner on my first practice climb thinking about the corner I had just left (a disastrous thing to do) and became so 'out of synch' that before the end of an absolutely hopeless climb I was actually lifting off on the straights! It took the rest of the day – fortunately three practice climbs were possible on that occasion – to get back into a sensible frame of mind to go on the next day actually to reduce the times set at the previous meeting.

Aston Hill at around 1922.
NATIONAL MOTOR MUSEUM

Unchanging moment of truth.
Michael Christie leaves the line
at Shelsley Walsh in 1954,
driving Peter Bell's ERA R11B.
MIDLAND AUTOMOBILE CLUB

Hill climb machinery can be most varied. This is Jeremy Goodman's "Pubs 'n' Clubs" Championship winning Ginetta G4 Series IV.
JEREMY GOODMAN

With so many minutiae on which to concentrate, so many things to try to get right, and allowing for a natural concern for not damaging a valued friend's beautiful car on a course with even less margin for error than on a racing circuit, it is all remarkably tiring. On one occasion two practice runs were taken one after the other – allowing for waits at Paddock exits and down at the start line – on a rather warm day. The total time in the car, most of it spent in deep concentration and mounting tension and less than two minutes actually spent driving as hard as judgement and nerve would allow, was probably about 40 minutes. Yet when I got out of the car I felt absolutely drained. Four hours of uninterrupted driving on the road would not have been anything like as debilitating.

To one man that is the complete answer to anyone who thinks that you don't get much value for money in hill climbing. Everyone has his own taste of course but such is the concentration of effort in hill climbing, to say that it is not good value is about as valid as saying that scotch is a poorer drink than beer because one gets so much less of it for the same money.

After experiencing the sport from the driving seat I declare that hill climbing's resilience and continued survival seems less surprising. Long may it continue evolving in exactly the same way as it has done for so many years!

Cathy Cooper, sister of hill climber Maggie Blankstone, took the Ladies Award at Shelsley in her Ginetta G4.
via TREVOR PYMAN

Park's Vauxhall takes BTD.
(undated).
NATIONAL MOTOR MUSEUM

W. Short(?) at Dean Hill Climb.
(undated).
NATIONAL MOTOR MUSEUM

*1922 Vauxhall TT car at
Shelsley Walsh, October 1923.*
NATIONAL MOTOR MUSEUM

*A view of Kop Hill in the early
nineteen-twenties.*
NATIONAL MOTOR MUSEUM

*Basil Davenport's spider at
Shelsley Walsh (undated).*
NATIONAL MOTOR MUSEUM

Early nineteen-twenties hill climb.
NATIONAL MOTOR MUSEUM

Wonderful action shot of Vauxhall at Shelsley Walsh in October 1923.
NATIONAL MOTOR MUSEUM

*Tony Lambert's Ginetta G4R
screams up Doune during
June 1971.*
viaTREVOR PYMAN

POSTSCRIPT

As this book was going to press the final stages of the 1990 season were unfolding. Most of the headlines had been monopolised by the struggle for Championship supremacy between two vastly experienced men: Martyn Griffiths and Roy Lane. Refreshed after a year's sabbatical from Championship-chasing, Martyn and Max Harvey returned with a gleaming new Pilbeam MP58, fitted with a 580 bhp, ex-Benetton Formula 1 3.5 Cosworth DFR engine and Hewland HGB transaxle. This magnificent Chase Web Offset/Severn Advertising car, maintained by Ian Tilsley, was soon sorted and Martyn overhauled Roy Lane's early Guyson Beadblast RAC British Championship lead to clinch his fourth RAC title at Prescott early in September. Highlight of a superb season was a new Shelsley Walsh course record in August, in 25.86s, thus breaking Alister Douglas-Osborn's seven year old record. Further records fell to Martyn at Prescott (38.67s), a shortened, 1,700 yards Craigantlet (39.25s) and at Wiscombe Park (35.03s).

Although Ray Rowan won the RAC rounds at Bouley Bay and September Prescott in the further revised Roman – denuded of body panels again, as in 1988 – Ray again had his own efforts hampered by the necessity to give early season priority to customer cars. By season's end though, his methanol-fuelled, 2.5 Hart-engined machine was virtually on a par with the two highly expensive, and immensely powerful, Cosworth V8-engined Pilbeams which dominated the season. At least, Rowan's amazing car control made it so.

Roy Lane, whose 600 bhp, 4.0 Cosworth DFL had powered him to an early season Wiscombe record in 35.56s, and also to four RAC wins, had consolation in winning the *Birmingham Post* Top Ten series.

Rob Stevens (1.7 Caterham Super 7) lifted the important Pound Garden Buildings Midland title by a single point from John Corbyn, who enjoyed another highly successful year in his little Jedi. John also narrowly missed out on the RAC Leaders' title. This was won by Graham Hickman's brutal 6.2 Skoda-Donovan/Chevrolet, which was based on a Sports 2000 Royale. Since Martyn Brake's Imp 'clone' was also in the running for a top Leaders' place, this Championship provided something of a swansong for these Silhouette 'saloons', for new regulations will force them to run as Sports Libre cars in 1991. It certainly seemed bizarre that these thinly-disguised sports-racers could run as Special Saloons, whereas Tom Hammonds' crowd-pleasing Pike's Peak-specification Audi had to compete against Mallocks and Pilbeam sports-racers.

THE CHAMPIONS

RAC British Hill Climb Championship

Year	Driver	Car	Championship Sponsor
1947	Raymond Mays	ERA R4D	
1948	Raymond Mays	ERA R4D	
1949	Sydney Allard	Steyr-Allard	
1950	Dennis Poore	Alfa Romeo 8C-35	
1951	Ken Wharton	Cooper-JAP	
1952	Ken Wharton	Cooper-JAP	
1953	Ken Wharton	Cooper-JAP	
1954	Ken Wharton	Cooper-JAP/ERA R4D	
1955	Tony Marsh	Cooper-JAP	
1956	Tony Marsh	Cooper-JAP	
1957	Tony Marsh	Cooper-JAP	
1958	David Boshier-Jones	Cooper-JAP	
1959	David Boshier-Jones	Cooper-JAP	
1960	David Boshier-Jones	Cooper-JAP	
1961	David Good	Cooper-JAP	
1962	Arthur Owen	Cooper-Coventry Climax T53	
1963	Peter Westbury	Felday-Daimler	
1964	Peter Westbury	Ferguson-Coventry Climax P99	
1965	Tony Marsh	Marsh-GM	
1966	Tony Marsh	Marsh-GM	
1967	Tony Marsh	Marsh-GM/Marsh-GM 4WD	
1968	Peter Lawson	BRM 670P 4WD	
1969	David Hepworth	Hepworth-GM 4WD	Shell
1970	Sir Nicholas Williamson	McLaren-Chevrolet M10A/B	Shell
1971	David Hepworth	Hepworth-GM 4WD	Shell
1972	Sir Nicholas Williamson	March-Hart 712S	Shell
1973	Mike MacDowel	Brabham-Repco BT36X	
1974	Mike MacDowel	Brabham-Repco BT36X	
1975	Roy Lane	McRae-Chevrolet GM1	
1976	Roy Lane	McRae-Chevrolet GM1	
1977	Alister Douglas-Osborn	Pilbeam-Cosworth DFV MP22	
1978	David Franklin	March-BMW 772	
1979	Martyn Griffiths	Pilbeam-Hart MP40	
1980	Chris Cramer	March-Hart 782/79B	
1981	James Thomson	Pilbeam-Hart MP40K	
1982	Martin Bolsover	Pilbeam-Hart MP51	Pace Petroleum
1983	Martin Bolsover	Pilbeam-Hart MP51	Pace Petroleum
1984	Martin Bolsover	Pilbeam-Hart MPB43/MP51	Pace Petroleum
1985	Chris Cramer	Gould-Hart 84/2	
1986	Martyn Griffiths	Pilbeam-Hart MP53/04	Guyson USA

1987	Martyn Griffiths	Pilbeam-Hart MP53/04	Guyson USA
1988	Charles Wardle	Pilbeam-Repco MP47/RB	Guyson USA
1989	Ray Rowan	Roman-Hart IVH	Guyson Beadblast
1990	Martyn Griffiths	Pilbeam MP58	Guyson Beadblast

RAC British Leaders Hill Climb Championship

1970	Chris Cramer	Mini-Cooper S	Shell
1971	'S M Smith' (Tony Bancroft)	Ford GT40	Shell
1972	Chris Cramer	Mallock U2-BL Mk11	Shell
1973	Alex Brown	Ginetta-Imp/G17	Woking Motors
1974	Martyn Griffiths	Mallock U2-TC Mk8B	Woking Motors
1975	Alan Richards	Gryphon-Ford AR3	Woking Motors
1976	Russ Ward	Austin Healey Sprite s/c	
1977	John Meredith	Mini-Cooper S	
1978	Charles Barter	Davrian-Imp Mk 7	Haynes Publishing Group
1979	John Meredith	Mini-Imp	Haynes Publishing Group
1980	Charles Barter	Davrian/Imp Hartwell	Haynes Publishing Group
1981	Barrogill Angus	Stiletto-BMW	Haynes Publishing Group
1982	Charles Wardle	Mallock U2-BDA Mk20	Haynes Publishing Group
1983	Brian Walker	Skoda-Hart S110R	Aston Martin
1984	Ken Snailham	Lotus-Ford TC 7	Aston Martin
1985	Russ Ward	Saracen-BDJ M85	Aston Martin
1986	Dave Whitehead	Stiletto-BDH	AWS Group
1987	Mike Kerr	Skoda-Rover S110R	Bratt
1988	Simon Frost	Lotus-Ford TC7	Edwards Catering Company
1989	John Whyte	Stiletto-BDH	Audi
1990	Graham Hickman	Skoda-Donovan/Chevrolet	

RAC British Award of Merit

1979	Ted Williams	March-Hart 772/752	
1980	Dave Harris	Pilbeam-Hart MP42	
1981	James Thomson	Pilbeam-Hart MP40K	
1982	Max Harvey	Pilbeam-Hart MP53	
1983	Jim Thomson	Pilbeam-Hart MP50	
1984	Tim Thomson	Pilbeam-Hart MP50	Guyson International
1985	Chris Cramer	Gould-Hart 84/2	Guyson International
1986	Charles Wardle	Pilbeam-Repco MP47RB	Chase Web Offset
1987	Chris Knapman	Ralt-Hart RT4HCS	
1988	Steve Allen	Pilbeam-Hart MP40	
1989	Rob Turnbull	Roman-Hart IVH/Pilbeam-Hart MP40	

Midland Automobile Club
Junior Hill Climb and Sprint Championship

1956	Jimmy Stuart	ERA R14B/Lotus-Coventry Climax
1957	Bill Moss	ERA R5B
1958	(Tie) Edward Willmott/	Cooper-Norton
	Peter Cottrell	Cooper-JAP/Lotus-Bristol Mk10
1959	Peter Hughes	Cooper-Norton
1960	NOT RUN (insufficient entries)	
1961	Gordon March	Djinn/Mezzolitre
1962	Tony Griffiths	Jaguar E-type
1963	Ray Terry	Lotus-Coventry Climax 7
1964	Bryan Brown	Kieft-Ford

Motor Racing/Sports Car & Lotus Owner
Sports Car Championship

1959	Phil Scragg	HWM-Jaguar
1960	Ray Fielding	Cooper-Coventry Climax
1961	Phil Scragg	Lister-Jaguar
1962	Josh Randles	Cooper-Coventry Climax Monaco T49
1963	Josh Randles	Cooper-Maserati Monaco T49

BARC Hill Climb Championship

1968	Jeff Goodliff	Mini-Cooper S s/c	
1969	Jeff Goodliff	MiniSprint GT s/c	Castrol
1970	Jeff Goodliff	Lotus Elan	Castrol
1971	Jim Thomson	Vauxhall Viva GT	Castrol
1972	Chris Seaman	MG Midget/Biota-BL Mk1C GT	Castrol
1973	Mike Flather	Mini-Cooper S s/c	Castrol
1974	Peter Voigt	Voigt-Renwick Special	Castrol
1975	David Franklin	Ensign-Holbay BDA LNF3	Guyson
1976	Charles Barter	Hillman Imp	Guyson
1977	Charles Barter	Hillman Imp	Guyson
1978	Charles Barter	Davrian-Imp Mk7	Euroblast
1979	Josh Sadler	Porsche 911	Guyson
1980	Charles Barter	Davrian/Imp-Hartwell	Guyson
1981	Josh Sadler	Porsche 911	Guyson
1982	Paul Tankard	TVR Tuscan	Guyson
1983	Paul Tankard	TVR Tuscan	
1984	Mike Kerr	Vauxhall Chevette HSR	
1985	Graham Oates	Lotus Europa-Ford TC	

BARC FTD Awards Championship

1973	Richard Thwaites	McLaren-Chevrolet M10B	Castrol
1974	Roy Lane	McRae-Chevrolet GM1	Castrol
1975	Roy Lane	McRae-Chevrolet GM1	Guyson
1976	Alister Douglas-Osborn	Pilbeam-Cosworth DFV MP22	Guyson
1977	Alister Douglas-Osborn	Pilbeam-Cosworth DFV MP22	Guyson
1978	Chris Cramer	March-Cosworth GA 76A	Euroblast
1979	Chris Cramer	March-Hart 782/79B	Guyson
1980	Martyn Griffiths	Pilbeam-Hart MP40	Guyson
1981	James Thomson	Pilbeam-Hart MP40K	Guyson
1982	Martin Bolsover	Pilbeam-Hart MP51	Guyson
1983	Jim Thomson	Pilbeam-Hart MP40RX	
1984	John Istead	Mallock U2-Ford Mk14/18	
1985	Alister Douglas-Osborn	Pilbeam-Hart MP54	

Scottish Hill Climb Championship

1970	Ted Clark	Lotus-Ford 51	Burmah
1971	Iain McLaren	Chevron-Ford B15	Burmah
1972	Iain McLaren	Brabham-Cosworth FVC BT35X	Burmah
1973	Iain McLaren	Brabham-Cosworth FVC BT36	Burmah
1974	Doug Thomson	GRD-BDA 273	Burmah
1975	Alan Thomson	Chevron-Holbay TC B17	Burmah
1976	Alan Thomson	Chevron-Holbay TC B17	Burmah
1977	Norrie Galbraith	Mallock U2-Ford TC Mk8/16	Grampian Television
1978	Jim Campbell	Brabham-BDA BT35	Grampian Television
1979	Jim Campbell	Brabham-BDA BT35	Grampian Television
1980	Norrie Galbraith	March-Hart 782A	Grampian Television
1981	Jimmy Jack	March-Hart 782/79B	Grampian Television
1982	Norrie Galbraith	March-BMW 782	Grampian Television
1983	Kenny Allen	Mallock U2-Ford Mk21	Grampian Television
1984	Alex Graham	Mallock U2-Ford Mk20	Grampian Television
1985	Kenny Allen	Vision-Ford V84H	Grampian Television
1986	Kenny Allen	Vision-Ford V84H	Grampian Television
1987	Kenny Allen	Vision-BDG V86H	Grampian Television
1988	(Tie) Tim Thomson/ Kenny Allen	Pilbeam-Hart MP50/ Vision-BDG V86H	Grampian Television
1989	George Ritchie	Chevron-Hart B34	Grampian Television

Midland Hill Climb Championship

1980	Charles Barter	Davrian/Imp-Hartwell	Bradburn & Wedge
1981	Martin Bolsover	Pilbeam-BDA MP51	B&W/Beacon Radio
1982	Josh Sadler	Porsche 911	Swinford Motors/Beacon Radio
1983	Brian Walker	Skoda-Hart S110R	Swinford Motors/Beacon Radio
1984	Martin Bolsover	Pilbeam-Hart MPB43	Castrol/Beacon Radio
1985	Russ Ward	Saracen-BDJ M85	Rydale BMW
1986	Nigel Garland	Porsche 911	Rydale BMW/Shell Oils
1987	Phil Jefferies	Trakstar-Rotax ZK86	Shell Oils
1988	Adrian Hopkins	Sark-BDA IIIH	Pound Garden Buildings
1989	Allan Warburton	Caterham Super 7	Pound Garden Buildings
1990	**Rob Stevens**	**Caterham Super Seven**	**Pound Garden Buildings**

Birmingham Post Top Ten Challenge

1981	James Thomson	Pilbeam-Hart MP40K
1982	Martyn Griffiths	Pilbeam-Hart MP53
1983	Martyn Griffiths	Pilbeam-Hart MP53
1984	Martin Bolsover	Pilbeam-Hart MPB43
1985	Roy Lane	Pilbeam-BMW MP53
1986	Martyn Griffiths	Pilbeam-Hart MP53/04
1987	Roy Lane	Pilbeam-Cosworth DFL MP58
1988	Martyn Griffiths	Pilbeam-Hart MP53/04 Turbo
1990	**Roy Lane**	**Pilbeam MP58**

WATERING HOLES

by Jim Thomson

Partaking in and following the sport of hill climbing mean that most weekends are spent travelling around the country to the various hill climb venues. During the years after the Second World War until about the nineteen-seventies it was usual for entrants, mechanics and friends to stay at local pubs or hotels in the area where some very interesting parties took place: these further generated the excellent spirit of comradeship known in the sport.

However, the advent of better caravans (and latterly the American-style motor home) has meant that a lot of people now stay at the hill climb venues overnight, but of course they still visit local pubs and restaurants, but fewer of them now stay overnight at hotels.

The following covers the more interesting hotels or pubs around each hill climb venue in the British Isles and will perhaps be found of benefit to supporters of the sport:

Barbon

Located 2½ miles North East of Kirkby Lonsdale, in Cumbria, on the edge of the small village of Barbon, where the *Barbon Inn* has outstandingly good food and an excellent bar which is really the main meeting place at each Barbon event. There are other pubs in Kirkby Lonsdale, such as the *Royal*, a nice old coaching inn, and the *Red Dragon* in the centre of town, which offers accommodation.

It is difficult to recommend anywhere better than the *Barbon Inn*.

Bouley Bay JERSEY

Located on the North East Coast, the *Water's Edge Hotel* at Bouley Bay has excellent accommodation and food and is possibly the best place to stay for the hill climb, although the *Bouley Bay Hotel* at the top of the hill climb is also a popular place. There are many attractive hotels and restaurants on the island and top-quality food may be had at *Longueville Manor* and *L'Horizon*, with prices in keeping, but there is the excellent *Bistro Roc*, and *Les Couperons Restaurant and Bar* at Rozel Bay which is very attractive and of excellent quality. Most places on the island are good value.

Craigantlet NORTHERN IRELAND

Just outside Belfast, the *Stormont Hotel* is really the only place where the visiting hill climbing fraternity stay.

Doune SCOTLAND

Located 1½ miles West of Doune on the Callender Road, near Stirling, where the gathering place is the *Woodside Hotel* in Doune village. There are also the excellent *Highland Hotel* and the *Red Lion* which offer commendable refreshment and food. There is top-class accommodation and probably the nicest food in the UK at *Cromlix House Hotel* just outside Dunblane, and of course the excellent *Dunblane Hydro* in Dunblane is a traditional larger Scottish hotel.

There are a few hotels in Callender where the *Roman Camp* is first class and there is an excellent small Inn at Kilmahog, the *Lade Inn*, about 2 miles West of Callender, where there is draught beer and top-quality food.

Gurston Down

Located one mile West of Broadchalke, near Salisbury. The *Rose & Crown* at Harnham, just outside Salisbury, is an excellent place to stay, has good food and a nice bar. Also the *Red Lion Hotel* in Salisbury offers good accommodation, and there is good eating at the *Haunch of Venison*, again in Salisbury, and top-class food at the *Yew Tree* in Oddstock – French Cordon Bleu cookery. The local pub, the *Queens* at Broadchalke, has excellent food and beers, and being quite close to the hill climb course is extremely popular with competitors.

Harewood

Located 7½ miles East North East of Leeds, Harewood is in some of the nicest Yorkshire countryside in the area. Close by is the *Harewood Arms* which is a first-class modernised hotel, restaurant and pub, where there is excellent food and drink, with often a good gathering on the Saturday night of any Harewood event.

There is also the *Ladbroke Hotel* at Wetherby which is a modern hotel and the *Scott's Arms* at Sicklinghall which has good food and Younger's beer. The *Windmill* at Linton is an old pub used as a meeting place for car enthusiasts. Not too far away, of course, is the town of Harrogate where there are many fine hotels and restaurants.

Loton Park

Located 8½ miles West of Shrewsbury in Shropshire, being part of the Loton Park Estate, kindly loaned for hill climb events by the owner, Sir Michael Leighton. The nearest pub is the *Hand & Diamond Inn* over the border in Wales (only 2 miles away) and dispenses food and ale of excellent quality. There are good hotels in Shrewsbury such as the *Lion* (Trusthouse Forte), the *Lord Hill*, and the *Prince Rupert*, all of which have good food and accommodation. Nearby is the renowned *Hawkstone Park Hotel* which provides all the amenities of a leisure complex and also golf.

Prescott

Located 8 miles North East of Cheltenham, once again amongst beautiful countryside with lots of small pubs and hotels. Amongst these the most popular is the *Oak* on the road to Winchcombe: it has hand-pulled draft beer and an amazing range of bar snacks. There is also the *Bugatti* on the same road which has a small restaurant and an excellent bar. There are also one or two restaurants in Winchcombe, and of course many hotels in Cheltenham such as the *Golden Valley* on the Gloucester Road which is modern and convenient for users of the motorway, and the *Queens* in the town (Trusthouse Forte).

Rumster SCOTLAND

Located 3 miles North West of Lybster off the A9 and approximately 14 miles South of John O'Groats, this is the most northerly hill climb in the UK where the meeting place for competitors and followers is *McKays Hotel* at Wick, a fairly simple, rugged establishment where the warmth of welcome has to be experienced to be believed and party time is instant. A nice small hotel is the *Pentland Arms* at Lybster, quite close to the hill climb: here the food is very good.

Shelsley Walsh

Probably the most famous venue in hill climbing, located 10 miles West of Worcester and set in a beautiful valley close by the village of Shelsley Beauchamp where the *Birche Hotel* has an outstanding reputation for good food and party time. The *Hundred House* nearby has good food and ale at reasonable prices. An outstanding hotel, the *Elms* at Abberley, has long had a fine reputation for excellent food and wines.

Not to be forgotten, of course, is the *Lion* at Clifton-on-Teme which has a very good small dining room and good beers.

Val des Terres GUERNSEY

Located half a mile from St. Peter Port, a top-quality hotel is the *St. Pierre Park*, but *Old Government House* and *Le Frigate* are well recommended. There is an excellent small hotel, *The Atlantic*, on the coast and a fine restaurant virtually next to the hill climb paddock which has Cajun style food. An interesting recent innovation is a new restaurant located alongside the start of the hill climb, run by the well-known local hill climber, Graham Priaulx.

Wiscombe Park

Located 6 miles South of Honiton in Devon, and close to the coastal village of Branscombe, where the *Masons Arms* is a beautiful old inn with excellent accommodation either in the inn or in the surrounding cottages in the village – the food is first-class. Another popular pub/restaurant is the *Three Horseshoes* located on the Lyme Regis-Sidmouth road. There are many hotels in Sidmouth, the local seaside resort, and the *Salston Hotel* at Ottery St. Mary nearby is recommended.

This is by no means a complete list of the hotels, pubs and restaurants in the vicinity of hill climb events, but will certainly serve to give the reader an idea of where to meet his/her fellow enthusiasts.

INDEX

1991 Hill Climb
NOTES

The following six pages are inserted to allow the reader,
if he/she so wishes, to keep his/her full record of the forthcoming
1991 hill climb season